Vedic Astrology

An Integrated Approach

Vedic Astrology

An Integrated Approach

P.V.R. Narasimha Rao

SAGAR PUBLICATIONS
72, Janpath, Ved Mansion, New Delhi-110 001
Tel.: 23320648, 23328245
Mob.: +91 9312237900 (WhatsApp)
E-mail: s.sagarpublications@gmail.com
Website: www.sagarpublications.com

First Published:2001
Reprinted 2004, 2017, 2020

Published and Printed by:
Saurabh Sagar for **Sagar Publications** New Delhi-110001

and

Printed at:
The Artwaves, New Delhi-110019
Telefax: +91 11 41609709
E-mail: theartwaves@gmail.com

ॐ श्री महागणाधिपतये नमः

ॐ श्री जगन्नाथस्वामी नयनपथगामी भवतु मे

विश्वेशो मधुसूदनो यदुवरो गीतागुरुर्ज्ञानदो।
गोपालो मदनान्तकादिविनुतो गोपीप्रियो मोहनः।
कृष्णो वृष्णिकुलोद्भवोऽपरगुरुः पूर्णावतारो हरिः।
गोविन्दस्सुरनायकोऽवतु सदा मां नारसिंहं नतम्।।

Lord of the Universe, destroyer of demon Madhu, beacon of Yadu community, preceptor of Gita, giver of Knowledge, cowherd, one who is prayed by Shiva – the destroyer of Love God, beloved of Gopis, one who is filled with tempting charm, Krishna, born in Vrishni lineage, the Final Preceptor with nothing beyond or after, a complete Incarnation, Vishnu, Govinda, leader of Gods — may He always bless me, Narasimha (Rao), who is bowed before Him.

Dedication

This book is humbly dedicated to the lotus feet of three great men from whom I learnt Jyotish:

1. **Sri P. Venkata Subrahmanyachalapathi Rao** (my father and my first guru),
2. **Dr. B. V. Raman** (immortal author who rendered yeoman service to Jyotish), and,
3. **Pt. Sanjay Rath** (author, my guru and founder of "Sri Jagannath Vedic Centre").

My only qualification for writing this book, apart from great enthusiasm to share my little knowledge with others, is the little knowledge I gained from the above three gurus. Whatever flows from my pen (or rather computer keyboard) is due to the knowledge and blessings I received from Mahavishnu and the above three great men. This book really belongs to them and not to me[1].

---

1 But any mistakes in this book are *mine*.

About the author

P.V.R. Narasimha Rao is an engineer by profession. He did his B.Tech in Electrical & Electronics Engineering from Indian Institute of Technology, Madras (1987-1991). He did his masters at Rice University, Houston, US (1991-1993). He works as a software engineer near Boston, USA

He is seriously interested in Jyotish and Sanskrit literature. His academic record includes two diplomas equivalent to Bachelor's degree in Sanskrit at a young age: *Sanskrita Bhaashaa Kovida* diploma from Bharatiya Vidya Bhavan at an age of 10 and *Sanskrita Bhaashaa Visaarada* diploma, with distinction, from a board in Baroda at an age of 11. He is an ardent student of Jyotish and a designated Jyotish Guru at "Sri Jagannath Vedic Centre".

Preface

With the Creator said to be one of its eighteen great preceptors, Jyotish or Vedic astrology is thought to be as old as this creation is. There are many excellent books on Jyotish written in Sanskrit language by great Maharshis and brilliant scholars. Thanks to the yeoman service rendered by Dr. B.V. Raman and the efforts of other Indian astrologers to follow him, today we have a fair amount of Jyotish literature in English language too.

Considering the wealth of Vedic astrology literature in Sanskrit and English, another book may not really be needed. Even if another book is needed, there are many erudite scholars who are better equipped than me to write. Nevertheless, I wanted, like a parrot that enthusiastically repeats the few words learnt by it, to share with fellow students the little knowledge I received from classics and from my gurus.

In this book, I have covered divisional charts, special ascendants, arudhas, argalas, yogas, ashtakavarga, avasthas, a few nakshatra dasas, a few rasi dasas, several techniques of transit analysis, Tajaka analysis and a few miscellaneous topics.

I have tried to give prominence to special ascendants, divisional charts and arudhas, because contemporary literature doesn't seem to give them the kind of importance that Sage Parasara gave. Understanding the primacy Parasara gave to all these concepts is a must for a renaissance in Vedic astrology.

Unfortunately, some people think today that Parasara and Jaimini taught two totally different approaches to astrology. When we talk about arudha padas, argalas, chara karakas, chara dasa and other rasi dasas, people think of them as "Jaimini astrology". People even use terms like "Jaimini karakas" and "Jaimini dasas". However, all these concepts were covered by Parasara also (please read "Brihat Parasara Hora Sastram"). The "Parasari vs Jaimini" distinction is based on unfortunate misconceptions that we can do away with.

In this book, I have de-emphasized these wrong distinctions and emphasized an *integrated* approach – a holistic approach – that looks at Vedic astrology as a whole. I really think that this is the right approach.

In the part on dasas, I covered Vimsottari dasa and Ashtottari dasa, as they are the most commonly used nakshatra dasas. Kalachakra dasa was termed the "most respectable dasa" by Parasara and a discussion on dasas cannot be complete without it. In the galaxy of dasas, rasi dasas taught by Parasara and Jaimini have their own place and I covered two rasi dasas used for timing material success – Lagna Kendradi Rasi dasa and Sudasa. I also covered Narayana dasa, which is the most versatile rasi dasa taught by maharshis. For the spiritually inclined, I included Drigdasa, which can help us in timing events in one's spiritual evolution. Because of the importance of the topic of longevity, I covered two ayur dasas – Shoola dasa and Niryaana Shoola Dasa.

In the part on transits, I covered the interpretation of transits based on the natal positions of planets in rasi chart and divisional charts. I covered some techniques based on ashtakavarga and sodhya pindas. I also covered several techniques related to transits in nakshatras.

In the part on Tajaka, I covered the casting of Tajaka annual, monthly and sixty-hour charts, their interpretation, Tajaka yogas and three dasas used for timing events in Tajaka charts. Some scholars may validly question why Tajaka system is being covered in a book on Vedic astrology. There are no references to it in the works of Parasara, Jaimini and other maharshis. The oldest reference to these techniques to be found in the works of a respected authority on Vedic astrology is in *Tajaka Neelakanthi*, a work by Neelakantha who also wrote a celebrated commentary on "Jaimini Sutras". His coverage of Tajaka system lends some authenticity to the system. One can only *speculate* whether Parasara talked about this system in parts that are possibly missing today. I simply followed the precedent set by illustrious scholars of Vedic astrology, like Neelakantha and Dr. B.V. Raman.

When we rely on finer techniques of Vedic astrology – such as divisional charts and special lagnas – for finer predictions, it is crucial to have an accurate birthtime. The chapter "Impact of Birthtime Error" shows how to cope with birthtime inaccuracies.

While I am upset with the dismissal of astrology by some critics as a 'superstition', I am equally, if not more, upset with the irrational and unscientific attitude of some astrologers. In an effort to promote rational thinking in the astrological community, I included a chapter on "Rational Thinking".

A very brief introduction to some special topics such as remedial measures, mundane astrology and muhurtas is provided in this book and it is hoped that interested readers will pursue these topics further by referring to other textbooks.

Vedic astrology is considered a sacred subject and Maharshi Parasara warned us against sharing this knowledge with unworthy people. Ancient sages laid down some rules for the ethical behavior of a Vedic astrologer. I earnestly hope that all the readers of this book will appreciate those rules.

To that end, I added a chapter on "Ethical Behavior of a Jyotishi".

While no particular topic has been covered in great depth, key fundamentals are covered in this book. Most fundamental concepts and computations are clearly defined with examples and their uses are briefly outlined. But I do not want to bill this as a comprehensive introduction for beginners. There are parts of this book that can be followed even by beginners, but an average beginner may find it overwhelming in many places. For most part, this book is for intermediate level students who already have a good background, but are in need of integrating and consolidating their knowledge. However, there are some points *in some places* that can be appreciated only by advanced scholars. So I will not make any claims on who will find this book useful. Rather than targeting readership with a specific level of knowledge, I tried to write a more or less *self-sufficient* book that covers a *wide spectrum* of topics. Beginners should read this book very carefully, and more than once, to completely understand various concepts. Though I have tried to maintain some level of clarity, I squeezed in a lot of material and beginners should patiently read, re-read and practice.

Due to my background in engineering, I tried to adopt a style somewhat similar to the one used in mathematics and physics textbooks. I tried to be concise and always to the point. I gave plenty of examples and even some exercises. I hope that students will read the material and examples carefully and attempt the exercises sincerely. I hope that the astrological community will accept this new style of astrology teaching.

In this book, I did not try to steer clear of the controversies plaguing Vedic astrology. As my purpose in writing this book is to chronicle my broad understanding of Jyotish in a clear and concise fashion and to give clear guidance to fellow students, I stated my views clearly except in issues in which I do not have a firm opinion.

This book probably contains some fine knowledge, due to the blessings I received from my gurus, and some wrong knowledge as well, due to the limitations of my intelligence. Giving fine knowledge to unworthy students and feeding wrong knowledge to worthy students are both mistakes and I am aware that I may be committing both. I beg for the forgiveness of my gurus, maharshis and gods.

A free computer software program written by me called "Jagannatha Hora Lite" is available for a *free* download on SJVC website (http://www.sjvc.net). It can compute the positions of all planets, upagrahas, lagna, special lagnas, arudha padas and ashtakavarga for twenty divisional charts. It supports several popular ayanamsas. It gives Shadbalas, Vimsottari, Ashtottari and Kalachakra dasas and also gives Tajaka annual charts,

Patyayini dasa, Mudda dasa, Panchavargeeya Bala and Sahams. Those who have a computer with a Microsoft operating system (Windows 95 or later) can download and use this software.

As I devoted most of my free time in the last few years to astrology reading, research and writing, my wife Padmaja, my daughter Sriharini and my son Sriharish made a personal sacrifice and co-operated with my astrological activities. I am thankful to them for their co-operation.

I cannot possibly conclude this preface without expressing my deep gratitude for my guru Pt. Sanjay Rath, who has been a constant source of enlightenment, encouragement and inspiration. I am eternally grateful to him. I express my gratitude to all the elders and well-wishers whose blessings gave me the energy to finish this book. I hope that I will be forgiven for any mistakes and that I will continue to receive their kind blessings. I will always be eager to correct my mistakes.

May Jupiter's light shine on us,

P.V.R. Narasimha Rao

3 Baron Park Lane #13
Burlington, MA 01803 (USA)
e-mail: pvr108@yahoo.com
July 15, 2000 (Guru Pournima)

Contents

Part 1:
Chart Analysis

Several important principles and techniques of chart analysis are explained in this part. This part forms the basis for the rest of the book.

Based on the positions of all the planets at the time of birth, several charts are prepared. They go by the names – "rasi chart" and "divisional charts". Based on the analysis of these charts, several conclusions can be drawn regarding the results that can be given by different planets to the native. This part covers the analysis and judgment of these charts.

It can help if the reader has basic understanding and prior knowledge of Vedic or western astrology, but it is not really required. This part is intended to be self-sufficient. However, bear in mind that extra reading can only do good!

1. Basic Concepts

1.1 What is astrology

Planets in the skies are constantly in motion with respect to earth . The positions of Sun, Moon and some planets close to earth can give important clues about the fortunes of individual human beings and groups of human beings. *That* is the basic premise of astrology. How exactly we can make guesses about the fortunes of individual human beings and groups of human beings based on the positions of those planets in the skies is the question that we will attempt to answer in this book. While astrology is the subject that deals with this question, there are many theories and philosophies in vogue and they are significantly different from each other.

Sunsign astrology, for example, is based on categorizing people into twelve groups based on the solar month of birth. Some people may be convinced, based on their experiences, that people born in the same month share certain qualities. It is, however, not very logical from a rational perspective – there are just too many people in this world, who are totally different from each other. So the month of one's birth is totally inadequate for guessing one's nature or fortune. Even the date and the hour of birth are not enough. We know that there are many **twins** in this world, who are significantly different from each other!

What we mentioned just now is, by the way, a very important question to be answered – it is like an "acid test" for any astrological doctrine. It is a known fact that there are many twins in this world, who are significantly different from each other and who lead totally different lives. Of course, some twins may have some common qualities between them, but the fact remains that several twins are significantly different. An astrological doctrine should be capable of explaining this fact in order to be considered as a meaningful subject.

Most astrological doctrines of the world fail this acid test. If an astrological doctrine assumes, like in the case of many popular astrological theories of the world, that two persons born within a couple of hours in nearby towns will have the same fortune, then that doctrine is obviously lacking in completeness and inadequate for confident use in real-life. It fails the acid test of twins.

1.2 Indian Astrology

Materialistically speaking, India may not be a rich country today, but India has an extremely rich cultural heritage. The depth of some of India's ancient knowledge (like astrology) is just amazing and it makes one wonder if the history of this great civilization is correctly represented in the pages of modern history. Indian Astrology is the most comprehensive and complete system of astrology available today and it is the only one that comes close to answering the just mentioned "twins puzzle". It can explain how twins can be different. The principles used in India's astrology are so sensitive to changes in birthtime that people born within 1-2 minutes can be significantly different in some aspects and similar in some others. This approach distinguishes between what a person truly is, what a person wants to be, what he thinks he is and what the world thinks he is. It has enough parameters, tools, techniques and degrees of freedom to model the extremely complicated human life.

This astrological approach is known in the world by many names. Early pioneers of modern Indian astrology, like Dr. B.V. Raman, called it "Hindu astrology", because this system was first taught by ancient Hindu sages. However, some people do not like this expression because "Hindu" is not a Sanskrit word. This word was later coined by the western invaders from the name of a river flowing on the northwestern border of India (river "Sindhu" or "Indus"). They used the word "Hindu" to describe the land and the people on the eastern side of this river.

The religion practiced by a majority of Indians is known as "Hindu" religion today, but the fact is that there is no name for this religion in India's Sanskrit language, the language in which most of the literature of this religion – and astrology – appeared! Most other religions are known by the name of their main propagator, but India's ancient religion had no single propagator or prophet. This religion consisted of knowledge that revealed itself to spiritual masters of many generations. So there was no name for this religion and the word "Hindu" coined by western invaders was accepted by the world. However, as already stressed, this word finds no place in Sanskrit literature. Some people do not like using a non-Sanskrit word to describe India's astrology, considering that most of India's classical literature in astrology appeared in Sanskrit.

Later day authors came up with the name – "Vedic astrology". The word "Vedic" means "pertaining to Vedas". Vedas are the sacred scriptures of, what is known today as, Hinduism and they are supposed to contain knowledge of *all* subjects. Moreover, astrology in particular is supposed to be a "Vedaanga" (which means a limb of Vedas). In particular, it is said to be the eye of the Vedas. So the name "Vedic astrology" is becoming popular these days. This author also suggests using "Vedic astrology" or "Jyotish" (meaning "science of light"). Jyotishi is a practitioner of Jyotish, *i.e.* a Vedic astrologer.

1.3 Basics

1.3.1 *Grahas (planets)*

The words "planet" and "star" are used in a slightly different sense in astrology than in astronomy. For example, Sun (a star) and Moon (a satellite of earth) are called planets in astrology, along with Mars etc. Basically, a *graha* or a planet is a body that has considerable influence on the living beings on earth. Distant stars have negligible influence on us, but Sun, Moon and planets in the solar system have a great influence on our activities. So the word *graha* (or planet) is used to describe them.

Seven planets are considered in Indian astrology. They are – **Sun, Moon, Mars, Mercury, Jupiter, Venus** and **Saturn**. In addition, two "chaayaa grahas" (shadow planets) are considered in Indian astrology – **Rahu** and **Ketu**. These are also called "the north node" and "the south node" respectively (or the head and tail of dragon). Rahu and Ketu are not real planets; they are just some mathematical points.

Apart from these 9 planets, there are 11 moving *mathematical points* known as **Upagrahas** (sub-planets or satellites). We also have **lagna** (ascendant), which is the point that rises on the eastern horizon as the earth rotates around itself. In addition, we have some mathematical points known as "**special ascendants**".

1.3.2 *Rasis (signs)*

The positions of all these planets, upagrahas, lagna and special lagnas in the zodiac are measured in degrees, minutes and seconds from the start of the zodiac (which is a fixed point in the sky). These positions are measured as seen from earth and they are called "geocentric positions". For the positions (calculated in degrees, minutes and seconds) of planets, lagna, special lagnas and upagrahas, we also use the words **longitude** and **sphuta**. When watched from earth, the longitude of any planet in the skies can be from 0°0'0" (0 degrees 0 minutes 0 seconds) to 359°59'59". It should be noted that 0°0'0" corresponds to the beginning of the zodiac. Many western astrologers consider *Sayana* or tropical (moving) zodiac, whereas *Nirayana* or sidereal (fixed) zodiac is considered in Vedic astrology.

The zodiac (sky) lasts 360° as mentioned above and it is divided into 12 equal parts. They are called "**rasis**" (signs). English names, Sanskrit names, two-letter symbols and values of the start longitude and the end longitude (in degrees, minutes and seconds) of all twelve rasis are given in Table 1.

Table 1: Definition of Rasis

Rasi name	Sanskrit name	Symbol	Start	End
Aries	Mesha	Ar	0°0'0"	29°59'59"
Taurus	Vrishabha/Vrisha	Ta	30°0'0"	59°59'59"
Gemini	Mithuna	Ge	60°0'0"	89°59'59"
Cancer	Karkataka/Karka	Cn	90°0'0"	119°59'59"
Leo	Simha	Le	120°0'0"	149°59'59"
Virgo	Kanya	Vi	150°0'0"	179°59'59"
Libra	Tula	Li	180°0'0"	209°59'59"
Scorpio	Vrischika	Sc	210°0'0"	239°59'59"
Sagittarius	Dhanus	Sg	240°0'0"	269°59'59"
Capricorn	Makara	Cp	270°0'0"	299°59'59"
Aquarius	Kumbha	Aq	300°0'0"	329°59'59"
Pisces	Meena	Pi	330°0'0"	359°59'59"

Notation: If a planet is at 221°37', then you can find from Table 1 that it is between 210°0'0'' and 239°59'59''. So, that planet is in Scorpio (or Vrischika). Its advancement from the start of the rasi occupied by is 11°37'. Its position in the zodiac (221°37') is shown by some people by the notation **11°37' in Sc** or simply **11 Sc 37**. This means "advanced by 11°37' from the start of Sc (Scorpio)". Some people show it as **7s 11° 37'**. This means "after completing 7 signs, advanced by 11°37' in the 8th sign (which is Scorpio)".

Exercise 1:

Jupiter is at 94°19'. Mercury is at 5s 17° 45'. Venus is at 25 Li 31. For each of these planets, find (*a*) the rasi occupied and (*b*) the advancement from the start of the rasi occupied

Each rasi again has many kinds of divisions and they are called "**vargas**". They will be defined in detail later.

1.3.3 *Bhavas (houses)*

Another important concept is "**house**" (Sanskrit name: **bhava**). In each chart, houses can be found with respect to several *reference points* and the reference points most commonly employed are lagna and special lagnas. Starting from the rasi occupied by the selected reference point and proceeding in the regular order across the zodiac, we associate each rasi with a house (first, second *etc*). Always the rasi containing the reference point chosen is the 1st house. Next rasi is the 2nd house. The rasi after that is the 3rd house.

We proceed until the 12th house like that. Just remember that when we encounter Pisces, we go to Aries after it. If no reference point is specified when houses are mentioned, it means that **lagna** is used as the reference.

If, for example, horalagna is in Cn, first house with respect to horalagna is in Cn. Second house is in Le (see Table 1). Third house is in Vi. Ninth house is in Pi. Tenth house is in Ar. Eleventh house is in Ta. Twelfth house is in Ge.

Exercise 2:

---

(1) Lagna is in Cn, Sun is in Ar, Moon is in Ta and Mars is in Cp. Find the houses occupied by Sun, Moon and Mars.

---

(2) Repeat the exercise, taking Moon as the reference point when finding houses.

Different houses stand for different matters. Looking at the rasis and houses occupied by various planets, we can say a lot of things about the person. How exactly this is done will become clear in the coming chapters.

1.3.4 *Chakras (charts)*

A "**chart**" (Sanskrit name: **chakra**) is prepared with the information of rasis occupied by all planets. For preparing any chart, we need to first determine the rasis occupied by all planets, upagrahas, lagna and special lagnas. In the visual representation of a chart, there are 12 boxes (and some other visual areas) with each representing a rasi. All planets, upagrahas and lagnas are written in the boxes corresponding to the rasis they occupy.

There are 3 popular ways of drawing charts in India: (1) South Indian style chart ruled by Jupiter, (2) North Indian style diamond chart ruled by Venus and (3) East Indian style Sun chart ruled by Sun. In this book, all the charts will be given in formats (1) and (2).

Out of the three chart formats, (1) and (3) are rasi-based and (2) is bhava-based. In rasi-based chart drawing formats, a rasi is always at a fixed position. Ar is always in one particular position and Ta is in another position and so on. Planets, lagna etc are placed in the box (or the visual area) representing the rasi occupied by it. In bhava-based chart drawing formats, a bhava (house) is always at a fixed position. Lagna (denoted by "Asc" for ascendant) is always in a particular visual area of the chart and the 2nd, 3rd etc houses are in fixed positions.

Example 1: Let us take Lord Sree Rama's rasi chart. The rasis occupied by planets and lagna are given below.

Ar – Sun; Ta – Mercury; Ge – Ketu; Cn – Ascendant (lagna), Moon & Jupiter; Li – Saturn; Sg – Rahu; Cp – Mars; Pi – Venus.

Figure 1: Indian Chart Styles

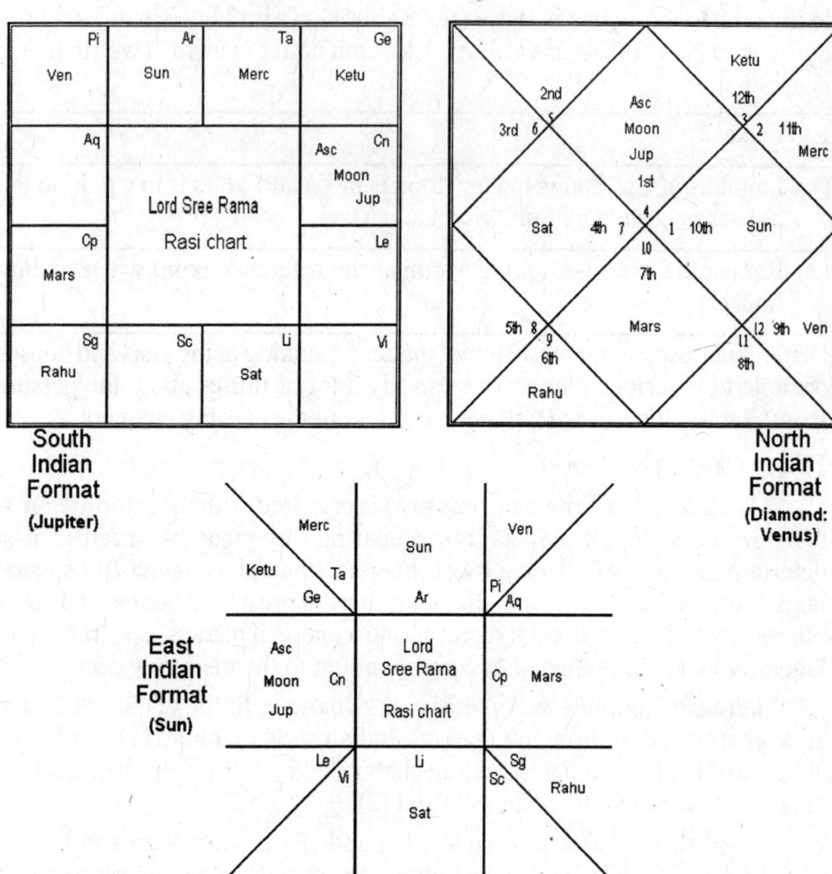

Rasi chart for the above data is drawn in South Indian, North Indian and East Indian formats in Figure 1. In the South Indian chart, notice the boxes containing Ar, Ta, Ge etc. In this format, these rasis will always be in the same positions. The same holds for the East Indian format. The North Indian format is different. Note the box containing "Asc" (ascendant – lagna). The same box will show the house containing lagna in all north Indian format charts. It may be Ar in one chart, Ta in another and Ge in yet another. The number corresponding to the rasi (1 for Ar, 2 for Ta, 3 for Ge and so on) is shown in the box. For example, the box with "Asc" has 4 in it and it shows Cn. So the 1st house is in Cn. Please note the order in which houses are visually arranged in this chart. The same pattern will be used in all charts.

NOTE: Some people draw the east Indian format charts with an enclosing rectangle.

1.3.5 *Varga chakras (divisional charts)*

We saw that charts can be drawn with the information of which planet occupies which rasi. Based on the longitude of a planet, we can find the rasi occupied by it and mark its position in rasi chart.

In addition, we have what are known as "divisional charts" (Sanskrit name: varga chakras). These are based on dividing rasis into 2 parts, 3 parts, 4 parts and so on. We divide each rasi into *n* parts and map each part to a rasi again. Based on the rasis occupied by planets in these divisional mappings, we draw divisional charts (or harmonic charts). Each divisional chart throws light on a specific area of one's life. In each divisional chart, we find houses and analyze the chart as if it were an independent chart. The science of Vedic astrology stands on the basis of 4 pillars – (1) *grahas* or planets, (2) *rasis* or signs, (3) *bhavas* or houses, and, (4) *varga chakras* or divisional charts.

1.3.6 *Nakshatras (constellations)*

In Vedic astrology, the zodiac is divided into 27 nakshatras. Each nakshatra has a length of 360°/27 = 13° 20'. The first nakshatra, for example, stretches from the beginning of Aries to 13° 20' in Aries. The second nakshatra stretches from there to 26° 40' in Aries. The third nakshatra stretches from there to 10° in Taurus. The list of nakshatras with the respective starting and ending points is given in Table 2. The table also gives the "Vimsottari lords" of all nakshatras. This will be used later.

Each nakshatra is again divided into 4 quarters. They are called padas (legs/feet). The length of a nakshatra pada is 3° 20'.

Table 2: Nakshatras

Name of Nakshatra	Starts at	Ends at	Vimsottari Lord	Ruling Deity
Aswini	00 Ar 00	13 Ar 20	Ketu	Aswini Kumara
Bharani	13 Ar 20	26 Ar 40	Venus	Yama
Krittika	26 Ar 40	10 Ta 00	Sun	Agni
Rohini	10 Ta 00	23 Ta 20	Moon	Bramha
Mrigasira	23 Ta 20	6 Ge 40	Mars	Moon
Aardra	6 Ge 40	20 Ge 00	Rahu	Shiva
Punarvasu	20 Ge 00	03 Cn 20	Jupiter	Aditi
Pushyami	03 Cn 20	16 Cn 40	Saturn	Jupiter
Aasresha	16 Cn 40	30 Cn 00	Mercury	Rahu
Makha	00 Le 00	13 Le 20	Ketu	Sun
Poorva Phalguni	13 Le 20	26 Le 40	Venus	Aryaman
Uttara Phalguni	26 Le 40	10 Vi 00	Sun	Sun
Hasta	10 Vi 00	23 Vi 20	Moon	Viswakarma
Chitra	23 Vi 20	6 Li 40	Mars	Vaayu
Swaati	6 Li 40	20 Li 00	Rahu	Indra
Visaakha	20 Li 00	03 Sc 20	Jupiter	Mitra
Anooraadha	03 Sc 20	16 Sc 40	Saturn	Indra
Jyeshtha	16 Sc 40	30 Sc 00	Mercury	Nirriti
Moola	00 Sg 00	13 Sg 20	Ketu	Varuna
Poorvaashaadha	13 Sg 20	26 Sg 40	Venus	Viswadeva
Uttaraashaadha	26 Sg 40	10 Cp 00	Sun	Brahma
Sravanam	10 Cp 00	23 Cp 20	Moon	Vishnu
Dhanishtha	23 Cp 20	6 Aq 40	Mars	Vasu
Satabhishak	6 Aq 40	20 Aq 00	Rahu	Varuna
Poorvaabhaadra	20 Aq 00	03 Pi 20	Jupiter	Ajacharana
Uttaraabhaadra	03 Pi 20	16 Pi 40	Saturn	Ahirbudhanya
Revati	16 Pi 40	30 Pi 00	Mercury	Pooshan

For the purpose of some special charts like Kota Chakra and Sarvatobhadra Chakra, we consider 28 nakshatras. The last quarter of Uttarashadha is known as "Abhijit". However, we consider 27 nakshatras for all other purposes.

1.3.7 *Solar Calendar*

In solar calendar, one year is the time in which Sun moves by 360° and one month is the time in which Sun moves by 30°. These are called "solar year" and "solar month" respectively. Each solar month has 30 days, where one day stands for exactly 1° motion of Sun). This calendar will be used in dasas and in Tajaka analysis.

1.3.8 *Tithis and Lunar Calendar*

1.3.8.1 Tithis

In lunar calendar, one day stands for one tithi. Tithi or lunar day is a period in which the difference between the longitudes of Moon and Sun changes by exactly 12°.

Table 3: Names of Tithis

Sukla/Suddha Paksha (brighter fortnight)	Krishna/ Bahula Paksha (darker fortnight)	Name of tithi	Planet (Lord)
1st	16th	Pratipat/Pratipada/Padyami	Sun
2nd	17th	Dwitiya/Vidiya	Moon
3rd	18th	Tritiya/Tadiya	Mars
4th	19th	Chaturthi/Chaviti/Chauth	Mercury
5th	20th	Panchami	Jupiter
6th	21st	Shashti	Venus
7th	22nd	Saptami	Saturn
8th	23rd	Ashtami	Rahu
9th	24th	Navami	Sun
10th	25th	Dasami	Moon
11th	26th	Ekadasi	Mars
12th	27th	Dwadasi	Mercury
13th	28th	Trayodasi	Jupiter
14th	29th	Chaturdasi	Venus
15th	—	Paurnami/Paurnimasya/ Poornima (Full Moon)	Saturn
—	30th	Amavasya (New Moon)	Rahu

When Sun and Moon are at the same longitude, a new lunar month of 30 tithis starts. As time progresses, Moon will go ahead of Sun. When Moon's longitude is exactly 12° greater than Sun's longitude, the first tithi or lunar day finishes and the second tithi starts. When Moon's longitude is exactly 24° greater than Sun's longitude, the second tithi finishes and the third tithi starts. When Moon's longitude is exactly 36° greater than Sun's longitude, the third tithi finishes and the fourth tithi starts. And so on. You can see that Sun-Moon longitude differential will be $(12 \times n)°$ after exactly n tithis.

A lunar month consists of 30 tithis. Each month is divided into two fortnights (*pakshas*). During Sukla/Suddha paksha or the brighter fortnight, Moon is waxing. During this paksha, Moon is ahead of Sun by an amount that is between 0° and 180°. During Krishna/Bahula paksha or the darker fortnight, Moon is waning. During this paksha, Moon is ahead of Sun by an amount that is between 180° and 360°.

At the end of a month, Sun-Moon longitude differential will be (12 x 30)°, *i.e.*, 360°. That means that Moon will finish one cycle around the zodiac and catch up with Sun again. So Sun and Moon will be at the same longitude again. Then a new month starts.

We can find the tithi running on a day from the longitudes of Sun and Moon using the following procedure.

(1) Find the difference: (Moon's longitude – Sun's longitude). Add 360° if the result is negative. The result will be between 0° and 360° and will show how advanced Moon is with respect to Sun.

(2) Divide this result by 12°. Ignore the remainder and take the quotient.

(3) Add 1 to the quotient. You get a number from 1 to 30. That will give the index of the tithi running.

(4) Refer to Table 3 and find the name of the tithi. There are 15 tithis and the same tithis repeat in the brigher and darker fortnights. For example, it can be seen from the table that the 22th tithi out of the 30 tithis is in Krishna paksha and it is Saptami. So the 22nd tithi is "Krishna Saptami". We write the classification of fortnight (Sukla or Krishna) first and then write tithi name. "Sukla Saptami" stands for "Saptami" in the brighter fortnight (sukla paksha), *i.e.* the 7th tithi. "Krishna Saptami" stands for "Saptami" in the darker fortnight (krishna paksha), *i.e.* the 22nd tithi.

Example 2:

Let us say that Moon is at 24°12' in Gemini. This is (2 x 30°) + 24° 12' = 84° 12' from the beginning of the zodiac.

Let us say that Sun is at 17°46' in Scorpio. This is (7 x 30°) + 17° 46' = 227° 46' from the beginning of the zodiac.

Moon – Sun = 84° 12' – 227° 46' = –(143° 34'). It is negative because Sun is at a higher longitude. We have to add 360° to it to make it positive. It becomes 216° 26'. So this is the advancement of Moon with respect to Sun.

Converting this to a decimal number, we get 216.43°. We have to divide it by 12°. We find 216.43 ÷ 12 and the quotient is 18. So 18 tithis are over.

Adding 1 to it, we get 19 and so the 19th tithi is running. Referring to Table 3, we see that this is "Chaturthi" tithi of Krishna paksha (darker fortnight). So it is "Krishna Chaturthi".

Exercise 3: Moon is at 14°43' in Leo. Sun is at 28°13' in Capricorn. Find the running tithi.

1.3.8.2 Lunar Months

We said that a new lunar month starts whenever Sun and Moon are at the same longitude. Then Moon will go ahead of Sun and, after about 29-30 days, he will catch up with Sun again. A new lunar month will start again.

These lunar months go by special names. The name of a lunar month is decided by the rasi in which Sun-Moon conjunction[2] takes place. If Sun-Moon conjoin in Pisces, for example, it starts Chaitra maasa. These names come from the constellation that Moon is most likely to occupy on the full Moon day. In the month that starts when Sun and Moon conjoin in Pisces, Moon is likely to be in Chitra constellation (23°20' in Virgo to 6°40' in Libra) on the full Moon day (15th tithi – Pournimasya). So the month is called Chaitra.

Table 4: Lunar Months

Rasi of Sun-Moon conjunction that starts the month	Name of the month	Most likely constellation of Full Moon	Approx when?
Pisces	Chaitra	Chitra	Mar/Apr
Aries	Vaisaakha	Visaakha	Apr/May
Taurus	Jyeshtha	Jyeshtha	May/June
Gemini	Aashaadha	Poorva/Uttara Aashaadha	June/July
Cancer	Sraavana	Sravana	July/Aug
Leo	Bhaadrapada	Poorva/Uttara Bhadrapada	Aug/Sept
Virgo	Aaswayuja	Aswini	Sept/Oct
Libra	Kaarteeka	Krittika	Oct/Nov
Scorpio	Maargasira	Mrigasira	Nov/Dec
Sagittarius	Pushya	Pushyami	Dec/Jan
Capricorn	Maagha	Makha	Jan/Feb
Aquarius	Phaalguna	Poorva/Uttara Phalguni	Feb/Mar

---

2 Two planets are said to be in "conjunction" if they are exactly at the same longitude.
NOTE: However, we sometimes use this term approximately. If two planets are in the same sign, but not exactly at the same longitude, we still say that they are in conjunction.

A solar year has about 365.2425 days, but a lunar year only has about 355 days. Once in every 3 years, this difference accumulates to one month and an extra lunar month comes. This results in Sun-Moon conjunction coming twice in the same rasi. For example, Sun-Moon conjunction took place at 0°23' in Taurus on May 15, 1999 at 5:35:32 pm (IST) and again at 28°29' in Taurus on June 14, 1999 at 12:33:27 am (IST). Sun-Moon conjunction in Taurus starts Jyeshtha maasa (maasa = month) as per Table 4. So 1999 had 2 Jyeshtha maasas. One is called "Nija" Jeshtha maasa and the other is called "Adhika" Jyeshtha maasa. Nija means real and adhika means extra. An adhika maasa (extra month) comes once in every 3 years and that synchronizes the lunar years with solar years. This calendar has been in use in India for millennia.

1.3.9 *Yogas*

Add the longitudes of Sun and Moon. Remove 360° from the sum if it is greater than 360°. Divide the sum by the length of one nakshatra (13°20' or 800'). Ignore fractions and take the integer part. Add 1 to it and the result is the index of the yoga running. Refer to Table 5 and find the yoga corresponding to the index.

Table 5: Sun-Moon Yogas

Index	Yoga	Meaning
1	Vishkambha	Door bolt/supporting pillar
2	Preeti	Love/affection
3	Aayushmaan	Long-lived
4	Saubhaagya	Long life of spouse (good fortune)
5	Sobhana	Splendid, bright
6	Atiganda	Great danger
7	Sukarman	One with good deeds
8	Dhriti	Firmness
9	Shoola	Shiva's weapon of destruction (pain)
10	Ganda	Danger
11	Vriddhi	Growth
12	Dhruva	Fixed, constant
13	Vyaaghaata	Great blow
14	Harshana	Cheerful
15	Vajra	Diamond (strong)
16	Siddhi	Accomplishment
17	Vyatipaata	Great fall

Index	Yoga	Meaning
18	Variyan	Chief/best
19	Parigha	Obstacle/hindrance
20	Shiva	Lord Shiva (purity)
21	Siddha	Accomplished/ready
22	Saadhya	Possible
23	Subha	Auspicious
24	Sukḷa	White, bright
25	Brahma	Creator (good knowledge and purity)
26	Indra	Ruler of gods
27	Vaidhriti	A class of gods

Example 3: Suppose Sun is at 23°50' in Cp and Moon is at 17°20' in Li. Then Sun's longitude is 23°50' + 9 x 30° = 293°50' and Moon's longitude is 17°20' + 6x 30° = 197°20'. The sum is 293°50' + 197°20' = 491°10'. By subtracting 360°, we get 131°10'. This is equivalent to 131 x 60 + 10 = 7870'. By dividing this with 800', we get 9.8375. Ignoring the fraction, we get 9. Adding 1 to it, we get 10. From Table 5, we see that the 10th yoga is "Ganda yoga".

Exercise 4: Moon is at 14°43' in Leo. Sun is at 28°13' in Capricorn. Find the running Sun-Moon yoga.

1.3.10 *Karanas*

Each tithi is divided into 2 karanas. There are 11 karaṇas: (1) Bava, (2) Balava, (3) Kaulava, (4) Taitula, (5) Garija, (6) Vanija, (7) Vishti, (8) Sakuna, (9) Chatushpada, (10) Naga, and, (11) Kimstughna. The first 7 karanas repeat 8 times starting from the 2nd half of the first lunar day of a month. The last 4 karanas come just once in a month, starting from the 2nd half of the 29th lunar day and ending at the 1st half of the first lunar day.

1.3.11 *Hora*

Each day starts at sunrise and ends at next day's sunrise. This period is divided into 24 equal parts and they are called horas. A hora is almost equal to an hour. These horas are ruled by different planets. The lords of hora come in the order of decreasing speed with respect to earth: Saturn, Jupiter, Mars, Sun, Venus, Mercury and Moon. After Moon, we go back to Saturn and repeat the 7 planets.

The first hora of any day (*i.e.* a period of one hour following sunrise) is ruled by the lord of the weekday (Sun for Sunday, Moon for Monday, Mars for Tuesday, Mercury for Wednesday, Jupiter for Thursday, Venus for Friday and Saturn for Saturday). After that, we list planets in the order mentioned above.

For example, let us take 9:40 pm on a Wednesday on which sunrise was at 6:10 am. The time elapsed since sunrise is 21:40 – 6:10 = 15:30. So the 16th hour since sunrise was running then. This is ruled by the 16th planet from Mercury. After subtracting multiples of 7 from 16, we get 2. So the hora (hour) is ruled by the 2nd planet from Mercury. From the list given above, we see that the 2nd planet from Mercury is Moon. So Moon's hora runs at 9:40 pm.

1.3.12 *Panchaanga*

Panchaanga means "one with 5 limbs". Almanacs published in India with planetary positions are traditionally called panchaangas. Along with the planetary positions, they give the start and end times of tithi, vaara (week day – Sunday, Monday *etc*), nakshatra, yoga and karana running on each day. These five are the limbs of panchaanga.

When we choose a muhurta (an auspicious time for starting a venture), we should choose an auspicious tithi, vaara, nakshatra, yoga and karana.

1.3.13 *Ayanamsa*

Because of the movement in earth's precession, the starting point of the tropical zodiac changes slowly (with respect to fixed stars). Tropical (sayana) zodiac is analogous to measuring the positions of trees and buildings sitting in a slowly moving bus. Sidereal (nirayana) zodiac, on the other hand, considers a fixed zodiac. It considers the motion of the tropical zodiac (bus in our analogy) and makes an adjustment accordingly. We use the sidereal zodiac in Vedic astrology. The difference between the tropical zodiac and the sidereal zodiac is of great importance. What modern ephemeris gives us is the tropical positions of planets. To convert these positions, we have to subtract the difference between the two zodiacs. This difference varies with time. As earth's precession changes every year, the difference between the tropical zodiac and the sidereal zodiac changes. This difference is called "ayanamsa" (sidereal difference). There are many opinions on the correct value of ayanamsa, because nobody knows exactly which star is supposed to be the starting point of the real zodiac. We will use Chitrapaksha/Lahiri ayanamsa in this book, which is accepted by most Vedic astrologers of India.

1.4 Dasa Systems

Dasa systems are a hallmark of Vedic astrology. Vedic astrology has hundreds of dasa system. Each dasa system divides one's life into periods, sub-periods, sub-sub-periods and so on. All the periods are *ruled* by different planets or rasis. Some dasa systems are planet-based and some are rasi-based. Each dasa system is good at showing events of a specific nature. For each dasa system, we have some standard rules, based on which we analyze the natal chart and attribute different results to different periods and sub-periods. Each dasa system comes with rules for dividing one's life into periods and sub-periods and rules for attributing different results to different periods, based on the planetary positions in the natal chart. These periods are called "dasas" or "mahadasas" (MD). Sub-periods are called "antardasas" (AD). Sub-sub-periods are called "pratyantardasas" (PD).

Some dasas are good at showing matters related to longevity and death. They are called "ayur dasas" (dasas of longevity). Some dasas are good at showing general results. They are called "phalita dasas" (dasas of general results).

Mind is a very important part of our existence and Moon governs it. Some dasas are computed based on the nakshatra occupied by Moon and they are called "nakshatra dasas". Some dasas are based on the rasis occupied by planets and they are called "rasi dasas".

We will learn 10 different dasa systems in this book. Readers should not look at these 10 dasas as ten different alternatives to look at the same life event. They should instead be looked at as ways to look at 10 different aspects of the same life event. In fact, some of the dasas taught in this book are limited to specific matters. For example, we should look at Drigdasa for spiritual progress and we should look at Sudasa for money and wealth. Like that, some dasas are limited to specific matters.

1.5 Conclusion

The content of this chapter may be too rudimentary for most readers. However, for beginners, it may be confusing.

The content of the first several chapters of this book may seem to be disjoint, but things will fall in place as we go on. Readers should patiently go through the material in the order presented. One has to work hard on the basics. Once the basics are clear, Vedic astrology is a very systematic subject.

Some Western astrologers mix Western astrology with Vedic astrology and bring in progressions, extra-Saturnine planets etc into Vedic astrology. It is silly to suggest that the Sages who taught such brilliant and superfine techniques did not consider some planets because they did not know about them. Vedic astrology is a very logical and systematic subject and **there is no need to corrupt it**. There are some techniques of western astrology that are not used by most contemporary Vedic astrologers but were taught by seers. We can accept those techniques. An example is progressions. They were not taught by Parasara, but they were taught by Manu. So we can accept them. But the use of Uranus, Neptune and Pluto were not taught by any seers of Vedic astrology. We should first strive to clearly understand the teachings of maharshis. There is a lot of width and depth in the knowledge taught by maharshis. Our focus should be on understanding their teachings correctly and *not* on adding new things to the knowledge that we only superficially understand.

Western astrologers reading this book may have to *unlearn* some things they learnt before, as they read this book.

1.6 Answers to Exercises

Exercise 1: Jupiter: (*a*) Cancer and (*b*) 4°19'. Mercury: (*a*) Virgo and (*b*) 17°45'. Venus: (*a*) Libra and (*b*) 25°31'.

Exercise 2: (1) No reference is mentioned. So reference is lagna (Cn). Sun in Ar: 10th house. Moon in Ta: 11th house. Mars in Cp: 7th house.

(2) Sun: 12th house. Moon: 1st house. Mars: 9th house.

Exercise 3: Krishna Dwitiya (17th tithi or the 2nd tithi in the darker fortnight).

Exercise 4: Atiganda yoga.

2. Rasis

2.1 Introduction

We learnt that the zodiac of 360° is divided into 12 equal parts of 30°. We learnt these are called rasis (signs). We learnt the definition of rasis in Table 1. Different rasis have different properties and they stand for different things. We will learn them in this small chapter.

2.2 Characteristics of Rasis

2.2.1 *Limbs of Vishnu*

The whole zodiac is nothing but a manifestation of Lord Vishnu's body. Aries is the head. Taurus is the face. Gemini is the arms. Cancer is the heart. Leo is the stomach. Virgo is the hip. Libra is the space below navel. Scorpio is the private parts. Sagittarius is the thighs. Capricorn is the knees. Aquarius is the ankles. Pisces is the feet.

These are the limbs that rasis in the natural zodiac stand for. Because we are all part of the Supreme energy governing this world, the above mapping applies to us too. For example, we should pay attention to Leo for analyzing stomach problems and to Pisces for analyzing problems related to feet and so on.

2.2.2 *Odd and Even*

(1) Ar, Ge, Le, Li, Sg and Aq are called *odd* rasis or *vishama* rasis or *oja* rasis. They are also known as *male* rasis.

(2) Ta, Cn, Vi, Sc, Cp and Pi are called *even* rasis or *sama* rasis or *yugma* rasis. They are also known as *female* rasis.

This division is used in some dasas and in the determination of the sex of children.

2.2.3 *Odd-footed and Even-footed*

(1) Ar, Ta, Ge, Li, Sc and Sg are called *odd-footed* rasis or *vishamapada* rasis or *ojapada* rasis.

(2) Cn, Le, Vi, Cp, Aq and Pi are called *even-footed* rasis or *samapada* rasis or or *yugmapada* rasis.

This division is used in some dasas.

2.2.4 *Movable, Fixed and Dual*

(1) Ar, Cn, Li and Cp are known as *chara* rasis or *movable* rasis. They are ruled by Brahma, the Creator. Their nature is to move and to be dynamic.

(2) Ta, Le, Sc and Aq are known as *sthira* rasis or *fixed* rasis. They are ruled by Shiva, the Destroyer. Their nature is to be stable and constant.

(3) Ge, Vi, Sg and Pi are known as *dwiswabhava* rasis or *dual* rasis. They are ruled by Vishnu, the Sustainer.[3] They are stable sometimes and dynamic sometimes.

2.2.5 *Rasis & Five Elements*

According to Hindu philosophy, this world is made up of five elements – fire, water, air, earth and ether. Water is a substance with a flexible state. Air is a substance with a varying state. Earth is a substance with a constant and solid state. Fire is a substance that transforms the state of things. Ether is something that is present everywhere.

For example, suppose one has a good memory and remembers something he learnt 10 years back. It involves a skill of earthy nature. Suppose a poet's imagination creates a nice poem that appeals to one's aesthetic sense. This involves watery skills. Suppose one is in a bad mood and his mind is wandering aimlessly. This shows airy state of the mind. These 5 elements are behind every material substance, every action, every thought, every emotion and every happening in this universe.

(1) Ar, Le and Sg are called *agni* rasis or *fiery* rasis.

(2) Ta, Vi and Cp are called *bhoo* rasis or *earthy* rasis.

(3) Ge, Li and Aq are called *vaayu* rasis or *airy* rasis.

(4) Cn, Sc and Pi are called *jala* rasis or *watery* rasis.

(5) The 5th element of *aakaasa* or *ether* is present in every rasi.

Let us see how these may be used. For example, the 5th house in one's chart shows one's emotional nature. The 5th house in a fiery sign may show a normally angry, aggressive or determined person. The 5th house in an earthy sign may show a balanced, logical and stable person. The 5th house in an airy sign may show someone with unstable and wandering emotions. The 5th house in a watery sign may show one with an imaginative and creative mind.

2.2.6 *Pitta, Vaata and Kapha*

Ayurveda is India's Vedic medical system that recognizes human body and everything else in the universe as having 3 natures that are formed with the above 5 elements:

Pitta or *bilious* nature is a combination of the elements of fire and

---

3 Brahma, Vishnu and Shiva together form the Trinity of Hindu Gods. Brahma creates the world. Vishnu sustains it. Shiva destroys it.

water. It shows things that result in tranformation in a system. In a human body, for example, it may show digestion *etc*.

Vaata or *windy* nature is a combination of the elements of air and ether. It shows things that move in and out of a system. In a human body, for example, it may show breathing *etc*.

Kapha or *phlegmatic* nature is a combination of the elements of earth and water. It shows things that bind a system together. In a human body, for example, it may show bones, muscles, fat *etc*. It shows things that give a structure to a system.

Ar, Le and Sg are of pitta nature. Ta, Vi and Cp are of vaata nature. Cn, Sc and Pi are of kapha nature. Ge, Li and Aq are of a mixed nature.

2.2.7 *Sattwa, Rajas and Tamas*

In Hindu philosophy, everything in this universe has one of 3 gunas (qualities). They are called trigunas. *Sattwa* (purity) is a quality that gives truthfulness and purity. *Rajas* or *rajo* guna (energy) is a quality that makes one energetic and passionate. *Tamas* or *tamo* guna (darkness) is a quality that makes one depraved.

As an example, let us say a saint is living in a small hermitage. Let us say a man living in a local forest comes, makes fun of the saint and abuses him for no reason. Let us say a king fights with that man after finding out about this. Let us say that the saint tells him to leave the man and yet the king punishes him.

The saint shows sattva guna and he is not bothered by petty things. He ignores the abuse. He is a pure person. The man abusing the saint for no reason shows tamo guna, as he is in the dark. Abusing a saattwik person for no reason is a pathetic thing to do and only a depraved person in darkness can do it. The king acts appropriately and shows his energy by defeating the man. So far it is sattwa guna (the state of being true). But the king punishes the man ignoring the advice of the saint to forgive him. His passionate response makes him a person with rajo guna.

(1) Saattwik signs, *i.e.* signs with sattwa guna, are – Cn, Le, Sg, Pi.

(2) Raajasik signs, *i.e.* signs with rajo guna, are – Ar, Ta, Li, Sc.

(3) Taamasik signs, *i.e.* signs with tamo guna, are – Ge, Vi, Cp, Aq.

2.2.8 *Rasis and Directions*

(1) Ar, Le and Sg show east.
(2) Ta, Vi and Cp show south.
(3) Ge, Li and Aq show west.
(4) Cn, Sc and Pi show north.

2.2.9 *Rasis and Colors*

Ar shows blood-red color. Ta shows white. Ge shows grass green. Cn shows pale red. Le shows white. Virgo is variegated. Libra shows black. Scorpio shows reddish brown. Sagittarius shows the color of the husk of grass. Capricorn is variegated. Aquarius shows brown color (that of a mongoose). Pisces shows cream color or the color of fish.

2.2.10 *Day and Night*

(1) Ar, Ta, Ge, Cn, Sg and Cp are *night time* rasis – they are strong during the night time. They are *nishaa* rasis.

(2) Le, Vi, Li, Sc, Aq and Pi are *day time* rasis – they are strong during the day time. They are *divaa* rasis.

Out of the two rasis owned by a planet, one is a day sign and one is a night sign. Moon governs all the nishaa rasis and Sun governs all the divaa rasis.

2.2.11 *Rising of rasis*

Some rasis rise with their head. They are called "Seershodaya rasis". Some rasis rise with their feet[4]. They are called "Prishthodaya rasis".

(1) Ge, Le, Vi, Li, Sc, Aq are Seershodaya rasis.

(2) Ar, Ta, Cn, Sg, Cp are Prishthodaya rasis.

(3) Pi rises with both its head and feet.

It is said that planets in Seershodaya rasis give their results in the first half of their dasas and planets in Prishthodaya rasis give their results in the second half of their dasas.

2.2.12 *Varna or Class*

In Hinduism, people are divided into 4 *varnas* or classes – (1) Brahmanas, (2) Kshatriyas, (3) Vaisyas and (4) Sudras. Brahmanas pursue knowledge and work as priests or ministers. Kshatriyas are valiant and they become kings, army chiefs and soldiers. Vaisyas are the traders and suppliers of various services. Sudras execute various menial tasks.

(1) Brahmanas (scholars) are represented by watery signs – Cn, Sc, Pi.

(2) Kshatriyas (warriors) are represented by fiery signs – Ar, Le, Sg.

(3) Vaisyas (traders) are represented by earthy signs – Ta, Vi, Cp.

(4) Sudras (workers) are represented by airy signs – Ge, Li, Aq.

---

4 Many scholars have interpreted "prishthodaya" as "rising with the feet". So we will use the same interpretation. However, strictly speaking, one should note that "prishtha" means "back".

2.3 Indications of Rasis

Aries: Dynamic, enterprising, valiant, ruddy, head, forests, large forehead, hasty, impulsive, restless, thick eyebrows, leadership, overbearing, dry, lean, tall.

Taurus: Beautiful, face, stable, sluggish, loyal, meadows, plains, luxury halls, dining halls, eating places, fine teeth, large eyes, luxurious, faithful, thick hair, stout.

Gemini: Chest, garden, communication, journalism, schools, colleges, study rooms, cables, telephone, newspapers, tall, well-built, prominent cheeks, thick hair, broad chest, curious, learned, jovial.

Cancer: Heart, breast, watery fields, rivers, canals, kitchen, food, attractive, small build, emotional, deeply attached, mother-like, sensitive.

Leo: Stomach, digestion, navel, mountains, forests, caves, deserts, palaces, parks, forts, boilers, steel factories, thin, dry, hot, royal, self-pride, insolent, domineering.

Virgo: Hip, appendix, lush gardens, fields, orchards, libraries, bookstores, farms, intelligent, sharp, orator, nervous, physically weak, discretion, tactfulness.

Libra: Groins, Businessmen, markets, trade centers, banks, hotels, amusement parks, entertainment, toilets, cosmetics, balanced, wise, good talker.

Scorpio: Private parts, holes, deep caves, mines, garrages, small build, dusky complexion, bright eyes, secretive, scheming, occult, best friend or a worst enemy, peevish, sensitive.

Sagittarius: Thighs, royal, attorneys, government offices, aircraft, falling, sparse hair, muscular, deep eyes, uproght, honest, genial, gambler.

Capricorn: Knees, marsh lands, watery places, alligators, beasts, bushes, slender buils, long neck, prominent teeth, witty, perfectionist, patient, organizer, cautious, secretive, pragmatic.

Aquarius: Ankles, charity, philosophy, tall, bony, small eyes, mountain spring, places with water, ill-formed teeth, coarse hair, hard-working, stoic, honest.

Pisces: Feet, oceans, seas, prisons, hospitals, hermitages, short, plump, large eyes, large eyebrows, lazy, emotional, timid, honest, irresolute, talkative, intuitive.

3. Planets

3.1 Introduction

There are 7 grahas (planets) in Vedic astrology: Sun, Moon, Mars, Mercury, Jupiter, Venus and Saturn. There are two more chaayaa grahas (shadow planets): Rahu and Ketu. Rahu and Ketu are mathematical points. They are also called the north and south nodes or the head and tail of dragon. They are based on the points at which the orbit of Moon around earth cuts the orbit of earth around Sun.

Rasis represent situations that develop in one's life and influences that enter one's life. Planets in a chart represent human beings that play a role in one's life.

Just as the whole zodiac represents Lord Vishnu and rasis represent His limbs, planets represent Vishnu's avataras (incarnations).

3.2 Characteristics of Planets

3.2.1 *Vishnu's Avataras*

This world contains two essences – *jeevaamsa* (living essence) and *paramaatmaamsa* (absolute and supreme essence). Planets are the manifestations of different aspects of these essences. Vishnu's incarnations happened with these essences taken from various planets.

Meena/Matsya avatara (fish) came from Ketu. Koorma avatara (tortoise) came from Saturn. Varaaha/sookara avatara (boar) came from Rahu. Narasimha/Nrisimha avatara (half-man, half-lion) came from Mars. Vaamana avatara (learned dwarf) came from Jupiter. Parasu Rama/ Bhaargava Rama came from Venus. Rama came from Sun. Krishna came from Moon. Buddha came from Mercury.

All these incarnations came into being with a significant percentage of paramaatmaamsa (supreme essence) than *jeevaatmaamsa* (living essence). Rama, Krishna, Narasimha and Varaha avataras had only *paramaatmaamsa*.

Other living beings are born with a significant percentage of jeevaamsa and a little of paramaatmaamsa from the planets.

3.2.2 *Benefics and Malefics*

(1) Jupiter and Venus are *natural benefics* (saumya grahas or subha grahas). Mercury becomes a natural benefic when he is alone or with more natural benefics. Waxing Moon of Sukla paksha is a natural benefic.

(2) Sun, Mars, Rahu and Ketu are *natural malefics* (kroora grahas or paapa grahas). Mercury becomes a natural malefic when he is joined

by more natural malefics. Waning Moon of Krishna paksha is a natural malefic.

This information is important because the results given by planets are based on their inherent nature.

3.2.3 *Main Governance*

Sun governs soul. Moon governs mind. Mars governs strength. Mercury governs speech. Jupiter governs knowledge and happiness. Venus governs potency. Saturn governs grief.

3.2.4 *Planets and Colors*

Sun shows blood-red color. Moon shows tawny color. Mars shows blood-red color. Mercury shows grass green color. Jupiter shows tawny color. Venus is variegated. Saturn shows black color.

These colors can be useful, for example, when predicting the color of one's car. For now, readers should just memorize these characteristics.

3.2.5 *Planetary Cabinet*

Sun and Moon are kings. Mars is the leader (army chief). Mercury is the prince. Jupiter and Venus are the ministers. Saturn is the servant. Rahu and Ketu form the army.

3.2.6 *Planetary Deities*

Ruling deities of various planets are as given below: Agni (fire god) for Sun, Varuna (rain god) for Moon, Subrahmanya (army chief of gods) for Mars, Maha Vishnu (supreme sustaining force) for Mercury, Indra (ruler of gods) for Jupiter, Sachi Devi (Indra's wife) for Venus, Brahma (Creator) for Saturn.

3.2.7 *Sex of Planets*

Sun, Mars and Jupiter are male. Moon and Venus are female. Saturn and Mercury are eunich.

This information can be used for predicting the sex of children based on one's chart. For example, if the house ruling the first child is influenced by Jupiter, Mars and Mercury, we may predict a son. If it is influenced by Moon and Mercury, we may predict a daughter.

3.2.8 *Planets and Five Elements*

(1) Agni tattva (fiery element) is ruled by Mars. Sun also has the same nature.
(2) Bhoo tattva (earthy element) is ruled by Mercury.
(3) Vaayu tattva (airy element) is ruled by Saturn.
(4) Aakaasa tattva (ethery element) is ruled by Jupiter.

(5) Jala tattva (watery element) is ruled by Venus. Moon also has the same nature.

These rulerships throw light on the basic nature of planets. Being a fiery planet, Mars governs leadership, enterprise *etc*. Being an earthy planet, Mercury governs memory, logical abilities *etc*. Being an airy planet, Saturn governs wandering and free spirit. Being a watery planet, Venus governs imaginative and creative work. Being an ethery planet, Jupiter governs wisdom, intelligence and perceiving knowledge.

3.2.9 *Planets and Varnas*

Jupiter and Venus are Brahmanas (learned). Sun and Mars are Kshatriyas (warriors). Moon and Mercury are Vaisyas (traders). Saturn is a Sudra (worker).

Learning and intelligence is the forte of the learned class. Bravery is the forte of the warrior class. Getting along with others well is the forte of the trader class. Hard work is the forte of the working class. In this manner, we should understand varnas to show one's basic nature rather than the caste of one's family.

It should be noted that Moon, who was earlier classified in the planetary cabinet as a king, is said here to be of Vaisya varna. Sun is a king who is also a warrior. He is a brave king, who asserts himself. But Moon is a king who gets along well with everyone.

3.2.10 *Planets and Gunas*

Sun, Moon and Jupiter are *saattwik* planets. Mercury and Venus are *raajasik* planets. Mars and Saturn are *taamasik* planets.

NOTE: There is a misconception today that *sattwa* guna means patience and not hurting others. An aggressive response to an offender is often thought to be *raajasik*. However, *sattwa* simply means "the state of being true". Pleasing others with artificial goodness is *not* sattwa guna. Punishing a person for his mistakes is not necessarily rajo guna. If there is some passion and impurity in one's energetic response, then it shows rajo guna. But, if a warrior fights a sinning person with no passion or ego, it can still be a saattvic act. Lord Sri Rama and Sun are examples for this. Sun is a king of the warrior class and yet he is saattwik. Lord Rama, who was born with his amsa, is a saattwik person despite killing Ravana and other demons.

Sattva guna simply means purity and truthfulness in one's thoughts and action. Rajo guna shows some passion, energy and impurity in thoughts and actions. Tamo guna shows a dark, mean and depraved spirit in thoughts and actions.

3.2.11 *Planetary Abodes*

Sun lives in a temple. Moon lives in a watery place. Mercury lives in a sports ground. Jupiter lives in a treasure house. Venus lives in the bedroom. Saturn lives in a filthy area.

This description should give one an idea of the nature of planets.

3.2.12 *Seven Dhaatus*

Sapta dhaatus or 7 matters make up human body. The planetary rulerships are as follows: Sun rules bones. Moon rules blood. Mars rules marrow. Mercury rules skin. Jupiter rules fat. Venus rules semen (materials related to the reproductive system). Saturn rules muscles.

If Sun is afflicted, it can show some problems related to bones. Weakness of Moon may give blood related problems. And so on.

3.2.13 *Planets and Time Periods*

Sun rules an ayana[5] . Moon rules a minute. Mars rules a week. Mercury rules a ritu[6]. Jupiter rules a month. Venus rules a fortnight. Saturn rules a year.

These periods are very use ful in prasna or horary astrology.

3.2.14 *Planets & Tastes*

Sun governs the pungent taste (*e.g.* onion, ginger, pepper). Moon governs the saline taste (*e.g.* sea salt, rock salt). Mars governs the bitter taste (*e.g.* karela/bitter melon, dandelion root, rhubarb root, neem leaves). Mercury governs a mixed taste. Jupiter governs sweetness (*e.g.* sugar, dates). Venus governs the sour taste (*e.g.* lemon, tamarind). Saturn governs the astringent taste (*e.g.* plantain, pomegranate).

The 2nd house shows one's preference in food. The planets influencing it may decide one's favorite taste. In addition, one should avoid the tastes of the planets who are likely to bring disease. Suppose one is running a dasa or antardasa of a sign containing Moon as per Shoola dasa (a dasa that shows suffering). Then some suffering related to Moon is possible. Moon can give problems related to blood pressure as he governs blood. So eating too much salty food during such a period may result in high blood pressure. Similarly,

---

5 There are 2 ayanas in a year. During Sun's transit from Cp to Ge, we have Uttara (north) ayana. During Sun's transit from Cn to Sg, we have Dakshina (south) ayana.

6 Ritu roughly means a "season". There are 6 ritus in a year. They are – vasanta (spring), greeshma (summer), varsha (rain), hemanta (dew), seeta (winter), sisira (fall). Each ritu consists of 2 months.

one should cut down on sweets during a period in which Jupiter related troubles are indicated. Or, one may develop too much fat (Jupiter) or get other Jupiter related diseases.

3.2.15 *Planetary Strengths*

Mercury and Jupiter are strong in the eastern direction (lagna). Sun and Mars are strong in the southern direction (meridian – 10th house). Moon and Venus are strong in the northern direction (nadir – 4th house). Saturn is strong in the west (7th house). These are the *digbalas* (strengths associated with direction) of planets. These show the direction taken by one in one's life, as we will see later.

Moon, Mars and Saturn are strong in the night time. Sun, Jupiter and Venus are strong in the daytime. Mercury is always strong.

Natural malefics are strong in Krishna paksha. Natural benefics are strong in Sukla paksha.

Natural malefics are strong in Dakshina ayana[7]. Natural benefics are strong in Uttara ayana.

3.2.16 *Planets & Ritus*

Planetary rulerships over *ritus* (seasons) are as follows: Venus governs *vasanta ritu* (spring). Mars governs *greeshma ritu* (summer). Moon governs *varsha ritu* (rainy season). Mercury governs *hemanta ritu* (season of dew). Jupiter governs *sheeta ritu* (winter). Saturn governs *sisira ritu* (fall).

3.2.17 *Dhatu, Moola and Jeeva*

(1) Rahu, Mars, Saturn and Moon rule over *dhaatus* (metals and materials).

(2) Sun and Venus rule over *moolas* (roots and vegetables).

(3) Mercury, Jupiter and Ketu rule over *jeevas* (living beings).

3.3 Planetary Dignities

Each planet has a sign where it is exalted (*uchcha*), a sign where it is debilitated (*neecha*), a sign that is called its *moolatrikona* and one or two rasis that are *owned* by it. A planet is said to be strong in its own rasi or exaltation rasi or moolatrikona.

Table 6 shows own rasis, exaltation rasis, the degree of deep exaltation, debilitation rasi, the degree of deep debilitation and the moolatrikona of each planet.

---

7 For the meaning of ayanas, see footnote 5.

Table 6: Dignities of Planets

Planet	Own rasis	Exaltation rasi (deep exaltation point)	Debilitation rasi (deep debilitation point)	Mool-atri - kona
Sun	Le	Ar (10°)	Li (10°)	Le
Moon	Cn	Ta (3°)	Sc (3°)	Ta
Mars	Ar & Sc	Cp (28°)	Cn (28°)	Ar
Mercury	Ge & Vi	Vi (15°)	Pi (15°)	Vi
Jupiter	Sg & Pi	Cn (5°)	Cp (5°)	Sg
Venus	Ta & Li	Pi (27°)	Vi (27°)	Li
Saturn	Cp & Aq	Li (20°)	Ar (20°)	Aq
Rahu	Aq	Ge	Sg	Vi
Ketu	Sc	Sg	Ge	Pi

Some special points regarding the results given by planets:

(1) Sun gives the results of being in moolatrikona in the first 20° of Le and the results of being in own rasi in the remaining 10°.

(2) Moon gives the results of being in exaltation rasi in the first 3° of Ta and the results of being in moolatrikona in the remaining 27°.

(3) Mars gives the results of being in moolatrikona in the first 12° of Le and the results of being in own rasi in the remaining 18°.

(4) Mercury gives the results of being in exaltation rasi in the first 15° of Vi, the results of being in moolatrikona in the next 5° and the results of being in own rasi in the remaining 10°.

(5) Jupiter gives the results of being in moolatrikona in the first 10° of Sg and the results of being in own rasi in the remaining 20°.

(6) Venus gives the results of being in moolatrikona in the first half of Li and the results of being in own rasi in the second half of Li.

(7) Saturn gives the results of being in moolatrikona in the first 20° of Aq and the results of being in own rasi in the remaining 10°.

An analogy may help one understand the subtle difference between own rasi, exaltation rasi and moolatrikona.

Own rasi of a planet (*e.g.* Pisces of Jupiter) is like one's home. One is most *natural* and *comfortable* at home. That is exactly what a planet in own rasi is. Moolatrikona of a planet (*e.g.* Sagittarius of Jupiter) is like one's office. One executes one's formal job and performs one's duty at office. One is powerful and duty-minded at office. Exaltation sign of a planet (*e.g.* Cancer of Jupiter) is like a favorite party/picnic. One is excited to be at one's favorite party/picnic. So an exalted planet is like an excited person at his favorite picnic spot. Debilitation sign of a planet (*e.g.* Capricorn of Jupiter) is like one's worst party. A debilitated planet is like an unhappy person stuck at a place he hates.

Jupiter is a saattwik and dharmik Brahmin. Ethery Jupiter, planet of perception, intelligence and wisdom, is most comfortable in saattwik Pisces, which is the 12th house of the natural zodiac. That is his home. However, he also has to uphold dharma. Upholding dharma is his *duty*. Whether he likes it or not, he has to do it. So fiery Sagittarius, 9th house in the natural zodiac, is his moolatrikona. Jupiter is like a "raaja purohit" (chief priest of a king) in Sagittarius. He has to sometimes take strong decisions to uphold dharma (like sentencing someone to death). In Pisces, he is like a peaceful Brahmin doing pooja at his home. In watery Cancer, the 4th house of the natural zodiac, Jupiter is excited to do some imaginative (watery) learning (4th house matter). In taamasik and earthy Capricorn, the 10th house of the natural zodiac, Jupiter hates doing tamasik and well-defined karma (action, 10th house matter). It is against his nature. Executing well-defined taamasik karma may be fine with taamasik planets Mars and Saturn, but Jupiter is unhappy with it. So Jupiter is debilitated in Cp.

Take Mercury as another example. He is an intellectual planet and significator of communications. "Intelligent communication" is the most comfortable activity for him. So his home is intellectual Gemini, the 3rd house (communications) of the natural zodiac. However, intelligent debates and arguments are the formal job assigned to him. Virgo is the 6th house (arguments) of the natural zodiac and it is Mercury's moolatrikona!

While saattwik and ethery Jupiter doesn't quite love the job of fiercely and fierily upholding dharma (by punishing demon king Bali in Vaamana avatara, for example), he does it with a sense of duty. But Mercury loves his official job! He loves engaging in intellectual debates. So Virgo (6th house of the natural zodiac) is not only his moolatrikona (office), but also his exaltation sign (favorite picnic spot). Still, "intelligent communications" (Gemini) is what he is most comfortable with (home).

Let us take one final example – Ketu. Ketu is most comfortable with occult activity, which are shown by the 8th house. So he owns the 8th house of the natural zodiac, *i.e.* Scorpio. His official duty, however, is giving upaasana (meditation) and moksha (liberation), which are shown by the 12th house. So his moolatrikona is in the 12th house of the natural zodiac, *i.e.* Pisces.

One should remember the above and understand the mood of a planet based on whether it is in own rasi or exaltation rasi or moolatrikona. Though all the three are good placements, there is a subtle difference in the mood of the planet and the results given by it.

3.4 Planetary Relationships

3.4.1 *Natural Relationships*

For each planet, its friends and enemies are found as follows: Take the moolatrikona of the planet. Lord of the rasi where it is exalted is its friend. Lords of 2nd, 4th, 5th, 8th, 9th and 12th rasis from it are also its natural friends. Lords of other rasis are its natural enemies. If a planet becomes a friend and an enemy on account of owning two rasis, then it is a neutral planet. The list of friends, neutral planets and enemies of all planets is listed in Table 7.

Table 7: Natural relationships

Planet	Friends (mitra)	Nuetral (sama)	Enemies (satru)
Sun	Moon, Mars, Jupiter	Mercury	Venus, Saturn
Moon	Sun, Mercury	Mars, Jupiter, Venus, Saturn	—
Mars	Sun, Moon, Jupiter	Venus, Saturn	Mercury
Mercury	Sun, Venus	Mars, Jupiter, Saturn	Moon
Jupiter	Sun, Moon, Mars	Saturn	Mercury, Venus
Venus	Mercury, Saturn	Mars, Jupiter	Sun, Moon
Saturn	Mercury, Venus	Jupiter	Sun, Moon, Mars

3.4.2 *Temporary Relationships*

In addition to the permanent relationship, we have temporary relationships based on the planetary position in a chart. These temporary (*tatkaala*) relationships are specific to a chart.

Planets occupying the 2nd, 3rd, 4th, 10th, 11th and 12th rasis counted from the rasi occupied by a planet are its temporary friends. Planet occupying other rasis are its temporary enemies.

Example 4: Let us consider Lord Sree Rama's chart given in Figure 1 and find the temporary friends and temporary enemies of Sun and Moon.

Sun: Sun is in Ar. The 2nd, 3rd, 4th, 10th, 11th and 12th rasis counted from Ar are Ta, Ge, Cn, Cp, Aq and Pi. Planets in those rasis are Mercury,

Moon, Jupiter, Mars and Venus. They are temporary friends of Sun in this chart. Saturn is the only temporary enemy.

Moon: Moon is in Cn. The 2nd, 3rd, 4th, 10th, 11th and 12th rasis counted from Cn are Le, Vi, Li, Ar, Ta and Ge. Planets in those rasis are Saturn, Sun and Mercury. They are temporary friends of Moon in this chart. Temporary enemies are Mars, Jupiter, Venus.

Exercise 5: Consider Lord Sree Rama's chart given in Figure 1 and find the temporary friends and temporary enemies of Jupiter and Venus.

Note that Moon and Jupiter have the same temporary friends and temporary enemies. That is because they occupy the same rasi and temporary relationships are based on the rasis occupied by planets.

3.4.3 *Compound Relationships*

We get the compound relationships between planets by combining permanent and temporary relationships as shown in Table 8.

Table 8: Compound Relationships

	Temporary friend	**Temporary enemy**
Natural friend	Adhimitra (good friend)	Sama (neutral)
Natural neutral	Mitra (friend)	Satru (enemy)
Natural enemy	Sama (neutral)	Adhisatru (bad enemy)

Example 5: Let us continue from Example 4 and find the friends and enemies of Sun and Moon in Lord Sree Rama's chart given in Figure 1.

Sun: We found in Example 4 that Sun's temporary friends are Mercury, Moon, Jupiter, Mars and Venus. Of these, Moon, Mars and Jupiter are natural friends and they become adhimitras (good friends). Mercury is a neutral planet in natural relationship and he becomes a mitra (friend) in compound relationship. Venus is a natural enemy. Being a temporary friend, Venus becomes a sama (neutral) planet in compound relationship.

Saturn is the only temporary enemy of Sun. Being a natural enemy too, he becomes an adhisatru (bad enemy) of Sun.

Moon: We found in Example 4 that Moon's temporary friends are Sun, Mercury and Saturn. Of these, Sun and Mercury are natural friends and they become adhimitras (good friends). Saturn is a neutral in natural relationship and he becomes a mitra (friend) in compound relationship.

Moon's temporary enemies are Mars, Jupiter and Venus. They are all natural neutrals and they become satru (enemies) in compound relationship.

Exercise 6: Continue from Exercise 5 and find the friends and enemies of Jupiter and Venus in Lord Sree Rama's chart given in Figure 1.

Whenever we refer to a planet being in a friendly house or an inimical house in the rest of this book, we mean the compound relationships. A planet occupying a rasi owned by a mitra or adhimitra is in a friendly house. A planet occupying a rasi owned by a satru or adhisatru is in an inimical house.

3.5 Answers to Exercises

Exercise 5:

Jupiter: Jupiter is in Cn. The 2nd, 3rd, 4th, 10th, 11th and 12th rasis counted from Cn are Le, Vi, Li, Ar, Ta and Ge. Planets in those rasis are Saturn, Sun and Mercury. They are temporary friends of Jupiter in this chart. Temporary enemies are Moon, Mars, Venus.

Venus: Venus is in Pi. The 2nd, 3rd, 4th, 10th, 11th and 12th rasis counted from Pi are Ar, Ta, Ge, Sg, Cp and Aq. Planets in those rasis are Sun, Mercury and Mars. They are temporary friends of Venus in this chart. Temporary enemies are Moon, Jupiter, Saturn.

Exercise 6:

Jupiter: We found in Exercise 5 that the temporary friends of Jupiter are Sun, Mercury and Saturn. Being a natural friend, Sun becomes an adhimitra (good friend). Being a natural neutral, Saturn becomes a mitra (friend). Being a natural enemy, Mercury becomes a neutral planet in compound relationship.

Temporary enemies of Jupiter are Moon, Mars and Venus. Being natural friends of Jupiter, Moon and Mars become sama (neutral) planets in compound relationship. Being a neutral planet in natural relationship, Venus becomes an enemy in compound relationship.

Venus: We found in Exercise 5 that the temporary friends of Venus are Sun, Mars and Mercury. Being a natural friend, Mercury becomes an adhimitra (good friend). Being a neutral planet in natural relationship, Mars becomes a mitra (friend). Being an enemy in natural relationship, Sun becomes a sama (neutral) in compound relationship.

Temporary enemies of Venus are Moon, Jupiter, Saturn. Of these, Saturn is a natural friend and he becomes a sama (neutral) in compound relationship. Jupiter is a natural neutral and he becomes a satru (enemy) of Venus in compound relationship. Moon is a natural enemy of Venus and he becomes an adhisatru (bad enemy) in compound relationship.

4. Upagrahas

4.1 Introduction

There are **11** upagrahas (sub-planets or satellites) defined by Sage Parasara. They do not appear to correspond to any physical bodies (planets, stars *etc*). From Sage Parasara's definition, they appear to be some significant mathematical points. They will be defined in two groups.

4.2 Sun-based Upagrahas

Five upagrahas called **Dhuma, Vyatipaata, Parivesha, Indrachaapa** and **Upaketu** are defined based on Sun's longitude. The exact formulas are given in Table 9. All these upagrahas are very *malefic* in nature. Any houses occupied by them in rasi chart or divisional charts are spoiled by them.

Table 9: Sun-based Upagrahas

Upagraha	Longitude Formula
Dhuma	Sun's longitude + 133°20'
Vyatipaata	360° – Dhuma's longitude
Parivesha	Vyatipaata's longitude + 180°
Indrachaapa	360° – Parivesha's longitude
Upaketu	Indrachaapa's longitude + 16°40'
	= Sun's longitude – 30°

It may be noted that Dhuma and Indrachaapa are apart by 180° and Vyatipaata and Parivesha are apart by 180°.

Example 6:

Let us say Sun is at 9Sg36. Sg is the 9th rasi and so Sun's longitude can be expressed as 8s 9°36' (based on the notation introduced in 1.3.2). The length of each of the 8 rasis before Sg is 30°. So we can find the longitude of Sun (*i.e.*, distance traversed by Sun from the beginning of the zodiac) as 8x30°+9°36' = 249°36'.

---

8 When adding or subtracting longitudes, we should subtract 360° if we get more than 360° and we should add 360° if we get less than 0°. Adding or subtracting 360° means going around the zodiac once and coming to the same position. We should finally reduce all longitudes to a value between 0° and 360°, by adding or subtracting 360° as many times as needed.

Adding 133°20' to it, we get 382°56'. This can be rewritten[8] as 22°56'. That is the longitude of Dhuma. So Dhuma is at 22°56' in Ar. Because Dhuma and Indrachaapa are 180° apart, you can say without further computation that Indrachapa is in the 7th sign from Ar, which is Li. His advancement from the start of Li is also 22°56'.

NOTE: You can verify that Aries and Libra, Taurus and Scorpio, Gemini and Sagittarius, Cancer and Capricorn, Leo and Aquarius, Virgo and Pisces are the signs that are 180° apart. So, if Dhuma is at 11°36' from the start of Aquarius, Indrachapa will be at 11°36' from the start of Leo.

Vyatipata is obtained by subtracting Dhuma from 360°. We see that 360° – 22°56' = 337°4'. So Vyatipata is at 337°4', *i.e.* at 7°4' from the start of Pi. Since Parivesha is at 180° from Vyatipata, he is at 7°4' in Vi.

Exercise 7: If Sun is at 13°19' from the start of Ta, find the positions of all the five upagrahas defined so far.

4.3 Other Upagrahas

Six upagrahas called **Kaala, Mrityu, Arthaprahaara, Yamaghantaka, Gulika and Maandi** are more difficult to compute. Kaala is a malefic upagraha similar to Sun. Mrityu is a malefic upagraha similar to Mars. Arthaprahaara is similar to Mercury. Yamaghantaka is similar to Jupiter. Gulika and Maandi are similar to Saturn.

A day starts at the time of sunrise and ends at the time of sunset. A night starts at the time of sunset and ends at the time of next day's sunrise. Depending on whether one is born during the day or the night, we divide the length of the day/night into 8 equal parts.

Daytime births: The first part is ruled by the lord of weekday and then we cover planets in the order of weekdays. The part after the one ruled by Saturn is lord-less. After that, Sun's part comes. For example, the first 1/8th of the daytime on a Thursday is ruled by Jupiter. Next part is ruled by Venus. The 3rd part is ruled by Saturn. The 4th part is lord-less. The 5th part is ruled by Sun. The 6th part is ruled by Moon. The 7th part is ruled by Mars. The 8th part is ruled by Mercury.

Table 10: Ruling planets

Rulers of the 8 parts of the Day

Weekday	1st	2nd	3rd	4th	5th	6th	7th	8th
Sun	Sun	Moon	Mars	Merc	Jup	Ven	Sat	—
Mon	Moon	Mars	Merc	Jup	Ven	Sat	—	Sun
Tue	Mars	Merc	Jup	Ven	Sat	—	Sun	Moon
Wed	Merc	Jup	Ven	Sat	—	Sun	Moon	Mars
Thu	Jup	Ven	Sat	—	Sun	Moon	Mars	Merc
Fri	Ven	Sat	—	Sun	Moon	Mars	Merc	Jup
Sat	Sat	—	Sun	Moon	Mars	Merc	Jup	Ven

Rulers of the 8 parts of the Night

Weekday	1st	2nd	3rd	4th	5th	6th	7th	8th
Sun	Jup	Ven	Sat	—	Sun	Moon	Mars	Merc
Mon	Ven	Sat	—	Sun	Moon	Mars	Merc	Jup
Tue	Sat	—	Sun	Moon	Mars	Merc	Jup	Ven
Wed	Sun	Moon	Mars	Merc	Jup	Ven	Sat	—
Thu	Moon	Mars	Merc	Jup	Ven	Sat	—	Sun
Fri	Mars	Merc	Jup	Ven	Sat	—	Sun	Moon
Sat	Merc	Jup	Ven	Sat	—	Sun	Moon	Mars

Night time births: The first part is ruled by the 5th planet from the lord of weekday and then we cover planets in the order of weekdays. For example, the first 1/8th of a Thursday night is ruled by the 5th planet from Jupiter, *i.e.* Moon (Jupiter, Venus, Saturn, Sun, Moon – that's the 5th one). Next part is ruled by Mars. The 3rd part is ruled by Mercury. The 4th part is ruled by Jupiter. The 5th part is ruled by Venus. The 6th part is ruled by Saturn. The 7th planet is lord-less. The 8th part is ruled by Sun.

Table 10 gives the list of the ruling planets of all the eight parts of the daytime and night time on all weekdays.

Once we divide the day/night of birth into 8 equal parts and identify the ruling planets of the 8 parts, we can find the longitudes of Kaala etc upagrahas using the following procedure:

(1) Kaala rises at the middle of Sun's part[9]. In other words, we find the

9 Some scholars suggest that Kaala rises at the *beginning* of Sun's part. The same thing applies to others.

time at the middle of Sun's part and find lagna rising then. That gives Kaala's longitude.

(2) Mrityu rises at the middle of Mars's part.

(3) Artha Praharaka rises at the middle of Mercury's part.

(4) Yama ghantaka rises at the middle of Jupiter's part.

(5) Gulika rises at the middle of Saturn's part.

(6) Maandi rises at the beginning of Saturn's part.

Suppose one is born on Thursday night and we want Yamaghantaka's longitude in his chart. Suppose night starts at 6 pm and ends at 6 am on the next day. We see from the table that Jupiter rules the 4th part of a Thursday night. Each part is 12/8 = 1.5 hours. The 4th part starts 4.5 hours after sunset, *i.e.* at 10:30 pm, and ends 1.5 hours later. So Jupiter's part extends from 10:30 pm to midnight. The middle point of this part is at 11:15 pm. We find lagna rising at 11:15 pm and that will be Yama ghantaka's longitude.

4.4 Answer to Exercise

Exercise 7:

Dhuma:	At 26°39' from the start of Vi
Vyatipaata:	At 3°21' from the start of Li
Parivesha:	At 3°21' from the start of Ar
Indrachaapa:	At 26°39' from the start of Pi
Upaketu:	At 19°1' from the start of Sc'

5. Special Lagnas

5.1 Introduction

There are some special lagnas defined by Parasara. In this book, we will widely use **Hora lagna** and **Ghati lagna** and it is time to define them and other special lagnas.

5.2 Bhaava Lagna

Bhaava lagna is at the position of Sun at the time of sunrise. It moves at the rate of **one rasi per 2 hours**. In the rest of this book, bhava lagna will be denoted by **BL.**[10]

If sunrise takes place at 6:00 am and Sun is at 6s 4°47' then, horalagna is at 6s 4°47' at 6:00 am, at 6s 19°47' at 7:00 am, at 7s 4°47' at 8:00 am, 8s 4°47' at 10:00 am and so on. Bhavalagna moves at the rate of 1° per 4 minutes (*i.e.*, 15° per hour).

The following method may be used for computing bhavalagna.

(1) Find the time of sunrise and sun's longitude at sunrise.

(2) Find the difference between the birthtime (or the event time) and the sunrise time found in (1) above. Convert the difference into minutes. The result is the advancement of bhavalagna since sunrise, in degrees.

(3) Add Sun's longitude at sunrise (in degrees) to the above number. Expunge multiples of 360° and reduce the number to the range 0°–360°.

(4) This is the longitude of bhavalagna (BL).

Example 7:

A gentleman was born at 7:23 pm. Sunrise at his birthplace was at 6:37 am on his birthday. At 6:37 am, Sun was at 24°17' in Capricorn. Let us find BL.

(1) 19:23–6:37=12 hr 46 min=12x60 + 46 min = 766 min

(2) Sun's longitude at sunrise is 270°+24°17'=294°17'. Add 766° to it. The result is 1060°17'. Subtracting 360° twice, we get 340°17'. So BL is at 10°17' in Pisces.

5.3 Hora Lagna

Hora lagna is at the position of Sun at the time of sunrise. It moves at the rate of **one rasi per hora (hour)**. In the rest of this book, horalagna will be denoted by **HL**.

10 BL is defined only for the sake of completeness. We will not use it in this book.

If sunrise takes place at 6:00 am and Sun is at 6s 4°47' then, horalagna is at 6s 4°47' at 6:00 am, at 6s 19°47' at 6:30 am, at 7s 4°47' at 7:00 am, 8s 4°47' at 8:00 am and so on. Horalagna moves at the rate of 1/2° per minute (*i.e.*, 30° per hour).

The following method may be used for computing horalagna.

(1) Find the time of sunrise and sun's longitude at sunrise.

(2) Find the difference between the birthtime (or the event time) and the sunrise time found in (1) above. Convert the difference into minutes.

(3) Divide the number by 2. The result is the advancement of horalagna since sunrise, in degrees.

(4) Add Sun's longitude at sunrise (in degrees) to the above number. Expunge multiples of 360° and reduce the number to the range 0°–360°.

(5) This is the longitude of horalagna (HL).

Example 8:

A gentleman was born at 7:23 pm. Sunrise at his birthplace was at 6:37 am on his birthday. At 6:37 am, Sun was at 24°17' in Capricorn. Let us find HL.

(1) 19:23–6:37=12 hr 46 min=12x60 + 46 min = 766 min

(2) 766/2=383

(3) Sun's longitude at sunrise is 270°+24°17'=294°17'. Add 383° to it. The result is 677°17'. Subtracting 360°, we get 317°17'. So HL is at 17°17' in Aquarius.

5.4 Ghati Lagna

Ghati lagna is at the position of Sun at the time of sunrise. It moves at the rate of **one rasi per ghati** (ghati=1/60th of a day, *i.e.*, **24 minutes**). In the rest of this book, ghatilagna will be denoted by **GL**. Ghati lagna is also called "ghatika lagna".

If sunrise takes place at 6:00 am and Sun is at 6s 4°47' then, ghatilagna is at 6s 4°47' at 6:00 am, at 6s 19°47' at 6:12 am, at 7s 4°47' at 6:24 am, 8s 4°47' at 6:48 am and so on. Ghatilagna moves at the rate of 1°15' per minute (*i.e.*, 30° per 24 minutes).

The following method may be used for computing ghatilagna.

(1) Find the time of sunrise and sun's longitude at sunrise.

(2) Find the difference between the birthtime (or the event time) and the sunrise time found in (1) above. Convert the difference into minutes.

(3) Multiply the number by 5. Divide the result by 4. The result is the advancement of ghatilagna since sunrise, in degrees.

(4) Add Sun's longitude at sunrise (in degrees) to the above number. Expunge multiples of 360° and reduce the number to the range 0°–360°.

(5) This is the longitude of ghatilagna (GL).

Example 9:

Let us find GL for the data in Example 8.

(1) 19:23–6:37=12 hr 46 min=766 min

(1) 766x5/4=957.5

(2) Sun's longitude at sunrise is 294°17'. Add 957°30' to it. The result is 1251°47'. Subtracting 360° three times, we get 171°47'. So GL is at 21°47' in Virgo.

Exercise 8:

A lady was born at 3:11:48 am (hr, min, sec) in the early hours of May 28, 1961. Sun was at 13°1' in Taurus then. Sunrise was at 6:19:18 am on May 27, 1961 at her birthplace. At that time, Sun was at 12°11' in Taurus. Find the longitudes of HL and GL in her chart.

5.5 Comments

(1) If the birthtime changes by one minute, GL will change by 1.25° (*i.e.*, 1°15'). This is quite large and it can cause some error in the position of GL in some divisional charts. So, ghati lagna is more sensitive to birthtime errors than normal lagna. When using GL in divisional charts, we should keep this in mind and try to correct the birthtime based on known events first. Wrong data produces wrong results. Our analysis can only be as good as our data!

(2) Some astrologers don't like dealing with it, but birthtime errors are a *fact of life* and we have to live with them. If we prefer to choose methods that work in spite of deviation in birthtime by a few minutes, we are ignoring a key fact – there *are* many people in this world who are born a few minutes apart in nearby places and yet lead significantly different lives. Still some people *hide* from this fact and stick to methods that give the *same results* to *everyone* born in a 15-minute or one-hour or two-hour period, because they don't have to deal with the complicated issue of birthtime errors then! But that's not the right approach – we should give importance to finer techniques. After all, Sage Parasara must have written about all these fine techniques only because he thought they were useful.

(3) Some people define sunrise as the time when the **center** of the visual disk representing Sun rises on the eastern horizon, *i.e.*, the time when

lagna and Sun are exactly at the same longitude. Some other people consider sunrise as the time when the **upper tip** of the visual disk representing Sun appears to be rising on the eastern horizon, *i.e.*, the time when the first ray of Sun is seen. The latter approach is recommended.

Exercise 9:

Suppose (just suppose) that a key event from the known past of the lady of Exercise 8 makes us think that her GL has to be between 16°15' and 17°30' in Virgo. Correct the given birthtime accordingly.

5.6 Use of Special Lagnas

Use of special lagnas will become clearer in future chapters. For now, it will suffice to say that hora lagna shows money and ghati lagna shows power.

In any chart, normal lagna shows self. Hora lagna shows self, from the point of view of money, wealth and prosperity. Ghati lagna shows self, from the point of view of fame, power and authority. For example, when we time good and bad periods for a businessman, hora lagna may be very important. When we time good and bad periods for a politician, ghati lagna may be very important.

5.7 Sree Lagna

In Sanskrit, the word "Sree" means wealth. It also means Lakshmi, wife of Lord Narayana and goddess of wealth. Sree Lagna will be denoted by SL in the rest of this book. Sree Lagna is important for prosperity. Its use will be shown in the chapter on Sudasa. Computation of Sree Lagna will be explained for now.

(1) Find the constellation occupied by Moon.

(2) Find the fraction of the constellation traversed by Moon.

(3) Find the same fraction of the zodiac (360°).

(4) Add this amount to the longitude of lagna. Subtract multiples of 360° if necessary. The resulting amount is the longitude of Sree Lagna (SL).

Example 10:

Let us take a native with Moon at 13 Li 06 and lagna at 25 Vi 05. Moon's longitude is 180° + 13°6' = 193°6'. Lagna's longitude 150°+25°5' is 175°5'.

(1) Moon is in Swathi constellation, which runs from 6°40' to 20°0' in Libra.

(2) Moon's advancement in his constellation is 13°6' – 6°40' = 6°26'. As

fraction of the whole constellation, this is (6°26')/(13°20') = 386'/800' = 0.4825.

(3) The same fraction of the zodiac is 0.4825 x 360° = 173.7° = 173°42'.

(4) Adding this amount to the longitude of lagna, we get 175°5' + 173°42' = 348°47. This is the longitude of SL. So SL is in Pisces at 18°47'.

Exercise 10:

Suppose someone has Moon at 15 Le 29 and lagna at 14 Sc 19. Find the longitude of SL (Sree Lagna).

Warning: There are some more special lagnas defined by Parasara, but they are beyond the scope of this book. We will restrict ourselves to the ones defined in this book.

5.8 Answers to Exercises

Exercise 8:

HL: 8°26' in Aquarius.

GL: 17°48.5' in Virgo.

Exercise 9:

Birthtime has to be between 3:10:33 – 3:11:33 am.

[Hint: GL with given birthtime (3:11:48 am) is at 17°48.5' in Virgo. The error is between 18.5' and 1°33.5', *i.e.*, 0.3083° and 1.5583°. Find the corresponding error in birthtime in minutes and convert it to seconds. Then subtract the error from birthtime.]

Exercise 10:

SL is at 12°22' in Capricorn.

6. Divisional Charts

6.1 Divisions of A Rasi

Each rasi has many divisions. Divisions of rasis are again mapped to rasis. For example, a rasi may be divided into 4 parts and each part may be mapped to a different rasi. Ar may be divided into 4 parts and the 4 parts may be mapped to Ar, Cn, Li and Cp. Then the 4 parts of Ta may be mapped to Ta, Le, Sc and Aq. And so on. Like this, we may divide all rasis into 4 parts and map the 4 parts to different rasis. We may also divide rasis to 9 parts and map each part into a rasi. We can have many different divisions.

Sage Parasara defined 16 different divisions of rasis. Jaimini and Tajaka writers mentioned 4 more divisions. It is possible that Parasara also dealt with these 4 special divisions in sections that are perhaps missing today. In addition, there are more higher and finer divisions that are normally not used.

Based on the rasis occupied by planets in various divisions, "divisional charts" are drawn. As we have seen before, we need to know the rasis occupied by planets, upagrahas, lagna and special lagnas to draw any chart. In every division, we divide the rasi into different parts, find the part containing each planet and see the rasi to which that part is mapped. Then we place the planet in that rasi in the chart corresponding to that division. We can draw a chart for each division. A planet can occupy different rasis in different divisions.

Chart of each division is called a divisional chart. Each divisional chart can be treated as a different chart and interpreted differently. Different aspects of life are seen in different divisional charts. Rasi chart is simply a special case of divisional charts. If we divide each rasi into just one part (*i.e.* in effect, no division), we get rasi chart.

In the rest of this book, everything we describe will be applicable to all divisional charts, unless we explicitly state a chart. We can apply all the principles to all the divisional charts, but we should see only specific matters in a divisional chart. The list of matters to be seen in each divisional chart will be given after the details of computation are presented.

In this book, D-*n* will denote the divisional chart based on the nth division of rasis, *i.e.* based on dividing rasis into *n* parts.

6.2 Computing Divisional Charts

We will explain the computation of 20 divisional charts in this section.

Higher divisional charts like D-108 and D-150 and variations in charts like D-2, D-3, D-8 and D-11 will not be covered in this book.

6.2.1 *Rasi Chart (D-1)*

A simple example of divisions is **rasi chart** itself. It is also called "**kshetra chakra**". It is denoted by D-1. Longitudes in the range 0°-30° are mapped to Aries, 30°-60° to Taurus and so on, as mentioned earlier. Using Table 1, we can find the rasi occupied by a body based on its longitude. By "body" here, we mean planets, upagrahas, lagna or special lagnas – basically a physical or a mathematical point in the zodiac that has a longitude associated with it.

6.2.2 *Hora Chart (D-2)*

Each rasi is divided into 2 equal parts of 15° each. Bodies in the first 15° of odd rasis are in Sun's hora. Bodies in the second 15° of odd rasis are in Moon's hora. Bodies in the first 15° of even rasis are in Moon's hora. Bodies in the second 15° of even rasis are in Sun's hora.

NOTE: Though absolutely correct, the above is not quite complete. Proper use of hora chart is beyond the scope of this book. So we will ignore and not use hora chart in this book.

6.2.3 *Drekkana Chart (D-3)*

Each rasi is divided into 3 equal parts of 10° each. Bodies in the first 10° of a rasi are placed in drekkana chart in the same rasi. Bodies in the middle 10° of a rasi are placed in drekkana chart in the 5th from the rasi. Bodies in the last 10° of a rasi are placed in drekkana chart in the 9th from the rasi.

Example 11: Let us say Mercury, Jupiter and Venus are together in Gemini in rasi chart. Mercury is at 3°. Jupiter is at 19°. Venus is at 21°.

Then Mercury is in the first 10° (0°-10°), Jupiter is in the middle 10° (10°-20°) and Venus is in the last 10° (20°-30°). So Mercury is placed in Gemini itself in drekkana chart; Jupiter is placed in Libra (5th from Gemini) in drekkana chart; and, Venus is placed in Aquarius (9th from Gemini) in drekkana chart.

6.2.4 *Chaturthamsa Chart (D-4)*

Each rasi is divided into 4 equal parts of 7.5° each. Bodies in the first, second, third and fourth 7.5° arc of a rasi are in the 1st, 4th, 7th and 10th from that rasi (respectively) in chaturthamsa. In other words, planets in 0°-7.5° in a rasi go into 1st from that rasi; planets in 7.5°-15° go into 4th from that rasi; planets in 15°-22.5° go into the 7th from that rasi; and, planets in the 22.5°-30° go into the 10th from that rasi.

This chart is also known as **Chaturamsa** or **Turyamsa**.

Example 12: Let us say Mercury, Jupiter and Venus are together in Taurus. Mercury is at 3°, Jupiter is at 14° and Venus is at 23°.

Mercury is in 0°-7.5° arc, *i.e.* the first 7.5° arc, of Ta. So he is in Ta (1st from Ta) in D-4.

Jupiter is in 7.5°-15° arc, *i.e.* the second 7.5° arc, of Ta. So he is in Le (4th from Ta) in D-4.

Venus is in 22.5°-30° arc, *i.e.* the fourth 7.5° arc, of Ta. So he is in Aq (10th from Ta) in D-4.

6.2.5 *Panchamsa Chart (D-5)*

Each rasi is divided into 5 equal parts of 6° each. Bodies in the 5 parts of an odd rasi go into Ar, Aq, Sg, Ge and Li (respectively). Bodies in the 5 parts of an even rasi go into Ta, Vi, Pi, Cp and Sc (respectively).

6.2.6 *Shashthamsa Chart (D-6)*

Each rasi is divided into 6 equal parts of 5° each. Bodies in the 6 parts of a rasi go into the 6 rasis starting from Ar or Li, based on whether the rasi is odd or even.

Example 13: Let us say Mercury is at 11° in Ge and Jupiter is at 19° in Sc. We see that 11° is in the 3rd part of the rasi and 19° is in the 4th part of the rasi. Ge is an odd rasi and counting starts from Ar. The 3rd from Ar is Ge. So the 3rd part in Ge goes into Ge in D-6. On the other hand, Sc is an even rasi and counting starts from Li. The 4th from Li is Cp. So the 4th part of Sc goes into Cp in D-6. So Mercury is in Ge and Jupiter is in Cp in D-6 for this example.

6.2.7 *Saptamsa Chart (D-7)*

Each rasi is divided into 7 equal parts of 4° 17' 8.57". Bodies in the 1st, 2nd, 3rd, 4th, 5th, 6th and 7th parts of a rasi go into the 7 rasis starting from the rasi itself, if it is an odd rasi, or starting from the 7th sign from it, if it is an even rasi.

Example 14: Let us say Mercury is at 10° in Ge and Jupiter is at 19° in Vi. We see that 10° is in the 3rd part of the rasi and 19° is in the 5th part of the rasi. Because Ge is an odd rasi, the 3rd part in Ge goes into the 3rd from Ge, *i.e.* Le. On the other hand, Vi is an even sign and counting starts from the 7th from it, *i.e.* Pi. The 5th from Pi is Cn. So the 5th part of Vi goes into Cn. So Mercury is in Le and Jupiter is in Cn in D-7 for this example.

6.2.8 *Ashtamsa Chart (D-8)*

Each rasi is divided into 8 equal parts of 3° 45' each. Bodies in the eight parts of a rasi go into the 8 rasis starting from Ar, Sg or Le, based on whether the rasi is a movable, fixed or dual sign.

Example 15: Let us say Mercury is at 10° in Ge and Jupiter is at 19° in Sc. We see that 10° is in the 3rd part of the rasi and 19° is in the 6th part of the rasi. Because Ge is a dual rasi, counting starts from Le. The 3rd from Le is Li. So the 3rd part in Ge goes into Li in D-8. On the other hand, Sc is a fixed sign and counting starts from Sg. The 6th from Sg is Ta. So the 6th part of Sc goes into Ta in D-8. So Mercury is in Le and Jupiter is in Ta in D-8 for this example.

6.2.9 *Navamsa Chart (D-9)*

Each rasi is divided into 9 equal parts of 3° 20' each. Bodies in the 9 parts of a rasi go into the 9 rasis starting from Ar, Cp, Li or Cn, based on whether the rasi is a fiery, earthy, airy or watery sign.

This chart is also known as **Dharmamsa**. It is the most popular chart after rasi chart and some astrologers simply refer to it as "Amsa" (division).

Example 16: Let us say Mercury is at 11° in Ge and Jupiter is at 19° in Sc. We see that 11° is in the 4th part of the rasi and 19° is in the 6th part of the rasi. Because Ge is an airy rasi, counting starts from Li. The 4th from Li is Cp. So the 4th part in Ge goes into Cp in D-9. On the other hand, Sc is a watery sign and counting starts from Cn. The 6th from Cn is Sg. So the 6th part of Sc goes into Sg in D-9. So Mercury is in Cp and Jupiter is in Sg in D-9 for this example.

6.2.10 *Dasamsa Chart (D-10)*

Each rasi is divided into 10 equal parts of 3° each. Bodies in the 10 parts of a rasi go into the 10 rasis starting from the rasi itself or the 9th from it, based on whether the rasi is an odd or even sign.

This chart is also known as **Dasamaamsa** or **Karmamsa** or **Swargamsa**.

Example 17: Let us say Mercury is at 10° in Ge and Jupiter is at 19° in Sc. We see that 10° is in the 4th part of the rasi and 19° is in the 7th part of the rasi. Because Ge is an odd rasi, counting starts from Ge itself. The 4th from Ge is Vi. So the 4th part in Ge goes into Vi in D-10. On the other hand, Sc is an even sign and counting starts from the 9th from it, *i.e.* Cn. The 7th from Cn is Cp. So the 7th part of Sc goes into Cp in D-10. So Mercury is in Vi and Jupiter is in Cp in D-10 for this example.

6.2.11 *Rudramsa Chart (D-11)*

Each rasi is divided into 11 equal parts of 2° 43' 38" each. Count rasis from Ar to the rasi being divided, in the zodiacal order. Count the same number of rasis anti-zodiacally[11] from Ar. Bodies in the 11 parts of the rasi go into the 11 rasis starting from the rasi found thus.

This chart is also known as **Ekadasamsa**.

Example 18: Let us say Mercury is at 11° in Ge and Jupiter is at 19° in Sc. We see that 11° is in the 5th part of the rasi and 19° is in the 7th part of the rasi. In the case of Ge, it is the 3rd rasi from Ar. The 3rd rasi from Ar in the reverse order is Aq. So counting starts from the Aq. The 5th from Aq is Ge. So the 5th part in Ge goes into Ge in D-11. In the case of Sc, it is the 8th rasi from Ar. Counting the 8th rasi from Ar in the reverse order, we get Vi. So counting starts from Vi. The 7th from Vi is Pi. So the 7th part of Sc goes into Pi in D-11. So Mercury is in Ge and Jupiter is in Pi in D-11 for this example.

6.2.12 *Dwadasamsa Chart (D-12)*

Each rasi is divided into 12 equal parts of 2° 30' each. Bodies in the 12 parts of a rasi go into the 12 rasis starting from the rasi itself.

Example 19: Let us say Mercury is at 11° in Ge and Jupiter is at 19° in Sc. We see that 11° is in the 5th part of the rasi and 19° is in the 8th part of the rasi. The 5th from Ge is Li. So the 5th part in Ge goes into Li in D-12. The 8th from Sc is Ge. So the 8th part of Sc goes into Ge in D-12. So Mercury is in Li and Jupiter is in Ge in D-12 for this example.

6.2.13 *Shodasamsa Chart (D-16)*

Each rasi is divided into 16 equal parts of 1° 52' 30" each. Bodies in the 16 parts of a rasi go into the 16 rasis starting from Ar, Le and Sg, based on whether the rasi is movable, fixed or dual. When counting rasis from a given rasi, we go zodiacally. After going over the 12 rasis from a rasi, we get the same rasi as the 13th rasi. So the 13th, 14th, 15th and 16th rasis from a rasi are simply the 1st, 2nd, 3rd and 4th rasis.

This chart is also known as **Kalamsa**.

Example 20: Let us say Mercury is at 11° in Ge and Jupiter is at 19° in Sc. We see that 11° is in the 6th part of the rasi and 19° is in the 11th part of the rasi. Ge is a dual rasi and we start counting from Sg. The 6th from Sg is Ta. So the 6th part in Ge goes into Ta in D-16. On the other hand, Sc is a fixed

---

11 The zodiacal order is: Ar, Ta, Ge, Cn, Le, …
The anti-zodiacal order is: Ar, Pi, Aq, Cp, Sg, …

sign and we start counting from Le. The 11th from Le is Ge. So the 11th part of Sc goes into Ge in D-16. So Mercury is in Ta and Jupiter is in Ge in D-16 for this example.

6.2.14 *Vimsamsa Chart (D-20)*

Each rasi is divided into 20 equal parts of 1° 30' each. Bodies in the 20 parts of a rasi go into the 20 rasis starting from Ar, Sg and Le, based on whether the rasi is movable, fixed or dual.

Example 21: Let us say Mercury is at 11° in Ge and Jupiter is at 19° in Sc. We see that 11° is in the 8th part of the rasi and 19° is in the 13th part of the rasi. Because Ge is a dual rasi, we start counting from Le. The 8th from Le is Pi. So the 8th part in Ge goes into Pi in D-20. On the other hand, Sc is a fixed sign and the counting starts from Sg. The 13th from Sg is Sg itself (13th = 1st, after removing 12). So the 13th part of Sc goes into Sg in D-20. So Mercury is in Pi and Jupiter is in Sg in D-20 for this example.

6.2.15 *Chaturvimsamsa Chart (D-24)*

Each rasi is divided into 24 equal parts of 1° 15' each. Bodies in the 24 parts of a rasi go into the 24 rasis starting from Le or Cn, based on whether the rasi is odd or even.

This chart is also called **Siddhamsa**.

Example 22: Let us say Mercury is at 11° in Ge and Jupiter is at 19° in Sc. We see that 11° is in the 9th part of the rasi and 19° is in the 16th part of the rasi. Ge is an odd rasi and counting starts from Le. The 9th from Le is Ar. So the 9th part in Ge goes into Ar in D-24. On the other hand, Sc is an even rasi and counting starts from Cn. The 16th from Cn is Li (16th = 4th, after removing 12). So the 16th part of Sc goes into Li in D-24. So Mercury is in Ar and Jupiter is in Li in D-24 for this example.

6.2.16 *Nakshatramsa Chart (D-27)*

Each rasi is divided into 27 equal parts of 1° 6' 40'' each. Bodies in the 27 parts of a rasi go into the 12 rasis starting from Ar, Cn, Li and Cp based on whether the rasi is a fiery, earthy, airy or watery rasi.

This chart is also called **Saptavimsamsa** or **Bhamsa**.

Example 23: Let us say Mercury is at 11° in Ge and Jupiter is at 19° in Sc. We see that 11° is in the 10th part of the rasi and 19° is in the 18th part of the rasi. Because Ge is an airy rasi, counting starts from Li. The 10th from Li is Le. So the 10th part in Ge goes into Le in D-27. On the other hand, Sc is a watery sign and counting starts from Cp. The 18th from Cp is Ge (18th = 6th, after removing 12). So the 18th part of Sc goes into Ge in D-27. So Mercury is in Le and Jupiter is in Ge in D-27 for this example.

6.2.17 *Trimsamsa Chart (D-30)*

D-30 positions of planets are computed based on the following rules:

Odd Rasis:

- Bodies in 0°-5° in odd rasis are placed in Ar in D-30.
- Bodies in 5°-10° in odd rasis are placed in Aq in D-30.
- Bodies in 10°-18° in odd rasis are placed in Sg in D-30.
- Bodies in 18°-25° in odd rasis are placed in Ge in D-30.
- Bodies in 25°-30° in odd rasis are placed in Li in D-30.

Even Rasis:

- Bodies in 0°-5° in even rasis are placed in Ta in D-30.
- Bodies in 5°-12° in even rasis are placed in Vi in D-30.
- Bodies in 12°-20° in even rasis are placed in Pi in D-30.
- Bodies in 20°-25° in even rasis are placed in Cp in D-30.
- Bodies in 25°-30° in even rasis are placed in Sc in D-30.

6.2.18 *Khavedamsa Chart (D-40)*

Each rasi is divided into 40 equal parts of 45' each. Bodies in the 40 parts of a rasi go into the 40 rasis starting from Ar or Li, based on whether the rasi is odd or even.

This chart is also called **Chatvarimsamsa**.

Example 24: Let us say Mercury is at 11° in Ge and Jupiter is at 19° in Sc. We see that 11° is in the 15th part of the rasi and 19° is in the 26th part of the rasi. Because Ge is an odd rasi, counting starts from Ar. The 15th from Ar is Ge (15th = 3rd, after removing 12). So the 15th part in Ge goes into Ge in D-40. On the other hand, Sc is an even rasi and counting starts from Li. The 26th from Li is Sc (26th = 2nd, after removing multiples of 12). So the 26th part of Sc goes into Sc in D-40. So Mercury is in Ge and Jupiter is in Sc in D-40 for this example.

6.2.19 *Akshavedamsa Chart (D-45)*

Each rasi is divided into 45 equal parts of 40' each. Bodies in the 45 parts of a rasi go into the 45 rasis starting from Ar, Le or Sg, based on whether the rasi is a movable, fixed or dual rasi.

This chart is also called **Pancha-chatvarimsamsa**.

Example 25: Let us say Mercury is at 11° in Ge and Jupiter is at 19° in Sc. We see that 11° is in the 17th part of the rasi and 19° is in the 29th part of the rasi. Because Ge is a dual rasi, we start counting from Sg. The 17th from Sg is Ar (17th = 5th, after removing 12). So the 17th part in Ge goes into Ar in D-

45. On the other hand, Sc is a fixed rasi and counting starts from Le. The 29th from Le is Sg. So the 29th part of Sc goes into Sg in D-45. So Mercury is in Ar and Jupiter is in Sg in D-45 for this example.

6.2.20 *Shashtyamsa Chart (D-60)*

Each rasi is divided into 60 equal parts of 30' each. Bodies in the 60 parts of a rasi go into the 60 rasis starting the rasi itself.

To see the part occupied by a body, we can take its longitude from the beginning of the occupied rasi, multiply it by 2, take degrees and ignore minutes, add 1 to it.

Example 26: Let us say Jupiter is at 222° 58' , *i.e.* 12° 58' in Scorpio. Multiplying 12° 58' by 2, we get 25° 56'. Taking degrees and ignoring minutes, we get 25. Adding 1, we get 26. So 12° 58' is in the 26th part of rasi (where each part is 1/60th of rasi, *i.e.* 30'). So we have to count the 26th rasi from Sc. Removing multiples of 12 from 26, we get 2. The 2nd rasi from Sc is Sg. So Jupiter is in Sg in D-60 in this example.

6.3 Divisional Chart Significations

Each divisional chart signifies a particular area of life and throws light on it. Table 11 gives the list of these areas.

Table 11: Divisional Chart Significations

Divisional Chart	Symbol	Area of life to be seen from it
Rasi	D-1	Existence at the physical level
Hora	D-2	Wealth and money
Drekkana	D-3	Everything related to brothers and sisters
Chaturthamsa	D-4	Residence, houses owned, properties and fortune
Panchamsa	D-5	Fame, authority and power
Shashthamsa	D-6	Health troubles
Saptamsa	D-7	Everything related to children (and grand-children)
Ashtamsa	D-8	Sudden and unexpected troubles, litigation etc
Navamsa	D-9	Marriage and everything related to

Divisional Chart	Symbol	Area of life to be seen from it
		spouse(s), *dharma* (duty and righteousness), interaction with other people, basic skills, inner self
Dasamsa	D-10	Career, activities and achievements in society
Rudramsa	D-11	Death and destruction
Dwadasamsa	D-12	Everything related to parents (also uncles, aunts and grand-parents, *i.e.* blood-relatives of parents)
Shodasamsa	D-16	Vehicles, pleasures, comforts and discomforts
Vimsamsa	D-20	Religious activities and spiritual matters
Chaturvimsamsa	D-24	Learning, knowledge and education
Nakshatramsa	D-27	Strengths and weaknesses, inherent nature
Trimsamsa	D-30	Evils and punishment, sub-conscious self, some diseases
Khavedamsa	D-40	Auspicious and inauspicious events
Akshavedamsa	D-45	All matters
Shashtyamsa	D-60	*Karma* of past life, all matters

6.4 Insights on Divisional Charts

Divisional charts based on divisions between 1 and 12 operate in the **physical plane**. They show physical matters. Body, wealth, residence, wife, children, parents – these are all matters relating to the physical self.

Divisional charts based on divisions between 13 and 24 (*i.e.* D-16, D-20 and D-24) operate in the **mental plane**. They show matters that exist at the mental plane. Sense of pleasure and unhappiness, religiousness, learning and knowledge – these are all matters relating to the mind and intellect.

Divisional charts based on divisions between 25 and 36 (*i.e.* D-27 and D-30) operate in the **plane of sub-consciousness**. One's strengths, weaknesses, inherent nature, evils, certain psychological imbalances – these are all matters relating to the sub-conscious self.

Divisional charts based on divisions above 36 (*i.e.* D-40, D-45 and

D-60) operate in a **kaarmic** plane of existence that is **above** physical self, mind and sub-conscious self. Based on the *karma* from previous lives, we all have an existence at a level that goes beyond the levels of body, mind and sub-consciousness. Existence at that level has a considerable role in deciding the pattern of one's life, along with existence at the physical, mental and sub-conscious levels. Higher divisional charts like D-40, D-45 and D-60 throw light on this subtle aspect of chart analysis.[12]

6.5 Using Divisional Charts

It is very important to memorize Table 11. We should choose the divisional chart to analyze, based on the matter we are interested in. If we want to know something about one's career, for example, we should analyze one's dasamsa chart (D-10). If we want to know something about one's luxuries and pleasures, we should analyze one's shodasamsa (D-16). Based on the matter of interest, we decide which area of life is relevant and analyze the corresponding divisional chart.

We should remember which planets, rasis and houses show a particular matter and find links between them in the divisional chart of interest.

Suppose we want to see when one would go abroad. It is related to residence and fortune and we should analyze one's chaturthamsa (D-4). The 9th and 12th houses show foreign residence. Rahu signifies foreign residence. We should now look for links. If 12th lord is with Rahu in the 9th house in D-4, it can suggest that one would live abroad, probably during the periods of Rahu or 12th lord or 9th house.

Suppose we want to see when one would get a promotion at the office. Because D-10 shows one's career and achievements, we should analyze D-10. Because GL (ghati lagna) shows power and authority, planets or rasis giving a promotion are usually connected with GL. They are in GL or aspect GL. Because AL shows status, planets associating with AL or the5th or the 10th from it are favorable. If the lord of AL is in the 10th from it and aspects GL, probably his period will give a promotion.

In this manner, we should analyze the divisional chart that signifies the sphere of life that we are interested in and analyze the houses that show the matter of interest. This is the key to correct chart analysis. We will see many examples of this in coming chapters.

---

12 The content of this paragraph has philosophical undercurrents that may be difficult to understand for students without a good background in Hindu philosophy. This knowledge should be learnt directly from a competent guru. Readers are advised to leave these higher charts until they find one.

6.6 Varga Grouping and Amsabala

We have several varga groups, *i.e.* groups of divisional charts.

If a planet is in its moolatrikona or an own rasi or its rasi of exaltation in a chart, it makes the planet very strong in that chart. In each group of divisional charts, we can count the divisional charts in which a planet occupies its moolatrikona or an own rasi or its rasi of exaltation. Based on the count of such good divisional charts for the planet, we say that the planet is in a particular amsa (the higher this number is, the stronger the planet is).

6.6.1 *Shadvarga*

"Shadvarga" literally means "six divisions". Shadvarga is a group of the following divisional charts: (1) Rasi chart, (2) D-2, (3) D-3, (4) D-9, (5) D-12, and, (6) D-30.

The amsa said to be occupied by a planet and the corresponding count of divisional charts – from the above list – in which it occupies its moolatrikona, rasi of exaltation or an own rasi is listed below:

Kimsukaamsa – 2, Vyanjanaamsa – 3, Chaamaraamsa – 4, Chatraamsa – 5, Kundalaamsa – 6.

6.6.2 *Sapta varga*

"Sapta varga" literally means "seven divisions". Sapta varga is a group of the following divisional charts: (1) Rasi chart, (2) D-2, (3) D-3, (4) D-7, (5) D-9, (6) D-12, and, (7) D-30.

The amsa said to be occupied by a planet and the corresponding count of divisional charts – from the above list – in which it occupies its moolatrikona, rasi of exaltation or an own rasi is listed below:

Kimsukaamsa – 2, Vyanjanaamsa – 3, Chaamaraamsa – 4, Chatraamsa – 5, Kundalaamsa – 6, Mukutaamsa – 7.

6.6.3 *Dasa varga*

"Dasa varga" literally means "ten divisions". Dasa varga is a group of the following divisional charts: (1) Rasi chart, (2) D-2, (3) D-3, (4) D-7, (5) D-9, (6) D-10, (7) D-12, (8) D-16, (9) D-30, and, (10) D-60.

The amsa said to be occupied by a planet and the corresponding count of divisional charts – from the above list – in which it occupies its moolatrikona, rasi of exaltation or an own rasi is listed below:

Paarijaataamsa – 2, Uttamaamsa – 3, Gopuraamsa – 4, Simhaasanaamsa – 5, Paaraavataamsa – 6, Devalokaamsa – 7, Brahmalokamsa – 8, Airaavataamsa – 9, Sreedhaamaamsa – 10.

NOTE: This group is very important and some yogas – special combinations – make use of these amsas. For example, lagna lord or ghati lagna lord in Simhaasanaamsa would make one very famous. A quadrant lord with good amsabala in dasavarga makes one very successful. Readers should memorize the above amsas.

6.6.4 *Shodasa varga*

"Shodasa varga" literally means "sixteen divisions". Shodasa varga is a group of the following divisional charts: (1) Rasi chart, (2) D-2, (3) D-3, (4) D-4, (5) D-7, (6) D-9, (7) D-10, (8) D-12, (9) D-16, (10) D-20, (11) D-24, (12) D-27, (13) D-30, (14) D-40, (15) D-45, and, (16) D-60.

The amsa said to be occupied by a planet and the corresponding count of divisional charts – from the above list – in which it occupies its moolatrikona, rasi of exaltation or an own rasi is listed below:

Bhedakaamsa – 2, Kusumaamsa – 3, Nagapurushaamsa – 4, Kandukaamsa – 5, Keralaamsa – 6, Kalpavrikshaamsa – 7, Chandanavanaamsa – 8, Poornachandraamsa – 9, Uchchaisravaamsa – 10, Dhanvantaryamsa – 11, Sooryakaantaamsa – 12, Vidrumaamsa – 13, Indraasanaamsa – 14, Golokaamsa – 15, Sree Vallabhaamsa – 16.

Example 27: Let us look at the chart of Bill Cosby. He is a famous TV and film actor in USA. He is one of the greatest theatrical personalities of the world and a natural actor. He is known as a charitable person who donated huge amounts of money for the education of African American kids. His birthdata is: 12th July 1937, 12:30 am (Time Zone: 5:00 west of GMT), 75 W 10, 39 N 57.

The 9th house shows charitable nature and the 12th house shows expenditure. Jupiter owns the 9th and 12th houses and occupies the 9th house here. This may be the reason for Mr. Cosby's charitable nature. Let us see the amsabala of Jupiter. Jupiter is at 29° 49' in Sg. The signs occupied by him in various charts are shown below:

Rasi: Sg, *D-2:* Cn, *D-3:* Li, *D-4:* Vi, *D-7:* Ge, *D-9:* Sg, *D-10:* Vi, *D-12:* Sc, *D-16:* Pi, *D-20:* Pi, *D-24:* Cn, *D-27:* Ge, *D-30:* Li, *D-40:* Cn, *D-45:* Le, *D-60:* Sc.

Jupiter owns Sg and Pi. His moolatrikona is Sg. He is exalted in Cn. So we have to count the charts in which he is in Cn, Sg or Pi.

(1) Out of the 6 divisional charts of shadvarga, Jupiter is in Cn, Sg or Pi in 3 charts –Rasi, D-2 and D-9. So Jupiter is in **Vyanjanaamsa**.

(2) Out of the 7 divisional charts of sapta varga, Jupiter is in Cn, Sg or Pi in 3 charts –Rasi, D-2 and D-9. So Jupiter is in **Vyanjanaamsa**.

(3) Out of the 10 divisional charts of dasa varga, Jupiter is in Cn, Sg or Pi in 4 charts –Rasi, D-2, D-9 and D-16. So Jupiter is in **Gopuraamsa**.

(4) Out of the 16 divisional charts of shodasa varga, Jupiter is in Cn, Sg or Pi in 7 charts –Rasi, D-2, D-9, D-16, D-20, D-24 and D-40. So Jupiter is in **Kalpavrikshaamsa**.

Being in Gopuramsa and Kalpavrikshamsa makes Jupiter very strong.

6.7 Conclusion

The science of Vedic astrology stands on the basis of 4 pillars – grahas (planets), rasis (signs), vargas (divisional charts) and bhavas (houses). This chapter covered the third pillar – divisional charts. If readers have an accurate software program that gives all the divisional charts for any chart, it may be acceptable to ignore the details of computation. However, it is good to be aware of the details.

For D-8 and D-11, there are different versions. For D-2 and D-3 also, there are variations. Different variations of divisional charts show different spheres of activities. However, we will ignore the variations in this book.

Twenty divisional charts are covered here. Each divisional chart throws light on a specific sphere of activity. For example, D-10 shows career, D-9 shows marital life and D-7 shows the fortune of children. Choosing the correct divisional chart for analyzing the matter of interest is the key to correct analysis.

7. Houses

7.1 Introduction

The zodiac consists of 12 rasis. Each rasi is said to form a house. When we talk about houses, we always have a point of reference. The rasi containing the point of reference is the 1st house. The next rasi is the 2nd house. The rasi after that is the 3rd house. Suppose Moon is in Aquarius and suppose we want houses with respect to Moon. Then Aquarius is the 1st house, Pisces is the 2nd house, Aries is the 3rd house, Taurus is the 4th house and so on. As we go around the zodiac, we reach Capricorn when we find the 12th house.

In the same chart, Sun may be in Taurus. When we find houses with respect to Sun, Taurus contains the 1st house, Gemini contains the 2nd house, Cancer contains the 3rd house and so on. If Ghati Lagna is in Virgo in the same chart, then the 1st, 2nd and 3rd houses with respect to Ghati Lagna are in Virgo, Libra and Scorpio respectively.

Thus we can find houses with respect to different references. The same sign may contain the 2nd house with respect to one reference and the 6th house with respect to another reference. If we mention houses without clearly specifying the reference used, it means that the reference used is lagna (ascendant). Lagna is the default reference when finding houses.

Different houses stand for different matters. The matters signified by a house also depend on the reference used. Each reference throws light on matters of a specific nature and that colors the meaning of a house. For example, the 11th house from lagna may stand for something and the 11th house from arudha lagna may stand for something else. It depends on the kind of matters shown by the two references – lagna and arudha lagna.

In addition, the matters signified by a house depend on the divisional chart in which we are finding houses. Each divisional chart throws light on matters of a specific nature. Again, that colors the meaning of a house. The 4th house from lagna in D-16 may mean something and the 4th house from lagna in D-24 may mean something else. We have already listed the areas of life seen from various divisional charts in the chapter on "Divisional Charts".

7.2 Significations of Houses

The matters signified by various houses are listed below. For further discussion on the results of various houses, readers may refer either to the ancient classics or to the modern classic – *How to Judge a Horoscope* (Vols I & II) by Dr. B.V. Raman.

First House: Physical body, complexion, appearance, head, intelligence, strength, energy, fame, success, nature of birth, caste.

Second House: Wealth, assets, family, speech, eyes, mouth, face, voice, food.

Third House: Younger co-borns, confidants, courage, mental strength, communication skills, creativity, throat, ears, arms, father's death (7th from 9th), expenditure on vehicles and house (12th from 4th), travels.

Fourth House: Mother, vehicles, house, lands, immovable property, motherland, childhood, wealth from real estate, education, relatives, happiness, comforts, pleasures, peace, state of mind, heart.

Fifth House: Children, poorvapunya (good deeds of previous lives), intelligence, knowledge & scholarship, devotion, mantras (prayers), stomach, digestive system, authority/power, fame, love, affection, emotions, judgment, speculation.

Sixth House: Enemies, service, servants, relatives, mental tension, injuries, health, diseases, agriculture, accidents, mental affliction, mother's younger brother, hips.

Seventh House: Marriage, marital life, life partner, sex, passion (and related happiness), long journeys, partners, business, death, the portion of the body below the navel.

Eighth House: Longevity, debts, disease, ill-fame, inheritance, loss of friends, occult studies, evils, gifts, unearned wealth, windfall, disgrace, secrets, genitals.

Ninth House: Father, teacher, boss, fortune, religiousness, spirituality, God, higher studies & high knowledge, fortune in a foreign land, foreign trips, diksha (joining a religious order), past life and the cause of birth, grandchildren, principles, dharma, intuition, compassion, sympathy, leadership, charity, thighs.

Tenth House: Growth, profession, career, karma (action), conduct in society, fame, honors, awards, self-respect, dignity, knees.

Eleventh House: Elder co-borns, income, gains, realization of hopes, friends, ankles.

Twelfth House: Losses, expenditure, punishment, imprisonment, hospitalization, pleasures in bed, misfortune, bad habits, sleep, meditation, donation, secret enemies, heaven, left eye, feet, residence away from the place of birth, moksha (emancipation/liberation).

We can find houses from houses and concatenate the meanings in some places. For example, the 3rd house shows younger brother. The 2nd house from the 3rd house is the 4th house (count 1, 2 from 3rd and get 3rd, 4th). So the 4th house shows the wealth, speech etc of younger brother. The 7th house from the 3rd house is the 9th house and it can show younger sibling's spouse. The 11th house from lagna shows friends and the 4th house from lagna is nothing but the 6th house from the 11th house. So the 4th house stands for enemies, diseases and debts of friends. In this manner, we can deduce many additional meanings of various houses.

7.3 Common References for Houses

It may be noted from the list above that each house shows many matters. It may be confusing at first to pick the right meaning that is relevant in a particular analysis. It becomes easier with experience. We have to note the area of life seen in the divisional chart under examination. We have to choose the meanings of houses that are relevant in that area of life. For example, the 4th house shows education, vehicle, house and mother (among other things). A list of the areas of life seen in various divisional charts is given in the chapter on "Divisional Charts". We see from it that learning is seen from D-24, pleasures and comforts from D-16, house and immovable property from D-4 and parents from D-12. So the 4th houses in D-24, D-16, D-4 and D-12 show education, vehicle, house and mother (respectively).

We should also take cognisance of the kind of matters shown by various references and interpret the meaning of a house accordingly. The 4th house from lagna, the 4th house from arudha lagna and the 4th house from paaka lagna can mean different things, depending on the matters shown by lagna, arudha lagna and paaka lagna. Now we will learn about the most common references used in finding houses and the matters shown by them.

Depending on the matter we are analyzing, we should look at the correct divisional chart, the correct reference and the correct house. Then only good results can be obtained. All this complexity may be perplexing to new students. However, there is something we should realize. Human existence is a very complicated thing and it is silly and unscientific to expect a simplistic model for the complicated human life. Though Vedic astrology has too many parameters used in chart analysis, they are all important as they give us the degrees of freedom necessary for modeling something as complicated as human life. However, if we do not understand what each parameter means and end up using them in a mixed-up way, we will get nowhere. So readers should strive to understand these basics very clearly.

7.3.1 *Lagna*

Lagna is the most commonly used reference when finding houses. If no reference is mentioned when houses are listed, it means that lagna – the default reference – was used. Lagna shows true self. If we are trying to understand someone's status in society, lagna may not be the correct reference. Status does not relate to "true self". It is a part of the illusion of this world. However, if we are trying to understand someone's intentions in doing something or someone's knowledge or someone's persistence, it relates to "true self". So they are seen from the houses counted from lagna. Lagna shows true self. It shows the overall spirit of "I" (self).

7.3.2 *Chandra Lagna (Moon lagna)*

Chandra lagna means Moon taken as a reference. We can find houses from Moon. Because Moon is the significator of mind, these houses show things from the perspective of mind. For example, someone may be working in a routine job, but he may have an active and enterprising mind and he may be using it in his career. In that case, the 10th house (career) from lagna may have the influence of Saturn (routine job) and the 10th house from Moon may have the influence of Mars (active and enterprising).

Houses counted from Moon are useful in looking at things from the point of view of mind. When we judge how happy one is, how ambitious one is and how one views one's career, the role of mind is paramount. So Chandra lagna should not be ignored.

7.3.3 *Ravi Lagna (Sun lagna)*

Ravi lagna means Sun taken as a reference. We can find houses from Sun. Because Sun is the significator of soul, these houses show things from the perspective of soul. For things related to physical vitality also, Sun is an important reference.

7.3.4 *Arudha Lagna*

Computation of arudha lagna (AL) will be explained in the chapter on "Arudha Padas". For now, the readers should remember that arudha lagna shows how a native is perceived in the world. It also shows the status of a native.

A planet in the 10th house from lagna may give some important developments in one's profession. A planet in the 10th house from Chandra lagna may give some important mental activity in one's profession. A planet in the 10th house from arudha lagna may give some important developments in one's professional status.

7.3.5 *Paaka Lagna*

Paaka lagna is important when analyzing the natal chart, dasas and transits. Paaka lagna is nothing but lagna lord taken as a reference. If someone with Pisces lagna has Jupiter in Cancer, then Cancer becomes paaka lagna. If someone with Leo lagna has Sun in Virgo, Virgo becomes paaka lagna.

Rasis represent situations and forces influencing the course of a native's life and planets represent individual beings. Lagna lord represents the physical self of a native. So that is what paaka lagna shows. Houses counted from paaka lagna throw light on matters related to the physical self of a native.

Lagna shows the *concept* of self and it deals with one's true *personality*. The physical *existence* of the person is different from this conceptual self. This applies to all divisional charts. Let us take an example. The 5th house shows scholarship, memory and success in competition. All these are related to learning and they are seen in D-24, the chart of learning. But they are better seen from different references. Let us find the best reference for each.

Success in competition is related to the illusions and perceptions of the world and so the most appropriate reference is arudha lagna. The 5th house from arudha lagna shows success in competition. Scholarship is not a measurable attribute of the physical existence. It is a property of one's true personality and one's conceptual self. So the 5th from lagna shows scholarship. If we take the self that exists physically and take its part as applicable to the area of life shown by D-24 (*i.e.* learning), memory is a direct attribute of that self. Memory is a property of one's self that physically exists. So the 5th house from paaka lagna shows memory the best.

Saturn's transit[13] over the rasi containing one's lagna may throw obstructions and hamper one's activities. Saturn's transit over the rasi containing one's Chandra lagna may create frustration and mental depression. Saturn's transit over the rasi containing one's paaka lagna may leave one feeling sick all the time and attack the physical vitality.

7.3.6 *Karakamsa Lagna*

Atma karaka stands for the soul of the person. Atma karaka is an important reference point in a chart. Because the soul is an important factor in deciding the nature of inner self than the physical existence, atma karaka is an important reference point in navamsa chart. Navamsa chart throws light on the inner self and the rasi occupied by atma karaka in it is called "Karakamsa". We can analyze navamsa chart with respect to Karakamsa. The 12th house from Karakamsa shows the liberation of the soul and the situation of Ketu there is conducive to moksha. Propitiation of the deities corresponding to the strongest planet in the 12th house in navamsa from Karakamsa lagna can take one's soul towards moksha.

---

13 If a planet occupies, on a given day, a particular rasi, then it is said to "transit" in that sign on that day. Transit positions refer to the positions of planets on a given day and natal positions refer to the positions of planets at the time of one's birth. This will be dealt with in detail in the part "Transit Analysis".

7.3.7 *Ghati Lagna*

Ghati lagna (GL) shows self, from the point of view of power, authority and fame. When we analyze promotions in career or political power of politicians, this reference is very important.

7.3.8 *Hora Lagna*

Hora lagna (HL) shows self, from the point of view of wealth. This reference is important when analyzing one's wealth.

7.3.9 *Graha Lagnas*

Apart from the above references, we use several "graha lagnas" or planetary references. For each house, a planet works as the natural significator. To see matters signified by a house, we can take the relevant planet as the reference. The list of houses that can be seen from each planet is given in Table 12.

Table 12: Houses signified by planets

Planet	Houses
Sun	9th, 10th, 11th
Moon	4th, 1st, 2nd, 11th, 9th
Mars	3rd
Mercury	6th
Jupiter	5th
Venus	7th
Saturn	8th, 12th

When we analyze courage or persistence or weapons or younger brothers or the expenditure on house or the expenditure on car, we have to analyze the 3rd house in the relevant divisional chart. In all those cases, we can see the 3rd house from lagna and the 3rd house from Mars and draw conclusions based on the strength of both. If Mars is stronger than lagna, then the 3rd house from Mars may be more important than the 3rd house from lagna. Similarly, we see the 4th from lagna and the 4th from Moon for mother. We see the 9th from Sun and the 9th from lagna for father. We see the 12th from lagna and the 12th from Saturn for losses. We see the 5th from lagna and the 5th from Jupiter for progeny. We see the 7th from lagna and the 7th from Venus for marriage.

In addition to the above list, we can find a house with respect to the *naisargika karaka* (natural significator) who signifies the matter shown by a house. For example, Venus signifies vehicles. D-16 is the chart that shows vehicles and pleasures. So the 4th from Venus in D-16 can show one's happiness from vehicles and other luxuries. As Mercury is the natural significator of speech, the 2nd house from lagna and the 2nd house from Mercury show speech (in rasi, D-9 and D-27[14]). A complete list of naisargika karakas of different matters can be found in the chapter on "Karakas".

7.4 Special Categories

There are some special categories of houses:

(1) The 1st, 5th and 9th houses form a triangle and they are known as "konas" or "trikonas" or **"trines"**.

(2) The 1st, 4th, 7th and 10th houses are called "kendras" or **"quadrants"** or "angles".

(3) The 2nd, 5th, 8th and 11th houses are called **"panapharas"** or "succedants". These are basically the quadrants from the 2nd house.

(4) The 3rd, 6th, 9th and 12th houses are called **"apoklimas"** or "precedants". These are basically the quadrants from the 3rd house.

(5) The 3rd, 6th, 10th and 11th houses are called **"upachayas"**.

(6) The 6th, 8th and 12th houses are called "trik sthanas" or **"dusthanas"** (bad/evil houses).

(7) The 4th and 8th houses are called **"chaturasras"**.

We can find trines, quadrants *etc* from lagna or other references or even from houses. We can find houses with respect to a reference and then find trines, quadrants *etc* with respect to *those houses*. For example, let us take the 3rd house from lagna. Trines from it are the 1st, 5th and 9th houses from it. The 5th house from the 3rd house is the 7th house (count 1, 2, 3, 4, and 5 starting from the 3rd house. We get 3rd, 4th, 5th, 6th and 7th. So the 5th from 3rd is 7th). The 9th house from the 3rd house is the 11th house. So 3rd, 7th and 11th houses are the trines from the 3rd house. Similarly, the 3rd, 6th, 9th and 12th houses are the quadrants from the 3rd house. And the 5th, 8th, 12th and 1st houses are the upachayas from the 3rd house. The 8th, 10th and 2nd houses are the dusthanas from the 3rd house. Thus we can find trines, quadrants *etc* from any house.

14 Rasi chart shows the overall picture and the manifestation at the physical level. Navamsa shows basic skills and the way one interacts with others. D-27 shows one's strengths and weaknesses. All the three charts are important. One may have strong benefics in the 2nd from lagna in rasi and navamsa charts, but malefics in the 2nd from Mercury in D-27. In such a case, one will be a skilled speaker, but harsh speech may be his weakness. D-27 throws light on the sub-conscious self and shows one's inherent strengths and weaknesses.

7.4.1 *Trines*

Trines are the abode of Goddess Lakshmi, who rules prosperity. Trines from any reference are houses that are beneficial to the reference. They bring prosperity and well-being to the reference. For example, trines from lagna shows prosperity of self.

In Hinduism, there are 4 purushaarthas (purposes/goals of man) – (1) *Dharma*: righteousness and adherence to one's duty, (2) *Artha*: money and career, (3) *Kaama*: desiring things and getting them, and, (4) *Moksha*: final liberation of soul.

Dharma is shown by the trines from the 1st house – 1st, 5th and 9th – and they show prosperity of self, intelligence and dharma[15]. They are called "dharma trikonas" (trines of duty). The character of a person, his intelligence and his righteousness decide how one follows *dharma* – the first purpose of human existence.

Trines from the 2nd house are called "artha trikonas" (trines of money) and they show money related activities. The 2nd house shows wealth. The 6th house shows service. The 10th house shows career and activities in society. These three houses show money related activities and how one follows *artha* – the second purpose of human existence.

Trines from the 3rd house are called "kaama trikonas" (trines of desire) and they show one's desires and how one gets them. The 3rd house shows one's persistence. The 7th house shows relations and sex. The 11th house shows gains. These three houses show how one follows *kaama* – the third purpose of human existence.

Trines from the 4th house (4th – harmony, 8th – occult studies and spiritual awakening and 12th – moksha) are called "moksha trikonas" (trines of liberation) and they show how one follows *moksha* – the fourth purpose of human existence.

Digbala of planets who attain full digbala in various of these trines shows the strength of different purushaarthas in one's life. Dasas like "Trikona Dasa" which are based on trines show how one follows the four purushaarthas in life.

Planets in mutual trines[16] make each other prosper.

7.4.2 *Quadrants*

Quadrants are the abode of Sri Maha Vishnu, the Supreme Lord who sustains this universe as per Hinduism. Quadrants from any reference show

15 Dharma literally means duty. However, it has come to mean righteousness.

16 We say that two planets are in "mutual trines", if one planet is in a trine from the other.

its sustenance. The 1st house (self), 4th house (comforts), 7th house (marriage and relations with others) and the 10th house (profession) sustain each other.

Planets in mutual quadrants[17] have a sustaining effect on each other.

7.4.3 *Upachayas*

Upachayas from a reference show forces causing gains and growth to the matters signified by the reference. For example, arudha lagna shows one's status and the upachayas from arudha lagna show improvement of status.

7.4.4 *Dusthanas*

Dusthanas from a reference show forces causing setbacks to the matters signified by it. If a dusthana is fortified or afflicted by malefics, it may show serious obstacles. If a dusthana is weak, it shows that obstacles will be easily overcome. For example, exalted 8th lord may show a lot of troubles and debilitated 8th lord may show easy sailing.

7.4.5 *Visible Half and Invisible Half*

The zodiac is divided into two halves in every chart: The 7th, 8th, 9th, 10th, 11th and 12th houses form the "visible half" of the zodiac. The 1st, 2nd, 3rd, 4th, 5th and 6th houses form the "invisible half" of the zodiac. The houses in the visible half of the zodiac with respect to a reference give results that can be seen in the material world and the houses in the invisible half of the zodiac give results that cannot be easily seen. It is for this reason that the bases of dharma trikona (1st house) and moksha trikona (4th house) are in the invisible half and the bases of artha trikona (10th house) and kaama trikona (7th house) are in the visible half.

7.4.6 *Quick Summary*

Trines:	Prosperity and flourishing
Quadrants:	Sustenance and vital activity
Upachayas:	Gains and growth
Dusthanas:	Setbacks and obstacles
Argala sthanas[18]:	Decisive influences

7.5 A Controversy

Houses are found with respect to lagna, special lagnas and some planets. Houses are found in rasi chart and in all the divisional charts. Some scholars

17 We say that two planets are in "mutual quadrants", if one planet is in a quadrant from the other.

18 This will be covered in the chapter on "Aspects and Argalas".

ignore all these and take houses only with respect to lagna and only in rasi chart. They prepare something called "bhaava chakra" or "chalit chakra", in which houses can start in one rasi and end in another. They take lagna's longitude to be the mid-point of the first house and construct all the houses accordingly. In the "equal house method", they take a 30° arc with center at lagna as the 1st house. The next 30° arc is taken as the 2nd house and so on. This method is popular among Indian astrologers. Another method taught by Sripathi is more complicated and it is also popular. However, this author recommends neither. Each rasi is a house. The rasi containing the reference point chosen is the 1st house and the next rasi is the 2nd house.

Though there are some *indirect* references in BPHS[19] suggesting that Parasara supported house divisions placing houses in 2 rasis, there are quite a few *direct* references making it amply clear that each house falls in one rasi. Parasara taught us to find houses by counting rasis from the reference chosen. Moreover, only this approach is logical as we go to divisional charts. Parasara's treatment does not differentiate between rasi and divisional charts, as far as the basic techniques go.

So readers are advised to ignore all the discussions found in other textbooks on house division methods, "bhaava chakra" and "chalit chakra". It may do good to follow the instructions in this chapter.

19 "Brihat Paaraasara Hora Saastram" is a classic by Sage Parasara. It is the most *authentic* and *final* treatise on Vedic astrology. It was written more than 5,000 years ago.

8. Karakas

8.1 Introduction

The word karaka [20] means "one who causes". Karaka of a matter is the significator of the matter. He is the one who causes events related to that matter.

There are 3 kinds of karakas:

(1) **Naisargika karakas** (*natural* significators, 9 in number).

(2) **Chara karakas** (*variable* significators, 8 in number), and,

(3) **Sthira karakas** (*fixed* significators, 7 in number),

One should not use the three types of karakas in a mixed-up way. Karakas of each type have a specific purpose. One should understand the distinction between chara, sthira and naisargika karakas clearly and use them accordingly.

Naisargika karakas shows everything that exists in the creation. They include Rahu, Ketu and the seven planets. They are presided by **Brahma**. Naisargika karakas show not only human beings, but they show various impersonal things and matters. They show everything that exists in Brahma's creation and affects a person. Naisargika karakas are very useful in phalita Jyotish, *i.e.* analysis of general results.

Chara karakas include Rahu and the seven planets. They do not include Ketu, as Ketu stands for moksha (emancipation) and does not stand for any person who affects one's sustenance. Chara karakas are presided by **Vishnu** and they show people who play a role in one's life. As Vishnu presides over activities related to sustenance, achievements and spiritual progress, chara karakas show these aspects of one's life. Chara karakas show people who play an important role in one's sustenance and achievements. Examples are – mother, father, wife, advisors *etc*. Chara karakas are very useful in Raja Yogas and in spiritual progress. They also show how our karma (cumulative sum of actions) is carried from one life to another.

Sthira karakas include only 7 planets because only they have physical bodies. They are presided by **Shiva**. As Shiva presides over death[21], they show the destruction of body. Sthira karakas are useful in timing the death of various near relatives.

---

20 This is pronounced as "kaaraka".

21 In Indian philosophy, death is nothing but praana (life) becoming *sthira* (fixed).

8.2 Chara Karakas

We use the following procedure to find chara karakas:

(1) Take the eight planets – Sun, Moon, Mars, Mercury, Jupiter, Venus, Saturn and Rahu. For each planet, find its advancement from the beginning of the rasi occupied by it. For Rahu, measure the advancement from the end of his rasi.

(2) Arrange them in the decreasing order of advancement.

(3) The planet with the highest advancement is Atma Karaka (significator of self). We will denote him by AK. Find other chara karakas using Table 13.

Table 13: Chara karakas

Advancement	Order	Karaka	Symbol	Persons shown[22]
Highest	1	Atma Karaka	AK	Self
	2	Amatya Karaka	AmK	Ministers[23]
	3	Bhratri Karaka	BK	Siblings
	4	Matri Karaka	MK	Mother
Lowest	5	Pitri Karaka	PiK	Father
	6	Putra Karaka	PK	Children
	7	Jnaati[24] Karaka	GK (JK)	Rivals[25]
	8	Dara Karaka	DK	Spouse

If two planets have the same degrees, we should compare minutes. If minutes are same, we should compare the seconds. If two planets are exactly at the same longitude, then they will hold a karakatwa (signification) together and the next karakatwa will have no ruler. We should use the corresponding sthira karaka in that case. However, this rarely becomes necessary, as two planets are rarely at exactly the same longitude.

Example 28: Consider the following planetary position – Sun: 12Ge47, Moon: 20Ar28, Mars: 13Ge51, Mercury: 25Ge18, Jupiter: 5Ta40, Venus: 17Ge21, Saturn: 2Ta28, Rahu: 1Cn43. Advancements of planets in respective

22 PK can also show subordinates and followers. PiK can show a boss.

23 In practical terms, this means people who give advice (advisors and counsellors).

24 In the symbol "jn" here, 'j' is the voiced palatal consonant and 'n' is the palatal nasal. This is a tough sound to pronounce correctly. Some people approximate it as as "gnaati" or "gyaati".

25 This karaka is commonly used for enemies or rivals. However, the literal meaning of "jnaati" is "paternal cousin".

rasis are found and arranged in the decreasing order in Table 14. Based on it, chara karakas are listed.

Table 14: Chara karakas in Example 28

Planet	Advancement in rasi	Order	Chara karaka
Rahu	30° – 1°43' = 28°17'	1	AK
Mercury	25°18'	2	AmK
Moon	20°28'	3	BK
Venus	17°21'	4	MK
Mars	13°51'	5	PiK
Sun	12°47'	6	PK
Jupiter	5°40'	7	GK (JK)
Venus	2°28'	8	DK

So Rahu represents the self of the native for the purpose of raja yogas, analysis of sustenance, achievements and spiritual evolution. AK throws light on the inner self of a native. Rahu can show a spiritually advanced person or a saint on one hand and a revolutionary or an outcast on the other. Mercury represents the native's advisors and he shows intellectuals when strong and indecisive people when weak.

Exercise 11: Consider the following planetary position – Sun: 9Sg36, Moon: 15Le29, Mars: 13Ar40, Mercury: 21Sc00, Jupiter: 2Aq06, Venus: 17Sg42, Saturn: 9Sc41, Rahu: 14Ge30. Find chara karakas. Guess the nature of the inner self of the native.

8.3 Sthira Karakas

The following is the list of sthira karakas:

Sun or *Venus (stronger)* [26]: Father

Moon or *Mars (stronger)*: Mother

Mars: Younger siblings, brother-in-law and sister-in-law (spouses of siblings)

Mercury: Maternal relatives (uncles and aunts)

---

26 For methods to compare the strengths of planets, one may refer to the chapter "Strength of Planets and Rasis". Some people opine that Sun should be taken as the fixed significator of father for *daytime* births and Venus for *nighttime* births. Similarly, Moon is taken as the fixed significator of mother for *nighttime* births and Mars for *daytime* births.

Jupiter: Husband, sons, paternal grandparents and other paternal relatives (uncles and aunts)

Venus: Wife, father-in-law, mother-in-law & maternal grandparents

Saturn: Elder siblings[27]

The use of sthira karakas has already been explained. They are presided by Shiva and they are used in the timing of death of the above relatives. They should not be used in general predictive astrology in the place of naisargika karakas. For example, some astrologers use the 7th from Jupiter instead of the 7th from Venus to predict marriage. However, Venus is the natural significator of marriage and the 7th from Venus should be used for predicting marriage, both in male and female charts. When predicting the death of spouse, we use Jupiter in female charts and Venus in male charts.[28]

Another difference between sthira and naisargika karakas is that sthira karakas themselves represent the physical bodies of the relatives. In the case of naisargika karakas, we must take the relevant house from the karaka. For example, Jupiter represents the physical body of husband in a female chart, for the purpose of timing death. For the purpose of timing marriage, the 7th from Venus (and not Venus himself) shows husband.

Chara karakas are also similar to sthira karakas in this aspect. We do not take the 7th from DK for spouse, but DK himself shows spouse.

8.4 Naisargika Karakas

We have seen that chara karakas are used in analyzing the influences of various persons on a native, from the point of view of sustenance, achievements and spiritual evolution. We have seen that sthira karakas are used in analyzing the death of relatives. In addition, we have naisargika karakas, who are the natural significators of various matters. These significations are used in general Phalita Jyotish. Table 15 gives a list of naisargika karakas. For example, the 4th house from Moon shows mother. The 5th house from Jupiter shows sons. If we want to analyze the birth of children or analyze some simple events from their lives, we should take the 5th from Jupiter. If we want to analyze some children-related troubles that punish one's soul or if we want to analyze some achievements and happiness related to children, they will be more closely related to PK (putra karaka of chara karakas). If we want to time the death of a child, sthira karaka for children (Jupiter) should be used.

---

27 Some scholars give Saturn as the sthira karaka for children instead of elder siblings.

28 Some scholars take Jupiter as the sthira karaka of spouse in male charts also.

Table 15: Primary Naisargika Karakas

House	From Planet	Matters signified
1st	Sun	Self, physical constitution, soul, health
2nd	Jupiter	Family, wealth
3rd	Mars	Younger siblings, courage
4th	Moon	Mother
5th	Jupiter	Children
6th	Mars	Enemies
7th	Venus	Wife, husband, marital bliss, relationships
8th	Saturn	Longevity, troubles
9th	Jupiter	Teacher, religion, fortune
10th	Mercury	Work, achievements, honors
11th	Jupiter	Elder siblings
12th	Saturn	Losses

In addition, we have various other matters allotted to different planets in classics. The list of the natural significations of various planets is listed in Table 16. For example, Mercury and 5th house show memory and so the 5th house from Mercury shows memory.

Table 16: List of Naisargika Karakatwas

Planet	Matters signified and associated houses
Sun	Self, soul, constitution, health (1st); fame, power (5th); father, boss (9th); career, achievements (10th)
Moon	Mind (1st); mother, peace of mind (4th); friends (11th)
Mars	Courage, younger siblings (3rd); real estate (4th); schol arship in Nyaya sastra, speculation (5th); enemies, diseases, accidents, loans (6th)
Mercury	Speech (2nd); learning (4th); memory, scholarship, students (5th); work, achievements, honors (10th); credits (11th)
Jupiter	Family, wealth (2nd); traditional learning (4th); children, intelligence (5th); teacher, religion, fortune (9th); elder brother, gains (11th)
Venus	Vehicles (4th); wife, husband, marital bliss (7th); bed pleasures (12th)

Planet	Matters signified and associated houses
Saturn	Following (5th); servants (6th), Longevity, troubles (8th); losses, hospitalization (12th)
Rahu	Accidents (6th); occult knowledge (8th); pilgrimages, going abroad (9th)
Ketu	Occult knowledge (8th); pilgrimages, going abroad (9th); moksha (12th)

8.5 Answer to Exercise

Exercise 11:

Table 17: Chara karakas in Example 28

Planet	Advancement in rasi	Order	Chara karaka
Mercury	21°0'	1	AK
Venus	17°42'	2	AmK
Rahu	30° – 14°30' = 15°30'	3	BK
Moon	15°29'	4	MK
Mars	13°40'	5	PiK
Saturn	9°41'	6	PK
Sun	9°36'	7	GK (JK)
Jupiter	2°6'	8	DK

Mercury is AK. Mercury shows intellectuals, orators, journalists, good communicators, people who can move with anyone, people who are liked by everyone, and, fickle-minded people. The native can be one of these types.

9. Arudha Padas

9.1 Introduction

Lagna shows true self. However, people's perceptions of a person can be different from reality. Usually, how one is perceived by others is more important in material life than who one really is. A political leader perceived by people as a powerful and influential person may in reality be a coward and a confused man always in doubt. But the reality does not matter in deciding his material life. Perceptions matter more. People perceive him as a strong leader and that matters the most in deciding his political career.

A political leader generally perceived as an honest man may in reality be badly corrupt. A person generally perceived as an intelligent person may in reality be of average intelligence. An intelligent person may score poorly in examinations and people may not know his intelligence.

If someone studied at IIT (a top engineering institute of India), people may think that he is very knowledgable. If someone studied at an obscure university, people may not get the same impression. But it is possible that people's perceptions are wrong and the person who studied at IIT is less knowledgable. If an astrologer is frequented by a top politician, people may get an impression that the astrologer is good. If an astrologer maintains a low profile, people may think that he is average. But the latter astrologer may be more learned in reality.

What people perceive about a person can often be different from reality. **However, perceptions and reality are both important to an astrologer.** For predicting some matters, we need knowledge of the perceptions (*e.g.* success of a politician in elections, success in a competitive examination, promotion at office *etc*). For predicting some internal matters, on the other hand, true self should be clearly understood.

So we, astrologers, should be able to separate reality from perceptions and understand both correctly. We should understand the true nature of a person and also how he is perceived by the world. Arudha padas are a very important concept of Vedic astrology and they help us with that tough, but important, task.

9.2 Computation of Bhava Arudhas

Arudha padas of all the 12 houses (bhavas) in all the divisional charts are defined as follows:

(1) Take sign containing the house of interest in the divisional chart of interest.

(2) Find the sign occupied by the lord of that house.

NOTE: Aquarius is owned by Saturn and Rahu. Scorpio is owned by Mars and Ketu. Take the stronger lord in the case of houses falling in these two signs. The chapter on “Strength of Planets and Rasis” will explain the rules used in comparing the strengths of planets.

(3) Count signs from the house of interest to the sign containing its lord. Counting is in the zodiacal direction always. For example, if the house we are interested in is in Gemini and its lord Mercury is in Aquarius, we count signs from Gemini to Aquarius and get 9.

(4) Count the same number of signs from the sign containing the lord and find the ending sign. In the above example, we count 9 signs from Aquarius and we end up in Libra.

(5) Exception: If the sign found thus in step (4) is in the 1st or 7th from the original sign in step (1), then we take the 10th sign from the sign found in step (4). Otherwise we don’t make any change.

(6) The resulting sign contains the arudha pada of the house of interest.

Arudha pada of a house is simply called arudha or pada also. In this book, we will denote the arudha pada on *n*th house with A*n*. For example, arudha pada of 4th house is A4 and arudha pada of 9th house is A9.

There are two special cases: Arudha pada of lagna is denoted as AL (arudha lagna) and arudha pada of 12th house is denoted as UL (upapada lagna).

Example 29: Consider Chart 1 and find the arudha padas of all the 12 houses.

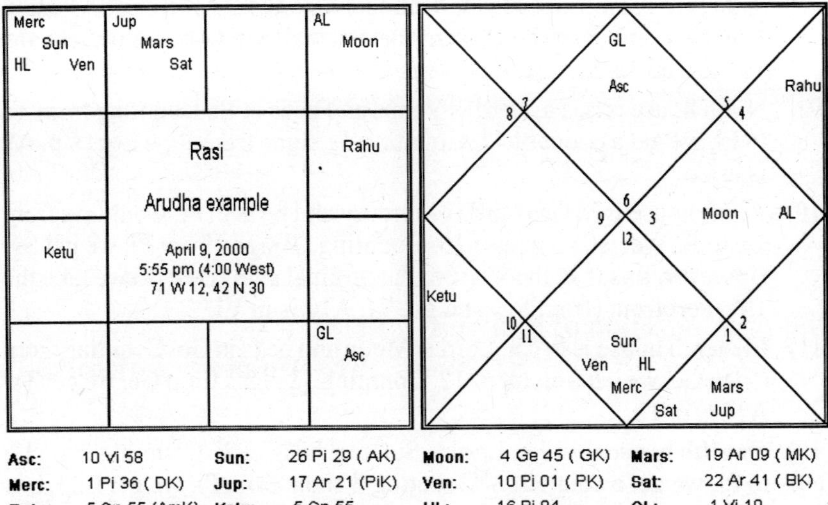

Asc:	10 Vi 58	**Sun:**	26 Pi 29 (AK)	**Moon:**	4 Ge 45 (GK)	**Mars:**	19 Ar 09 (MK)
Merc:	1 Pi 36 (DK)	**Jup:**	17 Ar 21 (PiK)	**Ven:**	10 Pi 01 (PK)	**Sat:**	22 Ar 41 (BK)
Rahu:	5 Cn 55 (AmK)	**Ketu:**	5 Cp 55	**HL:**	16 Pi 04	**GL:**	1 Vi 10

(1) First house is in Vi. Lord is Mercury and he is in Pi. Counting from Vi to Pi, we get a count of 7. Counting 7 signs from Pi, we get Vi. However, this is in the 1st from the original sign (Vi). So we take the 10th therefrom and get Ge. AL is in Ge.

(2) Second house is in Li. Lord is Venus and he is in Pi. Counting from Li to Pi, we get a count of 6. Counting 6 signs from Pi, we get Le. A2 is in Le.

(3) Third house is in Sc. Lord is Mars – he is stronger than Ketu, being with 2 other planets – and he is in Ar. Counting from Sc to Ar, we get a count of 6. Counting 6 signs from Ar, we get Vi. A3 is in Vi.

(4) Fourth house is in Sg. Lord is Jupiter and he is in Ar. Counting from Sg to Ar, we get a count of 5. Counting 5 signs from Ar, we get Le. A4 is in Le.

(5) Fifth house is in Cp. Lord is Saturn and he is in Ar. Counting from Cp to Ar, we get a count of 4. Counting 4 signs from Ar, we get Cn. However, this is in the 7th from the original sign (Cp). So we take the 10th therefrom (from Cn) and get Ar. A5 is in Ar.

(6) Sixth house is in Aq. Lord is Saturn – he is stronger than Rahu, being with 2 other planets – and he is in Ar. Counting from Aq to Ar, we get a count of 3. Counting 3 signs from Ar, we get Ge. A6 is in Ge.

(7) Seventh house is in Pi. Lord is Jupiter and he is in Ar. Counting from Pi to Ar, we get a count of 2. Counting 2 signs from Ar, we get Ta. A7 is in Ta.

(8) Eighth house is in Ar. Lord is Mars and he is in Ar. Counting from Ar to Ar, we get a count of 1. Counting 1 sign from Ar, we get Ar itself. However, this is in the 1st from the original sign (Ar). So we take the 10th therefrom and get Cp. A8 is in Cp.

(9) Ninth house is in Ta. Lord is Venus and he is in Pi. Counting from Ta to Pi, we get a count of 11. Counting 11 signs from Pi, we get Cp. A9 is in Cp.

(10) Tenth house is in Ge. Lord is Mercury and he is in Pi. Counting from Ge to Pi, we get a count of 10. Counting 10 signs from Pi, we get Sg. However, this is in the 7th from the original sign (Ge). So we take the 10th therefrom (from Sg) and get Vi. A10 is in Vi.

(11) Eleventh house is in Cn. Lord is Moon and he is in Ge. Counting from Cn to Ge, we get a count of 12. Counting 12 signs from Ge, we get Ta. A11 is in Ta.

(12) Twelfth house is in Le. Lord is Sun and he is in Pi. Counting from Le to Pi, we get a count of 8. Counting 8 signs from Pi, we get Li. UL is in Li.

Some terms used specifically to describe various arudha padas are given below:

Table 18: Specific names of arudha padas

Arudha	Specific
A1	Arudha lagna, Pada lagna, Arudha, Pada
A2	Dhanarudha, Vittarudha, Dhana pada, Vitta pada
A3	Bhatrarudha, Bhratri pada, Vikramarudha, Vikrama pada
A4	Matri pada, Vahana pada, Sukha pada, Matrarudha, Vahanarudha, Sukharudha
A5	Mantra pada, Mantrarudha, Putrarudha, Putra pada, Buddhi pada
A6	Roga pada, Satru pada, Rogarudha, Satrarudha
A7	Dara pada, Dararudha
A8	Mrityu pada, Kashta pada, Kashtarudha, Randhrarudha
A9	Bhagya pada, Bhagyarudha, Pitri pada, Pitrarudha, Dharma pada, Guru pada
A10	Karma pada, Karmarudha, Swarga pada, Swargarudha, Rajya pada
A11	Labha pada, Labharudha
A12	Upapada lagna, Upapada, Gaunapada, Vyayarudha, Moksha pada

Exercise 12: Find arudha padas of all the 12 houses in Chart 2.

Hint: Mars is with 2 other planets and Ketu is with only one planet. So Mars is stronger than Ketu and works as the lord of Sc. Saturn is alone and Rahu is with another planet. So Rahu is stronger and works as the lord of Aq.

9.3 Use of Arudha Lagna

While lagna stands for true self, arudha lagna (AL) stands for the maya associated with self. It shows how the native is perceived in the material world. It shows the status of the native. A timid and confused individual may be perceived in the world as a strong leader. In that case, that is the maya associated with his personality and AL shows it.

Because arudha lagna deals with maya, illusions, perceptions and impressions, it is very important in judging various materialistic things. For example, Parasara and Jaimini taught that the 11th and 12th houses from AL show financial gains and expenditures. Natural malefics in the 3rd and 6th houses from AL show someone who is perceived as a bold person who hits

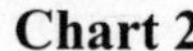

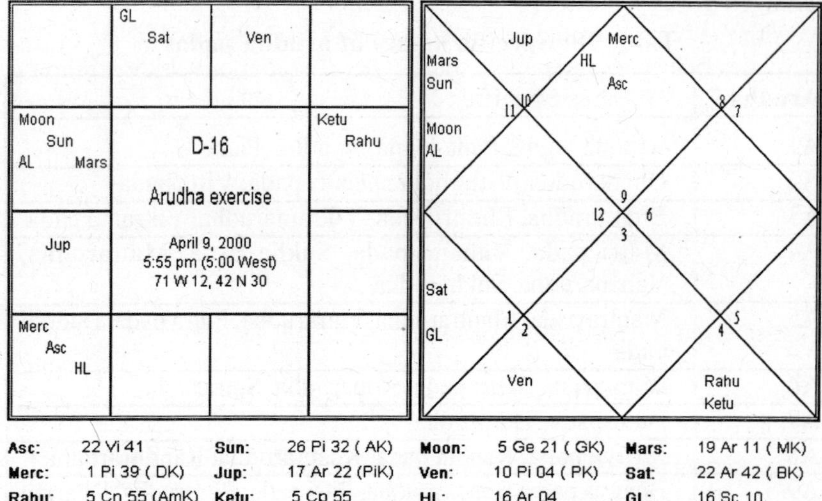

enemies hard. Since such impressions are usually formed about materially successful people, malefics in the 3rd and 6th from AL make one bold and materially successful. Natural benefics in the 3rd and 6th houses from AL make one very gentle and restrained in public behavior. Such a person does not fight with others boldly. This combination is usually found in the charts of saints and saintly and mild-natured people.

The 10th house from lagna in D-10 shows one's true conduct in society. It shows the one's career and the true nature of one's karma (work). The 10th house from AL in D-10 shows perceptions about one's conduct in society. It deals more with one's status in career.

9.4 Use of Bhava Arudhas

Arudha padas show the maya (illusion) of material world. Arudha pada of *n*th house shows the maya associated with the matters signified by of *n*th house.

For example, 1st house stands for self. While the first house from lagna stands for true self, its arudha pada (AL) stands for the maya associated with self. It shows the how the native is perceived in the material world. It shows the status of the native.

The 4th house in D-16 shows happiness from vehicle. It shows true happiness from a vehicle.

One may be very happy with a Bajaj Chetak (an inexpensive two-wheel vehicle popular in India) or even a bicycle and one owning three

Mercedes Benz cars may be unhappy with them and always dreaming of owning a better vehicle. One's true happiness from vehicle has nothing to do with the type of vehicle owned. However, people perceive one with 3 Mercedes Benz cars as a happier person in the matter of vehicle, compared to a Chetak owner. This is the maya associated with "happiness from vehicle" in this material world. So this is shown by A4.

Benefics influencing the 4th house in D-16 show someone who is happy with his vehicle(s). Benefics influencing A4 in D-16 show someone who is perceived to be happy with his vehicle(s). So planets influencing A4 in D-16 shed light on the physical vehicle owned by a person. Someone with Venus in own sign in A4 and Saturn in 4th (in D-16) may own luxurious vehicles (*i.e.* perceived to be happy with respect to vehicle) but not be happy. Someone with Saturn in A4 and Venus and Jupiter in 4th (in D-16) may own a small vehicle (*i.e.* perceived to be unhappy with respect to vehicles), but be happy with it.

As shown above, 4th house in D-16 deals with happiness from vehicles. In D-24, 4th house deals with learning and education. A4 in D-24 deals with the maya (illusion) associated with learning. What is it?

If someone studied at IIT (a top engineering institute of India), people may think that he is very knowledgable. If someone studied at an obscure university, people may not get the same impression. But it is possible that people's perceptions are wrong and the person who studied at IIT is less knowledgable.

So A4 in D-24 shows the school or university and the environment in which one's learning takes place. Usually that decides what impression people form about one's learning.

Similarly, A10 in D-10 shows the maya associated with one's karma (action – career). We form an impression about one's career based on the place and environment where one's work takes place. So A10 in D-10 shows one's workplace. One with Mars in A10 in D-10 may work at dynamic places or engineering companies. One with Jupiter in A10 in D-10 may work at a university or college or a court of law or a temple.

One important arudha pada used in Jyotish is upapada lagna (UL) – the arudha pada of the 12th house. This shows one's marriage and spouse. Planets in UL show the kind of marriage one has and the kind of spouse one gets. For example, Mercury in UL can show intelligent (when good) or indecisive (when bad) spouse. Ketu in UL can show spiritual (when good) or short-tempered (when bad) spouse. Sun in UL can show a charming spouse from a respectable family. It can also show an authoritative spouse. Mars in UL may show a bold spouse (when good) and a quarrelsome spouse (when bad).

The 8th house from UL shows the longevity of marriage and the 2nd and 7th houses from UL show the end of marriage. Malefics like Mars, Saturn and nodes in these houses from UL can result in troubles for the marriage and even a divorce.

Nature of spouse and the length of the marriage are two different issues. If Mars and Saturn are in UL and Jupiter is in the 8th from UL, it may show a long marriage to an argumentative and mean spouse. If Jupiter is in UL and Mars and Saturn in the 8th from it, one may have a noble spouse but the marital life will be very rough and there can even be a divorce. In such a case, propitiating Saturn and Mars can help (for more, see the chapter on "Remedial Measures").

The 7th house shows relations and A7 (darapada) shows the illusion associated with them, *i.e.* the kind of people one usually interacts with. Based on the kind of people one deals with, we perceive the nature of one's relations. If one has a friend who is a prostitute, people may get a negative impression about one's dealings. If one has a friend who is a famous film star, there is some glamour associated with one's relations. Thus darapada shows the kind of people one associates with and that plays an important role in forming people's impressions about one's relations. In D-10, darapada may show professional associates. In D-24, it may show friends at college or colleagues in the pursuit of knowledge. In D-20, it may show colleagues or friends in religious activities.

The 3rd house shows one's boldness. The 3rd house from lagna and the 3rd house from Mars show one's true boldness and the 3rd house from AL shows how bold one is perceived. In addition, A3 shows the maya surrounding one's boldness. It shows what drives the perceptions of people about one's boldness. The weapons one possesses may drive those perceptions and A3 may show one's weapons.

The 3rd house also shows one's communication skills. The 3rd house in D-24 (chart of learning and knowledge) and D-10 (achievements in society) may show one's writing skills. A3 shows the maya associated with one's writing skills. One may have excellent writing skills, but not write any book. In such a case, people may not really appreciate one's writing skills. One may be an average writer, but end up writing 20 books. In such a case, people may perceive him as a great writer. Thus the exact books written by one decide the perceptions of the world about one's writing skills. So A3 in D-24 and D-10 may show the books or articles written by him. In this author's D-10, for example, A3 is in Pisces. This can mean that he will be known for some books on saattwik and traditional subjects and astrology certainly fits the bill.

Let us take the 5th house as another example. It shows intelligence, following, devotion *etc*. The 5th house in D-20, the chart of religious activities, shows one's devotion (*bhakti*) in religious activities. A5 in D-20 shows the things based on which the world forms an impression about one's devotion. The mantras one recites, the *poojas* and the religious rituals one performs control the impression of the world about one's devotion in religious matters. So A5 shows them.

The 5th house in D-10, the chart of career, shows the following one has. The world forms an impression about one's following based on the power wielded by one. A political leader in a position of power is assumed to have a lot of following. So A5 can show the trappings of power enjoyed by one. It can also show awards.

In D-24, the chart of learning, the 5th house may show intelligence. A5 in D-24 shows the things based on which the world forms an impression about one's intelligence in learning. These impressions are usually formed based on one's performances in examinations, one's scores in tests and one's academic distinctions. So that is what A5 in D-24 shows.

Similarly, the 9th house shows one's fortune. In D-24, it may show fortune related to learning. It can show the guidance received by one (*i.e.* guru – teacher). But the world forms an impression about one's fortune in learning, based on the degrees received by one. One with an advanced degree is assumed to be more fortunate with respect to learning than one with a simple degree. So A9 can show one's higher degrees.

In this manner, intelligent and blessed students can clearly understand the meanings of various arudha padas in various divisional charts. One cannot become a good Vedic astrologer by memorizing a lot of tables. One needs to understand the basics clearly and apply them intelligently.

All the principles of Vedic astrology should be understood and applied in the context of "desa" (country – place), "kaala" (time – age) and "paatra" (nature and class of the persons involved). When we interpret arudha padas, we are talking about the things based on which the world forms an impression about an aspect of the native. The things that drive the world's perceptions can be different based on which world we are living in. They vary significantly from one place to another, from one age to another and from one class to another. Intelligent use of arudhas requires an astrologer to understand the world that the native lives in.

9.5 Computation of Graha Arudhas

Just as arudha padas of all houses (bhavas) are defined, arudha padas of all the nine planets (grahas) are also defined and they are called graha arudhas. They are computed as follows:

(1) Take the sign containing the planet of interest in the divisional chart of interest.

(2) Find the sign owned by that planet.

NOTE: Mars, Mercury, Jupiter, Venus and Saturn own 2 signs each. In their case, take the stronger sign owned by the planet. The chapter on "Strength of Planets and Rasis" will explain the rules used in comparing the strengths of signs. Take the two signs, apply those rules and find the stronger sign.

(3) Count signs from the sign containing the planet of interest to the stronger sign owned by it. Counting is in the zodiacal direction always. For example, if the planet we are interested in is Sun and he is Gemini, we count signs from Gemini to Leo and get 3.

(4) Count the same number of signs from the stronger sign owned and find the ending sign. In the above example, we count 3 signs from Leo and we end up in Libra.

(5) **Exception:** If the sign found thus in step (4) is in the 1st or 7th from the original sign containing the planet, then we take the 10th sign from the sign found in step (4). Otherwise we don't make any change.

(6) The resulting sign contains the arudha pada of the planet of interest.

Example 30: Find the arudha padas of all the planets in Chart 1.

(1) Sun is in Pi. From Pi, Sun's own sign Le is the 6th sign. Counting 6 signs from Le, we get Cp. So Cp contains Sun's arudha pada.

(2) Moon is in Ge. From Ge, Moon's own sign Cn is the 2nd sign. Counting 2 signs from Cn, we get Le. So Le contains Moon's arudha pada.

(3) Mars is in Ar. He owns 2 signs – Ar and Sc. Ar is stronger as it contains more planets. From Ar, Ar is the 1st sign. Counting 1 sign from Ar, we get Ar. Because this is the 1st house from the sign containing Mars, we take the 10th therefrom and get Cp. So Cp contains the arudha pada of Mars.

(4) Mercury is in Pi. He owns 2 signs – Ge and Vi. Ge is stronger as it has Moon and Vi is empty. From Pi, Ge is the 4th sign. Counting 4 signs from Ge, we get Vi. Since Vi is the 7th from Pi, we take the 10th from Vi and get Ge. So Ge contains Mercury's arudha pada.

(5) Jupiter is in Ar. He owns 2 signs – Sg and Pi. Pi is stronger as it has 3 planets and Sg is empty. From Ar, Pi is the 12th sign. Counting 12 signs from Pi, we get Aq. So Aq contains Jupiter's arudha pada.

(6) Venus is in Pi. He owns 2 signs – Ta and Li. Li is stronger (it will

become clear after reading the chapter on "Strength of Planets and Rasis".). From Pi, Li is the 8th sign. Counting 8 signs from Li, we get Ta. So Ta contains the arudha pada of Venus.

(7) Saturn is in Ar. He owns 2 signs – Aq and Cp. Cp is stronger as it has Ketu and Aq is empty. From Ar, Cp is the 10th sign. Counting 10 signs from Cp, we get Li. Since Li is the 7th from Ar, we take the 10th from Li and get Cn. So Cn contains Saturn's arudha pada.

(8) Rahu is in Cn. From Cn, Rahu's own sign Aq is the 8th sign. Counting 8 signs from Aq, we get Vi. So Vi contains Rahu's arudha pada.

(9) Ketu is in Cp. From Cp, Ketu's own sign Sc is the 11th sign. Counting 11 signs from Sc, we get Vi. So Vi contains Ketu's arudha pada.

Exercise 13: Find arudha padas of all the nine planets in Chart 2.

Hint: Out of the 2 signs owned by Mars, Mercury, Jupiter, Venus and Saturn, Ar, Ta, Vi, Sg and Aq are stronger (respectively).

NOTE: In divisional charts in which Ketu is in the 7th from Rahu, his maya (arudha pada) is with Rahu's maya. In divisional charts in which Rahu and Ketu are together, their mayas are in opposite rasis. The readers may ponder over the philosophical significance of this.

9.6 Use of Graha Arudhas

Just as arudha padas of various houses show the illusions of the world related to the matters signified by various houses, arudha padas of various planets show the illusions of the *native* related to the matters signified by various planets. Houses show various aspects of the person's life and their arudhas show how they are perceived in the world. Planets show various persons, forces and situations that impact various aspects of a person's life and their arudhas show the related perceptions by the person.

Just as the perceptions of the world about a native can be totally different from the reality, perceptions of a native about himself, about the world and about the situations that (s)he goes through can be totally different from the reality. Graha arudhas throw light on these perceptions.

Example 31:

Let us consider Moon's periods for the native in Chart 1. Because Moon is in the 10th house, his periods will give important details of developments related to career. Because Moon owns the 2nd from AL and occupies AL, status of the native in the eyes of people will increase in Moon's periods. However, Moon's arudha pada is in the 12th from lagna. This will make the native feel frustrated. The native will be unhappy and under the illusion that things are going bad for him. But people will think that his status is increasing and in reality there will be some good developments in career.

Example 32:

Let us consider India's Prime Minister Sri A.B. Vajpayee's rasi chart given in Chart 3. Jupiter's period ran in 1980's and 1990's. With Jupiter in the 2nd house from AL, his dasa can give a rise in material fortune. With Jupiter being a functional benefic for Scorpio lagna and occupying a quadrant, Jupiter dasa should give comforts in reality. However, Jupiter's arudha pada is in Libra, the 12th house from lagna. This can make the native feel unhappy, uncomfortable and alienated. Graha arudhas show how the native feels.

In Rahu's sub-period in Jupiter's period, the native became India's Prime Minister. Rahu is in the 8th house from lagna and his periods should cause discomfort, frustration and health troubles in reality. However, being a natural malefic in the 6th house from AL, Rahu can give material success and victory over enemies and rivals. That is how the world perceives him. Rahu's arudha pada is in Libra, *i.e.* the 12th house from lagna. This can again make the native frustrated and unhappy. However, if we are interested in the native's material success, Rahu's 6th house placement from AL is the most important factor and success is ensured.

Chart 3

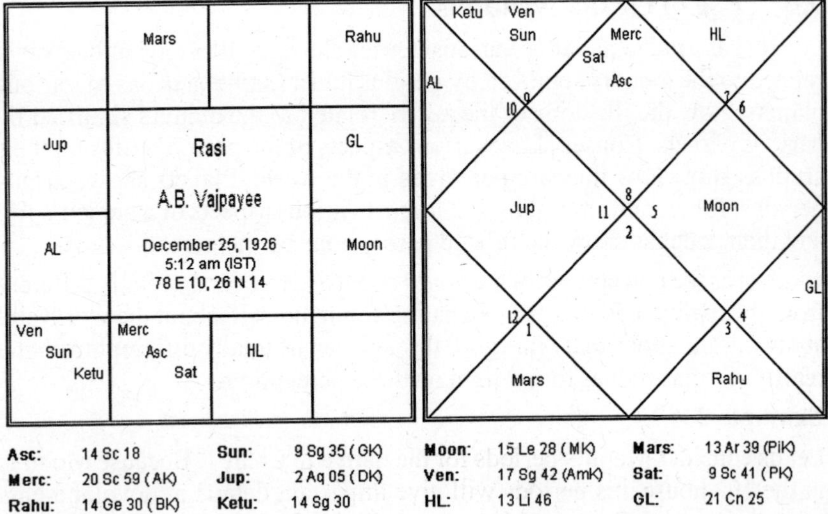

Asc:	14 Sc 18	**Sun:**	9 Sg 35 (GK)	**Moon:**	15 Le 28 (MK)	**Mars:**	13 Ar 39 (PiK)
Merc:	20 Sc 59 (AK)	**Jup:**	2 Aq 05 (DK)	**Ven:**	17 Sg 42 (AmK)	**Sat:**	9 Sc 41 (PK)
Rahu:	14 Ge 30 (BK)	**Ketu:**	14 Sg 30	**HL:**	13 Li 46	**GL:**	21 Cn 25

Example 33:

Consider the native of Chart 4. Let us see what results Ketu's period can give him. Ketu is in lagna. Ketu in lagna can make one spiritual. In Ketu dasa, this native joined a spiritual movement and started meditating regularly.

From AL, Ketu is in 3rd. As a natural malefic in the 3rd from AL, Ketu can give boldness and material success. He was indeed materially successful.

How did the native feel in this dasa? Look at Ketu's arudha pada. It is in Capricorn, the 5th house from lagna. Ketu in 5th gives proficiency in mathematics and abstract analysis and makes one do intelligent work. This may be how the native felt about his activities in that period.

In this manner, we can use graha arudha to understand the illusions the native is under. Illusion should not be looked at as a bad word here. We are all constantly under illusion. Basically graha arudhas show the perceptions of the native. They show how the native feels.

Judging the positions of planets with respect to lagna, we can understand the real situation. Judging the positions of planets with respect to AL, we can understand the perceptions of people and the situation at a materialistic level. Judging the positions of the arudha padas of planets with respect to lagna, we can understand how the native perceives the situation and how the native feels. Unless we understand this aspect correctly, we cannot offer good astrological counselling. When we counsel a person, we must understand how the person feels and what drives those feelings. So, each of these 3 aspects of chart analysis is important in its own right. A good student of Vedic astrology will master all the 3 aspects.

Chart 4

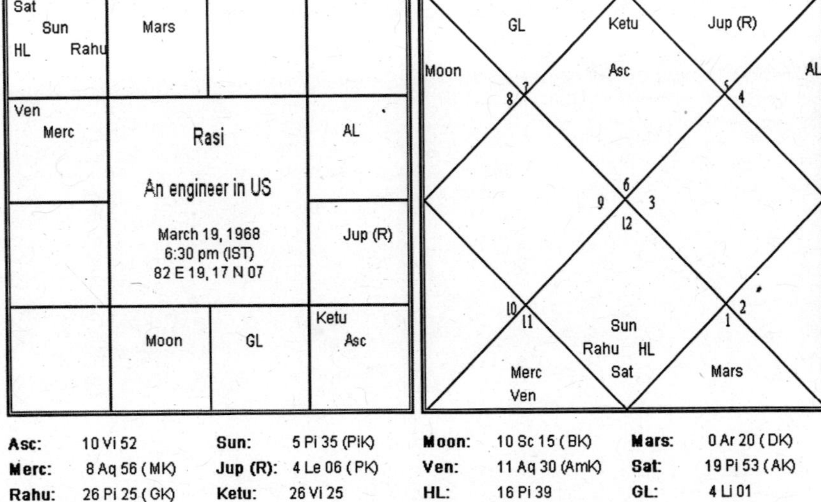

9.7 Summary

Arudha pada of a house shows the maya surrounding the matters signified by that house. It shows the factors based on which the impressions of people are formed. Arudha lagna or AL shows people's impressions about a native. It shows one's status in the material world. Darapada or A7 shows one's relationships. Upapada (UL) shows one's marriage and spouse. A4 in D-16 shows one's vehicle. A4 in D-24 shows one's school or college or university (place of education). A10 in D-10 shows one's workplace.

Arudha padas of planets show the perceptions of the native about the world, about himself or herself and about the situations developing in his or her life.

Analysis of the positions of planets with respect to lagna shows reality. Analysis of the positions of planets with respect to AL shows perceptions of the world and material situation. Analysis of individual bhava arudhas throws light on various things based on which world forms impressions about a native. Analysis of the positions of the arudha padas of planets with respect to lagna shows the perceptions of the native.

9.8 Answers to Exercises

Exercise 12: AL in Aq, A2 in Ar, A3 in Sg, A4 in Sc, A5 in Sg, A6 in Aq, A7 in Pi, A8 in Vi, A9 in Ta, A10 in Sg, A11 in Sg, UL in Aq.

Exercise 13: Arudha padas of planets are in the following signs: Sun – Sc, Moon – Sg, Mars – Ge, Mercury – Pi, Jupiter – Sc, Venus – Aq, Saturn – Sg, Rahu – Vi, Ketu – Pi.

10. Aspects and Argalas

10.1 Introduction

Planets aspect other planets, rasis and houses in astrology. A planet aspecting a house or a planet has some influence on the matters signified by that house or planet. The nature of the influence exerted and the degree to which that influence succeeds depends on the individual situation.

There are 2 kinds of aspects: (1) graha drishti and (2) rasi drishti. Drishti means aspect. Each planet aspects certain houses from it with graha drishti (planetary aspect). The houses aspected are fixed based on the planet. In addition, rasis aspect each other and a planet aspects the rasis aspected by the rasi occupied by it. This is called rasi drishti (sign aspect).

10.2 Graha Drishti

All planets aspect the 7th house from them. For example, Sun in Ta aspects Sc. Mars in Ge aspects Sg. Moon in Le aspects Aq. Jupiter in Pi aspects Vi. Saturn in Cp aspects Cn. Find the 7th house from the planet and the planet aspects that house.

In addition to the 7th house, Mars, Jupiter and Saturn have special aspects:

- Jupiter aspects the 5th and 9th houses from him.
- Mars aspects the 4th and 8th houses from him.
- Saturn aspects the 3rd and 10th houses from him.

We can decide the signs and houses aspected by a planet as above. If any planet occupies the aspected houses, then the planet is also aspected. For example, Jupiter in Ta will aspect Saturn in Cp, because Cp is the 9th house from Ta and Jupiter aspects the 9th from him.

Example 34:

Let us say Jupiter is in Ge, Mars in Le and Saturn in Sg. Jupiter in Ge will aspect the 5th, 7th and 9th from Ge. So Jupiter in Ge will aspect Li, Sg and Aq. Mars in Le will aspect the 4th, 7th and 8th from Le. So Mars in Le will aspect Sc, Aq and Pi. Saturn in Sg will aspect the 3rd, 7th and 10th from Sg. So Saturn in Sg will aspect Aq, Ge and Vi.

Look at a few charts and figure out which planets are aspecting which houses and which planets are aspecting which planets. With experience, you can become good at it and this is an important skill required in interpreting charts.

Chart 5

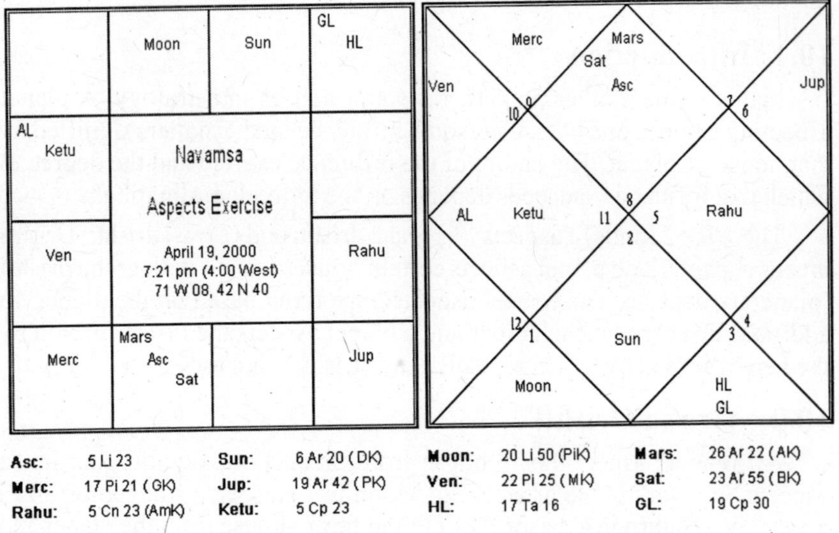

Exercise 14: Find the rasis, houses and planets aspected with *graha drishti* by Sun, Moon, Mars, Mercury, Jupiter, Venus and Saturn in Chart 5.

10.3 Rasi Drishti

Rasis aspect other rasis based on the following rules:

- A *movable* rasi aspects all *fixed* rasis except the one adjacent to it.
- A *fixed* rasi aspects all *movable* rasis except the one adjacent to it.
- A *dual* rasi aspects all other *dual* rasis.

For example, Ar is a movable sign. It aspects all the fixed signs except the one adjacent to it, *i.e.* Ta. So Ar aspects Le, Sc and Aq.

Ta is a fixed sign. It aspects all the movable signs except the one adjacent to it, *i.e.* Ar. So Ta aspects Cn, Li and Cp.

Ge is a dual sign. It aspects all other dual signs. So Ge aspects Vi, Sg and Pi.

Figure 2: Rasi Aspects

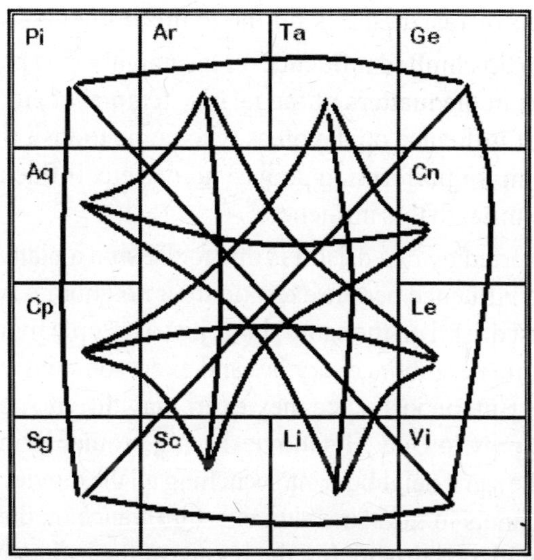

It may be noted that sign Y will aspect sign X if sign X aspects sign Y. A visual representation of rasi aspects is given in Figure 2. A line is drawn between every pair of signs that aspect each other. A planet aspects the signs aspected by the sign it occupies. It also aspects the houses and planets in those signs. This aspect is called rasi drishti (sign aspect). For example, a planet in Libra will aspect the houses and planets in Aq, Ta and Le.

Exercise 15: Find the rasis, houses and planets aspected with *rasi drishti* by Sun, Moon, Mars, Mercury, Jupiter, Venus, Saturn, Rahu and Ketu in Chart 5.

10.4 Graha Drishti vs Rasi Drishti

A simple analogy will make things clearer. Look at planets as people. Let us take a priest as an example. Will he have some influence on his neighbors? Probably. Because he lives there, gets up early in the morning and recites mantras, it may influence his neighbors also. Because of the houses they live in, his neighbors come under his influence. How pious and god-fearing his influence makes his neighbors depends on other factors. If one of the neighbors is a dreaded criminal, he is not going to be influenced.

Let us take a dreaded criminal as another example. He may also have an influence on his neighbors. Youngsters living in the neighboring houses may enter the criminal world because of him. Ladies in the neighboring houses may stay inside their houses at night and not come out after certain time.

Thus we are influenced by people in neighboring houses. Influence exerted by planets by rasi drishti is similar to this influence.

Compared to this limited influence on the neighbors, a priest may have greater influence in the matters of the nearby temple where he works. He may have a lot of influence on devotees who come to visit the temple and who approach him for performing poojas, homas etc. Influence exerted by graha drishti is similar to this influence.

Influence exerted by rasi drishti is due to the sign a planet is in. This is analogous to the influence people exert on their neighbors. All planets in a sign will have rasi drishti on the same signs, just as people living in the same house see the same neighbors everyday and exert some influence over the same neighbors. But the influence they exert may differ. A priest may tell his neighbors to pray to God. His movie-loving brother living in the same house may talk the same neighbors into watching all the movies of a particular actress. Thus, planets in the same sign exert influence on the same houses and planets through rasi drishti, but the nature of the influence varies from planet to planet.

Influence exerted by graha drishti is due to the inherent nature of a planet. Different planets in the same sign may aspect different houses and planets with graha drishti. A priest may have great influence over the devotees at the temple he works at and his movie-loving brother living in the same house may have great influence over his movie-loving classmates and co-members of the fan club of an actress, of which he is president. Similarly, planets in the same sign may influence planets in different houses. However, everyone in a house may have a strong influence over friends of the family who visit the house frequently. Similarly, all planets aspect the 7th house from them and have an influence over it.

10.5 Argala (Intervention)

In addition to the influence caused by planets with graha drishti and rasi drishti, there is another influence called "argala".

Argala is a very important concept in Vedic astrology. Literally speaking, argala means "a bolt". Argala on a house shows the influences that intervene in its affairs, decide some parts of it and close the bolt on it, so to speak. Planet having rasi drishti have a small influence. Planets having graha drishti have a more concrete influence. Planets with argala simply decide some parts of the matter signified by the house. The influence caused by argala is decisive.

A planet or house in the 2nd, 4th and 11th houses from a planet or house causes primary argala on the latter. Argala by a benefic planet is called a "subhaargala" (benefic intervention) and argala by a malefic planet is called a "paapaargala" (malefic intervention). This simple concept can be better appreciated if some examples are given.

The 4th house stands for education. The 2nd, 4th and 11th from the 4th house are 5th, 7th and 2nd houses respectively. One's intelligence (5th), interaction with others (7th) and overall character and *samskara* (2nd) make or break one's education. If Jupiter is in 5th house, he will give intelligence and his subhaargala (benefic intervention) on 4th will help one's education. If Rahu is in 5th house, his paapaargala (malefic intervention) on 4th will cause obstacles in one's education by way of poor intelligence. Similarly, benefics and malefics in the houses causing argala cause good and bad intervention. Basically, the point is that intelligence, interaction and samskara are the things that decide one's education. They have a decisive role.

Let us take another example. Short journeys are seen from the 3rd house. What are the things necessary for a journey? One needs a vehicle (4th). One may need someone to serve one by driving the vehicle. Servants are seen from 6th. So, no wonder the 4th and 6th houses cause argala on the 3rd house, being the 2nd and 4th from it respectively! If one has papargala on 3rd from 4th, it may show trouble to the journey because of the vehicle. If one has papargala on 3rd from 6th, it may show trouble to the journey because of the driver.

Let us take another example. Domestic harmony, comfort, well-being and happiness are seen from the 4th house. What are the things that can make or break domestic harmony? Of course, wife, children and other family members! Each of them can intervene in one's domestic harmony. No wonder the 5th, 7th and 2nd houses have an argala on the 4th house (being the 2nd, 4th and 11th respectively from the 4th house)! If a malefic in 5th has paapaargala on 4th, it may show domestic clashes and lack of sukha (comfort/happiness) on account of a child. If a benefic in 7th has subhaargala on 4th, it may show domestic happiness due to a caring partner.

Apart from the 2nd, 4th and 11th houses from a house, the 5th house from a house has a *secondary* argala on it. In the case of learning, argala of 8th house on 4th (8th is the 5th from 4th) shows the influence of hard work in learning. Hard work is another decider. In the case of journey, argala of 7th house on 3rd house (7th is the 5th from 3rd) shows the influence of partners in a journey.

10.6 Virodhaargala (Obstruction)

Virodhaargala shows the obstruction of argala. Planets and houses in the 12th, 10th, 3rd and 9th houses from a house or planet cause virodhaargala and obstruct the argala on it from the 2nd, 4th, 11th and 5th houses from it (respectively). For example, let us say Mercury, Jupiter, Venus and Saturn are in Ge, Pi, Ar and Vi respectively. Saturn is in the 4th from Mercury and Ge and he causes argala on them. With Saturn being a malefic, this is a paapaargala (malefic intervention). But Jupiter is in the 10th from Mercury and Ge. So he obstructs Saturn's argala and averts the troubles. Venus is in the 11th from Mercury and Ge and so he causes argala on them. With Venus being a benefic, it is a subhaargala (benefic intervention). If Le (3rd from Ge) is empty, this argala is unobstructed.

NOTE: If a sign contains Ketu, argalas and virodhargalas on it are counted anti-zodiacally. For example, let us say Ketu is in Vi. Then Le, Ge, Sc and Ta are the 2nd, 4th, 11th and 5th from Vi (counted anti-zodiacally) and planets in those signs cause argala on Vi and on the planets in Vi. Virodhaargala is also counted similarly.

Exercise 16: Find the planets causing argalas and virodhaargalas on all the 12 houses in Chart 5.

There is a special principle regarding the 3rd house obstruction. If there are several malefics in the 3rd house from a house or a planet, they cause argala instead of virodhargala on that house or planet.

10.7 Use of Argala

Depending on the matter of interest, take the relevant house or the relevant karaka. Find argalas and virodhaargalas on it. If there are both, see if more planets cause argala or virodhaargala. If they are caused by the same number of planets, compare the strengths and decide whether argala dominates or virodhaargala. Based on the signs, houses and planets involved, guess the meaning of the argala or virodhaargala.

Argala from the 2nd house shows the basic ingredient for the sustenance of a matter. For example, the 2nd house shows food and it is a basic ingredient for the sustenance of self (1st). The 5th house shows intelligence and it is a basic ingredient for the sustenance of learning (4th).

Argala from the 4th house shows the basic factor that drives the mood, state and progress of a matter. For example, the 4th house shows comfort and it drives the mood and state of self (1st). The 7th house shows interaction and that drives one's learning (4th).

Argala from the 11th house shows the catalyst that can result in gains for a matter. For example, the 2nd house shows character, grooming and *samskara* and it is a catalyst in the process of learning (4th).

Secondary argala from the 5th house shows the additional contributing factors. For example, the 5th house shows emotional situation and that contributes to the state of self (1st). The 8th house shows hard work and that contributes to one's learning (4th).

Using the above guidelines, we can understand the meaning of argalas on houses and karakas.

Chart 6

Moon	Ketu Ven		Mars Sun Merc (R)
	Rasi P.V. Narasimha Rao		
HL	June 28, 1921 12.49 pm (5:17 East) 79 E 09, 19 N 26		Sat Jup
AL GL		Rahu	Asc

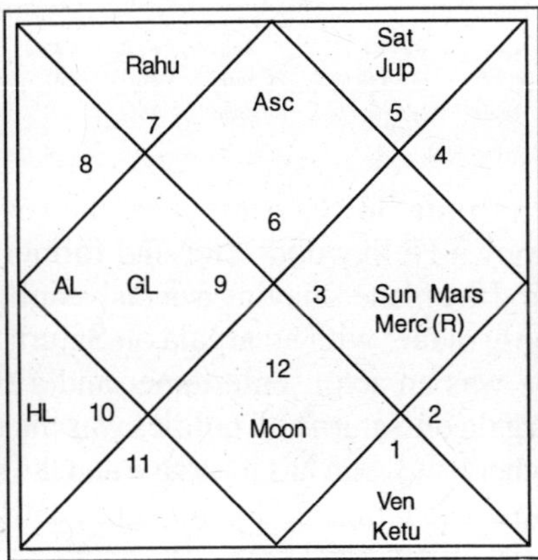

Asc	: 24 Vi 19	**Sun**	: 13 Ge 16 (GK)	**Mars**	: 13 Ge 33 (PK)
Merc (R)	: 27 Ge 40 (AmK)	**Jup**	: 20 Le 06 (PiK)	**Sat**	: 26 Le 26 (MK)
Rahu	: Li 47 (AK)	**Ketu**	: 0 Ar 47	**GL**	: 25 Sg 59

Example 35: Consider India's former Prime Minister Sri P.V. Narasimha Rao's chart, shown in Chart 6. Let us find the planets having a decisive influence on his livelihood and *karma* (action) in society.

Saturn is the significator of livelihood and karma. Argalas on him denote decisive influences on livelihood and karma. Mercury, Mars and Sun have an argala on Saturn, as they are in the 11th from him. Mercury's influence indicates writing and scholarliness. Sun and Mars suggest politics.

Chart 7

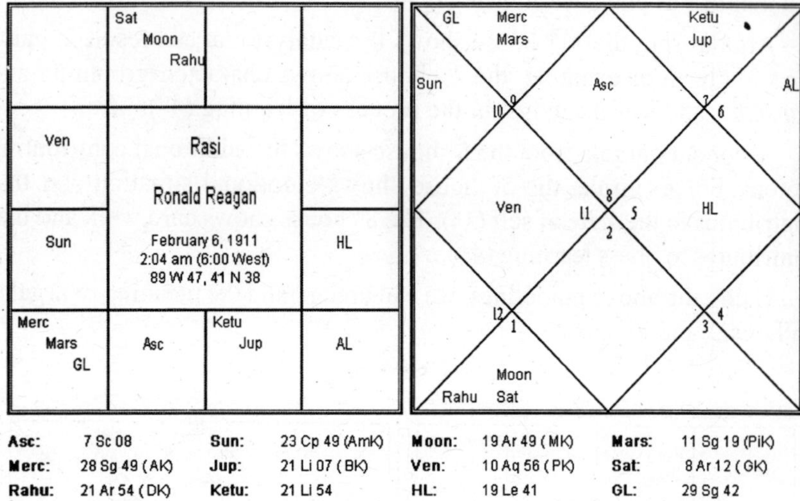

Example 36: Consider the chart shown in Chart 7. It belongs to well-known Hollywood actor and former US President Ronald Reagan. Let us find the planets having a decisive influence on his livelihood and karma. The only planet with an argala on Saturn is Venus in the 11th from Saturn. Thus he was an actor, entertainer and a showman. In Example 35, Sun has an argala on Saturn and politics was the native's livelihood. In this chart, on the other hand, Sun has no argala and the native entered politics late. His political power is indicated by Sun's unobstructed argala on GL.

Exercise 17: Try to guess the nature of livelihood and karma (action) of the native in Chart 8. Don't look at the answer until you think a lot.

Hint: Being in own house, Venus dominates over Jupiter and Mercury. Being the most advanced planet, Mercury is also strong. Mars dominates over Sun and Ketu, being in own house and being more advanced than Ketu – the other owner of Sc.

Chart 8

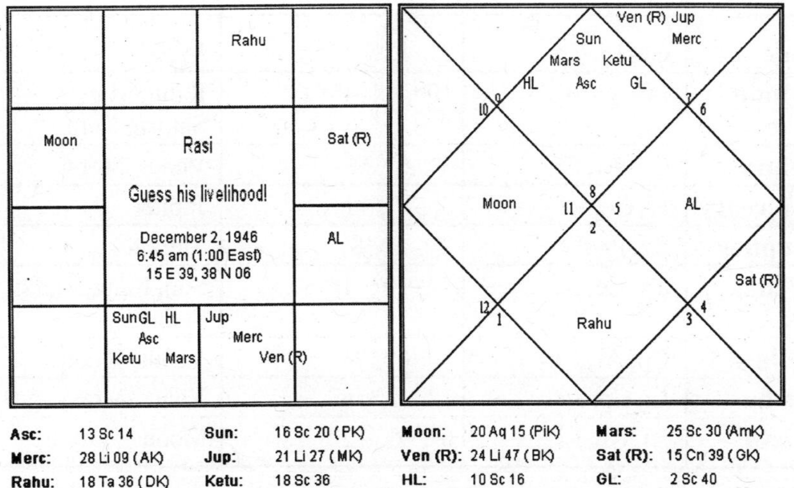

10.8 Answers to Exercises

Exercise 14: Rasis, houses and planets aspected with graha drishti are listed below.

Planet	Aspected Rasis	Aspected Houses	Aspected Planets
Sun	Sc	1st	Mars, Saturn
Moon	Li	12th	—
Mars	Aq, Ta, Ge	4th, 7th, 8th	Ketu, Sun
Mercury	Ge	8th	—
Jupiter	Cp, Pi, Ta	3rd, 5th, 7th	Venus, Sun
Venus	Cn	9th	—
Saturn	Cp, Ta, Le	3rd, 7th, 10th	Venus, Sun, Rahu

Exercise 15: Rasis, houses and planets aspected with rasi drishti are listed below:

Planet	Aspected Rasis	Aspected Houses	Aspected Planets
Sun	Cn, Li, Cp	9th, 12th, 3rd	Venus
Moon	Le, Sc, Aq	10th, 1st, 4th	Rahu, Mars, Saturn, Ketu
Mars	Cp, Ar, Cn	3rd, 6th, 9th	Venus, Moon
Mercury	Pi, Ge, Vi	5th, 8th, 11th	Jupiter
Jupiter	Sg, Pi, Ge	2nd, 5th, 8th	Mercury
Venus	Ta, Le, Sc	7th, 10th, 1st	Sun, Rahu, Mars, Saturn
Saturn	Cp, Ar, Cn	3rd, 6th, 9th	Venus, Moon
Rahu	Li, Cp, Ar	12th, 3rd, 6th	Venus, Moon
Ketu	Ar, Cn, Li	6th, 9th, 12th	Moon

Exercise 16: List of planets causing argalas and virodhargalas is given below.

House	Argalas from				Virodhargalas from			
	2nd	4th	5th	11th	12th	10th	9th	3rd
1st (Sc)	Merc	Ketu	—	Jup	—	Rahu	—	Ven
2nd (Sg)	Ven	—	Moon	—	Mars Sat	Jup	Rahu	Ketu
3rd (Cp)	Ketu	Moon	Sun	Mars Sat	Merc	—	Jup	—
4th (Aq)*	Ven	Mars Sat	—	Moon	—	Sun	—	Merc
5th (Pi)	Moon	—	—	Ven	Ketu	Merc	Mars Sat	Sun
6th (Ar)	Sun	—	Rahu	Ketu	—	Ven	Merc	—
7th (Ta)	—	Rahu	Jup	—	Moon	Ketu	Ven	—
8th (Ge)	—	Jup	—	Moon	Sun	—	Ketu	Rahu
9th (Cn)	Rahu	—	Mars Sat	Sun	—	Moon	—	Jup
10th (Le)	Jup	Mars Sat	Merc	—	—	Sun	Moon	—

House	Argalas from				Virodhargalas from			
	2nd	4th	5th	11th	12th	10th	9th	3rd
11th (Vi)	—	Merc	Ven	—	Rahu	—	Sun	Mars Sat
12th (Li)	Mars Sat	Ven	Ketu	Rahu	Jup	—	—	Merc

∗ Ketu is in Aq and the counting is in reverse.

Exercise 17:

Saturn is the significator of livelihood and karma. He shows what kind of activity a native engages in. Being in a watery sign, he shows something flexible and fluid. By studying the argalas on him, we can see the decisive influences on the nature of his karma.

Venus is in the 4th from Saturn. His argala on Saturn shows creative and aesthetic work (*e.g.* actor, poet etc). Though Venus is in own sign, Mercury is more advanced and Mercury also has influence over Saturn through his argala. Mercury and Venus together show intelligent and logical work of an aesthetic nature. Being the 4th house argala, this influence is the basic driving factor of the native's karma.

Mars is very strong in the 5th house from Saturn and he also has a secondary argala. Martian influence gives discipline, systematicity and enterprise. He can denote some design work. Mars engineers things.

Rahu is in the 11th from Saturn and he has a malefic argala on Saturn. Rahu stands for pathbreaking innovation and also shady elements of society. His 11th house argala can denote gains in his livelihood with those factors working as catalysts.

The final answer: The native was a very famous and successful fashion designer. He had mafia connections. He was finally shot dead.

11. Yogas

11.1 Introduction

We have seen in previous chapters the use of divisional charts, houses, karakas, arudha padas, aspects and argalas. Using all these tools, we can interpret charts and draw various conclusions about a native's fortune.

In addition to these general guidelines, there are several particular combinations that give specific results. These are very important and called "Yogas". Readers are advised to refer to classics such as "Brihat Parasara Hora Sastram" and acquaint themselves with as many yogas as possible. Dr. B.V. Raman's "Three Hundred Important Combinations" is an excellent compendium on yogas.

Some software programs list the yogas present in a chart. However, they are sometimes erroneous and one should be familiar with important yogas and be able to judge yogas by oneself, without relying on software. Many yogas are applicable in divisional charts. When we use yogas in divisional charts, we should interpret the results ascribed to a yoga based on the matters signified by the divisional chart.

A few key yogas will be listed in this chapter, but the reader is urged to do more reading. In this book, yogas are divided into the following classes for convenience:

- Ravi Yogas (solar combinations)
- Chandra Yogas (lunar combinations)
- Mahaapurusha Yogas (combinations producing 5 kinds of great men)
- Naabhasa Yogas (classified celestial combinations)
- Other Popular Yogas
- Raaja Yogas (combinations giving power)
- Raaja Sambandha Yogas (combinations for association with kings)
- Dhana Yogas (combinations giving wealth)
- Daridra Yogas (combinations giving poverty)

11.2 Ravi Yogas

Ravi yogas are the solar combinations. There are several yogas based on Sun.

Because Mercury and Venus are with Sun or a sign away from him most of the time, the following yogas are very common in rasi chart.

However, they are less common in divisional charts. One can apply these yogas in D-9 and D-10 in particular.

11.2.1 *Vesi Yoga*

Definition: If there is a planet other than Moon in the 2nd house from Sun, then this yoga is present. For example, if Sun is in Gemini and Jupiter and Mercury are in Cancer, then this yoga is present.

Results: One born with this yoga has a balanced outlook. He is truthful, tall and sluggish. He is happy and comfortable even with little wealth.

11.2.2 *Vosi Yoga*

Definition: If there is a planet other than Moon in the 12th house from Sun, then this yoga is present. For example, if Sun is in Aries and Jupiter and Venus are in Pisces, then this yoga is present.

Results: One born with this yoga is skilful, charitable, famous, learned and strong.

11.2.3 *Ubhayachara Yoga*

Definition: If there are planets other than Moon in the 2nd and 12th houses from Sun, then this yoga is present. For example, if Sun is in Cancer, Mars is in Leo and Venus is in Gemini, then this yoga is present.

Results: One born with this yoga has all comforts. He is a king or an equal.

11.2.4 *Budha-Aaditya Yoga (Nipuna Yoga)*

Definition: Budha means Mercury, Aaditya means Sun and yoga means togetherness. If Sun and Mercury are together (in one sign), this yoga is present.

Results: One born with this yoga is intelligent and skilful in all works. He is well-known, respected and happy. Nipuna means an expert.

Note: If Mercury is too close to Sun, he is combust (*asta* or *astangata*). Yogas formed by combust planets lose some of their power to do good. This yoga is the most powerful in divisional charts like D-10. In rasi chart also, it can give results if Mercury is not combust. Suppose someone has Sun and Mercury together in Leo in D-10. Then that person has a powerful Budha-Aditya yoga in career. The results will be felt throughout one's life and the periods of Sun, Mercury and Leo will give those results in particular.

11.3 Chandra Yogas

Chandra yogas are the lunar combinations. There are several yogas based on Moon.

General Guidelines:

(1) If Moon is in a quadrant from Sun, then one may possess little wealth, intelligence and skills. If Moon is in a panapara from Sun, then one may possess average wealth, intelligence and skills. If Moon is in an apoklima from Sun, then one may possess a lot of wealth, intelligence and skills.

(2) If Moon is in own navamsa or that of an adhimitra (good friend), that is good. In such a situation, aspect of Jupiter on Moon beings wealth and comforts in the case of daytime birth (respectively). The same result is given by Venusian aspect on Moon in the case of night birth. On the other hand, Jupiter's aspect on Moon in a night birth and Venusian aspect on Moon in a daytime birth are detrimental to one's wealth and comforts.

(3) If all the natural benefics occupy upachayas (3rd, 6th, 10th and 11th) from Moon, one has great wealth. If two benefics occupy upachayas from Moon, the native has medium wealth. If only one benefic occupies an upachaya from Moon, the native has little wealth.

11.3.1 *Sunaphaa Yoga*

Definition: If there are planets other than Sun in the 2nd house from Moon, this yoga is present. For example, if Moon is in Gemini and Jupiter and Mercury are in Cancer, then this yoga is present.

Results: One born with this yoga becomes a king or an equal. He is intelligent, wealthy and famous. He has self-earned wealth.

11.3.2 *Anaphaa Yoga*

Definition: If there are planets other than Sun in the 12th house from Moon, this yoga is present. For example, if Moon is in Aries and Jupiter and Venus are in Pisces, then this yoga is present.

Results: One born with this yoga becomes a king with good looks. His body is free from disease. He is a man of character and has great reputation. He is surrounded by comforts.

11.3.3 *Duradhara Yoga*

Definition: If there are planets other than Sun in the 2nd *and* 12th houses from Moon, this yoga is present. For example, if Moon is in Cancer, Mars is in Leo and Venus is in Gemini, then this yoga is present.

Results: One born with this yoga enjoys many pleasures. He is charitable. He owns wealth and vehicles. He has good servants.

11.3.4 *Kemadruma Yoga*

Definition: If there are *no* planets other than Sun in the 1st, 2nd and 12th houses from Moon *and* if there are *no* planets other than Moon in the quadrants from lagna, this bad yoga is present. For example, if lagna is in Taurus, Moon is in Virgo, no planets other than Sun in Leo, Virgo and Libra and no planets in Taurus, Leo, Scorpio and Aquarius, then this yoga is present.

Results: One born with this yoga is unlucky, bereft of intelligence and learning and afflicted by poverty and trouble. This bad yoga kills the results of other good yogas in the chart, especially Chandra yogas. One with this yoga has to work hard and succeed through great efforts.

11.3.5 *Chandra-Mangala Yoga*

Definition: If Moon and Mars are together (in one sign), then this yoga is present.

Results: One born with this yoga is worldly wise and materially successful. He may earn money through unscrupulous means. He may treat mother or other women badly.

11.3.6 *Adhi Yoga*

Definition: If the natural benefics occupy 6th, 7th and 8th from Moon, this yoga is present. For example, if Moon is in Taurus, Mercury and Jupiter in Virgo and Venus is Leo, then this yoga is present.

Results: One born with this yoga becomes a king or a minister or an army chief, depending on the strength of the planets involved.

11.4 Pancha Mahapurusha Yogas

Pancha means five and mahapurusha means a great person. Pancha mahapurusha yogas give the combinations that produce 5 kinds of great persons.

There are 5 basic elements of which this universe is made of. These are called pancha bhootas (five existences) or pancha tattvas (five natures). They are:

- Agni tattva (fiery nature)
- Bhoo tattva (earthy nature)
- Vaayu tattva (airy nature)
- Jala tattva (watery nature)
- Aakaasa tattva (ethery nature)

Mars, Mercury, Saturn, Venus and Jupiter (respectively) represent these

5 elements. Pancha mahapurusha yogas produce five kinds of great persons with one of these 5 elements playing a predominant role in their personalities.

11.4.1 *Ruchaka Yoga*

Definition: If Mars is in a quadrant in own sign or exaltation sign, it is called Ruchaka yoga. In other words, Mars should be in Ar, Sc or Cp and he should be in 1st, 4th, 7th or 10th from lagna. This yoga does not apply from Moon and it applies mainly in rasi chart. As an example, a native with lagna in Li and Mars in Ar will have this yoga.

Results: One born with this yoga is a great man of fiery nature. He has a lot of enthusiasm. He is a natural leader. He loves to fight wars and he is victorious over enemies. He is discriminative and a devotee of learned people. He is well-versed in occult sciences. He has good taste. He is always successful.

11.4.2 *Bhadra Yoga*

Definition: If Mercury is in a quadrant in own sign or exaltation sign, it is called Bhadra yoga. In other words, Mercury should be in Ge or Vi and he should be in 1st, 4th, 7th or 10th from lagna. This yoga does not apply from Moon and it applies mainly in rasi chart. As an example, a native with lagna in Ge and Mercury in Vi will have this yoga.

Results: One born with this yoga is a great man of earthy nature. He is lion-like. He is learned in all respects. He has a good build of body and a deep voice. He has sattwa guna. He knows yoga well. He is always surrounded by relatives, friends and family and enjoys his wealth with them. He maintains cleanliness in everything and he is very systematic. He has a spirit of independence. He is religious.

11.4.3 *Sasa Yoga*

Definition: If Saturn is in a quadrant in own sign or exaltation sign, it is called Sasa yoga. In other words, Saturn should be in Cp, Aq or Li and he should be in 1st, 4th, 7th or 10th from lagna. This yoga does not apply from Moon and it applies mainly in rasi chart. As an example, a native with lagna in Cp and Saturn in Li will have this yoga.

Results: One born with this yoga is a great man of airy nature. He is rabbit-like[29]. He is wise and enjoys wandering. He is comfortable in forests, mountains and forts. He is valorous and has a slender build. He knows the weaknesses of others. He is lively, but has some vacillation. He is charitable.

---

29 "Sasa" means a hare or a rabbit.

11.4.4 *Maalavya Yoga*

Definition: If Venus is in a quadrant in own sign or exaltation sign, it is called Maalavya yoga. In other words, Venus should be in Ta, Li or Pi and he should be in 1st, 4th, 7th or 10th from lagna. This yoga does not apply from Moon and it applies mainly in rasi chart. As an example, a native with lagna in Ge and Venus in Pi will have this yoga.

Results: One born with this yoga is a great man of watery nature. He emits a lustre akin to moonlight. He enjoys tasty food. He has luxuries. He has excellent health. He is well-versed in arts.

11.4.5 *Hamsa Yoga*

Definition: If Jupiter is in a quadrant in own sign or exaltation sign, it is called Ruchaka yoga. In other words, Jupiter should be in Sg, Pi or Cn and he should be in 1st, 4th, 7th or 10th from lagna. This yoga does not apply from Moon and it applies mainly in rasi chart. As an example, a native with lagna in Sg and Jupiter in Pi will have this yoga.

Results: One born with this yoga is a great man of ethery nature. He is swan-like[30]. He has spiritual strength and purity. He is respected by everyone. He is very passionate. He becomes a king. He has all comforts. He enjoys life fully. He is a clever conversationalist and endowed with good speech.

11.5 Naabhasa Yogas

Naabhasa yogas are classified celestial combinations. These are classified as follows:

Aasraya Yogas (3): Rajju, Musala and Nala yogas

Dala Yogas (2): Maalaa, Sarpa yogas

Aakriti Yogas (20): Gadaa, Sakata, Sringaataka, Vihangama, Hala, Vajra, Yava, Kamala, Vaapi, Yoopa, Sara, Sakti, Danda, Naukaa, Koota, Chatra, Chaapa, Ardhachandra, Chakra and Samudra yogas

Sankhya Yogas (7): Veenaa, Daama, Paasa, Kedaara, Soola, Yuga and Gola yogas.

Results of other yogas may be felt primarily during the dasas of the planets and signs involved. But the results of Naabhasa yogas are felt in all dasas.

11.5.1 *Aasraya Yogas*

Aasraya means dwelling or asylum. Aasraya yogas are based on the

30 "Hamsa" means a swan.

signs occupied by planets. If all the planets are in movable signs or in fixed signs or in dual signs, these yogas arise.

Rajju Yoga: If all the planets are exclusively in movable signs, this yoga is formed. One born with this yoga likes to travel. He has good looks and flourishes in foreign countries. He is cruel. Rajju means a rope.

Musala Yoga: If all the planets are exclusively in fixed signs, this yoga is formed. One born with this yoga has honor, wisdom and wealth. Kings like him. He is famous. He has many children. He has a firm spirit. Musala means a pestle.

Nala Yoga: If all the planets are exclusively in dual signs, this yoga is formed. One born with this yoga has a poor physique. He accumulates money. He has good looks and helps relatives. He is skilful.

11.5.2 *Dala Yogas*

Maalaa Yoga: If three quadrants are occupied by natural benefics, this yoga is formed. One born with this yoga is always happy. He has nice clothes, vehicles, luxuries and friendship of many women. Maalaa means a garland.

If a malefic also occupies one of the quadrants, this yoga may not operate well.

As an example, let us say lagna is in Ar, Jupiter is in Cn, Venus is in Cp and Mercury is in Li. This gives Maalaa yoga.

Sarpa Yoga: If three quadrants are occupied by natural malefics, this yoga is formed. One born with this yoga is miserable, unhappy, cruel, poor and dependent on others for food. This is a very bad combination. Sarpa means a serpant.

If a benefic also occupies one of the quadrants, this yoga may not operate well.

As an example, let us say lagna is in Sc, Mars is in Ta, Rahu is in Le and Ketu is in Aq. This gives Sarpa yoga.

11.5.3 *Aakriti Yogas*

Aakriti means a shape and the many of these yogas are based on the shape of the arrangement of planets in a chart. In all these yogas, Rahu and Ketu are not counted as planets by many authors.

Gadaa Yoga: If all the planets occupy two successive quadrants from lagna, this yoga is formed. For example, this yoga is formed if all the planets occupy 4th and 7th (or 10th and 1st). One born with this yoga possesses wealth, gold and gems. He performs yajnas (sacrificial rites). He knows sastras (sciences) and songs. Gadaa means a mace or a bludgeon.

Sakata Yoga: If all the planets occupy 1st and 7th houses from lagna, this yoga is formed. One born with this yoga suffers from diseases. He has ugly nails. He is foolish. He doesn't have friends and family. He lives pulling carts. Sakata means a cart.

Vihanga Yoga: If all the planets occupy 4th and 10th houses from lagna, this yoga is formed. One born with this yoga loves to wander. He works as a messenger. He likes sex. He has no shame and he likes to quarrel. Vihanga means a bird. Some authors call this Vihaga yoga.

Sringaataka Yoga: If all the planets occupy trines (1st, 5th and 9th) from lagna, this yoga is formed. One born with this yoga is happy and liked by kings. He has a noble wife and hates women. He is wealthy. Sringaataka means a cross-road junction. It has some other popular meanings too.

Hala Yoga: If all the planets occupy mutual trines but not trines from lagna, this yoga is formed. In other words, if all the planets are in 2nd, 6th and 10th or if all the planets are in 3rd, 7th and 11th or if all the planets are in 4th, 8th and 12th, then this yoga is formed. One born with this yoga becomes a farmer. He eats a lot of food. He is poor. He is deserted by friends and relatives. He is unhappy and worried. Hala means a plough.

Vajra Yoga: If lagna and the 7th houses are occupied by natural benefics and the 4th and 10th houses are occupied by natural malefics, this yoga is formed. One born with this yoga is happy in the early and late parts of life. He has valour. He is not fortunate, but he has no desires either. He fights. Vajra means a diamond.

Yava Yoga: If lagna and the 7th houses are occupied by natural malefics and the 4th and 10th houses are occupied by natural benefics, this yoga is formed. One born with this yoga observes religious rules. He is happy in the middle part of life. He has wealth and good children. He is charitable. He is strong-minded. Yava means a grain among other things.

Kamala Yoga: If all the planets are in quadrants from lagna, this yoga is formed. One born with this yoga becomes a king. He has a strong character. He is famous and long-lived. He is pure and performs many good deeds. Kamala means a lotus.

Vaapi Yoga: If all the planets are panaparas or in apoklimas, this yoga is formed. One born with this yoga has a mind capable of amassing wealth. He has all the comforts. He becomes a king. Vaapi means a pond or a water tank or a well.

Yoopa Yoga: If all the planets are in 1st, 2nd, 3rd and 4th houses from lagna, this yoga is formed. One born with this yoga has spiritual knowledge and knowledge of yajnas (sacrificial rites). His wife is with him always. He has sattwa guna. He observes all the religious rules. Yoopa means a pillar and in particular a sacrificial post.

Sara Yoga: If all the planets are in 4th, 5th, 6th and 7th houses from lagna, this yoga is formed. One born with this yoga makes arrows. He heads prisons. He is a hunter. He eats meats. He tortures people. Sara means an arrow.

Sakti Yoga: If all the planets are in 7th, 8th, 9th and 10th houses from lagna, this yoga is formed. One born with this yoga is unhappy, poor, unsuccessful, unworthy, lazy, long-lived and firm. He has sharp minds in war. Sakti means energy and it is also a powerful weapon.

Danda Yoga: If all the planets are in 10th, 11th, 12th and 1st houses from lagna, this yoga is formed. He has born with this yoga loses wife and children and their people will desert them. He is unhappy and serve mean people. Danda means a stick used to punish people.

Naukaa Yoga: If all the planets occupy the 7 signs from lagna, this yoga is formed. One born with this yoga makes money on things related to water. He has many desires and is well-known. He is wicked, rough and miserly. Naukaa means a ship.

Koota Yoga: If all the planets occupy the 7 signs from the 4th house, this yoga is formed. One born with this yoga becomes a jailer. He is a liar. He lives in hills and forts. He is poor and cruel. Koota means a group. It has several other meanings.

Chatra Yoga: If all the planets occupy the 7 signs from the 7th house, this yoga is formed. One born with this yoga will help his people. He is kind and liked by many kings. He is intelligent. He is happy in the early and late parts of life. He is long-lived. Chatra means an umbrella.

Chaapa Yoga: If all the planets occupy the 7 signs from the 10th house, this yoga is formed. One born with this yoga becomes a liar, thief and a protector of secrets. He wanders in forests. He is unfortunate. He is happy in the middle part of his life. Chaapa means a bow.

Ardha Chandra Yoga: If all the planets occupy the 7 signs starting from a panapara or an apoklima, this yoga is formed. One born with this yoga becomes an army chief. He has a good physique. Kings like him. He is strong and possesses gems, gold and many ornaments. Ardha Chandra means half-Moon.

Chakra Yoga: If all the planets occupy 1st, 3rd, 5th, 7th, 9th and 11th houses, this yoga is formed. One born with this yoga becomes a great emperor. Diamond-studded crowns of many kings touch his feet (*i.e.* many kings prostate before him). Chakra means a wheel. Chakravarti means an emperor.

Samudra Yoga: If all the planets occupy 2nd, 4th, 6th, 8th, 10th and 12th houses, this yoga is formed. One born with this yoga owns a lot of wealth and many gems. He has luxuries. He likes people. Their fortune and greatness are stable. They are soft-natured. Samudra means a sea or an ocean. Samudra is also the name of the God of Ocean, who has a lot of wealth and many gems with him.

11.5.4 *Sankhya Yogas*

Sankhya means a number. Sankhya yogas are based on the number of distinct signs occupied by the seven planets combined. Rahu and Ketu are not included. As an example, let us take the chart of Lord Sri Rama (see Figure 1). The signs occupied by the seven planets are: Ar, Ta, Cn, Li, Cp and Pi. There are six signs. This forms Daama yoga, as can be seen below.

These yogas apply if no other Naabhasa yogas mentioned previously are applicable in a chart. These are the least important of all Naabhasa yogas.

Veenaa Yoga: If the seven planets occupy exactly 7 distinct signs among them, this yoga is formed. One born with this yoga likes music, dance and songs. He has many servants. He is wealthy, skilful and a leader of men. Veenaa is a stringed musical instrument. This is also called Vallaki yoga by some authors.

Daama Yoga: If the seven planets occupy exactly 6 distinct signs among them, this yoga is formed. One born with this yoga is very rich and famous. He has many children. He has many gems. He helps others. Daama means a wreath. Some authors call this Daamini yoga.

Paasa Yoga: If the seven planets occupy exactly 5 distinct signs among them, this yoga is formed. One born with this yoga has the risk of being imprisoned. He is capable in his work. He is talkataive. He has many servants. He lacks character. Paasa means a noose.

Kedaara Yoga: If the seven planets occupy exactly 4 distinct signs among them, this yoga is formed. One born with this yoga is an agriculturist. He is happy wealthy and helpful to others. Kedaara means a field.

Soola Yoga: If the seven planets occupy exactly 3 distinct signs among them, this yoga is formed. One born with this yoga is sharp, lazy, violent, poor, prohibited and valiant. They win accolades in wars. Soola is Shiva's weapon.

Yuga Yoga: If the seven planets occupy exactly 2 distinct signs among them, this yoga is formed. One born with this yoga is a heretic. He is poor and discarded in the world. He is irrelegious. He has no happiness from children and mother. Yuga means a pair.

Gola Yoga: If the seven planets are in one sign, this yoga is formed. One born with this yoga is strong, poor, dirty and uneducated. He is always sad. Gola means a sphere or a globe.

11.6 Other Popular Yogas

Some other important combinations will be listed below. Sometimes the results of a dasa may be felt even if all the required combinations are not present. But, for a yoga to be fully present, all the required combinations must be present and the participating planets must be strong.

Subha Yoga: If lagna has benefics or has "subha kartari"[31] – benefics in 12th and 2nd – then this yoga is present. One born with this yoga has eloquence, good looks and character.

Asubha Yoga: If lagna has malefics or has "paapa kartari" – malefics in 12th and 2nd – then this yoga is present. One born with this yoga has many desires. He is sinful and enjoys the wealth of others.

Gaja-Kesari Yoga: If (1) Jupiter is in a quadrant from Moon, (2) a benefic planet conjoins or aspects Jupiter, and, (3) Jupiter is not debilitated or combust or in an enemy's house, then this yoga is present. One born with this yoga is famous, wealthy and intelligent. He has great character and he is liked by kings. For virtuousness and ever-lasting fame, this is a key yoga.

Some authors consider Gaja-Kesari yoga to be present even when Jupiter is in a quadrant from lagna and not Moon. If he is strong, this yoga can be present even without a benefic's aspect or conjunction.

Guru-Mangala Yoga: If Jupiter and Mars are together or in the 7th house from each other, then this yoga is present. One born with this yoga is righteous and energetic. His energies are channelled in dharmic paths.

---

31 Kartari literally means "scissors". The 12th and 2nd houses from a house cast kartari on it. If the 2nd and 12th from a house have benefics, it is said to have a subha (benefic) kartari. Malefics in the same places cause paapa (malefic) kartari. Subha kartari on any house does good to the matters of that house and paapa kartari does harm. Subha kartari and paapa kartari are also known as "subha kartari yoga" and "paapa kartari yoga" and they can be seen with reference to any house or planet.

Amala Yoga: If there are only natural benefics in the 10th house from lagna or Moon, then this yoga is present. One born with this yoga has ever-lasting fame. He is respected by kings. He has luxuries and he is virtuous. He helps others. Amala means pure. Because the 10th house shows one conduct in society, situation of only benefics there makes one's conduct in the society very pure.

Parvata Yoga: If (1) quadrants are occupied only by benefics and (2) the 7th and 8th houses are either vacant or occupied only by benefics, then this yoga is present. One born with this yoga is fortunate, eloquent, famous, charitable, easy-going and likes humour. Parvata means a mountain.

Kaahala Yoga: If (1) the 4th lord and Jupiter[32] are in mutual quadrants and (2) lagna lord is strong, then this yoga is present. Alternately, this yoga is present if the 4th lord is exalted or in own sign and the 10th lord joins him. One born with this yoga is strong, bold, cunning and leads a large army. He owns a few villages. Kaahala means excessive. It also means mischievous.

Chaamara Yoga: If the lagna lord is exalted in a quadrant with Jupiter's aspect *or* two benefics join in 7th, 9th or 10th, then this yoga is present. One born with this yoga is a king or someone respected by kings. He is long-lived, scholarly, eloquent and learned in many arts. Chaamara means something akin to the plume on the head of a horse. By waving it, servants give relief to kings from heat (like a fan). It basically stands for the trappings of power.

Sankha Yoga: If (1) lagna lord is strong and (2) 5th and 6th lords are in mutual quadrants, then this yoga is present. Alternately, this yoga is present if (1) lagna lord and 10th lord are together in a movable sign and (2) the 9th lord is strong. One born with this yoga is blessed with wealth, spouse and children. He is kind, pious, intelligent and long-lived. Sankha means a conch shell.

Bheri Yoga: If (1) the 9th lord is strong and (2) 1st, 2nd, 7th and 12th houses are occupied by planets, then this yoga is present. Alternately, this is yoga is present if (1) the 9th lord is strong and (2) Jupiter, Venus and lagna lord are in mutual quadrants. One born with this yoga is blessed with wealth, spouse and children. He can be a king. He has fame and character. He is virtuous and religious. He enjoys pleasures. Bheri means a kettledrum.

Mridanga Yoga: If (1) there are planets in own and exaltation signs in quadrants and trines and (2) lagna lord is strong, then this yoga is présent. One born with this yoga is a king or an equal and he is happy. Mridanga is a rich and elegant percussion instrument popular in south India.

---

32 Some say "9th lord" instead of Jupiter

Sreenaatha Yoga: If (1) the 7th lord is exalted in 10th[33] and (2) 10th lord is with 9th lord, then this yoga is present. One born with this yoga becomes a great king equal to Indra – king of gods. Sreenaatha means the lord of great wealth and prosperity. It also means Vishnu.

Matsya Yoga: If (1) benefics are in lagna and 9th, (2) some planets are in 5th, and, (3) malefics are in chaturasras (4th and 8th houses), then this yoga is present. One born with this yoga becomes an astrologer or a seer. He is a personification of kindness, character and intelligence. He is strong and good-looking. He is famous and learned. He is a *tapasvi* (austere pursuer). Matsya means a fish.

Koorma Yoga: If (1) the 5th, 6th and 7th houses are occupied by benefics who are in own, exaltation or friendly signs and (2) the 1st, 3rd and 11th houses are occupied by malefics who are in own or exaltation signs, then this yoga is present. One born with this yoga becomes a king. He has piety and character. He is happy, helpful and famous. Koorma means a tortoise.

Khadga Yoga: If (1) the 2nd lord is in the 9th house, (2) the 9th lord is in the 2nd house, and, (3) lagna lord is in a quadrant or a trine, then this yoga is present. One born with this yoga is skilful, wealthy, learned, happy, fortunate, intelligent, grateful and mighty. Khadga means a sword.

Kusuma Yoga: If (1) lagna is in a fixed sign, (2) Venus is in a quadrant, (3) Moon is in a trine with a benefic, and, (4) Saturn is in the 10th house, then this yoga is present. One born with this yoga becomes a king or an equal. He is charitable. He is endowed with pleasures and happiness. He is a leader of his community. He has character and scholarship. Kusuma means a flower.

Kalaanidhi Yoga: If (1) Jupiter is in the 2nd house or the 5th house and (2) he is conjoined or aspected by Mercury and Venus, then this yoga is present. One born with this yoga is endowed with character, happiness, good health, wealth and learning. He is respected by kings. Kalaanidhi means a treasure of arts and skills.

Kalpadruma Yoga: Consider (1) lagna lord, (2) his dispositor, (3) the latter's dispositor in rasi and (4) in navamsa. If all the four planets are all in quadrants, trines or exaltation signs, then this yoga is present. An example will make this clearer.

One born with this yoga becomes a king. He likes wars[34]. He is very

---

33 If this is to be applied strictly, 7th lord can be exalted in 10th only for Sagittarius lagna.

34 This is not meant negatively. War and curbing bad elements are a king's duty. The results of this yoga include the words "principled" and "kind". So the expression "likes wars" (yuddhapriyah) should be taken in a positive sense. Shivaji's example may explain it further.

prosperous, principled, strong and kind. Kalpadruma is a celestial tree of the heaven. This yoga is also known as Paarijaata yoga. Paarijaata is a celestial flower. Some authors have simplified this yoga and wrote that one of the last two planets mentioned can bring the yoga if in a quadrant or a trine or exaltation sign. Taking all the four planets make this a less common yoga, which it ought to be. Let us follow Parasara.

As an example, let us look at the rasi and navamsa charts of Chatrapati Shivaji, a great king of India (see Chart 9). Lagna lord is Sun. He is in Aq and his dispositor is Saturn (lord of Aq). Saturn is in Li and his dispositor is Venus. We also need Saturn's dispositor in navamsa. In navamsa, Saturn is in Aq and his dispositor is Saturn himself.

Chart 9

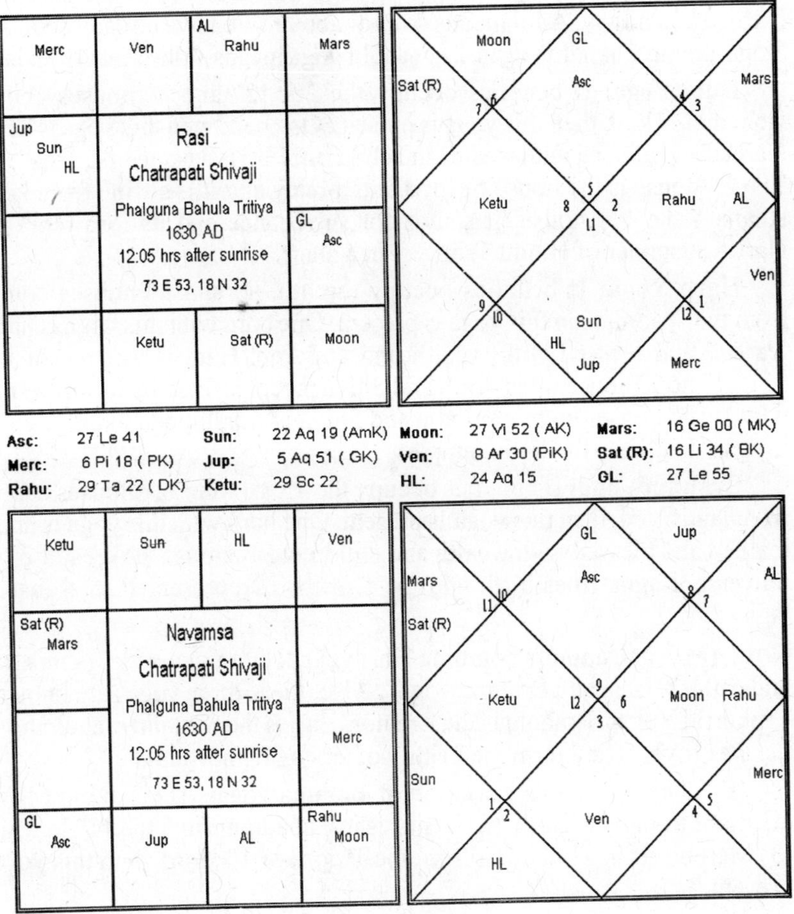

Asc:	27 Le 41	**Sun:**	22 Aq 19 (AmK)	**Moon:**	27 Vi 52 (AK)	**Mars:**	16 Ge 00 (MK)
Merc:	6 Pi 18 (PK)	**Jup:**	5 Aq 51 (GK)	**Ven:**	8 Ar 30 (PiK)	**Sat (R):**	16 Li 34 (BK)
Rahu:	29 Ta 22 (DK)	**Ketu:**	29 Sc 22	**HL:**	24 Aq 15	**GL:**	27 Le 55

Thus we get the four planets as — Sun, Saturn, Venus and Saturn. Sun is in a quadrant. Saturn is exalted. Venus is in a trine. Thus Shivaji had Kalpadruma yoga. In navamsa also, Sun is exalted, Saturn is in moolatrikona and Venus is in a lagna. This makes the yoga even more powerful. He was indeed a prosperous, principled, strong and kind king ever ready to take on powerful enemies. Even as he was fighting mighty Muslim emperors, he was open-minded and treated all his people equally. He respected every woman as a mother. He stood for every good thing that Hindu culture represented. About 400 years after his birth, name of this "dharma veera" (virtuous warrior) still inspires awe in Indians in general and Maharashtrians in particular.

Lagnaadhi Yoga: If (1) the 7th and 8th houses from lagna are occupied by benefics and (2) no malefics conjoin or aspect these planets, then this yoga is present. One born with this yoga becomes a great person. He is learned and happy. Adhi means over or above. We have already seen Adhi Yoga among Chandra yogas. Lagnaadhi yoga means Adhi Yoga from lagna.

Hari Yoga: If benefics occupy the 2nd, 12th and 8th houses counted from the 2nd lord, then this yoga is present. One born with this yoga is happy, learned and blessed with wealth and children. Hari is a name of Lord Vishnu. The 2nd house is the house of food and money and it is a trine from karma sthana – the 10th house. It stands for sustenance and its lord represents Hari – Sustainer of Hindu Trinity – in a chart.

Hara Yoga: If benefics occupy the 4th, 9th and 8th houses counted from the 7th lord, then this yoga is present. One born with this yoga is happy, learned and blessed with wealth and children. Hara is a name of Lord Shiva. The 7th house rules death and Shiva is represented by its lord. This is why the 7th house shows genitalia and Shiva is worshipped in the form of a Linga – Phallus – in Hindu temples.

Brahma Yoga: If benefics occupy the 4th, 10th and 11th houses counted from lagna lord, then this yoga is present. One born with this yoga is happy, learned and blessed with wealth and children. Brahma is the creator of this universe. Lagna rules birth and the Creator is represented in a chart by lagna lord.

NOTE: (a) Some authors combine Hari yoga, Hara yoga and Brahma yoga and call it "Hari Hara Brahma yoga". Also, these three yogas are known as Trimurthi Yogas. Brahma is the Creator; Hari is the Sustainer; and, Shiva is the Destroyer. They form the Trinity of Gods (Trimurthis).

(b) There is another variation of Brahma yoga: "If (1) Jupiter is in a quadrant from the 9th lord, (2) Venus is in a quadrant from the 11th lord, and, (3) Mercury is in a quadrant from the 1st lord or 10th lord, then this yoga is present."

Vishnu Yoga: If (1) the 9th and 10th lords are in the 2nd house and (2) the lord of the sign occupied in navamsa by the 9th lord in rasi chart is also in the 2nd house, then this yoga is present. One born with this yoga is fortunate, learned, long-lived and liked by kings. He is a worshipper of Vishnu.

Siva Yoga: If (1) the 5th lord is in the 9th house, (2) the 9th lord is in the 10th house, and, (3) the 10th lord is in the 5th house, then this yoga is present. One born with this yoga is wise and virtuous. He is a conqueror. He can be an army chief or a businessman. Lord Siva is one of the Trinity of Gods.

Trilochana Yoga: If Sun, Moon and Mars are in mutual trines, then this yoga is present. One born with this yoga is wealthy, intelligent, long-lived and victorious over enemies. He achieves everything without many obstacles. Trilochana means "one with three eyes". It is another name of Lord Siva, who has a hidden eye in His forehead.

Gouri Yoga: If the lord of the sign occupied in navamsa by the 10th lord is exalted in the 10th house and lagna lord joins him, then this yoga is present. One born with this yoga is from a respectable family and he is religious and virtuous. He is blessed with happiness from family. Gouri is a form of Parvati – Lord Siva's wife. She is an epitome of marital bliss and purity.

Chandikaa Yoga: If (1) lagna is in a fixed sign aspected by 6th lord and (2) Sun joins the lords of the signs occupied in navamsa by 6th and 9th lords, then this yoga is present. One born with this yoga is aggressive, charitable, wealthy, famous and long-lived. Chandika is an aggressive form of Parvati. She kills demons mercilessly.

Lakshmi Yoga: If (1) the 9th lord is in an own sign or in his exaltation sign that happens to be quadrant from lagna and (2) lagna lord is strong, then this yoga is present. One born with this yoga becomes a king. He is blessed with good looks, character, wealth and many children. He is principled and famous. Lakshmi is Vishnu's wife. She is the goddess of prosperity.

Saarada Yoga: If (1) the 10th lord is in the 5th house, (2) Mercury is in a quadrant, (3) Sun is strong in Leo, (4) Mercury or Jupiter is in a trine from Moon, and, (5) Mars is in 11th, then this yoga is present. One born with this yoga is blessed with wealth, spouse and children. He is happy, learned, principled and liked by kings. He is a tapaswi (autere pursuer of knowledge). Saarada is another name of Saraswathi, the goddess of learning.

Bhaarathi Yoga: If the lord of the sign occupied in navamsa by 2nd, 5th or 11th lord exalted and joins the 9th lord, then this yoga is present. One born with this yoga is a great scholar. He is intelligent, religious, good-looking and famous. Bhaarathi is another name of Saraswathi, the goddess of learning.

Saraswathi Yoga: If (1) each of Mercury, Jupiter and Venus occupies a quadrant or a trine or the 2nd house (not necessarily together) and (2) Jupiter is in an own or friendly or exaltation sign, then this yoga is present. One born with this yoga is very learned, skilful, intelligent, rich and famous. He is praised by all. Saraswathi is the goddess of learning.

Amsaavatara Yoga: If Jupiter, Venus and exalted Saturn are in quadrants, then this yoga is present. One born with this yoga becomes a king or an equal. He is learned and pleasure-loving. He has unsullied reputation. Amsaavatara means one who is an incarnation of a part of the Lord.

Devendra Yoga: If (1) lagna is in a fixed sign, (2) 2nd and 10th lords have an exchange[35], and, (3) lagna and 11th lords have an exchange, then this yoga is present. One born with this yoga is a leader of men. He is handsome, romantic, long-lived and famous. Devendra is the ruler of gods.

Indra Yoga: If (1) the 5th and 11th lords have an exchange and (2) Moon occupies the 5th house, then this yoga is present. One born with this yoga becomes a king. He is bold, famous and long-lived. Indra is the ruler of gods.

Ravi Yoga: If (1) Sun is in the 10th house and (2) the 10th lord is in the 3rd house with Saturn, then this yoga is present. One born with this yoga is learned, passionate and respected by kings. Ravi means Sun.

Bhaaskara Yoga: If (1) Moon is in the 12th from Sun, (2) Mercury is in the 2nd from Sun, and, (3) Jupiter is in the 5th or 9th from Moon, then this yoga is present. One born with this yoga is wealthy, valorous and aristocratic. He is learned in sastras, astrology and music. He has a good personality. Bhaaskara means "one with bright rays". It is a name of Sun.

Kulavardhana Yoga: If each planet occupies the 5th house from either lagna or Moon or Sun, then this yoga is present. One born with this yoga is happy, wealthy and brings name to his lineage and community. He has an unbroken line of worthy successors. Kula means "lineage or community". Vardhana means "one who makes it grow and prosper".

Vasumati Yoga: If benefics occupy upachayas, then this yoga is present. For it to give full results, malefics should not occupy upachayas and the benefics occupying upachayas should be strong. One born with this yoga has abundant wealth. Vasumati means earth.

Gandharva Yoga: If (1) the 10th lord is in a trine from the 7th house, (2) lagna lord is conjoined or aspected by Jupiter, (3) Sun is exalted and strong,

---

35 That means that the 2nd lord is in the 10th house and the 10th lord is in the 2nd house. Exchange is called "parivartana" in Sanskrit.

and, (4) Moon is in the 9th house, then this yoga is present. One born with this yoga is skilful and famous in fine arts. Gandharvas are a class of gods with excellent skills in singing and other fine arts.

Go Yoga: If (1) Jupiter is strong in his moolatrikona, (2) the lord of the 2nd house is with Jupiter, and, (3) lagna lord is exalted, then this yoga is present. One born with this yoga is from a respectable family. He is wealthy and respected by all. Go means a cow.

Vidyut Yoga: If (1) the 11th lord is in deep exaltation, (2) he joins Venus, and, (3) the two of them are in a quadrant from lagna lord, then this yoga is present. One born with this yoga becomes a king or an equal. He is wealthy, pleasure-loving and charitable. Vidyut means a lightning bolt or electricity.

Chapa Yoga: If (1) the 4th and 10th lords have an exchange and (2) lagna lord is exalted, then this yoga is present. One born with this yoga works for a king and commands a lot of wealth. Chapa means a bow.

Pushkala Yoga: If (1) lagna lord is with Moon, (2) dispositor of Moon is in a quadrant or in the house of an adhimitra (good friend), (2) dispositor of Moon aspects lagna, and, (4) there is a planet in lagna, then this yoga is present. One born with this yoga is eloquent, wealthy, famous and respected by kings. Pushkala means abundant.

Makuta Yoga: If (1) Jupiter is in the 9th house from the 9th lord, (2) the 9th house from Jupiter has a benefic, and, (3) Saturn is in the 10th house, then this yoga is present. One born with this yoga is a powerful leader of men. He often manages unruly activities. Makuta means crown.

Jaya Yoga: If (1) the 10th lord is in deep exaltation and (2) the 6th lord is debilitated, then this yoga is present. One born with this yoga is happy, successful, victorious over enemies and long-lived. Jaya means victorious.

Harsha Yoga: If the 6th lord occupies the 6th house, then this yoga is present. One born with this yoga is happy, strong, good-natured and invincible. Harsha means joyous.

Sarala Yoga: If the 8th lord occupies the 8th house, then this yoga is present. One born with this yoga is long-lived, fearless, learned, celebrated and prosperous. He is a terror to his enemies. Sarala means straight-forward.

Vimala Yoga: If the 12th lord occupies the 12th house, then this yoga is present. One born with this yoga is noble, frugal, happy and independent. Vimala means pure.

11.7 Raaja Yogas

Raaja means a king. Raaja yogas are the combinations that give power and prosperity to a native. They make one the best in something.

11.7.1 *Basics*

Basic Raaja Yoga: In any chart, Lord Vishnu sits in the quadrants and Goddess Lakshmi sits in the trines. If the lord of a quadrant is associated with the lord of a trine, that association brings the combined blessings of Lakshmi and Vishnu. This is called a Raaja Yoga. The native is powerful and prosperous.

What do we mean by "association" here? There are 3 important associations:

(1) The two planets are conjoined,

(2) The two planets aspect each other with graha drishti, or,

(3) The two planets have a parivartana (exchange). For example, if the 4th lord is in the 5th house and the 5th lord is in the 4th house, then we say that there is a parivartana between the 4th and 5th lords. This is an association.

If the lord of a quadrant and the lord of a trine have one of the three kinds of associations mentioned above, it forms a Raaja Yoga. Lagna can be taken as a quadrant or a trine here. It is both.

Dharma-Karmadhipati Yoga: This is a special case of the above yoga. If the lords of dharma sthana (9th) and karma sthana (10th) form a raja yoga, it is known by this special name. The 9th house is the most important trine and the 10th house is the most important quadrant. Raaja yoga involving the lords of these two houses is excellent. One born with this yoga is sincere, devoted and righteous. He is fortunate and.

Vipareeta Raaja Yoga: The 6th, 8th and 12th houses are known as trik sthanas or dusthanas (bad houses). If their lords occupies dusthanas or conjoin dusthanas, it results in this yoga. One having this yoga experiences tremendous success, typically after an initial struggle. Vipareeta means extreme.

Because dusthanas show the obstacles one faces in life, situation of dusthana lords in dusthanas shows that obstacles will run into obstacles themselves. One experiences tremendous success in the face of obstacles.

In the ideal case, the lords of the 6th, 8th and 12th houses will all be together in one of the three houses (or the 3rd house or the 11th house), with no other planets conjoining them. But the results of this yoga may be experienced with just one or two dusthana lords occupying a dusthana.

11.7.2 *Magnitude of a Raaja Yoga*

We find the conjunction of the lords of a quadrant and a trine in many charts. The magnitude to which this raaja yoga fructifies depends on the strength of the two planets. The key factors that come into play are:

(1) The two planets should be free from afflictions from functional malefics.

(2) The conjunction or aspect responsible for the Raaja Yoga should be close (say, within 6° or so).

If Mercury and Venus are at 2° and 26° in Ta for a native with Cp lagna, for example, their conjunction brings a Raaja Yoga (Dharma-Karmadhipati Yoga in particular). However, the two planets are too far apart for this yoga to give its full results. They are still associated, but the association is not very strong. If Venus is at 3° in Ta in instead of 26°, the conjunction is very close and the yoga can give its full results, if other factors are favorable.

(3) The two planets should not be combust, debilitated or in an inimical house or in bad avasthas (states).

Any blemishes here will considerably reduce the magnitude of the yoga. In addition to the above factors, Sage Parasara recommended looking at the amsas occupied by the 2 planets as per Dasa Varga (ten division) scheme. Count the divisional charts – out of the ten charts of Dasa Varga scheme – in which a planet occupies an own, exaltation or moolatrikona sign. Based on the count of divisional charts with such a good placement for the planet in question, we say that it is in a particular amsa. Please see the chapter "Divisional Charts" for details.

If the two planets giving raaja yoga have a count of one or zero, the yoga is ordinary and gives good results depending on the factors already outlined.

If the two planets are in Paarijaataamsa (count of 2), then one becomes a king who rules his people well. If the two planets are in Uttamsaamsa (count of 3), then one becomes a good king with tremendous assets. If the two planets are in Gopuraamsa (count of 4), then one becomes a great king respected by many kings.

If the two planets are in Simhaasanaamsa (count of 5), then one becomes a great emperor who rules the whole world. Parasara said that several great emperors of Indian mythology – like Harischandra, Manu, Bali, Vaiswaanara, Yudhisthira (also known as Dharmaraja) and Saalivaahana[36] – were born with this combination.

Two planets giving Raaja Yoga can be in Paaraavataamsa (count of 6), Devalokamsa (count of 7), Brahmalokaamsa (count of 8) and Airaavataamsa

36 Saalivaahana was yet to be born when Parasara wrote his classic "Brihat Paaraasara Horaa Saastram". He referred Dharmaraja of Mahabharata as "King Yudhisthira of this Yuga" and made a prediction about the birth of Saalivaahana with Raaja Yoga giving planets in Simhaasanaamsa.

(count of 9) only for divine persons such as Svaayambhuva Manu (Manu who was born by Himself), Brahma (Creator!!) and Vishnu's incarnations such as Sri Rama and Sri Krishna.

Final Judgment: None of the above factors influences the end result completely. We should look at all the factors and make the final judgment.

Chart 10

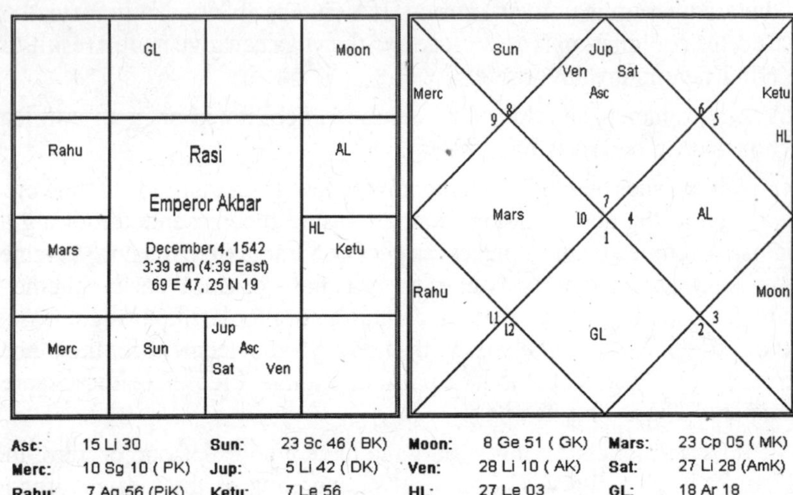

India's former Prime Minister Rajiv Gandhi[37] had lagna lord Sun and 5th lord Jupiter in lagna giving a Raaja Yoga. Both were in Simhaasanaamsa. However, they were more than 8° apart[38] and functional malefics were with them. Saturn had a very close aspect on Jupiter. So the Yoga is pretty weak. However, the two planets are in Simhaasanaamsa and that raises the level of the Yoga. In the end, he only became India's prime minister and not an "emperor of the whole world".

Let us look at India's emperor Akbar[39] (see Chart 10). His chart has Libra lagna. Lagna lord Venus and 4th and 5th lord Saturn are in lagna. They give Mahapurusha yogas (Maalavya and Sasa) as well as a Raja Yoga. Moon and Mercury own 10th and 9th and they have a close aspect. They

---

37 Birthdata: August 20, 1944, 7:11:40 am (IST), 72 E 49, 18 N 58

38 Anything greater than 5 or 6 degrees is too large for a Raaja Yoga to give its full results.

39 Birthdata: December 4, 1542, 3:39 am (LMT), 69 E 47, 25 N 19. This date may be written by some as November 24, 1542 based on the old calendar.

also form a Raja Yoga. But they are not even in Paarijaataamsa. Venus and Saturn are only in Uttamaamsa and Paarijaataamsa.

However, Venus and Saturn are very strong and take part in other Yogas. Both the Raaja Yogas are very close. Venus and Saturn are less than a degree apart. They are afflicted by a functional malefic (Jupiter), but Jupiter is 22° away from them. Moreover, lord of GL is Mars and he gives another Mahapurusha Yoga – Ruchaka Yoga – and he is in Simhaasanaamsa.

Due to all these reasons, Akbar was a great emperor of India although Raaja Yoga giving planets weren't in Simhaasanaamsa. We should always make the final judgment after looking at all the factors.

11.7.3 *More Raaja Yogas*

Some advanced Raaja Yogas will be listed below.

(1) If (*a*) chara putra karaka (PK) and chara atmaka karaka (AK) are conjoined and (*b*) lagna and 5th lords conjoin, then Raaja Yoga is present and the native enjoys power and prosperity. If only one condition is satisfied, still the results may be felt, but not fully.

(2) If (*a*) lagna lord is in 5th, (*b*) 5th lord is in lagna, (*c*) AK and PK are in lagna or the 5th house, and (*d*) those planets in owns rasi or amsa or in exaltation or aspected by benefics, then this yoga is present and the native becomes a great king (Maharajah) loved by his associates.

(3) If the 9th lord and AK are in lagna, 5th or 7th, aspected by benefics, then Raaja Yoga is present.

(4) If the 2nd, 4th and 5th houses from lagna lord and AK are occupied by benefics, one becomes a king.

(5) If the 3rd and 6th houses from lagna lord and AK are occupied or aspected by malefics, one becomes a king.

(6) If lagna, HL and GL are joined or aspected by the same planet, then that planet gives a Raaja Yoga. One may add "owned" to "joined or aspected".

Planets aspecting or joining HL and GL give wealth and power respectively. If such a planet is associated with lagna also, its potential to do good increases.

Results of this yoga may be experienced if the conditions are not strictly met, but a planet has an association with lagna (or lagna lord), HL (or HL lord) and GL (or GL lord). Association here can mean ownership, conjunction or aspect. If lagna lord is in HL and aspects GL lord, for example, results of this Raaja Yoga may be experienced to some extent.

(7) If the same planet aspects lagna in the six divisional charts of shad vargas – Rasi, Navamsa, Hora, Drekkana, Dwadasamsa, Trimsamsa – then that planet gives a Raaja Yoga.

(8) If lagna, HL and GL are occupied by a planet in own or exaltation sign, then the native becomes a king. [NOTE: It can be different planets.]

(9) If lagna in Rasi, Navamsa and Drekkana charts is occupied by a planet in own or exaltation sign, then the native becomes a king. [NOTE: It can be different planets.]

(10) If (*a*) the 3rd, 6th and 8th houses are occupied by one or two planets in debilitation and (*b*) lagna lord is in an own or exaltation sign and aspects lagna, it forms a Raaja Yoga.

(11) If (*a*) the 6th, 8th and 12th lords are debilitated or combust or in inimical signs and (*b*) lagna lord is in an own or exaltation sign and aspects lagna, it forms a Raaja Yoga.

(12) If the 5th and 9th lords are in a conjunction or a mutual aspect, it makes one prosperous.

(13) If (*a*) the 4th lord is in the 10th house and the 10th lord is in the 4th house and (*b*) both of them are aspected by the 5th lord or the 9th lord, then a Raaja Yoga is formed.

(14) If (*a*) the 5th lord is in the 1st, 4th or 10th house and (*b*) lagna lord or the 9th lord joins him, then the native becomes a king.

(15) If (*a*) Moon is strong and occupies vargottamamsa[40] and (*b*) four or more planets aspect him, then one becomes a king.

(16) If 4 or more planets occupy moolatrikonas or exaltation signs, one becomes a king even if he is from a lowly family.

(17) If benefics are in quadrants and malefics are in the 3rd, 6th and 11th houses, one becomes a king even if he is from a lowly family.

(18) If arudha lagna and darapada (arudha pada of the 7th house) are *not* in mutual 2nd/12th or 6th/8th positions, then Raja Yogas in the chart will be more effective.

11.8 Raaja Sambandha Yogas

Raaja means a king. Sambandha means relation or association. Raaja sambandha yogas are the combinations that give association with rulers. Those who have these yogas are typically powerful ministers, secretaries, counsellors and bureaucrats, associated with the rulers and powerful men. However, these yogas are very common. The magnitude of success depends

---

40 A planet is in vargottamaamsa if it occupies the same sign in Rasi and Navamsa charts.

on the strength of the planets involved in raja yoga.

(1) If the 10th lord is conjoined or aspected by AmK (chara amaatya kaaraka) or his dispositor, one becomes an important person in the court of a king.

(2) If the 11th lord aspects the 11th house and there are no malefic planets joining or aspecting the 10th and 11th houses, one becomes an important person in the court of a king.

(3) If AK (chara aatma kaaraka) and AmK conjoin, one is very intelligent and becomes a minister.

(4) If AmK is very strong in own sign or his exaltation sign, then also one becomes a minister.

(5) If AmK is in a trine from lagna, one becomes a famous minister.

(6) If AmK is in a quadrant or a trine from AK, one is an associate liked by a king.

(7) If malefics occupy the 3rd and 6th houses from lagna, AL *and* AK, then one becomes a powerful chief of army.

(8) If AK is in an own or exaltation sign in a quadrant or a trine and the 9th lord is conjoined or aspected by AK, one becomes a minister.

(9) If AK happens to be Moon's dispositor and he occupies lagna along with a benefic, one becomes a minister at an old age.

(10) If AK is in the 5th,7th, 9th or 10th houses with a benefic, one will be associated with kings and earn money thus.

(11) If bhagyapada (A9 – arudha pada of the 9th house) is in lagna or AK is in 9th, one is fortunate and associates with kings.

(12) If the 11th lord is in the 11th house without aspects from any malefics and AK is with benefics, then one has gains from a king.

(13) If lagna lord is in the 10th house and the 10th lord is in lagna, one is powerful and associated with kings.

(14) If Moon and Venus are in the 4th house from AK, one is endowed with royal insignia.

(15) If lagna lord or AK conjoins the 5th lord in a quadrant or a trine, one becomes a king's friend.

11.9 Dhana Yogas

Dhana means wealth. Dhana yogas are combinations that give one abundant riches.

Basic Principle: The 5th and 9th lords and planets joining them are capable of giving money. They give dasas in their dasas. The 11th house is also important for material gains and it should be strong. The 2nd house is also important. If Moon, Mercury, Jupiter or Venus is exalted in the 2nd house, it makes the native very rich.

In addition to these general principles, Parasara listed specific combinations for various lagnas. In all these combinations, the strength of the participating planets decides the magnitude of results experienced.

(1) **For Ar lagna:** If Sun is in the 5th house and Saturn, Moon and Jupiter are in the 11th house, one becomes very affluent. If Mars occupies lagna conjoined or aspected by Mercury, Venus and Saturn, then also one becomes very rich.

(2) **For Ta lagna:** If Mercury is in the 5th house and Moon, Mars and Jupiter are in the 11th house, one becomes very affluent. If Venus occupies lagna conjoined or aspected by Mercury and Saturn, then also one becomes very rich.

(3) **For Ge lagna:** If Venus is in the 5th house and Mars is in the 11th house, one becomes very affluent. If Mercury occupies lagna conjoined or aspected by Jupiter and Saturn, then also one becomes very rich.

(4) **For Cn lagna:** If Mars is in the 5th house and Venus is in the 11th house, one becomes very affluent. If Moon occupies lagna conjoined or aspected by Mercury and Jupiter, then also one becomes very rich.

(5) **For Le lagna:** If Jupiter is in the 5th house and Mercury is in the 11th house, one becomes very affluent. If Sun occupies lagna conjoined or aspected by Mars and Jupiter, then also one becomes very rich.

(6) **For Vi lagna:** If Saturn is in the 5th house and Sun and Moon are in the 11th house, one becomes very affluent. If Mercury occupies lagna conjoined or aspected by Jupiter and Saturn, then also one becomes very rich.

(7) **For Li lagna:** If Saturn is in the 5th house and Sun and Moon are in the 11th house, one becomes very affluent. If Venus occupies lagna conjoined or aspected by Mercury and Saturn, then also one becomes very rich.

(8) **For Sc lagna:** If Jupiter is in the 5th house and Mercury is in the 11th house, one becomes very affluent. If Mars occupies lagna conjoined or aspected by Mercury, Venus and Saturn, then also one becomes very rich.

(9) **For Sg lagna:** If Mars is in the 5th house and Venus is in the 11th house, one becomes very affluent. If Jupiter occupies lagna conjoined or aspected by Mars and Mercury, then also one becomes very rich.

(10) For Cp lagna: If Venus is in the 5th house and Mars is in the 11th house, one becomes very affluent. If Saturn occupies lagna conjoined or aspected by Mars and Jupiter, then also one becomes very rich.

(11) For Aq lagna: If Mercury is in the 5th house and Moon, Mars and Jupiter are in the 11th house, one becomes very affluent. If Saturn occupies lagna conjoined or aspected by Mars and Jupiter, then also one becomes very rich.

(12) For Pi lagna: If Moon is in the 5th house and in the 11th house, one becomes very affluent. If Jupiter occupies lagna conjoined or aspected by Mars and Mercury, then also one becomes very rich.

11.10 Daridra Yogas

One experiences poverty if the following yogas (combinations) are present in one's chart:

(1) Lagna lord is in 12th and 12th lord is in lagna. They are conjoined or aspected by a maraka planet.

Note: The 2nd and 7th houses are maraka (killer houses). Their lords are marakas (killers). Any malefics occupying 2nd and 7th or associating with 2nd and 7th lords also become malefics.

(2) Lagna lord is in 6th and 6th lord is in lagna. They are conjoined or aspected by a maraka planet.

(3) Lagna or Moon is with Ketu. Lagna lord is in 8th. A maraka planet conjoins or aspects lagna lord.

(4) Lagna lord is with a malefic in a dusthana (6th, 8th or 12th) and 2nd lord is debilitated or in an enemy's sign. Even a royal scion with this combination becomes poor.

(5) The 5th lord is in 6th and 9th lord is in 12th, with aspects from marakas.

(6) Malefics occupy lagna without 9th and 10th lords, aspected or conjoined by marakas.

(7) Lords of the signs occupied by 6th, 8th and 12th lords are in 6th, 8th and 12th houses, conjoined or aspected by malefics.

(8) Lord of the sign occupied by Moon in navamsa is with a maraka or occupies a maraka house (2nd and 7th).

(9) Lords of lagna in rasi and navamsa are conjoined or aspected by marakas.

(10) Benefics are in malefic houses and malefics are in benefic houses.

(11) Planets conjoined by 6th, 8th and 12th lords give loss of wealth in their

dasas, if they are *not* conjoined or aspected by the lords of trines.

(12) Mars and Saturn are in 2nd and Mercury doesn't aspect them. (*Exception*: If Mercury aspects Mars and Saturn in 2nd, great wealth is generated.)

(13) Sun in 2nd is aspected by Saturn. (*Exception*: If Saturn doesn't aspect, Sun in 2nd gives wealth.)

The **general principles** emerging from the above combinations are:

Dusthanas (6th, 8th and 12th) and their lords are detrimental to wealth. If lagna, lagna lord and trine lords are afflicted by them, one may be poor. Conjunction or aspect of marakas clinches the issue. However, conjunction or aspect of trine lords is a saving factor. In addition, the planets in the 2nd house and the strength of 2nd lord matter.

11.11 Conclusion

A lot of combinations and results have been given in this chapter. Readers are advised to read more literature and practice yogas on real charts. One should be able to find with a quick glance the yogas present in a chart. Experience certainly helps there. In the rest of this book, we will see some examples of yogas.

When looking at the results ascribed to various yogas, try to fit them in today's world. For example, one with Kamala yoga may not really become a king, but probably become the Prime Minister of a nation or the Governor of a state. When using yogas in divisional charts, adapt the results to the matters signified by the chart.

All the great results ascribed to some yogas may not materialize in reality, due to weaknesses in them. Unless a yoga is very strong, all the results cannot expected. Just one yoga cannot make or break a personality, unless it is very powerful.

In the case of yogas with many conditions, partial results may sometimes be experienced if all the conditions are not satisfied.

12. Ashtakavarga

12.1 Introduction

Analyzing a chart and making correct predictions requires mixing many different principles and making fine compromises and judgments. Sage Parasara said that it is difficult for even great Maharshis. In Kali Yuga[41], human beings become sinful and the sins kill their intelligence. Parasara said that the intellectual pygmies of Kali Yuga cannot cope with too many complicated principles and presented ashtakavarga as a simple technique that lets them make reasonable predictions without much fuss. Ashtaka means "consisting of eight" and varga means "a group". Ashtakavarga is the system of analyzing a chart with respect to a group of 8 reference points.

When we analyze the positions of planets with respect to lagna, we have the concept of good and bad placements. For example, Jupiter in the 9th from lagna will be well placed and Jupiter in the 3rd will be badly placed. Mars in the 3rd from lagna will be well placed and Mars in the 9th will be badly placed.

However, lagna is not the only reference point in a chart. We have Sun and Moon. In fact, all the planets serve as reference points in a chart and they represent the sources of various energies that are present in a native. Based on the houses in which different planets are placed in transit, they can be benefic with respect to some energy sources and malefic with respect to some. If a transiting planet is benefic with respect to more energy sources, then it brings good results.

So ashtakavarga is essentially a system that tells us the benefic positions of lagna and seven planets with respect to each other. This can be used to analyze the strength of a natal chart, but it is much more important in analyzing transits.

12.2 Benefic and Malefic Houses

The benefic and malefic houses for Sun with respect to all the 8 references are given in Table 19.

---

41 As per Vedic science, time is divided into a cycle of four Yugas that keep repeating. Those are: Krita yuga (1,728,000 years), Treta yuga (1,296,000 years), Dwapara yuga (864,000 years) and Kali yuga (432,000 years). In Krita yuga, religiousness and virtuosity of human beings is exemplary. It is the worst in Kali yuga. It gradually worsens from Krita yuga to Kali yuga. We are currently in Kali yuga. It started about 5,000 years back.

Table 19: Definition of Sun's Ashtakavarga

From House	Sun	Moon	Mars	Merc	Jup	Ven	Sat	Lag
1st	1	0	1	0	0	0	1	0
2nd	1	0	1	0	0	0	1	0
3rd	0	1	0	1	0	0	0	1
4th	1	0	1	0	0	0	1	1
5th	0	0	0	1	1	0	0	0
6th	0	1	0	1	1	1	0	1
7th	1	0	1	0	0	1	1	0
8th	1	0	1	0	0	0	1	0
9th	1	0	1	1	1	0	1	0
10th	1	1	1	1	0	0	1	1
11th	1	1	1	1	1	0	1	1
12th	0	0	0	1	0	1	0	1

In Table 19, an entry of **0** denotes a malefic position or a "karana" or a **bindu** (dot). An entry of **1** denotes a benefic position or a "sthana" or a **rekha** (line)[42]. To understand how to read this table, let us go to the column titled "Merc" in Table 19. This shows benefic houses for Sun to occupy, with respect to Mercury. The 1st and 2nd houses have 0 and the 3rd house has 1. So the first 2 houses from Mercury are malefic for Sun and the 3rd house is benefic for Sun. Table 20-Table 26 give the benefic and malefic houses of Moon, Mars, Mercury, Jupiter, Venus, Saturn and lagna (respectively).

---

42 Some astrologers (especially south Indian astrologers) use a different notation. They use "bindu" to describe a benefic house (1) and "rekha" to describe malefic house (0). Let us follow Parasara.

Table 20: Definition of Moon's Ashtakavarga

From House	Sun	Moon	Mars	Merc	Jup	Ven	Sat	Lag
1st	0	1	0	1	1	0	0	0
2nd	0	0	1	0	1	0	0	0
3rd	1	1	1	1	0	1	1	1
4th	0	0	0	1	1	1	0	0
5th	0	0	1	1	0	1	1	0
6th	1	1	1	0	0	0	1	1
7th	1	1	0	1	1	1	0	0
8th	1	0	0	1	1	0	0	0
9th	0	1	0	0	0	1	0	0
10th	1	1	1	1	1	1	0	1
11th	1	1	1	1	1	1	1	1
12th	0	0	0	0	0	0	0	0

Table 21: Definition of Mars's Ashtakavarga

From House	Sun	Moon	Mars	Merc	Jup	Ven	Sat	Lag
1st	0	0	1	0	0	0	1	1
2nd	0	0	1	0	0	0	0	0
3rd	1	1	0	1	0	0	0	1
4th	0	0	1	0	0	0	1	0
5th	1	0	0	1	0	0	0	0
6th	1	1	0	1	1	1	0	1
7th	0	0	1	0	0	0	1	0
8th	0	0	1	0	0	1	1	0
9th	0	0	0	0	0	0	1	0
10th	1	0	1	0	1	0	1	1
11th	1	1	1	1	1	1	1	1
12th	0	0	0	0	1	1	0	0

Table 22: Definition of Mercury's Ashtakavarga

From House	Sun	Moon	Mars	Merc	Jup	Ven	Sat	Lag
1st	0	0	1	1	0	1	1	1
2nd	0	1	1	0	0	1	1	1
3rd	0	0	0	1	0	1	0	0
4th	0	1	1	0	0	1	1	1
5th	1	0	0	1	0	1	0	0
6th	1	1	0	1	1	0	0	1
7th	0	0	1	0	0	0	1	0
8th	0	1	1	0	1	1	1	1
9th	1	0	1	1	0	1	1	0
10th	0	1	1	1	0	0	1	1
11th	1	1	1	1	1	1	1	1
12th	1	0	0	1	1	0	0	0

Table 23: Definition of Jupiter's Ashtakavarga

From House	Sun	Moon	Mars	Merc	Jup	Ven	Sat	Lag
1st	1	0	1	1	1	0	0	1
2nd	1	1	1	1	1	1	0	1
3rd	1	0	0	0	1	0	1	0
4th	1	0	1	1	1	0	0	1
5th	0	1	0	1	0	1	1	1
6th	0	0	0	1	0	1	1	1
7th	1	1	1	0	1	0	0	1
8th	1	0	1	0	1	0	0	0
9th	1	1	0	1	0	1	0	1
10th	1	0	1	1	1	1	0	1
11th	1	1	1	1	1	1	0	1
12th	0	0	0	0	0	0	1	0

Table 24: Definition of Venus's Ashtakavarga

From / House	Sun	Moon	Mars	Merc	Jup	Ven	Sat	Lag
1st	0	1	0	0	0	1	0	1
2nd	0	1	0	0	0	1	0	1
3rd	0	1	1	1	0	1	1	1
4th	0	1	1	0	0	1	1	1
5th	0	1	0	1	1	1	1	1
6th	0	0	1	1	0	0	0	0
7th	0	0	0	0	0	0	0	0
8th	1	1	0	0	1	1	1	1
9th	0	1	1	1	1	1	1	1
10th	0	0	0	0	1	1	1	0
11th	1	1	1	1	1	1	1	1
12th	1	1	1	0	0	0	0	0

Table 25: Definition of Saturn's Ashtakavarga

From / House	Sun	Moon	Mars	Merc	Jup	Ven	Sat	Lag
1st	1	0	0	0	0	0	0	1
2nd	1	0	0	0	0	0	0	0
3rd	0	1	1	0	0	0	1	1
4th	1	0	0	0	0	0	0	1
5th	0	0	1	0	1	0	1	0
6th	0	1	1	1	1	1	1	1
7th	1	0	0	0	0	0	0	0
8th	1	0	0	1	0	0	0	0
9th	0	0	0	1	0	0	0	0
10th	1	0	1	1	0	0	0	1
11th	1	1	1	1	1	1	1	1
12th	0	0	1	1	1	1	0	0

Table 26: Definition of Lagna's Ashtakavarga

From House	Sun	Moon	Mars	Merc	Jup	Ven	Sat	Lag
1st	0	0	1	1	1	1	1	0
2nd	0	0	0	1	1	1	0	0
3rd	1	1	1	0	0	1	1	1
4th	1	0	0	1	1	1	1	0
5th	0	0	0	0	1	1	0	0
6th	1	1	1	1	1	0	1	1
7th	0	0	0	0	1	0	0	0
8th	0	0	0	1	0	1	0	0
9th	0	0	0	0	1	1	0	0
10th	1	1	1	1	1	0	1	1
11th	1	1	1	1	1	0	1	1
12th	1	1	0	0	0	0	0	0

Readers without a computer program should memorize these tables. To the modern reader who is overly dependent on computers, memorizing these tables may seem like a daunting task. As our dependency on technology increases, several skills of our brain are left either unused or undeveloped and those skills slowly vanish. Computing ashtakavarga by hand is not as difficult as it may seem to be. In fact, even today, some people in India compute all the ashtakavarga tables by hand in a matter of a few minutes.

Example 37: Let us say Venus is in Ge. Find the rasis in which Jupiter is benefic with respect to Venus.

To find the rasis in which Jupiter is benefic, we should look at Jupiter's ashtakavarga (see Table 23). To find the rasis in which Jupiter is benefic with respect to Venus, we should look at the column of Venus. Only the 2nd, 5th, 6th, 9th, 10th and 11th houses have a 1 (rekha – benefic point) against them. Venus is in Ge and finding these houses with respect to Venus, we get Cn, Li, Sc, Aq, Pi and Ar. So Jupiter is benefic with respect to Venus in these rasis.

Exercise 18: Consider the rasi chart in Chart 6. Find the rasis in which Mercury is benefic with respect to different planets and lagna.

12.3 Bhinna Ashtakavarga

In this book, we will denote ashtakavarga with AV. We prepare what is known as "Bhinna Ashtakavarga" for each planet. It is denoted with BAV. Bhinna means "separate". When preparing the BAV of a planet, we count the number of references from which the planet is benefic in each rasi and put that count in that rasi. For each planet, we prepare a different BAV. Sometimes we may simply use the word "ashtakavarga" (AV) to represent a BAV.

The count in each rasi is between 0 to 8. It is called the number of rekhas (benefic points) in that rasi. If a planet is in a sign with a count of 5, 6, 7 or 8, it means that the planet is benefic in that rasi with respect to more references. So the planet is favorable. If a planet is in a sign with a count of 3, 2, 1 or 0, it means that the planet is malefic in that rasi with respect to more references. So the planet is unfavorable. If the count is 4, the planet is neutral. We can use this analysis in natal charts and also transit charts.

Example 38: Let us go further with Exercise 18 now. After finding the rasis in which Mercury is benefic with respect to various references, let us count the references with respect to which Mercury is benefic in each rasi. From the answer to Exercise 18, we see that Mercury is benefic in Ar with respect to Sun, Moon, Mars, Mercury, Venus, Saturn and lagna. In other words, Mercury is benefic in Ar with respect to 7 references. So we write 7 in Ar. We see that Mercury is benefic in Ta with respect to Sun, Mercury, Venus and Saturn. In other words, Mercury is benefic in Ta with respect to 4 references. So we write 4 in Ta. We find the count of references for each rasi and prepare a chart. This is called Mercury's BAV or simply Mercury's AV. Readers may complete the calculations and verify with Chart 11.

In Ar and Ge, we have 7 rekhas. So Mercury is benefic in those rasis with respect to 7 references out of 8. In Aq, we have 6 rekhas. So these three rasis are particularly favorable for Mercury. In Vi and Cp, we have 3 rekhas and that is the lowest. So Mercury is particularly unfavorable in Vi and Cp. We can use this information to interpret how favorable Mercury is in the natal chart or in a transit chart. Here Mercury is in Ge in the natal chart and Ge has 7 rekhas in Mercury's AV. That means that Mercury is a very favorable planet. Being the lagna lord and being in a quadrant from lagna in own sign (*i.e.* Bhadra yoga) makes him even stronger. Because of this, Mercury is extremely favorable in this chart. No wonder Sri P.V. Narasimha Rao is a brilliant scholar, well versed in many languages. He is an excellent writer and he won a prestigious literary award for a literary work in a language that is not his mother tongue.

Chart 11

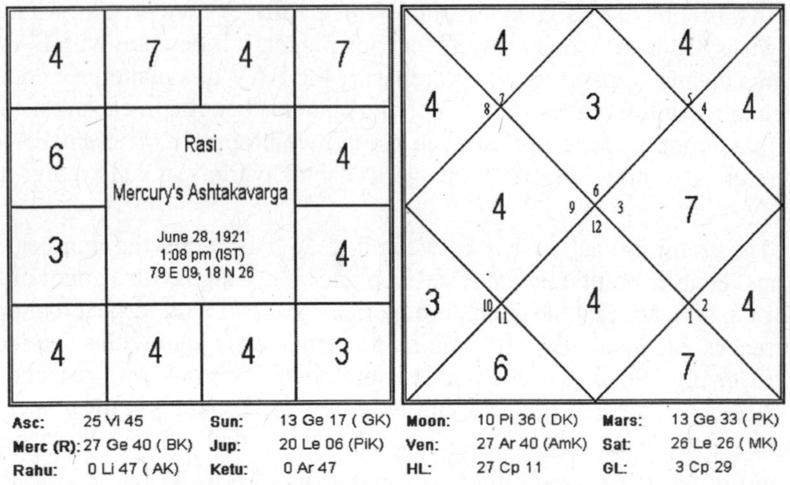

Exercise 19: Find the number of rekhas in all the rasis in the BAVs of Sun, Moon, Mars, Mercury, Jupiter, Venus and Saturn for the same rasi chart (see Chart 6).

12.4 Samudaaya Ashtakavarga

Samudaaya means "group". Samudaaya Ashtakavarga is nothing but the sum of the ashtakavargas of seven planets. In each rasi, we add the number of rekhas in the BAVs of Sun, Moon, Mars, Mercury, Jupiter, Venus and Saturn. The sum denotes the number of rekhas in that rasi in Samudaaya Ashtakavarga. It will be denoted with SAV. It is also called "Sarva Ashtakavarga" (sarva = all).

Let us continue with the rasi chart in Chart 6. From the answer to Exercise 19, we see that the BAVs of Sun, Moon, Mars, Mercury, Jupiter, Venus and Saturn have 5, 3, 4, 7, 4, 8 and 3 rekhas in Ar (respectively). Adding them all, we get 34. So SAV has 34 rekhas in Ar and we write 34 in Ar. We can find the number of rekhas in all the rasis in the same manner and prepare a chart with the number of rekhas written in each rasi.

Exercise 20: Find the number of rekhas in all the rasis in SAV for the same rasi chart (see Chart 6).

A rasi with 30 or more rekhas becomes strong. Matters signified by the house falling in such a rasi flourish and planets transiting in such a rasi bring good results. A rasi with 25-30 rekhas is average. A rasi with less than 25 rekhas becomes weak. Matters signified by the house falling in such a rasi suffer and planets transiting in such a rasi bring bad results.

When choosing muhurtas[43] for auspicious activities like a wedding or housewarming, one should look at the strengths, as per SAV of the natal chart, of the rasis containing lagna, Moon and Sun in the muhurta chart. Rasis containing 30 or more rekhas in SAV are favorable.

12.5 Divisional Charts

There is a misconception that ashtakavarga is applicable only to rasi charts. Parasara does not say it. Parasara lists the divisional charts in which different areas of life are seen, at the very beginning of BPHS. So all the analysis in the rest of his classic applies to all the divisional charts, unless Parasara explicitly mentions rasi chart. For example, Parasara says that D-12 shows matters related to father. So any principles based on ashtakavarga and sodhya pindas that let us predict matters related to father must use D-12. This is a logical deduction and Parasara does not have to mention it explicitly each time.

If we can judge the benefic positions of various planets with respect to 8 references in rasi chart, there is no reason why we should not do it in all the divisional charts. In fact, this becomes invaluable when we interpret transits in rasi chart with respect to the natal positions in divisional charts and transits in divisional charts with respect to the natal positions in rasi chart.

Ashtakavarga of divisional charts is prepared in the same manner as that of rasi chart. The benefic houses for each planet with respect to the 8 references are the same. We can apply the same rules and find the BAVs of all planets. In fact, we can find SAV of a divisional chart too.

Example 39: Let us consider the rasi chart and D-10 of India's Prime Minister Sri A.B. Vajpayee (see Chart 3 for birthdata).

Readers may find SAV of rasi and D-10 and verify the following:

SAV of Rasi chart:

	Ar	Ta	Ge	Cn	Le	Vi	Li	Sc	Sg	Cp	Aq	Pi
Rekhas	29	22	27	29	28	38	29	26	23	34	28	24

SAV of D-10 chart:

	Ar	Ta	Ge	Cn	Le	Vi	Li	Sc	Sg	Cp	Aq	Pi
Rekhas	23	26	33	20	28	33	26	35	28	31	24	30

43. Muhurta is an auspicious pre-set time at which one begins important activities.

In rasi chart, the 11th house has the maximum number of rekhas (38) showing excellent gains. The 3rd house of communication has 34 rekhas. With the significator of communication Mercury and the artistic Moon in the 3rd house, he is an excellent communicator, great orator and poet. Though Sri Vajpayee's career wasn't a bed of roses – he struggled in the opposition parties for most of his career – he finally became India's Prime Minister and one must agree that he had a very successful career. He is known as a man of great character. With lagna and the 10th house in the SAV of rasi chart containing only 26 and 28 rekhas – which is just average – why did he have such a successful career?

The answer lies in the SAV of D-10. Lagna in D-10 is Sc and it contains 35 rekhas – maximum in D-10's SAV. Arudha lagna also contains more than 30 rekhas. These factors explain his success and good name. The 3rd house in D-10 also has more than 30 rekhas – like in the rasi chart – and that increases the chance of being an excellent communicator in public life. Though D-10 is powerful with lagna and arudha lagna containing more than 30 rekhas, one may notice that the 8th house in D-10 (Ge) has 33 rekhas in D-10's SAV. This explains the struggle in Vajpayee's career.

Chart 12

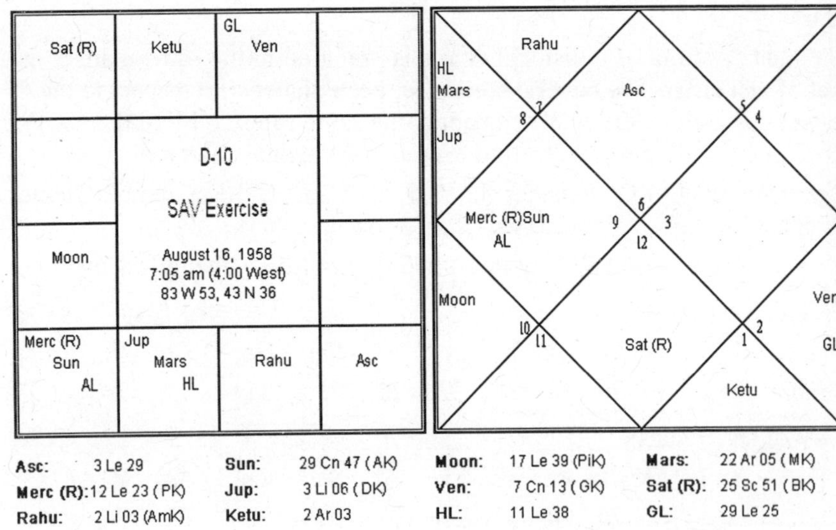

12.6 Prastaara Ashtakavarga

Using the Bhinna Ashtakavarga (BAV) of a planet, we can find out the rasis in which it is benefic with respect to more references and the rasis in which it is malefic with respect to more references. To interpret transits, this is sometimes not enough. For example, if we know that a planet is benefic in Ta with respect to 5 references, that may not be enough. We may need to know exactly what those 5 references are. If we are looking for Jupiter's transit that brings marriage, for example, we may want Jupiter to be benefic in his transit rasi with respect to certain planets (Venus or DK or 7th lord in navamsa, for example). In such situations, we need to know exactly which references a planet is benefic from.

For this purpose, we prepare "Prastaara Astakavarga". It will be denoted with PAV. Prastaara means "spread-out". PAV is a spreadsheet that shows the exact references from which a planet is benefic in a rasi. We prepare one PAV for each planet. Different people may represent PAV differently. Some people may cast a chart and write the list of benefic references in each rasi. For some people, the answer to Exercise 18 may qualify as Mercury's PAV. Some people may prefer to represent the same information as shown in Table 27.

Table 27: Mercury's PAV for Exercise 18

From	Ar	Ta	Ge	Cn	Le	Vi	Li	Sc	Sg	Cp	Aq	Pi
Sun	1	1	0	0	0	0	1	1	0	0	1	0
Moon	1	0	1	0	1	0	1	0	1	1	0	0
Mars	1	0	1	1	0	1	0	0	1	1	1	1
Merc	1	1	1	0	1	0	1	1	0	0	1	1
Jup	0	0	1	1	0	0	0	0	0	1	0	1
Ven	1	1	1	1	1	0	0	1	1	0	1	0
Sat	1	1	1	0	1	1	0	1	0	0	1	1
Lagna	1	0	1	1	0	1	1	0	1	0	1	0
Total (BAV)	7	4	7	4	4	3	4	4	4	3	6	4

The basic purpose of a planet's PAV is to show the references with respect to which the planet is benefic in each rasi.

NOTE: From PAV, we can construct BAV easily. From Table 27, we may note that the sum of all the entries in each column – rasi – in a PAV gives the number of rekhas in that rasi in BAV. This is shown in the last row.

12.7 Sodhya Pindas

We discussed the computation of BAV before. By applying some reductions on the values in BAV, we get "Sodhita Ashtakavarga" (SoAV). Using it, we find Sodhya Pindas of different planets. These pindas are very important in predicting key events and we will talk about them again in the part "Transit Analysis".

12.7.1 *Trikona Sodhana (Trinal Reduction)*

Consider the BAV of a planet. Look at different sets of mutual trines separately (*e.g.* First set: Ar, Le and Sg, Second set: Ta, Vi and Cp) and apply the following rules on each set:

(1) If atleast one rasi has zero, no reduction is necessary.[44]

(2) If the three rasis have the same value, make them all zero.

(3) Take the lowest value out of the three. Subtract it from all the values.

Example 40: As an example, let us take Mercury's BAV given in Chart 11. Let us takes fiery trines. Ar, Le and Sg have 7, 4 and 4 rekhas. Rules (1) and (2) don't apply and we go to (3). The lowest value is 4. Subtracting it from the three values, we write 3, 0 and 0 in Ar, Le and Sg respectively. Let us take the watery trines now. Cn, Sc and Pi have 4 rekhas each. Rule (2) applies and we write zero in all the three rasis. Readers may carry out the reduction for the remaining two sets of trines and verify that we get the following table after Trikona Sodhana:

	Ar	Ta	Ge	Cn	Le	Vi	Li	Sc	Sg	Cp	Aq	Pi
Mercury	3	1	3	0	0	0	0	0	0	0	2	0

12.7.2 *Ekaadhipatya Sodhana (Co-owned Reduction)*

After we carry out Trikona Sodhana, we carry out another reduction on the pairs of signs that are owned by the same planet. Ar and Sc are owned by Mars; Ta and Li are owned by Venus; Ge and Vi are owned by Mercury; Sg and Pi are owned by Jupiter; and, Cp and Aq are owned by Saturn. We

---

44 Some authors suggest that this applies only if there is zero in exactly one rasi. If two rasis have a zero, they suggest making the third one also zero. But this is inconsistent with the spirit of the other rules. The idea is to subtract the lowest value from others. In that sense, (1) and (2) are special cases cases of (3). The change suggested by these authors is inconsistent with this. Let us follow Parasara.

apply a reduction on these pairs of rasis separately, using the following rules:

(1) If atleast one of the rasis has a zero in it, no reduction is necessary and stop here.

(2) If both the rasis are occupied by a planet (or planets), again no reduction is necessary and stop here.

(3) If one rasi is occupied by a planet (or planets) and the other is empty, then do the following:

(a) If the empty rasi has a lower value, replace the value with a zero.

(b) If the empty rasi has a higher value, replace the value with the value in the other rasi.

(4) If both the rasis are empty, then do the following:

(a) If both the rasis have the same value, replace both with zero.

(b) If they have different values, replace the higher value with the lower value.

Example 41: Let us continue with Example 40. Let us take Ar and Sc. Sc has zero in it and (1) applies. So there is no reduction. In fact, (1) applies to all pairs and so all the values remain unchanged after Ekaadhipatya reduction.

Example 42: Let us consider some other hypothetical examples to understand all the rules correctly.

(a) Let us say Ta and Li have 4 and 2 rekhas after Trikona reduction. Let us say Ta is occupied by Mars and Li by Jupiter and Saturn. In this case, rule (2) applies and we do not alter the values.

(b) Let us say Ta and Li have 4 and 2 rekhas after Trikona reduction. Let us say Ta is occupied by Mars and Li is empty. In this case, rule (3*a*) applies and we write zero in Li, as Li is empty and it has a lower value than Ta.

(c) Let us say Ta and Li have 4 and 2 rekhas after Trikona reduction. Let us say Ta is empty and Li is occupied by Jupiter and Saturn. In this case, rule (3*b*) applies and we write 2 in Ta, as Ta is empty and it has a higher value than Li.

(d) Let us say Ta and Li have 4 and 2 rekhas after Trikona reduction. Let us say Ta and Li are empty. In this case, rule (4*b*) applies and we replace the higher value 4 with the lower value 2. So we write 2 in Ta.

(e) Let us say Ta and Li have 2 and 2 rekhas after Trikona reduction. Let us say Ta and Li are empty. In this case, rule (4*a*) applies and we write zero in Ta and Li.

12.7.3 *Sodhya Pindas*

After carrying out Trikona sodhana and then Ekaadhipatya sodhana on the BAV of a planet, we get the "Sodhita Ashtakavarga" of that planet. We denote Sodhita Ashtakavarga with SoAV.[45] From it, we find "Sodhya Pinda" of each planet. This will be used in transit analysis.

For each rasi, we multiply the number in that rasi in SoAV with the multiplier of that rasi (shown in Table 28). We find such a product for all the 12 rasis. We find the sum of the products of all the 12 rasis and the sum is called rasi pinda.

For each planet, we multiply the number in the rasi containing that planet with the multiplier of that planet (shown in Table 29). We find such a product for all the 7 planets. We find the sum of the products of all the 7 planets and the sum is called graha pinda.

Table 28: Multipliers in Rasimana

From	Ar	Ta	Ge	Cn	Le	Vi	Li	Sc	Sg	Cp	Aq	Pi
Multiplier	7	10	8	4	10	6	7	8	9	5	11	12

Table 29: Multipliers in Grahamana

Planet	Sun	Moon	Mars	Merc	Jup	Ven	Sat
Multiplier	5	5	8	5	10	7	5

By adding rasi pinda and graha pinda, we get "Sodhya Pinda" of the planet whose SoAV we are working with.

Example 43: Let us continue with Mercury's SoAV found in Example 40 and Example 41.

	Ar	Ta	Ge	Cn	Le	Vi	Li	Sc	Sg	Cp	Aq	Pi
SoAV:	3	1	3	0	0	0	0	0	0	0	2	0

45 This chart has several purposes which will not be covered in this book. An example is Vaastu or Sthaapatya Veda or the Vedic Science of Architecture. The direction signified by the rasis containing most rekhas in the SoAV of a planet should contain the room in which the activity related to the planet takes place. For example, we should look at the SoAV of Venus to decide where bedroom should be. We should look Jupiter's SoAV to decide where money and jewels should be kept. We should look at Moon's SoAV to decide the living room (hall). Mercury is important for the study room. Sun is important for the pooja room.

Rasi Pinda: Product for Ar is 3 x 7 = 21. Product for Ta is 1 x 10 = 10. Product for Ge is 3 x 8 = 24. Product for Aq is 2 x 11 = 22. Product for other rasis is zero, because they contain zero and we get zero by multiplying zero with any number. The sum of all the products is 21 + 10 + 24 + 22 = 77. So rasi pinda is 77.

Graha Pinda: Sun, Mars and Mercury are in Ge, which has 3 rekhas in SoAV. Product of Sun is 3 x 5 = 15. Product of Mars is 3 x 8 = 24. Product of Mercury is 3 x 5 = 15. Venus is in Ar, which has 3. Product of Venus is 3 x 7 = 21. Other planets are in rasis with zero in them. So the product is zero for them. The sum of all the products is 15 + 24 + 15 + 21 = 75. So graha pinda is 75.

We get sodhya pinda of Mercury by adding rasi pinda and graha pinda. We get 77 + 75 = 152. So Mercury's sodhya pinda in this chart is 152.

Exercise 22: Find BAV, SoAV and sodhya pinda of all planets in Chart 7.

12.8 Controversies

With some authors using the term bindu (dot) to denote a benefic house and the term rekha (line) to denote a malefic house – which is the opposite of what we learnt in this chapter – readers may be confused when reading other books. So they should keep in mind that there are different conventions in vogue. We are following Parasara's conventions in this book.

The above is merely a problem of different naming conventions. It is not a serious issue at all. It is just a matter of getting used to different nomenclature. But there is another issue, which is far more serious. There are a few inconsistencies between the lists of benefic houses of Moon and Venus as given by Maharshi Parasara and the great astrologer Varahamihira, who is relatively modern, as he belongs to 600 AD. These inconsistencies may have arisen due to corruption of texts in time[46].

To define a planet's ashtakavarga, Parasara first gives the count of references from which the planet is malefic in the 1st house and then he lists the references. He does the same thing for all houses. So we can crosscheck. As if this isn't enough, the Sage then lists the references from which the planet is benefic. He does it in all the houses again. Just as "checksum" values are transmitted in today's digital communication schemes to provide resilience to transmission errors, the Sage, who normally uses words sparingly, takes plenty of care to ensure that his teachings on ashtakavarga remain

46 In India, books seldom existed on paper and classics were transmitted from one generation to the other, mostly by word of mouth. People got the classics by heart and recited them to their children and students. Books were written in poetry, using nice meters, to facilitate memorization.

difficult to corrupt. To corrupt one house value in Parasara's account of ashtakavarga, one has to *consciously* re-write the verses in *three* different places in a *consistent* fashion. With the direct approach adopted by other authors, one can change the table just by changing one word. For example, changing "sukha" (comfort – 4th) to "suta" (son – 5th) changes one value without affecting the meter used in the verses. With Parasara's indirect approach, consistent changes in multiple places are required for a single value change. So Parasara's indirect approach is superior in corruption resistance. We will follow Parasara in this book.

Just for the information of the reader, the places of conflict will be mentioned below:

(1) Moon's ashtakavarga: As per Parasara, Moon is benefic in the 9th from Moon and malefic in the 9th from Mars. As per Varahamihira, Moon is malefic in the 9th from Moon and benefic in the 9th from Mars.

(2) Moon's ashtakavarga: As per Parasara, Moon is benefic in the 2nd from Jupiter and malefic in the 12th from Jupiter. As per Varahamihira, Moon is malefic in the 2nd from Jupiter and benefic in the 12th from Jupiter.

(3) Venus's ashtakavarga: As per Parasara, Venus is benefic in the 4th from Mars and malefic in the 5th from Mars. As per Varahamihira, Venus is malefic in the 4th from Mars and benefic in the 5th from Mars.

The definitions and calculations given in this chapter strictly follow Parasara for the reasons already mentioned. However, readers are welcome to experiment and draw their own conclusions. Until authentic and conclusive researches are conducted into the use of sodhya pindas in the timing of events, we cannot conclusively resolve the above controversy.

Apart from this, there is another needless controversy related to ashtakavarga. Some people prepare "bhava chakra" or "chalit chakra" using Sripathi's (or Porphyry's) house devision method and use that chart to cast ashtakavarga. If Saturn is at 3° in Vi and lagna is at 27° in Le, they are very close and these people argue that Saturn is in the 1st house from lagna and not in the 2nd house. These people make a bhava chakra accordingly and use it in ashtakavarga. However, if lagna is at 15° in Le, Saturn is at 3° in Vi and Jupiter is at 27° in Le, they may take Saturn to be in the 2nd house from Jupiter. They compute a bhava chakra with multi-sign houses only with respect to lagna and not with respect to all the references used in ashtakavarga. So their approach is *neither here nor there*.

The stand of this book is very clear – each bhava (house) with respect to one reference can only be in one rasi. Even if Saturn is at 1° in Vi and lagna is at 29° in Le, we still say that the 1st house is in Le, the 2nd house is in Li and Saturn is in the 2nd house (though he is only 2° away from lagna). We do not recognize the house division methods of Porphyry and others in this book. Each rasi is a house and the 1st house is the rasi containing the reference. Readers will do well to follow Maharshi Parasara and ignore the creations and borrowings of later day Indian astrologers.

12.9 Answers to Exercises

Exercise 18:

See Table 22 for Mercury's ashtakavarga. Looking at the columns of different planets, find the houses from the planets in which Mercury is benefic. Count those houses from the respective planets and find the rasis.

Sun: Ar, Ta, Li, Sc, Aq
Moon: Ar, Ge, Le, Li, Sg, Cp
Mars: Ar, Ge, Cn, Vi, Sg, Cp, Aq, Pi
Mercury: Ar, Ta, Ge, Le, Li, Sc, Aq, Pi
Jupiter: Ge, Cn, Cp, Pi
Venus: Ar, Ta, Ge, Cn, Le, Sc, Sg, Aq
Saturn: Ar, Ta, Ge, Le, Vi, Sc, Aq, Pi
Lagna: Ar, Ge, Cn, Vi, Li, Sg, Aq

Exercise 19:

	Ar	Ta	Ge	Cn	Le	Vi	Li	Sc	Sg	Cp	Aq	Pi
Sun	5	3	5	3	4	4	2	3	5	4	5	5
Moon	3	2	5	3	6	3	4	5	5	5	3	5*
Mars	4	3	4	3	4	3	2	5	1	3	3	4
Mercury	7	4	7	4	4	3	4	4	4	3	6	4
Jupiter	4	3	5	6	3	7	4	3	5	6	5	5
Venus	8	7	4	3	3	2	4	6	4	4	4	3
Saturn	3	3	4	3	2	3	2	3	4	5	3	4

Using the above values, one can prepare a chart for each planet's BAV, as shown in Chart 11.

Exercise 20:

	Ar	Ta	Ge	Cn	Le	Vi	Li	Sc	Sg	Cp	Aq	Pi
Sum	34	25	34	25	26	25	22	29	28	30	29	30

Using the above values, one can prepare a chart for SAV, as shown in Chart 11.

Exercise 21:

SAV of D-10 is as given below:

	Ar	Ta	Ge	Cn	Le	Vi	Li	Sc	Sg	Cp	Aq	Pi
Rekhas	24	25	31	28	27	39	33	29	26	22	28	25

Lagna is in Vi in Chart 12. Vi it has 39 rekhas. That's a lot more than 30! The 10th house (Ge) also has more than 30 rekhas. So this D-10 is very powerful and it possibly cannot belong to an unsuccessful waiter at a small restaurant. This has to be someone pretty successful.

Now let us guess her career.

Apart from the 1st and 10th houses, the 2nd house is strong in D-10's SAV, with 33 rekhas. This shows the importance of speech and voice in her career. Ghati lagna is in Taurus and its lord Venus occupies it. This makes ghati lagna and 9th house very powerful. This shows a fortunate (9th) and famous (GL) entertainer (Venus). Saturn's 11th house argala on GL suggests popular mass support as a catalyst in her success. Rahu's unobstructed 2nd house argala on lagna shows unconventional behavior in public life.[47]

Final Answer: The chart belongs to Madonna, a pop diva of USA.

Exercise 22:

Readers should carefully go through the examples given in this chapter and understand the calculations. This exercise covers most of the calculations defined in this chapter and it will be a good idea to attempt this exercise and verify the calculations.

Bhinna Ashatakavarga (BAV):

	Ar	Ta	Ge	Cn	Le	Vi	Li	Sc	Sg	Cp	Aq	Pi	
Sun	4	2	3	4	6	5	5	3	2	6	6	2	
Moon	6	3	5	3	5	5	6	3	3	4	4	2	
Mars	3	2	3	4	2	5	4	3	3	4	3	3	
Merc	4	6	4	3	4	7	4	5	6	3	5	3	
Jup	4	4	3	5	6	5	6	4	6	4	3	6	
Ven	3	5	5	4	6	2	3	6	5	2	7	4	
Sat	3	2	2	3	5	6	3	4	1	3	6	1	
Total	27	24	25	26	34	35	31	28	26	26	34	21	← SAV

47 Argalas on lagna show decisive influences on one's nature and argalas on GL show decisive influences on one's fame.

Sodhita Ashatakavarga (SoAV):

	Ar	Ta	Ge	Cn	Le	Vi	Li	Sc	Sg	Cp	Aq	Pi
Sun	2	0	0	2	4	3	2	1	0	4	3	0
Moon	3	0	1	1	2	1	2	1	0	1	0	0
Mars	1	0	0	1	0	3	1	0	1	2	0	0
Merc	0	3	0	0	0	4	0	2	2	0	1	0
Jup	0	0	0	1	2	1	3	0	2	0	0	0
Ven	0	3	2	0	3	0	0	2	2	0	4	0
Sat	2	0	0	2	4	4	1	3	0	1	4	0

	RasiPinda	GrahaPinda	SodhyaPinda
Sun	152	81	233
Moon	85	55	140
Mars	52	43	95
Merc	95	33	128
Jup	68	56	124
Ven	154	54	208
Sat	162	63	225

13. Interpreting Charts

13.1 Introduction

In the previous chapters, we have learnt various parameters and tools available in Vedic astrology. When it comes to putting them all together and interpreting charts, there is no substitute for experience. One should also refer to classics and "How to Judge a Horoscope" (Vols I & II) by Dr. B.V. Raman, to become familiar with the standard results attributed to different planets being in different houses and the lords of different houses being in various houses. In this chapter, we will cover some topics not covered yet and go through a couple of examples of interpreting charts. We will see many more examples in the rest of this book.

13.2 Functional Nature

We learnt that Jupiter, Venus, waxing Moon and well-associated Mercury are natural benefics. We learnt that Sun, Mars, Saturn, Rahu, Ketu, waning Moon and ill-associated Mercury are natural malefics. In addition, we have the concept of *functional benefics* and *functional malefics*.

The lords of trines from lagna are functional benefics. The lords of 3rd, 6th and 11th are functional malefics. The lord of a quadrant is a functional malefic if he is a natural benefic and functionally neutral if he is a natural malefic. The lords of 2nd, 8th and 12th are functionally neutral. Of these, the 8th house is more malefic than the other two.

Planet owning a quadrant and a trine becomes a yogakaraka (excellent planet).

In the case of planets owning two rasis, we need to judiciously combine the two indications. The list of yogakarakas, functional benefics, functional neutrals and functional malefics for each lagna is given in Table 30. Moon is not listed for movable rasis, because his functional nature depends on whether he is waxing or waning. Waxing Moon is a natural benefic and he becomes a functional malefic with quadrant ownership. Waning Moon, on the other hand, is a natural malefic and quadrant ownership makes him functionally neutral.

Table 30: Functional nature of planets

Lagna	Yoga karaka	Functional Benefics	Functional neutrals	Functional malefics
Ar	—	Sun, Mars, Jupiter	—	Mercury, Venus, Saturn
Ta	Saturn	Sun, Mercury, Saturn	Mars	Moon, Jupiter, Venus
Ge	—	Venus	Moon, Mercury, Saturn	Sun, Mars, Jupiter
Cn	Mars	Moon, Mars, Jupiter	Sun, Saturn	Mercury, Venus
Le	Mars	Sun, Mars, Jupiter	Moon	Mercury, Venus, Saturn
Vi	—	Mercury, Venus	Sun, Saturn	Moon, Mars, Jupiter
Li	Saturn	Mercury, Venus, Saturn	—	Sun, Mars, Jupiter
Sc	—	Moon, Jupiter	Sun, Mars	Mercury, Venus, Saturn
Sg	—	Sun, Mars	Moon, Mercury, Jupiter	Venus, Saturn
Cp	Venus	Venus, Mercury, Saturn	Sun	Mars, Jupiter
Aq	Venus	Venus, Saturn	Sun, Mercury	Moon, Mars, Jupiter
Pi	—	Moon, Mars	Jupiter	Sun, Mercury, Venus, Saturn

A functional benefic is a favorable planet in a chart. Placement of a functional benefic in quadrants (sustenance) and trines (prosperity) brings good results. Placement of a functional malefic in these houses is not good, unless it is very strong. A functional malefic placed in the 3rd house and dusthanas (6th, 8th and 12th houses) brings good results, by spoiling the significations of the bad houses.

If a planet aspects or conjoins or owns HL *and* lagna, it becomes a yogada (giver of yoga) in money matters. If a planet aspects or conjoins or owns GL *and* lagna, it becomes a yogada in the matters of power and authority. Irrespective of their functional nature, planets that become yogada bring goodluck. Similarly, planets involved in important yogas also bring good luck.

We should consider the inherent nature and the functional nature of planets. Whether a planet is a natural benefic or a natural malefic is analogous to whether a person is inherently good or bad. Whether a planet is a functional benefic or a functional malefic is analogous to whether a person does good or bad to one. Just as a nice person may harm one and a bad person may do good, natural benefics can become functional malefics and natural malefics can become functional benefics.

13.3 Baadhakas

For a house falling in a movable/fixed/dual rasi, the 11th/9th/7th house (respectively) from there becomes baadhaka sthaana (troubling spot). Its lord is called a "baadhaka" (troublemaker) for the original house. The list of baadhaka sthaanas and baadhakas corresponding to each rasi is given in Table 31.

For example, suppose lagna in someone's D-10 is in Ge. Then Jupiter is baadhaka for lagna. The periods of Jupiter and planets in Sg can create some obstructions and troubles in career. Let us take another house. Aq is the 9th house and the 9th house in D-10 shows the guidance one gets in one's career. It can show manager and elders giving guidance. Baadhaka sthana for Aq is Li. So the periods of Venus and occupants of Li can create some troubles related to the guidance one gets. There may be some troubles related to manager. Thus we can consider baadhaka from every house and arudha pada in every divisional chart.

13.4 Analyzing Charts

13.4.1 *Basic Guidelines*

When we analyze the charts, we should remember all the concepts we have learnt in the previous chapters. The following factors must be remembered:

(1) Divisional Chart: Use the correct divisional chart for the matter of

Table 31: Baadhakas

Rasi	Baadhaka sthaana	Baadhaka
Ar	Aq	Saturn & Rahu
Ta	Cp	Saturn
Ge	Sg	Jupiter
Cn	Ta	Venus
Le	Ar	Mars
Vi	Pi	Jupiter
Li	Le	Sun
Sc	Cn	Moon
Sg	Ge	Mercury
Cp	Sc	Mars & Ketu
Aq	Li	Venus
Pi	Vi	Mercury

interest. Suppose we are looking at happiness from a vehicle. D-16 is the best chart. Suppose we are trying to analyze a criminal's psychology. D-30 is the best chart. Suppose we are analyzing marriage. D-9 is the best chart. Suppose we are analyzing marriage in a culture where marriage is not a dharma (duty) and a union of souls, but it is merely living together of two people, then rasi chart may be better than D-9. Suppose we want to study one's religious activities. Then D-20 is the chart. If we want to study one's learning, D-24 is the chart. Suppose we want to study one's career and achievements in society, D-10 chart is the correct chart. In this manner, we should choose the correct divisional chart.

(2) House: We should choose the correct house after choosing the correct divisional chart. Let us say that we are analyzing someone's learning related activities and decided to look at D-24. If we want to see his education, we see the 4th house. If we want to see his intelligence, scholarship, academic reputation, academic distinctions/awards, students *etc*, we should look at the 5th house. If we want to see how one, in one's pursuit of knowledge, interacts with others and what kind of people one interacts with, then we should see the 7th house. Like that, we choose the correct house for the matter of interest.

(1) **Reference:** We should choose the correct reference for counting houses. In the above example of D-24, academic reputation is related more to the perceived self (AL) than the true self (lagna). So it is seen from the 5th from arudha lagna (AL). Intelligence and scholarship, on the other hand, are related to the true self and they are seen from the 5th from lagna. When the relevant karakas are stronger, we can use them as references instead of lagna. So scholarship can be seen from the 5th from Mercury. Students can be seen from the 5th lord. Intelligence can be seen from the 5th from Jupiter. Academic reputation can be seen in D-24 from the 5th from Sun.

(2) **House *vs* Arudha:** Sometimes, an arudha pada is more appropriate to see a matter than a house. For example, we can see darapada (A7) in D-24 to figure out what kind of people one typically interacts with in one's learning related activities. We can see one's academic distinctions/ awards in A5, because they are maya (illusion) related to intelligence and scholarship. The world forms an impression about one's intelligence and scholarship based on one's scores, ranks, grades, distinctions and awards.

(3) **Influences:** After we choose a house/arudha in a divisional chart to represent the matter of interest, the next step is to analyze the influences on it. Planets influence it with rasi drishti and graha drishti. We should also check for argala. We should judge the meaning of each influence. We can also judge the influences on a house by finding houses *with respect to* that house. Planets in the quadrants from a house sustain it. Planets in trines from a house let it prosper. Planets in upachayas let it grow. Planets in dusthanas bring obstacles. Suppose we are analyzing A3 in an author's D-10. While the 3rd house shows one's writing skills, it is A3 that shows one's books. If a planet is in a quadrant from A3, its periods may result in book writing. If a planet is in the 8th house from A3, its periods may bring obstacles in book writing. If a planet is a baadhaka from A3, it can create troubles in book-writing.

(4) **Standard Results:** There are many standard results given in literature for various planets and house lords in various houses. These results should be mastered.

Attention should be paid to the strength and avasthas of various planets and ashtakavarga strength of various houses. The presence of yogas should also be noted.

13.4.2 *Family Members*

We can analyze the fortunes of family members from one's chart. For parents, grandparents, uncles and aunts, we should see D-12. For children, children-in-law and grandchildren, we should see D-7. For brothers, sisters, brothers-in-law and sisters-in-law, we should see D-3. For spouse and his/her family members, we should see D-9.

In each of these charts, we should look at the house that shows the person of interest and consider the rasi containing the lord of that house as lagna. We can consider the corresponding arudha pada also. For example, the 9th lord or the arudha pada of 9th house in D-12 shows father. The 4th lord or the arudha pada of 4th house in D-12 shows mother.

In D-3, we see siblings. The 3rd house shows younger sibling and the 11th house shows elder sibling. Being the 3rd from the 3rd house, the 5th house shows younger brother's younger brother, *i.e.* second younger brother. Being the 11th from the 11th house, the 9th house shows elder brother's elder brother, *i.e.* second elder brother. We take the 3rd lord, 5th lord, 7th lord *etc* as lagnas of first (immediate) **younger** sibling, second younger sibling, third younger sibling etc. We take the 11th lord, 9th lord, 7th lord etc as lagnas of first (immediate) **elder** sibling, second elder sibling, third elder sibling etc.

Similarly, the 5th house house shows children in D-7. The 7th house is the 3rd from 5th and shows one's child's younger sibling. So the 5th lord shows the first child, the 7th lord shows the second child, the 9th house shows the third child and so on.

When we count houses corresponding to siblings and children in D-3 and D-7, we count in the forward or backward direction based on whether lagna is odd or even (respectively). If lagna in D-7 is in Ge, Venus (lord of Li) shows first child, Jupiter (lord of Sg) shows the second child and so on. On the other hand, if lagna in D-7 is in Cn, Jupiter (lord of Pi) shows the first child, Saturn (lord of Cp) shows the second child and so on.

NOTE: After covering all the odd or even signs, we move from odd to even signs or even to odd signs, instead of coming back to where we started.

13.5 Examples

After going through a couple of examples, readers may be able to appreciate the process of interpreting charts.

Example 44: Let us consider the rasi chart given in Chart 13 and start making some observations.

Lagna in Leo can show someone royal and authoritative. Lagna lord Sun is in the 10th house with 5th lord Jupiter. This forms a raaja yoga. With

Jupiter in Uttamaamsa, this yoga is powerful. Moreover, this yoga takes place in the 7th from AL. That makes it more powerful.

However, we note that debilitated Moon occupies AL in a Martian sign and Saturn aspects him. Debilitated Moon in AL shows that the mind is turned away from the material world. Saturn is the significator of hard-work, service and austerity and he also signifies renunciation. His aspect on Moon can give renunciation. Moreover, Saturn is with Ketu here. Overall, there are parivraaja yogas[48] here. So this native is likely to have renounced the world.

Chart 13

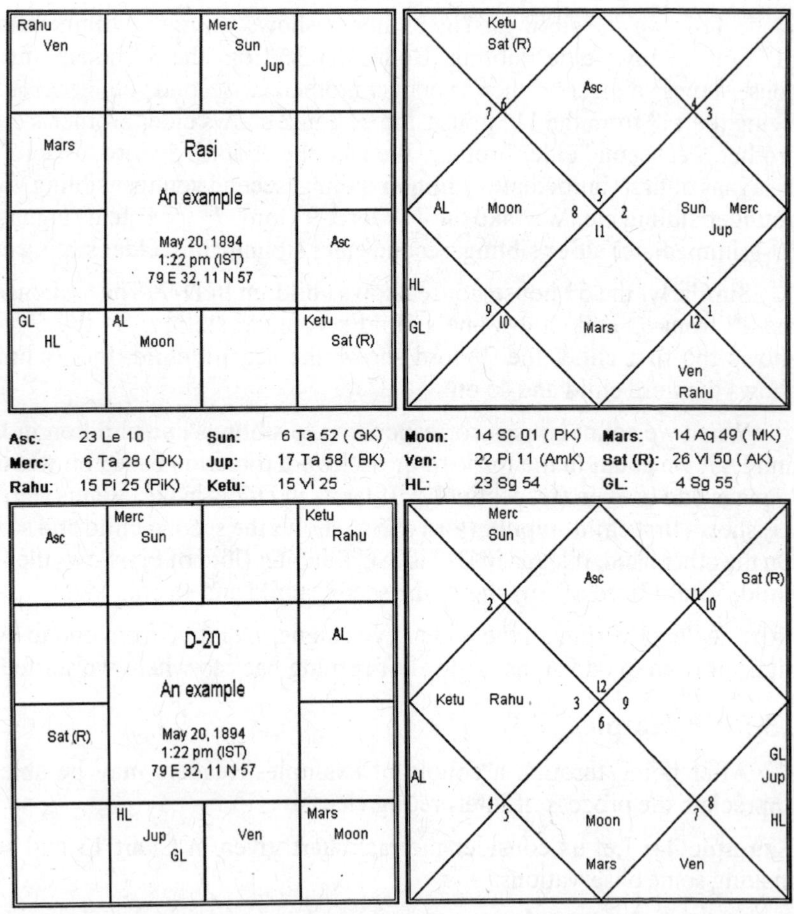

48 Parivraaja yogas are combinations that give renunciation of the material world.

Saturn is the planet of hard-work. Ketu is the planet of selflessness, evolution and rising above the shackles of the material world. Venus is the planet of passion. If two of these planets are together and the third planet aspects them, it gives Tapaswi[49] yoga. If AK (chara atma karaka – soul) also aspects or conjoins the planets involved in Tapaswi yoga, this tapas will be more fruitful and will be a continuation of the efforts of the past lives (AK is one's link with the past lives).

Here Saturn and Ketu are together in Virgo and exalted Venus aspects them from Pisces. This gives Tapaswi yoga. Tapaswi yoga is particularly powerful when formed with a planet in the 8th house (hard-work, research, discovery and occult knowledge). Here Venus is in the 8th house. AK is also involved in Tapaswi yoga.

So this native is likely to be a renunciate who did tapas in something and dedicated his life to it. His soul is likely to have found its purpose in his tapas. However, at the same time, there is a powerful rajayoga involving lagna lord and GL lord in the 7th from AL. That yoga cannot go waste. So this native must've enjoyed some power and influence in the society.

Let us consider his D-20 now (see Chart 13). D-20 shows religious and spiritual activities. Lagna is in Pisces and lord Jupiter is in the 9th house. This shows religiousness and also being guided by a brilliant guru/parampara. GL in D-20 is in Sc and Jupiter occupies it. It shows a powerful position in religion.

If the 5th and 9th lords conjoin and aspect lagna, we learnt that it forms a rajayoga. Here 5th lord Moon and 9th lord Mars join in Vi and aspect lagna in Pi. This shows a powerful rajayoga giving a powerful and prosperous position related to religious matters. Venus, the planet of passion, is in the 8th house in own rasi. That shows sincere efforts and hard-work in religious matters. The 2nd house has Sun and Mercury in it. The 2nd house shows speech among other things. Mercury is the planet of speech and he has 6 rekhas in his D-20 BAV. Sun is a charismatic planet and he has 5 rekhas in D-20 BAV. They together give Budha-Aaditya yoga in the house of speech. The native is likely to be an excellent orator of religious matters.

This chart belongs to Swami Chandrasekhara Saraswathi, who was the chief pontiff of Kanchi Kama Koti Peetham. He was a great scholar and a keen student of many subjects. He was a true tapaswi and made a Herculean

49 Tapaswi is a person who performs *tapas*. He forgets everything and pursues something single-mindedly. Tapaswis usually dedicate themselves to research and uncover the secrets of the world. A tapaswi can be into yoga, mantra, tantra, astrology or even physics or chemistry.

contribution in restoring the place of Vedic knowledge in Indian society. He was a brilliant orator. He commanded the respect of presidents, prime ministers, chief ministers and millions of Indians.

Chart 14

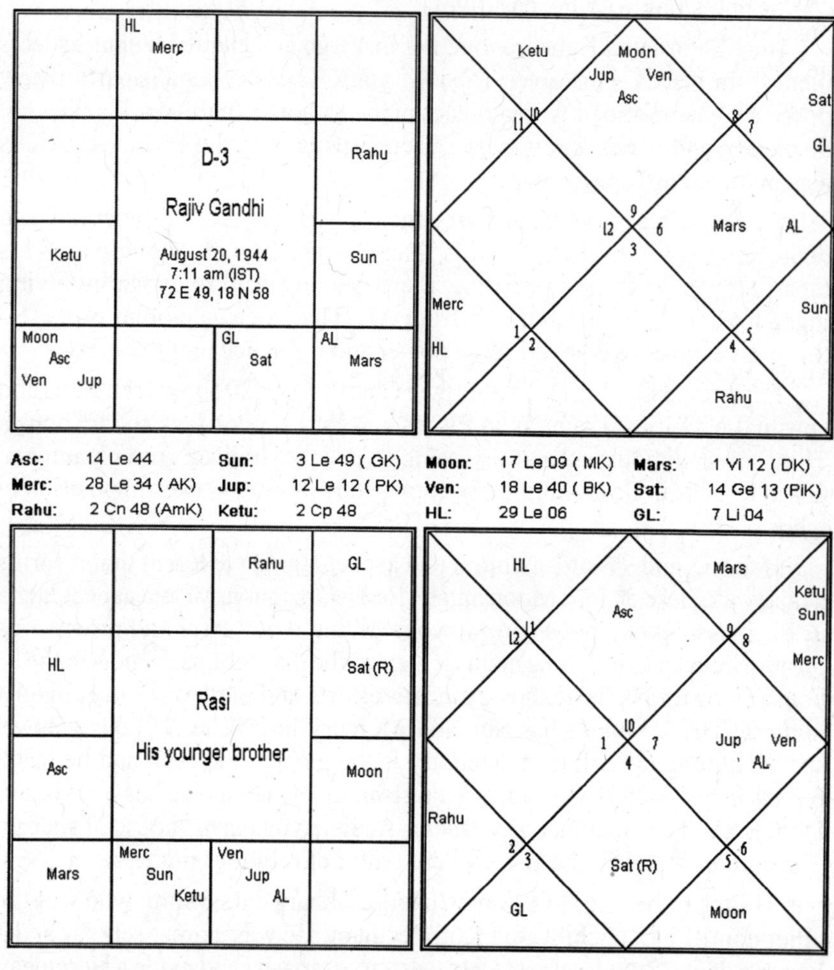

Example 45: Let us consider the D-3 chart of Late Rajiv Gandhi (see Chart 14).

Based on his D-3, let us try to say something about his younger Sanjay Gandhi. Lagna in D-3 is in Sg, an odd sign. So we count houses normally.

The 3rd house is Aq. Saturn is its lord and we should take Li as lagna in Rajiv Gandhi's D-3 to analyze Sanjay Gandhi's fortune.

Lagna has exalted Saturn in it. This shows Sasa yoga. This shows someone with many loyal followers. The 10th house has 5th lord Rahu. If the 5th lord is in 10th, it can show power. Because it is Rahu, it can show forceful nature in career. However, the 10th lord Moon is in a fiery sign in the 3rd house with Jupiter and Venus, two rank benefics. The 3rd house shows one's parakrama (boldness and initiative). This shows a very positive and pro-active attitude. It shows a doer.

It may be interesting to note the similarities between Rajiv Gandhi's D-3 and Sanjay Gandhi's rasi chart (shown in Chart 14). In both, Saturn is on the lagna axis. In the former, Saturn is in lagna and Saturn owns lagna in the latter. In the former, Moon owns 10th and joins Jupiter and Venus. In the latter, Jupiter and Venus are in 10th, aspected by Moon. In the former, 5th lord Rahu is in 10th. In the latter, Rahu is in 5th and aspects 10th. In the former, Sun is in own sign in 11th, aspected by Mercury, Saturn and Ketu. In the latter, Sun, Mercury and Ketu are in 11th and Saturn aspects them. In both, Mars is in the 12th house.

Usually, we have such links between the charts of related people.

Example 46: Let us consider the D-24 charts (see Chart 15) and D-27 charts (see Chart 16) of twins Satyam Gaur and Shivam Gaur, who were born just 2 minutes apart. They have the same rasi chart, but Satyam Gaur was a brilliant student and Shivam Gaur was a mediocre student. Satyam studied commerce and accountancy and scored well. Shivam was a mediocre student except in mathematics. Satyam is jovial, amicable and optimistic. Shivam is a skeptic. He does not believe in astrology and always seeks rational explanations. Let us try to explain these facts.

Chart 15

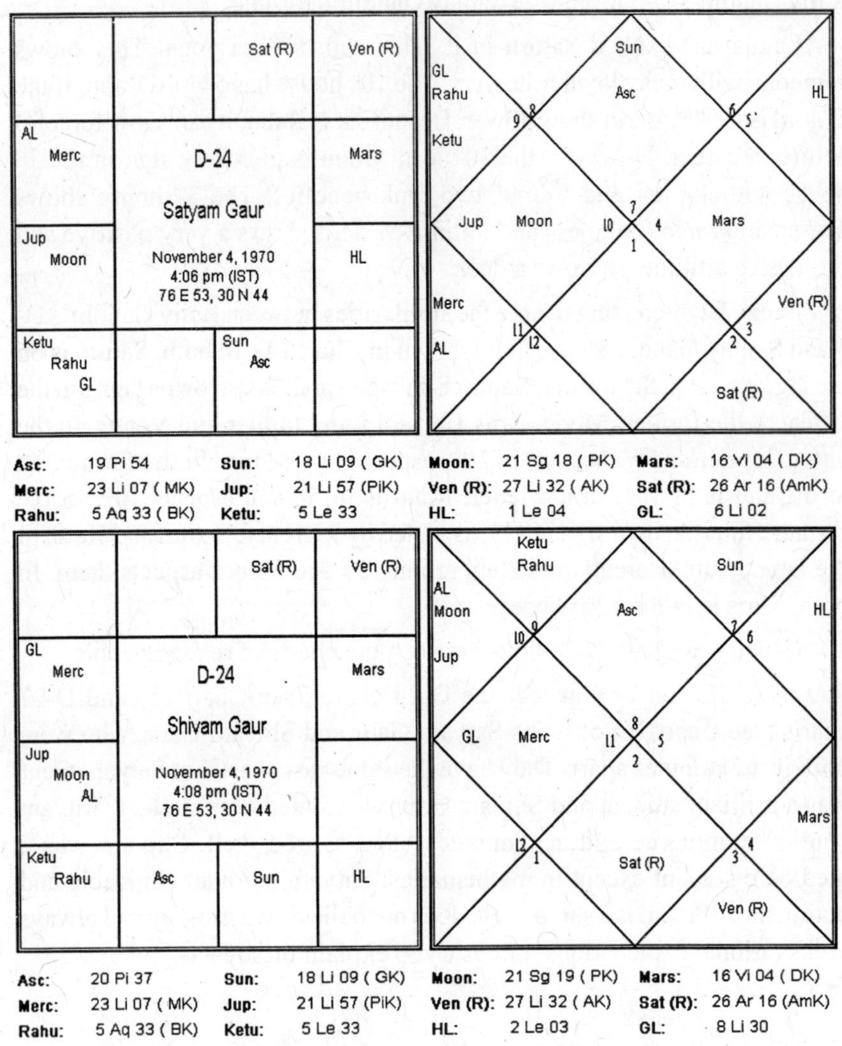

D-24 is the chart that shows education. In Satyam's case, lagna is in Li and lagna lord Venus is well-placed in a trine in a friendly house. Moreover, the sign occupied by lagna lord is Ge, an intellectual sign. Mercury is in the 5th house and that gives good memory and intelligence. It also gives skills in commerce and accounting.

Chart 16

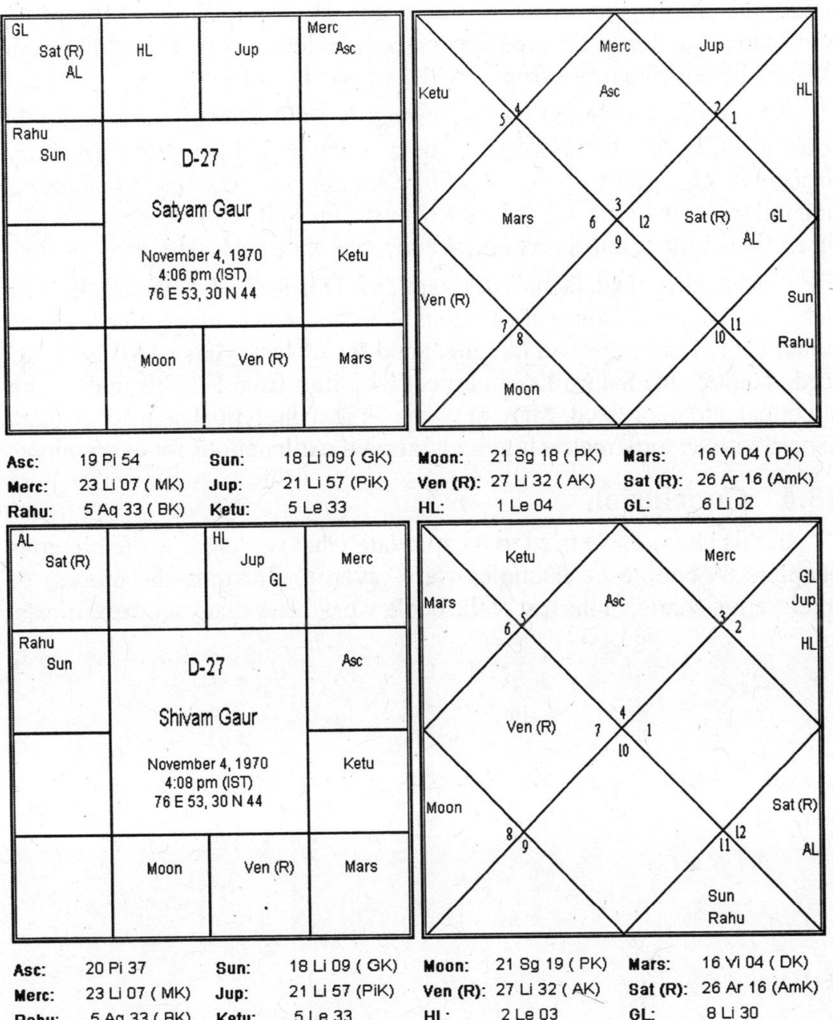

Moreover, AL has Mercury and it shows a person who is perceived as an intellectual person as far as learning goes. Mars in 6th, Venus in 5th and nodes in 11th are well-placed from AL.

In Shivam's D-24, lagna moved to Sc and lagna lord is debilitated. The strength of lagna and lagna lord is very important in any chart. Moreover,

5th lord Jupiter is also debilitated. Still, exalted Ketu's aspect on Pi, the 5th house, gave him some skills in mathematics. But the debilitation of lagna lord and 5th lord makes him a mediocre student. From AL also, Mars in 7th, Venus in 6th, nodes in 12th are badly placed. Malefics in 3rd, 6th and 11th from AL and benefics in trines from it will give good results.

To see one's inherent nature, strengths and weaknesses, we should look at D-27. In Satyam's D-27, lagna is in Ge and lagna lord Mercury aspects it. This gives Bhadra yoga like results. The 5th house of emotions and judgment is Libra and its lord Venus occupies it. This strength of lagna and 5th house made him a very jovial, amicable, cheerful and balanced person.

On the other hand, lagna in Shivam's D-27 is in Cn. Lagna lord Moon is debilitated in the 5th house of emotions. This gives an unhappy spirit. The 5th house shows emotions and judgment and the 5th lord Mars is in Vi. The 8th lord (skepticism) Saturn has an aspect with him from Pi. This makes him skeptical and depressed. Mars in taamasik and analytical sign Vi, with an aspect with 8th lord, makes him seek rational explanations for everything.

13.6 Conclusion

In this chapter, we tried to recapitulate what we learnt in the previous chapters. A couple of examples were given to illustrate the process of interpreting charts. In the rest of the book, we will see many more examples.

14. Topics Related to Longevity

14.1 Introduction

Many human beings are curious about how long they will live. An ethical astrologer will not scare a client by predicting death, but he may caution a client gently before critical periods and suggest some remedial measures to ward off an impending danger. An estimation of longevity is also helpful in matchmaking. After all, if one person will live for 81 years and the other only for 36 years, it is not advisable to approve a match between those two people. In matchmaking, it is desirable that the bridegroom and the bride have comparable longevity.

In this chapter, we will study some basic tools that are used in longevity determination techniques. There are formulas for determining longevity, based on ashtakavarga. But they do not always work and they will not be covered in this book. We will cover the estimation of longevity based on natal chart and dasas. Though there are many dasas that help us in timing death, we will cover only Shoola dasa in this book.

14.2 Marakas (Killers)

Each chart has some rasis and planets that are called marakas (killers). Since death is an event relating to the physical existence, rasi chart is of utmost importance in seeing death. Rudramsa (D-11) shows the forces of death and destruction and it can also give insight into death. D-30 shows one's evils and punishment for the evils. Death can be a punishment for one's evils and so we should look at D-30 also. However, the most important chart is the rasi chart.

The 3rd and 8th houses are the houses of life. The 3rd house shows the vitality of one's existence and the 8th house shows the longevity. The 12th house from any house shows losses related to the matters signified by that house. So the 12th house from these two houses shows death. **So the 2nd and 7th houses are the houses of death.** For good longevity, the 3rd and 8th houses and their lords should be strong and the 2nd and 7th houses and their lords should be weak.

The rasis containing the 2nd and 7th houses are called **maraka sthanas** (killer stations). When we use rasi-ruled dasas that can show death, dasas of these rasis can bring death. Lords of the 2nd and 7th houses are called **maraka grahas** (killer planets). When we use planet-ruled dasas that can show death, dasas of these planets can bring death.

There are other maraka grahas too. If a malefic planet powerfully conjoins or aspects, using graha drishti, the 2nd and 7th houses or their lords, then it qualifies as a maraka graha. Let us look at an example. Suppose lagna is in Le, Saturn is in Sg and Mars is in Ge. Then Saturn is a maraka on account of owning the 7th house (Aq). Mars is a malefic and he is in Ge. He aspects the 2nd house (Vi, with the 4th house aspect) and the 7th lord (Saturn in Sg – with the 7th house aspect). Because of these two factors, Mars is a maraka. Let us take another example. Suppose lagna is in Pi, Mars is in Ge, Mercury is in Cp and Saturn is in Ar. On account of owning the 2nd and 7th houses, Mars and Mercury are marakas. Look at Saturn. He is in the 2nd house and aspects the 2nd lord Mars (with the 3rd house aspect) and the 7th lord Mercury (with the 10th house aspect). So Saturn is also a maraka and he may in fact be a stronger maraka than Mars and Mercury.

When we time one's death using a dasa, we should look for the involvement of maraka sthanas and maraka grahas. We can also use marakas when timing death using the transits of planets.

14.3 Rudra, Trishoola and Maheswara

In Indian mythology, there are eleven Rudras. They are all different forms of Lord Shiva. They bring suffering and death to a native. Trishoola or trident is the weapon of Lord Shiva. Maheswara is the Supreme form of Lord Shiva and he gives emancipation to the soul.

For every person, there are eleven rasis that represent the eleven Rudras. These rasis bring suffering related to various areas of life.

Out of all the eleven Rudras, the one who brings suffering to the physical self is the most important one. In each chart, there is one planet that plays this role. That planet is simply called "Rudra". That planet stands for the suffering and destruction of the native. There are three rasis designated as Trishoola rasis and they bring death. Let us see the astrological defintions.

Table 32: Eighth House for Rudra Calculation

Rasi	Ar	Ta	Ge	Cn	Le	Vi	Li	Sc	Sg	Cp	Aq	Pi
The 8th house	Sc	Ge	Cp	Sg	Cn	Aq	Ta	Sg	Cn	Ge	Cp	Le

Rudra

Consider the lord of the 8th house from (*i*) lagna and (*ii*) the 7th house. Find the 8th house using Table 32 and not in the normal way[50]. The stronger of the two planets becomes Rudra. If the weaker planet is afflicted, it can also become Rudra. We say that a planet is stronger if it conjoins more planets. If both planets conjoin the same number of planets, a planet in exaltation or own rasi is stronger. A planet joining exalted planets is stronger. A planet aspected by many planets (rasi aspect) is stronger. Finally, a planet which is more advanced in its rasi is stronger. We find the stronger planet in this manner and it becomes Rudra. However, if the weaker planet is debilitated or in an inimical sign and conjoined/aspected by malefics like Mars, Saturn, Rahu and Ketu, then it becomes Rudra.

Trishoola Rasis

The three trines from the rasi occupied by Rudra in rasi chart represent the three spikes of Shiva's Trishoola/trident. They are called Trishoola rasis. Depending on whether a native has short life or middle life or long life, one of the three Trishoola rasis kills the native during its Shoola dasa.

Maheswara

The lord of the 8th house from AK (chara atma karaka) is called Maheswara. AK stands for the soul and the 8th lord from him stands for the liberation of soul. He represents the channels through which one's soul strives for liberation.

There are a couple of exceptions:

(1) If the 8th lord from AK is in own rasi or exaltation rasi, then take the stronger of the 8th and 12th lords from him. Suppose AK is Mars and he is in Ge. Then the 8th house from AK is Cp and Saturn is Maheswara. Now let us say that Saturn is exalted in Li. From Saturn (Li), Venus owns the 8th house (Ta) and Mercury owns the 12th house (Vi). The stronger of Mercury and Venus becomes Maheswara.

(2) If Rahu or Ketu joins AK or the 8th from him, then we find the 6th lord from AK instead of the 8th lord. Please note that this is equivalent to taking the 8th lord in the anti-zodiacal order. Suppose AK is Mars and he is in Taurus. Then Sg is the 8th house from Mars and Jupiter, lord of Sg, becomes Maheswara. Now, suppose Ketu is in Ta or Sg. Because

50 For odd rasis, we count houses zodiacally. For even rasis, we count houses anti-zodiacally. For Brahma and Vishnu rasis, we use the regular motion. For Shiva rasis, we use Shiva's motion. That is how Table 32 is constructed. Shiva's rasis and Shiva's motion will be discussed in "Narayana Dasa".

of Ketu's presence, we find the 6th house from Mars instead of the 8th house. It is Li. Venus owns it and he becomes Maheswara.

(3) If Rahu becomes Maheswara, we take Mercury instead. If Ketu becomes Maheswara, we take Jupiter instead.

14.4 The Method of Three Pairs

This method allows us to determine the approximate range of one's longevity. In this method, we look at 3 pairs of planets/mathematical points. In each pair, we look at the two planets and see if they occupy a movable or fixed or dual rasi. Using Table 33, we look at the longevity category corresponding to the combination.

(1) Lagna lord and 8th lord (find the 8th house and its lord using Table 32)
(2) Moon and Saturn
(3) Lagna and Horalagna (HL)

Table 33: Longevity Category for Each Pair

Combination 1	Combination 2	Result
Fixed + Dual	Movable + Movable	Long life
Movable + Fixed	Dual + Dual	Middle life
Movable + Dual	Fixed + Fixed	Short life

Long life means 72-108 years. Middle life means 36-72 years. Short life means 0-36 years. We learnt how to find the longevity category corresponding to each pair. Now, we should learn how the results of the three pairs can be combined for one final result.

If all the three pairs result in the same longevity category, that will be the combined classification. If two pairs give one result and the third pair gives a different result, then the result given by two pairs dominates. Parasara gave further hints regarding this case and suggested finding the maximum longevity (paramaayush) of a person using Table 34.

Table 34: Paramaayush Reckoner

Two Pairs / Third Pair	Short life	Middle life	Long life
Short life	32 years	64 years	96 years
Middle life	36 years	72 years	108 years
Long life	40 years	80 years	120 years

If all the three pairs give three different results (*i.e.* one giving short life, one giving middle life and one giving long life), then we should give preference to the third pair of lagna and horalagna. However, if Moon is in lagna or the 7th house, then the second pair of Moon and Saturn should be given preference.

Example 47: Let us say that lagna is in Ta, HL is in Ar, Moon is in Ta, Mercury is in Cn, Venus is in Cp, and Saturn is in Ge.

Pair 1: Lagna lord Venus is in Cp, a movable rasi. The 8th house is in Ge (see Table 32) and Mercury owns it. He is in Cn, another movable rasi. Looking for the combination "Movable + Movable" in the table, we see that "long life" is the result.

Pair 2: Moon is in Ta, a fixed rasi. Saturn is in Ge, a dual rasi. Looking for the combination "Fixed + Dual" in the table, we see that "long life" is the result.

Pair 3: Lagna in Ta, a fixed rasi. Horalagna is in Ar, a movable rasi. Looking for the combination "Movable + Fixed" in the table, we see that "middle life" is the result.

We see that two pairs indicate long life and one pair indicates middle life. So "long life" dominates and the native has long life. Using Table 34, we see that the paramaayush for this case is 108 years.

14.5 The Eighth Lord Method

Parasara and Jaimini prescribed another method for estimating the longevity category. Find the stronger of lagna and 7th house and take it as the reference. Find the 8th lord from it and see where he is placed from it. If he is in a quadrant, long life is indicated. If he is in a panaphara, middle life is indicated. If he is in an apoklima, short life is indicated.

Example 48: Let us say that lagna is in Ar and Li is stronger than Ar. Then we take Li as the reference. The 8th lord is Venus. If Venus is in Li, Cp, Ar or Cn (*i.e.* a quadrant from Li), it shows long life. If Venus is in Sc, Aq, Ta or Le (*i.e.* a panaphara from Li), it shows middle life. If Venus is in Sg, Pi, Ge or Vi (*i.e.* an apoklima from Li), it shows short life.

Exercise 23: Consider the rasi chart shown in Chart 8. Identify the maraka planets in this chart. Find Rudra, Trishoolas and Maheswara. Finally estimate the longevity category of the native using the method of three pairs and the eighth lord method.

14.6 Conclusion

The definitions and methods given in this chapter will be useful in timing death using dasas. The two methods of outlined here for determining the longevity category are not infallible. There are some exceptions not covered in this book. So one should not be biased by these calculations.

It is worthwhile to emphasize once more that this knowledge should not be misused for fame or for scaring clients. One should only gently caution clients and prescribe remedial measures. Sages have warned that one misusing the knowledge of astrology will live in misery and distress.

14.7 Answer to Exercise

Exercise 23:

Marakas: Jupiter and Venus own the 2nd and 7th houses. Rahu is in the 7th house. These three planets are the main marakas. Mercury owns 8th and joins Jupiter and Venus. So he may also be considered a maraka.

Rudra & Trishoola: The 8th house from lagna is Sg (see Table 32) and its lord is Jupiter. The 8th house from Ta (the 7th house) is Ge and its lord is Mercury. Mercury is stronger, as he is more advanced in his rasi. He is Rudra. Rudra is in Libra. So Trishoola (Destroyer Shiva's trident) has spikes in Ge, Li and Aq.

Maheswara: Mercury is AK. The 8th from him is Ta. The 8th from him has Rahu. So we take the 6th from Li and get Pi. Its lord Jupiter is Maheswara.

Method of Three pairs: Lagna lord and 8th lord show middle life (fixed+movable). Moon and Saturn show middle life (fixed+movable). Lagna and horalagna show short life (fixed+fixed). So the longevity category is "middle life" (36-72 years). The native died at the age of 50 years.

The Eighth Lord Method: Lagna is stronger than the 7th house. So let us take Sc as the reference. The 8th lord from it is Mercury. He is in an apoklima from Sc (12th). So the result is "short life". This method did not work here.

15. Strength of Planets and Rasis

15.1 Introduction

When judging the results given by houses and planets, we have to judge their strength. Sometimes we have to compare the strength of two planets and see which one will dominate. For example, when finding the arudha pada of a house falling in Scorpio, we learnt that we have to take the stronger of Mars and Ketu as the lord of Scorpio. In several rasi dasas, dasas start from the stronger of lagna and the 7th house. We need to be able to compare them and judge which is stronger. A house may be influenced by several planets and they may suggest contradictory results. In such a case, we need to decide which influence dominates.

There are different ways of measuring the strengths of planets and rasis for different purposes. We will learn some of them in this section.

15.2 Why Different Strengths

Why do we need different strengths for different purposes? Why can't we use the same strength? To understand this, let us consider an analogy.

Suppose X is an engineer. Suppose Y is another engineer with exactly the same background and suppose Y comes to the house of X for a few days. Suppose Y sleeps in the afternoon and X doesn't. Suppose it is 1 pm and Y is ready for his afternoon nap. Suppose the two engineers have promised a charity in town that they would give a big donation together and suppose someone from the charity comes to X's house. Because it is not his house and because he is sleepy, Y is probably not going to play a prominent role and X is probably going to talk pleasantries and then give a cheque on behalf of Y and himself. The money is both his and Y's, but X is in a better position to handle it. Shadbalas are similar to this. When two or more planets take part in a yoga, the one that is stronger as per shadbala ends up giving the results.

Both X and Y may have to deal with contractors, workers and vendors for their professional work. If Y has better relations with the people he deals with, he will be more productive at his work as an engineer. Similarly, strength as per ashtakavarga shows the ability of planets to deliver their goods in harmony with other planetary forces at work in a chart. Even if a planet has good shadbala, it will be unable to deliver its goods if it is at odds with other planets in the chart, *i.e.* has a low ashtakavarga strength.

An engineer who has good relations with workers, vendors and contractors related to one project may not go along well with people involved in another project. In that case, he will produce excellent results in the former project and he may not be effective in the latter. Similarly, a planet may have good ashtakavarga strength in one divisional chart and poor ashtakavarga strength in another divisional chart. Then it will give its results more effectively in the area of life related to the first chart.

Despite good capabilities and potential to get work done, Y may be unable to get his work done if he is depressed about something or if he is absent-minded for some reason. If he is in a cheerful state, he may get his work done well. Thus the state one is in decides one's final output. Similarly, a planet must be in a good "avastha" (state) to give good results. There are different kinds of states – states related to age, states related to alertness, states related to mood and states related to activity.

When one hires an engineer as an employee or when one assigns a project to an engineer, one is concerned about how effective he will be in the project. But suppose one is considering the same engineer as a partner in business. Then his effectiveness in a particular project does not matter much. What matters now is how well rounded he is. He should have good overall knowledge of various projects. Vimsopaka bala is analogous to this. When we consider the *overall effectiveness* of a planet in one's life, we no longer look at its effectiveness to give results in a specific area of life. Instead, we look at Vimsopaka bala. It shows the overall strength of a planet and its ability to play an important role in one's life (rather than a specific area of life).

If X and Y have to decide who eats a cake first or who gets to drink the only can of soft drink left in the refrigerator, they are probably not going to argue about it. Their qualifications or productivity at work or mental state or overall ability are not going to matter. For something so trivial, they will probably toss a coin or have a friendly arm-wrestling or simply do what their friends present in the room suggest. If Y has more friends in the room and they say "let Y have it", then Y is going to have it. Similarly, for trivial things like determining who initiates dasas, antardasas *etc*, we have very simple rules that are different from shadbala, ashtakavarga bala, avastha bala, Vimsopaka bala *etc*.

As it has been emphasized many times in this book, Vedic astrology has a rich variety of parameters, tools and techniques. Attempting to use various techniques in an interchangable manner only leads to confusion. One should strive to understand the meanings of various parameters and tools and use the right set of parameters and tools for the occasion. Though we have different ways of measuring a planet's strength, their meanings are different and accordingly they are used for different purposes. We will learn the most common ones in this chapter.

15.3 Shadbala and Astakavarga Bala

There are six sources of strength – strength due to placement, strength due to time, strength due to directions, strength due to aspects, strength due to motion and strength due to inherent nature. **Shadbala** is a measure of the strength of a planet based on these six sources of strength. Explaining the computation of shadbalas is beyond the scope of this book. For the details of its computation, one may refer to "Brihat Parasara Hora Sastram" by Parasara or "Graha and Bhava Balas" by Dr. B.V. Raman. Most computer software programs give shadbala, though there are minor differences between the definitions used by them.

When two or planets influence the same house or when they participate in a yoga, then the planet with the highest shadbala is the most likely give the results. The planet with the strongest shadbala is like a group leader who acts on the group's behalf.

On the other hand, ashtakavarga bala shows how other planets support or oppose a planet. It does not show how capable the planet is of leading and giving the results of a group of planets, unlike shadbala. It shows how capable a planet is of giving its own results, in harmony with other planetary forces.

15.4 Avasthas (States)

Avastha literally means "state". There are different possible states of a planet and we will learn them in this section.

15.4.1 *State Related to Age*

One of the states of a planet has to do with its age. Just as a 10-year old child or an 80-year old man have their limitations and cannot execute certain tasks efficiently, a planet in childhood or old age may not be very effective.

Table 35: Avasthas related to age

In odd rasis	In even rasis	Avastha	Meaning	Results
0°–6°	24°–30°	Saisava	Child	Quarter
6°–12°	18°–24°	Kumaara	Adolescent	Half
12°–18°	12°–18°	Yuva	Youth	Full
18°–24°	6°–12°	Vriddha	Old	Some
24°–30°	0°–6°	Mrita	Dead	None

A planet at 23° in Cn will be in Kumaara avastha (adolescence) and it will give half of its results. A planet at 19° in Li will be in Vriddha avastha (old age) and it will not be very effective. A planet at 14° in Sg will be in Yuva avastha (young age) and it will give all of its results. A planet at 27° in Pi will be at Saisava avastha (childhood) and it will give one quarter of its results.

One should not be carried away with these avasthas. Just as there are some child prodigies and wizards with wrinkles, a planet can give good results irrespective of its age-related state. Age is *just one* of the factors deciding a person's productivity. Similarly, age-related state is *just one* of the factors deciding a planet's effectiveness.

15.4.2 *State Related to Alertness*

We have 3 alertness-related states of planets:

(1) A planet in its exaltation rasi or an own rasi is said to be in "Jaagrita" avastha (awake). It gives full results.

(2) A planet in a rasi owned by a neutral or friendly planet is said to be in "Swapna" avastha (dreaming). It gives medium results.

(3) A planet in its debilitation rasi or a rasi owned by an enemy is said to be in "Sushupta" avastha (asleep). The results it gives are negligible.

15.4.3 *State Related to Attitude and Mood*

We have 9 states of planets that are related to attitude and mood :

(1) A planet in its exaltation rasi is said to be in "Deepta" avastha (bright).

(2) A planet in its own rasi is said to be in "Swastha" avastha (doing well, contented, comfortable, natural).

(3) A planet in a good friend's rasi is said to be in "Mudita" avastha (delighted).

(4) A planet in a friend's rasi is said to be in "Saanta" avastha (peaceful).

(5) A planet in a neutral planet's rasi is said to be in "Deena" avastha (sad, depressed).

(6) A planet in an enemy's rasi is said to be in "Dukhita" avastha (distressed, miserable).

(7) A planet joined by malefic planets is said to be in "Vikala" avastha (crippled, confused).

(8) A planet in a malefic planet's rasi is said to be in "Khala" avastha (mischievous, scheming).

(9) A planet joined closely by Sun is said to be in "Kopita" avastha (angry).

We have 6 additional states of planets that are related to attitude and mood:

(1) A planet in the 5th house joined by Sun, Mars, Saturn, Rahu and Ketu is said to be in "Lajjita" avastha (ashamed).

(2) A planet in its exaltation rasi or moolatrikona rasi is said to be in "Garvita" avastha (proud).

(3) A planet is in an enemy's rasi or conjoined by enemies or aspected by enemies or conjoined by Saturn, it is said to be in "Kshudhita" avastha (hungry).

(4) A planet stationed in a watery rasi and aspected by enemies without the aspect of benefics is said to be in "Trishita" avastha (thirsty).

(5) A planet in a friend's sign, conjoined or aspected by friends and conjoined by Jupiter, is said to be in "Mudita" avastha (delighted).

(6) A planet conjoined by Sun and aspected by malefics or enemies is said to be in "Kshobhita" avastha (shaken, agitated).

Planets give results based on the state they are in. If a house contains planets in Kshudhita or Kshobhita avasthas, the significations of the house are affected. If a planet in the 5th house is in Lajjita avastha, there may be losses related to progeny. If a planet in the 7th house is in Kshobhita avastha, there may be loss of spouse.

15.4.4 *States Relates to Activity*

There are 12 possible states of a planet related to its activity. This state is the most important of all states. For each planet, we use the following formula to find its avastha.

Suppose C is the number of the constellation occupied by the planet (1 for Aswini, 2 for Bharani and so on). Suppose P is the index of the planet whose avastha we are finding (1 for Sun, 2 for Moon). Suppose A is the index of the amsa (navamsa) occupied by the planet in its rasi[51]. Suppose M is the constellation occupied by Moon. Suppose G is the ghati running at birth.[52] Suppose L is the rasi occupied by lagna (1 for Ar, 2 for Ta and so on). Then we compute (C x P x A) + M + G + L, divide it by 12 and take the

51 For example, let us say Mercury is in 22Ge14. Each navamsa has a length of 3°20' (1/9th of 30°) and 22°14' in Ge is in the 7th navamsa of Ge (please note that we are not talking about the rasi occupied by the planet in navamsa). Then we use A = 7 for Mercury.

52 Suppose sunrise was at 6 am and someone was born at 11 pm. So 17 hours were over. Each hour has 2.5 ghatis and 17 hours = 17 x 2.5 = 42.5. So the 43rd ghati was running at birth.

remainder. Using the resulting number as the avastha index and referring to Table 36, we find out the avastha of the planet.

Table 36: Sayanaadi Avasthas

Avastha Index	Avastha name	Meaning
1	Sayana	Lying down, resting
2	Upavesana	Sitting down
3	Netrapaani	Eyes and hands
4	Prakaasana	Shining
5	Gamana	Going (on the move)
6	Aagamana	Coming, returning
7	Sabhaa (Sabhaa vasati)	Being at an assembly
8	Aagama	Coming/Acquiring
9	Bhojana	Eating
10	Nriyalipsaa	Longing to dance
11	Kautuka	Being eager
12	Nidraa	Sleeping

After we find the avastha index, we can multiply it with itself and add the number corresponding to the first sound in the first syllable of the name, as found from Table 37. We can take the remainder when that number is divided by 12. Then we can add a planetary adjustment to the remainder. We use 5 for Sun and Jupiter, 2 for Moon and Mars, 3 for Mercury, Venus and Saturn and 4 for Rahu and Ketu. We divide the sum by 3 and take the remainder. This gives the strength of the activity. A value of 1 means "drishti" and medium results. A value of 2 means "cheshta" and full results. A value of 3 (or 0) means "vicheshta" and gives very little results. Based on the activity-related state of a planet, we can guess the results given by it. Based on whether it is in Cheshta, Drishti or Vicheshta, the results will be full, medium or little. An example will clarify this computation.

Table 37: Numbers of the Sounds

Number	Sounds	Roman transliteration
1	अ क छ ड ध भ व	a, ka, chh, d (alveolar), dh (dental), bh, v
2	इ ख ज ढ न म श	i, kh, j, dh (alveolar), n (dental), m, s/sh (palatal)
3	उ ग झ त प य ष	u, g, jh, t, p, y, sh (alveolar)
4	ए घ ट थ फ र स	e, gh, t (alveolar), th (dental), ph, r, s (dental)
5	ओ च ठ द ब ल ह	o, ch, th (alveolar), d (dental), b, l, h

Results in Sayana avastha:

Sun: Digestive troubles, diseases, stout legs, bile, piles, heart troubles.

Moon: Honorable, sluggish, lustful, spoils finances.

Mars: Troubled, wounded, ulcers, itches.

Mercury: Addicted to pleasures, licentious, wicked, always hungry; [in lagna] lame, eyes like a bee.

Jupiter: Strong, but weak voice, tawny complexion, prominent cheeks, afraid of enemies.

Venus: Strong, troubles of teeth, short-tempered, poor, licentious.

Saturn: Hungry, thirst, dieases in childhood, wealthy later.

Rahu: Many miseries; [in Ar, Ta, Ge, Vi] wealth.

Ketu: Many diseases; [in Ar, Ta, Ge, Vi] wealth.

Results in Upavesana avastha:

Sun: Poor, fond of quarrels, hard-hearted, loses money.

Moon: diseases, unintelligent, poor, merciless, does misdeeds, steals money.

Mars: Strong, sinful, liar, eminent, wealthy.

Mercury: [in lagna] good character; [conjoined/aspected by malefics] poor; [conjoined/aspected by benefics] wealthy and happy.

Jupiter: Talkative, troubled by enemies and kings, ulcers on feet, hands, feet.

Venus: Endowed with gems and gold, destroys enemies, honored by kings, happy.

Saturn: Self-respect, punished by kings, troubles by enemies, faces dangers, ulcers.

Rahu: Distressed due to ulcers, royal association, honorable, but financial troubles.

Ketu: Distressed due to ulcers, troubles from enemies, snakes and thieves, windy (vaata-related) diseases.

Results in Netrapaani avastha:

Sun: Ever happy, wise, helps others, strong, wealthy, pleasures, favorite of kings.

Moon: Great diseases, garrulous, wicked, always bad actions.

Mars: [in lagna] penury; [elsewhere] ruler of a town.

Mercury: Honorable, no wisdom, no learning, no well-wishers; [in 5th] no happiness from wife and children, many daughters, gains money from royal patronage.

Jupiter: Devoid of health and wealth, libidinous, likes entertainment, tawny complexion, moves with people of a different class.

Venus: [in lagna, 7th or 10th] troubles to eyes and loss of wealth; [else] large house.

Saturn: Charming wife, learned in arts, royal favors, friends, intelligent, good speaker.

Rahu: Eyes troubles, financial losses, troubles from wicked men, snakes and thieves.

Ketu: Eyes troubles, troubles from wicked men, snakes, thieves and rulers.

Results in Prakaasana avastha:

Sun: Charitable, wealthy, good orator in assemblies, strong, good-looking.

Moon: Famous in world, virtuous, royal patronage, royal insignia, wealth, luxuries, regular visits to shrines, many ornaments.

Mars: Virtuous and honored by kings; [in 5th] loss of children; [in 5th with Rahu] faces a severe fall.

Mercury: Charitable, kind, good deeds, scholar of many subjects, wise and destroyer of groups of wicked men.

Jupiter: Virtuous, pure happiness and comfort, splendorous, visits holy places of Krishna; [if exalted] excellent fame in the whole world, very opulent.

Venus: [exalted or in own/friendly rasi] has a conduct similar to a mighty elephant; equal to a king, interested in poetry, arts and music.

Saturn: Virtuous, intelligent, opulent, likes entertainment, kind, devotee of Shiva.

Rahu: Prosperous in foreign places, virtuous, wealthy, high position, good deeds, a chief in king's court, charming.

Ketu: Wealthy, righteous, lives abroad, enthusiastic, genuine, serves the king.

Results in Gamana avastha:

Sun: Lives in foreign lands, unhappy, lazy, unwise, poor, disturbed by fears, angry.

Moon: [if waning] sinful, cruel, eye troubles; [if waxing] troubled by fear.

Mars: Wanderer, boils, itches, quarrels with women, many wounds and ulcers.

Mercury: Visits the courts of kings frequently, wealthy.

Jupiter: Brave, many friends, scholar, wealthy.

Venus: Mother doesn't live long, separated from own people, fear from enemies.

Saturn: Rich, good sons, scholar at a king's court, grabs other people's land.

Rahu: Many children, scholarly, wealthy, charitable and honored by a king.

Ketu: Many children, scholarly, wealthy, charitable, virtuous, great man.

Results in Aagamana avastha:

Sun: Affairs with the wives of others, deserted by people, likes travels, cheat, dirty.

Moon: Honorable, diseases of feet, secret sins, poor, unintelligent, sad.

Mars: Good character, endowed with gems, has weapons, destroyer of enemies.

Mercury: Visits the courts of kings frequently, wealthy.

Jupiter: Servants, excellent women and wealth always adore his abode.

Venus: Wealthy, visits holy shrines, enthusiastic, diseases of hands and feet.

Saturn: Separated from family, foolish, wanderer, miserable.

Rahu: Irritable, unintelligent, poor, wicked, miserly, libidinous.

Ketu: Diseases, loss of wealth, tale-bearer, hurts others.

Results in Sabhaa avastha:

Sun: Helps others, possesses wealth, gems and lands, virtuous, very strong, affectionate and kind.

Moon: Eminent, honored by kings, sexual pleasures, good character.

Mars: A scholar in a king's court, wealthy, honorable, charitable; [if exalted] skilled at wars, successful, upholds dharma; [in trines] unlearned; [in 12th] devoid of happiness from wife and children.

Mercury: [if exalted] highly wealthy and good deeds; wealthy, king or a minister, devotion to Vishnu and Shiva, saattwik, obtains moksha.

Jupiter: Excellent speech, superior gems and wealth, royal insignia, supremely learned.

Venus: Eminent in a king's court, virtuous, destroyer of enemies, wealthy and charitable.

Saturn: Displays excellent judicial knowledge in assemblies, excellent wealth and gems, exceedingly brilliant.

Rahu: Scholarly, miserly, many virtues, wealthy, happy.

Ketu: Garrulous, proud, miserly, licentious, skilful in evil subjects.

Results in Aagama avastha:

Sun: Troubled by enemies, fickle-minded, cheat, emaciated, doesn't follow good dharma and karma, wanton.

Moon: [if waxing] Garrulous, virtuous; [if waning] two wives, sick, cheat, wicked.

Mars: Bad character and deeds, ear troubles, timid, friendly with evil-minded people.

Mercury: Serves mean people and makes money, two sons, one daughter who brings good name.

Jupiter: Many conveyances, comforts, honors, servants, happiness from progeny, knowledge, friends, learning and noble path.

Venus: No wealth, troubles from enemies, separation from children, diseases, unhappiness from spouse.

Saturn: Diseases, not skilful, no royal patronage.

Rahu: Financial losses, fear of enemies and litigation, depressed, separated from own people, emaciated, manipulative.

Ketu: Notorious, sinful, litigation with own men, diseases, enemies.

Results in Bhojana avastha:

Sun: Pains in joints, loss of wealth over opposite sex, loss of strength, lies, headaches, spreading lies, bad path.

Moon: [if waxing] Social status, honor, conveyances, wife and daughters, servants; [if waning] these results will be hard to get.

Mars: [if strong] sweet food; [if weak] means acts, dishonorable.

Mercury: Financial losses in litigations, wrath of kings, no marital happiness.

Jupiter: Excellent food, wealth, royal insignia.

Venus: [debilitated] wealthy, respected by scholars; [else] Distressed due to hunger, dieases, fear from enemies.

Saturn: Weak-sighted, delusion, enjoys tasty food.

Rahu: No happiness from wife and children, bereft of good food, timid.

Ketu: Hungry, sick, wanderer, poor.

Results in Nrityalipsaa avastha:

Sun: Learned, scholar, good at discussing poetry, reverred by kings.

Moon: [if waxing] strong, knowledge of poetry and music, connoisseur of arts; [if waning] sinful.

Mars: Wealthy through royal connections, has gold, diamonds and corals.

Mercury: Honor, conveyances, gems, valorous, friends, progeny, learned in assemblies; [in a malefic rasi] licentious, goes to prostitutes.

Jupiter: Honored by kings, wealthy, learned in dharma sastra and tantra, revered by powerful men, respected by learned men, a scholar and faultless in grammar and etymology.

Venus: Skilful in literature, arts, music, meritorious and opulent.

Saturn: Righteous, opulent, honored by kings, brave and heroic at wars.

Rahu: Great disease, eye problems, fear from enemies, financial losses.

Ketu: Diseases, eye troubles, wicked, sinful.

Results in Kautuka avastha:

Sun: Happy, learned, performs yajnas (rites), stays at a king's palace, good at discussing poetry, good-looking.

Moon: King, wealthy, skilful in sexual acts.

Mars: Curious, friends and children; [if exalted] honored by king and virtuous.

Mercury: [in lagna] skilful in music; [in 7th or 8th] addicted to courtesans; [in 9th] good deeds and character, goes to heaven.

Jupiter: Curious, very kind, happy, honored, sons, famous.

Venus: Opulent, learned, famous and respected in assemblies.

Saturn: Endowed with lands, wealthy, happy, pleasures from charming ladies, learned in poetry and arts.

Rahu: Wanderer, after other men's wives, steals other men's wealth.

Ketu: Goes after courtesans, losses in profession, sinful, wanderer.

Results in Nidraa avastha:

Sun: Drowsy, lives abroad, troubles to wife.

Moon: [if with Jupiter] eminent; [without Jupiter] loses wealth on females, troubles.

Mars: Angry, unintelligent, poor, wicked, fallen from the virtuous path, sick.

Mercury: Uncomfortable sleep, troubles of neck, miseries, litigation with own men, loses wealth.

Jupiter: Poor, unintelligent, foolish, no righteous acts.

Venus: Serves others, criticizes others, garrulous, wanderer.

Saturn: Rich, charming, good character, brave, destroys all enemies, skilful in dealing with women.

Rahu: Virtuous, good wife and children, happy, proud, bold, wealthy.

Ketu: Virtuous, endowed with wealth and agricultural products, whiles away time with entertainment.

Example 49: Let us take a native born at 5:50 pm (IST) on 4th April 1970 at Machilipatnam, India (81E12, 16N15). Let us find the activity-related states of Mercury, Jupiter and Venus for this native. The native's given name starts with "V".

Moon is in Poorvabhadrapada, *i.e.* the 25th constellation. So M = 25. The native was born at 5:50 pm and sunrise was at 6 am. So 11:50 hours passed since sunrise. In minutes, this is 710 minutes. Because a ghati contains 24 minutes, this is 29.6 ghatis. So the 30th ghati after sunrise was running at birth. So G = 30. Lagna is in Virgo, the 6th rasi from Aries and so L = 6. The native's given name starts with "V" and the number corresponding to this sound is 1.

Mercury: Mercury is at 3Ar08. He is in Aswini, i.e. 1st constellation. So C = 1. Because Mercury is the 4th planet from Sun, P = 4. Mercury is in the first 1/9th of Ar and so A = 1. Using the formula, we get (C x P x A) + M + G + L = (1 x 4 x 1) + 25 + 30 + 6 = 65. Dividing it by 12, we get a remainder of 5. From Table 36, we see that an avastha index of 5 means "Gamana" avastha (going/on the move). We see that 5 x 5 is 25. Adding 1 (corresponding to the sound), we get 26. Remainder when this is divided by 12 is 2. Adding 3 (Mercury's planetary adjustment), we get 5. When we divide it by 3, remainder is 2. It shows "Cheshta". So Mercury's results due to "Gamana" avastha are given in full. We see that the standard results are "visits the courts of kings frequently, wealthy".

Jupiter: Jupiter is at 9Li46. He is in Swaati, i.e. 15th constellation. So C = 15. Because Jupiter is the 5th planet from Sun, P = 5. Jupiter is in the third 1/9th of Li and so A = 3. Using the formula, we get (C x P x A) + M + G + L = (15 x 5 x 3) + 25 + 30 + 6 = 286. Dividing it by 12, we get a remainder of 10. From Table 36, we see that an avastha index of 10 means "Nriyalipsaa" avastha (urge for dance). We see that 10 x 10 is 100. Adding 1 (corresponding to the sound), we get 101. Remainder when this is divided by 12 is 5. Adding 5 (Jupiter's planetary adjustment), we get 10. When we divide it by 3, remainder is 1. It shows "Drishti". So Jupiter's results due to "Nriyalipsaa" avastha are given only to a medium extent. We see that the standard results are: "honored by kings, wealthy, learned in dharma sastra and tantra, revered by powerful men, respected by learned men, a scholar and faultless in grammar and etymology".

Venus: Venus is at 7Ar55. He is in Aswini, i.e. 1st constellation. So C = 1. Because Venus is the 6th planet from Sun, P = 6. Venus is in the third 1/9th of Ar and so A = 3. Using the formula, we get (C x P x A) + M + G + L = (1 x 6 x 3) + 25 + 30 + 6 = 79. Dividing it by 12, we get a remainder of 7. From Table 36, we see that an avastha index of 7 means "Sabhaa" avastha (assemby/council). We see that 7 x 7 is 49. Adding 1 (corresponding to the sound), we get 50. Remainder when this is divided by 12 is 2. Adding 3 (planetary adjustment of Venus), we get 5. When we divide it by 3, remainder is 2. It shows "Cheshta". So Venus's results due to "Sabhaa" avastha are given in full. We see that the standard results are "eminent in a king's court, virtuous, destroyer of enemies, wealthy and charitable".

Exercise 24: Consider a gentleman born at 8:30 am (LMT) on 8th November 1927 at 67E03, 24N52. Find the activity-related states of Sun, Mars and Jupiter and interpret them. His name starts with the sound "L".

Importance of Sayanaadi Avasthas:

Sayanaadi (Sayana *etc*) avasthas are the most important of all avasthas. In addition to the results listed above, Parasara listed some special results. If a benefic is in Sayana avastha, the house benefits from his presence. If a malefic is in Nidraa avastha in the 7th house without the conjunction or aspect of another malefic, it is auspicious. If a malefic is in Bhojana avastha, the house containing it is destroyed. If a malefic is in the 5th house in Sayana or Nidraa avastha, it is auspicious. If a malefic is in the 8th house in Sayana or Nidraa avastha, it brings death by royal wrath. If a malefic occupies the 10th house in Bhojana or Sayana avastha, all kinds of miseries may be expected. If a benefic or a planet in own or exaltation rasi occupies in the 1st, 5th, 7th or 10th house in Prakasana, Nrityalipsaa or Kautuka avasthas, it brings Raja Yoga. Parasara specifically mentioned Moon in the 10th house in Kautuka or Prakaasana avasthas.

However, **one should not be carried away with avasthas** and one should remember that they are only the "states" of the planet. The state of a planet related to age, alertness, mood and activity will have a role in the results given by it, but the houses influenced by it in various divisional charts are more important in deciding the results. We should avoid the temptation to make predictions based on thumbrules and look-up tables.

15.5 Other Simple Strengths

15.5.1 *Stronger Co-Lord*

When we find the arudha pada of a house falling in Scorpio or Aquarius, we need to find the stronger of Mars & Ketu (co-lords of Sc) and Saturn & Rahu (co-lords of Aq). The stronger lord acts its lord and decides the arudha pada. The stronger lord of Sc (or Aq) is also used in finding the duration of its dasa in many rasi dasas (*e.g.* Narayana dasa).

Basic rule: If one of the co-lords is in the rasi, take the other planet. For example, if Saturn is in Aq and Rahu is in a rasi other than Aq, Rahu becomes the primary lord of Aq. If not, we find the stronger of the 2 planets and the stronger planet becomes the primary lord.

The stronger planet of two planets is determined using the following rules. We go from one rule to the next, only if we do not have a winner. If we have a winner in one step, we do not go through the remaining steps.

(1) If one planet is joined by more planets than the other, it is stronger. Suppose Saturn is in Pi with Mars and Sun and Rahu is in Ar with Jupiter. Then Saturn is stronger than Rahu, because he is with 2 planets and Rahu is only with one planet. So Saturn becomes the primary lord of Aq.

(2) We find how many of the following planets conjoin/aspect a planet: (1) Jupiter, (2) Mercury, and, (3) dispositor. A planet conjoined/aspected by more of these 3 planets is stronger. We must use rasi aspects here. Suppose Saturn is in Ge with Mercury, Rahu is in Ar, Mars is in Le, Jupiter is in Ta. Saturn is conjoined by Mercury and his dispositor (who is Mercury again). His count is 2. Rahu in Ar is aspected by Mars, his dispositor, from Le. Neither Jupiter nor Mercury aspects or conjoins Rahu. So Rahu's count of 1 loses to Saturn's count of 2 and Saturn is the stronger planet. He becomes the lord of Aq.

(3) If one planet is exalted and the other not, then the exalted planet is stronger. Suppose Saturn is in Li and Rahu is in Cn, with the same number of planets. Suppose we have a tie after step (2). Then we note that Saturn is exalted in Li and declare him as the stronger planet. He becomes the primary lord of Aq.

(4) If we have a tie after (3), we consider the natural strength of the rasi containing the planet. Dual rasis are stronger than fixed rasis and fixed rasis are stronger than movable rasis. Suppose Mars is in Ge and Ketu is in Aq and we have a tie between them after step (3). Then we declare Mars as the stronger planet and the primary lord of Sc, because he is in a dual rasi and Ketu is in a fixed rasi.

(5) (*a*) *When finding dasa duration*: If we have a tie after (4), we take the planet giving a larger length for dasa. Suppose Saturn is in Ge and Rahu is in Vi and suppose we have a tie after (4). Suppose we want to find the stronger lord for Narayana dasa. Rahu in Vi gives 5 years and Saturn in Ge gives 8 years[53]. So Saturn is used instead of Rahu.

(*b*) *When finding the lord for arudha padas etc*: If we have a tie after (4), we take the planet that is more advanced in its rasi. We measure the advancement of Rahu and Ketu from the *end* of the rasi. Suppose Mars is at 23Li17 and Ketu is at 5Cn54. Suppose we have a tie after (4). Advancement of Mars in Li is 23°17'. Advancement of Ketu from

53 We will learn the computation of dasa years in Narayana dasa later.

the end of Cn is 30° – 5°54' = 24°6'. Because Ketu is more advanced, Ketu is stronger than Mars and becomes the primary lord of Sc.

Exercise 25: Find the primary lord of Aq and Sc in Chart 12 for the purpose of arudha padas.

15.5.2 *Stronger Rasi*

When computing rasi dasas, we sometimes need to find the strongest rasi out of 2 or 3 or 4 rasis. In this book, we will mainly use Narayana dasa and we will only need to compare the strengths of 2 rasis. To conclude that one rasi is stronger than another rasi for the purpose of rasi dasas, we use the following rules. We use the same rules for finding the stronger rasi owned by a planet, when computing its graha arudha. We go from one rule to the next only if there is no winner after the rule. When we have a winner, we stop and do not go to the next rule.

(1) If one rasi contains more planets than the other rasi, then it is stronger. Suppose we are comparing the strengths of Ar and Li. Suppose Ar contains Saturn and Jupiter and Li contains Venus. Then Ar is stronger, as it contains more planets.

(2) We find how many of the following planets occupy/aspect a rasi: (1) Jupiter, (2) Mercury, and, (3) the rasi's lord. A rasi occupied/aspected by more of these 3 planets is stronger. We must use rasi aspects here. Suppose we are comparing the strengths of Ar and Li. Suppose Jupiter is in Ar, Mercury and Venus are in Ta and Mars is in Vi. Then Ar is occupied by Jupiter and not by the other two (Mercury and lord Mars). Its count is 1. Li is aspected by two (Mercury and lord Venus) and only Jupiter doesn't aspect it (we are using rasi aspects). So Li's count of 2 beats Ar's count of 1 and Li is stronger than Ar.

(3) If one rasi contains an exalted planet and the other does not, then the former rasi is stronger. Suppose we are comparing the strengths of Ar and Li. Suppose Saturn and Mercury are in Li and Jupiter and Venus are in Ar. Suppose we have a tie between Ar and Li after rule (2). Then we note that Saturn is exalted in Li and declare Li as the stronger rasi.

(4) A rasi whose lord is in a rasi with a different oddity (odd/even) is stronger than a rasi whose lord is in a rasi with the same oddity. Suppose we are comparing the strengths of Ar and Li and we have a tie after rule (3). Suppose Venus is in Cn, an even rasi and Mars is in Le, an odd rasi. Both Ar and Li are odd rasis. Because the lord of Li is in an even rasi (*i.e.* a rasi with a *different* oddity) and the lord of Ar is in an odd rasi (*i.e.* a rasi with *the same* oddity), Li is stronger.

NOTE: If we have a tie upto rule (3) when finding the stronger rasi owned by a planet for computing its graha arudha, this rule will surely resolve the tie, because the two rasis owned by each planet have a different oddity. So one of them will have the lord in a rasi with a different oddity.

(5) If we have a tie after rule (4), we use the natural strength of rasis. Dual rasis are stronger than fixed rasis and fixed rasis are stronger than movable rasis. This rule is not useful in Narayana dasa, because we always compare a rasi and the 7th from it. If a rasi is dual/fixed/movable, the 7th from it is also of the same type. However, this rule is useful in some other dasas.

(6) If we have a tie after rule (5), we look at the longitudes of the lords of the two rasis. We measure the advancement of each planet from the beginning of the rasi occupied by it (from the end of the rasi in the case of Rahu and Ketu) and compare them. The rasi owned by the planet with the higher advancement is stronger. Suppose we are comparing the strengths of Ar and Li. Suppose we have a tie after rule (5). Suppose Mars is at 23Ge17 and Venus is at 19Le51. Advancement of Mars (lord of Ar) in his rasi is 23°17'. Advancement of Venus (lord of Li) in his rasi is 19°51'. Because Mars is more advanced, his Ar is stronger than Li.

NOTE: In the case of Aq and Sc, we use the stronger lord. For Rahu and Ketu, advancement in rasi is measured from the end of the rasi. If Rahu is at 9Sc34, his advancement in Sc is 30° – 9°34' = 20°26'.

Exercise 26: Consider Chart 12. Identify the stronger rasi from each pair below:

---

(1) Ar & Li, (2) Ta & Sc, (3) Ge & Sg, (4) Cn & Cp, (5) Le & Aq, and, (6) Vi & Pi.

Warning: The above rules are too general. One should understand the meaning of each rule and adapt based on the situation. For example, aspect of Mercury, Jupiter and lord is important for Narayana dasa and other phalita dasas. In ayur dasas that show longevity, aspect of luminaries (Sun and Moon) are important. Aspect of all other planets is equally important. There is no significance for the aspect of lord. In dasas based on AK (*e.g.* Atmakaraka kendradi graha/rasi dasas), the sign containing AK is stronger than any other rasi. After we check for the aspects of Mercury, Jupiter and rasi lord, we should look at the placement of rasi lord from AK. A rasi who lord is in a quadrant from AK is stronger than a rasi whose lord is in a panaphara from AK. These rules, however, are not applicable to all dasas.

15.6 Anwers to Exercises

Exercise 24:

Sun is in "Sabhaa" avastha and his strength is "Cheshta". His results are "helps others, possesses wealth, gems and lands, virtuous, very strong, affectionate and kind". They are given in full.

Mars is in "Nidraa" avastha and his strength is "Drishti". His results are "angry, unintelligent, poor, wicked, fallen from the virtuous path, sick" and they are given to a medium degree.

Jupiter is in "Aagama" avastha and his strength is "Cheshta". His results are "many conveyances, comforts, honors, servants, happiness from progeny, knowledge, friends, learning and noble path" and they are given in full.

Exercise 25:

Rahu is alone and so is Saturn We have a tie after rule (1). Saturn is aspected by Mercury and not aspected/conjoined by Jupiter and his dispositor (Jupiter again). Rahu is aspected by Venus (his dispositor) and not aspected by Mercury and Jupiter. Both have a count of one and we have a tie after rule (2). Neither Saturn nor Rahu is exalted after rule (3). Now we use rule (4). Saturn is in a dual rasi and Rahu is in a movable rasi. So Saturn is stronger and he becomes the primary lord of Aq.

Mars is in Sc and Ketu is elsewhere (in Ar). So we don't even have to go through the rules to find the stronger planet. We use the "basic rule" and declare Ketu as the primary lord of Sc.

Exercise 26:

(1) Ar and Li have one planet each. There is a tie in rule (1). Ar is aspected by Jupiter & lord Mars. Li is aspected only by lord Venus. Ar is stronger than Li, from rule (2).

(2) Sc has 2 planets and Ta has 1. Sc is stronger than Ta, from rule (1).

(3) Sg has 2 planets and Ge is empty. Sg is stronger than Ta, from rule (1).

(4) Cp has 1 planet and Cn is empty. Cp is stronger than Cn, from rule (1).

(5) Le and Aq are empty. There is a tie after rule (1). Le is not aspected by any of Jupiter, Mercury and lord Sun. Aq is aspected by co-lord Rahu (though Saturn is the primary/stronger lord, Rahu's aspect also counts). Aq is stronger than Le, from rule (2).

(6) Pi has 1 planet and Vi is empty. Pi is stronger than Vi, from rule (1).

Part 2: Dasa Analysis

One unique feature of Vedic astrology is its concept of "dasa" systems. Dasa means "a period". One's lifetime is divided into several periods, sub-periods, sub-sub-periods and so on. These are ruled by different planets or rasis. Planets and rasis give their results in their respective periods and sub-periods. Each dasa system has a specific use. The nature of results given by planets and rasis in their respective periods and sub-periods depends on the dasa system being used.

There are many classifications of dasa systems:

(1) **Nakshatra dasas and Rasi dasas:** Nakshatra dasas are based on Moon's nakshatra (constellation). Rasi dasas are based on rasis occupied by planets and dasas are owned by rasis in rasi dasas.

(2) **Phalita dasas and Ayur dasas:** Phalita means results and ayur means longevity. Phalita dasas are used for general results and ayur dasas are used for predicting death.

Hundreds of dasa systems were enumerated by the seers of Vedic astrologey. Specific uses of these dasa systems weren't clearly mentioned in classics. These are hidden in remote corners of India as family secrets.

In this part, the use of the following dasa systems is explained in detail:

- **Vimsottari dasa:** Nakshatra dasa (phalita/ayur)
- **Ashtottari dasa:** Nakshatra dasa (ayur/phalita)
- **Narayana dasa:** Rasi dasa (phalita - general)
- **Lagna Kendradi Rasi dasa:** Rasi dasa (phalita – material fortune)
- **Sudasa:** Rasi dasa (phalita – material fortune)
- **Drigdasa:** Rasi dasa (phalita – spirituality)
- **Niryaana Shoola dasa:** Rasi dasa (ayur)
- **Shoola dasa:** Rasi dasa (ayur)
- **Kalachakra dasa:** Nakshatra dasa (phalita)

Sudarsana Chakra dasa is one of the most important dasas mentioned by Parasara. However, for reasons that will become clear later, we will learn it in the part "Tajaka Analysis".

16. Vimsottari Dasa

16.1 Introduction

Vimsottari dasa is the most popular dasa system among Vedic astrologers of today. Sage Parasara mentions in "Brihat Parasara Hora Sastram" that this dasa system is the most suitable dasa system in Kali yuga.

Vimsottari means 120. Vimsottari dasa is a dasa system where the total duration of the dasa cycle is 120 years. Dasas of different planets are for different number of years, but the sum of *all* dasas is 120 years.

In Kali yuga, *paramaayush* (maximum longevity) of human beings is supposed to be 120 years. Consequently, Vimsottari dasa is the most suitable dasa in Kali yuga.

Dasas are reckoned here based on the constellation occupied by Moon. There are other variations that are more applicable in some cases. Many contemporary Vedic astrologers ignore these variations and always reckon dasas from the lord of the constellation occupied by Moon. However, this may not result in the best predictions always. In this book, we will look at some of the variations.

One's life is divided into dasas – periods – ruled by the nine planets. A dasa is also called a "mahadasa" (mahadasa = master period). Each mahadasa is again divided into 9 sub-periods ruled by 9 planets. These sub-periods in mahadasas are called "antardasas". We can have further divisions. Sub-periods in antardasas are called "pratyantardasas". Sub-periods in pratyantardasas are called "sookshma-antardasas" or simply sookshma dasas. Sub-periods in sookshma dasas are called "prana-antardasas" or simply prana dasas. Sub-periods in prana dasas are called "deha-antardasas". In this book, we will denote mahadasa with MD, antardasa with AD, pratyantardasa with PD, sookshma dasa with SD, prana-antardasa with PAD and deha-antardasa with DAD.

16.2 Dasa Computation

The lengths of the dasas (periods) of various planets are given in Table 38. The order of dasas is also as indicated in that table. For example, let us say that the first dasa is Sun's. It will be of 6 years. Then 10 years of Moon dasa will follow. Then 7 years of Mars dasa will follow. And so on. At the end of the table, we come back to the first entry. For example, let us say that the first dasa is of Jupiter. Then the order of dasas will be Jupiter, Saturn, Mercury, Ketu, Venus, Sun (go back), Moon, Mars and Rahu.

Table 38: Vimsottari Dasa Lengths

Planet	Dasa length (in years)
Sun	6
Moon	10
Mars	7
Rahu	18
Jupiter	16
Saturn	19
Mercury	17
Ketu	7
Venus	20
Total	120

In this manner, we can find the order of dasas and dasa lengths, given the first dasa.

For computing Vimsottari dasa, use the following steps:

(1) Find the constellation occupied by Moon.

(2) Find the advancement of Moon in the constellation.

(3) Find the part of the constellation that is yet to be traversed by Moon, as a fraction of the length of the constellation. [NOTE: Length of each constellation is 13°20'.]

(4) First dasa will belong to the lord of the constellation.

(5) Find the sequence of dasas and dasa lengths from Table 38.

(6) Multiply the length of the first dasa by the fraction found in step (3). Only this amount in the first dasa is left at birth. The rest was over before birth.

Controversy: Dasa length of each planet was given in years in Table 38. For example, Sun dasa is for 6 years. However, what is the meaning of "a year" here? Do we mean the normal solar year, *i.e.* 365.2425 days? Or, do we mean a *savana* year of 360 days that is used when finding the running year for calculating varsha bala (year strength) in shadbalas? Or, do we mean a period in which Moon traverses through 360 constellations? Or, do we mean a period of 360 tithis (luni-solar days)? Most scholars, including this author's guru Pt. Sanjay Rath, use solar years. However, this author prefers *savana* years based on the teachings of his father. Savana years will be used with nakshatra dasas in all the calculations given in this book. This is not meant to be a recommendation.

Example 50: Let us say someone was born at 5:50 am on 2000 April 28 (time zone: 4 hours west of GMT). Moon is at 2°23' in Aq at the time of birth.

(1) This is in the 3rd pada (quarter) of Dhanishtha constellation. Dhanishtha constellation starts at 23°20' in Cp and ends at 6°40' in Aq.

(2) Moon's advancement in Dhanishtha = 2Aq23 – 23Cp20 = 32°23' – 23°20' = 9°3'.

(3) The total length of the constellation is 13°20'. The length yet to be traversed in this constellation as a fraction of the total constellation length = (13°20' – 9°3')/13°20' = 4°17'/13°20' = (4x60+17)/(13x60+20) = 257/800 = 0.32125. This is the fraction of the constellation yet to be traversed by Moon.

(4) First dasa belongs to the lord of Dhanishtha. It is Mars.

(5) Let us start from Mars. From Table 38, dasa sequence is: Mars (7 years), Rahu (18 years), Jupiter (16 years), Saturn (19 years), Mercury (17 years), Ketu (7 years), Venus (20 years), Sun (6 years), Moon (10 years).

(6) First dasa needs a correction. Out of 7 years of Mars dasa, the amount left at birth = 7 x 0.32125 = 2.24875 years = 2 years 2 months 29 days 33 ghatis. [NOTE: Ghati = 1/60th of a day, *i.e.* 24 minutes.]

The native was born at 5:50 am on 2000 April 28. We can get the end date of Mars dasa by adding 2 years 2 months 29 days 33 ghatis to it. We get about 7 pm on 2002 July 15. Mars dasa will be over then and Rahu dasa will start. We get Rahu dasa's end date by adding 18 years to this date. Similarly, we can find the start and end dates of all dasas.

16.3 Antardasa Computation

Each mahadasa is divided into 9 antardasas. Take the planet ruling the mahadasa. First antardasa will belong to the same planet and antardasas go in the same sequence as dasas. The complete length of the mahadasa is ditributed among antardasas in the ratio of mahadasa years of planets.

For example, let us take Venus dasa of the native of Example 50. Venus dasa runs for 20 years. Antardasas in Venus dasa start from Venus and go in the order given in Table 38. So antardasa order in Venus dasa is — Venus, Sun, Moon, Mars, Rahu, Jupiter, Saturn, Mercury and Ketu. Length of Venus antardasa is 20/120 of the total dasa length, *i.e.* 20×20/120 years = 3 years and 4 months. Length of Sun antardasa is 6/120 of the total dasa length, *i.e.* 20×6/120 years = 1 year. Length of Moon antardasa is 10/120 of the total dasa length, *i.e.* 20x10/120 years = 1 year and 8 months. Length of Mars antardasa is 7/120 of the total dasa length, *i.e.* 20×7/120 years = 1 year and 2 months. In this manner, we proportionally divide the period of a mahadasa into 9 antardasas.

We use the same procedure to divide each antardasa into 9 pratyantardasas, each pratyantardasa into 9 sookshma dasas and so on.

In the case of the first dasa, we don't divide the remainder at birth (2.24875 years of Mars dasa remainder, for example, in Example 50) into 9 antardasas. Instead, we divide the complete duration of the first dasa (7 years of Mars dasa, for example, in Example 50) into 9 antardasas. So a few antardasas may be over before birth and only a few antardasas may be left at birth.

From now on, it will be assumed that the reader is familiar with the computations. If the reader does not have any software and needs to compute dasas by hand, he or she should practice with many charts.

16.4 Vimsottari Dasa Variations

16.4.1 *Computation of Variations*

We always compute the fraction left at birth in the first dasa based on the fraction of the constellation occupied by Moon, that is yet to be traversed by Moon. However, we need not always take the lord of Moon's constellation as the planet ruling the first dasa. We can take the lord of the 4th, 5th or 8th constellation from Moon's constellation to start the first dasa. These 3 stars are called kshema, utpanna and adhana stars.

Example 51: Let us consider the data of Example 50 and calculate Vimsottari dasa from 4th, 5th and 8th stars.

The 4th star from Moon's star is Uttarabhadrapada owned by Saturn. Using the 4th star to start Vimsottari dasa, we get the dasa sequence as — Saturn, Mercury, Ketu, Venus etc. Dasa lengths are the same as before, but the part of Saturn dasa left at birth is 19 x 0.32125 = 6.10375 years. Then Mercury dasa is for 17 years, Ketu dasa is for 7 years and so on.

In the same example, the 5th star from Moon's star is Revathi owned by Mercury. Using the 5th star to start Vimsottari dasa, we get the dasa sequence as — Mercury, Ketu, Venus, Sun *etc*. Mercury dasa left at birth is 17 x 0.32125 = 5.46125 years. Then Ketu dasa is for 7 years, Venus dasa is for 20 years and so on.

In the same example, the 8th star from Moon's star is Krittika owned by Sun. Using the 8th star to start Vimsottari dasa, we get the dasa sequence as — Sun, Moon, Mars, Rahu ect. Sun dasa left at birth is 6 × 0.32125 = 1.9275 years. Then Moon dasa is for 10 years, Mars dasa is for 7 years and so on.

16.4.2 *Dasa from Lagna*

Some authorities have also recommended Vimsottari dasa from the longitude of lagna instead of Moon. In practice, this will give better results only when lagna is considerably more powerful than Moon.

16.5 Using Vimsottari Dasa

16.5.1 *General Principles*

Vimsottari dasa is a very general phalita dasa that can also be used as an ayur dasa. All kinds of general results can be seen from it. A planet gives the results promised by its positions in various divisional charts. Here are just a few examples:

(1) Period of the 5th lord in D-7 can give a child.

(2) Period of the 8th lord in rasi chart can give some troubles and frustration.

(3) Period of a planet exalted in GL in D-10 can give power and authority in career.

(4) Period of an exalted planet in the 12th from AK in D-9 can give serious thoughts related to spiritual liberation.

(5) Period of the 7th lord in D-9 can give marriage.

(6) Period of a planet with Rahu in the 9th in D-4 can give foreign residence.

(7) Period of an exalted planet aspecting HL from the 11th from AL in rasi chart can give a lot of wealth.

(8) Period of a planet joined by Moon and Saturn in the 8th house in D-30 may give serious psychological problems and suicidal tendencies.

(9) Period of a well-disposed planet aspecting A3 in D-10 may make one write some books.

These are just a few examples. One should look at various divisional charts and figure out the results indicated by different planets. Each planet gives the results indicated by it in its dasas and antardasas. When analyzing antardasas, we can take the dasa lord as a temporary lagna and analyze the charts.

16.5.2 Using Dasa Variations

If the sign containing the 5th star from Moon is stronger than the sign containing Moon, Vimsottari dasa started from utpanna star may be preferred for general results. If the 5th star spans across 2 signs, take the sign containing the same quarter as occupied by Moon in birthstar. If Moon is in Makha 3rd pada (quarter), for example, 5th star is Chitra and it starts in Virgo and ends in Libra. So we should take the 3rd quarter of Chitra and we then get Libra. So Leo's strength should be compared to Libra's.

How do we know which sign is stronger? There are no clear guidelines in the literature to compare the strengths. A sign aspected by Jupiter and occupied by more planets may be taken to be stronger. We can also use known events to see which dasa is working better.

Vimsottari dasa started from the 4th and 8th stars is used mainly for the purposes of longevity determination. Look at the signs containing Moon and these 2 stars and find the strongest sign. Here a sign aspected by marakas and malefics becomes stronger. Start Vimsottari dasa from the star in the strongest of these 3 signs and use it in longevity analysis. If Moon is in Makha 3rd pada in Leo, 4th and 8th stars are Hasta (Virgo) and Anuradha (Scorpio). We should compare the strengths of Leo, Virgo and Scorpio.

16.5.3 *Rath's "Tripod of Life" Principle*

Sun, Moon and lagna form the "tripod of life". Parasara clearly said that we should analyze all charts with respect to the positions of Sun, Moon and lagna. He advised drawing Sudarsana chakra with the innermost chakra representing the houses with respect to lagna (body), next chakra representing the houses with respect to Moon (mind) and the outermost chakra representing the houses with respect to Sun (soul).

The results experienced due to soul (Sun) last long and change slowly. The results experienced due to mind (Moon) last shorter and change fast. The results experienced due to body (lagna) change even faster.

Sun is an important reference point in rasi and divisional charts when judging the results of a mahadasa. Moon is an important reference point when judging the results of an antardasa. Lagna is an important reference point when judging the results of a pratyantardasa.

If a planet takes part in a Ravi yoga (solar combination), it gives the results of the yoga in its mahadasa. If a planet takes part in a Chandra Yoga (lunar combination), it gives the results of the yoga in its antardasas. If a planet takes part in other yogas (*e.g.* a Raja Yoga), it gives the results of the yoga primarily in its pratyantardasas.

In addition, dasa lord can be taken as a reference point when interpreting antardasas.

16.6 Practical Examples

16.6.1 *As A Phalita Dasa*

Example 52: Consider the dasamsa chart of Pandit Sanjay Rath, a Vedic astrology author and founder of Sri Jagannath Vedic Centre (see Chart 17). Dasamsa shows one's achievements in society.

Chart 17

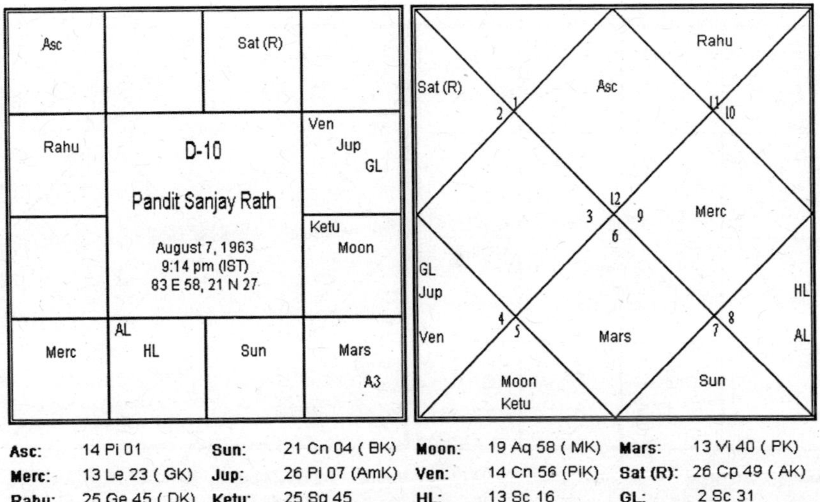

Just a few days of Rahu dasa were left at birth. Mercury dasa has been running since 1998. During Mercury dasa, he published a brilliant book "Crux of Vedic Astrology – Timing of Events" and he is writing more books. Why did Mercury give book writing?

Dasamsa shows achievements in society and A3 (arudha pada of 3rd house) shows the books authored by one. A3 is in Vi here. It has argalas from the 11th from it by Venus and Jupiter and that shows saattwik and brilliant traditional knowledge as the catalyst bringing gains in his book-writing. Mercury is the significator of writing and communication and he has argala on A3 from the 4th from it. This shows that good communication skills and scholarship (Mercury) are the basic driving factor in his book-writing.

In addition to containing A3, Virgo is the 3rd from GL. GL stands for power, authority and fame. The 3rd house from GL stands for fame as a communicator. Mercury owns and aspects it. In rasi chart, Mercury gives Vesi yoga being in the 2nd from Sun. So his dasa should bring the results of Vesi yoga.

Chart 18

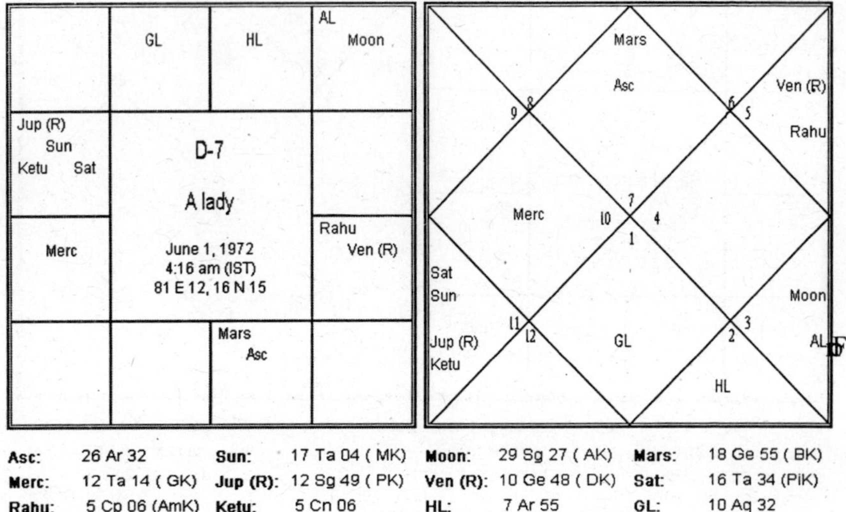

Asc:	26 Ar 32	**Sun:**	17 Ta 04 (MK)	**Moon:**	29 Sg 27 (AK)	**Mars:**	18 Ge 55 (BK)
Merc:	12 Ta 14 (GK)	**Jup (R):**	12 Sg 49 (PK)	**Ven (R):**	10 Ge 48 (DK)	**Sat:**	16 Ta 34 (PiK)
Rahu:	5 Cp 06 (AmK)	**Ketu:**	5 Cn 06	**HL:**	7 Ar 55	**GL:**	10 Aq 32

all these reasons, Mercury dasa can bring him book-writing activities and the fame that goes with it. He will author many more excellent books.

Example 53: Let us consider the D-7 chart of a lady who had her first child in November 1994 and second child in December 1996 (see Chart 18).

Moon is in Sun's constellation. First dasa belongs to Sun. About 1 year and 3 months of Sun dasa was over before birth and the remainder of Sun dasa at birth was about 4 years and 9 months. Rahu dasa started at the end of 1993. This dasa gave her children. Let us explain why Rahu gave children.

D-7 chart shows progeny. The 5th house shows children and it is in Aq here. It is owned by Saturn and Rahu. If one of the owners occupies the sign, the other owner acts as the main owner, according to Parasara. Saturn is in Aq. So Rahu acts as the 5th lord in this chart. He is in the 11th house of gains, with lagna lord Venus. His conjunction with Venus – conjunction of 1st and 5th lords – consists of a raja yoga in the house of gains. For these reasons, Rahu can give the happiness of getting a child. Antardasas at the time of childbirth belonged to Rahu and Jupiter. Jupiter is the naisargika and chara puttra karaka and he is in the 5th house here.

Rahu is the primary 5th lord here. But, after all, Saturn also owns 5th and moreover he occupies 5th with Jupiter. He is the strongest planet in 5th. Hence pratyantardasa at the time of both the childbirths belonged to Saturn.

Pratyantardasa running at the time of an event usually belongs to the most important planet influencing the house of interest in the divisional chart of interest.

Example 54: Let us consider the rasi chart of Sri Navin Patnaik (see Chart 19). He was elected as the Chief Minister of India's Orissa state in early 2000.

First dasa is of Mars and Mercury dasa started in July 1999. Mercury antardasa in Mercury mahadasa was running when he became Orissa's CM.

Mercury is in Libra. Rajya saham and GL are also in Libra. So Mercury has the potential to bring kingdom.

From AL, Mercury is in the 6th house. Upachayas from AL bring gains in status and a planet in the 6th from AL can bring an improvement in status.

Let us apply Rath's "tripod of life" principle. Sun is in Vi. We should judge mahadasa from Sun. Where is Mercury with respect to Sun? Mercury is Sun's dispositor and he is in the 2nd from Sun. This results in a powerful Vesi yoga.

Chart 19

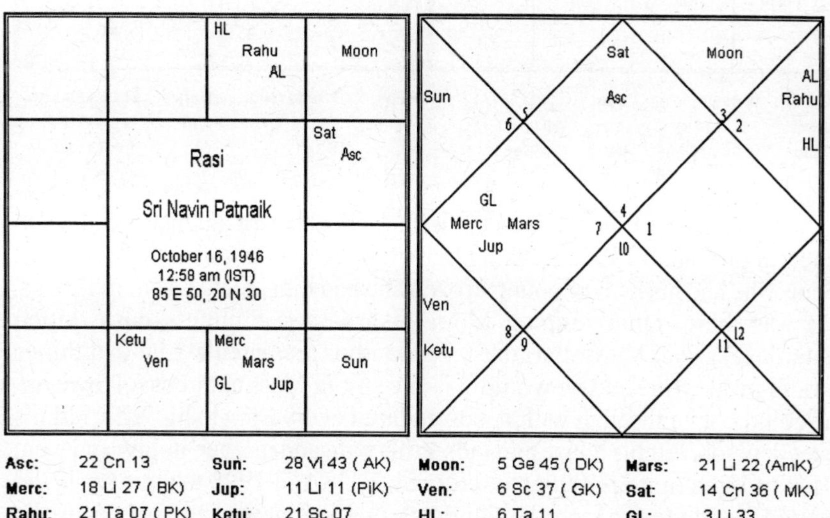

Asc:	22 Cn 13	**Sun:**	28 Vi 43 (AK)	**Moon:**	5 Ge 45 (DK)	**Mars:**	21 Li 22 (AmK)
Merc:	18 Li 27 (BK)	**Jup:**	11 Li 11 (PiK)	**Ven:**	6 Sc 37 (GK)	**Sat:**	14 Cn 36 (MK)
Rahu:	21 Ta 07 (PK)	**Ketu:**	21 Sc 07	**HL:**	6 Ta 11	**GL:**	3 Li 33

Even taking Moon as the reference, Mercury is 1st lord and he is in a trine. So he is favorably placed from Moon also. For this reason, Mercury's antardasa is a good antardasa and there was success in the very first AD of Mercury MD.

Of course, Mercury is a functional benefic in dasamsa, aspects GL and occupies rajya pada (A10) in a quadrant from lagna. These factors also contributed to success in Mercury dasa.

Example 55: Let us consider the rasi chart of an engineer who came from India to USA (see Chart 20). He studied at a reputed institution in India and had a good job at a big company in USA. He had a wife and two children.

Chart 20

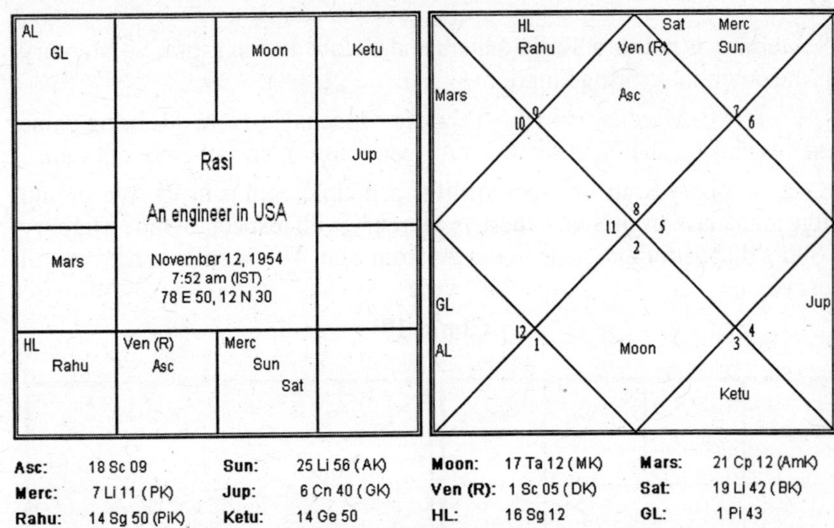

Asc:	18 Sc 09	**Sun:**	25 Li 56 (AK)	**Moon:**	17 Ta 12 (MK)	**Mars:**	21 Cp 12 (AmK)
Merc:	7 Li 11 (PK)	**Jup:**	6 Cn 40 (GK)	**Ven (R):**	1 Sc 05 (DK)	**Sat:**	19 Li 42 (BK)
Rahu:	14 Sg 50 (PiK)	**Ketu:**	14 Ge 50	**HL:**	16 Sg 12	**GL:**	1 Pi 43

He had a cruel shock when his wife filed a lawsuit against him in a US court at the end of 1995, accusing him of many wrong things that he hadn't done. She had his bank accounts frozen and had him evicted from his house. He was then running Jupiter-Moon antardasa (*i.e.* Jupiter dasa, Moon antardasa) as per Vimsottari dasa. This author predicted to him that things would just be fine and he would win the suit in Mars antardasa. However, he could not go through with it, surrendered everything to his wife, left his excellent job, left his house and kids to his wife and mother-in-law and went back to India in mid-1996. He returned to USA in 1998 to start fresh and started searching for a job. This author's prediction went wrong because he blindly used Vimsottari dasa started from Moon's star.

Why did Jupiter-Moon antardasa bring such a catastrophe? Why was his life turned upside down? Jupiter is an exalted functional benefic in a trine. Moon is an exalted functional benefic in a quadrant. Of course, we can give vague reasons to justify almost anything, but that's not the right approach. If we use the right variation of the dasa, we don't have to bend backwards or beat around the bush to explain events.

Let us consider utpanna star. Moon is in Rohini. The 5th star Pushyami is in Cancer and exalted Jupiter occupies it. Occupied by an exalted planet and owned by another exalted planet, Cancer is very strong. It is a tough call in this case, but dasas started from Pushyami explain the events better than dasas started from Rohini.

First dasa belongs to Saturn. Venus dasa of 20 years runs from February 1987 to October 2006. Venus is lagna lord and he gives Vesi yoga being in the 2nd from Sun. So his dasa is good. However, being the 8th lord from AL, he can also give a fall in status.

Rahu's antardasa runs during 1994-1997. As per Rath's "tripod of life" principle, we should give importance to Rahu's position from Moon. Rahu is in the 8th house from Moon and his antardasa is unfavorable. It can bring unexpected troubles and frustration. Debilitated Rahu's rasi aspect on AL can also cast a shadow on one's image and affect one's status.

Ketu's pratyantardasa ran during December 1995-February 1996 when a lot of this drama unfolded and he was evicted from house with his accounts frozen. That shook him up. We should give importance to lagna when judging pratyantardasas. Ketu is lagna lord in the 8th house. Again it is a bad period.

Sun's pratyantardasa was running when he went back to India, leaving everything he had behind – including his job at a big company. Sun is the 10th lord and he is debilitated in the 12th house, afflicted by Saturn and 8th lord. Moreover Sun is in the 8th house from AL and that adds to the indications of a fall in status. So Sun's pratyantardasa can bring losses and fall in status. During this pratyantardasa, he gave up everything he had and went back to India.

Jupiter is the 8th and 11th lord from Moon. He is in the 3rd from Moon. Jupiter in 3rd gives a positive spirit. Jupiter antardasa can inject some energy into his nearly destroyed life. He came back to US in Jupiter antardasa. Saturn is an exalted yogakaraka from Moon and his antardasa should bring gains again.

16.6.2 *As An Ayur Dasa*

We have so far seen examples of Vimsottari dasa used as a phalita dasa. We will now see its use as an ayur dasa.

Example 56: We will consider John F. Kennedy, Jr's rasi chart (see Chart 21). He passed away on the night of July 16, 1999.

Parasara mentioned that the 3rd and 8th houses are the houses of life and the 2nd and 7th houses are the houses of death. He said that the 2nd house is particularly a maraka (killer) house. Lords and occupants of these houses can kill a native.

Chart 21

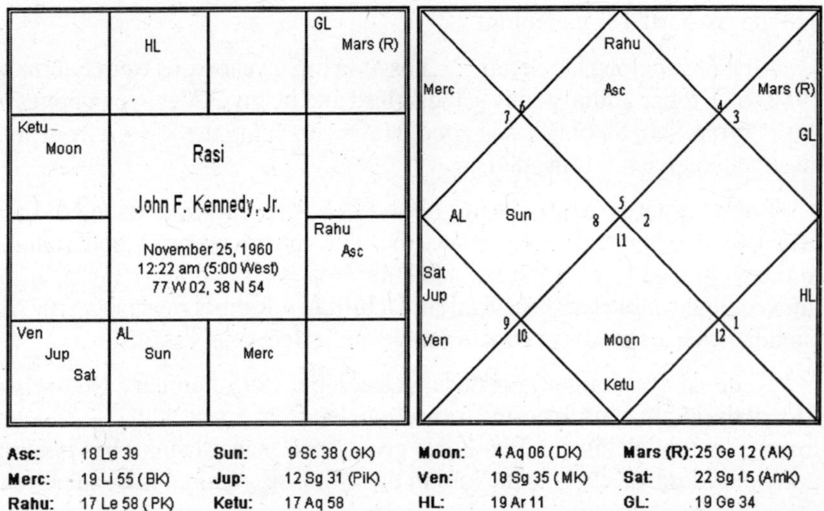

Here the 2nd house is Virgo. Its lord Mercury is in mrityu bhaga in the 3rd house. He is a strong maraka. Saturn is the 7th lord. He is also Maheswara, being the 8th lord from AK Mars. He joins Jupiter, who is Rudra. Saturn is also a strong maraka. Mr. Kennedy was running Saturn-Mercury antardasa when he passed away.

Example 57: Let us consider the rasi chart of a lady who committed suicide on April 6, 1988 (see Chart 22).

Jupiter is the 7th lord here and he is exalted. He is a very strong maraka. Venus is 2nd lord in 2nd and he can kill too.

Moon is in the 1st quarter of Bharani constellation. The 4th constellation is Mrigasira. Because the 1st quarter of Mrigasira is in Taurus, we should take Taurus as the sign of 4th star. The 8th star is Aasresha in Cancer. Cancer contains 7th lord Jupiter, a maraka. However, it is not aspected by 2nd lord. Taurus, on the other hand, has the rasi aspect of both Jupiter and Venus. Aspect of marakas makes a sign stronger. So start dasas from the 4th star.

Chart 22

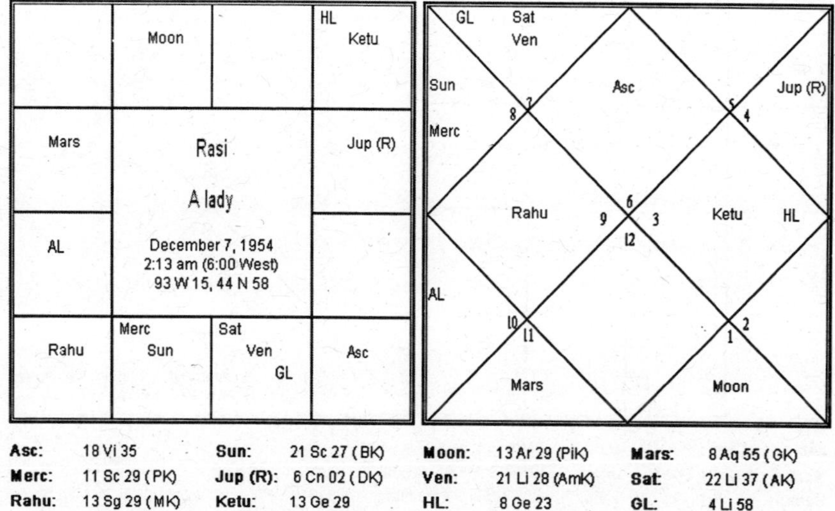

First dasa belongs to Mars and Jupiter-Venus antardasa was running at death. Both the planets are marakas.

Example 58: Let us consider the rasi chart of great astrologer Dr. B.V. Raman (see Chart 23). He passed away on 20th December 1998, leaving a void in the astrological community.

As per Vimsottari dasa reckoned from Moon's star, he passed away in Venus-Sun antardasa. Venus is a maraka being in the 7th house, but he is not a very strong maraka. Though Sun owns 7th, he is in 6th, *i.e.* in the 12th from 7th and the 11th from 8th. The likelihood of Sun killing the native is small.

Who are the strongest marakas in this chart? Certainly, Mercury is the strongest maraka. He owns 8th and occupies 7th. Malefics in the 2nd house are strong marakas. So Rahu in the 2nd is also a maraka. Mars is also a maraka, being the 3rd lord in 7th.

Let us consider the variations of Vimsottari dasa based on 4th and 8th stars. The 4th star is Pushyami in Cancer. The 8th star is Uttaraphalguni and its 1st quarter is in Leo. Because Leo is the strongest sign, we can start dasas from Sun who owns Uttaraphalguni (8th star from Moon's star).

Starting Vimsottari dasa from the 8th star, we can see that Mercury-Rahu antardasa was running in December 1998. Killership of both the planets has already been addressed.

Chart 23

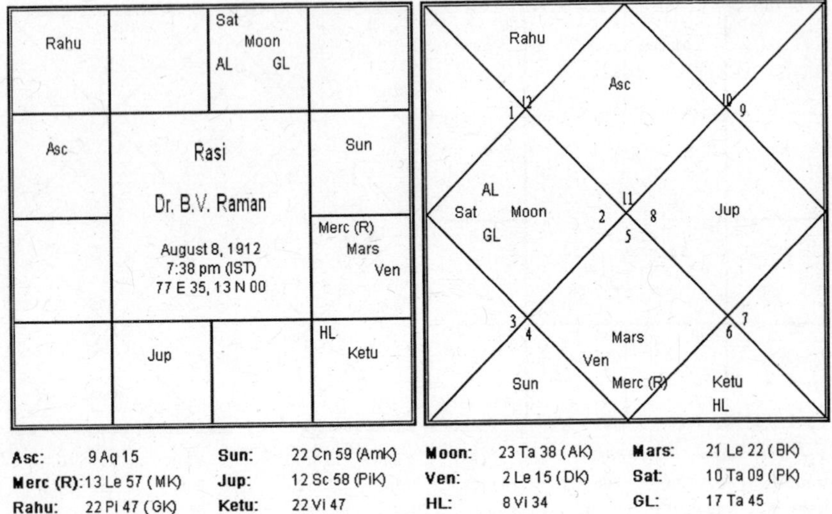

16.7 Conclusion

In this chapter, Vimsottari dasa and its variations are explained and their use is demonstrated. Use of Vimsottari dasa as a phalita dasa as well as an ayur dasa is demonstrated. As this is the most common constellation-based dasa system, readers should master its use through practical experience.

Though many people limit themselves to Vimsottari dasa started from the birthstar, one is advised to use the variations mentioned in this chapter for the best results.

If all the quadrants from the stronger of lagna and Moon are occupied by planets, "Kendradi Graha Dasa" is more appropriate than Vimsottari dasa. Results from Vimsottari dasa may not be very good in such cases.

In addition, it should be noted that the error in the start/end dates of dasas have an error of approximately $m.n/4$ days, if there is an error of m minutes in birthtime and the complete duration of the first dasa is n years.

For example, if the first dasa belongs to Venus, then $n = 20$. So an error of 5 minutes in the birthtime results in an error of 5x20/4 = 25 days in dasas (this is approximate). Considering this, we cannot use low level sub-periods of Vimsottari dasa (like sookshma dasas) confidently, unless we rectify the birthtime.

It is a good idea to allow a margin of error when we examine the dates on which dasas start and end.

17. Ashtottari Dasa

17.1 Introduction

Ashtottari dasa is perhaps the most popular dasa system in India after Vimsottari dasa. Sage Parasara listed it as a conditional dasa applicable only in some charts. The conditions for its applicability are highly controversial.

In this system, the sum of all dasas is 108 years. Ashtottari means "ashtottara sata", *i.e.* one hundred and eight. Because poornaayush (full life) of a man is 108 years, some scholars have suggested that ashtottari dasa is best used as an ayur dasa, *i.e.* a dasa that shows longevity.

Some other scholars suggest that Ashtottari dasa can be used as a phalita dasa. Because only chara karakas, *i.e.* Rahu and the seven planets, have dasas under the Ashtottari dasa scheme, it may also be suggested that it shows events related to sustenance, achievements, raja yogas and moksha (just like chara karakas do). Some people, however, prefer to see all matters in Ashtottari dasa.

17.2 Computation

17.2.1 *Dasas*

Order of dasas and the length of dasas is as shown in Table 39. Each planet covers an arc of either 53°20' (4 nakshatras) or 40°0' (3 nakshatras) in the zodiac, as shown in that table.

We note natal Moon's longitude and see which of the eight arcs it belongs to. The planet ruling the arc will rule the first dasa. The fraction of the arc that is yet to be traversed by natal Moon is calculated and the same fraction of the dasa length of the first dasa lord is left at birth. After that, dasas will come in the order shown in the table and the length of a planet's dasa is the full dasa length given in the table. After Venus, we come back to Sun at the beginning of the table.

Table 39: Ashtottari Dasa Table

No.	Nakshatra	Arc covered by planet	Arc length	Planet	Dasa Length
1	Aardra Punarvasu Pushyami Aasresha	66°40' – 120°0'	53°20'	Sun	6 years
2	Makha P.Phalguni U.Phalguni	120°0' – 160°0'	40°0'	Moon	15 years
3	Hasta Chitra Swaati Visaakha	160°0' – 213°20'	53°20'	Mars	8 years
4	Anooradha Jyeshtha Moola	213°20' – 253°20'	40°0'	Mercury	17 years
5	P.Ashadha U.Ashadha Sravanam	253°20' – 293°20'	40°0'	Saturn	10 years
6	Dhanishtha Satabhisha P.Bhadra	293°20' – 333°20'	40°0'	Jupiter	19 years
7	U.Bhadra Revati Aswini Bharani	333°20' – 386°40' (333°20' – 26°40')	53°20'	Rahu	12 years
8	Krittika Rohini Mrigasira	26°40' – 66°40'	40°0'	Venus	21 years

Example 59: Suppose Moon is at 24° in Leo. That is equivalent to 24°0' + 120°0' = 144°0'. We see that 144° is between 120°0' and 160°0'. So it is in the 2nd arc of Table 39, which is ruled by Moon. The full dasa length is 15 years. Here we have to find the fraction of the arc that is yet to be traversed. The arc starts at 120°0' and ends at 160°0'. So the part of the arc that is yet to be traversed by Moon is (160°0' – 144°0') = 16°. As a fraction of the arc length (40°), this is 16°/40° = 0.4. The same fraction of the full dasa length of Moon is 15 x 0.4 = 6 years. The native will run Moon dasa of 6 years from his birth. Then 8 years of Mars dasa will run. Then 17 years of Mercury dasa will run. Then 10 years of Saturn dasa will run. And so on.

NOTE: One has to be careful with the calculation if the first dasa is Rahu dasa. The arc ruled by Rahu starts at 333°20' and ends at 26°40'. The ending longitude 26°40' is equivalent to 386°40' and we should use either 26°40' or 386°40' based on Moon's longitude. For example, if Moon is at 10° in Aries, then the part of the arc that is yet to be traversed is 26°40' – 10° = 16°40'. If Moon is at 20° in Pisces, *i.e.* at 350°, then the part of the arc that is yet to be traversed is 386°40' – 350° = 36°40'.

17.2.2 *Antardasas*

The first antardasa belongs to the planet that comes in the table *after* the dasa lord. Then antardasas go in the same order as dasas and the last antardasa belongs to dasa lord. For example, antardasas in Jupiter dasa go as: Rahu, Venus, Sun, Moon, Mars, Mercury, Saturn and Jupiter. Antardasas in Moon dasa go as: Mars, Mercury, Saturn, Jupiter, Rahu, Venus, Sun and Moon.

The length of a dasa is divided into eight antardasas in the ratio of the dasa lengths. For example, Sun dasa is of 6 years. Moon antardasa in Sun dasa is of 6 x 15/108 = 0.8333 year = 10 months. Mars antardasa in Sun dasa is of 6 x 8/108 = 0.4444 year = 5 months 10 days. Mercury antardasa in Sun dasa is of 6 x 17/108 = 0.9444 years = 11 months 10 days. And so on.

17.2.3 *Application*

There are three different views on the applicability of Ashtottari dasa:

(1) Ashtottari dasa is applicable in all charts.

(2) Ashtottari dasa is applicable if Rahu, who is not in lagna, is in a quadrant or a trine from lagna lord.

(3) Ashtottari dasa is applicable for daytime births in Krishna paksha (darker fortnight) and night time births in Sukla paksha (brighter fortnight).

Some people use Ashtottari dasa as an ayur dasa and see longevity in it. Some other people use Ashtottari dasa as a phalita dasa. Because only chara karakas, *i.e.* Rahu and the seven planets, have dasas under the Ashtottari dasa scheme, it may also be suggested that it shows events related to sustenance, achievements, raja yogas and moksha (just like chara karakas do). Some people, however, prefer to see all matters in Ashtottari dasa.

17.3 Examples

Example 60: We saw the chart of great astrologer Dr. B.V. Raman in Example 58. We noted that his sad demise on 20th December 1998 makes better sense with Vimsottari dasa started from the 8th nakshatra from Moon's nakshatra than Vimsottari dasa started from Moon's nakshatra. As per the former, he passed away in Mercury-Rahu antardasa. Mercury is the 8th lord in the 7th house of death and Rahu is a malefic in the 2nd house of death.

One may compute Ashtottari dasa for the birthdata given in Chart 23 and find that Rahu-Mercury antardasa was running at the time of his death. For reasons already explained, Rahu and Mercury are the strongest marakas in this chart. It is significant that the same planets gave death in both dasas.

Example 61: Let us consider the assassination of Indira Gandhi. Her birthdata and assassination data are given in Example 110 (in a later chapter). Her rasi chart is given in Chart 61.

One may calculate Ashtottari dasa for her and find that Moon dasa ran from 1980-1995. Saturn antardasa was running at the time of her assassination.

Saturn is the 7th lord in lagna and Moon is in the 7th house. They are the only planets strongly associated with the 7th house of death. They can give death.

Example 62: Let us consider Sri P.V. Narasimha Rao's rasi chart given in Chart 6. He held important ministerial berths in Indian government during 1980-1989 and he was India's Prime Minister during 1991-1996.

If one calculates his Ashtottari dasa, one will find that Mercury dasa ran during 1981-1997. Mercury is lagna lord and he occupies an own sign. He is in the the 7th house from AL and GL and certainly promises power. The planet bringing a link between lagna and GL by way of aspect, ownership and occupancy brings power. Mercury is lagna lord and he has a rasi aspect on both lagna and GL. He can give power.

Moreover, Sri Rao's chart has a powerful Vipareeta Raja yoga (VRY) between 3rd and 8th lord Mars and 12th lord Sun, who are within a 17' from each other. If the planets involved in VRY have a conjunction or rasi aspect with lagna lord, then VRY can give permanent results and the power is transferred to lagna lord. Here Mercury is the dispositor of Mars and Sun and joins them in his own rasi. He has 7 rekhas in BAV and his rasi Gemini has 34 rekhas in SAV. Mercury is in Uttamamsa. For all these reasons, Mercury is a great yoga karaka. So his dasa (1981-1997) was excellent for Sri Rao.

17.4 Conclusion

Ashtottari dasa is a popular dasa, but its applicability as well as application are controversial. Readers should keep this in mind and keep their minds open to alternative views. What is taught in this book is not the final truth. Of course, this applies to everything taught in this book, but it is especially applicable to this chapter.

18. Narayana Dasa

18.1 Introduction

Narayana dasa is a very important rasi dasa. It is a phalita dasa. It shows general results. Narayana dasa is computed differently for different divisional charts and we can use Narayana dasa of a divisional chart to predict matters related to that divisional chart.

Narayana dasa is based on the progression of lagna in one's life. As one dasa ends and another starts, one rasi stops being the progressed lagna and another rasi becomes one's progressed lagna. Using the progressed lagna as the reference, we find out the events that happen in that dasa. Thus we get twelve charts for each person, with each chart applicable in one dasa.

This is a very versatile dasa system and readers sould pay attention to the details of calculation.

18.2 Computation

18.2.1 *Dasa Progression*

Dasas start from lagna or the 7th house, whichever is stronger. We use the rules of strength explained in the chapter "Strength of Planets and Rasis". Let us denote the stronger of lagna and 7th house by the expression "dasa seed".

Movable signs are governed by Brahma. Fixed signs are governed by Shiva. Dual signs are govenred by Vishnu.[54] Brahma is associated with the regular movement of 1st, 2nd, 3rd etc. Vishnu is associated with the trinal movement, *i.e.* 1st, 5th, 9th, then 10th, 2nd, 6th and so on. We cover the trines from dasa seed first, go to another quadrant and cover its trines and so on. Shiva, on the other hand, is associated with the 6th movment. We take dasa seed, 6th from there, 6th from there and so on.

The direction of reckoning these houses is based on the 9th house from dasa seed. If the 9th house from dasa seed is an odd-footed sign (Ar, Ta, Ge and Li, Sc, Sg), the direction is forward. If the 9th house from dasa seed is an even-footed sign (Cn, Le, Vi and Cp, Aq, Pi), the direction is backward.

Example 63: Suppose someone has lagna in Ta. Suppose Sc is stronger than Ta. Let us find the dasa progression.

---

54 Brahma is the God of creation. Vishnu is the God of sustenance. Shiva is the God of destruction. Brahma, Vishnu and Shiva are together known as "Trimurthis" (the "Trinity of Gods").

Because the 7th house is stronger than lagna, it becomes the dasa seed. So the dasa seed is Sc. Because it is a fixed sign, we use every 6th progression governed by Shiva. The 9th house from Sc is Cn. It is an even-footed sign. So the overall direction is backward. So we should count houses in the backward direction. The 6th house from Sc, counted backwards, is Ge. The 6th therefrom is Cp. We count the 6th house from every rasi in the backward direction and get the complete dasa sequence as:

Sc, Ge, Cp, Le, Pi, Li, Ta, Sg, Cn, Aq, Vi and Ar

This is the order of dasas for the native.

Example 64: Suppose someone has lagna in Pi. Suppose Pi is stronger than Vi. Let us find the dasa progression.

Because lagna is stronger than the 7th house, it becomes the dasa seed. So the dasa seed is Pi. Because it is a dual sign, we use the trinal progression governed by Vishnu. The 9th house from Pi is Sc. It is an odd-footed sign. So the overall direction is forward. So we should count houses in the forward direction. We count the 1st, 5th, 9th houses from dasa seed, then count the same houses from the 10th house, then from the 7th house and finally from the 4th house. Trines from Pi are Pi, Cn and Sc. Trines from the 10th (Sg) are Sg, Ar and Le. We get the complete dasa sequence as:

Pi, Cn, Sc, Sg, Ar, Le, Vi, Cp, Ta, Ge, Li and Aq.

This is the order of dasas for the native.

Example 65: Suppose someone has lagna in Cn. Suppose Cp is stronger than Cn. Let us find the dasa progression.

Because the 7th house is stronger than lagna, it becomes the dasa seed. So the dasa seed is Cp. Because it is a movable sign, we use the regular (1st, 2nd, 3rd) progression governed by Brahma. The 9th house from Cp is Vi. It is an even-footed sign. So the overall direction is backward. So we should count houses in the backward direction. We count the 1st, 2nd, 3rd *etc* houses from dasa seed backwards. We get the complete dasa sequence as:

Cp, Sg, Sc, Li, Vi, Le, Cn, Ge, Ta, Ar, Pi and Aq.

This is the order of dasas for the native.

Saturn exception:

If Saturn occupies dasa seed, dasa progression becomes regular and zodiacal. If Sc is dasa seed and it contains Saturn, dasa progression becomes Sc, Sg, Cp, Aq, Pi, Ar *etc*. If Pi is dasa seed and it contains Saturn, dasa progression becomes Pi, Ar, Ta, Ge, Cn, Le *etc*. We basically make the direction "forward" and use Brahma's progression.

Ketu exception:

If Ketu occupies dasa seed, the basic direction of dasa progression becomes reversed. If it is normally forward, it becomes backward. If it is normally backward, it becomes forward. If Sc is dasa seed and it contains Ketu, dasa progression becomes Sc, Ar, Vi, Aq, Cn, Sg etc (comparing this with Example 63, readers may note that the 6th house is counted in the forward direction instead of the backward direction). If Pi is dasa seed and it contains Ketu, dasa progression becomes Pi, Sc, Cn, Ge, Aq, Li etc (comparing this with Example 64, readers may note that the 5th, 9th, 10th etc house etc are counted in the backward direction instead of the forward direction.).

Dasa progressions for various dasa seeds are given in Table 40. Three cases are covered for each dasa seed — (*a*) the normal case, (*b*) with Saturn exception, and, (*c*) with Ketu exception.

Table 40: Dasa Progression in Narayana Dasa

	Dasa seed	**Dasa Progression**
Ar	(*a*) *Normal*:	Ar, Ta, Ge, Cn, Le, Vi, Li, Sc, Sg, Cp, Aq, Pi
	(*b*) *Saturn*:	Ar, Ta, Ge, Cn, Le, Vi, Li, Sc, Sg, Cp, Aq, Pi
	(*c*) *Ketu*:	Ar, Pi, Aq, Cp, Sg, Sc, Li, Vi, Le, Cn, Ge, Ta
Ta	(*a*) *Normal*:	Ta, Sg, Cn, Aq, Vi, Ar, Sc, Ge, Cp, Le, Pi, Li
	(*b*) *Saturn*:	Ta, Ge, Cn, Le, Vi, Li, Sc, Sg, Cp, Aq, Pi, Ar
	(*c*) *Ketu*:	Ta, Li, Pi, Le, Cp, Ge, Sc, Ar, Vi, Aq, Cn, Sg
Ge	(*a*) *Normal*:	Ge, Aq, Li, Vi, Ta, Cp, Sg, Le, Ar, Pi, Sc, Cn
	(*b*) *Saturn*:	Ge, Cn, Le, Vi, Li, Sc, Sg, Cp, Aq, Pi, Ar, Ta
	(*c*) *Ketu*:	Ge, Li, Aq, Pi, Cn, Sc, Sg, Ar, Le, Vi, Cp, Ta
Cn	(*a*) *Normal*:	Cn, Ge, Ta, Ar, Pi, Aq, Cp, Sg, Sc, Li, Vi, Le
	(*b*) *Saturn*:	Cn, Le, Vi, Li, Sc, Sg, Cp, Aq, Pi, Ar, Ta, Ge
	(*c*) *Ketu*:	Cn, Le, Vi, Li, Sc, Sg, Cp, Aq, Pi, Ar, Ta, Ge
Le	(*a*) *Normal*:	Le, Cp, Ge, Sc, Ar, Vi, Aq, Cn, Sg, Ta, Li, Pi
	(*b*) *Saturn*:	Le, Vi, Li, Sc, Sg, Cp, Aq, Pi, Ar, Ta, Ge, Cn
	(*c*) *Ketu*:	Le, Pi, Li, Ta, Sg, Cn, Aq, Vi, Ar, Sc, Ge, Cp
Vi	(*a*) *Normal*:	Vi, Cp, Ta, Ge, Li, Aq, Pi, Cn, Sc, Sg, Ar, Le
	(*b*) *Saturn*:	Vi, Li, Sc, Sg, Cp, Aq, Pi, Ar, Ta, Ge, Cn, Le
	(*c*) *Ketu*:	Vi, Ta, Cp, Sg, Le, Ar, Pi, Sc, Cn, Ge, Aq, Li

	Dasa seed	Dasa Progression
Li	(*a*) *Normal*: (*b*) *Saturn*: (*c*) *Ketu*:	Li, Sc, Sg, Cp, Aq, Pi, Ar, Ta, Ge, Cn, Le, Vi Li, Sc, Sg, Cp, Aq, Pi, Ar, Ta, Ge, Cn, Le, Vi Li, Vi, Le, Cn, Ge, Ta, Ar, Pi, Aq, Cp, Sg, Sc
Sc	(*a*) *Normal*: (*b*) *Saturn*: (*c*) *Ketu*:	Sc, Ge, Cp, Le, Pi, Li, Ta, Sg, Cn, Aq, Vi, Ar Sc, Sg, Cp, Aq, Pi, Ar, Ta, Ge, Cn, Le, Vi, Li Sc, Ar, Vi, Aq, Cn, Sg, Ta, Li, Pi, Le, Cp, Ge
Sg	(*a*) *Normal*: (*b*) *Saturn*: (*c*) *Ketu*:	Sg, Le, Ar, Pi, Sc, Cn, Ge, Aq, Li, Vi, Ta, Cp Sg, Cp, Aq, Pi, Ar, Ta, Ge, Cn, Le, Vi, Li, Sc Sg, Ar, Le, Vi, Cp, Ta, Ge, Li, Aq, Pi, Cn, Sc
Cp	(*a*) *Normal*: (*b*) *Saturn*: (*c*) *Ketu*:	Cp, Sg, Sc, Li, Vi, Le, Cn, Ge, Ta, Ar, Pi, Aq Cp, Aq, Pi, Ar, Ta, Ge, Cn, Le, Vi, Li, Sc, Sg Cp, Aq, Pi, Ar, Ta, Ge, Cn, Le, Vi, Li, Sc, Sg
Aq	(*a*) *Normal*: (*b*) *Saturn*: (*c*) *Ketu*:	Aq, Cn, Sg, Ta, Li, Pi, Le, Cp, Ge, Sc, Ar, Vi Aq, Pi, Ar, Ta, Ge, Cn, Le, Vi, Li, Sc, Sg, Cp Aq, Vi, Ar, Sc, Ge, Cp, Le, Pi, Li, Ta, Sg, Cn
Pi	(*a*) *Normal*: (*b*) *Saturn*: (*c*) *Ketu*:	Pi, Cn, Sc, Sg, Ar, Le, Vi, Cp, Ta, Ge, Li, Aq Pi, Ar, Ta, Ge, Cn, Le, Vi, Li, Sc, Sg, Cp, Aq Pi, Sc, Cn, Ge, Aq, Li, Vi, Ta, Cp, Sg, Le, Ar

We should choose the dasa progression based on dasa seed. If neither Saturn nor Ketu occupies dasa seed, we should use the normal progression. If Saturn occupies dasa seed, we should apply the Saturn exception. If Ketu occupies dasa seed, we should apply the Ketu exception.

18.2.2 *Dasa Length*

The length of a dasa is determined by the position of the lord of dasa rasi with respect to dasa rasi. Counting is forward if dasa rasi is odd-footed. Counting is backward if dasa rasi is even-footed. Count houses from dasa rasi to its lord. Subtract one from the count. That gives dasa length in years.

Exceptions:

(1) If the count of houses from dasa rasi to its lord is one, *i.e.* dasa rasi contains its lord, then we get zero by subtracting one from one. However, dasa length becomes 12 years then.

(2) If the lord of dasa rasi is exalted, add one year to dasa length.

(3) If the lord of dasa rasi is debilitated, subtract one year from dasa length.

Special Notes:

(1) If dasa rasi is Aq or Sc, it has two lords. We should take the stronger lord when computing Narayana dasa.

(2) After dasas of all the rasis are over, the second cycle starts. In the second cycle, dasa lengths of various rasis are obtained by subtracting the dasa length in the first cycle from 12 years.

Example 66: Let us take the rasi chart in Chart 23 and compute Narayana dasa. Because the 7th house (Le) is stronger than lagna (Aq), dasa seed is Le. Because it is a fixed sign, we use the "every 6th" progression governed by Shiva. Because the 9th from Le (Ar) is odd-footed, we count in the forward direction. Neither Saturn nor Ketu occupies Le and the exceptions don't apply. Dasa sequence is — Le, Cp, Ge, Sc, Ar, Vi, Aq, Cn, Sg, Ta, Li, Pi. Let us now find the lengths of various dasas.

Le is an even-footed sign. So we count houses from Le to its lord Sun in the backward direction. Sun is in Cn, *i.e.* the 2nd house from Le in the backward direction. So dasa length is 2–1=1 year. The native was born in August 1912. This dasa runs from Aug 1912 to Aug 1913.

Cp is an even-footed sign. So we count houses from Cp to its lord Saturn in the backward direction. Saturn is in Ta, *i.e.* the 9th house from Cp in the backward direction. So dasa length is 9–1=8 years. This dasa runs from Aug 1913 to Aug 1921.

Ge is an odd-footed sign. So we count houses from Ge to its lord Mercury in the forward direction. Mercury is in Le, *i.e.* the 3rd house from Ge in the forward direction. So dasa length is 3–1=2 years. This dasa runs from Aug 1921 to Aug 1923.

Sc is an odd-footed sign. So we count houses from Sc to its lord Mars in the forward direction. Mars is in Le, *i.e.* the 10th house from Sc in the forward direction. So dasa length is 10–1=9 years. This dasa runs from Aug 1923 to Aug 1932.

Ar is an odd-footed sign. So we count houses from Ar to its lord Mars in the forward direction. Mars is in Le, *i.e.* the 5th house from Ar in the forward direction. So dasa length is 5–1=4 years. This dasa runs from Aug 1932 to Aug 1936.

Vi is an even-footed sign. So we count houses from Vi to its lord Mercury in the backward direction. Mercury is in Le, *i.e.* the 2nd house from Vi in the backward direction. So dasa length is 2–1=1 year. This dasa runs from Aug 1936 to Aug 1937.

Aq is an even-footed sign. So we count houses from Aq to its lord Saturn in the backward direction. Saturn is in Ta, *i.e.* the 10th house from Aq in the backward direction. So dasa length is 10–1=9 years. This dasa runs from Aug 1937 to Aug 1946.

Cn is an even-footed sign. So we count houses from Cn to its lord Moon in the backward direction. Moon is in Ta, *i.e.* the 3rd house from Cn in the backward direction. So dasa length is 3–1=2 years. However, Moon is exalted and we add one year. We get 2+1=3 years. This dasa runs from Aug 1946 to Aug 1949.

Sg is an odd-footed sign. So we count houses from Sg to its lord Jupiter in the forward direction. Jupiter is in Sc, *i.e.* the 12th house from Sg in the forward direction. So dasa length is 12–1=11 years. This dasa runs from Aug 1949 to Aug 1960.

Ta is an odd-footed sign. So we count houses from Ta to its lord Venus in the forward direction. Venus is in Le, *i.e.* the 4th house from Ta in the forward direction. So dasa length is 4–1=3 years. This dasa runs from Aug 1960 to Aug 1963.

Li is an odd-footed sign. So we count houses from Li to its lord Venus in the forward direction. Venus is in Le, *i.e.* the 11th house from Li in the forward direction. So dasa length is 11–1=10 years. This dasa runs from Aug 1963 to Aug 1973.

Pi is an even-footed sign. So we count houses from Pi to its lord Jupiter in the backward direction. Jupiter is in Sc, *i.e.* the 5th house from Pi in the backward direction. So dasa length is 5–1=4 years. This dasa runs from Aug 1973 to Aug 1977.

Thus the first cycle of dasas ends in Aug 1977. The second cycle starts then. Dasas will come in the same order as in the first cycle. Let us compute the second cycle.

Because Le dasa is of 1 year in the 1st cycle, it is 12–1=11 years in the 2nd cycle. This dasa runs from Aug 1977 to Aug 1988.

Because Cp dasa is of 8 years in the 1st cycle, it is 12–8=4 years in the 2nd cycle. This dasa runs from Aug 1988 to Aug 1992.

Because Ge dasa is of 2 years in the 1st cycle, it is 12–2=10 years in the 2nd cycle. This dasa runs from Aug 1992 to Aug 2002.

Exercise 27: Calculate Narayana dasa for the rasi chart given in Chart 21. (*Hints*: Saturn is the stronger lord of Aq and Ketu is the stronger lord of Sc. Aq is stronger than Le.)

18.3 Antardasas

Each dasa is divided into 12 antardasas. All the antardasas have an equal length. If a dasa is of *n* years, then each antardasa in that dasa is for *n* months.

Antardasas start from the rasi containing the lord of dasa rasi or the rasi containing the lord of the 7th house from dasa rasi. Let us denote the stronger of dasa rasi and the 7th from it with the expression "antardasa seed". Antardasas start from the rasi containing the lord of antardasa seed and we take the 1st, 2nd, 3rd, 4th *etc* houses from there. The direction of counting houses is forward or backward based on whether the rasi from which antardasas start is an odd rasi or even rasi. (NOTE: We are talking about odd and even signs here and *not* about odd-footed and even-footed signs).

Example 67: Suppose Cp dasa of 5 years is running. Lords of Cp and Cn are Saturn and Moon respectively. Suppose Saturn is in Le and Moon is in Ta. Antardasas start from either Le or Ta. If Cp is stronger than Cn (or Saturn is much stronger than Moon), then we start from Le. If Cn is stronger than Cp (or Moon is much stronger than Saturn), then we start from Ta. Let us say Cn is stronger than Cp and Saturn is not much stronger than Moon. Then antardasas start from Ta, which contains Moon. Because Ta is an even sign, counting is backward. So antardasas go as — Ta, Ar, Pi, Aq, Cp, Sg, Sc, Li, Vi, Le, Cn and Ge. Each antardasa is of 5 months.

***Exceptions*:** If Saturn occupies antardasa seed rasi, antardasas go in the forward direction. If Ketu occupies antardasa seed rasi, antardasa direction is reversed (from forward to backward or from backward to forward). In the above example, antardasa sequence becomes Ta, Ge, Cn, Le, Vi, Li, Sc, Sg, Cp, Aq and Pi, if Ketu occupies Cn.

18.4 Interpretation

Narayana dasa gives the progression of lagna in life. During the dasa of a rasi, that rasi acts as lagna. If dasas are started from the 7th house from lagna, then Narayana dasa gives the progression of the 7th house. So the 7th from dasa rasi gives the progressed lagna, *i.e.* the rasi that acts as lagna during the dasa.

Treat the dasa rasi or the 7th from it – based on whether dasas start from lagna or the 7th house – as lagna and analyze the chart, to see fortune in a dasa. We will denote it with "dasa lagna". We will denote the rasi containing the lord of dasa lagna with "paaka rasi".

Just as the strength of lagna lord is very important in a natal chart, strength of the lord of dasa lagna is the key to interpreting a dasa. In addition, a lot of principles were mentioned by Parasara:

Natural malefics in the 3rd and 6th from dasa lagna give success in ventures. Natural benefics in those houses give failures. Natural benefics in trines and 8th from dasa lagna give happiness and success. Natural malefics in those houses give failures, obstructions and unhappiness. Situation of a planet – benefic or a malefic – in the 11th house ensures gains. Rahu in the 8th and 12th houses from dasa lagna gives constant fear. If the lord of dasa lagna or the lord of a trine or a quadrant from it is exalted or in own house, it gives excellent results. Debilitation, on the other hand, is bad. If the lord of a dusthana from dasa lagna is debilitated, it gives good results. If the 4th house from dasa lagna has malefics, there will be discomfort and lack of happiness. Benefics in the same house give happiness, well-being and pleasures. Benefics in the 2nd and 5th houses from dasa lagna give good name, fame and favors from authorities. Malefics in the same houses bring bad results in the same areas. If the 7th house from dasa lagna and paaka rasi is afflicted by malefics, there may be troubles in marriage. Raja yogas and dhana yogas with respect to dasa lagna bring success. If dasa lagna or paaka rasi is associated with an exalted planet or a planet in own house, there will be allround success and accumulation of wealth in that dasa.

In addition to interpreting dasas taking dasa lagna as lagna, we can interpret dasas from the natal references also. For example, dasa of raajya pada gives success in career. Dasa of upapada may bring marriage. Dasa of the 2nd house or the 7th house from upapada may bring troubles in marriage. Dasa of GL may bring power. In particular, antardasas aspected by GL may bring promotions. Antardasas aspecting upapada may bring marriage. Arudha padas aspected by antardasa rasi are important in deciding the results in an antardasa.

We also judge the results given in antardasas by looking at the house occupied by antardasa lord from dasa rasi.

Another approach is to divide each dasa into three equal parts. The rasi dominates in the first part. Its lord dominates in the second part and gives his results. Occupants of the rasi and those who aspect it dominate in the third part.

Example 68: Let us consider the rasi chart of Bill Gates, the well-known billionaire of computer software giant Microsoft Corporation (see Chart 24). Lagna is stronger than the 7th house as its exalted lord aspects it. So dasas start from Ge.

Chart 24

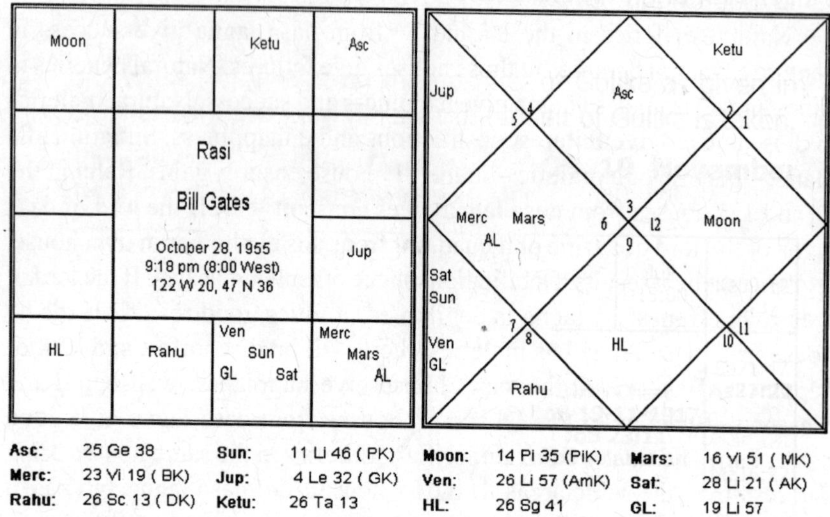

Narayana dasa calculations are given below:

Ge	(04 years)	:	Oct 1955	-	Oct 1959
Aq	(05 years)	:	Oct 1959	-	Oct 1964
Li	(12 years)	:	Oct 1964	-	Oct 1976
Vi	(12 years)	:	Oct 1976	-	Oct 1988
Ta	(05 years)	:	Oct 1988	-	Oct 1993
Cp	(04 years)	:	Oct 1993	-	Oct 1997
Sg	(08 years)	:	Oct 1997	-	Oct 2005

During Cp dasa, Mr. Gates had a phenomenal rise in stature and finances. His company Microsoft became the powerhouse of computer software. Why was Cp dasa such a good dasa?

(1) Cp contains raajya pada (A10 – arudha pada of the 10th house).

(2) During Cp dasa, dasa lagna is Cp and paaka rasi is Li. Lord of dasa lagna is Saturn. He is exalted in the 10th house with the 10th lord Venus (from dasa lagna). They form a powerful raja yoga *with respect to* dasa lagna as well as paaka rasi.

(3) Exalted Mercury is in a trine from dasa lagna and Jupiter is in 8th from dasa lagna. Rahu is in 11th. Two powerful planets are in 10th. All these are favorable placements.

(4) Sun owns the 8th house from dasa lagna and he is debilitated.

At the time of writing this book, Mr. Gates is going through Sg dasa. How will Sg dasa be?

(1) Dasa lagna is Sg and paaka rasi is Le. The lord of dasa lagna is not particularly strong (not as strong as the previous dasa's dasa lagna lord). But he is not weak either. So things can slow down.

(2) Dasa lagna lord Jupiter occupies the 9th house suggesting some noble acts of charity.

(3) Rahu occupies the 12th house. This shows constant fear. (Microsoft Corporation is facing law suits from the federal government and several state governments in US, for being a monopoly).

(4) Sun, the lord of the 9th house from dasa lagna, is debilitated. He is also the lord of paaka rasi. This can suggest some loss of fortune.

(5) However, other planets are favorably placed with respect to dasa lagna. The 10th and 11th houses from dasa lagna are particularly strong. Exalted Mercury occupies the 10th house from dasa lagna and he has a raaja yoga with Mars with respect to dasa lagna. So Mr. Gates may continue to be a successful and innovative entrepreneur.

Example 69: Let us consider the rasi chart of India's independence chart and look at the 1990's (see Chart 25). Narayana dasa calculations are given below:

Ta	(02 years)	:	Aug 1947	-	Aug 1949
Sg	(10 years)	:	Aug 1949	-	Aug 1959
Cn	(12 years)	:	Aug 1959	-	Aug 1971
Aq	(07 years)	:	Aug 1971	-	Aug 1978
Vi	(02 years)	:	Aug 1978	-	Aug 1980
Ar	(02 years)	:	Aug 1980	-	Aug 1982
Sc	(07 years)	:	Aug 1982	-	Aug 1989
Ge	(01 years)	:	Aug 1989	-	Aug 1990
Cp	(06 years)	:	Aug 1990	-	Aug 1996
Le	(01 years)	:	Aug 1996	-	Aug 1997
Pi	(05 years)	:	Aug 1997	-	Aug 2002

Chart 25

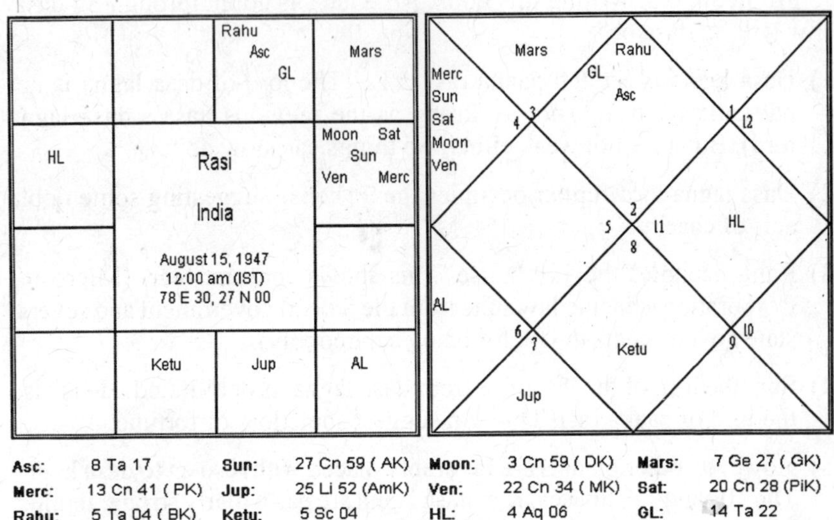

Capricorn dasa runs during 1990-1996. Mars in the 6th house, Jupiter in the 10th house and Ketu in the 11th house from dasa lagna are well-placed. Conglomeration of planets in the 7th house (relations with other nations) and Ketu in the 11th house gives gains from foreign sources. From paaka rasi also, Rahu is in the 11th house and it shows the same thing. So Indian economy was liberalized. Jupiter in the 10th house shows a versatile, intelligent and knowledgable Brahmin leader (Sri P.V. Narasimha Rao). Aspect of Mars on the analytical and tamasik rasi Vi containing the 9th house from dasa lagna made the judiciary system relatively aggressive. This resulted in the probe into hawala[55] scam that shook national politics.

While there was progress during 1990-1996 due to the good placement of most planets with respect to dasa lagna, India experienced disorder, confusion and instability during 1996-1997. During this time, India had a minority government formed by a conglomeration of minor parties that formed a "third force" in Indian politics. During this period, India ran Le dasa.

Dasa lagna during Le dasa is Le itself. Except Mars, no planet is well-placed with respect to Le. In particular, planetary conglomeration in the 12th house shows constant fear and turbulence. It signals instability. Rahu in the 10th house from dasa lagna denies stable and capable leadership.

---

55 Hawala means "bribes for favors"

During 1997-2002, India runs Pisces dasa. Most planets are well-placed with respect to Pisces. So Pisces dasa is a better dasa. As Pisces is a conservative rasi, conservative thought may be predominant in the nation. Jupiter owns the 10th house and Mars aspects it. So India has another learned and intelligent Brahmin leader who has Martian strength in his horoscope (Sri A.B. Vajpayee).

Chart 26

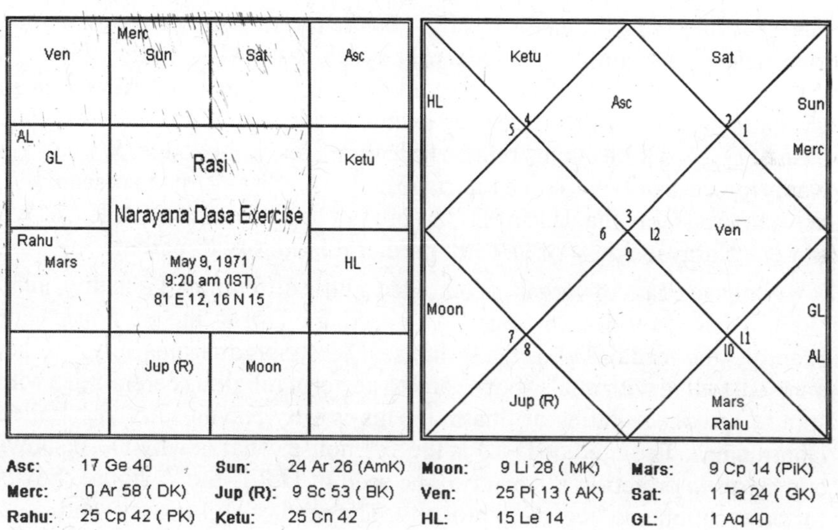

Ketu in the 9th house from dasa lagna may denote religious clashes and violence. Mars in the 4th house may denote lack of comfort and the absence of a feeling of well-being. These two are bad placements that stand out. Rahu in the 3rd house from dasa lagna makes India very bold and assertive. Rahu in the 3rd can also give aggressive weapon development, as the 3rd house shows weapons. India conducted nuclear tests in May 1998. Antardasas in Pisces dasa start from Libra and proceed in the forward direction. Antardasa at the time of nuclear tests was Sc. Sc aspects A3, which is in Ar. A3 shows the illusion related to boldness or the things based on which the world forms impression about one's boldness, *i.e.* one's weapons. Antardasas aspecting A3 can bring weapons, just as antardasas aspecting UL can bring marriage.

Exercise 28: The native of Chart 26 had an excellent career in India until 1997. Then he had to go to US with his wife, who is a software engineer. He could not find the right job for his qualifications in US. He could not succeed in his efforts to redeem his career. He had to depend on his wife and went through a lot of hard times. Calculate Narayana dasa and explain the events.

18.5 Narayana Dasa of Vargas

Narayana dasa may be calculated for vargas (divisional charts) also. Narayana dasa of a varga throws light on the progress of matters shown in that varga. For example, we can use Naryana dasa of D-4 to time changes in residence, happiness from home and stay in foreign countries. We can use Narayana dasa of D-10 to time events in career. We can use Narayana dasa of D-24 to time events related to learning and knowledge. We can use Narayana dasa of D-9 to time marriage and to predict events in marital life. We can use Narayana dasa of D-7 to predict happiness from children. We can use Narayana dasa of D-12 to predict relations with parents.

Narayana dasa of vargas is computed a little differently. Each divisional chart is based on a seed house. The seed for D-*n* is the nth house. For example, the seed of D-9 is the 9th house. D-9 shows dharma (duty). To get married, to live with one's spouse and to perform religious ceremonies with spouse are one's duties or dharma. This is why Navamsa is also called Dharmamsa. The seed of D-10 is the 10th house. That is why D-10 shows one's *karma* or action in society. The seed of D-7 is the 7th house. Sex is for procreation and begetting progeny. The seed of D-4 (house) and D-16 (vehicles and pleasures) is the 4th house. D-12 in the physical plane (it shows the lineage one belongs to) and D-24 in the mental plane (it shows one's learning) show the evolution of one's self in the respective planes. They are both based on the 12th house as the seed, which shows the evolution of self.

To get the seed of D-*n*, just take the nth house. For example, the seed of D-11 is the 11th house. If *n* is greater than 12, subtract multiples of 12 from *n*. For example, the seed of D-16 is 16–12=4th house. The seed of D-27 is 27–24=3rd house. The seed of D-30 is 30–24=6th house. The seed of D-24 is 24–12=12th house. The seed of D-40 is 40–36=4th house.

***Procedure*:**

(1) Find the seed house of the divisional chart of interest.

(2) Take that house in rasi chart.

(3) Find its lord. Take the stronger lord in the case of Aq and Sc.

(4) Take the rasi occupied by him in the divisional chart of interest as lagna and find Narayana dasa of the divisional chart just as if it were a rasi chart. Use the rules explained in the previous sections.

Warning on Interpretation: Narayana dasa of vargas is *not* the progression of lagna or the 7th house. So taking dasa rasi or the 7th from it as lagna and analyzing dasas has no technical basis. It applies only to the rasi chart.

Example 70: Suppose someone's rasi chart has lagna in Cn. Suppose we want Narayana dasa of D-10 to time some events in career. The 10th house is the seed of D-10. The 10th house in rasi chart is Ar. Its lord is Mars. Suppose D-10 has lagna in Ta and Mars in Vi. We ignore lagna in D-10 and treat the rasi containing Mars in D-10 as lagna and use the rules of Narayana dasa of rasi chart. So we treat Vi as lagna. We take the stronger of Vi and Pi as the dasa seed. Suppose Vi is stronger and it does not contain Saturn or Ketu. Then dasas go as Vi, Cp, Ta, Ge, Li, Aq etc. We find the lengths of dasas and antardasas taking D-10 and applying the rules taught for rasi chart.

Example 71: Let us time the foreign stay of the native of Chart 27 using Narayana dasa of D-4. Readers may recall that D-4 shows one's residence and fortune. It is the appropriate chart for timing foreign stay.

Chart 27

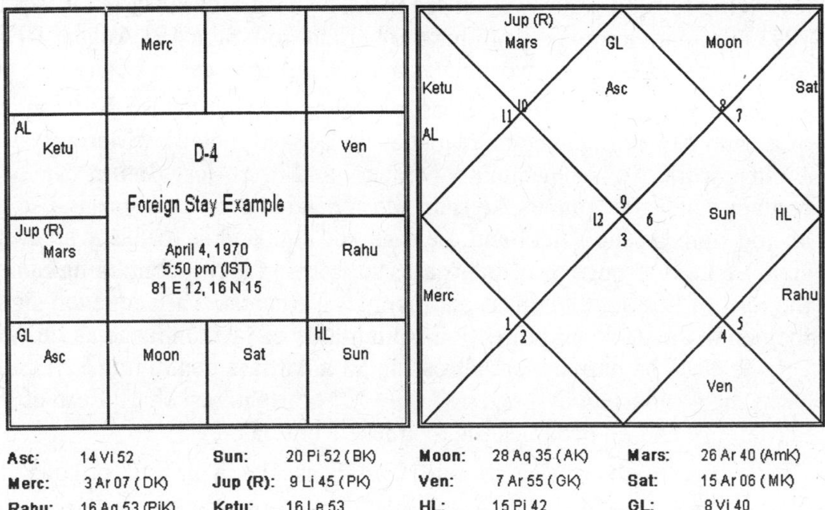

Asc:	14 Vi 52	**Sun:**	20 Pi 52 (BK)	**Moon:**	28 Aq 35 (AK)	**Mars:**	26 Ar 40 (AmK)
Merc:	3 Ar 07 (DK)	**Jup (R):**	9 Li 45 (PK)	**Ven:**	7 Ar 55 (GK)	**Sat:**	15 Ar 06 (MK)
Rahu:	16 Aq 53 (PiK)	**Ketu:**	16 Le 53	**HL:**	15 Pi 42	**GL:**	8 Vi 40

Lagna is at 14 Vi 52. The 4th house in rasi chart is Sg and Jupiter owns it. He occupies Cp in D-4. Let us treat Cp as lagna. So dasa seed is the stronger rasi of Cp and Cn (which is the 7th from Cp). As 2 planets occupy Cp, it is stronger than Cn. So dasas start from Cp. Narayana dasa calculations are given below:

Cp	(04 years)	:	Apr 1970	-	Apr 1974
Sg	(00 years)	:	—		
Sc	(03 years)	:	Apr 1974	-	Apr 1977
Li	(09 years)	:	Apr 1977	-	Apr 1986
Vi	(05 years)	:	Apr 1986	-	Apr 1991
Le	(11 years)	:	Apr 1991	-	Apr 2002

NOTES:

(1) Saturn is in the 4th house from Cp, reckoned in the backward direction because Cp is an even-footed rasi. We get 4–1=3. However, Saturn is exalted and we have to add one year. So Cp dasa is of 4 years.

(2) Jupiter is in the 2nd house from Sg. We get 2–1=1. However, Jupiter is debilitated and we have to subtract one year. So Sg dasa is of zero years. However, Sg dasa of 12 years will come in the second cycle.

We can see that Le is the 9th house. The 9th house shows prospering in a foreign land. Rahu signifies foreign things and he occupies Le. Exalted 12th lord Mars aspects Le. For these reasons, Le dasa is a natural candidate for giving foreign stay. We can see that 11-year Le dasa started in April 1991. The native moved from his motherland to US on 15th August 1991 for higher studies. He is working as a software engineer in US now.

Antardasa: To find antardasas in Le dasa, we should take the stronger of Le and Aq. Both have one planet each. Le is aspected by Mercury and Jupiter, while Aq is aspected by Mercury and its co-lord Saturn. Neither contains an exalted planet. Aq is an odd sign and its stronger lord is also in an odd sign. On the other hand, Le is an odd sign and its lord is in an even sign. So Le is stronger and antardasas start from the rasi containing Sun – the lord of Le. So antardasas start from Vi. Because Vi is an even sign, they go in the backward direction. Antardasas of 11 months go as Le, Vi, Cn, Ge etc. The native went abroad in Vi antardasa containing Sun. Sun owns the 9th house in D-4 and owns the 12th house in rasi chart. Lord of Vi is Mercury and he occupies the 9th house from dasa rasi.

Pratyantardasa: Vi is stronger than Pi, as it has a planet. Lord of Vi is Mercury. He is in Ar – an odd rasi. So pratyantardasas in Vi antardasa go as Ar, Ta, Ge, Cn, Le etc. Vi antardasa is of 11 months and it runs from 4th April 1991 to 4th March 1992. Dividing it into 12 equal parts, we see that the 5th pratyantardasa runs from 27th July 1991 to 25th August 1991. So Le pratyantardasa was running when the native landed in US. Le is the 9th house containing Rahu.

Example 72: Let us consider the navamsa chart of a lady who got married in mid-1993 (see Chart 28).

Lagna in rasi chart is Li. The seed for navamsa (D-9) is the 9th house. The 9th lord in rasi chart is Mercury. He is in Ge in navamsa and Ge is stronger than Sg. So dasas start from Ge. Narayana dasa calculations are given below:

Ge	(12 years)	:	Sep 1971	-	Sep 1983
Aq	(08 years)	:	Sep 1983	-	Sep 1991
Li	(02 years)	:	Sep 1991	-	Sep 1993

Chart 28

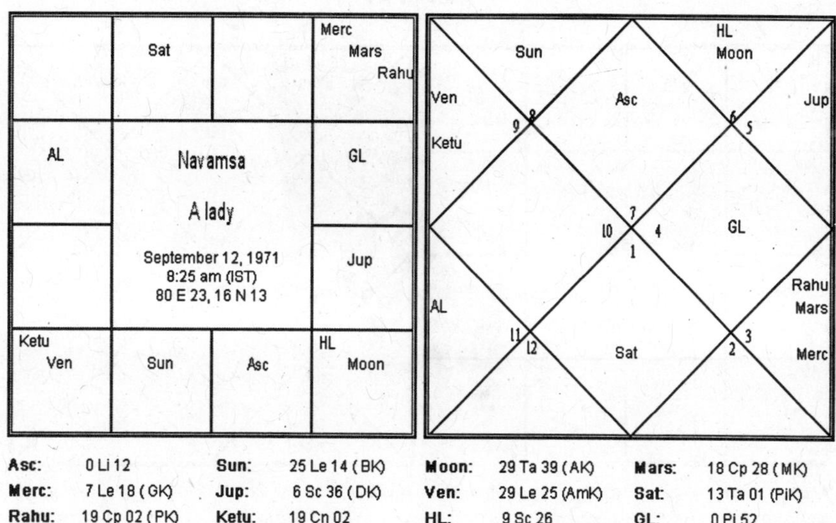

When she got married in August 1993, she was running Li's Navamsa Narayana dasa. Why did Li's dasa give marriage?

Lagna in navamsa shows self, from the point of view of dharma and marital life. So lagna's dasa is favorable for marriage. Dasas of the 1st, 3rd and 8th houses from upapada (UL) are also favorable for marriage. On the other hand, dasas of 6th house from lagna, dasas of the 2nd and 7th houses from UL can bring trouble in marriage and even a divorce when the chart has such indications. Because UL shows marriage, the 1st, 3rd and 8th houses from it show *its* birth, vitality and life (longevity). The 2nd and 7th houses from it show its end.

Here Li is lagna. So its dasa can certainly bring marriage.

Example 73: Let us consider the navamsa chart of another lady and guess when she got married. See Chart 29.

Lagna is at 4 Vi 08. So the 9th house in rasi chart is Ta. Lord is Venus. He is in Pi in Navamsa. Vi is stronger than Pi, as its lord Mercury aspects it. So dasas start from Vi. narayana dasa calculations are given below:

Vi	(09 years)	:	Jul 1969	-	Jul 1978
Cp	(05 years)	:	Jul 1978	-	Jul 1983
Ta	(11 years)	:	Jul 1983	-	Jul 1994
Ge	(06 years)	:	Jul 1994	-	Jul 2000

Chart 29

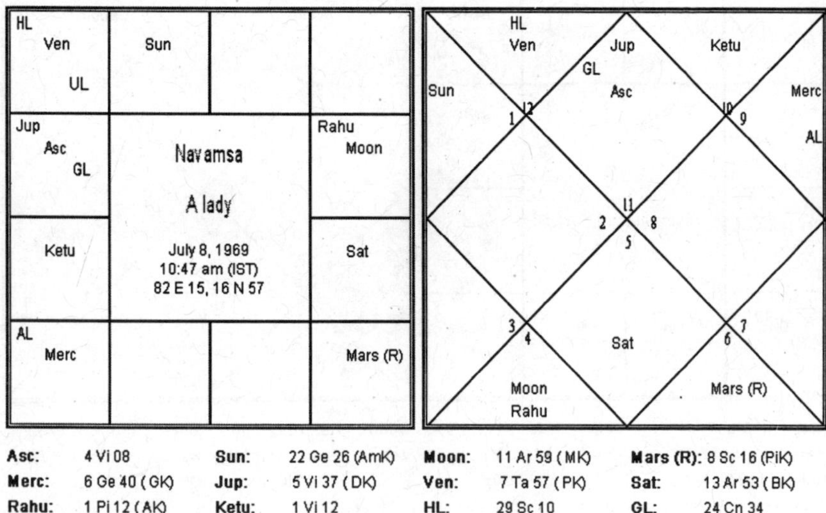

Dasas of lagna and UL do not run at the ages when marriage is likely. Dasa of Taurus runs from the age of 14 years to 25 years. Taurus is the 3rd from UL and its lord is exalted in UL. So Taurus dasa can give marriage. Which antardasa can give marriage? Certainly, Aq with lagna and UL lord is a strong candidate and Pi with UL and exalted Venus (significator of marriage) is an even stronger candidate.

As Sc is aspected by co-lord Ketu, it is stronger than Ta. However, Mars is the stronger lord of Sc, as he is aspected by Mercury and his dispositor (Mercury again). Ketu is aspected only by his dispositor (Saturn) and Mars' count of 2 beats Ketu's count of 1. So antardasas start from Vi. The 7th antardasa belongs to Pi. Each antardasa is of 11 months and the 7th antardasa starts after 5.5 years. It runs during Jan-Dec 1989. The lady got married in May 1989. So Pi antardasa brought marriage.

Exercise 29: Consider the lady whose Navamsa is given in Chart 30. Despite wise counsel by elders, this lady insisted on leaving her husband and ended her marriage in early June 2000. Find the antardasa running then as per Navamsa Narayana dasa and explain the event.

Chart 30

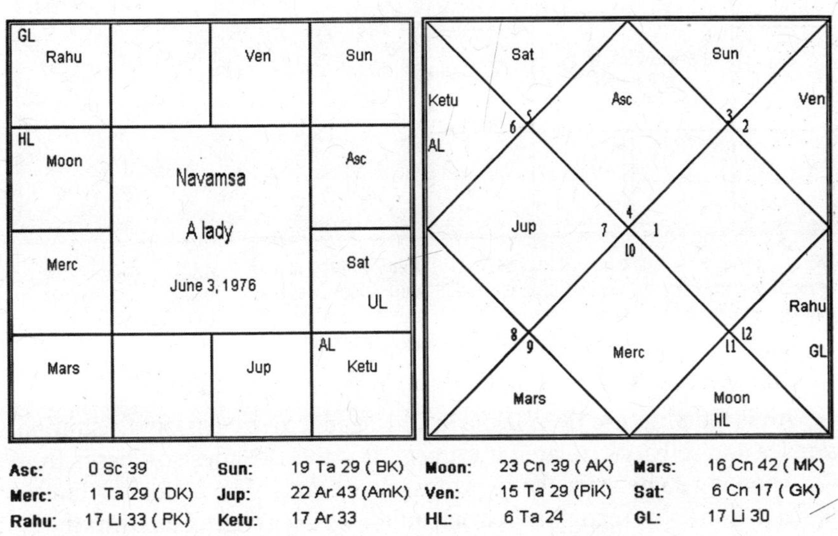

Example 74: Let us consider the D-10 of an electrical engineer who faced some setbacks in career during 1994-1996 (see Chart 31). His enemies conspired and laid a trap for him and he was suspended by the government from his job for a mistake he did not make. He had to suffer for a long time.

Lagna is at 16 Aq 50. The 10th house in rasi chart is Sc and Mars is its lord. Mars is in Cp in D-10. Cn is stronger than Cp, as Jupiter occupies it and its lord Moon aspects it. Narayana dasa starts from Cn and the calculations are given below:

Cn	(03 years)	:	Sep 1947	-	Sep 1950
Ge	(11 years)	:	Sep 1950	-	Sep 1961
Ta	(11 years)	:	Sep 1961	-	Sep 1972
Ar	(10 years)	:	Sep 1972	-	Sep 1982
Pi	(09 years)	:	Sep 1982	-	Sep 1991
Aq	(05 years)	:	Sep 1991	-	Sep 1996

Chart 31

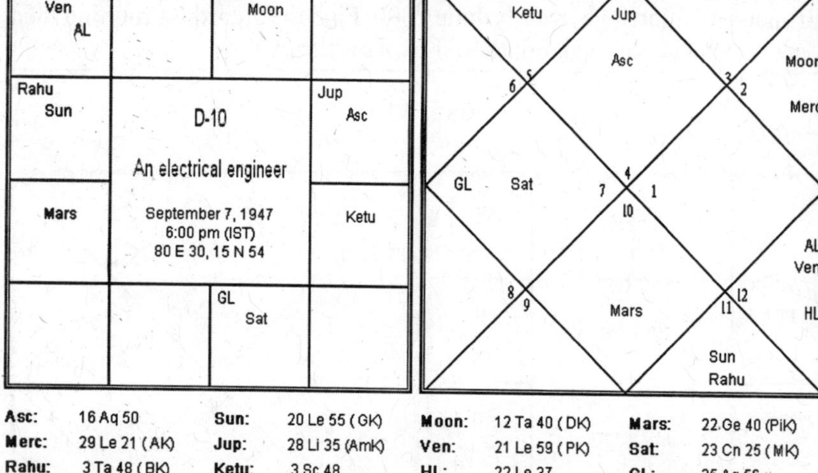

The setbacks occurred in Aq dasa. Why is Aq a bad dasa?

Aq is the 8th house from lagna in D-10 and it gives tension, frustration, worries and setbacks (related to career). It is the 12th house of losses from AL, showing some setbacks in professional status. The 2nd and 5th houses and also Sun show recognition from authorities in a chart. Sun owns the 2nd house here and he is in Aq, afflicted by enemy Rahu. Affliction of Sun by Rahu in dasa rasi can show scandals and making a bad name with authorities. Aquarius has Satru pada (arudha pada of 6th house) and it can show trouble from enemies. Because of the exaltation of Saturn in a quadrant, the middle part of this dasa must be good. Because the occupants of a rasi dominate the last one-third of a dasa, that was when Sun and Rahu gave the troubles.

Exercise 30: Consider the gentleman whose D-10 is given in Chart 32. Find Dasamsa Narayana dasa running in 1996-1998 and judge whether that period should be good or bad for his career.

Chart 32

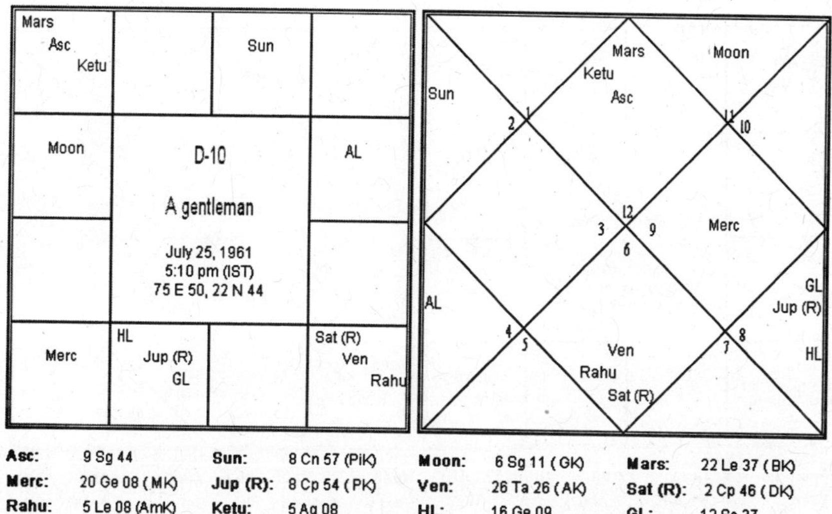

Example 75: Let us consider the native whose D-16 is given in Chart 33. D-16 shows vehicles, comforts and discomforts. The native had a vehicular accident in December 1996. Let us find the antardasa running then and see if the event makes sense.

Lagna is at 14 Vi 52. The seed of D-16 is the 4th house, as 16–12=4. The 4th lord in Rasi chart is Jupiter. In D-16, he is in Vi and Vi is stronger than Pi. So dasas start from Vi. Narayana dasa calculations of D-16 are given below:

Vi (04 years): Apr 1970 - Apr 1974

Cp (01 years): Apr 1974 - Apr 1975

Ta (03 years): Apr 1975 - Apr 1978

Ge (11 years): Apr 1978 - Apr 1989

Li (10 years): Apr 1989 - Apr 1999

Chart 33

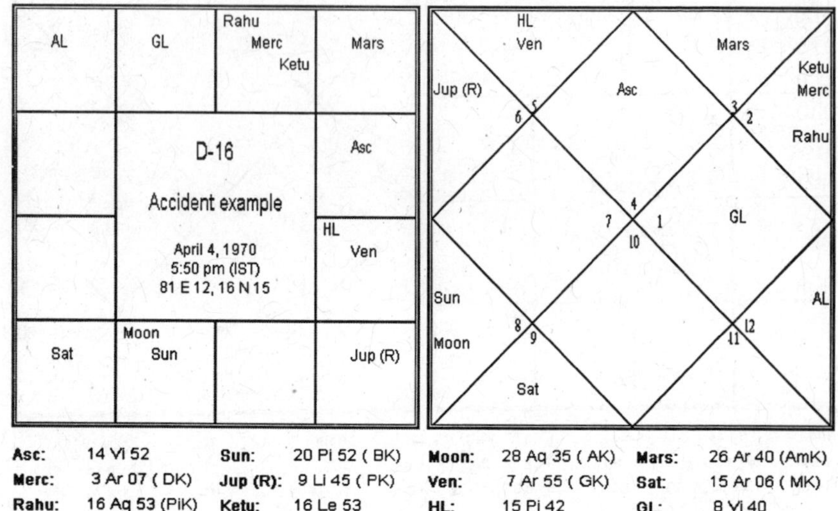

In Li dasa, antardasas start from the lord of Li or Ar. Li is aspected by Mercury and its lord Venus and it is stronger. Its lord Venus is in Le, an odd rasi. So antardasas start from Le and go in the forward direction. Li dasa started in April 1989 and this event happened in December 1996. From April 1989 to December 1996, a period of 7 years and 8 months (7x12+8=92 months) passed. Each antardasa is of 10 months as Li dasa is of 10 years. So 9 antardasas finish after 90 months and the 10th antardasa runs in the 92nd month. The 10th house from Le is Ta. Why did Ta antardasa bring an accident?

Ta is the 12th from vahanapada (A4 – arudha pada of the 4th house). It can give losses to the vehicle. Lord of A4 is Mercury and he is with Rahu and Ketu in Ta. So vehicle can be involved in an accident. Moreover, mrityu pada (A8) is in Ta and troubles related to vehicles can be expected. Nobody was hurt in the accident, but the car was badly damaged and the native was given a new car by his insurance company. In the next 6 months, his new car was damaged twice while parked in a parking lot. One of the damages was serious. So Ta antardasa continued to give vehicular troubles.

One may wonder why we are looking at antardasa and not mahadasa. Events shown by mahadasa suggest the overall mood of the whole 10 year period, while events shown by antardasa are applicable to 10 months here. With Li being the 4th house and having the argala of lord Venus, the native had the comfort of vehicles in Li dasa. However, Ta antardasa was bad due to Rahu and A8. Based on the event of interest, we should judiciously choose mahadasa or antardasa or pratyantardasa for examination. If an event plays a role in a native's life for just a week, it is probably shown in pratyantardasa. If an event plays a role in a native's life for a few months, it is probably shown in antardasa. Mahadasa shows the mood of longer periods. If we want to analyze a temporary activity that remains in a native's mind for just an hour, it is probably seen in the praana-antardasa or deha-antardasa running then. We should determine the effective period of an event and judiciously choose the dasa division in which it should be seen.

18.6 Sub-divisions of Narayana Dasa

Narayana dasa is a versatile rasi dasa. It is a general purpose phalita dasa. It can be computed separately for each divisional chart for precise timing of events related to the matters associated with that divisional chart. We can go down to the precision of a day or an hour by using fine sub-divisions of dasas. As in Example 71, we can divide each antardasa into 12 equal pratyantardasas. This is done in the same manner as each dasa is divided into 12 equal antardasas. In the same manner, we can divide each pratyantardasa into 12 equal sookshma-antardasas (or simply sookshma dasas), each sookshma-antardasa into 12 equal praana-antardasas (or simply praana dasas) and each praana-antardasa into 12 equal deha-antardasas.

When we say that a period is divided into 12 *equal* sub-periods, what do we mean by "equal"? We obviously mean that the twelve sub-periods have the same length. The next question is — how do we measure the length of a sub-period? In days, hours, minutes and seconds? No! We measure the length of a period (or a sub-period) by the angle of the arc traversed by Sun during that period (or sub-period). Two periods are said to be equal if and only if Sun moves by the same degrees, minutes and seconds during the two periods. In other words, we take 1 year=12 months and 1 month=30 days, where 1 day is the time in which Sun moves by 1°.

Motion of Sun is the basis for measuring time in rasi dasas. Suppose a dasa of 5 years starts after the native completes 37 years. If Sun is at 23° 50' 25" in Aq in the birthchart of a native born in 1960, he finishes 37 years when Sun reaches the same longitude in 1997. If the dasa is of 5 years, each antardasa is of 5 months. This corresponds to the time in which Sun moves by 5x30°=150°. When each antardasa divided into 12 equal pratyantardasas, Sun moves by exactly 150°/12=12°30' during each pratyantardasa.

Thus we should divide time in the space of Sun's longitude when dividing dasas upto praana-antardasas or deha-antardasas. Then only correct results will be obtained. A *free* software program for computers using Microsoft Windows operating systems can be downloaded at **http://www.sjvc.net**[56]. Given the birthdata and the start year and length of a mahadasa, this software program can divide the mahadasa upto the level of deha-antardasas using Sun's longitude as the measure of time. This software program is called "Rasi Dasa Division".

18.2 Conclusion

Narayana dasa may be said to be the most important phalita dasa. Its versatility lies in the fact that it can be computed separately for each divisional chart for precise timing of specific matters. In fact, we can compute more than one Narayana dasa for each divisional chart. Narayana dasa of D-12 seeded from the 12th lord is native-centric. It shows events in a native's life that are related to parents. Even when looking at the events in the lives of parents, it takes the native as the reference. To see events in the lives of parents directly, we can use different seeds. Similarly, 12th house used as the seed in D-24 Narayana dasa shows the learning from the point of view of one's evolution. One can use the 4th house (formal learning) as the seed in D-24 Narayana dasa to see formal education. By using a different seed, we can examine the events related to the chosen divisional chart from a different angle. Readers should try to master this fantastic dasa system.

18.3 Answers to Exercises

Exercise 27:

The 7th house has 2 planets and lagna has only one. So the 7th house acts as dasa seed. Progression for Aq is: every 6th. Because Li (9th from Aq) is odd-footed, direction is normally "forward". But Ketu's presence in Aq reverses it and makes it "backward". Saturn acts as the lord of Aq and Ketu as the lord of Sc. Dasas go as:

Aq (02 years): Nov 1960 - Nov 1962
Vi (11 years): Nov 1962 - Nov 1973
Ar (02 years): Nov 1973 - Nov 1975
Sc (03 years): Nov 1975 - Nov 1978
Ge (04 years): Nov 1978 - Nov 1982
Cp (01 years): Nov 1982 - Nov 1983
Le (09 years): Nov 1983 - Nov 1992

56 This is the address of the homepage of **"Sri Jagannath Vedic Centre" (SJVC)** on the Internet

Pi (03 years): Nov 1992 - Nov 1995
Li (02 years): Nov 1995 - Nov 1997
Ta (07 years): Nov 1997 - Nov 2004
Sg (12 years): Nov 2004 - Nov 2016
Cn (05 years): Nov 2016 - Nov 2021
Aq (10 years): Nov 2021 - Nov 2031
Vi (01 years): Nov 2031 - Nov 2032
Ar (10 years): Nov 2032 - Nov 2042
Sc (09 years): Nov 2042 - Nov 2051
Ge (08 years): Nov 2051 - Nov 2059
Cp (11 years): Nov 2059 - Nov 2070
Le (03 years): Nov 2070 - Nov 2073
Pi (09 years): Nov 2073 - Nov 2082

We stop here because 120 years is the paramayush of human beings.

Exercise 28:

Both Ge and Sg are unoccupied. Neither is occupied or aspected by Jupiter, Mercury or lord. Ge is an odd rasi and Mercury is also in an odd rasi. But Sg is an odd rasi and Jupiter is in an even rasi. So Sg is stronger. Narayana dasa calculations are given below:

Sg (11 years): May 1971 - May 1982
Le (05 years): May 1982 - May 1987
Ar (10 years): May 1987 - May 1997
Pi (04 years): May 1997 - May 2001
Sc (03 years): May 2001 - May 2004

Because we started dasas from the 7th house instead of lagna, Narayana dasa shows the progression of the 7th house instead of lagna. So dasa lagna is the 7th from dasa rasi. During Ar dasa, dasa lagna is Li. Due to the exaltation of dasa lagna lord Venus (among other things), it was a very good dasa. During Pi dasa, dasa lagna is Vi. Lord of Vi is Mercury and he is in the 8th house from it. Lords of two dusthanas – Mars and Sun – are exalted and that suggests hard times. Jupiter in the 3rd from dasa lagna suggests failures. There are no malefics in the 3rd or 6th from dasa lagna. Saturn in the 9th house suggests loss of fortune or struggle for fortune in far away places. Ketu in the 11th house shows gains from foreign sources. Exalted 9th lord Venus is in the 7th house. So he went abroad following his wife.

Exercise 29:

Lagna is at 0 Sc 39. Moon is the 9th lord in rasi chart. He is in Aq. Le is stronger than Aq because Sun is more advanced in his rasi than Saturn. Dasas start from Le. Because of the presence of Saturn in Le, they go in the regular zodiacal order. Narayana dasa calculations are given below:

Le (02 years): Jun 1976 - Jun 1978

Vi (08 years): Jun 1978 - Jun 1986

Li (07 years): Jun 1986 - Jun 1993

Sc (10 years): Jun 1993 - Jun 2003

Let us find antardasas in Sc dasa. Ta is stronger than Sc. Lord of Ta is Venus. He is in Ta itself. So antardasas start from Ta. Because Ta is an even rasi, antardasas go in the backward order. Each antardasa lasts 10 months. It takes 80 months (or 6 years and 8 months) for 8 antardasas to finish. So the 9th antardasa starts in February 2000 and runs for 8 months. The 9th antardasa belongs to the 9th house from Ta in the backward direction. It is Vi.

Vi is the 2nd house from UL and it shows the end of marriage. Ketu occupies it and Sun, Mars and Rahu aspect it. Because of these malefic influences, Vi periods can break her marriage. Sun's aspect on the 2nd from UL can denote father's influence in the break-up. This lady encountered resistance from mother and maternal relatives, but her father encouraged her to end the marriage.

Exercise 30:

Sg contains Mercury who owns the 10th house in rasi chart. Sg is stronger than Ge and dasas start from Sg. Dasamsa Narayana dasa calculations are given below:

Sg (11 years): Jul 1961 - Jul 1972

Le (03 years): Jul 1972 - Jul 1975

Ar (11 years): Jul 1975 - Jul 1986

Pi (04 years): Jul 1986 - Jul 1990

Sc (04 years): Jul 1990 - Jul 1994

Cn (05 years): Jul 1994 - Jul 1999

Cancer dasa was running in 1996-1998. Is it good or bad?

Cancer is the 5th house from lagna and it shows recognition. It contains AL in D-10 and shows status in career. Cancer has argalas and rasi aspects from lagna lord Jupiter and Sun. Moreover, it has bhaagya pada (A9 – arudha pada of the 9th house). A9 shows the illusion associated with fortune (in career, because this is D-10). It shows the things based on which people form impression about one's fortune. It essentially shows the trappings of fortune, like good position and money. Dasa of A9 in D-10 can give excellent position in career. So this period must have been excellent for the native's career.

In fact, it was. The native owned a private company specializing in computer software and hardware for a niche market. He sold his company to a large corporation for several millions of dollars in February 1997 and became a VicePresident of that corporation. It was predicted to him by this author in mid-1996 that a very important event in his professional and financial life would take place in the middle of February 1997.

19. Lagna Kendradi Rasi Dasa

19.1 Introduction

There is a dasa called "Kendradi Graha Dasa" or "Moola dasa", which goes through the dasas of planets in quadrants, panapharas and apoklimas from the stronger of lagna and Moon (some authors include Sun). Vimsottari dasa years with moolatrikona correction are used. According to some authors, this dasa is applicable to all people. In particular, if there are 4 planets in quadrants from the stronger of lagna and Moon, this dasa gives much better results than Vimsottari dasa.

Moola dasa is beyond the scope of this book. But we will cover a similar dasa, which belongs to rasis instead of planets. It is called "Kendradi Rasi Dasa". In particular, we will cover "Lagna Kendradi Rasi Dasa".

Kendra means "quadrants" and adi means "starting with". In this dasa, we cover the rasis in quadrants from lagna first and then cover panapharas and apoklimas.

This is a phalita dasa that shows material success well.

19.2 Computation

(1) Dasas start from the stronger of lagna and 7th house. Let us call this rasi "dasa seed".

(2) The direction of reckoning dasas is forward or backward based on whether lagna is in an odd sign or an even sign. If Saturn is in the stronger of lagna and 7th, dasa order is forward. If Ketu is in the stronger of lagna and 7th, dasa order is reversed.

    NOTE: We are talking about *odd* and *even* signs here and *not* about odd-footed and even-footed signs.

(3) First 4 dasas will belong to the kendras (1st, 4th, 7th and 10th) from dasa seed.

(4) Next 4 dasas will belong to the panapharas (2nd, 5th, 8th and 11th) from dasa seed.

(5) Last 4 dasas will belong to the apoklimas (3rd, 6th, 9th and 12th) from dasa seed.

(6) Dasa periods of various rasis in this dasa system are found just like in Narayana dasa.

Suppose lagna is in Ge and Ge is stronger than Sg. Then dasas start from Ge. Because Ge is an odd sign, we go in the forward order and get dasa order as:

Ge (1st), Vi (4th), Sg (7th) , Pi (10th), Cn (2nd), Li (5th), Cp (8th) , Ar (11th), Le (3rd), Sc (6th), Aq (9th) , Ta(12th).

Suppose lagna is in Ta and Ta is stronger than Sc. Then dasas start from Ta. Because Ta is an even sign, we go in the *backward* order and count houses in the backward direction. We get dasa order as:

Ta (1st), Aq (4th), Sc (7th) , Le (10th), Ar (2nd), Cp (5th), Li (8th) , Cn (11th), Pi (3rd), Sg (6th), Vi (9th) , Ge (12th).

19.3 Interpretation

Parasara taught that the quadrants are ruled by Sri Maha Vishnu and the trines are ruled by Sri Maha Lakshmi. If we cover the trines of lagna, then go to the trines of another quadrant and cover all the 12 signs in that fashion (*i.e.* as the trines from quadrants), that sequence is quadrant-based and hence Narayana rules it. This progression is seen for dual signs in Narayana dasa. On the other hand, if we cover the quadrants of lagna first, then go to the quadrants of 5th/9th and finally cover the quadrants of the 3rd trine, then the sequence is trine-based and Sri Lakshmi rules it.

In other words, the sequence 1st, 5th, 9th, 10th etc is quadrant-based and it is ruled by Narayana. The sequence 1st, 4th, 7th, 10th is trine-based and it is ruled by Lakshmi.

So Kendradi rasi dasa uses the movement ruled by Lakshmi. Lakshmi is the goddess of wealth and prosperity. So this dasa shows the periods of prosperity. It shows the progression of lagna using the movement ruled by Sri Lakshmi.

NOTE: We will learn Sudasa in a later chapter. Sudasa is also a Kendradi Rasi Dasa, but started from Sree Lagna instead of lagna. Sree Lagna is the Lakshmi sthana[57] in a horoscope. So its progression using the movement ruled by Sri Lakshmi is more important.

Example 76: Let us consider the horoscope of former US President Ronald Reagan (see Chart 34).

Lagna is in Sc. Ta is stronger than Sc, as it has Jupiter's aspect. So dasas start from Ta. Because Ta is an even rasi, we go anti-zodiacally. Dasas go as shown in Table 41.

57 Residence of Lakshmi, the goddess of prosperity

Chart 34

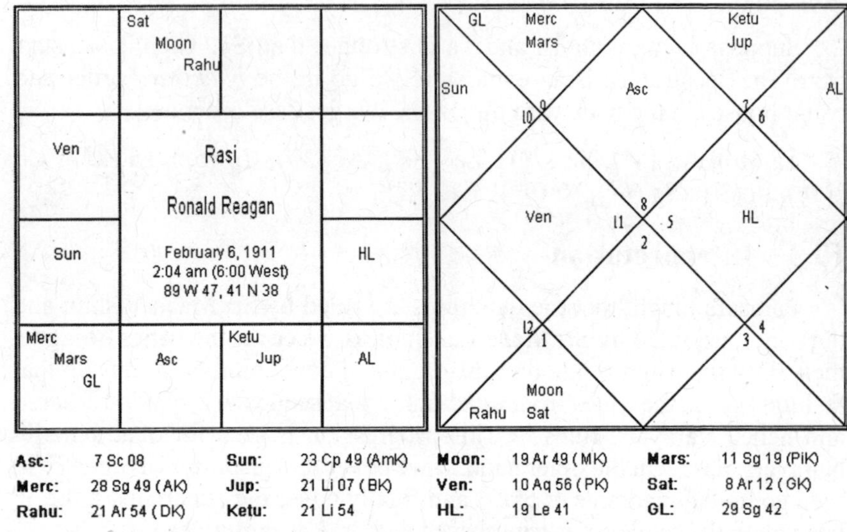

Table 41: Dasa years

Rasi	Ta	Aq	Sc	Le	Ar	Cp	Li	Cn	Pi	Sg	Vi	Ge
Dasa (years)	9	10	11	7	8	8	4	3	5	10	9	6

Dasas from Ta to Pi add up to 65 years and run during 1911-1976. Sg dasa runs during 1976-1986. Mr. Reagan became US President in 1980. Why did Sg dasa bring such success?

(1) Usually rasis containing AK give success. Sg has AK.

(2) Signs having a strong argala of AmK show coming under the decisive influence of good advisors, ministers and bureaucrats. We find in the charts of politicians that rasis having strong argalas from AmK give political power. That is because political power usually brings a leader in the company of excellent advisors, ministers, secretaries or bureaucrats. Here Sg has an unobstructed argala from AmK Sun, who is in the 2nd from Sg in Gopuramsa with 6 rekhas in ashtakavarga. This shows very capable political advisors.

(3) More than anything else, Sg has GL. GL is the seat of power in a chart.

(4) Lagna lord Mars is in Sg and he connects lagna to GL.

19.4 Conclusion

This dasa shows material success as it is based on a movement ruled by Sri Maha Lakshmi. It may be used in conjunction with Sudasa to predict material success. However, Sudasa is a superior dasa.

A noted author who wrote a book on "Mandooka dasa" made some changes to "Lagna Kendradi Rasi Dasa" and presented it as "Mandooka dasa". However the quadrants-panapharas-apoklimas movement is called "kendraadi gati" and certainly *not* mandooki gati. Mandooki gati was clearly explained by Parasara in his discussion on Kalachakra dasa and it is the 3rd/11th jump. Mandooka dasa is based on mandooki gati and Mandooka dasa of Rudramsa is used for predicting the results of wars and death. The dasa presented by the gentleman in question is certainly not Mandooka dasa. It is only a *variation* of the dasa discussed in this chapter.

20. Sudasa

20.1 Introduction

Sudasa is a rasi dasa. It is also called "Sree Lagna Kendradi Rasi Dasa" or simply "Rasi Dasa". Its computation is based on kendras *etc* from Sree Lagna. Sudasa is important for materialistic things like money, power and authority. It can be used to predict financial matters and matters related to status and power. If a political leader occupies a post of power, he must be enjoying a favorable dasa as per Sudasa. If a businessman sees increasing profits, he must be enjoying a favorable dasa as per Sudasa. If someone struggles with tight finances, he must be going through an unfavorable dasa as per Sudasa.

20.2 Computation

(1) In Sudasa, dasas start from the sign containing Sree Lagna (see the chapter on special lagnas).

(2) The direction of reckoning dasas is forward or backward based on whether SL is in an odd sign or an even sign.

NOTE: We are talking about *odd* and *even* signs here and *not* about odd-footed and even-footed signs.

(3) First 4 dasas will belong to the kendras (1st, 4th, 7th and 10th) from SL.

(4) Next 4 dasas will belong to the panapharas (2nd, 5th, 8th and 11th) from SL.

(5) Last 4 dasas will belong to the apoklimas (3rd, 6th, 9th and 12th) from SL.

(6) Dasa periods of various rasis in this dasa system are found just like in Narayana dasa.

(7) But there is an exception in the case of first dasa. Only a fraction of first dasa is left at birth. This fraction is found using the formula: (30° – SL's advancement in its sign)/30°.

Example 77: Consider Sri Vajpayee's rasi chart shown in Chart 3. His SL is at 12°21' in Capricorn.

(1) Dasas start from Capricorn, the sign containing SL.

(2) Because Capricorn is an even sign, the direction of reckoning dasas is *backward*.

(3) First 4 dasas will belong to kendras from Cp, reckoned in the backward direction. They are Cp, Li, Cn and Ar.

(4) Next 4 dasas will belong to panapharas from Cp, reckoned in the backward direction. They are Sg, Vi, Ge and Pi.

(5) Last 4 dasas will belong to apoklimas from Cp, reckoned in the backward direction. They are Sc, Le, Ta and Aq.

(6) Dasa periods are found as in Narayana dasa. We get dasa periods as:

Cp:	2 years
Li:	2 years
Cn:	11 years
Ar:	12 years
Sg:	2 years
Vi:	10 years
Ge:	5 years
Pi:	1 year
Sc:	2 years
Le:	8 years
Ta:	7 years
Aq:	3 years

(7) SL is at 12°21' in Capricorn. The fraction of the first dasa left at birth = (30° – 12°21'/30° = (1800 – 741)/1800 = 0.5883.

First dasa of Cp is of 2 years and 0.5883 of it is 1.1766 years, *i.e.*, 1 year 2 months 3 days 14 hours. So this is the remainder of Cp dasa at birth. After this, Li dasa of 2 years will start.

20.3 Interpretation

(1) Dasas of HL, 7th from HL and the signs aspecting HL bring financial prosperity.

If the lord of the dasa sign occupies or aspects HL, it will improve the chance of financial prosperity. Similarly, if the lord of HL occupies or aspects dasa sign, it will also improve the chances of financial prosperity.

For example, say HL is in Aries, Mars is in Leo and Sun is in Scorpio. Then (*a*) Leo aspects HL, (*b*) lord of Leo aspects HL and (*c*) lord of HL occupies Leo. So Leo dasa is triply likely to bring financial prosperity.

(2) Same thing holds for GL and the prescribed results are power and authority instead of financial prosperity.

(3) Upachayas from any house stand for the growth of matters signified by that house. AL stands for one's status. So dasas of upachayas from

AL bring growth of status. Dasa of the 11th house from AL is particularly favorable.

(4) The 8th and 12th houses from AL bring setbacks to one's status. Their dasas can be unfavorable.

Example 78: Consider Sri Vajpayee, whose Sudasa was calculated in Example 77. His GL is in Cancer. Capricorn is the 7th house from GL and it can bring power and authority. Its lord Saturn aspects GL. Moon is the lord of GL and he aspects Cp. So Cp dasa is very favorable for attaining a position of power and authority. Moreover, Cp contains AL and A5. AL shows status and A5 can show power. The 5th house shows one's following. A5 shows things based on which the world forms an impression about one's following. It can show the trappings of power. Capricorn dasa in the second cycle made him the Prime Minister of India.

Of course, Narayana is important for power, though Sri Lakshmi gives prosperity. So we should always check Narayana dasa along with Sudasa. Sri Vajpayee was running the Narayana dasa of Sc during the same time and so he became the Prime Minister. Scorpio is lagna and houses a powerful raja yoga between AK (Mercury) and PK (Saturn). We studied in the chapter "Yogas" that the conjunction of AK and PK is a raaja yoga, especially in 1st and 5th.

Example 79: Consider Indian political leader Jayalalita's chart shown in Chart 35. She was the Chief Minister of an important state in south India during 1991-1996.

Chart 35

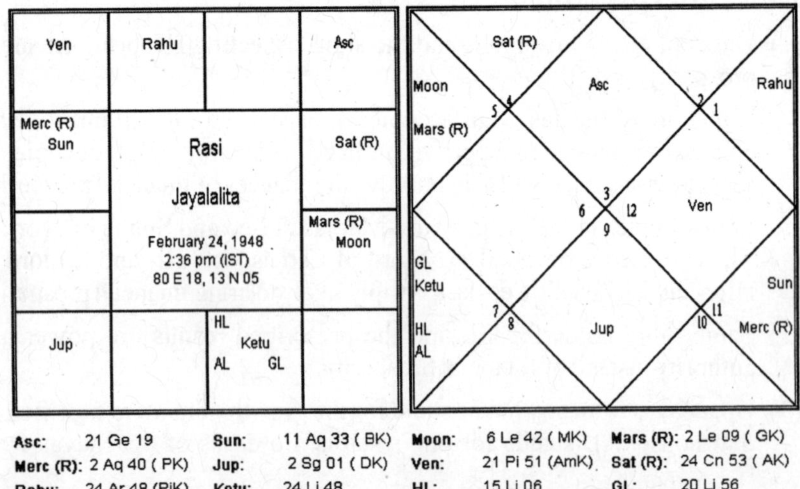

Her SL is in 22 Sg 22. So dasas start from Sg. Because Sg is an odd sign, counting of houses is in the zodiacal direction. Dasas go as Sg, Pi, Ge, Vi (quadrants); Cp, Ar, Cn, Li (panapharas); Aq, Ta, Le, Sc (apoklimas). The first dasa of Sg is of 12 years, because its lord Jupiter is in Sg. But SL is at 22°22' in Sg and the remainder in first dasa at birth is 12 x (30° – 22°22')/30° = 12 x 0.2544 years = 3 years 19 days. After that, 3 years of Pi dasa, 8 years of Ge dasa, 7 years of Vi dasa, 6 years of Cp dasa, 4 years of Ar dasa, 11 years of Cn dasa and 6 years of Li dasa follow. Li dasa ran during Feb 1990-Feb 1996.

As Libra contains AL, GL and HL, its dasa as per Sudasa must give status, power and wealth. No wonder the native became a powerful Chief Minister.

21. Drigdasa

21.1 Introduction

Drigdasa is a rasi dasa. Drik means vision and drigdasa is a dasa based on aspects. It shows how spiritual vision develops in a native and steers one's life. If a native's chart promises spiritual growth, this dasa shows religious and spiritual activities and the evolution of one's soul.

21.2 Computation

(1) Dasas start from the 9th house.

(2) First 4 dasas belong to the 9th house and the 3 signs aspected by it. Order of reckoning is forward or backward based on whether the 9th house is odd-footed or even-footed.

(3) Next 4 dasas belong to the next house (10th house) and the 3 signs aspected by it. Order of reckoning is forward or backward based on whether the 10th house is odd-footed or even-footed.

(4) Last 4 dasas belong to the house after that (11th house) and the 3 signs aspected by it. Order of reckoning is forward or backward based on whether the 11th house is odd-footed or even-footed.

(5) Dasa periods of various rasis in this dasa system are found just like in Narayana dasa.

Example 80: Consider the gentleman in Chart 36. His lagna is in Libra. Ge is the 9th house, Cn is the 10th house and Le is the 11th house.

(1) Dasas start from the 9th house, i.e., Ge.

(2) Because Ge is an odd-footed sign, we should go forward as Ge, Cn, Le, Vi, Li etc and find the signs that aspect Ge. We get Ge, Vi, Sg and Pi.

(3) Next 4 dasas will belong to the 10th house (Cn) and rasis aspected by it. Because Cn is an even-footed sign, we should go backward as Cn, Ge, Ta, Ar, Pi etc and find the signs that aspect Cn. We get Cn, Ta, Aq and Sc.

(4) Last 4 dasas will belong to the 11th house (Le) and rasis aspected by it. Because Le is an even-footed sign, we should go backward as Le, Cn, Ge, Ta, Ar etc and find the signs that aspect Le. We get Le, Ar, Cp and Li.

(5) So dasas go as Ge, Vi, Sg, Pi, Cn, Ta, Aq, Sc, Le, Ar, Cp and Li. Dasa periods of individual signs are found just as in Narayana dasa.

Chart 36

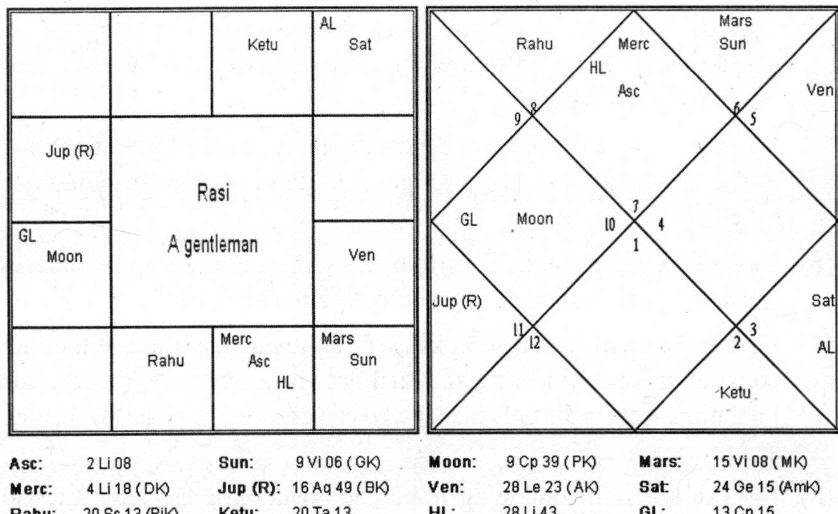

So we get the following as the dasa table:

Ge: 4 years
Vi: 11 years
Sg: 2 years
Pi: 1 year
Cn: 6 years
Ta: 3 years
Aq: 8 years
Sc: 10 years
Le: 11 years
Ar: 5 years
Cp: 7 years
Li: 10 years

21.1 Interpretation

(1) Dasa of arudha lagna can bring renunciation if there are parivraja yogas in the chart, indicating renunciation.

(2) Dasas of signs aspecting arudha lagna can bring external activities that are important for one's spiritual evolution.

(3) Dasa of lagna and the 7th house can bring internal awakening and self-realization.

(4) Dasa of lagna can also bring fame and power related to spreading spiritual knowledge. A monk may, for example, become the Chief Pontiff of a monastery.

(5) Dasas of signs containing or aspecting mantrapada (A5, arudha pada of the 5th house) can bring a religious initiation or sadhana (rigorous practice) of a mantra.

(6) Dasa of the sign containing mrityupada (A8, arudha pada of 8th house) can bring yogic sadhana. It can activate Kundalini sakti.

(7) Ketu is the significator of moksha (final liberation). Dasa of the sign containing Ketu can bring spiritual activities that take one towards liberation. Ketu is the only planet who can give real spiritual awakening and liberation.

(8) Dasa of the sign containing Rahu can create progress after internal turmoil if Rahu is favorable. If Rahu is unfavorable, it can take the native in the direction of materialism.

Example 81: Consider the gentleman in Chart 36, whose Drigdasa was computed in Example 80. Let us analyze Ta dasa that comes during 24-27 years of age. Ta has mokshakaraka Ketu in it. Lagna and mantrapada are in Li and Ta aspects both. Because of these reasons, Ta dasa can bring internal progress and spiritual evolution. It can make the native learn and use mantras.

Example 82: Chart 37 gives the rasi chart of an ISKCON[58] devotee who was disillusioned with the materialistic world, left his education in mathematics at a Russian university, wandered in the forests for a few months and then found ISKCON. He was introduced to ISKCON and moved to a monastery in 1990.

Lagna is in Aq. The 9th house is in Li. It is an odd-footed sign. So we start from Li, go zodiacally and list the rasis aspecting Li. They are Li, Aq, Ta and Le. The 10th house is in Sc. It is an odd-footed sign. So we start from Sc, go zodiacally and list the rasis aspecting Sc. They are Sc, Cp, Ar

58 ISKCON is an acronym for "International Society for Krishna Consciousness", which was founded by Srila Prabhupada for spreading Krishna consciousness and Vaishnava thought in the world.

Chart 37

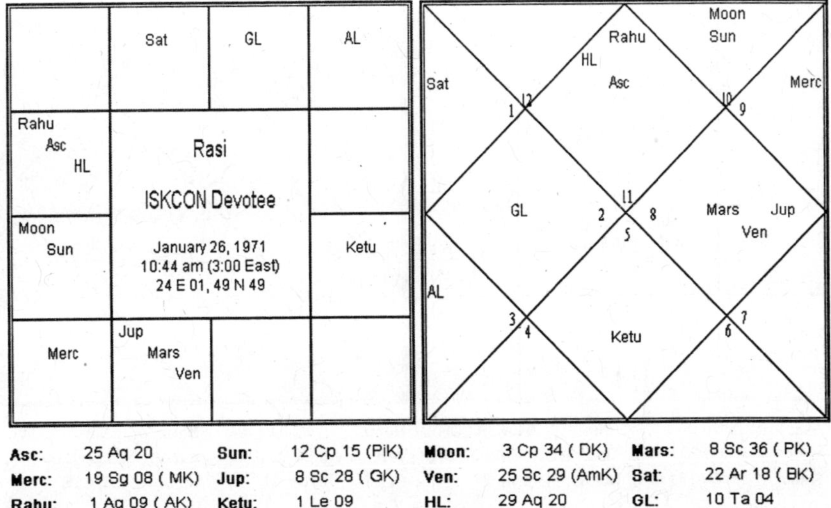

and Cn. The 11th house is in Sg. It is an odd-footed sign. So we start from Sg, go zodiacally and list the rasis aspecting Sg. They are Sg, Pi, Ge and Vi. So dasas go as

Li, Aq, Ta, Le, Sc, Cp, Ar, Cn, Sg, Pi, Ge, Vi

Lengths of dasas are found as in Narayana dasa. Dasa sequence is given below:

Li: 1 year
Aq: 9 years
Ta: 6 years
Le: 7 years

Leo dasa runs during Jan 1987-Jan 1994. Leo is the 7th from lagna and it contains Ketu. It can give spiritual awakening.

Example 83: Chart 38 shows the rasi chart of Sri Aurobindo Ghose. He was an Indian political activist, freedom fighter, yogi, spiritual teacher and a renowned author who wrote excellent commentaries on Vedas, Upanishats etc.

After his education in England, he returned to India to take part in India's freedom movement. He was imprisoned by the British in 1908. During his time in the prison, he went through a spiritual evolution. He realized that Indians had lost their independence not only politically, but also culturally

Chart 38

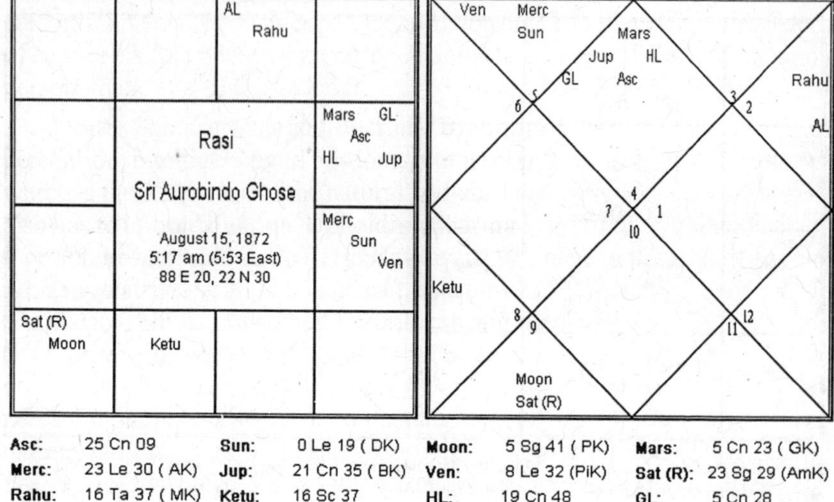

Asc:	25 Cn 09	**Sun:**	0 Le 19 (DK)	**Moon:**	5 Sg 41 (PK)	**Mars:**	5 Cn 23 (GK)
Merc:	23 Le 30 (AK)	**Jup:**	21 Cn 35 (BK)	**Ven:**	8 Le 32 (PiK)	**Sat (R):**	23 Sg 29 (AmK)
Rahu:	16 Ta 37 (MK)	**Ketu:**	16 Sc 37	**HL:**	19 Cn 48	**GL:**	5 Cn 28

and religiously[59]. He dedicated himself to spreading Indian culture and religion. When he was released in 1910, he withdrew from active politics and started an aashram (monastery) in Pondicherry, India. During 1906-1913, he was running Scorpio's dasa as per Drigdasa. Scorpio is the 7th house from AL; it aspects lagna; and, it contains its lord Ketu. For these reasons, Scorpio dasa can bring internal awakening and take one close to liberation. AL and the 7th from it can also play an important role in external activities such as renunciation and moving to (or starting) a monastery.

However, his aashram had only a handful of followers in the beginning. As his magazine and books were read by more people, he started becoming popular. In early 1920's, the number of students in his aashram grew manifold. During 1918-1925, he ran Cn dasa. As Cn contains lagna, its dasa brings true enlightenment and also recognition. During lagna's dasa, a monk can become a chief of a monastery. Here he got recognition and his aashram grew.

Libra's dasa started in August 1925. Sri Aurobindo left the material and spiritual charge of his aashram to the Mother and retired into seclusion to pursue yogic sadhana. Libra contains mrityupada and has the argala of Ketu. No wonder he wanted yogic sadhana in seclusion, rather than spreading religious learning in the world.

59 This is partly true even today. It is amazing to see how an average Indian intellectual undervalues the achievements of Indian culture and the wisdom in the teachings of ancient maharshis.

22. Niryaana Shoola Dasa

22.1 Introduction

Niryaana means death and shoola is a weapon of Lord Shiva, who is the lord of destruction. Niryaana Shoola dasa is one of the most reliable dasa systems for the timing of death. Parasara simply called it "Shoola dasa", but some scholars[60] use the name Shoola dasa to denote a different dasa. We will learn it in another chapter. In order to avoid confusion, we will call the dasa to be learnt in this chapter as "Niryaana Shoola dasa".

22.2 Computation and Interpretation

22.2.1 Computation

Find the stronger of the 2nd and 8th houses. Start from the rasi containing that house. If the rasi is odd, go in the forward (zodiacal) direction and cover the 12 rasis. If the rasi is even, go in the backward (anti-zodiacal) direction and cover the 12 rasis. Dasas of movable, fixed and dual rasis have 7, 8 and 9 years respectively.[61]

Classics are not clear about how we go about finding antardasas. This author suggests using the same rules used for Narayana dasa.

22.2.2 Interpretation

Dasa of strong maraka rasis and dasas of rasis containing strong maraka grahas can bring death. Usually death occurs in the dasa of a Trishoola rasi. There are three Trishoola rasis and we can identify the correct rasi based on the longevity category (short, middle or long life).

If Trishoolas don't bring death, the rasi containing Rudra in the 12th house can bring death.

Antardasa at the time of death can be the 6th, 7th, 8th or 12th rasi from dasa rasi. It can also be a rasi that aspects the rasi that, in navamsa, contains the owner of the 8th house from dasa rasi. Suppose dasa rasi at death is Ta and Jupiter is in Le in navamsa. Then the antardasas of the 6th, 7th, 8th and 12th houses from Ta (*i.e.* Li, Sc, Sg and Ar) can bring death. Also the antardasas of Ar, Le, Li and Cp – rasis that aspect Le, which contains

---

60 An example is my guru Pundit Sanjay Rath, author of "Jaimini Maharishi's Upadesa Sutras" and "Crux of Vedic Astrology: Timing of Events".

61 Sthira dasa, Mandooka dasa *etc* also use the same dasa years, though dasa sequences are different under those dasa systems.

Jupiter in navamsa – can bring death. If there is a common rasi between these two principles, it can be a strong candidate.

Example 84: Let us consider the native of Chart 8. Rudra, Trishoola *etc* were found for this native in Exercise 23. Let us calculate Niryaana Shoola dasa.

We have to find the stronger of 2nd (Sg) and 8th (Ge). Sg is stronger. It is an odd rasi. So dasas start from Sg and go as Sg (9 years), Cp (7 years), Aq (8 years), Pi (9 years), Ar (7 years), Ta (8 years), Ge (9 years) *etc*. It may be seen that Ge dasa starts after 9+7+8+9+7+8 = 48 years. It runs till the age of 57 years. The native died at an age of 50 years. So he died in Ge dasa. Why?

Well, we found in Exercise 23 that Ge, Li and Aq form Trishoola and the native has middle life. Ge is the only Trishoola rasi whose dasa comes in the middle life range (36-72 years).

Ge dasa ran during Dec 1994-Dec 2003. When he died in July 1997, the 4th antardasa was running (each antardasa is of 9 months). Antardasas in Ge dasa start from Li and go as Li, Sc, Sg, Cp *etc*. The 4th antardasa is Cp. It may be noted that Cp is the 8th house from Ge and Cp aspects Le, which contains Saturns in navamsa. Saturn is the 8th lord from dasa rasi. So Ge-Cp antardasa (Ge dasa, Cp antardasa) brought death.

Example 85: Let us consider Rajiv Gandhi's chart (see Chart 39). He was assassinated in May 1991.

Chart 39

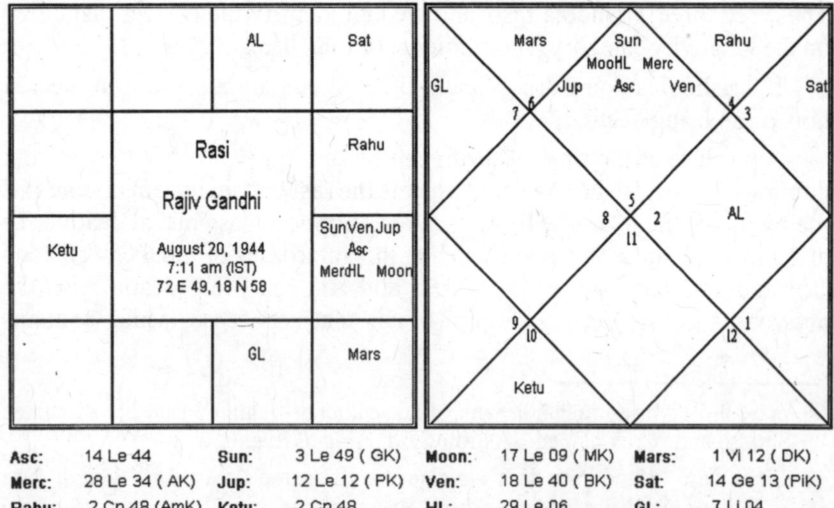

The 2nd house is stronger than the 8th house, as it is occupied by a planet (Mars). Dasas start from Vi. It is an even rasi and so dasas go backwards. We get Vi dasa of 9 years, Le dasa of 8 years, Cn dasa of 7 years, Ge dasa of 9 years, Ta dasa is of 8 years and Ar dasa of 7 years. Ar dasa ran during Aug 1985-Aug 1992. Mr. Gandhi died in this dasa. Why?

Rudra is the stronger of the 8th lords from Le and Aq. So Rudra is the stronger of Moon and Saturn (see Table 32). Moon is stronger and he becomes Rudra. He is in Le. So Trishoola spikes are in Ar, Le and Sg. Being a Trishoola rasi, Ar can kill.

In Ar dasa, each antardasa is of 7 months. During May 1991, the 10th antardasa was running. In Ar dasa, antardasas start from the lord of the stronger of Ar and Li. Li is stronger as its lord Venus aspects it. So dasas start from Le, which contains Venus. The 10th from Le is Ta. From Ar, the 8th lord is Ketu and he is in Cp with Mars in navamsa. Ta aspects Cp.

Example 86: Let us consider India Gandhi's rasi chart given in Chart 61 (in a later chapter). She was assassinated on October 31, 1984.

Because Saturn is in Cn, we take the 8th houses from Cn and Cp in the normal way, instead of using Table 32. The 8th lord Rahu is debilitated and he joins another planet. The 2nd lord Sun also joins another planet. But debilitated 8th lord is a better candidate for being Rudra. So Trishoola is in the trines from Sg, *i.e.* Ar, Le and Sg.

Because the 2nd house with a planet is stronger than the empty 8th house, dasas start from the 2nd house. As Le is an odd rasi, dasas go zodiacally. Dasas go as Le, Vi, Sc, Sg *etc*. It may be verified that Ar dasa runs during Nov 1982-Nov 1989. Ar is a Trishoola rasi.

Let us find antardasas in Ar dasa. Ar is stronger than Li, as its lord Mars aspects it. Antardasas start from Mars in Le and go as Le, Vi, Le, Sc *etc*. Each antardasa is of 7 months as Ar dasa is of 7 years. Nov 1982-June 1983 is the first antardasa of Le. June 1983-Jan 1984 is the second antardasaof Vi. Jan 1984-Aug 1984 is the third antardasa of Li. The fourth antardasa of Sc runs during Aug 1984-Mar 1985. This is the one that brought death.

Sc is the 8th from dasa rasi Ar. So the first antardasa principle we described is correct. Ketu owns the 8th from Ar and he is in Cp in navamsa. Sc aspects Cp and the second principle is also satisfied.

Example 87: Let us consider the rasi chart of a male given in Chart 40. He expired towards the end of 1949. Antardasa at the time of death does not follow the principles explained here, but dasa follows the Trishoola principle. Let us verify it.

The 8th lords from Ar and Li are Ketu and Venus. Venus is stronger than Ketu. So Venus is Rudra. He is in Cp and so Ta, Vi and Cp form Trishoola. Niryaana Shoola dasa starts from the stronger of Ta and Sc. Sc is stronger as it has one planet. Sc is an even rasi and normally dasas should go as Sc, Li, Vi etc. However, Saturn occupies Sc and the "Saturn exception" applies. So dasas go as Sc, Sg, Cp etc. Sc dasa of 8 years ran during 1927-1935. Sg dasa of 9 years ran during 1935-1944. Cp dasa of 7 years ran during 1944-1951 and it brought death. As we have seen, Cp is a Trishoola rasi.

Chart 40

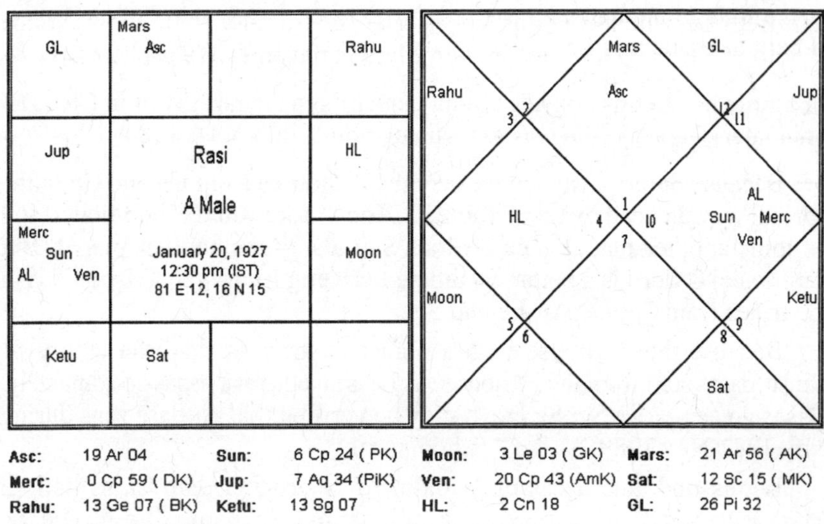

Asc:	19 Ar 04	**Sun:**	6 Cp 24 (PK)	**Moon:**	3 Le 03 (GK)	**Mars:**	21 Ar 56 (AK)
Merc:	0 Cp 59 (DK)	**Jup:**	7 Aq 34 (PiK)	**Ven:**	20 Cp 43 (AmK)	**Sat:**	12 Sc 15 (MK)
Rahu:	13 Ge 07 (BK)	**Ketu:**	13 Sg 07	**HL:**	2 Cn 18	**GL:**	26 Pi 32

Using the principle of three pairs, we get "short life" as the result (lagna and 8th lord show short life; Moon and Saturn show short life. Lagna and HL show long life). That is why death came in Cp dasa and not in Ta or Vi dasa.

In fact, this native was a brilliant scholar of many subjects and also a good astrologer. He knew that he might have a short life. He was sick and bed-ridden during his college days. He missed most of his classes at college, but he studied on his own and appeared at the exams with special permission from his university (there was a minimum attendance requirement and he needed a waiver). Despite chronic sickness, he graduated with distinction and first rank. He found a good job at a young age, but chose not to marry till an age of 24. At his time, people in India used to get married at a very young age. He thought that he had a *praanagandam* (danger to life) and decided to stay a bachelor till 24. He did not want to marry a lady knowing he might pass away in a few years. He is an example of the positive use of astrology.

Example 88: Let us consider the rasi chart of a gentleman shown in Chart 41. He passed away in 1967.

Chart 41

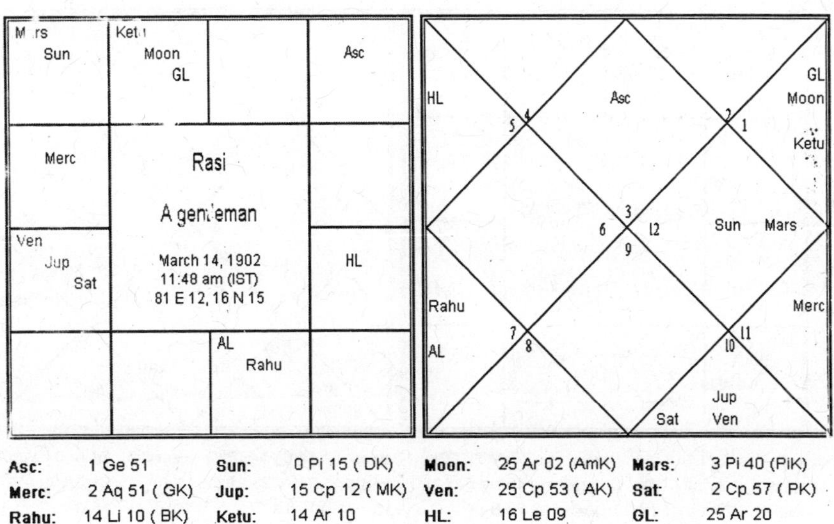

The 8th lords from Ge and Sg are Saturn and Moon. Saturn is stronger and becomes Rudra. Trishoola is in Ta, Vi and Cp. Shiva's Trishoola can strike the native (kill the native) in one of the three dasas. Let us find dasas now.

The 8th house is stronger than the 2nd house and it starts dasas. As Cp is an even rasi, dasas normally go as Cp, Sg, Sc etc. Here they go as Cp, Aq, Pi, Ar etc, due to Saturn's presence in Cp. We can see that Vi dasa starts after 63 years (7+8+9+7+8+9+7+8)[62]. So Vi dasa runs during March 1965-March 1974. Being a Trishoola rasi, Vi brought death in its Niryaana Shoola dasa.

62 One thumbrule that can help in calculating Niryaana Shoola dasa is that the sum of the first 3 dasas is always 24 years (7+8+9). The sum of the next 3 dasas is also 24 years.

Exercise 31: Consider the native whose rasi chart is shown in Chart 42. Using the method of three pairs, estimate his longevity category. Then identify the dasa of a Trishoola rasi falling in that longevity category. Try to guess the antardasa of death. Give the dates instead of just mentioning the dasa rasi and antardasa rasi.

Chart 42

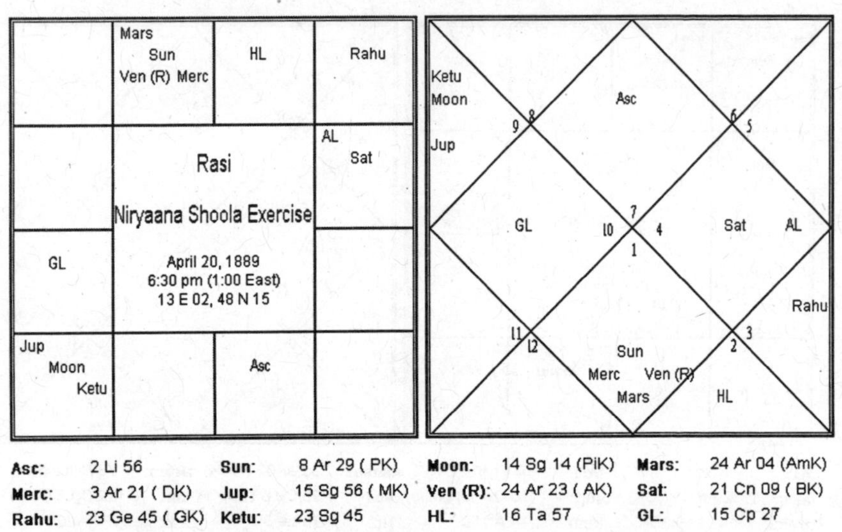

Asc:	2 Li 56	**Sun:**	8 Ar 29 (PK)	**Moon:**	14 Sg 14 (PiK)	**Mars:**	24 Ar 04 (AmK)
Merc:	3 Ar 21 (DK)	**Jup:**	15 Sg 56 (MK)	**Ven (R):**	24 Ar 23 (AK)	**Sat:**	21 Cn 09 (BK)
Rahu:	23 Ge 45 (GK)	**Ketu:**	23 Sg 45	**HL:**	16 Ta 57	**GL:**	15 Cp 27

22.3 Conclusion

Niryaana Shoola dasa is a dasa dedicated to timing one's death. Niryaana means death. In this author's humble opinion, this dasa is the best for timing death. Usually dasa of one of the three Trishoola rasis brings death. However, many special cases, exceptions and special rules mentioned by Maharshis were omited in this book. Timing of the antardasa of death wasn't given due attention. Readers should be aware that what is taught here is only the tip of an iceberg. Further details are beyond the scope of this book.

22.4 Answer to Exercise

Exercise 31:

Lagna lord and 8th lord is Venus. He is in a movable rasi. So we get "long life". Moon and Saturn are in dual and movable rasis. So we get "short life". Lagna and HL are in movable and fixed rasis. So we get "middle life". When there is a three-way tie, we use the Moon-Saturn pair if Moon is in lagna or 7th. That is not the case here. So we use the lagna and horalagna pair. This gives "middle life" as the longevity category (36-72 years).

The 8th lord, Venus, and 8th lord from 7th, Mars, are in Aries. So Rudra is in Aries. Trishoola rasis are Ar, Le and Sg. Death can happen in one of the three dasas.

As the 2nd house Sc is stronger due to the aspect of its lord, dasas start from Sc. As Sc is even, they go as Sc, Li, Vi, Le *etc*. Ar dasa starts after 56 years (56=24+24+8; 24 years for Sc, Li and Vi; 24 years for Le, Cn and Ge; 8 years for Ta). So Ar dasa starts on April 21, 1945 and runs for 7 years. The native is likely to pass away in this period.

Antardasa is tough to guess. The 8th lords from Ar are Mars and Ketu. They are in Sc in navamsa. The signs aspecting it are Ar, Cn, Sc and Cp. Of these, Sc is the strongest candidate as it is also the 8th from dasa rasi Aries. However, the native died in Aries antardasa itself (April 21, 1945-Nov 21, 1945), due to the strength of Aries in rasi chart. Aries not only contains Rudra, but it is also the 7th house and it contains 2nd, 7th and 8th lords. It is a strong maraka sthana.

This birthdata belongs to Adolf Hitler. History says that he committed suicide on April 30, 1945. Russian investigations after World War II supported this.

23. Shoola Dasa

23.1 Introduction

We looked at "Niryaana Shoola dasa" used for timing one's death. There is another dasa called Shoola dasa that can also be used for timing death. It shows death, diseases, suffering and death of relatives.

23.2 Computation

Find the stronger of lagna and the 7th house. Dasas start there and *always* go in the regular zodiacal order. For example, if lagna is in Sc and Ta is stronger than Sc, dasas go as Ta, Ge, Cn, Le etc. If lagna is in Le and Aq is stronger than Le, dasas go as Aq, Pi, Ar, Ta etc. Each dasa is of 9 years. Each dasa is divided into 12 equal antardasas. Antardasas are found using the same rules as dasas, but treating dasa rasi as lagna. If Cn dasa is running and Cn is stronger than Cp, then antardasas go as Cn, Le, Vi, Li etc and each antardasa will last 9 months.

Human beings live in the womb for an average of 9 months. For animals with an average of gestation period of *n* months, each dasa and antardasa will be of *n* years and *n* months respectively.

In mundane astrology, we can use Shoola dasa by compressing 108 years to the time period of effect of the chart. For example, suppose we want compressed Shoola dasa for the swearing-in chart of an Indian Prime Minister. Then, 108 years of Shoola dasa are compressed to 5 years or 60 months (which is the term of an Indian Prime Minister) and a dasa of 9 years is compressed 60/12 = 5 months.

23.3 Interpretation

Like in Niryana Shoola dasa, dasa of a Trishoola rasi can bring death. Because the 2nd and 8th rasis in the natural zodiac are owned by Mars and Venus, rasi aspect on either of them by Moon generates Rudra yoga and rasis aspected by Rudra yoga planets can give death.

This author found the following rules to hold true in many cases:

"AL or the trines from it can give death. If malefics or marakas occupy or aspect the 3rd from AL or the 8th from AL, those 2 houses can give death."

Lagna and 7th house both show the self of a person. They stand for the invisible and visible selves. Niryaana Shoola dasa starts from the 8th house from one of them. Niryaana Shoola dasa essentially shows the progress of the 8th house. It shows the motion of praana (life). That is why it has an uneven motion. It goes forward in some charts and backward in some charts. Also the lengths of dasas can be 7, 8 or 9 years. All this shows that different people have different motion of praana. When praana reaches Shiva's Trishoola or a powerful maraka rasi, the native can die. In Shoola dasa, however, the motion has a constant rate of 9 years per dasa and the order of dasas is always fixed. This fixed motion is like the motion of a quartz crystal. It is *not* the motion of praana and it must be a universal motion. It is suggested that Shoola dasas show the force of Lord Shiva. The force of Lord Shiva starts from one's self and moves at a *constant* rate in a *fixed* direction. So Shoola dasa rasi hitting Trishoola rasis is less significant than Niryaana Shoola dasa rasi hitting Trishoola rasis. In the case of Shoola dasa, death occurs when Shiva's motion hits AL or the trines from it or the houses of vitality from AL (3rd and 8th). AL is involved instead of lagna, because our existence is a maya (illusion) and what Lord Shiva destroys is the illusion of our existence. The physical body (lagna) simply merges with the material universe, when burnt or buried, and the perceived self or the maya of existence (AL) is what is completely destroyed by Lord Shiva.

Lesson: Niryaana Shoola dasa shows the motion of praana (life). Death occurs when praana hits maraka rasis and the trines from Rudra (Trishoola rasis). Shoola dasa is the reverse. It shows the motion of Shiva. Death occurs primarily when Shiva's motion hits the trines from AL or the 3rd house from AL or the 8th house from AL.

We have listed several rasis above. How do we choose one answer from the list? There are 2 criteria: (1) Usually a rasi occupied or aspected by AK or Jupiter does not kill a native, unless that planet happens to be Rudra. (2) Based on whether the native is of short/middle/long life, we are limited to just 4 dasas. The *first* 4 Shoola dasas (0-36 years) bring death to a person of the *short* life category. The *middle* 4 Shoola dasas (36-72 years) bring death to a person of the *middle* life category. The *last* 4 Shoola dasas (72-108 years) bring death to a person of the *long* life category. We should choose a good candidate from those dasas.

23.4 Examples

Example 89: Let us revisit Example 84 that we analyzed using Niryaana Shoola dasa.

Lagna is stronger and dasas start from Sc. They go as Sc, Sg, Cp, Aq etc. Each dasa is of 9 years. First 5 dasas are over after 45 years. The native died in the 50th year. From his 45th year, the 6th dasa was running. So the 6th dasa of Ar killed the native. One can see that Ar is a trine from AL. It is the only trine in the middle life range.

Example 90: Let us revisit Example 85 that we analyzed using Niryaana Shoola dasa.

Lagna is stronger and dasas start from Le. They go as Le, Vi, Li, Sc etc. Each dasa is of 9 years. First 5 dasas are over after 45 years. The native died in his 47th year. From his 45th year, the 6th dasa was running. So the 6th dasa of Cp killed the native. One can see that Cp is the only trine from AL in the middle life range.

Example 91: Let us revisit Example 86 that we analyzed using Niryaana Shoola dasa.

The 7th house Cp is stronger and dasas start from Cp. They go as Cp, Aq, Pi, Ar etc. Each dasa is of 9 years. First 7 dasas are over after 63 years. The native died in her 67th year. From her 63rd year, the 8th dasa was running. So the 8th dasa of Le killed the native. One can see that Le is a trine from AL and it contains the lord of AL. So Shiva destroyed the material existence of the native in Cp's Shoola dasa.

Example 92: Let us revisit Example 87 that we analyzed using Niryaana Shoola dasa.

Lagna is stronger and dasas start from Ar. They go as Ar, Ta, Ge, Cn *etc*. Each dasa is of 9 years. First 2 dasas are over after 18 years. The native died in the 23rd year. From his 18th year, the 3rd dasa was running. So the 3rd dasa of Ge killed the native. One can see that Ge is the 8th house from AL (see Table 32[63]) and it contains Rahu. In other words, Ge is afflicted and it is the house of longevity of material self. When Shiva's motion hit that rasi, the native died.

Exercise 32: Consider the native of Chart 43. Using the method of three pairs, estimate whether he has short or middle or long life. Then evaluate Shoola dasa and identify the four dasas in the estimated longevity range. Consider the trines from AL and the 3rd and 8th houses (using Table 32). Think hard and choose the dasa that must have given death.

23.5 Death of Near Relatives

Shoola dasa shows Shiva's punishment. It shows misfortune, suffering and death. Using it, death of near relatives can also be timed.

For each relative, we treat the house that shows him/her as lagna and find Shoola dasa based on it. Shoola dasa starts from the stronger of that rasi and the 7th from it. We have different names for Shoola dasas started

---

[63] The 8th house for the purpose of Rudra, the principle of 3 pairs and ayur dasa interpretation should be found from Table 32.

Chart 43

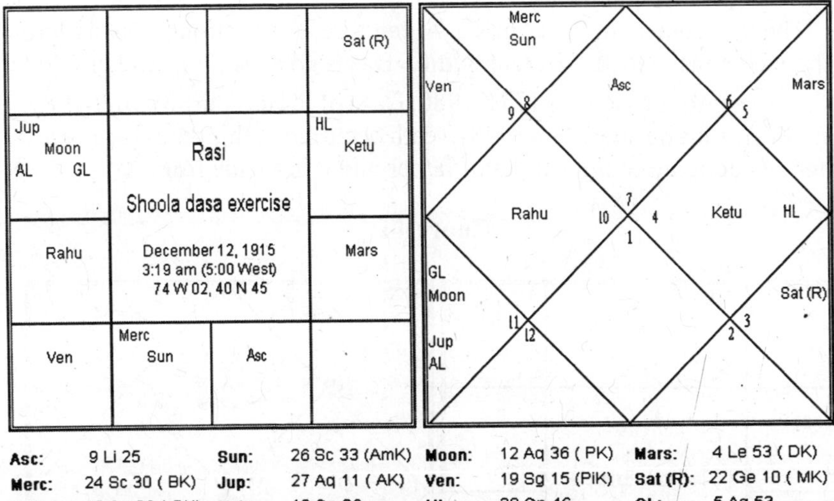

from different houses. For example, Pitri Shoola dasa (pitri = father) starts from the stronger of 9th and 3rd houses. It is used in the timing of father's death. Bhratri Shoola dasa (bhratri = brother) also starts from the stronger of 3rd and 9th houses and it shows the death of younger siblings. Matri Shoola dasa (matri = mother) starts from the stronger of 4th and 10th houses. Dara Shoola dasa (dara = wife) starts from the stronger of 7th and 1st houses and it shows the death of wife (this dasa will be identical to the native's normal Shoola dasa). Putra Shoola dasa (putra = son) starts from the stronger of 5th and 11th houses and it shows the death of a child.

We mentioned earlier that sthira karakas are useful in timing death. Sthira karaka of father represents father in a chart, for the purpose of matters controlled by Shiva (*i.e.* suffering and death). Pitri Shoola dasa shows the motion of Shiva's force for the father. When Shiva's force strikes trines from sthira karaka of father, father's death can take place. Trines from the corresponding arudha pada can also give death.

Similarly, we can time the death of other near relatives. Let us see a couple of examples.

Example 93: Let us consider the native of Chart 44. His father passed away in the second half of 1995.

Exalted Sun joins Mercury and Jupiter aspects him. So Sun is stronger than Venus. He becomes sthira pitri karaka (fixed significator of father).

Death can occur in trines from him, i.e. Ar, Le and Sg. Pitri pada (A9, arudha pada of 9th house) is in Sg. Trines from it are the same.

The 9th house is in Aq. Among Aq and Le, Aq is stronger as its lord Rahu is in a rasi with a different oddity. Dasas go as Aq, Pi, Ar etc.

Dasa of Aq runs during 1971-1980. Dasa of Pi runs during 1980-1989. Dasa of Ar runs during 1989-1998. Death occurred in this dasa. As already noted, Ar contains sthira karaka of father and it is a trine from A9.

Chart 44

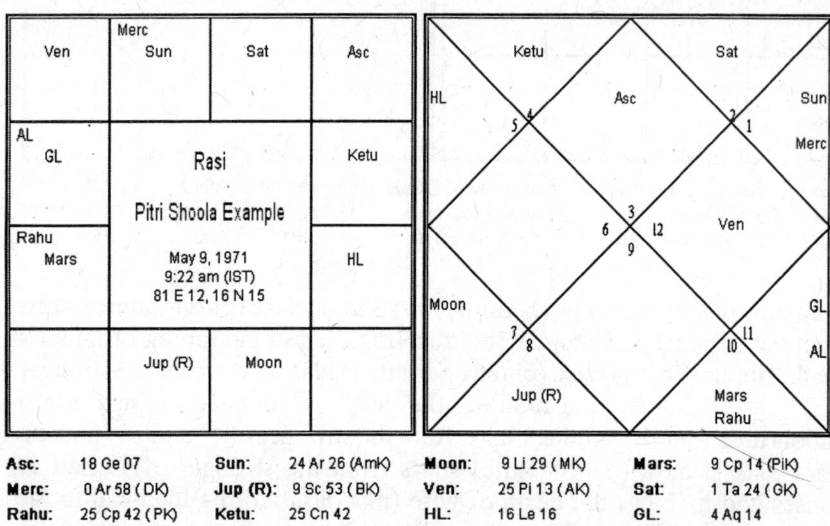

Example 94: Let us consider Indira Gandhi's birthdata given in Chart 61 (in a later chapter). Her father Jawaharlal Nehru died in May 1964. Her husband Feroze Gandhi died in 1960. Her son Sanjay Gandhi died in June 1980.

Sthira karaka of father is Venus here, as he is in a dual rasi. He shows father, for the purpose of matters ruled by Shiva. Death of father can occur in the trines from Venus, *i.e.* Sg, Ar and Le. Pitri Shoola dasa starts from Pi (9th house) and goes as Pi, Ar, Ta, Ge *etc*. Le dasa starts after 5 dasas, *i.e.* in 1917 + 45 = 1962. It runs till 1971. Her father died in 1964 in this dasa.

Jupiter is sthira karaka of husband. He shows husband, for the purpose of matters ruled by Shiva. Death of husband can occur in trines from Jupiter. Dara Shoola dasa starts from Cp and goes as Cp, Aq, Pi, Ar *etc*. Jupiter is in Ta and Ta dasa runs from 1917 + 36 = 1953. It ends in 1962. Her husband died in 1960 in this dasa.

Jupiter is also sthira karaka of children. He shows children, for the purpose of matters ruled by Shiva. Death of son can occur in trines from Jupiter. Putra Shoola dasa starts from Sc (5th house and stronger than Ta) and goes as Sc, Sg, Cp, Aq *etc*. Jupiter is in Ta and Ta dasa runs from 1917 + 54 = 1971. It ends in November 1980. Her son Sanjay Gandhi died in June 1980. He died in Ta dasa.

Exercise 33: Consider the rasi chart of a lady born in 1950, given in Chart 45. Compute Shoola dasa and identify the dasas that can give death to her husband. Looking at the 3rd from sthira karaka for husband, guess whether the death was violent or peaceful.

Chart 45

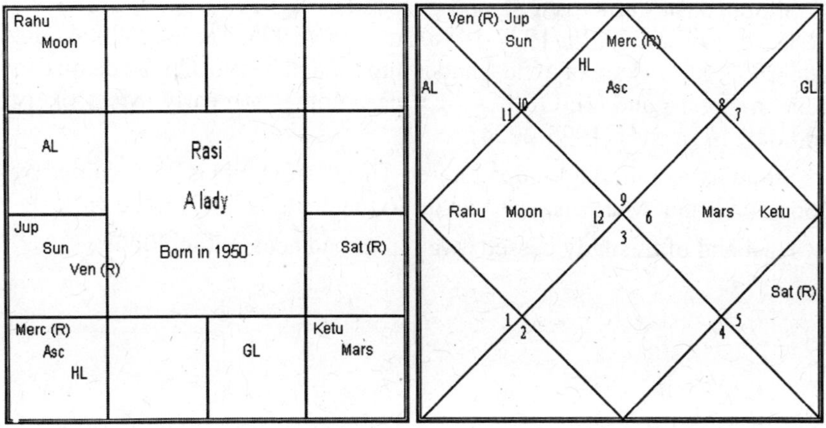

Rahu Moon			
AL	Rasi		
Jup Sun Ven (R)	A lady Born in 1950		Sat (R)
Merc (R) Asc HL		GL	Ketu Mars

Ven (R) Jup Sun
Merc (R)
HL
Asc
AL
GL
11 10 8 7
Rahu Moon
12 9 6 3
Mars Ketu
Sat (R)
1 2 4 5

23.1 Answers to Exercises

Exercise 32:

Method of three pairs: (1) Lagna lord and 8th lord is Venus and he is in dual rasi. Dual + Dual gives middle life. (2) Moon is in a fixed rasi and Saturn is in a dual rasi. Fixed + Dual gives long life. (3) Lagna and HL are in movable rasis. Movable + Movable gives long life. So the final result is "long life". This range covers 72-108 years. So the last 4 Shoola dasas can bring death.

Shoola dasa: The 7th house Aries is stronger as it has the aspect of Sun, Mercury and its lord Mars. Dasas start from Ar and go as Ar, Ta, Ge, Cn *etc*. The first 8 dasas are over after 72 years (8 x 9). The 9th dasa of Sg runs during 72-81 years of age. The 10th dasa of Cp runs during 81-90 years of age. The 11th dasa of Aq runs during 90-99 years of age. The 12th dasa of Pi runs during 99-108 years of age. These are the four dasas in the long life range.

Death when: Arudha lagna is in Aq. The trines are Aq, Ge and Li. The only trine in the long life range, *i.e.* among the 4 rasis mentioned above, is Aq. Its dasa can give death. However, it contains Jupiter who is also AK. So its dasa is unlikely to kill. We can try the 8th house from AL. From Table 32, we find that Cp is the 8th house from Aq. It is afflicted by Rahu here (just as in Example 92). So it is a good candidate.

Final Answer: This chart belongs to Frank Sinatra, a legendary singer and actor of US. He died of a heart attack on May 14, 1998. He died in his 83rd year. Shoola dasa of Cp was running then.

Exercise 33:

Shoola dasa starts from Sg and goes thus – Sg: 1950-1959, Cp: 1959-1968, Aq: 1968-1977, Pi: 1977-1986, Ar: 1986-1995, Ta: 1995-2004, Ge: 2004-2013. Sthira karaka of husband is Jupiter and he is in Cp. So death can occur in Cp, Ta and Vi. Of these, Cp dasa comes too early. Most likely candidate is Ta dasa (1995-2004).

Sthira karaka for husband is Jupiter. The 3rd from him is Pi, occupied by Moon and Rahu. Mars also aspects it. So the death is likely to be violent.

Husband of this lady passed away in a road accident in 2000.

24. Kalachakra Dasa

24.1 Introduction

Sage Parasara said in his classic "Brihat Parasara Hora Sastram":

कालचक्र चान्या मान्या सर्वदशासु या

It means, "there is another dasa called Kalachakra dasa, which is the most respectable of all dasa systems". Kalachakra literally means "the wheel of Time". It shows how the wheel of time unfolds events in the life of an individual. Parasara said that Lord Shiva explained this dasa to Goddess Parvati.

24.2 Computation

Nakshatras are divided into two groups – Savya (zodiacal) group and Apasavya (anti-zodiacal group), as shown in Table 42. Note that the first 3 nakshatras belong to the savya group, the next 3 constellations to the apasavya group and so on.

Table 42: Nakshatra Classification

Savya Group	Aswini, Bharani, Krittika Punarvasu, Pushyami, Aasresha Hasta, Chira, Swaati Moola, Poorvaashaadha, Uttaraashaadha Poorvabhaadrapada, Uttarabhaadrapada, Revati
Apasavya Group	Rohini, Mrigasira, Aardra Makha, Poorva Phalguni, Uttara Phalguni Visaakha, Anooraadha, Jyeshtha Sravanam, Dhanishtha, Satabhisha

Parasara taught that we can draw Kalachakra (wheel of Time) by drawing 2 sets of 12 houses for savya and apasavya groups of nakshatras, then repeating them and distributing them between nakshatras. Savya means "zodiacal" and apasavya means "anti-zodiacal".

We write the 12 rasis in one set (either zodiacally or anti-zodiacally). In the other set, we write their mirror images, *i.e.* the other sign owned by the same planet. The mirror image of Ar is Sc. The mirror image of Ta is Li. The mirror image of Cp is Aq. However, the mirror image of Cn is Cn itself and that of Le is Le itself, as they are the only signs owned by their lords.

The main sequence and the mirrored sequence together form **a sequence of 24 rasis**. We have two such sequences – one for the savya group and the other for the apasavya group (see Table 43). We find antardasas and dasas by repeating these 24-rasi sequences and going through them.

Table 43: Parasara's Kalachakra Basis

Savya Group

Main	Ar	Ta	Ge	Cn	Le	Vi	Li	Sc	Sg	Cp	Aq	Pi
Mirrored	Sc	Li	Vi	Cn	Le	Ge	Ta	Ar	Pi	Aq	Cp	Sg

Apasavya Group

Mirrored	Sg	Cp	Aq	Pi	Ar	Ta	Ge	Le	Cn	Vi	Li	Sc
Main	Pi	Aq	Cp	Sg	Sc	Li	Vi	Le	Cn	Ge	Ta	Ar

The *first* pada (quarter) of Aswini is associated with the *first* 9 rasis in the savya group above (Ar, Ta, Ge, Cn, Le, Vi, Li, Sc, Sg). The dasa running at birth will be one of these 9 rasis and one will run dasas of 9 rasis starting from *that* rasi. One born with Moon at the *beginning* of the first pada of Aswini will run Ar dasa at birth and run Ta, Ge, Cn, Le, Vi, Li, Sc and Sg dasas after it. One born with Moon in the *middle* of the first pada of Aswini may run Le dasa at birth and run Vi, Li, Sc, Sg, Cp, Aq, Pi and Sc dasas after it. One born with Moon towards the *end* of the first pada of Aswini may run Sg dasa at birth and Cp, Aq, Pi, Sc, Li, Vi, Cn and Le dasas after it. Based on the elapsed fraction of the 1st pada of Aswini, we choose the initial dasa from the 9 rasis associated with that nakshatra pada and then proceed along Kalachakra and list 9 rasis starting from it. The *second* pada of Aswini is associated with the *next* 9 rasis in the savya group above (Cp, Aq, Pi, Sc, Li, Vi, Cn, Le, Ge).

Like this, as we go from one nakshatra pada (constellation quarter) to the next in the savya group, we move from one set of 9 rasis to the next. When we reach the end of the 24 rasis, we go to the beginning. In this manner, we can find a set of 9 rasis associated with each nakshatra pada. The first of the nine rasis is called "Deha rasi" (body sign) and the last one is called "Jeeva rasi" (spirit/life sign).

At the end of the 4th quarter of Aswini, the 1st quarter of Bharani starts and we do the same thing. We go to the next 9 rasis in the set of 24 rasis.

We can do the same thing in the case of apasavya nakshatras and use the 24-rasi sequence given for the apasavya group in Table 43. In the case of apasavya nakshatras, the first rasi in the nine rasis corresponding to a nakshatra pada is called "Jeeva rasi" and the last one is called "Deha rasi" (note that the definition has reversed).

For the sake of those who do not understand the above logic well enough to list the nine rasis associated with each nakshatra pada, they are explicitly given in Table 44-Table 47. For the purpose of these tables, we will divide savya and apasavya groups of nakshatras into two sub-groups each.

Table 44: Savya-1 Nakshatras: Aswini, Krittika, Punarvasu, Aasresha, Hasta, Swaati, Moola, Uttarashadha, Poorvabhadrapada

Pada	Sequence of Rasis	Deha Rasi	Jeeva Rasi	Paramayush
1st	Ar, Ta, Ge, Cn, Le, Vi, Li, Sc, Sg	Ar	Sg	100 years
2nd	Cp, Aq, Pi, Sc, Li, Vi, Cn, Le, Ge	Cp	Ge	85 years
3rd	Ta, Ar, Pi, Aq, Cp, Sg, Ar, Ta, Ge	Ta	Ge	83 years
4th	Cn, Le, Vi, Li, Sc, Sg, Cp, Aq, Pi	Cn	Pi	86 years

Table 45: Savya-2 Nakshatras: Bharani, Pushyami, Chitra, Poorvashadha, Revati

Pada	Sequence of Rasis	Deha Rasi	Jeeva Rasi	Paramayush
1st	Sc, Li, Vi, Cn, Le, Ge, Ta, Ar, Pi	Sc	Pi	100 years
2nd	Aq, Cp, Sg, Ar, Ta, Ge, Cn, Le,Vi	Aq	Vi	85 years
3rd	Li, Sc, Sg, Cp, Aq, Pi, Sc, Li, Vi	Li	Vi	83 years
4th	Cn, Le, Ge, Ta, Ar, Pi, Aq, Cp, Sg	Cn	Sg	86 years

Table 46: Apasavya-1 Nakshatras: Rohini, Makha, Visakha, Sravanam

Pada	Sequence of Rasis	Deha Rasi	Jeeva Rasi	Paramayush
1st	Sg, Cp, Aq, Pi, Ar, Ta, Ge, Le, Cn	Cn	Sg	86 years
2nd	Vi, Li, Sc, Pi, Aq, Cp, Sg, Sc, Li	Li	Vi	83 years
3rd	Vi, Le, Cn, Ge, Ta, Ar, Sg, Cp, Aq	Aq	Vi	85 years
4th	Pi, Ar, Ta, Ge, Le, Cn, Vi, Li, Sc	Sc	Pi	100 years

Table 47: Apasavya-2 Nakshatras: Mrigasira, Ardra, Poorvaphalguni, Uttaraphalguni, Anuradha, Jyeshtha, Dhanishtha, Satabhisha

Pada	Sequence of Rasis	Deha Rasi	Jeeva Rasi	Paramayush
1st	Pi, Aq, Cp, Sg, Sc, Li, Vi, Le, Cn	Cn	Pi	86 years
2nd	Ge, Ta, Ar, Sg, Cp, Aq, Pi, Ar, Ta	Ta	Ge	83 years
3rd	Ge, Le, Cn, Vi, Li, Sc, Pi, Aq, Cp	Cp	Ge	85 years
4th	Sg, Sc, Li, Vi, Le, Cn, Ge, Ta, Ar	Ar	Sg	100 years

It may be noted in the tables above that there is a column called "paramaayush". This gives the sum of the dasas of the nine rasis associated with the constellation quarter. We now need to define the durations of various dasas. The duration of a dasa is based in its owner, as shown in Table 48. Two rasis owned by the same planet have the same duration.

Table 48: Dasa Years in Kalachakra Dasa

Rasi owner	Rasis	Dasa years
Sun	Le	5
Moon	Cn	21
Mars	Ar & Sc	7
Mercury	Ge & Vi	9
Jupiter	Sg & Pi	10
Venus	Ta & Li	16
Saturn	Cp & Aq	4

Let us go through the procedure used in finding dasas and antardasas, in case it is not yet obvious to the reader:

(1) Find the nakshatra pada occupied by natal Moon. Identify the 9-rasi sequence associated with it, using Table 44-Table 47. Also, note down the paramayush.

(2) Find the fraction of the nakshatra pada that was covered by Moon at birth.

(3) Find the same fraction of the paramayush. That represents the portion of the paramayush (dasas of the nine rasis) that was over before birth. Based on this, we can find which of the nine dasas runs at birth and how much of the dasa remains at birth.

(4) After this dasa, we go to the next rasi in the nine rasis. When we finish the nine rasis of the nakshatra pada, we go to the nine rasis of the next nakshatra pada. After the nine rasis of the 4th pada of a nakshatra, we go to the nine rasis corresponding to the 1st pada of the next nakshatra (*i.e.* 1st pada of the constellations belonging to the *other sub-group* in the *same group*). For example, after the nine rasis of the 4th pada of Savya-1 constellations, we go to the nine rasis of the 1st pada of Savya-2 constellations. After the nine rasis of the 4th pada of Apasavya-2 constellations, we go to the nine rasis of the 1st pada of Apasavya-1 constellations.

(5) In each dasa, antardasas start from dasa rasi itself. After the first antardasa, we go to the next rasi. After that, we go to the next rasi. And so on. We take 9 rasis *starting from* dasa rasi and antardasas will belong to those rasis. We distribute the dasa length among the 9 antardasas proportionally (in proportion to their respective dasa lengths as given in Table 48). If we reach the end of the nine rasis corresponding to the nakshatra pada when counting 9 rasis from dasa rasi, we proceed to the next nakshatra pada as described in rule (4) above.

All this may seem complicated to a casual reader, but it must be obvious to anyone who clearly understood Kalachakra shown in Table 43 and followed how Table 44-Table 47 are derived from it. A couple of examples may make this clearer.

Example 95: Suppose Moon is at 15Ta50 in someone's natal chart. Let us find Kalachakra dasa for him.

Moon is in Rohini 2nd pada, which runs from 13Ta20 to 16Ta40. From Table 46, we find that the 9 rasis associated with this nakshatra pada are: Vi, Li, Sc, Pi, Aq, Cp, Sg, Sc, Li.

Table 49: Calculation for Example 95

	Vi	Li	Sc	Pi	Aq	Cp	Sg	Sc	Li
Years	9	16	7	10	4	4	10	7	16
Cumulative	9	25	32	42	46	50	60	67	83

The amount of the nakshatra pada traversed by Moon is 15°50' – 13°20' = 2°30'. The fraction of the nakshatra pada[64] traversed by Moon is (2°30')/(3°20') = 150'/200' = 0.75. The same fraction of paramayush (83 years) is 0.75 x 83 = 62.25 years. So 62.25 years out of the 83 years were over before birth. We see from Table 49 that 60 years were over by the end of Sg dasa and 2.25 years of Sc dasa added to it makes it 62.25 years. So Sc dasa was running at birth and 7 – 2.25 = 4.75 years of Sc dasa were remaining at birth. By adding 4 years 9 months to the birthdate, we get the date on which Sc dasa ends. Then Li dasa of 16 years will run till an age of 20 years 9 months. With Li dasa, we finish the nine rasis associated with the 2nd pada of Rohini (Apasavya-1). So we go to the 3rd pada in the same table. The

64 The complete length of each nakshatra pada is 3°20'.

next 7 dasas[65] will be Vi, Le, Cn, Ge, Ta, Ar, Sg. Their lengths are as given in Table 48.[66]

Example 96: Suppose Moon is at 3Cn00 in someone's natal chart. Let us find Kalachakra dasa for him.

Moon is in Punarvasu 4th pada, which runs from 0Cn00 to 3Cn20. From Table 44, we find that the 9 rasis associated with this nakshatra pada are: Cn, Le, Vi, Li, Sc, Sg, Cp, Aq, Pi.

Table 50: Calculation for Example 96

	Cn	Le	Vi	Li	Sc	Sg	Cp	Aq	Pi
Years	21	5	9	16	7	10	4	4	10
Cumulative	21	26	35	51	58	68	72	76	86

The fraction of the pada traversed by Moon is (3°0')/(3°20') = 180'/200' = 0.9. The same fraction of paramayush (86 years) is 0.9 x 86 = 77.4 years. So 77.4 out of the 86 years were over before birth. We see from Table 50 that 76 years were over by the end of Aq dasa and 1.4 years of Pi dasa added to it makes it 77.4 years. So Pi dasa was running at birth and 10 – 1.4 = 8.6 years of Pi dasa were remaining at birth. By adding 8 years 7 months 6 days to the birthdate, we get the date on which Pi dasa ends. With Pi dasa, we finish the nine rasis associated with the 4th pada of Punarvasu (Savya-1). So we go to the 1st pada of Savya-2 nakshatras (Table 45). The next 8 dasas will be Sc, Li, Vi, Cn, Le, Ge, Ta, Ar. Their lengths are as given in Table 48.

Exercise 34: Suppose Moon is at 5Aq50 in someone's natal chart. Let us find Kalachakra dasa for him.

Example 97: Let us find the antardasa sequences in the 1st, 2nd, 3rd and 4th dasas in Example 95.

The 1st dasa is Sc (from the 2nd pada of Apasavya-1 constellations). We should start from Sc and find 9 rasis. After Sc, we have Li and the 9 rasis corresponding to the 2nd pada end there (see Table 46). So the next 7

65 Parasara suggested taking the dasas of nine rasis starting from the rasi whose dasa is running at birth. Sc dasa was running at birth and Sc and Li dasas belong to the set of nine rasis associated with Rohini 2nd pada. We already have 2 rasis. So we just need 7 rasis from the next pada.

66 We again have the issue of solar years vs savana years. This author prefers savana years with all nakshatra dasas. Kalachakra dasa is a nakshatra dasa.

rasis should be taken from the 9 rasis corresponding to the next pada, *i.e.* 3rd pada. So we get antardasas in Sc dasa as Sc, Li, Vi, Le, Cn, Ge, Ta, Ar, Sg.[67]

Similarly, one can see that antardasas in Li dasa (2nd dasa) go as Li, Vi, Le, Cn, Ge, Ta, Ar, Sg, Cp. Antardasas in Vi dasa (3rd dasa) go as Vi, Le, Cn, Ge, Ta, Ar, Sg, Cp, Aq. Antardasas in Le dasa (4th dasa) go as Le, Cn, Ge, Ta, Ar, Sg, Cp, Aq, Pi.

One can notice that dasa sequences and antardasa sequences all come from the two 24-rasi sequences given in Kalachakra (see Table 43). In the cases of dasas, the starting point in the 24-rasi sequence is determined by the nakshatra pada of Moon and the portion elapsed in it. In the case of antardasas, the starting point is based on dasa rasi.

To learn how the lengths of antardasas are computed, let us take Le dasa as an example. We found that antardasas in Le dasa are Le, Cn, Ge, Ta, Ar, Sg, Cp, Aq, Pi. By adding the dasa lengths of these 9 rasis (see Table 48), we get 86 years. So we divide Le dasa of 5 years into 86 parts and give 5 parts to Le antardasa, 21 parts to Cn antardasa, 9 parts to Ge antardasa and so on.

24.3 Interpretation

24.3.1 *Basics*

Dasa of a rasi gives the natural results of the rasi. For example, dasa of Pisces may give saattwik religious activities. Dasa of Aries may give enterprise or quarrels or wounds.

More importantly, dasa of a rasi gives the results of the house and planets in that rasi. If Aries has the 5th house in D-7, its dasa may give children. If Pisces has the 8th house in D-6, its dasa may give diseases. If Gemini has lagna in D-24, its dasa may give all-round progress in the accumulation of knowledge. If Sc has AL in D-10 and its lord Mars occupies it, its dasa may bring good developments related to career and status. Dasa of a rasi containing the 8th from AL in D-10 may give a fall in status at workplace. Dasa of a rasi may also give the results of its lord. If Mars is in the 5th house in D-7, Aries dasa may give children.

Samudaaya Ashtakavarga (SAV) plays an important role in deciding the results in a dasa. If a rasi has too many or too few rekhas in SAV of a

---

67 However, we see from Example 95 that 2.25 years of Sc dasa were over before birth. So some of these antardasas may be over before birth.

particular divisional chart, then its dasa may bring favorable or unfavorable results, respectively, relating to the significations of that house in that divisional chart. Usually dasas of rasis with 30 or more rekhas in D-10 SAV bring the best phases in one's career and dasas of rasis with 30 or more rekhas in in D-24 SAV bring the best periods for learning. One should keep SAV of various divisional charts with one when interpreting Kalachakra dasa.

24.3.2 *Deha and Jeeva Rasis*

In Table 44-Table 47, we listed the deha and jeeva rasis of different nakshatra padas. However, these hold for one born at the beginning of the nakshatra pada. One can have different deha and jeeva rasis based on the elapsed portion in the nakshatra pada.

Deha and **jeeva** rasis are simply the rasis of the *first* and the *ninth* dasas in the case of one born in a *savya* nakshatra. In the case of one born in an *apasavya* nakshatra, deha and jeeva rasis are the rasis of the *ninth* and the *first* dasas.

In Example 95, the first dasa is Sc and the ninth dasa is Sg. Since Rohini is an apasavya nakshatra, Sc becomes jeeva rasi and Sg becomes deha rasi. In Example 96, the first dasa is Pi and the ninth dasa is Ar. Since Punarvasu is a savya nakshatra, Pi becomes deha rasi and Ar becomes jeeva rasi.

Deha rasi shows body and jeeva rasi shows the spirit. Benefics and malefics transiting in them affect them positively and negatively (respectively). If Jupiter, Mercury and Venus are transiting in one's jeeva rasi, one may exhibit a positive spirit and be cheerful. If Mars, Sun, Saturn and Rahu are transiting in one's jeeva rasi, one may be without any enthusiasm. If Mars, Sun, Saturn and Rahu are transiting in one's deha rasi, one may face accidents or death.

24.3.3 Gatis (special movements)

We see that dasas progress in a regular fashion in Kalachakra dasa. We either go as Ar, Ta, Ge etc or as Pi, Aq, Cp etc. However, some irregularities can be found. The rasis whose dasas come after an irregular leap go by special names and special results are attributed to those dasas in classics.

(1) A trinal leap (from Sg to Ar or vice versa; from Pi to Sc or vice versa) is called **"Simhaavalokana gati"** (lion's leap)[68].

---

68 Simhavalokana doesn't really mean a lion. It strictly means a lion's view of the jungle from an elevated vantage point.

(2) Temporary reversal of the direction is called **"Markati gati"** (monkey's leap). When we go as Sc, Li, Vi, Cn, Le, Ge, Ta, Ar etc in savya nakshatras, we temporarily reverse the direction when we go from Cn to Le. So Le is a markati gati rasi. Similarly, when we go as Ar, Ta, Ge, Le, Cn, Vi, Li, Sc etc in apasavya nakshatras, we temporarily reverse the direction when we go from Le to Cn. So Cn is a markati gati rasi.

(3) Leaving one rasi and jumping over it is called **"Mandooki gati"** (frog's leap). When we go as Sc, Li, Vi, Cn, Le, Ge, Ta, Ar etc in savya nakshatras, we have 2 jumps – (*i*) from Vi to Cn and (*ii*) Le to Ge. So Cn and Ge are mandooki gati rasis. Similarly, when we go as Ar, Ta, Ge, Le, Cn, Vi, Li, Sc etc in apasavya nakshatras, we have 2 jumps – (*i*) from Ge to Le and (*ii*) Cn to Vi. So Le and Vi are mandooki gati rasis.

The results attributed to various leaps are given in Table 51.

Table 51: Results of gatis (leaps)

Leap	Savya nakshatras	Apasavya nakshatras
Lion	Fear of animals, loss of friends, distress to near relations, fall in dungeons, danger from poison and weapons, fall from a vehicle, fever, destruction of house	Death of father or elders, loss of position
Monkey	Loss of wealth, agriculture and animals, death of father or elders	Danger from water, distress to father, loss of position, anger of rulers, wandering in the forests
Frog	Distress to relatives, elders and father, trouble from poison, weapons, enemies, thieves. In Le-to-Ge leap, death of mother or, death of native, trouble from rulers and diseases are possible.	Distress to wife, loss of children, fever, sickness and loss of position

In addition, Parasara listed the directions to prefer and the directions to avoid, while travelling and relocating, during different leaps.

(1) In the leap from Vi to Cn, east will give great results. One can take up an auspicious journey in the northern direction.

(2) In the leap from Le to Ge, east should be avoided. A journey to the southwest will be fruitful.

(3) In the leap from Cn to Le, a move in the southern direction results in losses. West is favorable.

(4) In the leap from Pi to Sc and in the normal movement from Sg to Cp, there will be troubles in the northern direction.

(5) In the leap from Sg to Ar, journeys should be avoided, as they may result in sickness, imprisonment or death.

(6) In the normal movement from Sg to Sc, journeys will bring comforts, wealth and sexual pleasures.

(7) In the leap from Le to Cn, western direction should be avoided.

24.4 Practical Examples

Example 98: The navamsa chart of a male who got married in Dec 1994 is shown in Chart 46.

Readers can verify that the native had about 5 years of Sc dasa left at birth and the next dasas are Sg, Cp, Aq, Pi, Sc, Li, Vi, Cn. At the time of wedding, the native was running Pi-Pi (Pi dasa & Pi antardasa). Why did Pisces give marriage?

Well, it has lagna in navamsa and its lord Jupiter is in the 7th house! Naturally Pi and Vi are the front-runners for giving marriage. Moreover, Pi is the 2nd from Venus. Venus symbolizes domestic happiness and marital bliss. The 2nd from him in navamsa can show the sense of family happiness. It can show a new person coming into the family.

In addition, one may note that exalted Venus occupies Pi in rasi chart and he owns darapada, which is in Libra. So Pisces is conducive to physical relationship and marital pleasures.

Venus is in Aq in navamsa. While rasi shows what exists at the physical level, navamsa shows the inner self and the sense of connectedness. So Aq dasa can activate Venusian influence at navamsa level and give some romance. During Aq dasa (1990-1994), this native had a love affair with the lady he was to marry in December 1994.

Example 99: The D-24 shown in Chart 47 belongs to an astrologer. He learnt astrology at a young age, but he has been seriously into astrology since 1993. In particular, 1996-2000 was a very fruitful period. Knowledge came to him like rain from monsoon clouds. He never felt as fulfilled as he did with the knowledge that came to him in 1996-2000.

Chart 46

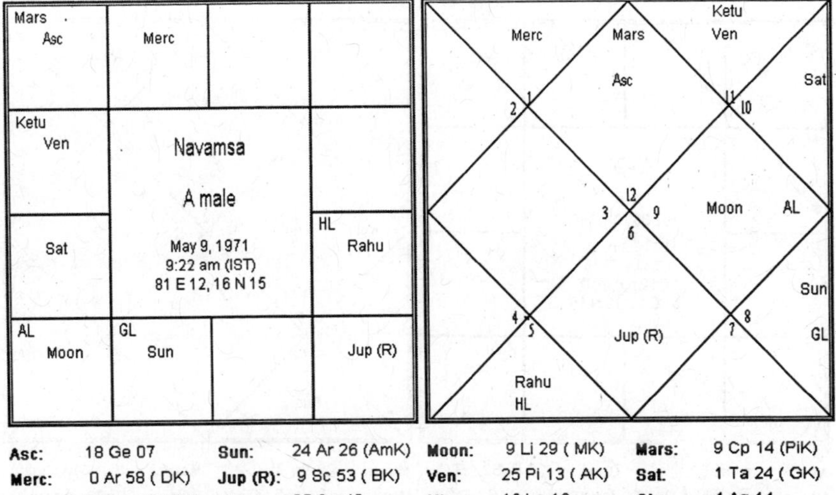

One may note that about 3 years and 2 months of Sg dasa was left at birth and Ar, Ta, Ge, Cn *etc* dasas run after it. One may find that Gemini dasa of 9 years started in 1996. This dasa brought fine knowledge and intellectual satisfaction. Why?

Gemini contains lagna in D-24. Lagna stands for all-round progress. This is D-24 and lagna in it shows all-round progress related to learning and knowledge. Its lord Mercury is in the 5th house of scholarship from lagna. So this dasa can increase scholarship. Mercury and Venus are in trines from Ge and they contribute to the prosperity of the indications of Ge. Moreover, Ge is very strong in D-24 with 34 rekhas in SAV. Any rasi with 30 or more rekhas brings favorable results related to that house in that divisional chart.

The strongest houses in this D-24 SAV are Le (36 rekhas), Ge (34 rekhas) and Pi (33 rekhas). They are the 7th, 5th and 2nd houses from AL. As these are the houses conducive to recognition and awards, this D-24 shows a person with academic achievements and associated recognition. With Ge being the 5th house from AL and also A5, this dasa can bring some reputation for his knowledge. So this dasa brings knowledge, scholarship and also recognition for it.

Example 100: Let us consider the native whose D-12 is given in Chart 48. Father passed away in 1967.

Chart 47

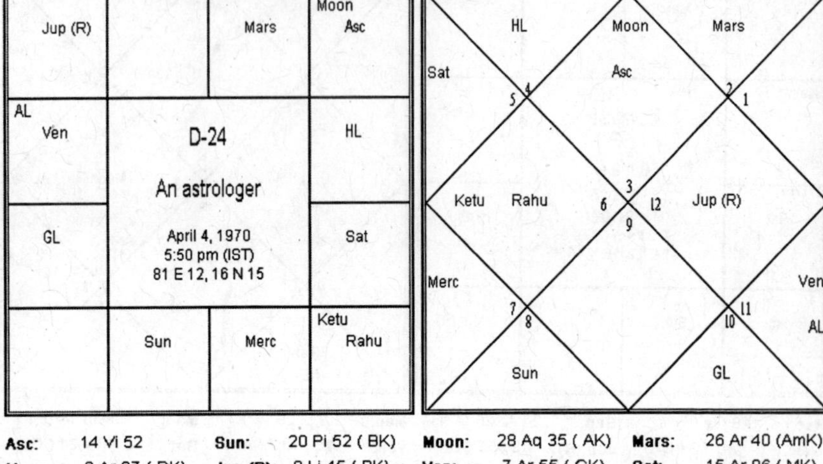

Asc:	14 Vi 52	**Sun:**	20 Pi 52 (BK)	**Moon:**	28 Aq 35 (AK)	**Mars:**	26 Ar 40 (AmK)
Merc:	3 Ar 07 (DK)	**Jup (R):**	9 Li 45 (PK)	**Ven:**	7 Ar 55 (GK)	**Sat:**	15 Ar 06 (MK)
Rahu:	16 Aq 53 (PiK)	**Ketu:**	16 Le 53	**HL:**	15 Pi 42	**GL:**	8 Vi 40

We can see that about 1 year and 8 months of Pi dasa was remaining at birth and the dasas coming after it are Sc, Li, Vi, Cn, Le, Ge, Ta and Ar. Cn dasa started in September 1966 and Cn-Cn antardasa was running at the time of his father's demise.

Chart 48

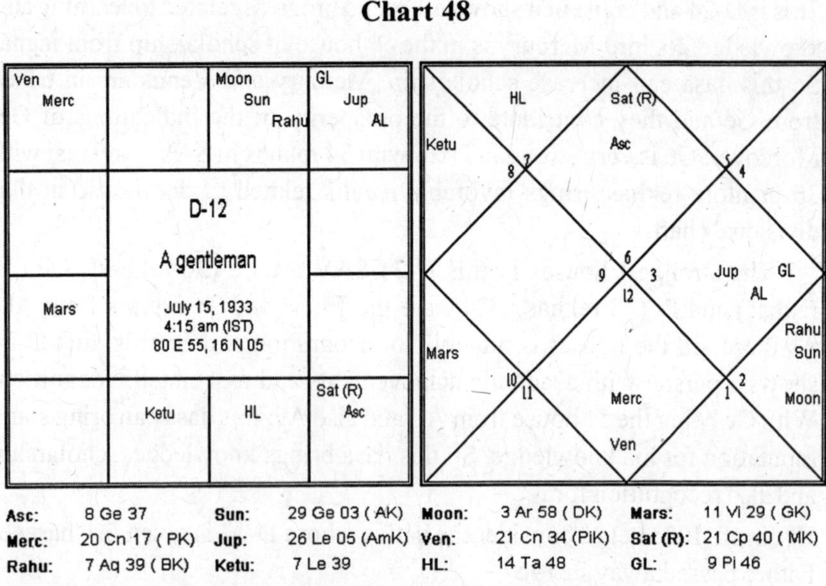

Asc:	8 Ge 37	**Sun:**	29 Ge 03 (AK)	**Moon:**	3 Ar 58 (DK)	**Mars:**	11 Vi 29 (GK)
Merc:	20 Cn 17 (PK)	**Jup:**	26 Le 05 (AmK)	**Ven:**	21 Cn 34 (PiK)	**Sat (R):**	21 Cp 40 (MK)
Rahu:	7 Aq 39 (BK)	**Ketu:**	7 Le 39	**HL:**	14 Ta 48	**GL:**	9 Pi 46

Lagna in D-12 is in Vi. The 9th house is in Ta. The 9th house in D-12 shows the relation with father and the associated happiness. It stands for the "concept" of father and paternal guidance. The "physical body" of the father is an *illusion* related to the concept of father and A9 represents it. So we can use the 9th lord or A9 to see the physical body of father. Here A9 is in Cp. Taking Cp as lagna, we see that Cn is the 7th house of death and its lord Moon is exalted. Moon is not only exalted, but he afflicts Sun, who owns the 8th house from Cp. So Cn-Cn antardasa can result in the death of father. Moreover, Cn dasa here comes after Vi and involves mandooki gati (frog's leap). We see from the previous discussions that mandooki gati in savya nakshatras can bring distress to father.

Exercise 35: The native of Example 100 lost his mother in Li-Li antardasa. Why?

Example 101: Sri A.B. Vajpayee's birthdata and D-10 chart is given in Chart 3. He has been India's Prime Minister since March 1998.

About 4.5 years of Vi dasa was left at birth. The dasas to follow are Le, Cn, Ge, Ta, Ar, Sg, Cp and Aq. His 4-year Cp dasa runs during 1998-2002.

We can see that Cp has 31 rekhas in the SAV of D-10 and 34 rekhas in the SAV of rasi chart. Because Cp is strong in both charts, Cp dasa must be good.

The houses having 30 or more rekhas are the 1st, 3rd, 5th, 7th and 10th houses from AL. Most of these houses are important for fame and recognition (and AL is the most appropriate reference for judging fame and recognition). The strength of these houses in D-10 SAV means that the native has a successful and famous career. Being the 5th house from AL, Cp can bring reputation and power. Moreover, the lord of Cp is exalted in GL. In addition, Cp contains A5 in rasi chart and D-10. A5 shows the illusion associated with the 5th house matters. In D-24, A5 shows the illusion associated with scholarship (5th house), *i.e.* one's degrees, academic distinctions and awards. In D-10, it shows the illusion associated with one's following (5th house), *i.e.* the positions held and the power wielded by one. For this reason, the presence of A5 in Cp adds to the probability of power in Cp dasa.

Example 102: Let us revisit Example 82. Chart 49 gives the D-20 chart of the devotee whose rasi chart was considered in that example.

Ta dasa of about 9.5 years was left at birth. The dasas to follow are Ar, Pi, Aq, Cp, Sg, Ar, Ta and Ge. Pi dasa started in July 1987 and Sg antardasa in it was running when he moved to the monastery.

Pi and Sg are owned by Jupiter and they can give religious knowledge. Pi is the 12th house in D-20 and Sg is the 9th house. The 12th house in D-20 shows spiritual evolution and activities related to moksha. It has 33 rekhas in SAV and hence it is strong. So its dasa can take in the direction of liberation from material bonds and evolution of soul.

Chart 49

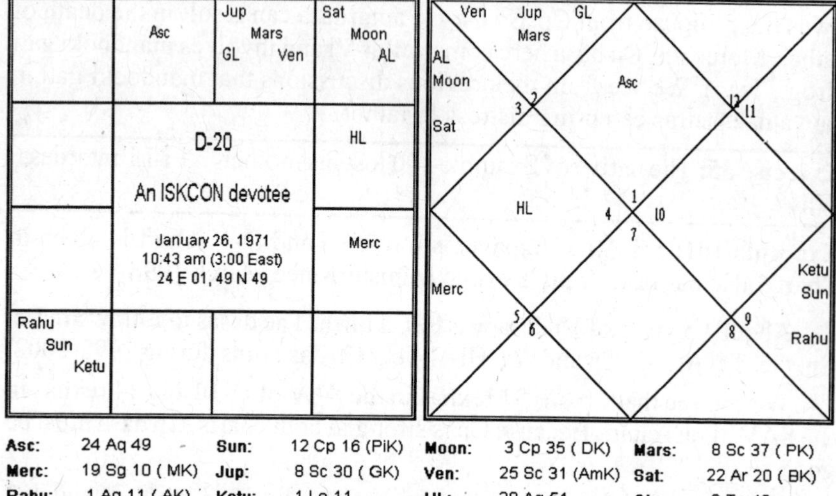

The antardasa sign Sg is the 9th house from lagna. The 9th house shows guidance. In D-20, it shows one's spiritual guru or organized religion or religious practices. It can also show pilgrimages. It can certainly show moving to a monastery. Darapada (A7) of D-20 is in Sg. The 7th house shows relations with others. Its arudha pada shows the illusion associated with relationships or the things based on which the world forms an impression about one's relationship with others. It shows the people one associates with. Darapada in D-20 shows the people one associates with, in one's spiritual life. So antardasa of the rasi containing darapada in D-20 can bring him to the people he will associate with for the rest of his religious life. With Sg containing Sun, natural significator of soul, and the nodes, his soul went through a churning during Sg antardasa and he wandered in forests thinking about what life is. But Sg is also the 9th house and its antardasa brought him to a monastery before its end.

The next antardasa belonged to Ar, which contains lagna. So there was all-round progress in spiritual matters. Ar has 33 rekhas in D-20 SAV and it is strong. In addition, Ar contains A5 (mantra pada, arudha pada of the 5th house) and this antardasa may have brought some religious initiation and practice of some mantras. It should be noted that the 5th house in D-20 shows one's devotion and *bhakti* in religious matters. A5 shows the maya relating to devotion, *i.e.* practice of mantras and religious rituals.

One may note that the 3rd house (Ge) and A3 (Li) have 30 or more rekhas in the SAV. The 3rd house shows one's communication skills. In D-20; it shows communication skills as applicable in religious activities. A3 shows the associated illusion, *i.e.* the things based on which the world forms impressions about one's communication skills. It can show the books and articles authored by one. In D-20, it shows one's religious works. If one casts D-10 of this native, one will see that the 3rd house and A3 have 30 or more rekhas, in D-10 SAV also. Houses with 30 or more rekhas in SAV are strengthened as per Parasara. So the 3rd house and A3 are strong in both D-20 and D-10. One can conclude that this native will be a good communicator and will be known for some religious literature. In fact, he is already authoring a translation of "Sreemadbhaagavatam" into his mother tongue and travels with some ISKCON gurus as an interpreter. A lot of worthy religious literature and translations will emerge from the pen of this blessed soul in the years to come.

Exercise 36: The lady whose rasi and navamsa charts are given in Chart 50 was married in Sg dasa and divorced in the same dasa. Sg contains Venus, the significator of marriage. However, Venus also owns the 2nd and 7th from upapada in rasi and navamsa. This dasa brought her marriage as well as divorce. Guess the antardasa that may have brought the marriage and the antardasa that may have brought the divorce.

Chart 50

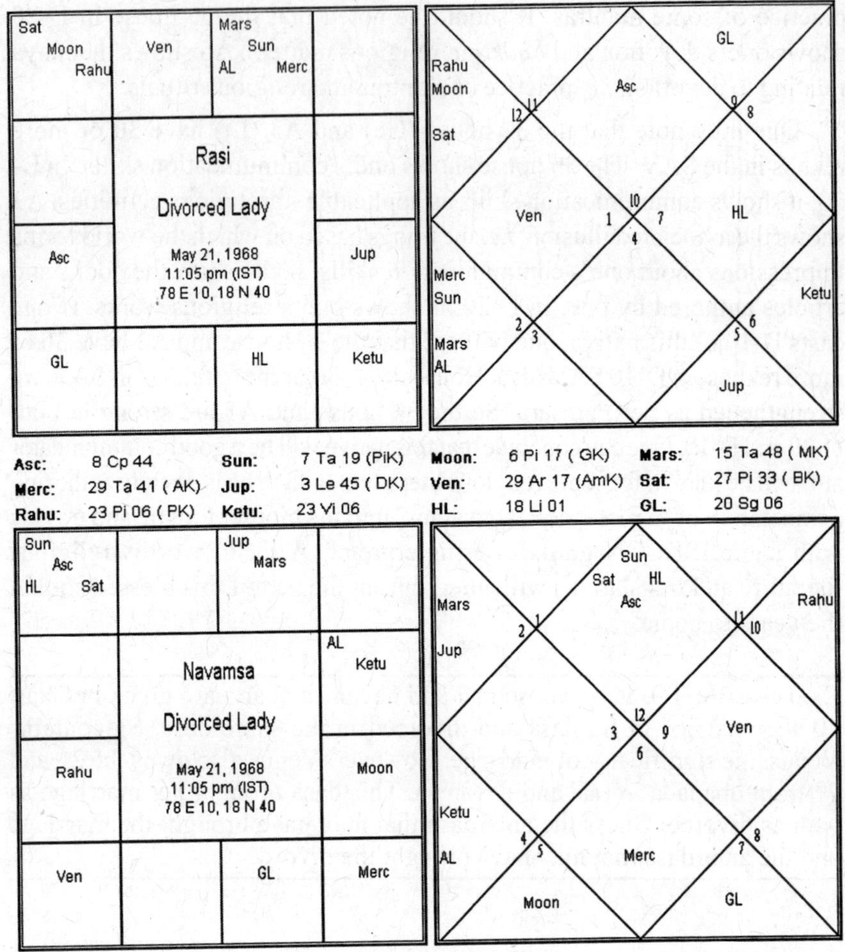

Exercise 37: Consider an actor's D-10 chart shown in Chart 51. Venus in Aries in the 10th house from AL shows a dynamic entertainer. Compute Kalachakra dasa and SAV of D-10. Estimate whether Cn dasa during 1964-1984 was poor or average or good.

Chart 51

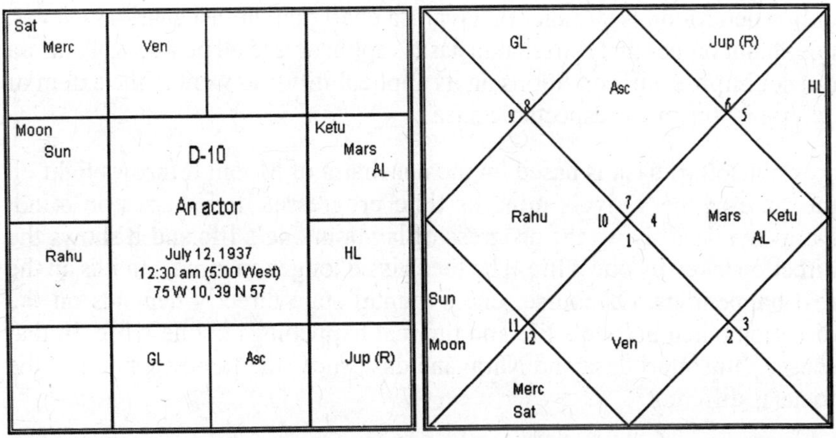

Sat Merc	Ven		
Moon Sun	D-10 An actor		Ketu Mars AL
Rahu	July 12, 1937 12:30 am (5:00 West) 75 W 10, 39 N 57		HL
	GL	Asc	Jup (R)

GL, Jup (R), Asc, HL, 9, 8, 6, 5, Rahu, 10, 7, 4, 1, Mars, Ketu, AL, Sun, Moon, 11, 12, Ven, 2, 3, Merc, Sat

Asc:	20 Ar 14	**Sun:**	26 Ge 29 (BK)	**Moon:**	19 Le 28 (MK)	**Mars:**	28 Li 00 (AmK)
Merc:	0 Cn 57 (DK)	**Jup (R):**	29 Sg 51 (AK)	**Ven:**	11 Ta 30 (PK)	**Sat:**	12 Pi 09 (PiK)
Rahu:	20 Sc 24 (GK)	**Ketu:**	20 Ta 24	**HL:**	19 Aq 33	**GL:**	10 Le 20

24.5 Conclusion

Kalachakra dasa was called "the most respectable dasa of all dasas" by Parasara. There are many controversies regarding its computation. This book follows the approach that this author found the most acceptable based on his study of "Brihat Parasara Hora Sastram" and his practical researches. A significant percentage of this author's successful long-range life-phase predictions were made using Kalachakra dasa[69] and that is his favorite dasa.

When we learn a new dasa, the first question we should ask is "when should it be applied and what results should be seen in it". It is illogical to use 10 different dasas interchangably. Mixing up various dasas without knowing the subtle differences between them results in vague explanations. An intelligent astrologer will realize that different dasas are good at showing different kinds of events. **Even when different dasas show the same event, they show it from different angles and focus on different aspects of the same event.** Without appreciating this, one cannot understand why maharshis described tens, if not hundreds, of dasa systems.

---

69 And, a significant percentage his successful short-term predictions (focussing on a period of one or two weeks) were made using Tajaka annual and monthly charts.

Hence it is important to learn when a dasa can be applied and what kind of results it shows. Some authors suggested that Kalachakra dasa applies only when Moon is stronger in navamsa chart than in rasi chart. However, this author opines that Kalachakra dasa is applicable to all people, as Parasara did not impose any conditions on its applicability and went to the extent of calling it "the most respectable dasa".

Vimsottari dasa is based on the nakshatra of Moon. It throws light on the state of the native's mind as time progresses. It focusses on mind. Narayana dasa shows the progress of lagna in one's life and it shows the direction taken by one's life. The focus is no longer on mind, but it is on the real happenings. Of course, one's mental state directly depends on the direction taken by one's life and the real happenings in one's life. In that sense, Vimsottari dasa and Narayana dasa show the same events. But the focus is different.

Kalachakra dasa depends on Moon's navamsa. Navamsa shows one's adherence of dharma or duty and throws light on the inner self. So the focus in Kalachakra dasa is state of the inner self and the sense of connectedness in one's mind. It shows how *connected* one is with respect to the events in one's life. For example, a political leader may be running D-10 Narayana dasa of a yogakaraka rasi and he may land political power. He may be running the Vimsottari dasa of Sun who may be exalted in D-10 and so he may be feeling powerful. However, if Kalachakra dasa of a weak and afflicted house in D-10 runs at the same time, his inner self may not feel connected with the events in his career and he may feel a void. On the other hand, if Kalachakra dasa rasi is strong and occupied by benefics in D-10, then one may be successfully involved in activities that keep his inner self engaged.

Narayana dasa specializes in showing what happens in one's life; Vimsottari dasa specializes in showing how one's mind *views* what happens in one's life; and, Kalachakra dasa specializes in showing how one *relates to* what happens in one's life and how connected one feels. These three are the most important of all general purpose phalita dasas.

Different dasas do not provide different alternatives that can be used *interchangeably* to understand what happens in one's life, but they provide different angles – or vantage points – to view the same kaleidoscope that life is.

24.6 Answers to Exercises

Exercise 34:

Moon at 5Aq50 is in Dhanishtha 4th pada, which runs from 3Aq20 to 6Aq40. From Table 47, we find that the 9 rasis associated with this nakshatra pada are: Sg, Sc, Li, Vi, Le, Cn, Ge, Ta, Ar.

Table 52: Calculation for Exercise 34

	Sg	Sc	Li	Vi	Le	Cn	Ge	Ta	Ar
Years	10	7	16	9	5	21	9	16	7
Cumulative	10	17	33	42	47	68	77	93	**100**

The fraction of the pada traversed by Moon is (2°30')/(3°20') = 150'/ 200' = 0.75. The same fraction of paramayush (100 years) is 0.75 x 100 = 75 years. So 75 years out of the 100 years were over before birth. We see from Table 52 that 68 years were over by the end of Cn dasa and 7 years of Ge dasa added to it makes it 75 years. So Ge dasa was running at birth and 9 – 7 = 2 years of Ge dasa were remaining at birth. By adding 2 years to the birthdate, we get the date on which Ge dasa ends. Then we run 16 years of Ta dasa and 7 years of Ar dasa. With Ar dasa, we finish the nine rasis associated with the 4th pada of Dhanishtha (Apasavya-2). So we go to the 1st pada of Apasavya-1 nakshatras (Table 46). The next 7 dasas will be Sg, Cp, Aq, Pi, Ar, Ta, Ge. So we get the following calculations:

Ge dasa (02 years): 00-02 years of age

Ta dasa (16 years): 02-18 years of age

Ar dasa (07 years): 18-25 years of age

Sg dasa (10 years): 25-35 years of age

Cp dasa (04 years): 35-39 years of age

Aq dasa (04 years): 39-43 years of age

Pi dasa (10 years): 43-53 years of age

Ar dasa (07 years): 53-60 years of age

Ta dasa (16 years): 60-76 years of age

Ge dasa (09 years): 76-85 years of age

Exercise 35:

The 4th house is in Sg. A4 or the arudha pada of 4th house is in Vi. From Vi, Li is the 2nd house. Its lord Venus is in exalted in the 7th house and afflicts the debilitated 1st lord (all from Vi). So Li is a strong maraka rasi from Vi. So Li-Li antardasa resulted in the death of mother.

Exercise 36:

Let us take navamsa. Ge contains A7 in navamsa and can show a relationship. It contains the 3rd from UL (upapada lagna) and can show the start of a marriage. It is the 7th house from Venus. It is the 4th house of harmony and bliss from lagna. Its lord Mercury is exalted in the 7th house. Ge has 33 rekhas in SAV. For all these reasons, Ge can be the antardasa. The 7th house Vi is also a candidate, but it is very weak with only 22 rekhas in SAV.

For divorce, the 6th and 8th houses from lagna and the 2nd and 7th houses from UL are good candidates. The 6th and 8th houses from lagna bring marital troubles and quarrels. The 2nd and 7th houses from upapada bring the end of marriage. Here Li is the 8th house from lagna and the 7th house from upapada. It is the 7th house from upapada in rasi also. In navamsa, it has 30 rekhas in SAV. While the 7th house has only 22 rekhas, the 8th house has 30 rekhas and so the 8th house is strong. Evil houses, when strong, only bring evil results.

Final Answer: The lady got married in Ge antardasa in Feb 1992 and got divorced in Li antardasa in late 1995.

Exercise 37:

Ta dasa of about 13 years was left at birth. Then Ge dasa of 9 years, Le dasa 5 years and Cn dasa of 21 years followed. Cn dasa ran during 1964-1984.

Cn is the 10th from lagna. Its lord Moon is in the 5th from lagna. Moreover, Cn contains AL and shows status in career. Its strength is decided by SAV. SAV of D-10 is shown below:

	Ar	Ta	Ge	**Cn**	Le	Vi	Li	Sc	Sg	Cp	Aq	Pi
Rekhas	24	28	21	**38**	34	21	26	26	37	31	25	26

In SAV, Cn has 38 rekhas. That is exceedingly strong. With the rasi containing AL having 38 rekhas in SAV, the status of this actor must be high. He must be a well-known actor. And, Cn dasa must've brought excellent results and increased his stature as an actor.

Final Answer: This chart belongs to Bill Cosby, one of the most gifted entertainers that the US television industry has ever seen. He had a successful acting career in films too. He came to limelight in 1965 with a lighthearted adventure TV serial called "I Spy". He was the first black American to star in a prime-time television drama series in US, and for his performances on the show he won the Emmy Award for best actor in 1966, 1967, and 1968. The onset of Cn dasa brought him status.

Part 3: Transit Analysis

The constant movement of planets in the skies is what is meant by the word "transits" in astrology. Planets keep moving. The relationship between (1) the positions of planets at a given time and (2) the positions of planets at a person's birthtime, will have a major impact on the kind of results that planets can give the person at the time.

Position of planets at any given time can be found out from computer programs/software or ephemeris or almanacs (panchangas). Judging the results for a person based on those, given the natal (birth) chart, is the subject of this part.

There are many special techniques in Vedic astrology for interpreting transits. Some of those techniques are explained in this part.

25. Transits and Natal References

25.1 Introduction

By transits or gochaara, we mean the motion of planets in the skies. By the **transit** or chaara or gochaara position of a planet, we mean the position occupied by a planet at a given time. By the **natal** or radical or birth or janma position of a planet, we mean the position occupied by a planet at the time of one's birth.

By correlating the transit positions on a given day with the natal positions of several reference points, we can draw some conclusions about the nature of results experienced by the native then. Some methods normally employed in such correlation will be studied in this chapter.

25.2 Transits from Moon

The most popular natal reference in transit analysis is Moon. Moon is the significator of mind and analysis of planetary positions with respect to Moon shows the mental state. Depending on the houses occupied by transit planets with respect to natal Moon, they exert different influences on one's mental state. The transit of Vimsottari dasa lord is particularly important, because he is the one who has the greatest influence on one's mental state during a period.

The rasi occupied by Moon in the natal chart is called "**janma rasi**" and planets give different results when transiting in different houses from janma rasi. The standard results given in literature are given in Table 53 – Table 59.

These results are given only for reference. In reality, not everyone with the same janma rasi experiences the same results on a given day (or week or month). The results given by planets depend on what they stand for in the natal chart. For example, if Mars is the 5th lord in a natal chart, then the worries given by him during his transit in the 8th house from janma rasi may pertain to children. If Mars is the 10th lord in natal chart, then the worries given by him during his transit in the 8th house from janma rasi may pertain to career.

Table 53: Sun's Transit from Janma Rasi

House	Snapshot	Typical results
1st	Bad	Financial loss, many travels, discomfort
2nd	Bad	Unhappiness, eye troubles, fear
3rd	Good	Wealth, good health, victory
4th	Bad	Marital disharmony, loss of name
5th	Bad	Bad health, fear from enemies
6th	Good	Success over enemies, good health
7th	Bad	Travels, physical pain
8th	Bad	Disease, setbacks in marriage
9th	Bad	Mental worries, obstacles
10th	Good	Success, honors, gains
11th	Good	Good health, prosperity, honors
12th	Bad	Expenditure, losses

Table 54: Moon's Transit from Janma Rasi

House	Snapshot	Typical results
1st	Good	Comfort, good spirits
2nd	Bad	Obstacles, losses
3rd	Good	Gains, happiness
4th	Bad	Lack of peace of mind, distrust
5th	Bad	Failures, disappointments, sadness
6th	Good	Happiness, health, wealth
7th	Good	Respect, gains
8th	Bad	Losses, tension, worries
9th	Bad	Mental uneasiness
10th	Good	Success, gains, authority
11th	Good	Prosperity, comforts, gains
12th	Bad	Injuries, expenditure, sadness

Table 55: Mars's Transit from Janma Rasi

House	Snapshot	Typical results
1st	Bad	Troubles, bodily afflictions
2nd	Bad	Accidents, losses, thefts, quarrels
3rd	Good	Gains, power, wealth
4th	Bad	Stomach problems, fevers, bad health
5th	Bad	Troubles from enemies, trouble with children
6th	Good	Success over enemies, wealth, success, well-being
7th	Bad	Quarrels, marital troubles, eye problems
8th	Bad	Worries, accidents, bad name, losses
9th	Bad	Losses, insults, illness
10th	Bad	Change of place, unexpected wealth
11th	Good	Authority, gains, good name
12th	Bad	Expenses, quarrels with wife, diseases

Table 56: Mercury's Transit from Janma Rasi

House	Snapshot	Typical results
1st	Bad	Quarrels, imprisonment, losses, poor advice
2nd	Good	Success, wealth, gains
3rd	Bad	Wandering, losses, trouble from authorities
4th	Good	Prosperity in family, gains
5th	Bad	Quarrels with wife and children, suffering
6th	Good	Renown, success, ornaments
7th	Bad	Quarrels, mental discomfort, addictions
8th	Good	Childbirth, happiness, gains, success
9th	Bad	Mental worries, obstacles
10th	Good	Money, happiness, domestic harmony, success
11th	Good	Childbirth, happiness, wealth
12th	Bad	Disease, domestic disharmony, disease, losses

Table 57: Jupiter's Transit from Janma Rasi

House	Snapshot	Typical results
1st	Bad	Loss of money and intelligence, Wandering
2nd	Good	Happiness, domestic harmony, success
3rd	Bad	Obstacles, loss of position, travels
4th	Bad	Troubles, defeat, losses
5th	Good	Childbirth, intelligence, prosperity, wealth
6th	Bad	Mental uneasiness, enemies, worries
7th	Good	Health, happiness, erotic pleasures, sense of well-being
8th	Bad	Disease, imprisonment, illness, grief
9th	Good	Success, wealth, childbirth, religiousness
10th	Bad	Loss of position and money, ill-health, wandering
11th	Good	Recovery of health and position, happiness
12th	Bad	Fall from grace, misconduct, grief

Table 58: Venus's Transit from Janma Rasi

House	Snapshot	Typical results
1st	Good	Comforts, pleasures, happiness, good spirits
2nd	Good	Money, fortune, erotic pleasures, childbirth
3rd	Good	Respect, wealth, good spirits
4th	Good	Prosperity, success of enemies, comforts
5th	Good	Fame, power, good name
6th	Bad	Loss of fame, bad name, quarrels
7th	Bad	Humiliation, disease, troubles
8th	Bad	Fears, mental worries, injuries, troubles from women
9th	Good	Fortune, luxuries, marital happiness
10th	Bad	Virtuous acts, troubles, unpleasant events, disgrace
11th	Good	Gains, happiness, prosperity, comforts
12th	Bad	New friends, money, pleasures, gains

Table 59: Saturn's Transit from Janma Rasi

House	Snapshot	Typical results
1st	Bad	Fear of incarceration, worries, foreign trips
2nd	Bad	Physical weakness, discomfort, wealth, unhappiness
3rd	Good	Wealth, health, happiness, all-round success
4th	Bad	Stomach problems, wickedness, separation from family
5th	Bad	Separation from children, uneasiness, quarrels
6th	Good	Freedom from disease and enemies, success
7th	Bad	Wandering, quarrels with spouse, trouble from authorities
8th	Bad	Suffering, loss of status and balance, impris onment
9th	Bad	Diseases, suffering, loss of status
10th	Bad	Loss of money, bad name, changes in career, laziness
11th	Good	Wealth, success, gains
12th	Bad	Grief, misery, losses, ill-health, frustration

Rahu's behavior is similar to that of Saturn's and Ketu's behavior to Mars's.

Chart 52

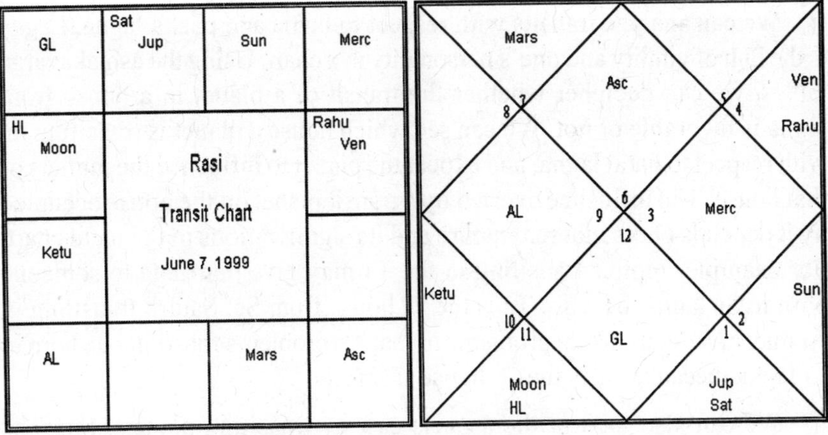

Example 103: Suppose someone has Moon in Ge in natal chart. Let us analyze the transits on June 7, 1999. The transit chart is shown in Chart 52.

Janma rasi is Ge. Transit Jupiter and Saturn are in Ar, the 11th house from janma rasi. This is a good transit and shows gains. The native may have gains in the matters signified by the houses ruled and occupied by Jupiter and Saturn in natal rasi chart and natal divisional charts. Because Jupiter signifies children and tradition and Saturn signifies livelihood, the gains may also be related to children, traditional cermemonies, livelihood etc.

Transit Sun is in Ta, the 12th house from janma rasi. That gives expenditure and losses. One may have losses in the matters signified by the houses ruled and occupied by Sun. Because Sun signifies authorities and health, it may also be related to those.

Mercury is in janma rasi (Ge). This suggests "quarrels, imprisonment, losses, poor advice". However, Mercury is strong being in own house (intellectual Gemini). So the results may be intellectual debates and arguments.

In this manner, we can analyze transits of all the planets. We can use the results given in literature, but we should adapt them intelligently to the chart at hand. We should understand what each planet stands for in a chart.

In addition, there are natal references other than Moon, though Moon is the most important natal reference when interpreting transits.

25.3 Other Natal References

We can analyze transits with respect to lagna and paaka lagna. Lagna is the hub of vitality and one's personality in a chart. Using the ashtakavarga tables, we can decipher whether the transit of a planet in a house from lagna is favorable or not. We can see which house a planet is transiting in, with respect to natal lagna, and expect the planet to influence the matters of that house. The influence exerted by a transit planet on the house occupied by it depends on its inherent nature and its significations in the natal chart. For example, Jupiter transiting in the Ta may give marriage to someone born in Sc lagna, because Ta is the 7th house from Sc. Saturn transiting in Ar may give relationship problems or marital problems for someone born in Li lagna, because Ar is the 7th house from Li.

We can also look at the aspects cast by transiting planets. Suppose

Jupiter is transiting in Vi and someone has lagna in Sc. Jupiter aspects Ta, the 7th house from Sc, when he is in Vi. So Jupiter can give marriage during his Vi transit also. We can look at the aspects cast by transiting planets on the rasis containing the natal houses and the natal planets. Suppose someone has lagna in Sc and Venus in Pi in natal chart. Then the 7th house is in Ta and Venus, the significator of marriage, is in Pi. Jupiter transiting in Vi aspects both Ta and Pi and hence he may give marriage.

Thus we should look at the rasis occupied and aspected by planets in their transit and find out which houses and planets occupy those rasis in the natal chart. Based on that, we should guess the results given by the planets. **A planet occupying or aspecting a rasi in transit *influences* the matters signified by the houses and planets stationed in that rasi in the natal chart.** The exact nature of the influence exerted by a planet depends on its inherent nature and the matters it stands for in the natal chart. For example, if the 5th lord in the natal chart is occupying the 8th house from natal lagna in transit, some troubles related to children may be expected. If Mars is the 8th lord in the natal chart and aspects, in transit, the rasis occupied by Venus and 7th lord in the natal chart, then some disturbances in marital life may be expected.

Sahams are useful in transit analysis. Sahams are the significant points in the zodiac. For example, when the 7th lord or Venus transits close to vivaha saham, one may get married. When the 6th lord or 8th lord or Mars or Rahu transits close to kali saham, one may have an accident.

A malefic planet transiting in janma rasi may give mental worries and a malefic planet transiting in natal lagna may affect the vitality of the native and create obstacles in his efforts. On the other hand, paaka lagna explicitly stands for the physical self and a malefic planet transiting in paaka lagna may give bodily complaints. Similarly planets occupying or aspecting arudha padas in transit may give relevant results. For example, Saturn's transit in A10 can be bad for career, Jupiter's transit in A9 is good for fortune and so on.

Example 104: Let us consider the natal chart of a lady and the transit chart at the time of her wedding (see Chart 53).

Chart 53

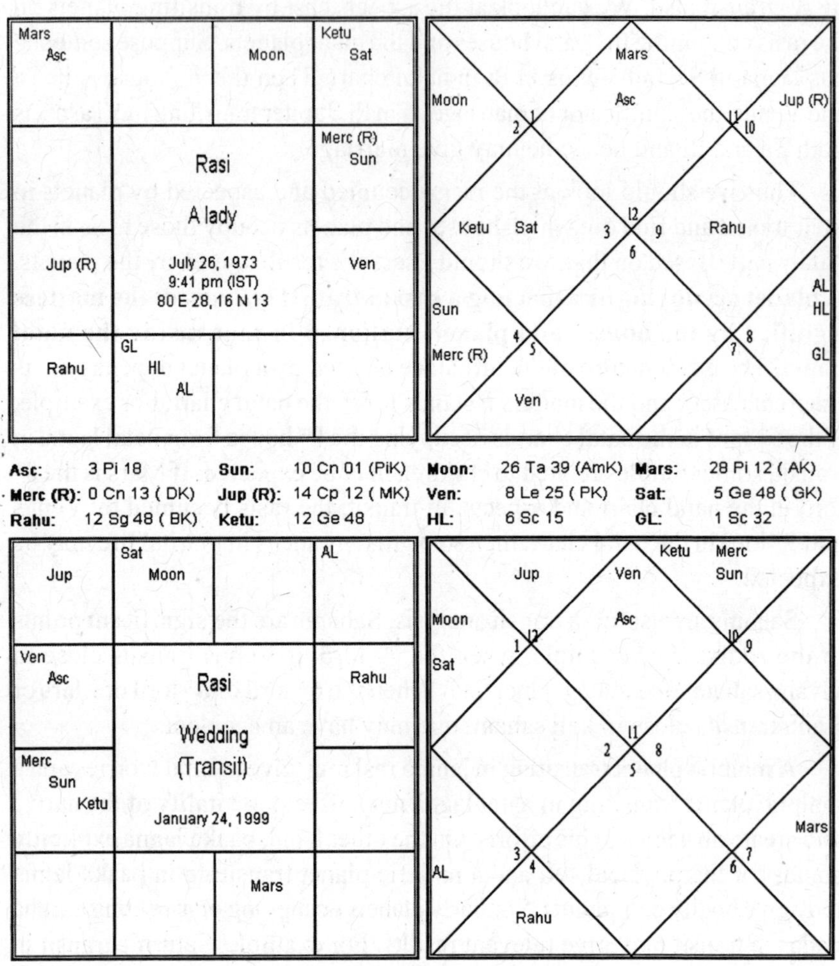

The 7th house in the natal chart is in Vi. Mercury is the 7th lord and he is in Cn in natal chart. Venus is the significator of marriage and he is in Le in the natal chart. Vivaha saham is at 1° in Cp in the natal chart. If important planets influence these reference points in transit, they can give marriage.

Jupiter is a natural benefic and also lagna lord here. His transit is important for timing auspicious events. On the day of wedding, Jupiter occupied Pi, aspecting Vi (natal 7th house) and Cn (has natal 7th lord). Natal 7th lord

Mercury occupied Cp in transit and aspected Cn, rasi occupied by him in the natal chart. In addition, transit Mercury was stationed about 1° away from natal vivaha saham. Venus also aspected his natal position in transit.

25.4 Transits and Divisional Charts

Though the *motivation* for the approach described here comes from some principles described in classics, the actual approach is essentially based on this author's own researches. This author heard about **"Bhrigu transits"**, which correlate the transit positions in navamsa chart with the natal positions in rasi chart. However, he does not know much about the tradition of Bhrigu transits to conclude whether or not his findings are loosely related to that tradition.

Though this author prefers to teach only those approaches that have the sanction of maharshis, he finds this particular approach superior to most other techniques of transit analysis. Moreover, this approach does not violate any teachings of maharshis. This is also a fertile area for research and deserves our attention. Hence it will be covered here. However, readers are advised to keep in mind that what follows is a product of the very limited intelligence of this author and hence prone to errors. Readers are encouraged to question and to conduct further researches in this area.

We said that a planet occupying or aspecting a rasi in transit influences the matters signified by the houses and planets stationed in that rasi in the natal chart. For example, we said that Jupiter transiting over Venus[1] may give marriage. However, we know that navamsa is the chart that shows marriage. So, is there any significance for Jupiter's rasi chart transit over the navamsa of Venus? In other words, if Venus is in Cancer in navamsa, can Jupiter transiting in Cancer in rasi chart bring marriage?

We do not have different zodiacs for different divisional charts. All the divisional charts use the same zodiac. So Cancer in natal navamsa chart and Cancer in transit rasi chart are not different. They are one and the same. If Jupiter transiting in Cancer can influence the house and planets stationed in Cancer in rasi chart, he should be able to influence the house and planets stationed in Cancer in navamsa chart too! We can extend this logic to all the divisional charts.

Rasi chart shows everything that exists at the physical level. Divisional charts show various areas of life. The interaction between the two decides how events in various areas of life materialize at the physical level. Natal chart shows the innate potential. Transit chart shows the temporary influences. The interaction between the two decides how temporary influences convert innate potential into actions and life events.

So the most important interactions are those between

(1) a natal divisional chart and the transit rasi chart, and,

(2) the natal rasi chart and a transit divisional chart.

Here (1) shows how innate potential in a particular area of life is influenced at a given time to result in action at the physical level. This helps us in *coarse* timing of events. We can *fine-tune* the timing of events with (2), which shows how the potential at the physical level is transformed into an event in a particular area of life.

Example 105: Let us consider the natal navamsa chart of a male engineer and the transit rasi chart at the time of his wedding (see Chart 54).

In natal navamsa, Pi contains the 7th house and its lord Jupiter is in Aq. When we look at navamsa, we should look at the 9th lord. The 9th lord in navamsa shows the dharma followed. In Hindu life, the marriage ceremony is an act of dharma. Here Venus shows dharma. So Venusian influence over the 7th house shows getting married. In the transit rasi chart of wedding, Venus occupies Aq, which is 7th lord Jupiter's natal navamsa position.

Chart 54

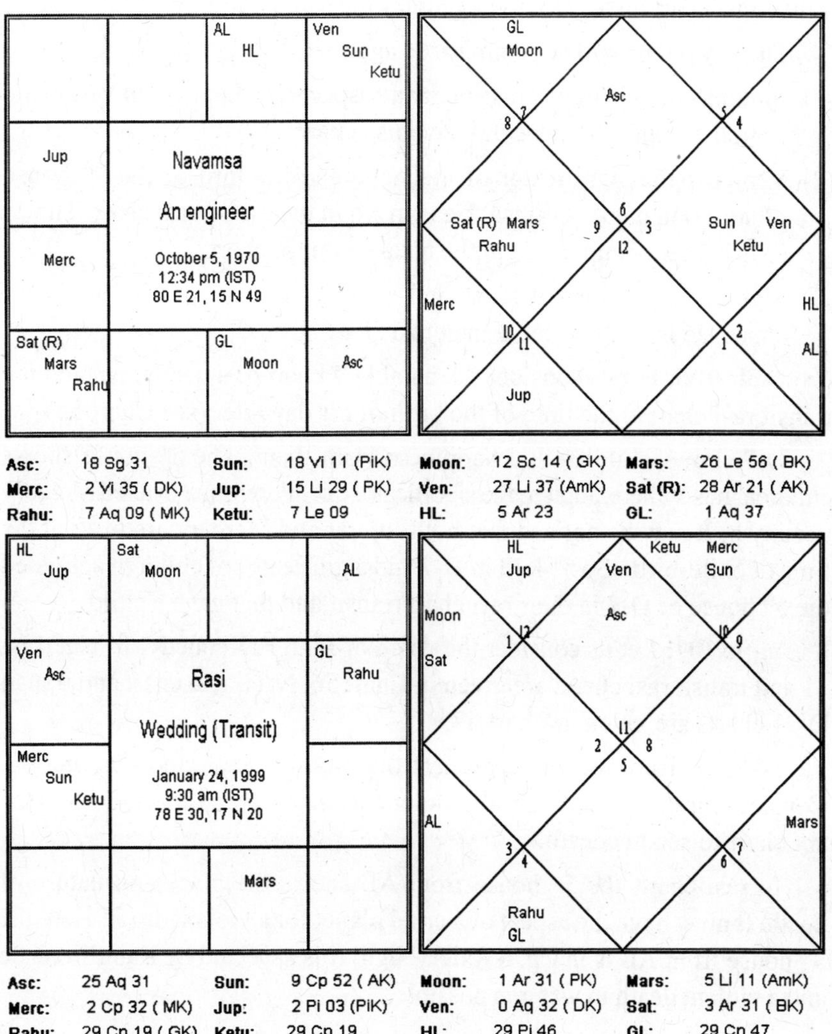

Asc:	18 Sg 31	**Sun:**	18 Vi 11 (PiK)	**Moon:**	12 Sc 14 (GK)	**Mars:**	26 Le 56 (BK)
Merc:	2 Vi 35 (DK)	**Jup:**	15 Li 29 (PK)	**Ven:**	27 Li 37 (AmK)	**Sat (R):**	28 Ar 21 (AK)
Rahu:	7 Aq 09 (MK)	**Ketu:**	7 Le 09	**HL:**	5 Ar 23	**GL:**	1 Aq 37

Asc:	25 Aq 31	**Sun:**	9 Cp 52 (AK)	**Moon:**	1 Ar 31 (PK)	**Mars:**	5 Li 11 (AmK)
Merc:	2 Cp 32 (MK)	**Jup:**	2 Pi 03 (PiK)	**Ven:**	0 Aq 32 (DK)	**Sat:**	3 Ar 31 (BK)
Rahu:	29 Cn 19 (GK)	**Ketu:**	29 Cp 19	**HL:**	29 Pi 46	**GL:**	29 Cn 47

Jupiter is in own sign in Pi in transit, which is the 7th house in natal navamsa. Moon owns the 11th house in natal navamsa and he shows gains in the matters of dharma and marriage. He is in Aries in the transit Rasi chart and Aries contains upapada in the natal navamsa chart. This shows the fructification, at the physical level, of gains in dharma due to marriage. Lagna lord Mercury is in Cp in the natal navamsa, showing dharmik self. In transit rasi chart also, Mercury occupies the same house.

The key points will be summarized again:

(1) Jupiter is in Pi in transit rasi chart and aspects Vi. Lagna is in Vi and the 7th house is in Pi in the natal navamsa chart.

(2) Venus is the significator of marriage and the lord of the 9th house (dharma) in natal navamsa. He is in Aq in the transit rasi chart. The 7th lord Jupiter occupies Aq in the natal navamsa chart.

(3) Mercury is the lord of lagna and occupies Cp, in the natal navamsa chart. He is in Cp in the transit rasi chart also.

Example 106: Let us consider the natal D-7 chart of a gentleman and the transit rasi chart at the time of the birth of his daughter (see Chart 55).

D-7 shows children and happiness from them. The 5th house shows children. It is Vi here. Jupiter, the significator of children, and exalted Mercury occupy it. It may be noticed that both Jupiter and Mercury are in Vi at the time of child-birth. So 5th lord in D-7 and significator of children activated the 5th house of D-7 in their rasi chart transit and that gave a child.

Example 107: Let us consider the death of John F. Kennedy, Jr. Natal D-11 and transit rasi charts are given in Chart 56. Natal rasi chart and transit D-11 charts are given in Chart 57.

D-11 or Rudramsa is the chart that shows death and destruction. Considering that the native had a violent death in a plane crash, D-11 is the apt chart to see his death.

In rasi chart, the 3rd house from AL shows the place and nature of death. It must have the aspect of a cruel planet for a violent death. Here the 3rd house from AL is in Cp, a watery sign. It is aspected by Rahu from Le and a violent death in water is possible.

Chart 55

Ketu
Asc
D-7
A gentleman
June 23, 1961
10:46 pm (IST)
81 E 48, 17 N 00
AL
Mars
Sun
HL
Sat (R)
Moon
Jup (R) GL
Merc (R)
Rahu Ven
Asc
Ketu
HL
Mars Sun
Sat (R)
Ven
Merc (R)
GL
Jup (R)
Rahu
AL
Moon
Asc: 14 Aq 59
Sun: 8 Ge 40 (PiK)
Moon: 5 Li 49 (PK)
Mars: 3 Le 36 (DK)
Merc (R): 14 Ge 25 (BK)
Jup (R): 12 Cp 32 (MK)
Ven: 23 Ar 00 (AmK)
Sat (R): 5 Cp 01 (GK)
Rahu: 6 Le 49 (AK)
Ketu: 6 Aq 49
HL: 15 Sc 51
GL: 12 Cp 40
AL
HL
Ketu
Mars
Rasi
Childbirth (Transit)
October 3, 1992
11:58 am (IST)
78 E 30, 17 N 29
Sat (R)
Moon
Asc
GL Rahu
Ven
Merc
Sun
Jup
Sat (R)
Moon
Rahu GL
Asc
Ven
AL HL
Sun Merc
Jup
Mars
Ketu
Asc: 6 Sg 06
Sun: 16 Vi 32 (PiK)
Moon: 12 Sg 55 (GK)
Mars: 17 Ge 26 (MK)
Merc: 29 Vi 49 (AK)
Jup: 4 Vi 41 (DK)
Ven: 16 Li 10 (PK)
Sat (R): 18 Cp 11 (BK)
Rahu: 1 Sg 24 (AmK)
Ketu: 1 Ge 24
HL: 11 Pi 56
GL: 5 Sg 24

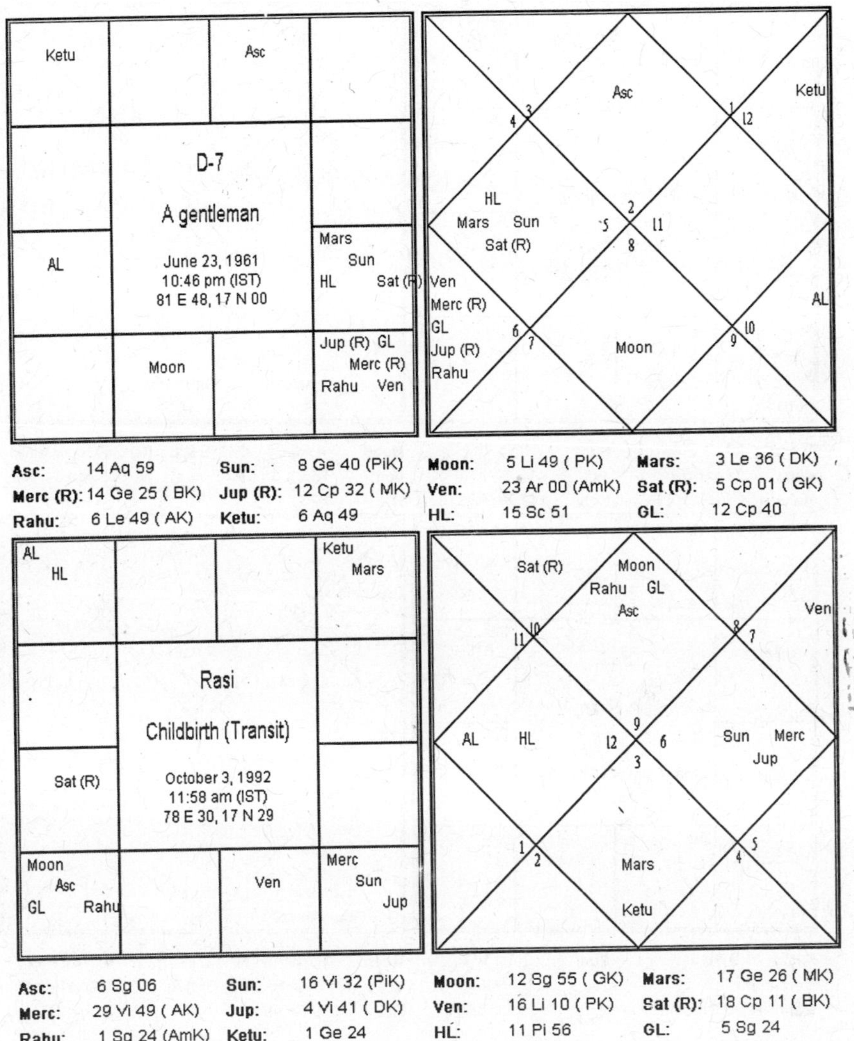

Chart 56

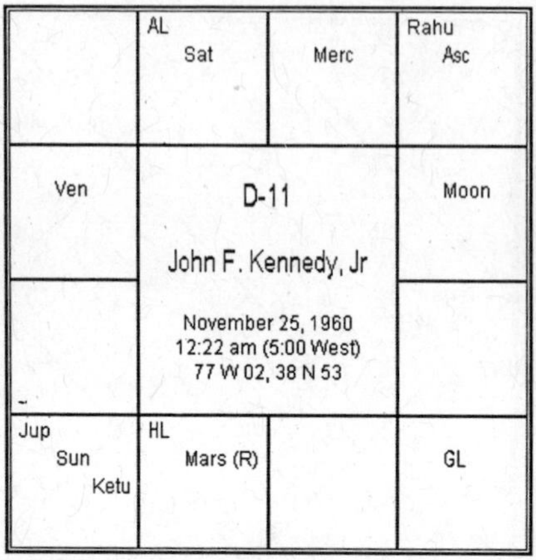

	AL Sat	Merc	Rahu Asc
Ven	D-11 John F. Kennedy, Jr November 25, 1960 12:22 am (5:00 West) 77 W 02, 38 N 53		Moon
Jup Sun Ketu	HL Mars (R)		GL

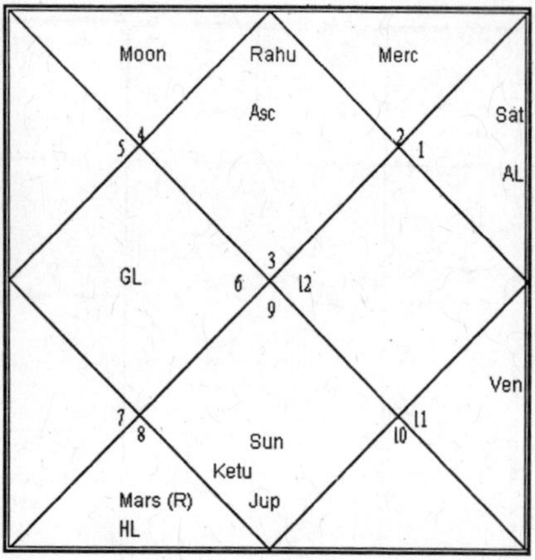

Moon Rahu Merc
Asc
5 4 2 1
Sat
AL
GL 6 3 12 9
Ven
7 8 11 10
Sun
Ketu
Mars (R) Jup
HL

Asc:	18 Le 39	**Sun:**	9 Sc 38 (GK)	**Moon:**	4 Aq 06 (DK)	**Mars (R):**	25 Ge 12 (AK)
Merc:	19 Li 55 (BK)	**Jup:**	12 Sg 31 (PiK)	**Ven:**	18 Sg 35 (MK)	**Sat:**	22 Sg 15 (AmK)
Rahu:	17 Le 58 (PK)	**Ketu:**	17 Aq 58	**HL:**	19 Ar 11	**GL:**	19 Ge 34

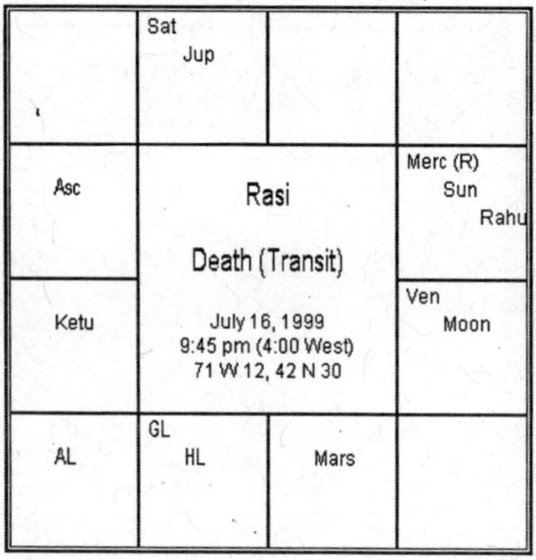

	Sat Jup		
Asc	Rasi Death (Transit) July 16, 1999 9:45 pm (4:00 West) 71 W 12, 42 N 30		Merc (R) Sun Rahu
Ketu			Ven Moon
AL	GL HL	Mars	

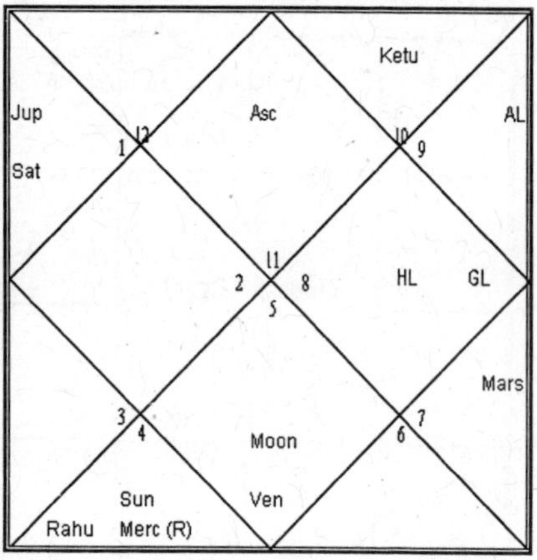

Ketu
Jup Asc AL
1 12 10 9
Sat
2 11 8 5
HL GL
Mars
3 4 7 6
Moon
Sun Ven
Rahu Merc (R)

Asc:	0 Aq 51	**Sun:**	0 Cn 14 (DK)	**Moon:**	21 Le 49 (AK)	**Mars:**	10 Li 37 (MK)
Merc (R):	14 Cn 58 (BK)	**Jup:**	8 Ar 45 (PK)	**Ven:**	8 Le 18 (GK)	**Sat:**	21 Ar 41 (AmK)
Rahu:	20 Cn 06 (PiK)	**Ketu:**	20 Cp 06	**HL:**	10 Sc 49	**GL:**	27 Sc 42

Chart 57

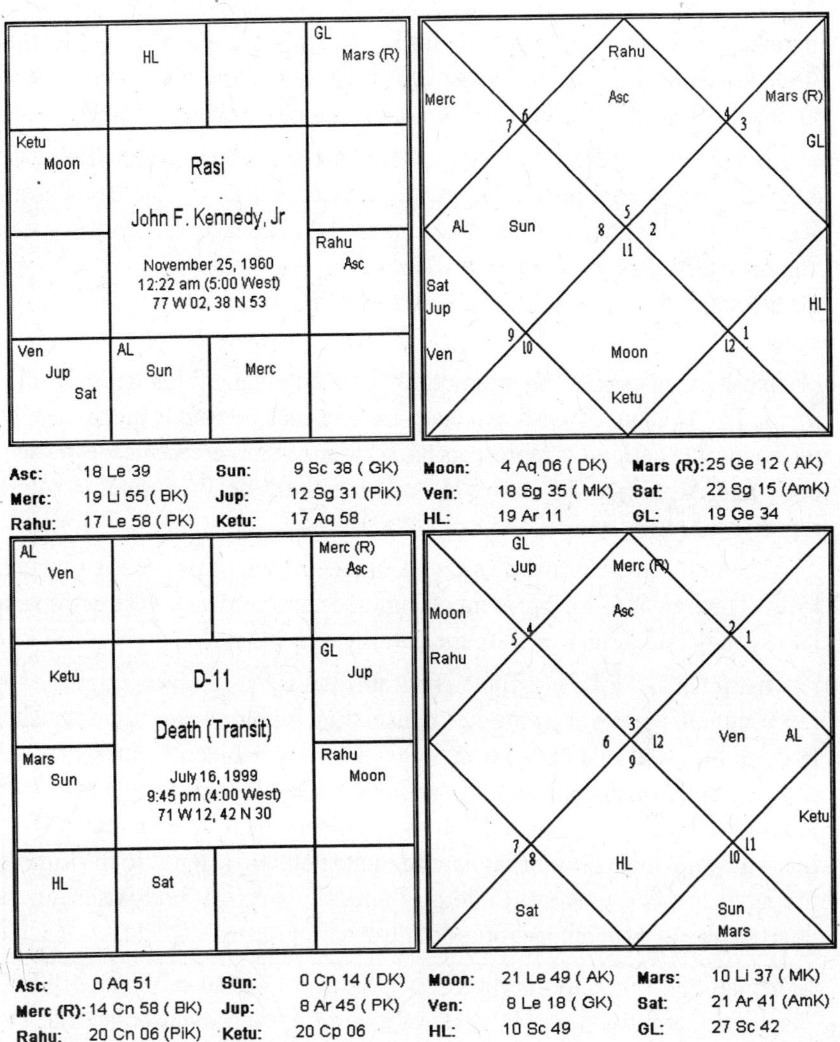

Now, we must analyze D-11 carefully for a violent death. Natal D-11 has lagna in Ge and Rahu occupies it. That is consistent with a violent death. The 2nd house in Cn is strong with its lord Moon occupying it. Sun is the 3rd lord – which shows physical vitality – and he joins the house of death, 7th, with 7th lord Jupiter. Mercury owns lagna and he is in 12th. This D-11 chart has unfavorable features. Now let us look at the houses occupied in transit rasi chart, with respect to this D-11, by the planets of life – Mercury (1st lord), Sun (3rd lord) and Saturn (8th lord) – and the planets of death – Jupiter (7th lord) and Moon (2nd lord) and Rahu (a malefic in lagna).

Two planets of life, Mercury and Sun, are in Cn, afflicted by Rahu. Cn is the 2nd house and stands for death in the natal D-11. Planet of death Moon is in Le (a house of life from natal D-11 lagna) and Jupiter aspects him, as well as his own 7th house (Sg). Saturn is debilitated. On the whole, the houses and planets of life in D-11 are afflicted or weak in the transit rasi chart.

Now let us look at the interaction between the natal rasi chart and the transit D-11 (Chart 57). In rasi chart, Le is lagna and Sun is lagna lord. Le represents the native, Cp represents his accidents, Sun represents the physical body and Aq (7th) and Saturn (7th lord) represent death. Jupiter (8th lord) represents longevity.

The natal rasi chart shows the existence of the native at the physical level. The transit D-11 represents the momentary forces of destruction and let us study its interaction with the natal rasi chart.

In transit D-11, Le is afflicted by Rahu and 12th lord Moon. Jupiter, who represents longevity is in the 12th house. Sun, who represents the physical body in the natal rasi chart, is in the 6th house of accidents in transit D-11 with exalted Mars, significator of accidents. The 7th lord in natal rasi chart, Saturn, represents the end of the native's life and he is in Sc in transit D-11, the same sign that contains lagna lord in the natal rasi chart. So the killer of the natal rasi chart (Saturn) interacts with the physical body (Sun) in the chart showing momentary forces of destruction (transit D-11).

Exercise 38: For a native born on 4th April 1970 at 5:50 pm (IST) at Machilipatnam, India (81e12, 16n15), an important event related to D-4 happened on 16th August 1991. Try to guess it based on the interaction between natal D-4 and transit rasi chart. Then analyze the interaction between natal rasi chart and transit D-4 also.

Exercise 39: The native of Exercise 38 had an important event related to D-24 on April 17, 1998. Try to guess it based on the interaction between the natal D-24 chart and the transit rasi chart.

25.5 Transits and Ashtakavarga

Though one of the purposes of ashtakavarga is to assess the strength of planets and houses in natal charts, its most important purpose is the interpretation of transits. Just as we look at the house occupied by a transit planet with respect to natal Moon and natal lagna, we can look at the houses occupied by a transit planet with respect to all the eight references used in ashtakavarga.

If a planet is benefic in its transit rasi with respect to 5 or more natal references, out of eight, then it will produce good results. If a planet is benefic in its transit rasi with respect to 3 or less natal references, out of eight, then it will produce bad results. Of course, the exact nature of the good or bad results given by a planet depend on its natural significations and its significations in the natal chart.

To see this, we look at the number of rekhas in the transit rasi in the transiting planet's BAV. If, for example, Saturn's BAV of the natal rasi chart has 5 rekhas in Ta, then that means that Saturn is benefic with respect to 5 out of 8 natal references in Ta. So he produces good results when he transits Taurus. The same logic can be extended to the divisional charts. If Jupiter has 8 rekhas in Ar in natal D-10 chart, then his transit in Aries in rasi chart invariably brings excellent results in career. The matters that benefit depend on Jupiter's placement and ownership in the natal D-10 chart. Basically, Jupiter's rasi transit in Aries activates the manifestation of Jovian energy at the physical level in Aries. If Jupiter has many rekhas in his D-10 BAV, it shows that Jovian energy in Aries goes well with most sources of energy in D-10 and thus it can have a significant impact on a native's career.

A planet with 6 or 7 rekhas in its transit rasi in its BAV invariably brings excellent results. A planet with 1 or 0 rekhas in its transit rasi in its BAV invariably brings very poor results.

25.5.1 *Samudaaya Ashtakavarga*

In addition to looking at the transit planet's natal BAV, we should also look at the natal SAV – Samudaaya Ashtakavarga. If, for example, SAV has 40 bindus in Pisces, then it means that Pisces is very strong in the chart. Planets transiting in Pisces, tend to give good results irrespective of their strength. Of course, if a planet with 6 rekhas in Pi in its own BAV and a planet with 2 rekhas in Pi in its own BAV are transiting Pi, the former planet will produce better results than the latter planet. Rekhas in the individual BAVs of planets also matter, but SAV will dominate over the BAVs if it has too many or too few rekhas.

Planets transiting in rasis with more than 30 rekhas in SAV usually bring favorable results. Planets transiting in rasis with less than 25 rekhas in SAV usually bring unfavorable results.

Chart 58

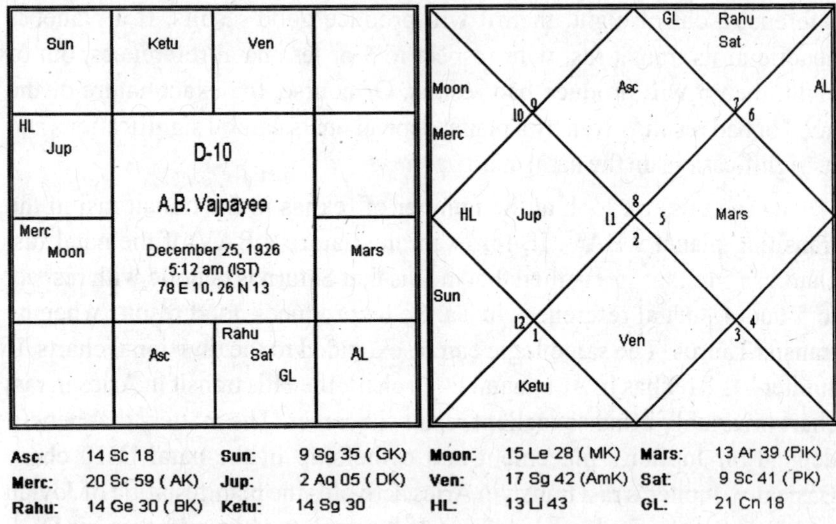

Example 108: Let us consider the D-10 chart of Sri A.B. Vajpayee, India's Prime Minister (see Chart 58). His D-10 ashtakavarga is given below:

	Ar	Ta	Ge	Cn	Le	Vi	Li	Sc	Sg	Cp	Aq	Pi
Sun	5	3	6	2	3	4	7	6	3	3	2	4
Moon	2	4	2	3	6	6	4	4	4	6	3	5
Mars	3	4	4	3	4	2	2	5	3	4	1	4
Merc	4	4	6	4	6	5	3	6	4	5	4	3
Jupi	4	6	4	2	3	8	3	6	4	3	7	6
Venu	2	4	6	4	3	5	3	5	5	6	5	4
Satu	3	1	5	2	3	3	4	3	5	4	2	4
SAV	23	26	33	20	28	33	26	35	28	31	24	30

He became India's Prime Minister on March 19, 1998 (see Chart 59).

Chart 59

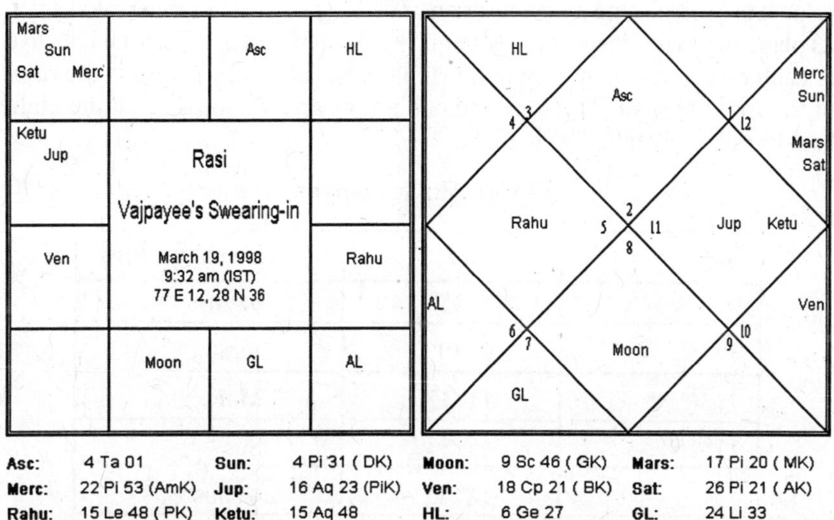

Sun, Mars, Mercury and Saturn are all in Pi and Pi has 30 rekhas in SAV. None of them is too weak in individual BAV. Venus is GL lord in natal D-10 and he is an important planet for power and authority. In the transit chart, he is in Cp. Cp has 31 rekhas and Venus has 6 rekhas. Moon is in Sc with 35 rekhas. Jupiter is in Aq. Though Aq is not strong in SAV, it is strong in Jupiter's BAV. It has 7 rekhas in Jupiter's natal D-10 BAV. Jupiter's strength is important, as he is the Vimsottari dasa lord.

So 6 out of 7 planets are in rasis that are very strong in D-10 SAV. And the 7th planet is extremely strong in its BAV. Vimsottari dasa lord and natal GL lord have 7 and 6 rekhas respectively.

So, as per ashtakavarga, transits are very favorable to Sri Vajpayee's career on March 19, 1998.

Exercise 40: Consider the D-10 chart of a gentleman and the transit rasi chart during a crucial week in his life, given in Chart 60. What are the prospects for his career at the time of the transit? Do you expect good results or setbacks?

25.5.2 *Kakshyas and Prastaara Ashtakavarga*

Each rasi is divided into eight kakshyas of 3° 45' each. Kakshya literally means "orbit". When a planet is in Saturn's kakshya, its placement with respect to Saturn is the most important. When a planet is in Jupiter's kakshya, its placement with respect to Jupiter is the most important. The first kakshya in each rasi starts from 0° in that rasi and ends at 3° 45'. Saturn is the ruler of the first kakshya. The start and end points and the lords of all the eight kakshyas are given in Table 60.

Table 60: Kakshyas

Start	End	Kakshya lord
0°	3° 45'	Saturn
3° 45'	7° 30'	Jupiter
7° 30'	11° 15'	Mars
11° 15'	15°	Sun
15°	18° 45'	Venus
18° 45'	22° 30'	Mercury
22° 30'	26° 15'	Moon
26° 15'	30°	Lagna

Example 109: Let us say Mercury is at 16° in Cn, Jupiter is it 24° in Vi and Venus is at 4° in Sc. Because 16° is between 15° and 18° 45', Mercury is in the kakshya of Venus. Because 24° is between 22° 30' and 26° 15', Jupiter is in the kakshya of Moon. Because 4° is between 3° 45' and 7° 30', Venus is in the kakshya of Jupiter.

In the above example, Venus is in the kakshya of Jupiter and hence the placement of Venus with respect to Jupiter is more important than his placement with respect to other planets. Suppose the BAV of Venus has 5 rekhas in Sc. Then Venus is benefic in Sc with respect to 5 out of 8 references and that is favorable. However, when Venus is at 4° in Sc, he is in Jupiter's kakshya and what matters the most is whether Venus is benefic in Sc with respect to Jupiter or not. If Jupiter is not one of the 5 references from which Venus is benefic in Sc, then Venusian transit between 3° 45' and 7° 30' in Sc will not be favorable.

Chart 60

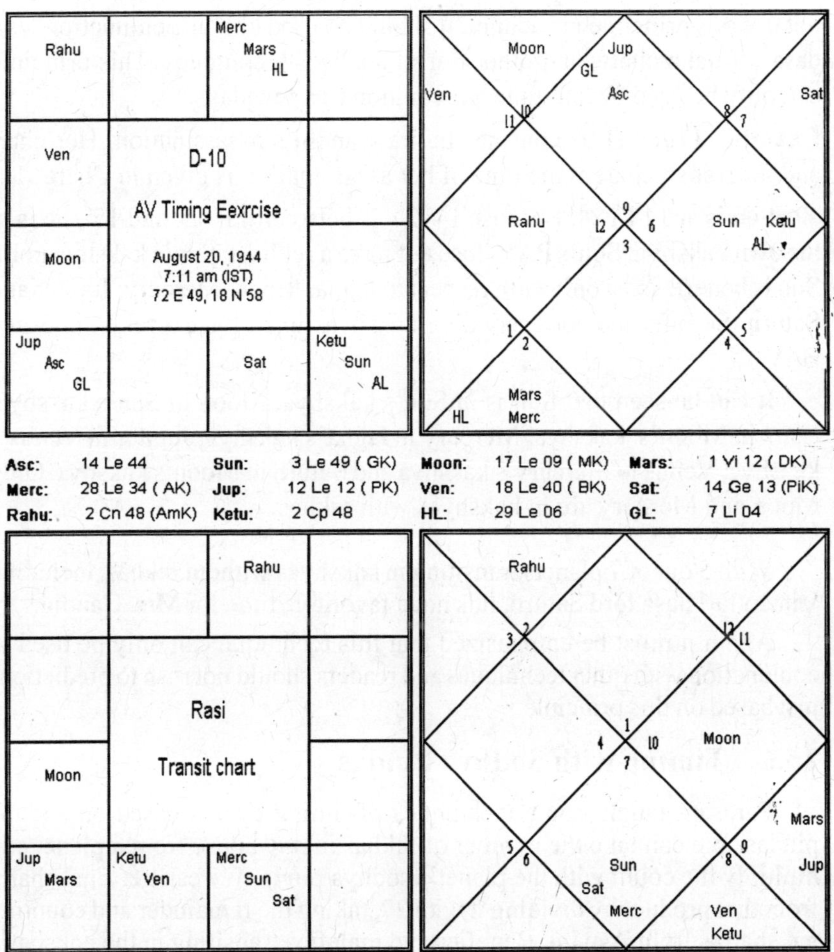

To find out whether Venus is benefic with respect to Jupiter in Sc or not, we can look at the Prastaara Ashtakavarga (PAV) of Venus. If we find that Venus is benefic with respect to Jupiter in Sc, we say that the PAV of Venus has a rekha in the kakshya of Jupiter in Sc. Each rasi has eight kakshyas and a kakshya has a rekha in a planet's PAV if that planet is benefic in that rasi with respect to the kakshya lord.

A popular method of delineating favorable and unfavorable days is to look at the number of planets that are in a kakshya with a rekha. If too many or too few planets are in a kakshya with a rekha, favorable or unfavorable results may be expected (respectively). However, one should not use this principle in vacuum. It should be used only in conjunction with dasas, Tajaka charts and other transit analysis techniques. This principle can only be used to fine-tune a prediction to a few days.

Example 110: Let us consider Indira Gandhi's assassination. Her chart and the transit chart at the time of her assassination is given in Chart 61.

Sun is at 14 Li 24. Because 14° 24' is between 11° 15' and 15°, he is in his own kakshya. Sun's PAV does not have a rekha in Sun's kakshya in Li. Sun is benefic in Li only with respect to lagna, Moon, Mercury, Jupiter and Saturn. So only the corresponding kakshyas in Li have a rekha in Sun's BAV.

It can be seen that Sun is in Sun's kakshya, Moon in Sun's kakshya, Mars in Moon's kakshya, Mercury in lagna's kakshya, Jupiter in Venus's kakshya, Venus in Mercury's kakshya and Saturn in Moon's kakshya. Only Moon and Mercury are in kakshyas with rekhas.

With 5 out of 7 planets transiting in kakshyas without rekhas, including Vimsottari dasa lord Saturn, it is not a favorable time for Mrs. Gandhi.

Again it must be emphasized that this technique can only be used in conjunction with other techniques and readers should not rush to predictions just based on this principle.

25.6 Timing with Sodhya Pindas

Parasara taught some techniques of timing events based on sodhya pindas. We can take the number of rekhas in *any* house from a planet and multiply the count with the planet's sodhya pinda. We can get a nakshatra from that product by dividing it with 27, taking the remainder and counting nakshatras from Aswini. Benefics and malefics transiting in the nakshatra will give good or bad results (respectively) relating to the original house. Especially Saturn's transit is important. Saturn's transit in the nakshatra corresponding to a particular house makes the signified matters suffer. Jupiter's transit is beneficial. Some people also take the 10th or 19th nakshatra from the nakshtra found above. A nakshatra and the 10th and 19th nakshatras from it are owned by the same planet under Vimsottari dasa scheme and they go together.

We can also find a rasi by dividing the product with 12 instead of 27 and counting rasis from Aries. Saturn's transit in the resultant rasi brings

Chart 61

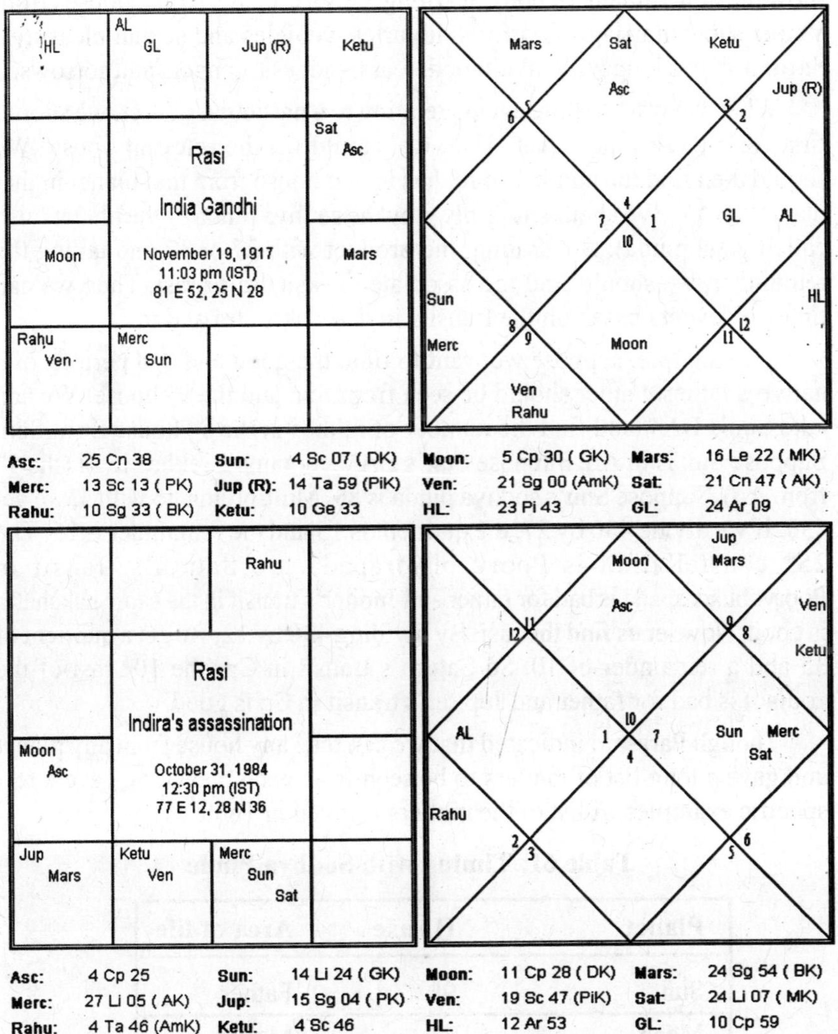

misfortune relating to the original house. However, nakshatras are more important.

When we find houses from **Sun**, we should look at matters related to soul, inherent nature, personality, will power and father. Houses from **Moon** show mind, wisdom, peace, happiness and mother. Houses from **Mars** show siblings, land and strength. Houses from **Mercury** stress on business, commerce, profession, friends and good behavior. Houses from **Jupiter** show the nourishment of body, learning, children and wealth. Houses from **Venus** show marriage, comforts, luxuries, vehicles and sexual pleasures. **Saturn** shows longevity, livelihood, fears, sadness, dangers and sorrows.

When we want to time events relating to a particular matter, we should first fix the relevant planet. Then we should fix the relevant house. We should then find the number of rekhas in that house from that planet in that planet's BAV. We should multiply it by the sodhya pinda of the planet (also called yoga pinda). By dividing the product with 27 or 12 and taking the remainder, we should find the associated nakshatra or rasi. Then we can time key events based on the transits in that nakshatra and rasi.

For example, suppose we want to time the good and bad periods of a native's father. Father should be seen from Sun and the 9th house. We can take Sun's BAV and find the number of rekhas in the 9th house from Sun. Suppose Sun is in Aq. Suppose Sun's BAV contains 5 rekhas in Li (the 9th from Aq). Suppose Sun's sodhya pinda is 86. Multiplying 86 with 5, we get 430. If we divide 430 by 27, the quotient is 15 and the remainder is 25. The 25th constellation is Poorvabhadrapada. So Saturn's transit in Poorvabhadrapada is bad for father and Jupiter's transit in the same nakshatra is good. Now let us find the rasi. By dividing 430 by 12, we get a quotient of 35 and a remainder of 10. So Saturn's transit in Cp (the 10th rasi of the zodiac) is bad for father and Jupiter's transit in Cp is good.

Though Parasara indicated that we can take any house from any planet and gave a long list of matters to be seen from each planet, he gave a few specific examples. A list of the matters is given in Table 61.

Table 61: Timing with Sodhya Pinda

Planet	House	Area of life
Sun	9th	Father
Moon	4th	Mother
Mars	3rd	Siblings
Mercury	10th	Profession
Jupiter	5th	Children
Venus	7th	Marriage
Saturn	8th	Longevity

Some examples will be given now. However, this approach does not give consistent results. Readers should realize that the topic of sodhya pindas is open to research. Most astrologers use these principles with only the rasi chart. If matters relating to father have to be seen from D-12, as taught by Parasara, should we use D-12 when timing events related to father? Should we use the sodhya pinda and rekha count from D-12? Should we take the 9th from Sun in rasi chart or take it in D-12? All these are issues that need to be researched. Moreover, as we have learnt, there are some inconsistencies between Parasara and Varahamihira in the definition of ashtakavarga and this can alter the sodhya pindas of Moon and Venus. In addition, we have some controversies in the exact definitions of the reductions to be done to get Sodhita Ashtakavarga from Bhinna Ashtakavarga. That can again alter sodhya pindas. Timing of events with sodhya pindas is a very important topic, but what the readers learn here may not be the final word. It is hoped that readers will experiment with an open mind and share their findings with other astrologers.

Example 111: Let us consider Princess Diana, who died in a fatal automobile crash when Saturn was in Revathi star (Pisces). Her rasi chart is given in Chart 62.

Chart 62

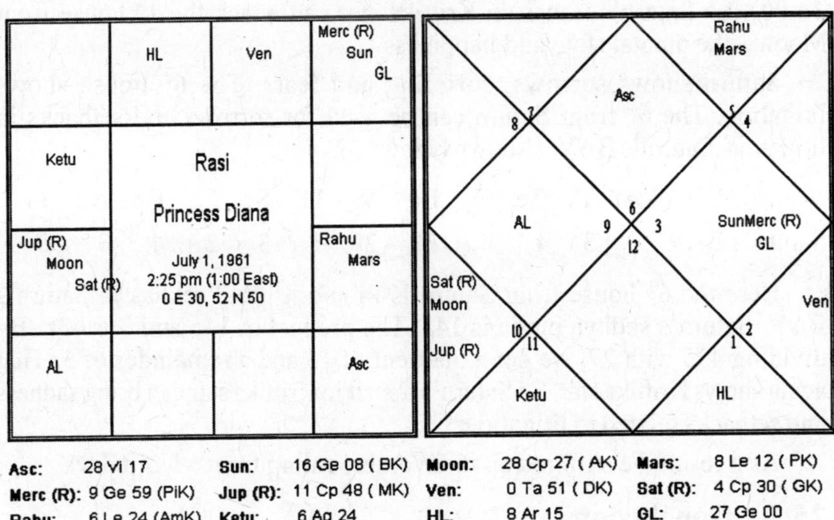

To see longevity, we should use the 8th house from Saturn and Saturn's BAV. The 8th house from Saturn is Le.

	Ar	Ta	Ge	Cn	Le	Vi	Li	Sc	Sg	Cp	Aq	Pi
Saturn's BAV	3	4	6	3	**0**	2	2	5	4	3	2	5

Le has 0 rekhas in Saturn's BAV. Saturn's sodhya pinda is 203. The product is 0. By dividing it with 27, we get 0 which is equivalent to 27. So we get Revathi star. By dividing 0 with 12, we get 0 which is equivalent to 12. So we get Pisces.

When Saturn was transiting in Revathi star in Pisces, she passed away.

Example 112: Let us look at the rasi chart of software tycoon Bill Gates (see Chart 24). Despite Jupiter's simultaneous transit, Saturn's transit in Krittika star brought some troubles. In a landmark ruling in June 2000, a US judge ruled that his company – software giant Microsoft Corporation – was a monopoly and ordered a breakup into two smaller companies.

Moon's BAV is shown below:

	Ar	Ta	Ge	Cn	Le	Vi	Li	Sc	Sg	Cp	Aq	Pi
Moon's BAV	4	3	4	4	6	3	1	5	5	4	4	**6**

•Moon is in Pisces and Pisces has 6 rekhas. Moon's sodhya pinda is 122. The product of 122 and 6 is 732. By dividing 732 with 27, we get a quotient of 27 and a remainder of 3. The 3rd star is Krittika (26 Ar 40 – 10 Ta 00). So Saturn's transit in Krittika star can attack the 1st house from Moon – the mental state and happiness.

Saturn shows sorrows, suffering and fears. The 6th house shows litigation. The 6th from Saturn can be used for sorrows and setbacks in litigation. Saturn's BAV is shown below:

	Ar	Ta	Ge	Cn	Le	Vi	Li	Sc	Sg	Cp	Aq	Pi
Saturn's BAV	3	3	4	4	7	2	1	3	2	4	3	**3**

Here the 6th house from Saturn is Pi and it has 3 rekhas in Saturn's BAV. Saturn's sodhya pinda is 145. The product of 145 and 3 is 435. By dividing 435 with 27, we get a quotient of 16 and a remainder of 3. That again shows Krittika star. So Saturn's transit in Krittika star can bring sadness and setbacks related to litigation.

As a result, he suffered an unfavorable ruling from a US judge.

25.7 Conclusion

Transit positions of planets are the positions occupied by them at a given time. Natal positions of planets are the positions occupied by them at the time of one's birth. Natal positions stand for the innate potential of a nativity and the transit positions show the temporary influences – planetary pulls and pushes. If their interaction is studied, some insight can be gained on the kind of results that are experienced at a given time. It is suggested that the interaction between the natal divisional charts and the transit rasi chart helps in coarse timing of events and the interaction between the natal rasi chart and transit divisional charts helps in fine timing of events. Some techniques based on ashtakavarga, kakshyas and sodhya pindas are also given in this chapter.

25.8 Answer to the Exercises

Exercise 38:

Natal D-4 chart and transit rasi chart are given in Chart 63. Lagna is in Sg in natal D-4. The 9th house of fortune in a foreign land is in Le and it contains Rahu, the significator of foreign things. So Le stands for life in a foreign land in this D-4. Four planets occupy it in the transit rasi chart, including Jupiter, Mercury and Mars. Jupiter owns lagna in natal D-4 and he shows the native from the point of view of residence and fortune. Mercury owns lagna in natal rasi chart and he shows the physical self of the native. Mars owns the 12th house in natal D-4 and he shows living in distant places. All these planets activate Le in their rasi chart transit. So foreign journey is a possibility. In addition, Rahu is in Sg in the transit rasi chart and Sg contains lagna in natal D-4. So foreign influence on residence is fortified.

Natal rasi chart and transit D-4 chart are given in Chart 64. Lagna in Vi shows the nativity. Rahu in Vi in transit D-4 shows foreign influence on Vi in the matter of residence. Since Vi represents the nativity in natal lagna, this D-4 transit supports going abroad.

Chart 63

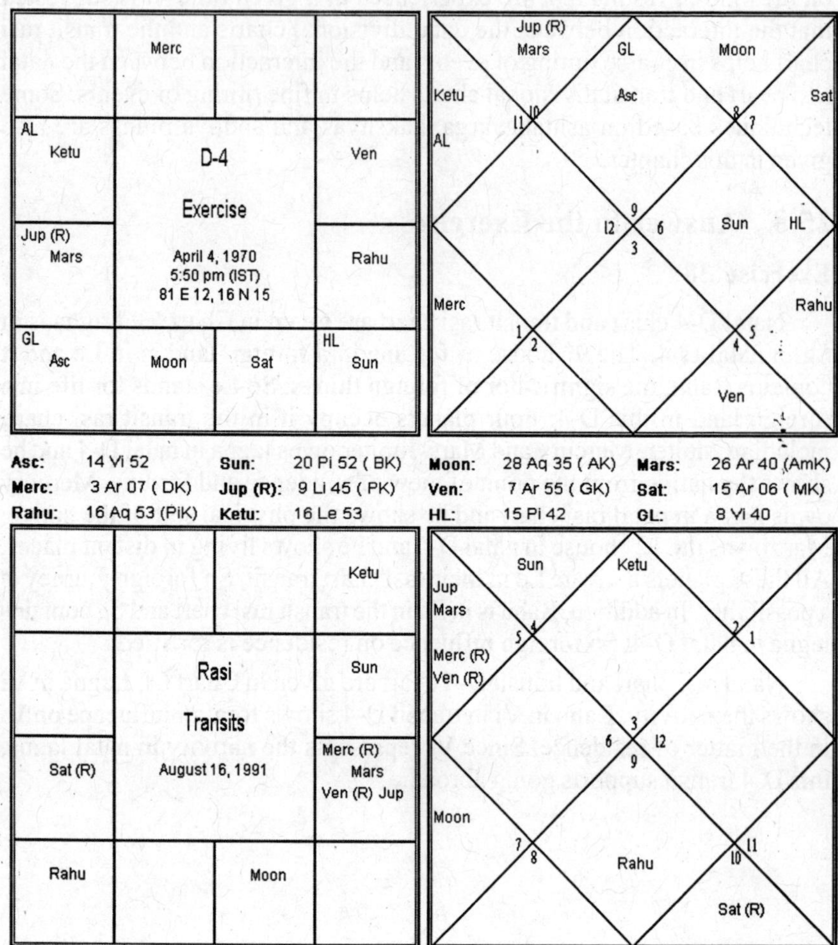

Merc
AL
Ketu
D-4
Ven
Exercise
Jup (R)
Mars
April 4, 1970
5:50 pm (IST)
81 E 12, 16 N 15
Rahu
GL
Asc
Moon
Sat
HL
Sun
Jup (R)
Mars
GL
Moon
Ketu
Asc
Sat
AL
Sun
HL
Merc
Rahu
Ven
Asc: 14 Vi 52
Sun: 20 Pi 52 (BK)
Moon: 28 Aq 35 (AK)
Mars: 26 Ar 40 (AmK)
Merc: 3 Ar 07 (DK)
Jup (R): 9 Li 45 (PK)
Ven: 7 Ar 55 (GK)
Sat: 15 Ar 06 (MK)
Rahu: 16 Aq 53 (PiK)
Ketu: 16 Le 53
HL: 15 Pi 42
GL: 8 Vi 40
Ketu
Sun
Rasi
Transits
August 16, 1991
Sat (R)
Merc (R)
Mars
Ven (R) Jup
Rahu
Moon
Sun
Ketu
Jup
Mars
Merc (R)
Ven (R)
Moon
Rahu
Sat (R)

Chart 64

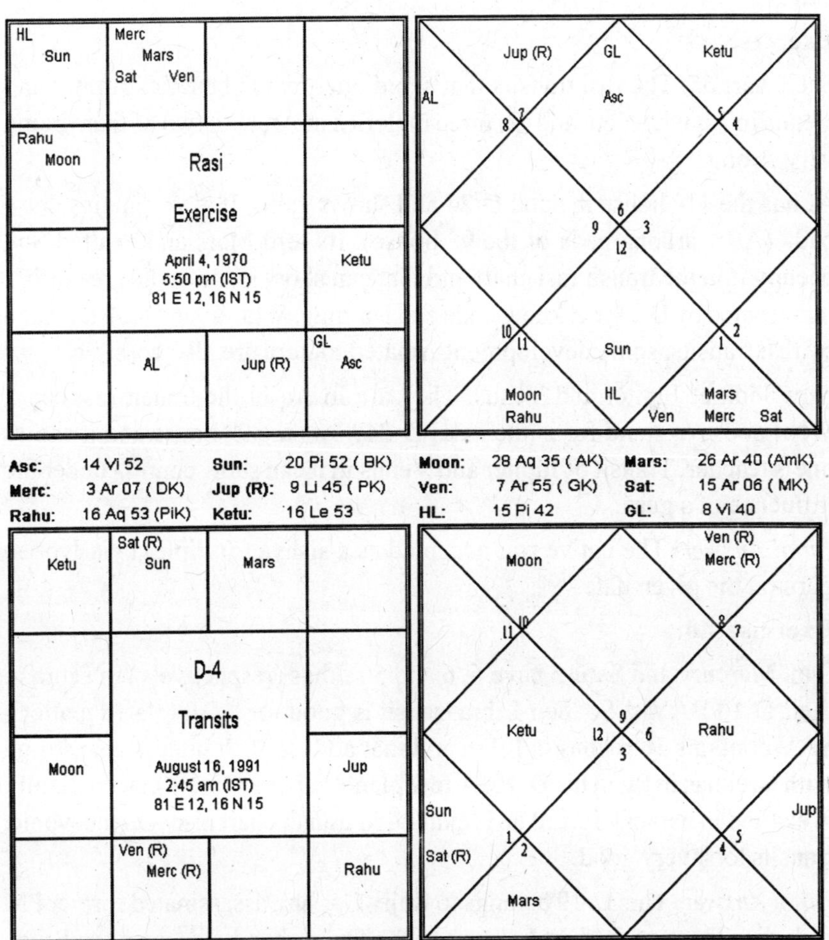

The 7th lord in the natal rasi chart is Jupiter and he is in Le in D-4. Le is the 12th house in the natal rasi chart. This shows a long trip. Aries (8th house) and Mars (8th lord) show changes in the natal rasi chart. Taurus (9th house) shows flourishing in a foreign land. Aries contains two malefics and Mars occupies Taurus, in transit D-4. This shows the changes in residence and the temporary troubles of adjusting to a foreign land. Interaction between the natal rasi chart and transit divisional charts shows finer and momentary details.

Final Answer: The native left his motherland and landed in USA on that date.

Exercise 39:

See Chart 65. The rasi transits that stand out are: (1) benefics Jupiter and Venus in Aq with Ketu and (2) three malefics in Ar, with two of them being very strong.

Ar has the 11th house in natal D-24 and shows gains. It also contains Guru pada (A9 – arudha pada of the 9th house). Its lord Mars and exalted Sun occupy it in the transit rasi chart and that can show gains in the area of life represented by D-24, *i.e.* knowledge and learning. With A9 in D-24 activated by rasi transits, some developments related to guru are also possible.

Now look at Jupiter and Venus. They are in Aq in the transit rasi chart. What does Aq stand for in the natal D-24? It is the 9th house and it shows one's teacher. Transit of Jupiter and Venus in it can show coming under the influence of a guru.

Final Answer: The native was accepted as a sishya (disciple) by a Jyotish guru on the given date.

Exercise 40:

Sun, Mercury and Saturn have 6, 6 and 5 rekhas (respectively) in Libra in their D-10 BAV's. So their Libra transit is good for D-10 related matters. SAV contains 36 rekhas in Libra and that adds to it. Jupiter is also strong with 6 rekhas in Sg in his D-10. A few planets are very well-placed. Saturn is exalted in natal D-10 and he is exalted in transit chart also. On the whole, transits look very good.

Final Answer: This D-10 belongs to Rajiv Gandhi, assassinated former PM of India. The transit chart belongs to the time when he became the Prime Minister of India.

Chart 65

Jup (R)		Mars	Moon Asc
AL Ven	D-24		HL
GL	D-24 Exercise April 4, 1970 5:50 pm (IST) 81 E 12, 16 N 15		Sat
	Sun	Merc	Ketu Rahu

HL, Moon, Mars, Sat, Asc, 5, 4, 2, 1, Ketu, Rahu, 6, 3, 12, 9, Jup (R), Merc, Ven, 7, 8, 10, 11, AL, Sun, GL

Asc:	14 Vi 52	**Sun:**	20 Pi 52 (BK)	**Moon:**	28 Aq 35 (AK)	**Mars:**	26 Ar 40 (AmK)
Merc:	3 Ar 07 (DK)	**Jup (R):**	9 Li 45 (PK)	**Ven:**	7 Ar 55 (GK)	**Sat:**	15 Ar 06 (MK)
Rahu:	16 Aq 53 (PiK)	**Ketu:**	16 Le 53	**HL:**	15 Pi 42	**GL:**	8 Vi 40

Merc (R) Mars Sun Sat			
Ven Jup Ketu	Rasi		
	Transit April 17, 1998 7:00 pm (IST) 81 E 12, 16 N 15		Rahu
Moon			

Moon, Rahu, 9, 8, 6, 5, 7, 10, 4, 1, Ketu, Jup, Ven, 11, 12, 2, 3, Sun, Sat, Merc (R), Mars

26. Transits: Miscellaneous Topics

26.1 Introduction

In the chapter "Transits and Natal References", we concentrated on correlating the natal chart and the transit chart using the rasis occupied by planets in both. There are some principles about rasi transits that we haven't yet covered. We will cover a couple of concepts in this chapter.

Nakshatras are also an important division of the zodiac and they are as important as rasis. By looking at the interactions between the nakshatras occupied by planets in the natal and transit charts, we can make some predictions about the results given by them at the time of the transit. We will look at a few principles.

26.2 Murthis (Forms/Idols)

To judge the results given by a planet during its transit in a particular rasi, find exactly when the planet enters the rasi. Find the house occupied by transit Moon at *that time* with respect to his own (Moon's) natal position. Based on the house, we say that the planet is in a golden or silver or copper or iron form during its transit in the rasi. The list of houses and murthis is given in Table 62.

Table 62: Murthis

House	Murthi	Meaning	Results
1st, 6th, 11th	Swarna	Golden form	Highly favorable
2nd, 5th, 9th	Rajata	Silver form	Favorable
3rd, 7th, 10th	Taamra	Copper form	Unfavorable
4th, 8th, 12th	Loha	Iron form	Highly unfavorable

Let us take Mercury's transit in Gemini during May 26, 2000 – Aug 3, 2000. Mercury entered Gemini at 3:06 pm (IST) on May 26, 2000. At that time, Moon was at 10° 29' in Aquarius. We should find which house Aquarius is with respect to natal Moon and then refer to Table 62 to find out which murthi Mercury is for a particular person during May 26-Aug 3, 2000.

Suppose someone has natal Moon in Aquarius. Then Moon at the time of Mercury's rasi entry is in the 1st house from natal Moon. So Mercury is a swarna murthi (golden form) for that person during his Ge transit and will give full results. Suppose someone has natal Moon in Pisces (*e.g.* Bill Gates, whose chart was considered earlier). Aquarius is the 12th house from Pisces.

So Mercury is a loha murthi (iron form) during his Ge transit. That is highly unfavorable. Even if it is a favorable transit otherwise, Mercury may not give his full results. If it is an unfavorable transit otherwise, then Mercury will make the native suffer much.

26.3 Rasi Gochara Vedha

We listed the good and bad houses for all planets to transit from natal Moon in a previous chapter. Even when a planet is transiting in a favorable house from natal Moon, it may be "obstructed" by another planet transiting in the vedha sthána (house of obstruction). In that case, the planet cannot give its good results. The vedha sthaanas of all good transits of all planets are listed in Table 63.

Table 63: Vedha Sthaanas

Transiting planet	Auspicious houses from natal Moon (Corresponding vedha sthanas in parantheses)
Sun	3 (9), 6 (12), 10 (4), 11 (5)
Moon	1 (5), 3 (9), 6 (12), 7 (2), 10 (4), 11 (8)
Mars	3 (12), 6 (9), 11 (5)
Mercury	2 (5), 4 (3), 6 (9), 8 (1), 10 (8), 11 (12)
Jupiter	2 (12), 5 (4), 7 (3), 9 (10), 11 (8)
Venus	1 (8), 2 (7), 3 (1), 4 (10), 5 (9), 8 (5), 9 (11), 11 (6), 12 (3)
Saturn	3 (12), 6 (9), 11 (5)

Let us take Bill Gates, who has natal Moon in Pisces. Natal lagna and arudha lagna lord Mercury transits in Gemini during June 2000. As Mercury transiting in the 4th house from natal Moon is auspicious, this transit should bring good results. We can find the vedha sthaana for the 4th house transit of Mercury from the above table. It is the 3rd house. If there are planets in Taurus, the 3rd house from Pisces, then they cause vedha (obstruction) on Mercury. There were several planets causing vedha on Mercury on June 8, 2000, when the company of Mr. Gates received a legal setback. With vedha from many planets, Mercury cannot give his good results. Moreover, Mercury is a loha murthi as we discussed earlier.

This is how one should use the above table. Only exceptions are the father and son pairs:

(1) Sun and Saturn do not cause vedha on each other.

(2) Moon and Mercury do not cause vedha on each other.

It is important to consider vedhas and murthis to understand why a planet expected to produce brilliant results gives only marginal results sometimes.

26.4 Taras (Stars)

26.4.1 *Basic Tara Classification*

We can count constellations from the constellation of natal Moon to the constellation occupied by a planet in transit. Suppose natal Moon is in Makha and transit Mars is in Swaati. Counting constellations from Makha, we get (1) Maksha, (2) Poorva Phalguni, (3) Uttara Phalguni, (4) Hasta, (5) Chitra and (6) Swaati. So Swaati is the 6th constellation from natal Moon's constellation.

Different constellations from the constellation of natal Moon stand for different things, as shown in Table 64. If a planet is in a bad tara in its transit, it cannot give its full results. If dasa lord and antardasa lord as per Vimsottari dasa are in bad taras, bad results can be expected.

Let us take an example. Bill Gates has natal Moon in Uttarabhadrapada constellation. His company received an adverse ruling from a judge who ordered a breakup of the company, on June 8, 2000. Saturn and Jupiter were transiting in Krittika, Sun, Venus and Mars were in Mrigasira. From Uttarabhadrapada, Krittika is the 5th star, *i.e.* pratyak tara (star of obstacles), and Mrigasira is the 7th star, *i.e.* naidhana tara (star of death). With 5 planets transiting in bad taras, tara bala (strength of stars) was weak.

Table 64: Taras

Constellation (from natal Moon's constellation)	**Name**	**Meaning**
1st, 10th, 19th	Janma Tara	Birth (mixed)
2nd, 11th, 20th	Sampat Tara	Wealth (good)
3rd, 12th, 21st	Vipat Tara	Danger (bad)
4th, 13th, 22nd	Kshema Tara	Well-being (good)
5th, 14th, 23rd	Pratyak Tara	Obstacles (bad)
6th, 15th, 24th	Saadhana Tara	Achievement (good)
7th, 16th, 25th	Naidhana/Vadha Tara	Death (bad)
8th, 17th, 26th	Mitra Tara	Friend (good)
9th, 18th, 27th	Parama Mitra Tara	Best friend (good)

Taras are also used in muhurtas. At the time of an auspicious effort or when a new project is launched, transit Moon should not be in a bad constellation with respect to the natal Moon's constellation.

26.4.2 *Special Nakshatras/Taras*

In addition to the above general classification, we have a few special nakshatras for each person:

(1) The constellation occupied by natal Moon is called **Janma** nakshatra. Janma means "birth" and this nakshatra shows general well-being.

(2) The 10th constellation from *janma* nakshatra is called **Karma** nakshatra. Karma means "profession" and this nakshatra shows profession and workplace.

(3) The 18th constellation from *janma* nakshatra is called **Saamudaayika** nakshatra. Saamudaayika roughly means "related to a crowd" and this nakshatra shows group activities.

(4) The 16th constellation from *janma* nakshatra is called **Sanghaatika** nakshatra. Sanghaatika roughly means "belonging to group" and this nakshatra shows group/social activities.

(5) The 4th constellation from *janma* nakshatra is called **Jaati** nakshatra. Jaati roughly means "community" and this nakshatra shows one's community. To be more correct, one's jaati shows people who belong to the same class, nature and profession.

(6) The 7th constellation from *janma* nakshatra is called **Naidhana** nakshatra. Naidhana means "death" and this nakshatra shows death and suffering.

(7) The 12th constellation from *janma* nakshatra is called **Desa** nakshatra. Desa means "country" and this nakshatra shows one's country.

(8) The 13th constellation from *janma* nakshatra is called **Abhisheka** nakshatra. Abhisheka means "coronation" and this nakshatra shows power and authority. This is also called **Raajya** nakshatra (kingdom).

(9) The 19th constellation from *janma* nakshatra is called **Aadhaana** nakshatra. Aadhaana means "epoch/conception" and this nakshatra shows well-being of family.

(10) The 22th constellation from *janma* nakshatra is called **Vainaasika/ Vinaasana** nakshatra. Vainaasika means "destructive" and this nakshatra shows one's destruction.

(11) The 25th constellation from *janma* nakshatra is called **Maanasa** nakshatra. Maanasa means "mind" and this nakshatra shows one's mental state.

Benefics or malefics situated in these constellations in their transit bring good or bad results related to the area covered by the nakshatra. However, it should be kept in mind that the results will be with respect to the native. For example, malefics transiting in desa nakshatra may not ruin one's country. After all, any country has almost the same number of people with desa nakshatra in each constellation. When many malefics are transiting in desa nakshatra, one may be driven away from one's country or start hating one's country. Similarly, many malefics transiting in jaati nakshatra may alienate one from one's community. Many benefics transiting in karma nakshatra may give success at workplace. This is how these special nakshatras should be used. Sometimes, using these nakshtras gives special insights that cannot be gained by looking at any divisional chart.

As an example, let us take Bill Gates who has natal Moon in Uttarabhadrapada. His jaati nakshatra is the 4th from Uttarabhadrapada, *i.e.* Bharani. His karma nakshatra is the 10th from Uttarabhadrapada, *i.e.* Pushyami. When Saturn was transiting in Bharani, several people in the software community turned against Bill Gates and gave damaging testimonies in a lawsuit to determine whether his company was a monopoly employing unfair tactics against competitors. He was more or less alienated in the community of software entrepreneurs. At the same time, Rahu was transiting in Pushyami and that brought tension related to litigation at his workplace.

Exercise 41: Consider a native born in Leo lagna. He has Moon also in Leo in Poorva Phalguni constellation. Let us say Jupiter is transiting in Sg in Poorvaashaadha constellation with Mars. Mars is a yogakaraka from natal lagna. Jupiter is transiting in his moolatrikona, in the 5th house from natal lagna and Moon. That's very favorable transit. Find out if transit Jupiter and transit Mars are in a special nakshatra. Based on it, try to guess the area in which the transit did good to the native.

Exercise 42: For a native with lagna in Leo, natal Moon is in the 4th quarter of Dhanishtha. When the transit chart contains Saturn in Bharani, identify a possible result.

Exercise 43: For a native with natal Moon in the 3rd quarter of Poorvabhadrapada and lagna in Virgo, transit of Mars in Aasresha constellation in Cancer brought material gains. Cancer is the 6th from natal Moon and 11th from natal lagna. Both are favorable transits and so it makes sense that this transit gave material gains. Now find out if Mars occupies a special constellation and, based on it, guess the nature of the gains.

26.5 Nakshatra-based Aspects

Sun and Moon aspect the 14th and 15th constellations from them. Mars aspects the 1st, 3rd, 7th, 8th and 15th constellations from him. Mercury and Venus aspect the 1st and 15th constellations from them. Jupiter aspects the 10th, 15th and 19th constellations from him. Saturn aspects the 3rd, 5th, 15th and 19th constellations from him.

A natural benefic gives good results related to the constellations aspected by it and a natural malefic gives bad results related to the constellations aspected by it.

Exercise 44: For the native of Exercise 42, transit Mars was in Swaati when transit Saturn was in Bharani. Identify the constellations aspected by Mars and see if any special constellations are included. If so, predict the possible result.

26.6 Constellations and Body Parts

When they are transiting in various constellations as counted from *janma nakshatra*, planets are said to dwell in different parts of one's body and correspondingly some standard results are attributed. These results are given in Table 65 – Table 69.

There are two different purposes for these tables:

(1) We can find the standard results for planetary transits in different constellations with respect to the constellation of natal Moon.

(2) If a native has a disease or problem in a particular body part, we may be able to use these tables and figure out the planet causing it. That can help us in deciding the right remedial measures. We can also take preventive measures before the transit.

Table 65: Body Parts in the Transit of Sun

Nakshatras (counted from janma nakshatra)	Body part dwelt by the planet	Standard Result
1st	Mouth/Face	Destruction
2nd, 3rd, 4th, 5th	Head	Influx of wealth
6th, 7th, 8th, 9th	Chest	Victory
10th, 11th, 12th, 13th	Right hand	Wealth
14th, 15th, 16th, 17th, 18th, 19th	Two feet	Poverty
20th, 21st, 22nd, 23rd	Left hand	Physical ailments
24th, 25th	Eyes	Gains
26th, 27th	Private parts	Death

Table 66: Body Parts in the Transit of Moon

Nakshatras (counted from janma nakshatra)	Body part dwelt by the planet	Standard Result
1st, 2nd	Face	Great fear
3rd, 4th, 5th, 6th	Head	Well-being
7th, 8th	Back	Victory over enemies
9th, 10th	Eyes	Money
11th, 12th, 13th, 14th, 15th	Heart	Comforts and peace
16th, 17th, 18th	Left hand	Quarrels
19th, 20th, 21st, 22nd, 23rd, 24th	Two feet	Going abroad
25th, 26th, 27th	Right hand	Financial gains

Table 67: Body Parts in the Transit of Mars

Nakshatras (counted from janma nakshatra)	Body part dwelt by the planet	Standard Result
1st, 2nd	Mouth/Face	Death
3rd, 4th, 5th, 6th, 7th, 8th	Two feet	Separation
9th, 10th, 11th	Chest	Victory
12th, 13th, 14th, 15th	Left hand	Poverty
16th, 17th	Head	Gains
18th, 19th, 20th, 21st	Face	Great fear
22nd, 23rd, 24th, 25th	Right hand	Well-being
26th, 27th	Eyes	Going abroad

Table 68: Body Parts in the Transit of Mercury, Jupiter and Venus

Nakshatras (counted from janma nakshatra)	Body part dwelt by the planet	Standard Result
1st, 2nd, 3rd	Head	Grief
4th, 5th, 6th	Face	Gains
7th, 8th, 9th, 10th, 11th, 12th	Two hands	Misfortune
13th, 14th, 15th, 16th, 17th	Stomach	Amassing of wealth
18th, 19th	Private parts	Destruction
20th, 21st, 22nd, 23rd, 24th, 25th, 26th, 27th	Two feet	Honor and fame

Table 69: Body Parts in the Transit of Saturn, Rahu and Ketu

Nakshatras (counted from janma nakshatra)	Body part dwelt by the planet	Standard Result
1st	Face	Grief
2nd, 3rd, 4th, 5th	Right hand	Comforts
6th, 7th, 8th	Right leg	Travels
9th, 10th, 11th	Left leg	Destruction
12th, 13th, 14th, 15th	Left hand	Gains
16th, 17th, 18th, 19th, 20th	Stomach	Pleasures
21st, 22nd, 23rd	Head	Comforts
24th, 25th	Eyes	Comforts
26th, 27th	Back	Death

If a planet dwells in the left hand in transit and some natural malefics aspect it or cause vedha on it, then the planet may give suffering related to the left hand. Some injuries to the left hand are possible then.

Let us consider a native who has natal Moon in the 1st quarter of Visakha. He had some persistent pain in his chest in February 2000. Let us determine the planet responsible for it.

One can find from Table 65 that Sun dwells in chest during his transit in the 6th, 7th, 8th and 9th nakshatras from janma nakshatra. From Visakha, they are Uttaraashaadha, Sravana, Dhanishtha and Satabhisha. Sun transited in these stars during Jan 11-Mar 3, 2000. The chest troubles when Sun was dwelling in chest can be related to Sun.

At the time Sun entered Capricorn in January 2000, Moon was in Ar and hence Sun is a taamra murthi (copper form) for people with natal Moon in Li. At the time Sun entered Aquarius in February 2000, Moon was in Ta and hence Sun is a loha murthi (iron form) for people with natal Moon in Li. Being a copper/iron form dwelling in the chest, Sun brought chest pains.

26.7 Latta (Kick)

Latta is a nakshatra-based planetary kick. Each planet has latta (kick) on a constellation based on its transit position. If a transit planet has latta on the constellation occupied by Moon (or lagna) in natal chart, then we may expect some unfavorable results related to the signification of the planet in natal chart.

Purolatta (forward kick):

(1) Sun has latta on the 12th nakshatra from him, reckoned in the forward direction. If Sun is in Mrigasira, for example, he has latta on the 12th nakshatra from Mrigasira, *i.e.* Visakha.

(2) Mars has latta on the 3rd nakshatra from him, reckoned in the forward direction. If Mars is in Mrigasira, for example, he has latta on the 3rd nakshatra from Mrigasira, *i.e.* Punarvasu.

(3) Jupiter has latta on the 6th nakshatra from him, reckoned in the forward direction. If Jupiter is in Krittika, for example, he has latta on the 6th nakshatra from Krittika, *i.e.* Pushyami.

(4) Saturn has latta on the 8th nakshatra from him, reckoned in the forward direction. If Saturn is in Krittika, for example, he has latta on the 8th nakshatra from Krittika, *i.e.* Makha.

Prishtha latta (backward kick):

(5) Moon has latta on the 22nd nakshatra from him, reckoned in the backward direction. If Moon is in Anuradha, for example, he has latta on the 22nd nakshatra (backwards) from Anuradha, *i.e.* Dhanishtha.

(6) Mercury has latta on the 7th nakshatra from him, reckoned in the backward direction. If Mercury is in Punarvasu, for example, he has latta on the 7th nakshatra (backwards) from Punarvasu, *i.e.* Aswini.

(7) Venus has latta on the 5th nakshatra from him, reckoned in the backward direction. If Venus is in Mrigasira, for example, he has latta on the 5th nakshatra (backwards) from Mrigasira, *i.e.* Aswini.

(8) Rahu has latta on the 9th nakshatra from him, reckoned in the backward direction. If Rahu is in Punarvasu, for example, he has latta on the 9th nakshatra (backwards) from Punarvasu, *i.e.* Uttarabhadrapada.

If the 6th lord has latta on janma nakshatra (nakshatra occupied by natal Moon) or lagna nakshatra (nakshatra occupied by natal lagna) in his transit, then some troubles related to litigation or disease or enemies may be expected. If the 7th lord has latta on janma nakshatra or lagna nakshatra in his transit, then some troubles related to marriage or spouse or relations can be expected. If an important planet in the 10th house in natal chart has a latta on janma nakshatra or lagna nakshatra in transit, then some troubles in career may be expected. We usually see some loss related to the natal significations of a planet having latta on janma nakshatra or lagna nakshatra in transit. This is an important concept and readers should memorize the latta formulas.

Example 113: Let us consider a native whose janma nakshatra is Poorvabhadrapada and lagna nakshatra is Hasta. Let us see if any bad result is possible, using lattas, on the evening of 5th December 1996.

Let us find if any planet has latta on Poorvabhadrapada or Hasta.

Table 70: Latta Calculation for Example 113

Planet	Constellation occupied in transit	Latta star count	Latta direction	Latta on
Sun	Jyeshtha	12th	Forward	Bharani
Moon	Hasta	22nd	Backward	Moola
Mars	Poorva Phalguni	3rd	Forward	*Hasta*
Mercury	Moola	7th	Backward	*Hasta*
Jupiter	Poorvaashaadha	6th	Forward	*Poorvabhadrapada*
Venus	Visaakha	5th	Backward	Uttaraphalguni
Saturn	Uttarabhadrapada	8th	Forward	Aardra
Rahu	Hasta	9th	Backward	Mrigasira

Natal lagna is in Virgo, as Hasta is in Virgo. There are two lattas on lagna nakshatra – Hasta. One is by 8th lord Mars and the other is by lagna lord Mercury. So bad results relating to 1st and 8th houses are possible. The 6th and 8th houses show accidents.

However, latta on janma nakshatra is more important. Here Jupiter has latta on Poorvabhadrapada. Jupiter owns the 4th and 7th houses in the natal chart. So some misfortune related to vehicle or house or marital life is possible.

The native had a vehicular accident on the evening of 5th December 1996, in which his car was totaled; *i.e.* it was so damaged that his insurance company found it cheaper to give a new car instead of repairing it.

Exercise 45: Consider the chart of Bill Gates (see Chart 24). On 8th June 2000, his company received an unfavorable ruling from a US judge in a landmark anti-trust lawsuit. Find if any planets had latta on janma nakshatra or lagna nakshatra at the time of the ruling. Find the common house related to those planets in the natal chart.

26.8 Sarvatobhadra Chakra

Definition: Sarvatah means "everywhere" or "entirely". Bhadra means "auspicious" or "well". Sarvatobhadra chakra is a chart that shows all-round well-being and all kinds of auspicious and inauspicious results.

Figure 3: Sarvatobhadra Chakra

NORTH

WEST

ई ee	Dhanishtha	Satabhisha	P.Bhadra	U.Bhadra.	Revati	Aswini	Bharani	अ a
Sravana	ऋ rii	ग g	स s	द d	च ch	ल l	उ u	Krittika
Abhijit	ख kh	ऐ ai	Aq	Pi	Ar	ऌ lu	अ a	Rohini
U.Shadha	ज j	Cp	अः ah	Rikta Friday	ओ o	Ta	व v	Mriga
P.Shadha	भ bh	Sg	Jaya Thursday	Poorna Saturday	Nanda Sunday Tuesday	Ge	क k	Ardra
Moola	य y	Sc	अं am	Bhadra Monday Wednesday	औ au	Cn	ह h	Punar
Jyeshtha	न n	ए e	Li	Vi	Le	ॡ luu	ड ḍ	Pushya
Anuradha	ऋ ri	त t	र r	प p	ट ṭ	म m	ऊ uu	Asresha
इ i	Visakha	Swaati	Chitra	Hasta	U.Pha.	Poo.Pha.	Makha	आ aa

EAST

SOUTH

There are 9 x 9 = 81 squares in the chart. Middle 7 squares on the outer borders contains 7 nakshatras each. Abhijit (the last quarter of Uttarashadha) is included among the nakshatras. The innermost 5 squares contains weekdays and tithis (lunar days). The notation regarding tithis is:

(1) The entry Nanda represents 1st, 6th, 11th, 16th, 21st and 26th tithis.

(2) The entry Bhadra represents 2nd, 7th, 12th, 17th, 22nd and 27th tithis.

(3) The entry Jaya represents 3rd, 8th, 13th, 18th, 23rd and 28th tithis.

(4) The entry Rikta represents 4th, 9th, 14th, 19th, 24th and 29th tithis.

(5) The entry Poorna represents 5th, 10th, 15th, 20th and 30th tithis.

Rasis are also included in the chart. Some consonants are listed in the squres just inside the border squares. All the squares lying on diagonals of the chart, except the central square of the chart, contain vowels. There are 16 vowels and 20 consonants that are covered. We see that 16 (vowels) + 20 (consonants) + 12 (rasis) + 28 (nakshtras) + 5 (tithis and weekdays) = 81.

Vedha: When a planet occupies a nakshatra, it causes vedha (obstruction) on the contents of the squares along 3 lines. We can draw one vertical or horizontal line and two crossward lines starting at the nakshatra. Contents of the squares on the lines have vedha from the planet.

Example 114: Let us say Saturn is in Punarvasu. We see that Punarvasu is on the eastern border.

Drawing a horizontal line to the west from it, we see that the consonant h, rasi Cn, vowel au, tithis Bhadra (2nd, 7th, 12th, 17th, 22nd and 27th), weekdays Monday and Wednesday, vowel am, rasi Sc, consonant y and constellation Moola are on this line. So Saturn in Punarvasu causes vedha on all these.

Drawing a crossward line to the northwest from it, we see that the consonant k, rasis Ta and Ar, consonant d and constellation Poorva Bhadrapada are on this line. So Saturn in Punarvasu causes vedha on all these.

Drawing a crossward line to the southwest from it, we see that the consonant d (alveolar), consonant m and constellation Uttara Phalguni are on this line. So Saturn in Punarvasu causes vedha on all these.

Exercise 46: Find all the consonants, vowels, tithis, weekdays, rasis and constellations on which Venus in Makha has vedha.

There are some special principles:

(1) A planet in the first quarter of Krittika or the last quarter of Bharani has vedha on the vowel "a" which is in the northeastern corner. A similar thing applies to all the vowels in corners.

(2) If an vowel has vedha, its similar vowel (*e.g.* a and aa, i and ee, u and uu) also has vedha from the same planet.

(3) Some consonants are not covered in this chart. Planets in Ardra have vedha on g, chh and ng (nasal). Planets in Hasta have vedha on h, n (alveolar) and th (alveolar). Planets in Poorvashadha have vedha on dh (dental), ph and dh (alveolar). Planets in Uttara Bhadrapada have vedha on th (dental), jh and nch (nasal).

(4) If a planet has vedha on one of the following pairs of consonants, it has vedha on the other one too: b & v; s & sh (palatal); kh & sh (alveolar); j & y; ng & tr.

Using Sarvatobhadra Chakra[71] **:** We should find the following in the ***natal*** chart:

(1) the constellation occupied by Moon or any special tara

(2) the rasi occupied by lagna or any house of interest

(3) the first/prominent consonant and vowel in the native's name

(4) the tithi of birth (janma tithi) or a special tithi

(5) the weekday of birth (janma vaara)

We should study the vedha caused on these by different planets in their transit. Vedha by benefics (Moon, Mercury, Jupiter and Venus) is favorable and vedha by malefics (Sun, Mars, Saturn, Rahu and Ketu) is unfavorable. If several transiting benefics have simultaneous vedha on several natal points listed above, then good results may be expected. Malefics, on the other hand, give bad results.

In addition to considering janma nakshatra, we can consider special nakshatras related to the matter of interest. Suppose we want to find the transit results related to career. Then we can take karma nakshatra of natal chart and see the vedhas on it in transit chart.

Similarly, we can take the tithi corresponding to the matter of interest. For example, we can take "karma tithi" (lunar day of profession) instead of janma tithi when finding transit results related to career.

Readers should refer to the first chapter for the procedure of finding tithis. Karma tithi is a little different from normal tithi. To find karma tithi, we multiply the difference between Moon's longitude and Sun's longitude with 10 and reduce the product to a value between 0° and 360° (by adding or subtracting multiples of 360°). We divide it by 12 and add 1 to the quotient. That gives a number between 1 and 30 and that represents "karma tithi". Karma tithi changes 10 times as fast as normal tithi. Similarly "dhana tithi" (lunar day of wealth) changes twice as fast as normal tithi. We can find a tithi for several matters. The tithi relevant to the matter of interest should be used when finding vedha of transiting planets on tithis (Nanda, Bhadra, Jaya, Rikta and Poorna).

Let us take an example. If the 10th house, karma nakshatra, karma tithi and janma vaara all have the vedha of a couple of transiting benefics, then some good developments may take place in the native's career. If they have the vedha of a couple of malefics (instead of benefics), then we can expect setbacks in the native's career. In this manner, we study the impact of transits on important tithis, janma vaara, important nakshatras and

71 This author's experience in the use of Sarvatobhadra Chakra is very very limited.

important houses in natal chart. If just one natal reference has vedha from just one planet, we cannot make any predictions. But, if 2-3 natal reference have vedha from a couple of benefic/malefic transit planets, then we can be more confident. However, a prediction should be made only if dasas and Tajaka charts also show an event.

Example 115: Let us consider the death of John F. Kennedy, Jr. The data of birth and death can be found in Example 107.

Janma tithi is Sukla Ashtami (8th tithi) and it belongs to the Jaya group. Janma vaara is Thursday[72]. Janma nakshatra is Dhanishtha. Vainasika nakshatra (destruction) is in Anooradha. Naidhana nakshatra (constellation of death) is in Bharani. If all these natal reference points have vedha from a couple of natural malefics, then death is more likely on other days. Of course, one will not die whenever this happens, but this will increase the chances of death.

In the transit chart, Saturn is in naidhana nakshatra Bharani. Mars is in Swati. Rahu is in Asresha. Ketu is in Sravanam.

If we draw crossward lines from Ketu in Sravanam and Saturn in Bharani, we can see that they intersect in the square containing Jaya and Thursday. So janma tithi (Jaya) and janma vaara (Thursday) have vedha from Ketu and Saturn. Janma nakshatra Dhanishtha has vedha from Ketu in Sravanam and Rahu in Asresha. Vainaasika nakshatra Anooradha also comes under the vedha of Saturn in Bharani and Rahu in Asresha. The house of accidents Cp, which is the 3rd house from AL in natal chart, comes under vedha from Ketu in Sravanam and Mars in Swati.

Considering that several key natal references are coming under the vedha of a couple of malefics, unfavorable results are possible. Considering the involvement of naidhana and vainaasika nakshatras, death is possible.

Example 116: Let us consider Rajiv Gandhi's ascension to power in India on October 31, 1984. It was covered in Exercise 40. Rasi chart of Mr. Gandhi can be found in Chart 39.

At the time of the event, Jupiter was in Poorvashadha, Venus was in Jyeshtha, Mercury was in Visakha and Moon was in Sravanam. Let us see if they have vedhas on any important natal references. Here are the vedhas:

(1) Jupiter and Mercury both have vedha on Nanda and Sunday. Sunday is the weekday of birth. The tithi of power (5th) is Sukla Shashthi (Nanda group).

72 As per the western calendar, Friday came at midnight and the native was born at 12:22 am. However, a new day starts at sunrise for Hindus. So it was still Thursday.

(2) Mercury and Moon both have vedha on Dhanishtha (abhisheka nakshatra – constellation of coronation).

(3) Jupiter and Venus both have vedha on Sg, which is the 5th house of power in natal chart.

(4) Mercury and Venus both have vedha on Libra, which contains GL in natal chart. GL is the seat of power.

So janma vaara, an important tithi, an important nakshatra and two important rasis in natal chart have vedha from two benefic planets each. This is conducive to getting political power.

Example 117: Let us continue with the same native. Rajiv Gandhi's party lost majority in the elections of November 22, 1989.

When he became India's Prime Minister in 1984, Jupiter was in Poorvashadha. Poorvashadha is karma nakshatra (constellation of profession). At the time of Mr. Gandhi's defeat in 1989, Saturn was in that constellation.

Let us find vedhas by transit planets on the same natal references considered in the last example:

(1) Nanda and Sunday have vedha from 3 malefics: Saturn in Poorvashadha, Rahu in Dhanishtha and Ketu in Asresha.

(2) Dhanishtha is Abhisheka nakshatra (constellation of coronation). It is occupied by Rahu and Ketu has vedha on it.

(3) The 5th house of power in the natal chart, Sg, has vedha from Mars and Saturn.

For these reasons, transits were unfavorable from the point of view of political power. So Mr. Gandhi's party lost power.

26.8 Conclusion

Several important topics related to transits in nakshatras were covered in this chapter. One should carefully learn and practice all these classical nakshatra-based techniques. However, new students should not make predictions just based on these techniques. Any technique that divides people into 27 groups and gives the same result for everyone in the same group can be correct only to a limited extent. These methods should be used in conjunction with other chart-sensitive methods.

26.9 Answers to the Exercises

Exercise 41:

Poorvaashaadha is the 10th constellation from Poorva Phalguni. So the favorable transit of Jupiter and Mars happens to be in the **Karma** nakshatra, which shows profession. So the good results to be experienced may be related to profession.

Final Answer: The details belong to Rajiv Gandhi. He suddenly became India's Prime Minister during the said transit. We gave his birthdata earlier.

Exercise 42:

Bharani is the 7th constellation from Dhanishtha, *i.e.* it is the naidhana nakshatra (death). Saturn is a malefic and the 7th lord – and hence a maraka – here. So this transit has the potential to bring death. Of course, not everyone with lagna in Leo and Moon in Dhanishtha dies then[73], but death is a possibility during the transit.

Final Answer: The details belong to John F. Kennedy, Jr. He died in a plane crash during the said transit. We gave his birthdata earlier.

Exercise 43:

Aasresha is the 12th constellation from Poorvabhaadrapada, i.e. Desa nakshatra. Being a debilitated malefic in desa nakshatra (country), Mars can drive him out of his country. That was indeed how Mars gave gains to the native of Chart 63 in the second week of November 1994. The native left his motherland India then.

Exercise 44:

Mars aspects the 1st, 3rd, 7th, 8th and 15th constellations from him. Mars in Swaati will aspect (1) Swaati, (2) Anooradha, (3) Uttaraashaadha, (4) Sravanam, and, (5) Bharani. Because natal Moon is in Dhanishtha, these are the 20th, 22nd, 26th, 27th and 7th constellations (respectively) from janma nakshatra. Out of these, 2 are special nakshatras. The 7th constellation is known as naidhana nakshatra and shows death. The 22nd nakshatra is known as vainaasika nakshatra and shows destruction. Mars aspects both. As seen in Exercise 42, maraka in the natal chart Saturn occupies naidhana nakshatra[74]. The predicted result is death.[75]

---

73 These transit principles based on nakshtra give good insight into future, but one cannot make predictions just based on them.

74 In the natal chart, Mars occupies his Mrityu Bhaga (part of death). So his aspect over the two special constellations is also significant.

75 It will be **very hasty** to predict someone's death just based on conjunctions and aspects on special nakshatras in transit. Out of the many people with the same nakshatra, only *those* people whose dasas and Tajaka charts also show death will die at the time of this death-inflicting transit.

Final Answer: As already mentioned, Mr. Kennedy passed away during this transit.

Exercise 45:

Rahu was in Punarvasu at that time. He had latta on the 9th from Punarvasu backwards, which is Uttarabhadrapada, *i.e.* janma nakshatra! So Rahu had latta on janma nakshatra. Mars was in Mrigasira at the time and he had latta on the 3rd from Mrigasira, which is Punarvasu, *i.e.* lagna nakshatra!

Rahu occupies the 6th house in the natal chart and Mars owns it. So the setbacks given by their lattas on janma nakshatra and lagna nakshatra were related to the 6th house matters – litigation and enemies.

Exercise 46:

(1) Verical line in the northern direction has uu, d (alveolar), h, k, v, a, u and Bharani.

(2) Crossward line in the northeastern direction has Asresha.

(3) Crossward line in the northwestern direction has m, Le, Bhadra (2nd, 7th, 12th, 17th, 22nd and 27th), Monday, Wednesday, Jaya (3rd, 8th, 13th, 18th, 23rd and 28th), Thursday, Cp, kh and Sravanam.

Part 4: Tajaka Analysis

A sub-system of Indian astrology, popularly known as "Tajaka system", is extremely useful in making precise and pointed predictions. It considers planetary aspects and yogas different from those employed in other classical methods of Vedic astrology and it is closer to western astrology in terms of aspects and yogas. In fact, some scholars may validly question why Tajaka system is being covered in a book on Vedic astrology. There are no references to it in the works of Parasara, Jaimini and other maharshis. The oldest reference to these techniques to be found in the works of a respected authority on Vedic astrology is in "Tajaka Neelakanthi", a work by Neelakantha who wrote a celebrated commentary on "Jaimini Sutras". His coverage of Tajaka system lends some authenticity to the system. One can only speculate whether Parasara talked about this system in parts that are possibly missing today. We will cover this system in this book, because some illustrious scholars of Vedic astrology, like Neelakantha and Dr. B.V. Raman, set the precedent by teaching this system.

This system is based on solar return charts. When Sun returns every year to the position he occupied in the zodiac at the time of a person's birth, a new year is said to commence for the person and a chart drawn for that time is called "Tajaka annual chart" or "Tajaka varsha chakra". Analysis of this chart can give insights into what may be in store during the one year following the solar return. Results suggested in the annual chart can take place only if they are 'possible' based on natal chart also. However, annual chart often gives a finer insight into the year in question than natal chart.

A few special dasa systems enable timing of events within the 365-day period of operation of an annual chart.

Similar to the annual charts, "monthly solar return charts" (Tajaka masa chakras) can also be drawn and they are useful in analyzing a one-month period in depth.

This part explains the casting and use of annual charts in giving precise predictions.

27. Tajaka Chart Basics

27.1 Casting Annual Charts

Sun moves with respect to earth at the rate of 30° per month. He takes one year to complete one cycle through the zodiac. He returns to the position occupied by him at the time of one's birth after every one-year period. *At the **exact moment** when Sun returns to the **exact position** he occupied at the time of a person's birth, a new year is said to commence in the life of that person.* A chart can be cast for the commencement of the new year. This is called a Tajaka varsha chakra or a Tajaka annual chart[76]. The longitude and latitude of the birthplace must be used in casting this chart, irrespective of the place of living at the commencement of the new year.

The commencement of a new year is called "varsha pravesh" by some people. Varsha means a year and pravesh means entry.

Example 118:

Let us take a native with this birthdata: 8th March 1967, 5:40 pm (IST), 73 E 04, 26 N 18. Sun occupies 23° 50' 25" in Aq in his birthchart. Suppose we want to analyze the one-year period of March 2000-March 2001 using Tajaka annual chart. Then we should find the date and time when Sun enters 23° 50' 25" in Aq in March 2000. We find that Sun enters this position at 4:41:21 am on 8th March 2000. The native finishes 33 years and enters his 34th year at that time.

We can erect a chart with the following data: 8th March 2000, 4:41:21 am (IST), 73 E 04, 26 N 18[77]. That chart is called the native's Tajaka annual chart for 2000-2001. Rasi chart erected with this data is shown in Chart 66. Along with this rasi chart, we can draw all the divisional charts at this time.

By analyzing this rasi chart and the associated divisional charts, we can find out the fortune of the native during the year. The matters shown by various divisional charts, houses, rasis, planets, arudha padas *etc* remain the same. To time events within this year, we have annual dasas. We will learn them in later chapters.

---

76 Western astrologers also use similar charts and call them "solar return" charts. Some Indian astrologers call these "varshaphal" charts. Varshaphal means "results for one year".

77 Even if the native is living on the other side of the globe, we must still cast the annual chart for birthplace co-ordinates. So we are using the longitude and latitude of his birthplace here.

Chart 66

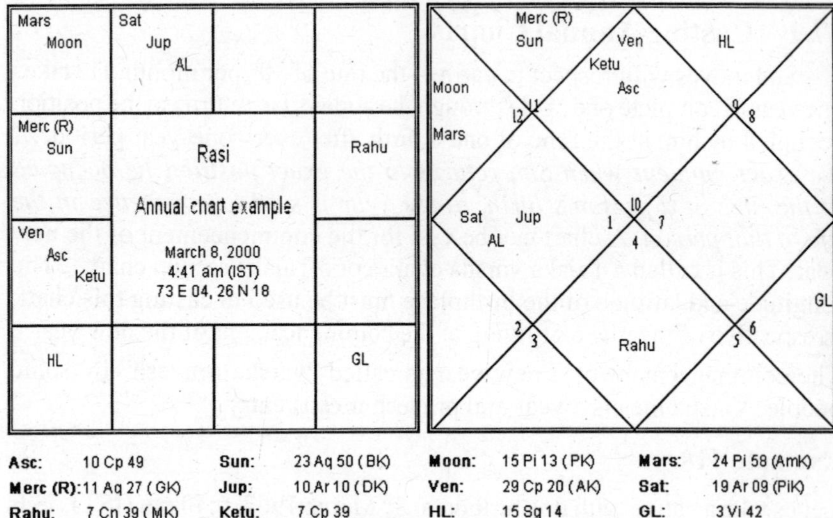

27.2 An Approximate Method

The exact time of the commencement of new year is determined by finding the exact time when Sun enters the exact position occupied by him at the time of one's birth. However, this can be a laborious calculation to do manually. To make this task less challenging, some scholars devised approximate methods based on the number of days in an average solar year. A sidereal solar year has 365 days 6 hours 9 minutes and 12 seconds. Based on this, the amount of time to be added to the birthdata to find the varsha pravesh data is given in Table 71.

Table 71: Approximate Annual Chart Data

Age (years)	Days	Hours	Minutes	Seconds
1	1	6	9	12
2	2	12	18	18
3	3	18	27	30
4	5	0	36	36
5	6	6	45	48
6	0	12	55	0
7	1	19	4	6
8	3	1	13	18

Age (years)	Days	Hours	Minutes	Seconds
9	4	7	22	30
10	5	13	31	36
20	4	3	3	12
30	2	16	34	54
40	1	6	6	30
50	6	19	38	6
60	5	9	9	42
70	3	22	41	24
80	2	12	13	0
90	1	1	44	36
100	6	15	16	12

Procedure:

(1) Find the birthday as per western calendar in the required year.

(2) Find the years completed. Find the corresponding days, hours, minutes and seconds from Table 71. If the age is not in the list, express it as a sum of entries found in the table and add their values. For example, suppose someone finished 46 years. Then add the values given for 40 years and 6 years.

(3) Add the days found above to the weekday[78] of birth and find the resulting weekday. Find the nearest date to the birthday found in (1) that falls on this weekday. A time equal to the birthtime on this date is taken as a reference.

(4) Add the hours, minutes and seconds found in (2) to the reference date and time found in (3). The result is the date and time of the commencement of new year.

(5) Find the planetary positions, lagna etc at this time for the longitude and latitude of the birthplace.

Let us now revisit Example 118 and calculate varsha pravesh data using this approximate method.

(1) Birthday is 8th March 1967. The 34th year starts in 2000. The birthday as per the western calendar is on 8th March 2000.

---

78 Remember that the weekday in Hindu calendar changes at sunrise and not at 12:00 midnight.

(2) Finished years are 33 = 30 + 3. Adding the entries of 30 years and 3 years, we get

	Days	*Hrs*	*Min*	*Sec*
30 years:	2	16	34	54 (from Table 71)
3 years:	3	18	27	30 (from Table 71)
33 years (sum):	6	11	02	24

(3) Birthday (8th March 1967) is a Wednesday. Adding 6 days to it, we get a Tuesday. We now have to find the Tuesday nearest to 8th March 2000. It is 7th March 2000. The time of birth on 8th March 1967 is 5:40 pm and we now take 5:40 pm on 7th March 2000 as the reference time.

(4) We have to add 11 hours, 2 minutes and 24 seconds found in (2) to the reference time in (3). We get 4:42:24 am on 8th March 2000.

(5) We find rasi chart and all divisional charts for the data: 8th March 2000, 4:42:24 am (IST), 73 E 04, 26 N 18.

Please note that the time found here is wrong only by 1 minute. In some examples, the error resulting from the approximation can be higher. However, this approximate method is very convenient and quick.

NOTE: Errors due to ayanamsa and approximations in the calculation of Sun's longitude cause greater errors than this approximation. As long as one takes the correct *nonlinear nature* of ayanamsa change into account, there will not be any appreciable discrepancy in the varsha pravesh times found by people using different ayanamsas. But ignoring the nonlinear nature of ayanamsa results in considerable errors in varsha pravesh time. This is because lagna moves 360 times faster than Sun. Any small errors in Sun's longitude result in errors in lagna which are 360 times as large.

Exercise 47: Find the varsha pravesh data for the 27th year of the native in Example 118 using (*a*) the approximate method and (*b*) the exact method.

27.3 Casting Monthly Charts

A year is divided into 12 months and a new chart can be cast at the commencement of every new month. This is called Tajaka maasa chakra or a Tajaka monthly chart.

The commencement of a new month is called "maasa pravesh" by some people.

A year is the period in which Sun moves by 360°. A month is the period in which Sun moves by 30°.

Let us take the native of Example 118. He was born on 8th March 1967.

Sun was at 23° 50' 25" in Aq when he was born. On 8th March 2000, Sun enters 23° 50' 25" in Aq at 4:41:21 am (IST) and a new year commences then. This is the 34th year in the life of the native.

Along with the new year, a new month commences then. This is the first month of the year. This month ends and a new month commences after Sun moves by exactly 30°. Sun enters 23° 50' 25" in Pi on 7th April 2000 at 10:38:06 am. The second month in the year commences then. We can cast rasi chart and divisional charts at that moment. Using those charts, we can predict events in the next one-month period. This month ends and the third month commences when Sun enters 23° 50' 25" in Ar.

Thus, when Sun enters 23° 50' 25" in different rasis, we cast different monthly charts and use them for predicting the events in a one-month period. The thing to remember here is that "one month" is the time when Sun moves by exactly 30°.

There isn't any good approximate method for casting monthly charts. Sun takes approximately the same time for moving by 360° and so we have an approximate method for annual charts. But the time Sun takes to move by 30° varies considerably from month to month. So there isn't any approximate method that gives decent results. It may be wise to exactly cast 12 monthly charts for the first year of the native and then find monthly charts in later years from them, using the approximate method given for annual charts.

27.4 Casting Sixty-hour Charts

A month is again divided into 12 shashti-horas. Each shashti-hora period consists of 60 hours, *i.e.* 2.5 days. At the beginning of every shashti-hora, a Tajaka shashti-hora chakra[79] (Tajaka sixty-hour chart) is cast. In the period corresponding to each Tajaka sixty-hour chart, Sun moves by 2°30'.

In other words, we can cast a chart after every 2°30' motion of Sun and use that Tajaka sixty-hour chart to predict events in the 2.5-day period commencing then. There are exactly 12 such charts in a one-month period.

For example, let us take the second month of the year 2000-2001 for the native of Example 118. The second month commences when Sun enters 23° 50' 25" in Pi, *i.e.* on 7th April 2000 at 10:38:06 am. The first shashti-hora of the month also starts then. It ends and the second shashti-hora or 60-hour period commences when Sun is advanced by 2°30', *i.e.* when Sun

79 This is popularly known as just "Tajaka Hora Chakra".

enters 26° 20' 25" in Pi. This happens at 11:40:51 pm (IST) on 9th April 2000. If we cast a chart for that moment, we can make some predictions for the next 2.5 days.

27.5 Conclusion

In this chapter, we learnt what Tajaka annual and monthly charts are and how they are cast. When Sun re-enters every year the same longitude occupied by him at the time of one's birth, it signals the commencement of a new year in the native's life. We can cast a chart for that exact moment and predict events in the next one year based on that chart. We can also cast monthly charts and sixty-hour charts.

These new years are based on the solar years and the commencement of new year is *around* one's birthday as per the modern western calendar. However, many Indians – especially south Indians – celebrate birthday as per the lunar calendar. In fact, most Hindu holidays are based on the lunar calendar. For example, birthdays of Lord Rama and Lord Krishna are celebrated based on the *tithi* and not based on the solar calendar. Lunar calendar is of great importance in Indian culture. Correspondingly, there are techniques based on the birthday as per lunar calendar. However, those techniques are beyond the scope of this book and we will restrict ourselves to solar birthday and Tajaka annual charts.

27.6 Answers to Exercises

Exercise 47:

(a) Approximate method:

(1) The approximate birthday of the 27th year is 8th March 1993. He completes 26 years then.

(2) Adding the entries of 20 years and 6 years, we get 4 days 15 hr 58 min 12 sec.

(3) Adding 4 days to Wednesday (weekday of birth), we get Sunday. The nearest Sunday to 8th March 1993 is 7th March 1993. So we take 5:40 pm on 7th March 1993 as the reference time.

(4) Add 15 hr 58 min 12 sec to this reference time. We get 9:38:12 am on 8th March 1993.

(b) Exact method:

Let us find the position of Sun at the above time. At 9:38:12 am (IST) on 8th March 1993, Sun is at 23° 50' 29" in Aq. Natal position is 23° 50' 25" in Aq. We have to subtract about 2 minutes of time to get Sun 4" behind. The correct varshapravesh data is – 9:36:18 am (IST) on 8th March 1993.

28. Techniques of Tajaka Charts

28.1 Muntha

Muntha is a concept specific to Tajaka charts. Progress lagna in the natal chart at the rate of one rasi per year to get muntha in an annual chart. Suppose someone finishes 31 years and starts the 32nd year on a given date. Suppose we are casting the annual chart of the 32nd year. Suppose the natal chart has lagna in Sc. Then muntha in the annual chart will be the 32nd house from Sc, *i.e.* the 8th house from Sc (after expunging multiples of 12 from 32). So muntha is in Ge.

Muntha is very important in Tajaka charts. Muntha is as important a reference point in an annual chart as lagna. The reason may be obvious in the chapter on "Sudarsana Chakra Dasa". Some people find muntha in monthly charts by progressing natal lagna by 2°30' per month. This author takes a different stand and the readers may be able to appreciate this after reading the same chapter.

Look at the planets in muntha. They tell us the nature of events in the year or month. For example, Jupiter in muntha may give good results, happiness from children and knowledge. Saturn in muntha may make one sluggish, unhealthy, frustrated and sorrowful. Of course, the strength of the planets influencing muntha also matters. For example, an afflicted and weak Jupiter in muntha may give loss of position, bad name and scandals.

Position of muntha in various houses with respect to lagna in the annual chart also tells us the nature of events in a year. Situation of muntha in the 9th, 10th and 11th houses is excellent. It gives prosperity, status and gains respectively. Situation of muntha in the 1st, 2nd, 3rd and 5th houses is also good. It gives health, wealth, success and fame respectively. Situation of muntha in the 6th, 8th and 12th houses is bad. It gives illness, troubles and expenditures respectively. Situation of muntha in the 4th house gives disputes and loss of position. Situation of muntha in the 7th house also gives troubles in marriage and many hardships.

28.2 Aspects

In Tajaka analysis, we consider the following aspects:[80]

---

80 These aspects are similar to the ones used in western astrology. Considering that graha and rasi aspects were mentioned by maharshis, the *exact* meaning and use of these special aspects needs to be further researched and correctly understood. The current understanding of scholars may be incomplete. *Rishi prokta* (words spoken by great sages) should form the basis of our knowledge.

(1) **Trinal aspect:** A planet has a strong benefic aspect on the 5th and 9th houses from it and on the planets in those houses.

(2) **Sextile aspect:** A planet has a weak benefic aspect on the 3rd and 11th houses from it and on the planets in those houses.

(3) **Square aspect:** A planet has a weak malefic aspect on the 4th and 10th houses from it and on the planets in those houses.

(4) **Conjunction:** A planet has a strong malefic aspect on the planets in the same house occupied by it.

(5) **Opposition:** A planet has a strong malefic aspect on the 7th house from it and on the planets in that house.

(6) **Semi-sextile aspect:** A planet has a neutral aspect on the 2nd and 12th houses from it and on the planets in those houses.

Deeptamsa is "the orb of an aspect". Deeptamsas of planets: Sun – 15°, Moon – 12°, Mars – 8°, Mercury – 7°, Jupiter – 9°, Venus – 7°, Saturn – 9°. If Venus is at 13° in Li, he will have a trinal aspect on Ge, but his aspect doesn't cover the entire rasi. Venusian aspect covers an angle of 7° from 13° in Gemini mainly, though Venus may have a moderate aspectual influence on the entire rasi. So Venus *mainly* influences 6°–20° in Ge by aspect. Deeptamsa is the same for all kinds of aspects.

28.3 Harsha Bala

Harsha bala[81] of seven planets is found by adding the strengths given by the following 4 sources of strength:

(1) Sun in the 9th house, Moon in the 3rd house, Mars in the 6th house, Mercury in the 1st house, Jupiter in the 11th house, Venus in the 5th house and Saturn in the 12th house get 5 units. They get zero units in other houses.

(2) A planet in exaltation or own sign gets 5 units (else zero units).

(3) Feminine planets (Moon, Mercury, Venus and Saturn) get 5 units in the 1st, 2nd, 3rd 7th, 8th and 9th houses. Masculine planets (Sun, Mars and Jupiter) get 5 units in the 4th, 5th, 6th, 10th, 11th and 12th houses.

(4) If the new year starts in the daytime, masculine planets get 5 units each. If the new year starts in the night time, feminine planets get 5 units each.

A planet with 20 units of strength is exceedingly strong. A planet with 15 units of strength is fully strong. A planet with 10 units of strength is of

---

81 Harsha means "cheerful" and bala means "strength". This is the strength of cheerfulness.

average strength. A planet with 5 units of strength has only a little strength. A planet with zero units of strength has no strength at all.

Example 119: Let us find Harsha bala of planets for the annual chart of Example 118.

(1) Only Moon is in the prescribed house (the 3rd house in Moon's case). He gets 5 units.

(2) No planet is in exaltation or own sign.

(3) Venus in 1st, Mercury in 2nd, Moon in 3rd are the feminine planets in prescribed houses. Jupiter in 4th is in the masculine planet in the prescibed house.

(4) Because the new year started at 4:42 am, *i.e.* during the night, we give 5 units each to the feminine planets – Moon, Mercury, Venus and Saturn.

Adding all the sources, we get 15 for Moon, 10 for Mercury and Venus, 5 for Jupiter and Saturn and zero for Sun and Mars.

28.4 Pancha Vargeeya Bala

Panchavargeeya[82] bala is found using the following procedure:

28.4.1 *Kshetra Bala*

Kshetra bala shows the strength in rasi chart. A planet in own rasi gets 30 units of Kshetra bala. A planet in a friend's rasi gets 15 units of Kshetra bala. A planet in an enemy's rasi gets 7.5 units of Kshetra bala.

28.4.2 *Uchcha Bala*

Uchcha bala shows how close a planet is from its exaltation point. A planet gets 20 units of uchcha bala if it is at its deep exaltation point (Sun: 10° Ar, Moon: 3° Ta, Mars: 28° Cp, Mercury: 15° Vi, Jupiter: 5° Cn, Venus: 27° Pi, Saturn: 20° Li). At 180° from its deep exaltation point, a planet is deeply debilitated and it gets 0 units of uchcha bala.

We can find the longitude difference between a planet's position and its deep debilitation point and divide it by 180° to get the fraction that shows how far away it is from its debilitation point. By multiplying 20 units with this fraction, we get uchcha bala.

For example, suppose Jupiter is at 8Vi30 (8°30' in Vi). So he is at 158°30' from the start of the zodiac. His debilitation point is 5° in Cp, *i.e.* 275°0'. The difference is 275°0' – 158°30' = 116°30'. Because this is less than 180°, we don't have to subtract it from 360°.

---

82 Pancha means "five". Pancha vargeeya means "from the group of five".

Now 116°30'/180° = 0.6472. Multiply 20 with this fraction, we get 12.94. So Jupiter's uchcha bala is 12.94 (out of 20).

28.4.3 *Hadda Bala*

Each rasi is divided into several haddas and different haddas have different lords. Hadda is similar to D-30. Table 72 can be used for finding the hadda lords of planets.

Hadda bala shows the strength in hadda. A planet in own hadda gets 15 units of Hadda bala. A planet in a friend's hadda gets 7.5 units of Hadda bala. A planet in an enemy's hadda gets 3.75 units of Hadda bala.

28.4.4 *Drekkana Bala*

Drekkana bala shows the strength in drekkana chart (D-3). A planet in own rasi in D-3 gets 10 units of Drekkana bala. A planet in a friend's rasi in D-3 gets 5 units of Drekkana bala. A planet in an enemy's rasi in D-3 gets 2.5 units of Drekkana bala.

Table 72: Hadda Lords

Ar	0°-6° Jupiter	6°-12° Venus	12°-20° Mercury	20°-25° Mars	25°-30° Saturn
Ta	0°-8° Venus	8°-14° Mercury	14°-22° Jupiter	22°-27° Saturn	27°-30° Mars
Ge	0°-6° Mercury	6°-12° Venus	12°-17° Jupiter	17°-24° Mars	24°-30° Saturn
Cn	0°-7° Mars	7°-13° Venus	13°-19° Mercury	19°-26° Jupiter	26°-30° Saturn
Le	0°-6° Jupiter	6°-11° Venus	11°-18° Saturn	18°-24° Mercury	24°-30° Mars
Vi	0°-7° Mercury	7°-17° Venus	17°-21° Jupiter	21°-28° Mars	28°-30° Saturn
Li	0°-6° Saturn	6°-14° Mercury	14°-21° Jupiter	21°-28° Venus	28°-30° Mars
Sc	0°-7° Mars	7°-11° Venus	11°-19° Mercury	19°-24° Jupiter	24°-30° Saturn
Sg	0°-12° Jupiter	12°-17° Venus	17°-21° Mercury	21°-26° Mars	26°-30° Saturn

Cp	0°-7° Mercury	7°-14° Jupiter	14°-22° Venus	22°-26° Saturn	26°-30° Mars
Aq	0°-7° Mercury	7°-13° Venus	13°-20° Jupiter	20°-25° Mars	25°-30° Saturn
Pi	0°-12° Venus	12°-16° Jupiter	16°-19° Mercury	19°-28° Mars	28°-30° Saturn

28.4.5 *Navamśa Bala*

Navamsa bala shows the strength in navamsa chart (D-9). A planet in own rasi in D-9 gets 5 units of Navamsa bala. A planet in a friend's rasi in D-9 gets 2.5 units of Navamsa bala. A planet in an enemy's rasi in D-9 gets 1.25 units of Navamsa bala.

28.4.6 *Final Computation*

We find the sum of kshetra bala, uchcha bala, hadda bala, drekkana bala and navamsa bala and divide the sum by 4. The result is called "Pancha Vargeeya Bala". If it is below 5, the planet is weak. If it is between 5 and 10, the planet has ordinary strength. If it is between 10 and 15, the planet is strong. If it is between 15 and 20, the planet is very strong. If it is above 20, the planet is extraordinarily strong.

28.5 Dwaadasa Vargeeya Bala

Consider the twelve divisional charts: D-1, D-2, D-3, D-4, D-5, D-6, D-7, D-8, D-9, D-10, D-11, and, D-12.

A planet is strong in a chart if it is in its exaltation rasi or its own rasi or a rasi owned by a friend. A planet is weak in a chart if it is in its debilitation rasi or a rasi owned by an enemy. Out of the 12 charts above, count the charts in which a planet is strong and count the charts in which a planet is weak. The difference gives Dwadasavargeeya[83] bala. If a planet is strong in more charts, it is strong overall. If a planet is weak in more charts, it is weak overall.

28.6 Lord of the Year

Varsheswara or lord of the year is the most important planet during the year. His dasa brings important results. The following are the candidates:

(1) Lord of the rasi occupied by Sun or Moon in the annual chart, based on whether the new year starts during the day or the night

83 Dwaadasa means "twelve". Dwaadasavargeeya means "from the 12 groups".

(2) Lord of natal lagna
(3) Lord of Muntha
(4) Lord of lagna in the annual chart
(5) Triraasi lord of lagna in the annual chart (see Table 73)

Table 73: Triraasi Lords

Lagna	Day	Night
Ar	Sun	Jupiter
Ta	Venus	Moon
Ge	Saturn	Mercury
Cn	Venus	Mars
Le	Jupiter	Sun
Vi	Moon	Venus
Li	Mercury	Saturn
Sc	Mars	Venus
Sg	Saturn	Saturn
Cp	Mars	Mars
Aq	Jupiter	Jupiter
Pi	Moon	Moon

If a candidate is strong as per panchavargeeya bala and has a benefic aspect on lagna, it becomes the lord of the year.

After the five candidates are found, the candidates having a benefic aspect on lagna are short-listed. Out of those, the planet having the highest panchavargeeya bala becomes the lord of the year. If two candidates have similar panchavargeeya bala, the one becoming a candidate in more of the five categories listed above becomes the lord of the year.

If none of the planet has a benefic aspect on lagna, even a malefic aspect may be accepted. If none of the planets has an aspect on lagna, we may take a candidate that is very strong as per panchavargeeya bala.

If none of the candidates has a strong aspect on lagna and none of the candidates is very strong as per panchavargeeya bala, then we may take the first candidate (lord of the rasi occupied by Sun or Moon in the annual chart, based on whether the new year starts during the day or the night).

Example 120: Let us consider the annual chart in Example 118. Let us find the candidates for the lord of the year:

(1) The new year started at 4:41 am, *i.e.* night time. So we should take Moon and find the lord of the rasi occupied by him. Moon is in Pisces owned by Jupiter. So Jupiter gets the first candidacy.

(2) Natal lagna is in Leo. So Sun gets the second candidacy.

(3) Muntha is in Taurus. So Venus gets the third candidacy.

(4) Lagna in the annual chart is in Capricorn. So Saturn gets the fourth candidacy.

(5) Triraasi lord for lagna in Cp at night time is Mars, from Table 73. So Mars gets the fifth candidacy.

The candidates are – Jupiter, Sun, Venus, Saturn and Mars. Of those, Venus occupies lagna and Jupiter and Saturn have a square aspect on lagna. All of them are malefic aspects. Sun has a semi-sextile aspect, which is neutral. Mars has a sextile aspect on Capricorn lagna from Pisces. He is also has the strongest panchavargeeya bala (13.7). So we conclude easily that Mars is the lord of the year.

28.7 Lord of the Month

We find the lord of the month in a monthly chart in the same manner. We have *six* candidates now:

(1) Lord of the rasi occupied by Sun or Moon in the monthly chart, based on whether the new month starts during the day or the night

(2) Lord of natal lagna

(3) Lord of Muntha

(4) Lord of lagna in the monthly chart

(5) Triraasi lord of lagna in the monthly chart (see Table 73)

(6) Lord of the year

The rest of the rules are the same.

28.8 Sahams

28.8.1 *Calculation*

Sahams are the significant points in the zodiac related to specific matters. For example, "raajya" means kingdom and "raajya saham" is a significant point in the zodiac related to obtaining kingdom. "Paradesa" means a foreign country and "paradesa saham" is a significant point in the zodiac related to going abroad. Each saham has a formula that looks like A – B + C. What this means is that we take the longitudes of A, B and C and find (A – B + C). This is equivalent to finding how far A is from B and then taking the same distance from C. However, if C is not *between* B and A (*i.e.* we start from B and go zodiacally till we meet A and we do *not* find C on the way), then we add 30° to the value evaluated above.

For example, finding (Moon – Sun + Lagna) is equivalent to finding how far Moon is *from* Sun and taking the same distance *from* lagna. If we start from the longitude of Sun and go zodiacally till the longitude of Moon and do *not* find lagna on the way, then we have to add 30°. The list of important sahams is given in Table 74. For most sahams, the formula given as (A – B + C) is for daytime charts. For nighttime charts, it changes to (B – A + C). This will not be explicitly mentioned for each saham and a mention will be made only when there is a difference.

Table 74: Sahams

No.	Saham	Meaning	Formula
1	Punya	Fortune/good deeds	Moon – Sun + Lagna
2	Vidya	Education	Sun – Moon + Lagna
3	Yasas	Fame	Jupiter – PunyaSaham + Lagna
4	Mitra	Friend	Jupiter – PunyaSaham + Venus
5	Mahatmya	Greatness	PunyaSaham – Mars + Lagna
6	Asha	Desires	Saturn – Mars + Lagna
7	Samartha	Enterprise/ability	Mars – Lagna Lord +Lagna (Jupiter – Mars + Lagna, if Mars owns lagna)
8	Bhratri	Brothers	Jupiter – Saturn + Lagna (same for day & night)
9	Gaurava	Respect/regard	Jupiter – Moon + Sun
10	Pitri	Father	Saturn – Sun + Lagna
11	Rajya	Kingdom	Saturn – Sun + Lagna
12	Matri	Mother	Moon – Venus + Lagna
13	Putra	Children	Jupiter – Moon + Lagna
14	Jeeva	Life	Saturn – Jupiter + Lagna
15	Karma	Action (work)	Mars – Mercury + Lagna
16	Roga	Disease	Lagna – Moon + Lagna
17	Kali	Great misfortune	Jupiter – Mars + Lagna

No.	Saham	Meaning	Formula
18	Sastra	Sciences	Jupiter – Saturn + Mercury
19	Bandhu	Relatives	Mercury – Moon + Lagna
20	Mrityu	Death	8th house – Moon + Lagna (same for day & night)
21	Paradesa	Foreign countries	9th house – 9th lord + Lagna (same for day & night)
22	Artha	Money	2nd house – 2nd lord + Lagna (same for day & night)
23	Paradara	Adultery	Venus – Sun + Lagna
24	Vanik	Commerce	Moon – Mercury + Lagna
25	Karyasiddhi	Success in endeavours	Saturn – Sun + Lord of sunsign (Night: Saturn – Moon + Lord of Moonsign)
26	Vivaha	Marriage	Venus – Saturn + Lagna
27	Santapa	Sadness	Saturn – Moon + 6th house
28	Sraddha	Devotion/sincerity	Venus – Mars + Lagna
29	Preeti	Love/attachment	SastraSaham – PunyaSaham + Lagna
30	Jadya	Chronic disease	Mars – Saturn + Mercury
31	Vyapara	Business	Mars – Saturn + Lagna (same for day & night)
32	Satru	Enemy	Mars – Saturn + Lagna
33	Jalapatana	Crossing an ocean	Cancer 15°– Saturn + Lagna
34	Bandhana	Imprisonment	PunyaSaham – Saturn + Lagna
35	Apamrityu	Bad death	8th house – Mars + Lagna
36	Labha	Material gains	11th house – 11th lord + Lagna (same for day & night)

Example 121: Let us consider the annual chart of Example 118 and find artha saham (money), samartha saham (enterprise/ability) and vanik saham (commerce).

Let us use the formulas given in Table 74. Formula of artha saham is: 2nd house – 2nd lord + Lagna. Because the chart is cast for the night time, we should reverse the formula. However, as the note in parantheses after the formula says, this formula should be used for both day & night. Lagna is at 10 Cp 50, *i.e.* 280°50'. The 2nd house is at 10 Aq 50, *i.e.* 310°50'. Lord of the 2nd house is Saturn and he is at 19 Ar 10, *i.e.* 19°10'. So artha saham = 310°50' – 19°10' + 280°50' = 572°30'. We can add or subtract multiples of 360° from a longitude to reduce it to the range 0° to 360°. By subtracting 360°, we get 212°30'. This means that artha saham is at 212°30'. This means 2°30' in Sc or simply 2 Sc 30. Now we have to check whether the C is between B and A in A – B + C. We have to check whether lagna (280°50') is between 2nd lord (19°10') and 2nd house (310°50'). It is – if we start from 19°10' and go till 310°50', we do encounter 280°50' on the way. So we don't have to add 30°.

Formula of samartha saham is: Mars – Lagna Lord + Lagna. Because this chart is cast for night time, we should make it Lagna Lord – Mars + Lagna. Lagna lord Saturn is at 19 Ar 10, *i.e.* 19°10'. Mars is at 24 Pi 58, *i.e.* 354°58'. Lagna is at 280°50'. So samartha saham = 19°10' – 354°58' + 280°50' + 360°. We added 360° to make the result positive. We can always add and subtract multiples of 360° from any longitude. So samartha saham is 305°2'. If we start from 354°58' and go zodiacally till we reach 19°10' (when we reach the end of Pisces, we go to Aries), we do *not* encounter 280°50'. So lagna is *not* between Mars and Lagna Lord. So we add 30°. Samartha saham is finally at 335°2', *i.e.* at 5°2' in Pi or simply 5 Pi 02.

Formula of vanik saham is: Moon – Mercury + Lagna. Because this chart is cast for night time, we should make it Mercury – Moon + Lagna. Moon is at 15 Pi 14, *i.e.* 345°14'. Mercury is at 11 Aq 28, *i.e.* 311°28'. Lagna is at 280°50'. So samartha saham = 311°28' – 345°14' + 280°50'. So vanik saham is 247°4'. If we start from 345°14' and go zodiacally till we reach 311°28' (when we reach the end of Pisces, we go to Aries), we cover a large arc of about 330°. On the way, we do encounter 280°50'. So lagna *is* between Moon and Mercury. So we don't have to add 30°. Vanik saham is at 247°4', *i.e.* at 7°4' in Sg or simply 7 Sg 04.

28.8.2 *Use of sahams*

If there are good yogas in an annual chart involving the lord of the rasi containing an important saham and lagna lord, then important events related to the matter of the saham may materialize during the year.

We can also use sahams in natal charts. When Saturn or Rahu transits close to natal paradesa saham or jalapatana saham, for example, one may go abroad. When Jupiter occupies or aspects natal vivaha saham in transit, one may get married. Thus we can use sahams in natal charts also.

NOTE: In western astrology, there are Arabian parts (*e.g.* part of fortune) which are similar to sahams. In fact, there are a lot of similarities between the techniques in Tajaka system and western astrology.

Some people may suggest that Indians learnt Tajaka system from Arabs. This is possible. However, one must note that astrology as practiced in India is much superior in width and depth to astrology practiced in any other part of the world. Indian astrology is a big *superset* of which different astrological traditions of the world are but small *subsets*. One may speculate that Vedic astrology as taught by Parasara, Jaimini, Manu *etc* was very exhaustive in scope and experts in different branches of it traveled to different parts of the world in ancient times to establish the knowledge there.

29. Tajaka Yogas

29.1 Introduction

Just as we have yogas in natal charts, we have special combinations with special results that are applicable to Tajaka annual/monthly charts. These are called Tajaka yogas. These yogas are applicable to Tajaka annual charts as well as prasna charts (horary charts). We will briefly go over their definitions in this chapter.

29.2 Definitions

29.2.1 *Ishkavala Yoga*

If planets occupy only kendras (1st, 4th, 7th and 10th houses) and panapharas (2nd, 5th, 8th and 11th houses) and if apoklimas (3rd, 6th, 9th and 12th houses) are empty, then this yoga is present. This yoga gives wealth, happiness and good fortune.

29.2.2 *Induvara Yoga*

If planets occupy only apoklimas (3rd, 6th, 9th and 12th houses) and if kendras (1st, 4th, 7th and 10th houses) and panapharas (2nd, 5th, 8th and 11th houses) are empty, then this yoga is present. This yoga gives disappointments, worries and illnesses.

29.2.3 *Ithasala Yoga*

If two planets have an aspect and if the faster moving planet[84] is less advanced in its rasi than the slower moving planet, then we have an ithasala yoga between the two. In western astrology, this is called an "applying aspect".

Results: This is a good yoga and this shows fulfilment of the matters represented by the two planets in ithasala. Suppose we want to analyze prospects for a particular matter. Then ithasala involving lagna lord, lord of the related house, lord of the related saham or the naisargika karaka (natural significator) will show good results related to the matter. For example, ithasala between lagna lord and 7th lord (or the lord of vivaha saham or Venus) shows that the native may get married in the year.

Example: Suppose Moon is at 14° in Le and Venus is at 19° in Li. They have a sextile aspect. Both the planets are within the deeptaamsa (orb) of the other. Moon's advancement in his rasi is 14° and Venus's advancement

---

84 In the increasing order of speed, planets can be listed as: Saturn, Rahu/Ketu, Jupiter, Mars, Sun, Venus, Mercury and Moon.

in his rasi is 19°. Faster planet (Moon) is less advanced than the slower planet (Venus). So we have ithasala yoga.

Types of Ithasala: There are 3 types of ithasala yoga.

(*i*) *Vartamaana ithasala yoga* results when the planets aspect each other and both are within the deeptaamsa (orb) of the other planet. Vartamaana means present (current). In the above example, Venus is at 19° and his deeptaamsa extends from 12° to 26°. Moon is within his deeptaamsa. Venus is also within Moon's deeptaamsa. So we have vartamaana ithasala.

(*ii*) *Poorna ithasala yoga* results when the planets aspect each other closely and their advancements in respective rasis are within 1° of each other. Poorna means complete. Poorna ithasala is the most powerful ithasala. It shows speedy fulfilment of the matter. In the above example, the difference between the advancements of Moon and Venus in respective rasis is 19°–14° = 5°. This is more than 1°. So we don't have a poorna ithasala. Now let us say that Moon is at 18°25' in Le (instead of 14° in Le). Then also we have an ithasala because Moon is behind Venus. The difference between the advancements is only 0°35', *i.e.* less than 1°. So we have a poorna ithasala now.

(*iii*) *Bhavishya ithasala yoga* is formed if vartamaana ithasala yoga is about to be formed when the faster moving planet moves by 1° or less. Bhavishya means future. Bhavishya ithasala shows fulfilment after some obstructions or delay. Suppose Moon is at 13°35' in Le and Venus is at 21°20' in Le. There is a sextile aspect. Moon's deeptaamsa is 12° and hence his sextile aspect on Li extends from 1°35' to 25°35' in Li (subtract and add 12°, Moon's deeptaamsa, from/to 13°35'). Venus is within Moon's deeptaamsa. However, Moon is just outside the deeptaamsa of Venus, as the deeptaamsa of Venus's sextile aspect on Le extends from 14°20' to 28°20' in Li (subtract and add 7°, Venus's deeptaamsa, from/to 21°20'). Moon is at 13°35' and this is outside Venus's deeptaamsa. So there is no vartamaana (present) ithasala. However, when Moon is the faster planet and he needs to move by just 0°45' (which is less than 1°) to come to 14°20'. Once he comes to 14°20', he is within the deeptaamsa of Venus's aspect on Le and we have a vartamaana ithasala yoga. So we have a bhavishya (future) ithasala yoga when Moon is at 13°35' in Le.

Special Notes: One should understand the meaning of these combinations and apply them intelligently. The main criterion of ithasala is that the faster moving planet should be behind. This means that the two planets will reach the same advancement in their rasis and have an *exact* aspect (sookshma drishti) very soon. If Moon is at 14° in Le and Venus is at 19° in Li, Moon is going to reach 19° very soon and Moon and Venus are going to have an *exact* sextile aspect. So the energies of Moon and Venus are soon going to work in unison.

That is the main idea behind ithasala. If the faster moving planet is retrograde, then the above is not going to happen and we no longer have ithasala. For example, suppose retrograde Mercury is at 18° in Ge and Mars is at 18°10' in Li. One may be tempted to think that there is an extremely powerful trinal aspect and a poorna ithasala yoga because the difference in advancements is merely 0°10'. However, that is not correct. Being retrograde, Mercury will go backward and Mars will go forward. They are *not* going to reach the same longitude anytime soon. Despite indications of success, one may be dogged with failure under this combination.

On the other hand, if the slower planet is retrograde, there is no problem. It, in fact, shows a faster realization, as the two planets will reach the same advancement faster. Suppose Moon is at 18° in Ar and retrograde Mercury is at 24° in Ge. Now both the planets move towards the other planet and they are going to reach the same advancement soon. So there is an ithasala yoga.

Suppose the faster moving planet is retrograde and it is *more* advanced in its rasi than the slower moving planet. In that case, one may be tempted to think that there is no ithasala yoga. However, both the planets move towards the other and so there is an ithasala yoga. However, a planet's speed reduces under retrogression and the difference in advancements has to be smaller. For example, suppose Mars is at 21° in Cp and retrograde Mercury is at 23° in Vi. They have a trinal aspect. One may be tempted to think that there is no ithasala here, because Mercury, who moves faster than Mars, is more advanced in his rasi. However, being retrograde, Mercury moves backward. Very soon, Mars and Mercury are going to have the same advancements in respective rasis (perhaps near 22°). They will have an exact aspect then. So we have an ithasala yoga.

Thus one should adapt the rules in the case of retrogression. Even when there is no retrogression, some changes may have to be made. Suppose Mercury is at 18° in Vi and Mars is at 18°45' in Cp and neither is retrograde. Then one may be tempted to think that there is a poorna ithasala yoga in their trinal aspect. Now suppose that Mercury is about to become retrograde and he will become retrograde after reaching 18°05'. In that case, Mercury and Mars are not going to have an *exact* aspect anytime soon, because Mercury will start going backward after reaching 18°05'. So there is no ithasala.

Thus an erudite astrologer should make proper modifications to the rules when a planet is retrograde or about to become retrograde.

29.2.4 *Eesarpha Yoga*

Eesarpha yoga is the opposite of ithasala. If two planets have an aspect and the faster moving planet has a *higher* advancement in its rasi than the slower moving planet, then we have eesarpha yoga.

Results: This is a bad yoga. This results in failures and disappointments. If lagna lord has eesarpha yoga with 5th lord or putra saham lord or Jupiter, some disappointments related to children are possible. If lagna lord has an eesarpha with 10th lord or 5th lord or raajya saham lord or Sun in the chart of a president or prime minister or king, loss of power is a possibility during the year.

Example: Suppose Moon is at 23° in Le and Venus is at 19° in Li. They have a sextile aspect. Both the planets are within the deeptaamsa (orb) of the other. Moon's advancement in his rasi is 23° and Venus's advancement in his rasi is 19°. Faster planet (Moon) is more advanced than the slower planet (Venus). So we have eesarpha yoga.

Special Notes: We made some comments under ithasala yoga about planets that are retrograde or about to become retrograde. If the faster moving planet is retrograde and less advanced in its rasi, then we have eesarpha yoga. If the faster moving planet in an aspect is retrograde and more advanced in its rasi, then we do not have eesarpha yoga. We have an ithasala yoga instead.

29.2.5 *Nakta Yoga*

Suppose two planets have an aspect, but there is no ithasala yoga or eesarpha yoga. Then, we say that there is Nakta yoga between the two planets, if a planet that moves faster than both the planets has an aspect with both and forms ithasala yoga with both. This shows fulfilment of the matters represented by the first 2 planets with the help of someone shows by the 3rd planet.

Example: Suppose lagna is in Ta and Venus is at 13° in Ge. Suppose 7th lord Mars is in Sc (7th itself) at 15°. They have no aspect. Now suppose Moon is at 11° in Cn. He has a semi-sextile aspect with Venus and a trinal aspect with Mars. He has a lower advancement in his rasi (11°) than the other two planets and hence he has an ithasala yoga with the two planets. Thus, Venus and Mars have Nakta yoga between them. Because Venus is lagna lord in 2nd (family) and Mars is the 7th lord in 7th, this yoga shows getting married in the year. This may happen with the help of someone shown by Moon. As Moon owns the 3rd house, this may show the involvement of younger brother or sister. For example, the native may marry a friend of his younger sister with her help.

29.2.6 *Yamaya Yoga*

Suppose two planets have an aspect, but there is no ithasala yoga or eesarpha yoga. Then, we say that there is Yamaya yoga between the two planets, if a planet that moves slower than both the planets has an aspect with both and forms ithasala yoga with both. This shows fulfilment of the matters represented by the first 2 planets with the help of someone shows by the 3rd planet, after obstacles and delays.

Example: Suppose lagna is in Ta and Venus is at 13° in Ge. Suppose 7th lord Mars is in Sc (7th itself) at 15°. They have no aspect. Now suppose Jupiter is at 16° in Cn. He has a semi-sextile aspect with Venus and a trinal aspect with Mars. He has a higher advancement in his rasi (16°) than the other two planets and hence he has an ithasala yoga with the two planets. Thus, Venus and Mars have Yamaya yoga between them. Because Venus is lagna lord in 2nd (family) and Mars is the 7th lord in 7th, this yoga shows getting married in the year. This may happen with the help of someone shown by Jupiter. As Jupiter owns the 11th house, this may show the involvement of elder siblings or friends.

29.2.7 *Manahoo Yoga*

Suppose two planets have an ithasala yoga. If Saturn or Mars is in conjunction with the faster moving planet and stays within the deeptaamsa of the latter, then Manahoo yoga results. This yoga cancels the ithasala yoga and gives failures, disappointments, quarrels, loss of wealth etc.

Suppose Jupiter is at 21° in Pi and Moon is at 18° in Cn, then they have a sextile aspect and an ithasala yoga, because Moon (18°) is behind Jupiter (21°). However, let us say that Saturn is at 19° in Cn. Then Saturn cancels the ithasala between Moon and Jupiter and gives bad results.

If Mars or Saturn is one of the two planets in ithasala yoga, then we obviously need the other planet to give Manahoo yoga.

Notes: Some people suggest that an aspect of Saturn or Mars within the deeptaamsa of the faster moving planet is sufficient to give Manahoo yoga. In the above example, Saturn need not be in Cn according to this. Saturn or Mars in 6°-30° (Moon's deeptaamsa) in Cn, Le, Vi, Li, Sc, Cp, Pi, Ar, Ta and Ge will have an aspect with Moon – faster moving planet in Moon-Jupiter ithasala – within Moon's deeptaamsa. So Manahoo yoga results. However, readers are advised to consider only conjunction. Some authors have suggested that both Mars and Saturn must be involved, but one of them is enough to spoil ithasala yoga and give Manahoo yoga.

29.2.8 *Kamboola Yoga*

Suppose two planets have an ithasala yoga. If Moon has an ithasala with one of the planets (or both), then we have Kamboola yoga. This yoga adds power to the ithasala yoga. The power added varies based on the strength of Moon and other planets.

Suppose Mars is at 23° in Sc and Jupiter is at 26° in Pi. Then they have a trinal aspect and an ithasala yoga. Now, suppose Moon is at 22° in Le. He has an ithasala yoga with Mars. So we have Kamboola yoga and Mars-Jupiter ithasala becomes more powerful because of it.

29.2.9 *Gairi-Kamboola Yoga*

If Moon is in the last degree of a rasi and he will form ithasala with one of the planets in an ithasala after moving to the next rasi, it is called Gairi-Kamboola yoga. It is essentially Kamboola yoga in waiting. Moon must also form an ithasala with a strong planet for this yoga to be effective. Moreover, Moon should not be exalted or debilitated or occupy his own navamsa, drekkana or hadda. This yoga shows realization of the matter with help from others, after some delay.

Suppose Mars is at 1° in Cp, Jupiter is at 2° in Pi and Venus is at 3° in Li. Mars and Jupiter have a sextile aspect and ithasala yoga. Suppose Moon is at 29°10' in Vi. Moon is in the last degree of Vi. Moon is in Mercury's navamsa (Vi), Venus's drekkana (Ta) and Saturn's hadda. Moon has no ithasala with Mars or Jupiter, but he will have ithasala with Mars as soon as he moves to Li. He also has ithasala with Venus, who is very strong. So we have Gairi-Kamboola yoga.

29.2.10 *Khallasara Yoga*

If lagna lord is in the rasi between Moon and another planet X without ithasala with either planet, then Khallasara yoga results. This yoga destroys the signification of X.

Suppose lagna is in Vi, Moon is at 1° in Ar, lagna lord Mercury is at 15° in Ta and Jupiter is at 29° in Ge, then Khallasara yoga is formed. Lagna lord Mercury is between Moon and Jupiter and there is no ithasala with Moon or Jupiter. The significations of Jupiter are destroyed and there may be some disappointments related to mother, education, house, vehicles or marriage.

29.2.11 *Radda Yoga*

If an ithasala yoga involves a planet in debilitation or retrogression or combustion or otherwise weak, it turns into Radda yoga. This yoga negates ithasala and gives bad results.

About planets in retrogression, one should remember the comments made under ithasala yoga. If retrograde Mercury is at 5° in Vi and Mars is at 7° in Sc, there is no ithasala. Whether one calls it Eesarpha or Radda yoga depends on one's interpretation, but the results are going to be bad in either case.

Suppose lagna is in Ar, Saturn is at 20° in Ar and Mars is at 15° in Sg. Then they have an ithasala yoga. However, Saturn is debilitated. So ithasala turns into radda and bad results are indicated. Because Saturn owns the 10th and 11th houses, they can be related to career and material gains.

29.2.12 *Duhphali-Kutta Yoga*

If (*a*) the faster planet in an ithasala is exalted or occupies own rasi or has a good panchavargeeya bala and (*b*) the slower planet is not exalted, not in own rasi and weak in panchavargeeya bala, then it goes by a special name – Duhphali-Kutta yoga. This yoga shows realization of ambitions and dreams.

Suppose Saturn is at 20° in Li with a good panchavargeeya bala and Mars is at 18° in Ge with a low panchavargeeya bala, then they have an ithasala yoga. Because Saturn, the slower planet, is exalted and strong and Mars, the faster planet, is weak, this becomes Duhphali-Kutta yoga.

29.2.13 *Duttota Yoga*

If two planets in an ithasala are weak (debilitated or occupying inimical rasis, having a low panchavargeeya bala) and one of them has an ithasala yoga with a strong planet (exalted or occupying own rasi, having a high panchavargeeya bala), then we have Duttota yoga.

This yoga gives good results.

Suppose lagna is in Ar, Saturn is at 20° in Ar and Mars is at 19° in Li. Then they have an ithasala yoga. However, Saturn is debilitated. So ithasala turns into radda and bad results are indicated. Now, suppose Venus is at 18° in Pi. Saturn has a semi-sextile aspect and an ithasala yoga with exalted Venus. So the final result is Duttota yoga and good results are promised. Because Saturn owns the 10th and 11th houses, they can be related to career and material gains.

29.2.14 *Thambira Yoga*

If a planet is in the last degree of a rasi and it forms ithasala yoga after moving to the next rasi with a slower moving planet, it is called Thambira yoga. This shows realization of hopes after delay and hard work.

Suppose lagna is in Ar, Mars is at 2° in Le and Venus is at 29°10' in Ta. Venus has no ithasala with Mars. However, when Venus moves to Ge, he will have an ithasala with Mars. So Venus forms Thambira yoga with Mars. This shows good events related to family and marital life after some hard work.

29.2.15 *Kutta Yoga*

If a planet occupying lagna is aspected by a planet in occupying own or exaltation rasi in a kendra or a panaphara, then this yoga is formed. The desires related to the matters signified by the planet in lagna are fulfilled.[85]

Suppose lagna is in Ta, Sun is at 21° in Ta and Mercury is at 16° in Vi. Mercury is exalted in a panaphara and aspects Sun in lagna. So Sun gives Kutta yoga and the 4th house matters receive a boost in the year.

29.2.16 *Durupha Yoga*

Ithasala given by two planets in dusthanas (6th, 8th and 12th house) in combustion or retrogression or debilitation turns into Durupha yoga. The planets are powerless to give any good results.

Suppose lagna is in Ar. Suppose Mars is at 15° in Cn and Saturn is at 17° in Ar. Because both Mars and Saturn are debilitated, their ithasala turns into Durupha yoga. Mars and Saturn cannot give good results related to career and gains.

29.3 Conclusion

One should remember the definitions of all the yogas and consider all of them. There is some overlap between some yogas here. An ithasala may be converted to another yoga if an additional combination is present and it may again turn into another yoga under yet another combination. So it is possible to overlook one planet and conclude the presence of a wrong yoga.

---

85 This yoga was interpreted differently by scholars.

30. Annual Dasas

30.1 Introduction

We have studied different dasa systems that enable us to time events in a person's life. In the previous few chapters, we have seen how Tajaka annual charts show the fortune in a one-year period. The next question is – how do we time events shown in a Tajaka annual chart? For example, an annual chart may show that the native will get married in the year. The question is – when in the year will (s)he get married?

All the dasas covered earlier are valid for natal charts and their *paramayush* is of the order of 100 years. On the other hand, an annual chart applies only for a period of one year. So we need dasas that are compressed to a one-year period. We will learn 3 dasas in this chapter: (1) Patyayini dasa[86] mentioned by Tajaka writers, (2) Mudda dasa or Varsha Vimsottari dasa, and, (3) Varsha Narayana dasa.

In Vimsottari dasa and Narayana dasa, paramayush of 120 years is compressed to one year. One may try finding compressed Vimsottari dasa based on Moon's constellation in the annual chart, but the best results are obtained by progressing Moon's constellation in the natal chart at the rate of one constellation per year and using it to initiate dasas. Similarly, one may try finding compressed Narayana dasa based on lagna in the annual chart, but the best results are obtained by progressing lagna in the natal chart at the rate of one sign per year and using it as lagna for the purpose of Narayana dasa[87].

Example 122: Let us consider a lady born on 1st June 1972 at 4:16 am (IST) at 81 E 12, 16 N 15. She got married on 24th July 1993. Let us time this event from 1993-94 annual chart using all the 3 dasas.

Varsha pravesh data: 1st June 1993, 1:30:04 pm (IST), 81 E 12, 16 N 15. Rasi and navamsa charts of this data are given in Chart 67.

---

86 Dr. B.V. Raman simply called this "Varsha dasa" (annual dasa).

87 This is a result of the author's own researches.

Chart 67

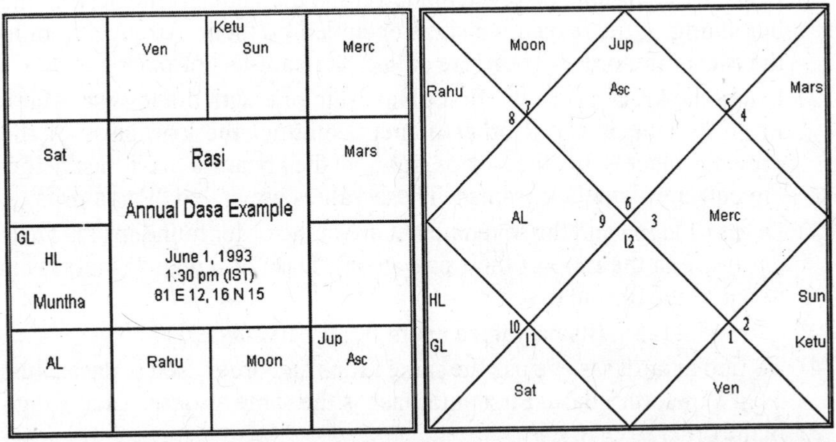

	Ven	Ketu Sun	Merc
Sat	Rasi Annual Dasa Example June 1, 1993 1:30 pm (IST) 81 E 12, 16 N 15		Mars
GL HL Muntha			
AL	Rahu	Moon	Jup Asc

Moon Jup Asc Rahu 8 7 5 4 Mars
AL 9 6 3 12 Merc
HL Sun
10 11 2 1 Ketu
GL Sat Ven

Asc:	7 Vi 13	**Sun:**	17 Ta 04 (AmK)	**Moon:**	4 Li 48 (PK)	**Mars:**	23 Cn 53 (AK)
Merc:	4 Ge 47 (GK)	**Jup:**	10 Vi 59 (MK)	**Ven:**	1 Ar 37 (DK)	**Sat:**	6 Aq 29 (PiK)
Rahu:	18 Sc 38 (BK)	**Ketu:**	18 Ta 38	**HL:**	15 Cp 32	**GL:**	13 Cp 42

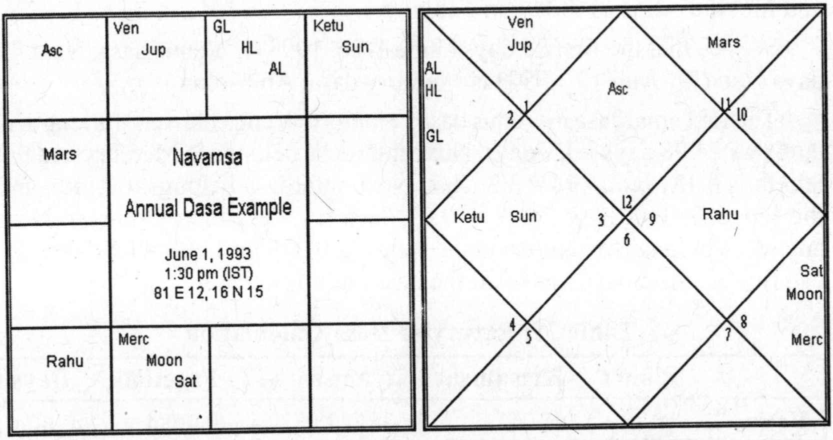

Asc	Ven Jup	GL HL AL	Ketu Sun
Mars	Navamsa Annual Dasa Example June 1, 1993 1:30 pm (IST) 81 E 12, 16 N 15		
Rahu	Merc Moon Sat		

Ven Jup Mars
AL HL Asc
2 1 11 10
GL
Ketu Sun 12 3 9 Rahu
6
Sat Moon
4 5 7 8
Merc

Marriage in this year: Vivaha saham is at 2°22' in Sg. Lagna has 7th lord and vivaha saham lord Jupiter in it. Lagna lord Mercury is in own sign and has ithasala with Jupiter. In navamsa, 7th lord Mercury is well-placed. Lagna lord Jupiter joins Venus in the 2nd house of family. All these factors brought marriage in the year. We will time it using different dasas now.

30.3 Patyayini Dasa

This dasa is based on the longitudes of lagna and all planets and it is specifically meant for Tajaka charts.

Procedure:

(1) Consider lagna and the seven planets. Find their advancement from the beginning of the respective signs occupied by them. Arrange them in the ascending order. These are called "Krisamsas" of planets.

(2) Leave the krisamsa of the first planet (the one with the lowest value). From krisamsas of all other planets, subtract the krisamsas of the previous planets. In other words, subtract the krisamsa that is just below the current planet's krisamsa. These values are called "Patyamsas".

(3) Dasas of lagna and the seven planet are in the order found in (1). Their dasas are in the ratio of their patyamsas. Dasa of a planet (in days) is given by the formula:

365.2425 x (its patyamsa / sum of all patyamsas[88])

(4) To find antardasas, we use the same ratios and order used in dasas, just as in Vimsottari dasa. First antardasa is the same as dasa. Then we go in the order.

For the annual chart in Example 122, we can find the longitudes of planets and lagna in Chart 67. We can arrange them in the ascending order and find the ratios as shown in Table 75.

We see that the first 25 days (June 1-26, 1993) is Venus dasa. Next 48 days (June 26-Aug 13, 1993) is Mercury dasa. And so on.

The first antardasa in Venus dasa belongs to Venus himself. Its length is 0.0684 x 24.98 days = 1.7 days. Next antardasa belongs to Mercury and the length is 0.1319 x 24.98 = 3.3 days. Next antardasa belongs to Moon and the length is 0.0014 x 24.98 = 0.03 days (*i.e.* less than an hour). Next antardasa belongs to Saturn and the length is 0.0705 x 24.98 = 1.8 days. We can find all the antardasas in all the dasas in this manner.

Table 75: Patyayini Dasa Calculation

	Planet	Krisamsa	Patyamsa	Fraction	Days
Venus	1° 38'	1° 38'	1° 38'/23° 53' =	0.0684	24.98
Mercury	4° 47'	3° 9'	3° 9'/23° 53' =	0.1319	48.17
Moon	4° 49'	0° 2'	0° 2'/23° 53' =	0.0014	0.51
Saturn	6° 30'	1° 41'	1° 41'/23° 53' =	0.0705	25.74
Lagna	7° 14'	0° 44'	0° 44'/23° 53' =	0.0307	11.21
Jupiter	10° 59'	3° 45'	3° 45'/23° 53' =	0.1570	57.35
Sun	17° 5'	6° 6'	6° 6'/23° 53' =	0.2554	93.29
Mars	23° 53'	6° 48'	6° 48'/23° 53' =	0.2847	103.99

88 It may be noted that the sum of all patyamsas is nothing but the largest krisamsa.

Timing of marriage:

Mercury dasa ran during June 26-Aug 13, 1993. This was the dasa that was running when she got married on 24th July 1993. Why did Mercury give marriage?

(1) Mercury is lagna lord.
(2) He is very strong as per panchavargeeya bala.
(3) He is varsheswara (lord of the year).
(4) He aspects vivaha saham within 3°.
(5) In navamsa, which is the right chart for marriage, he is the 7th lord. He is strong in a trine. Lagna and 7th lords in navamsa can certainly give marriage.

30.4 Mudda Dasa (Varsha Vimsottari Dasa)

Dasa length

This is essentially Vimsottari dasa with 120 years[89] compressed to a solar year. If we take a solar year to be of 360 days, with each day corresponding to the time period in which Sun moves by exactly 1°, we get the dasa of days of a planet by multiplying normal dasa years by 3. For example, Sun dasa is normally for 6 years. By compressing 120 years to 360 solar days, we find Sun's Varsha Vimsottari dasa to be 6 x 3 = 18 days. Durations of all dasas are given in Table 76 (in solar days).

Table 76: Varsha Vimsottari Dasa Days

Planet	Sun	Moon	Mars	Rahu	Jupiter	Saturn	Mercury	Ketu	Venus
Days	18	30	21	54	48	57	51	21	60

Dasa order

To initiate dasas, we should progress Moon's natal constellation at the rate of one constellation per year and use the resulting constellation. Instead of progressing the constellation, we can also do the following:

Consider (1) Sun, (2) Moon, (3) Mars, (4) Rahu, (5) Jupiter, (6) Saturn, (7) Mercury, (8) Ketu and (9) Venus.

Take the number corresponding to the lord of Moon's natal constellation (*i.e.* the lord of the first Vimsottari dasa in natal chart). Add the number of

89 Sum of the 2 cycles of Narayana dasa for natal charts is 12 x 12 = 144 years. However, only the first 120 years of this is valid, as the paramayush of human beings is 120 years.

completed years to this number. Divide the number by 9 and take the remainder. See the planet corresponding to that number. First dasa belongs to that planet. After that, dasas will follow the normal order. Remainder of 0 is equivalent to 9 and hence shows Venus.

In Example 122, natal Moon is in Uttaraashaadha constellation. So the first dasa belongs to Sun. The number corresponding to Sun is 1. Number of completed years is 1993-1972=21. Adding 1 and 21, we get 22. Dividing it by 9, we get a quotient of 2 and a remainder of 4. That shows Rahu.

Dasa balance

For finding the dasa balance, the fraction of the natal Moon's constellation yet to be traversed is taken.

In Example 122, natal Moon is at 29 Sg 28. About 0.79 of the constellation is yet to be traversed by natal Moon. So the balance in Rahu's Varsha Vimsottari dasa of 1994-94 is 0.79 x 54 solar days = 42.66 solar days. So June 1-July 14, 1993 is Rahu dasa. Jupiter dasa runs for 48 days then.

Timing of marriage

Jupiter is 7th lord and vivaha saham lord in rasi chart. He is in lagna. In navamsa, he is lagna lord and occupies the 2nd house of family with Venus.

It may, however, be noted that Mercury is a better candidate for giving marriage, for the reasons mentioned earlier. Patyayini dasa shows the event better than Mudda dasa.

30.5 Varsha Narayana Dasa

Dasa durations

This is essentially Narayana dasa compressed from 120 years[2] to 360 solar days. If a rasi's dasa is of n years, it becomes $3 \times n$ solar days after compression, *i.e.* a period in which Sun moves by $(3 \times n)^\circ$.

Dasa order

We find the dasa order in Narayana dasa of rasi chart and Narayana dasa of divisional charts just as in natal charts. The only difference is that we should progress natal lagna and use it, instead of lagna in the annual chart.

Just as we progress Moon by one constellation per year when finding Varsha Vimsottari dasa, we progress lagna by one rasi per year when finding Varsha Narayana dasa. In other words, we take muntha as lagna when finding Varsha Narayana dasa. This is the link between the natal chart and the Tajaka chart.

Let us take Example 122 and find Varsha Narayana dasa of D-9. Natal lagna is in Aries. Because the native started the 22nd year in 1993, we find the 22nd house, *i.e.* the 10th house (after removing 12), from Ar and get muntha in Cp.

We now find Varsha Narayana dasa assuming that lagna in rasi chart is in Cp. To find Narayana dasa of D-9, we need the 9th lord in rasi chart. Vi is the 9th from Cp and Mercury owns it. He is in Sc in navamsa and Sc is stronger than Ta. So we start dasas from Sc. Normally the dasa order should have been Sc, Ge, Cp, Le, Pi, Li *etc*. But Saturn is in Sc and the "Saturn exception" applies. So dasas go as Sc, Sg, Cp, Aq, Pi, Ar *etc*.

Sc, Sg, Cp and Aq dasas are of 7, 4, 2 and 3 years respectively. After compressing to one year, they are of 21, 12, 6 and 9 solar days respectively. This covers 48 solar days and these dasas run from June 1-July 20, 1993. Pisces dasa of 33 days started then and it brought marriage.

Why Pisces dasa? Well, it contains lagna in D-9 and has subhaargala from lagna lord Jupiter and Venus. Navamsa lagna's dasa as per Varsha Narayana dasa of navamsa is an ideal candidate for bringing marriage.

Exercise 48: A native born on 4th April 1970 at 5:50 pm (IST) at 81 E 12, 16 N 15 got married on 1st August 1993. Verify that navamsa lagna's dasa as per Varsha Narayana dasa of navamsa was running at the time of marriage. Verify that the running dasa and antardasa as per Patyayini dasa and Mudda dasa – at the time of wedding – belonged to lagna/7th lord in rasi/navamsa.

Usually Patyayini dasa gives better results than Mudda dasa. Varsha Narayana dasa is, however, the best dasa for Tajaka annual charts. So we will see more examples of Varsha Narayana dasa.

Example 123: The native of Exercise 48 went from India to US for his masters degree in engineering, on 15th August 1991. He went on a fellowship from a University in US. Let us time his foreign trip using Varsha Narayana dasa of D-4.

Varsha pravesh data: 5th April 1991, 3:05:33 am (IST), 81 E 12, 16 N 15

In rasi chart, lagna has Saturn and Rahu. Both the planets show living away from the place of birth. Jupiter owns 12th – living away from homeland – and he is exalted in 7th – a long trip. In D-4 (see Chart 68), 9th and 12th lord Mercury is in 7th showing a long trip to a foreign land. Mars owns 7th (long trips) and he is in 9th. Sun owns paradesa saham and jalapatana saham and he is in 12th – foreign lands – in D-4. For all these reasons, the native went abroad during the year.

Chart 68

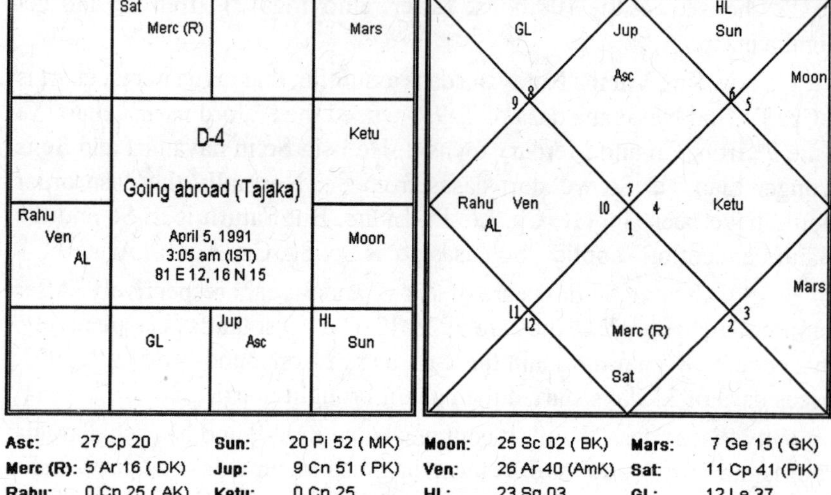

Asc:	27 Cp 20	**Sun:**	20 Pi 52 (MK)	**Moon:**	25 Sc 02 (BK)	**Mars:**	7 Ge 15 (GK)
Merc (R):	5 Ar 16 (DK)	**Jup:**	9 Cn 51 (PK)	**Ven:**	26 Ar 40 (AmK)	**Sat:**	11 Cp 41 (PiK)
Rahu:	0 Cp 25 (AK)	**Ketu:**	0 Cn 25	**HL:**	23 Sg 03	**GL:**	12 Le 37

Though rasi chart has lagna in Cp, muntha or annual progressed ascendant is in Ge. We should use Ge as lagna for Varsha Narayana dasa. The 4th house from Ge is Vi and Mercury owns it. He is in Ar in D-4. Ar with two planets is stronger than Li with one planet. Dasas go as Ar, Ta, Ge Cn etc.

Virgo dasa was running during August 10-26, 1991. The native went abroad on 15th/16th August 1991, during Virgo dasa, Gemini antardasa as per Varsha Narayana dasa of D-4. Virgo is the 12th house containing the lord of padesa saham and jalapatana saham. Gemini is the 9th house containing 7th lord. Lord of both Virgo and Gemini is Mercury and he is in the 7th house.

Example 124: The native of Exercise 48 stood First in Intermediate (Secondary School) examinations in the AP state of India on 28th May 1987 and he was selected fcr Indian Institute of Technology (India's top engineering school) on 1st June 1987. Let us time this academic success using Varsha Narayana dasa of D-24.

Varsha pravesh data: 5th April 1987, 2:15:41 am (IST), 81 E 12, 16 N 15

Vidya saham lord Mars is in the 5th house in rasi chart. He is in own sign in D-24, which shows education (see Chart 69). He is in the 3rd house from AL in D-24, showing material success (in education, as this is in D-24).

Chart 69

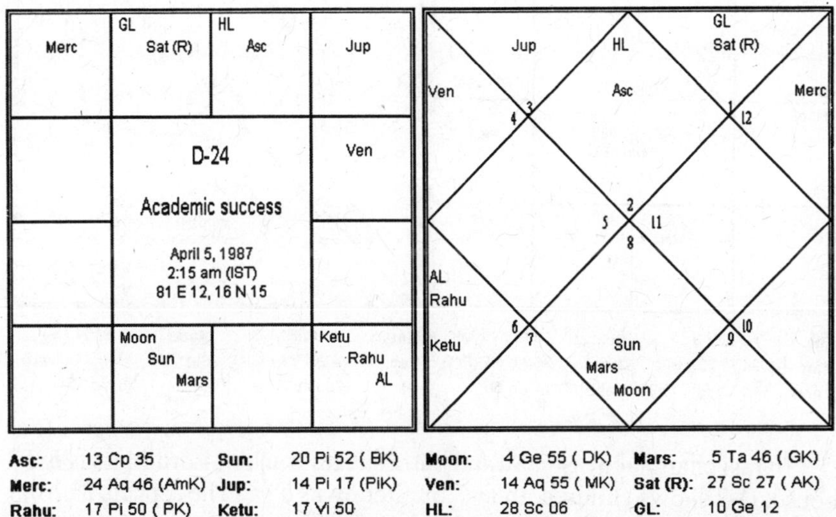

Asc:	13 Cp 35	**Sun:**	20 Pi 52 (BK)	**Moon:**	4 Ge 55 (DK)	**Mars:**	5 Ta 46 (GK)
Merc:	24 Aq 46 (AmK)	**Jup:**	14 Pi 17 (PiK)	**Ven:**	14 Aq 55 (MK)	**Sat (R):**	27 Sc 27 (AK)
Rahu:	17 Pi 50 (PK)	**Ketu:**	17 Vi 50	**HL:**	28 Sc 06	**GL:**	10 Ge 12

Muntha is in Aq in rasi chart. Taking Aq as lagna, 12th house is Cp. Its lord is Saturn. He is in Ar in D-24 and Ar is stronger than Li. So Varsha Narayana dasa of D-24 goes as Ar, Ta, Ge, Cn *etc*. Cn dasa runs during May 26-June 17, 1987. This dasa brought academic success. Why?

(1) Cn contains lagna lord and shows prosperity to the matters signified by the chart, *i.e.* education.

(2) It is the 11th from AL and shows gains in status (of course, only in the field of education).

(3) Its lord Moon is in the 5th house from it.

(4) The 5th house from it has a very strong Mars, who is in own sign. Moreover, Mars owns vidya saham and occupies 5th in rasi chart.

Example 125: The native of Exercise 48 had a son on 21st August 1998. Let us time this using Varsha Narayana dasa of D-7.

Varsha pravesh data: 4th April 1998, 9:59:49 pm (IST), 81 E 12, 16 N 15

Chart 70

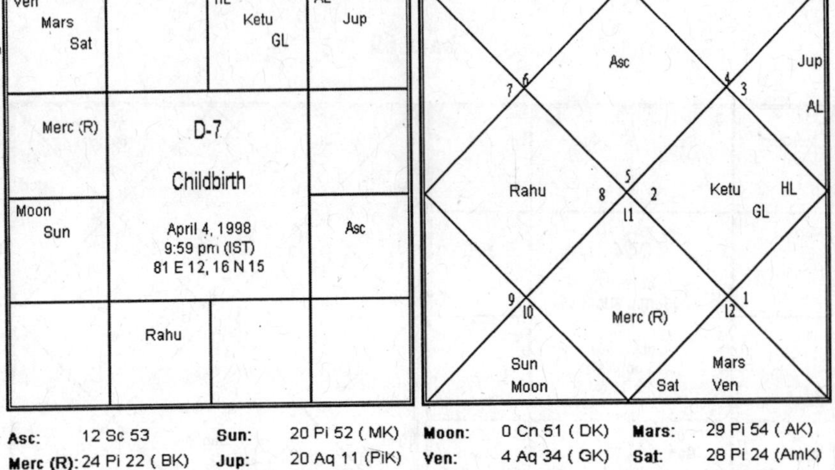

Asc:	12 Sc 53	**Sun:**	20 Pi 52 (MK)	**Moon:**	0 Cn 51 (DK)	**Mars:**	29 Pi 54 (AK)
Merc (R):	24 Pi 22 (BK)	**Jup:**	20 Aq 11 (PiK)	**Ven:**	4 Aq 34 (GK)	**Sat:**	28 Pi 24 (AmK)
Rahu:	14 Le 56 (PK)	**Ketu:**	14 Aq 56	**HL:**	20 Cn 30	**GL:**	20 Cn 55

In rasi chart, lagna is in Sc and putra saham is in Ar. Lord Mars is in 5th house. D-7 shows children. In D-7, Jupiter owns 5th and he aspects 5th from 11th (see Chart 70). This resulted in a son in the year.

Muntha is in Cp in rasi chart. The 7th house is in Cn. Moon owns it. Moon is in Cp in D-7 and Cp is stronger than Cn. So Narayana dasa of D-7 starts from Cp and goes as Cp, Sg, Sc, Li *etc.*

Ge dasa of 24 solar days started just before the birth of son. Why did Ge give a child in its D-7 Varsha Narayana dasa?

(1) Ge is the 11th house in D-7, showing happiness related to children.

(2) Ge has Jupiter, the significator of children.

(3) Ge has Jupiter, the 5th lord who aspects 5th.

(4) The 3rd house is the 11th from 5th and shows childbirth. Its exalted lord Venus aspects Ge.

(5) Mars owns putra saham and he aspects Ge.

(6) Putra pada (arudha pada of 5th) aspects Ge from Vi.

Gemini is a clear candidate simply because it is 11th and 5th lord Jupiter occupies it.

Exercise 49: Given that the native of Exercise 48 bought a car in 1995-96, try to time it using Varsha Narayana dasa of D-16.

30.5 Conclusion

In this chapter, we learnt three dasa systems that are applicable to Tajaka annual charts. Patyayini dasa is applicable to Tajaka monthly charts also. For annual charts, Varsha Narayana dasa and Patyayini dasa give the best results. If a result seems likely in an annual chart, we can find the exact month or week of the event using these dasas.

30.6 Answers to Exercises

Exercise 48:

Try yourself. Varsha pravesh: 4th April 1993, 3:19:03 pm (IST), 81 E 12, 16 N 15

Exercise 49:

[Varsha pravesh data: 5th April 1995, 3:28:36 am (IST), 81 E 12, 16 N 15]

Chart 71

Moon	Ven	Merc	GL HL
Mars	D-16 Bought a car April 5, 1995 3:28 am (IST) 81 E 12, 16 N 15		AL Jup (R)
	Sun	Rahu Asc Ketu	Sat

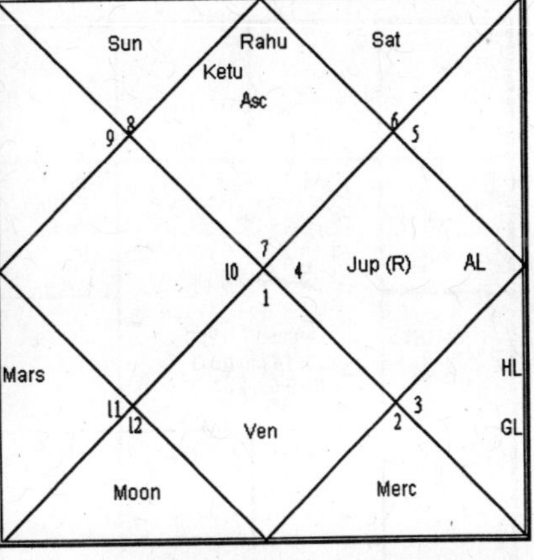

Asc:	3 Aq 59	**Sun:**	20 Pi 52 (BK)	**Moon:**	14 Ta 40 (GK)	**Mars:**	20 Cn 06 (MK)
Merc:	11 Pi 04 (DK)	**Jup (R):**	21 Sc 34 (AmK)	**Ven:**	15 Aq 26 (PK)	**Sat:**	24 Aq 48 (AK)
Rahu:	13 Li 00 (PiK)	**Ketu:**	13 Ar 00	**HL:**	4 Cp 31	**GL:**	11 Vi 19

Look at D-16 of the annual chart. The 4th from lagna is not strong. If the native bought a vehicle, it must be due to the strength of the 4th from Venus. Exalted Jupiter is in the 4th from Venus. Jupiter owns 3rd and shows expenditure on 4th, *i.e.* expenditure on account of happiness from vehicle. He is exalted in the 4th from Venus showing a good vehicle. Muntha is in Li and Cp is the 4th. Saturns owns it and occupies Vi in D-16. Pi is stronger than Vi. So dasas go as Pi, Cn, Sc, Sg, Ar, Le *etc*.

Cancer dasa in the second cycle ran during Jan 16-Feb 9, 1996. The native bought a car in this dasa.

31. Sudarsana Chakra Dasa

31.1 Introduction

Parasara said that Sudarsana Chakra dasa was taught by Brahma – the Creator – Himself and that it is a great tool for predicting daily, monthly and annual fortune. Because the calculations necessary for Sudarsana Chakra dasa interpretation are an integral part of casting Tajaka annual, monthly and sixty-hour charts, this dasa is being covered in the part on "Tajaka Analysis" rather than the part on "Dasa Analysis". However, it should be borne in mind that this is a dasa applicable to natal charts. This is just a natal dasa like Vimsottari dasa, Narayana dasa and Kalachakra dasa.

Chart 72

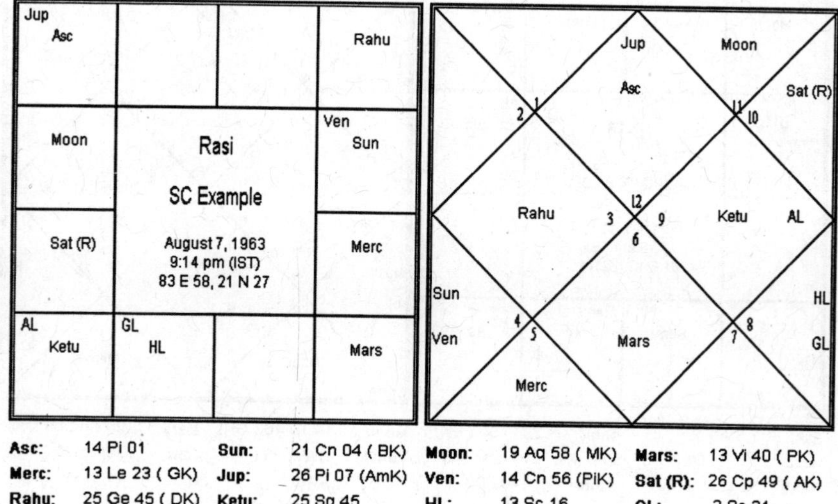

31.2 Sudarsana Chakra

In each chart, there are 3 important reference points: (1) lagna, (2) Moon, and, (3) Sun. Lagna represents the physical body. Moon represents the mind. Sun represents the soul. The three together represent one's self. We should consider houses from all the three reference points when judging a chart. For example, we need to look at the 10th house from lagna, Moon and Sun to see career. Though we generally give importance to lagna, all the three references are important.

To symbolically represent this, we can draw Sudarsana Chakra (SC) as taught by Parasara. We should draw 3 concentric circles. We should write down the bhava chakra with respect to lagna, Moon and Sun in the inner, middle and outer charts. To illustrate this, let us take the rasi chart given in Chart 72. Sudarsana Chakra for this chart is given in Figure 4.

The 10th house from lagna is in Sg and it has Ketu. The 10th house from Moon is Sc and it is empty. The 10th house from Sun is Aries and it is empty. We should analyze all the 3 factors together to draw conclusions.

31.3 Dasa Computation

Dasas of the 12 houses run in cycles throughout a native's life. Each dasa is for one year. For example, dasa of the 1st house runs in the 1st year of one's life. Dasa of the 2nd house runs in the 2nd year of one's life. After 12 years, dasa of the 1st house will return in the 13th year. Dasa of the 2nd house will return in the 14th year. After every 12 years, the same dasas keep coming.

One year stands for a solar year here. A new dasa starts after every one year. The exact date and time when a new SC dasa starts can be found by casting Tajaka annual chart. Look at the number of years completed. Adding one to it, you get the year that starts. Divide it by 12 and find the remainder (if the remainder is zero, make it 12). This remainder gives the house whose dasa runs in the year.

For example, let us take a native who finishes 44 years and starts the 45th year of his life on a particular date. Because the remainder when 45 is divided by 12 is 9, SC dasa of the 9th house runs in the 45th year.

When we say dasa of the 9th house here, we mean the 9th house from lagna, Moon and Sun. If lagna is in Pi, Moon is in Aq and Sun is in Cn, then the 9th house is in Sc, Li and Pi.

However, analyzing with 3 signs becomes difficult. So one may conveniently choose the strongest reference out of lagna, Moon and Sun and take dasas from it. This is only an approximation, but it simplifies analysis.

Figure 4: Sudarsana Chakra

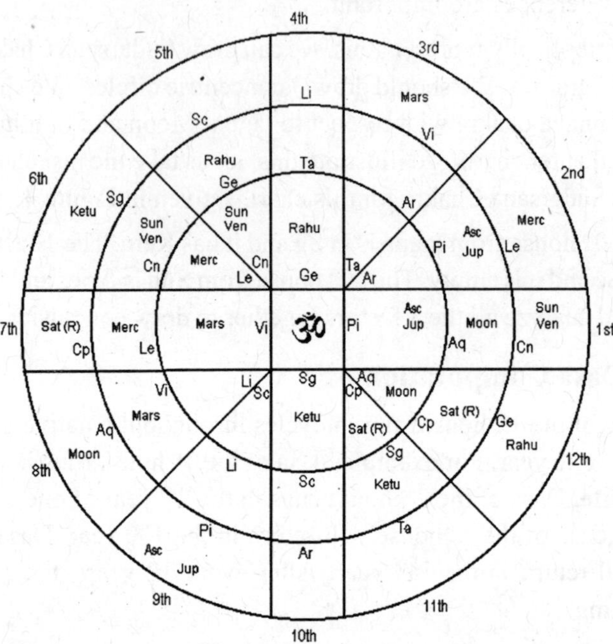

Antardasas

Each dasa is divided into 12 antardasas. Take the dasa sign as lagna and give the 1st, 2nd, 3rd etc houses from it to antardasas.

If Pi is natal lagna, dasa in the 45th year belongs to the 9th house, *i.e.* Sc. Antardasas in this dasa go as Sc, Sg, Cp, Aq etc.

We can use Tajaka monthly charts to find the date and time when an antardasa starts.

Similarly, we can find pratyantardasas from antardasas and use Tajaka sixty-hour charts to find the date and time when a pratyantardasa starts.

In short, Tajaka annual, monthly and sixty-hour charts are nothing but the *entry charts* of dasas, antardasas and pratyantardasas as per Sudarsana Chakra dasa. Muntha in Tajaka annual charts is nothing but the dasa sign as per Sudarsana Chakra dasa, but always reckoned from lagna. If we redefine muntha to be the progressed from the strongest of lagna, Moon and Sun (instead of always from lagna), it exactly becomes the SC dasa sign.

We can find Sudarsana Chakra dasa for divisional charts also. We take the strongest of lagna, Moon and Sun and then start SC dasa from there. It moves at the rate of one house per year. Examples will make this clear.

31.4 Dasa Interpretation

To interpret a dasa (or antardasa or pratyantardasa), we have to take the dasa sign (or antardasa sign or pratyantardasa sign) as lagna and analyze the planetary positions with respect to it. What planetary positions do we mean – natal or transit?

Some people may prefer to analyze the natal positions, but that would suggest that one gets the same results after every 12 years. That is not logical.

Parasara clearly advised that we have to analyze the planetary positions *at the commencement* of a dasa (or antardasa or pratyantardasa) with respect to the dasa sign (or antardasa sign or pratyantardasa sign). This is where Tajaka charts fit in.

If benefics are in quadrants, trines and 8th from dasa sign, favorable results can be expected. Benefics in houses other than the 6th and 12th houses produce good results for the houses they occupy. Malefics in the 3rd, 6th and 11th houses bring good results. Malefics in other houses spoil the results of the houses they occupy. In particular, Rahu destroys the house he occupies.

Example 126: Let us revisit Example 124. In the natal chart, lagna and Moon are in Ge in D-24. In 1987-88, the native ran the 18th year of his life. So SC dasa of the 6th house was running. The 6th house from Ge is Sc. So Scorpio dasa was running as per Sudarsana Chakra dasa of D-24. We should look at planetary positions *w.r.t.* Sc at the time this dasa started, i.e. in Tajaka annual chart of the year (see Chart 69).

Benefics Mercury, Jupiter and Venus are in 5th, 8th and 9th respectively and all of them are good placements. Malefics Saturn, Rahu and Ketu are in 6th, 11th and 11th respectively and all of them are good placements. Moreover, dasa sign Sc houses a powerful raja yoga involving the 1st, 9th and 10th lords from it.

For all these reasons, this year was excellent for matters shown in D-24.

Though Sudarsana Chakra dasa can be found for all divisional charts, pay special attention to rasi chart. Here is an example.

Example 127: Indira Gandhi's natal rasi chart and Tajaka annual chart of 1976-77 are given in Chart 73. During that year, Indira Gandhi's party lost the Parliamentary Elections and she was removed from the post of India's Prime Minister.

Because the finished years are 1976-1917 = 59, we should add 1 and divide 60 by 12. Remainder is 12 and Sudarsana Chakra dasa during the year belongs to the 12th house. Compared to lagna and Moon, Sun with Budha-Aaditya yoga is stronger. Let us take the 12th from Sun. It is Libra.

Libra's SC dasa runs during the year and we should look at the planetary positions from Libra in the Tajaka annual chart (or dasa commencement chart). Benefic Venus is in 3rd giving failures. Rahu afflicts the 1st house. Mars, Sun and Mercury are not well-placed in the 2nd house. Saturn afflicts the 10th house showing troubles in career.

Chart 73

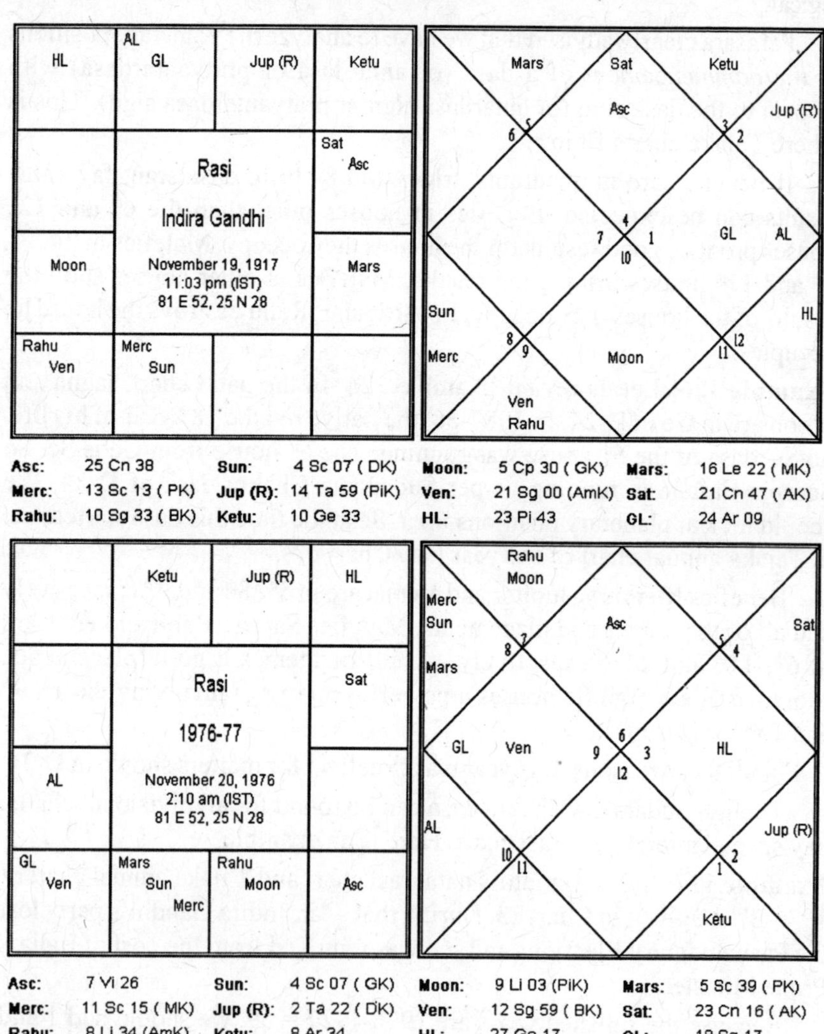

Because of bad placement of planets (especially Saturn and Rahu), Sudarsana Chakra does not promise a good year. No wonder Mrs. Gandhi fell from power.

Example 128: Let us consider the lady of Chart 74. She got married in January 1999. Let us analyze her Sudarsana Chakra dasa of navamsa for 1998-99.

She was born in 1973 and she started her 26th year in July 1998. If we divide 26 by 12, we get a remainder of 2. So SC dasa in 1998-99 belongs to the 2nd house. In natal navamsa, lagna is in Cn and it is stronger than Moon and Sun. The 2nd house from Cn is Le. So Le dasa was running in 1998-99. Is it a good dasa?

Three benefics are in quadrants and 3 malefics are in 3rd/11th. Though Mars is in 9th, he is strong being in own house. Most planets are favorably placed and, more importantly, lagna and 7th are strong with Jupiter and Venus in them (respectively). So this was a favorable year for matters shown by D-9. No wonder she got married.

31.5 Conclusion

Parasara called Sudarsana Chakra dasa a very important dasa. It, however, needs to be understood better.

Sudarsana Chakra dasa is interpreted based on the planetary positions at the commencement of a dasa or an antardasa or a pratyantardasa. Those planetary positions can be found from Tajaka annual or monthly or sixty-hour charts. In addition, muntha defined in Tajaka texts is nothing but Sudarsana Chakra dasa rasi reckoned from lagna. So there may be some missing links between Sudarsana Chakra dasa and Tajaka analysis.

Sudarsana chakra dasa is good at showing favorable and unfavorable periods in a general sense.

Chart 74

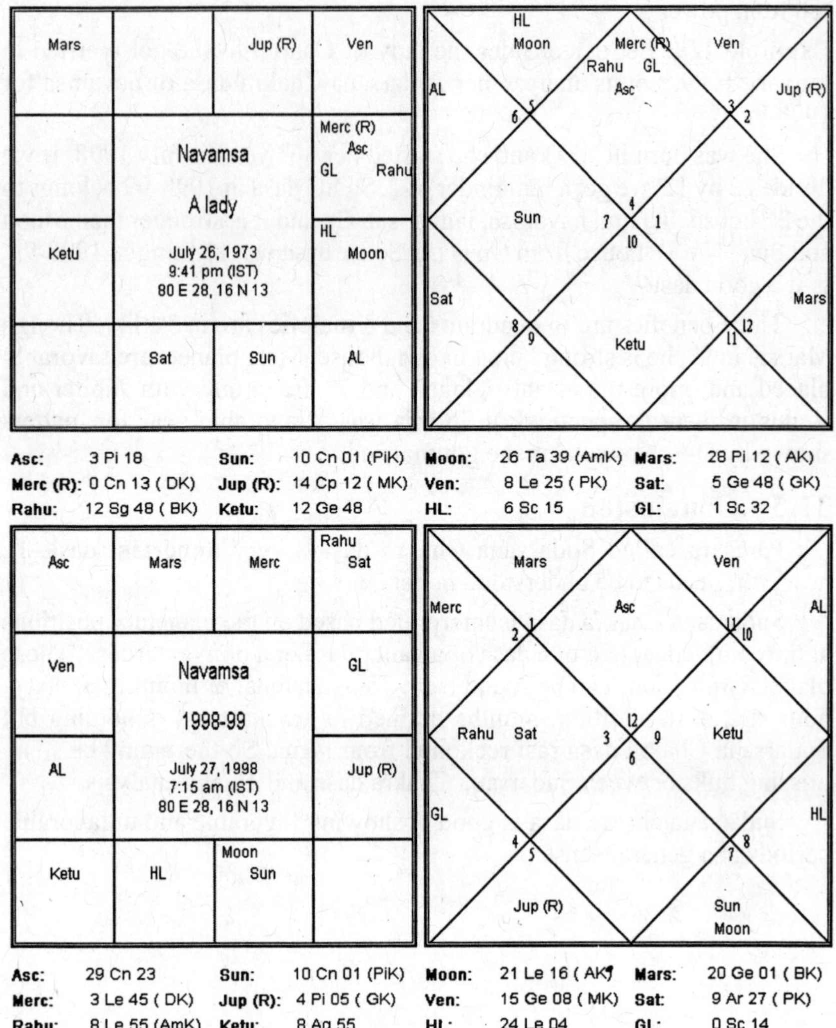

Asc:	3 Pi 18	**Sun:**	10 Cn 01 (PiK)	**Moon:**	26 Ta 39 (AmK)	**Mars:**	28 Pi 12 (AK)
Merc (R):	0 Cn 13 (DK)	**Jup (R):**	14 Cp 12 (MK)	**Ven:**	8 Le 25 (PK)	**Sat:**	5 Ge 48 (GK)
Rahu:	12 Sg 48 (BK)	**Ketu:**	12 Ge 48	**HL:**	6 Sc 15	**GL:**	1 Sc 32

Asc:	29 Cn 23	**Sun:**	10 Cn 01 (PiK)	**Moon:**	21 Le 16 (AK)	**Mars:**	20 Ge 01 (BK)
Merc:	3 Le 45 (DK)	**Jup (R):**	4 Pi 05 (GK)	**Ven:**	15 Ge 08 (MK)	**Sat:**	9 Ar 27 (PK)
Rahu:	8 Le 55 (AmK)	**Ketu:**	8 Aq 55	**HL:**	24 Le 04	**GL:**	0 Sc 14

Part 5: Special Topics

Some speical topics will be covered in this part.

When one uses Vedic astrology at its fullest glory, it is very systematic and leads to very precise predictions. However, we need a very accurate birthtime. In real life, however, we often get erroneous data. Coping with birthtime errors is a very important topic.

In an effort to promote rational thinking in the astrological community, a chapter on rational thinking is included.

What is the use of diagnosing one's disease, if the diease cannot be remedied? Similarly, what is the use of making intelligent guesses about future, if we cannot do something about undesirable events that are likely to happen? The basics of remedial measures are introduced in the chapter on remedial measures.

Making predictions about groups of people, like nations, is much more complicated than making predictions about individuals. Some basic techniques are introduced in the chapter on mundane astrology.

Muhurta or electional astrology is an important branch of astrology. It lets us choose an auspicious time for starting new ventures. A small chapter is dedicated to it.

Vedic astrology is not a mundane subject like mathematics and subject. For its believers, it is a divine subject. Vedic astrologers are required to be spiritually aware and observe some ethics. These are addressed in a small chapter.

All these topics are covered for the sake of completeness. Justice is not done to any topic and readers should do further reading on these interesting topics.

32. Impact of Birthtime Error

32.1 Introduction

There are twins in this world who are born 1-2 minutes apart, but live significantly different lives. There may be some similarities between closely born twins, but there can be significant differences too.[90] So this *proves* that divisional charts and special lagnas, which change very fast, have a great bearing on a native's fortune. If one's birthtime is wrong by 2 minutes, lagna and special lagnas in some divisional charts change and so the results change. This is how we can explain the differences between twins.

Now the question is — if changes in lagna and special lagnas in divisional charts explain the different fortunes of twins, what about people who don't have a twin? Well, the same thing applies to them. If we analyze the chart cast with a birthtime that is wrong by 2 minutes, we are no longer examining the chart of the native – we are simply looking at the chart of his hypothetical twin! The results predicted need not be true.

Lagna in D-1 changes rasi once in 2 hours. Some people make predictions only using D-1, but that is unscientific and against the teachings of maharshis. Due to divine powers and God-given intuition, one can be successful in one's predictions only using D-1, but that is clearly unscientific. We should see different areas of life in different divisional charts, as taught by Maharshi Parasara. When we do that, we need an accurate birthtime. If one's birthtime is between 9:02 am and 9:08 am, can we make accurate predictions using an average of 9:05 am? No! Many people are born within the small span of 6 minutes (between 9:02 and 9:08) and they can be significantly different from each other (*e.g.* twins). Applying precise techniques is pointless when we only have an approximate time. So let us conclude that **we must first make sure that we are working with an accurate birthtime**. Readers should remember that our analysis could be only as accurate as our data!

We are often told by clients that their birthtime is very accurate. However, it is this author's experience that birthtimes reported by people

90 In order to explain the differences between twins, some astrologers take the lagna of the second twin in the 3rd house (younger brother) from the first twin. If Aquarius is rising at the birth of both, they take Aries (3rd from Aquarius) as the lagna of the younger twin. This is, however, illogical, irrational and against the teachings of maharshis. One who understands what lagna means and what the rasi chart shows will reject such theories.

are seldom accurate. There can be various reasons behind a birthtime error: (1) using an unadjusted clock/wristwatch showing a slightly incorrect time, (2) forgetting to note the birthtime exactly after birth and noting down it a little later with some manual correction applied to compensate for the lapse, (3) wrong memory of mother or father when giving the correctly noted birthtime to an astrologer, (4) using the wrong definition of 'birth'.

Birthtime rectification is the process of correcting the reported birthtime before proceeding to make predictions based on the birthtime. There are some formulas in literature for birthtime rectification, but these assume that human births happen in certain quanta. For example, an approach may assume that nobody is born during a period of 3 minutes and people can be born in a period of half a minute then. Then again, nobody is born for 3 minutes and people can be born in a period of half a minute following it. Like this, time is divided into certain quanta in which people can be born. Then we find the nearest "human birth can happen now" quantum from the reported birthtime and use it as the rectified (corrected) birthtime.

Out of these methods, some of the reasonable methods are the ones based on (*a*) Tattva siddhaanta, (*b*) Pranapada lagna in navamsa, and, (*c*) Kunda. The first method beyond the scope of this book and the other two fail the acid test of twins. If we were to apply those methods to the charts of twins born 2 minutes apart, the rectified birthtimes of the two twins would be either the same or too far apart.

In essence, most of the birthtime rectification techniques described in literature do not work. The only correct way to rectify a birthtime is to find a time in the neighborhood of the reported birthtime so that we can explain the nature, credentials, attitude and aptitude of the native and the known events from the native's past. This is a laborious process, but there is no other way.

Suppose we are told that one was born between 9:02 and 9:08 am and suppose we are looking at his chart. Because we don't know the exact birthtime, we can look at a range. If we do that, we are potentially looking at thousands of people born during that time. Our native could be anyone among thousands of people born in that range. But all those thousands of people have significant differences. We want to identify our native among those thousands of people and the only way is to look at the known past. That's the only thing that distinguishes him from others born closely.

So we should look at 9:02, 9:03, 9:04 etc and see which one explains the known past better. The rectified birthtime is the birthtime with which the known life events of the native make sense.

32.2 Robustness of Computations

When we try different birthtimes, all the computations change. If we know how various computations are altered based on small changes in the birthtime, we can approach the problem of birthtime rectification intelligently. We will discuss the **approximate** impact of birthtime change on various computations.

32.2.1 *Divisional Charts*

Planets

Positions of planets in rasi chart and divisional charts change very slowly. For example, Sun stays in one rasi for 30 days. He changes rasi in D-10 once in 30/10=3 days. He changes rasi in D-24 once in every 30/24=1.25 days. The speed of Mercury, Venus and Mars is comparable to Sun's. Jupiter and Saturn are even slower. Moon is faster than all these planets. He stays in one rasi for 2.5 days or 60 hours. He changes rasi in D-10 once in 60/10=6 hours. He changes rasi in D-24 once in every 60/24=2.5 hours.

If the uncertainty in birthtime is of the order of 5 minutes or 10 minutes, one may think that there is no problem with these planets as they stay in the same rasi in all divisional charts for a lot longer time than 5-10 minutes. However, if a planet is at a border and changes rasi in a divisional chart during those 5 minutes, we have to take that into consideration. Suppose Moon is at 23Sc59. That places him in the 8th dasamsa of Sc, *i.e.* Aq. Suppose lagna in D-10 is Cn. So D-10 has lagna lord in 8th. This makes the D-10 chart weak. On the other hand, if Moon is at 24Sc00 or above, he will be in the 9th dasamsa of Sc, *i.e.* Pi. This puts lagna lord in 9th in D-10 and the chart is strengthened. Because Moon moves by one quarter of a nakshatra (or 200 arc-min) in 6 hours (or 360 min), he takes 360/200=1.8 min to move by 1 arc-min. For Moon to go from 23Sc59 to 24Sc00, it only takes about 2 minutes.[91] If we cannot rule out an error of 2 minutes, we should consider Moon in both Aq and Pi and see which one explains the native's career better.

Thus, we should pay attention if any planet is at a rasi border in the divisional chart of interest. If so, we must consider both the positions and see which one makes better sense based on known past.

91 We are assuming here that our computation of Moon's longitude is very accurate. There are some unresolved controversies like (1) ayanamsa and (2) geocentric positions vs topocentric positions. Due to these controversies, we cannot be confident of our calculations. It is prudent to consider both the rasis in border-line situations.

Lagna

Lagna changes rasi in divisional charts much faster than planets. So it is the most important consideration in birthtime rectification.

Lagna moves by one rasi (30°) in 2 hours or 120 min. To move by 1°, lagna takes about 4 min.

***Lesson*:** Lagna moves by 1° in 4 min. Lagna moves by 10' in 2/3 min (or 40 seconds). Lagna moves by 1' in 4 sec. Lagna moves by 10" in 2/3 sec.

We can see that lagna changes rasi in D-10 in 12 min. It changes rasi in D-24 in 5 min.

Example 129: Suppose we are told that someone was born at 9:05 am. Suppose lagna is at 4Sg39. Suppose we have events related to D-10 (career), D-12 (parents) and D-24 (education). Lagna at 4Sg39 puts lagna in these 3 charts in Cp, Cp and Sc (respectively). Suppose the birthtime is reasonably accurate and the maximum error is 5 minutes (*i.e.* birthtime can be 9:00-9:10). Let us find the possible lagnas in the 3 charts.

An error of 5 min changes lagna by about 5/4=1.25° or 1°15'. So, instead of being 4Sg39, it can be as low as 3Sg24 or as high as 5Sg54. So we should consider all lagnas between 3Sg24 and 5Sg54. In D-10, lagna changes rasi at multiples of 3°. So the whole range we have for lagna results in the same D-10 lagna (Cp). In D-12, lagna changes rasi at multiples of 2°30'. So we have a transition at 5°. So there are two possibilities for lagna – one in 3Sg24-5Sg00 and the other in 5Sg00-5Sg54. So lagna in D-12 can be Cp or Aq. Lagna in D-24 changes rasi at multiples of 1°15'. It changes rasi at 3°45' and 5°00'. So we have 3 possibilities for lagna – (1) 3Sg24-3Sg45: Li, (2) 3Sg45-5Sg00: Sc, (3) 5Sg00-5Sg54: Sg.

Using these sets of lagnas, we should analyze the charts and see which one makes sense. Suppose Sg lagna in D-24 and Aq lagna in D-12 explain known events. But suppose we cannot explain his career. Suppose Aq lagna instead of Cp lagna explains his career well. Then what do we do?

To get the next rasi as D-10 lagna (Aq instead of Cp), we should cross the next D-10 border, which is 6Sg00. So the lagna should become 6Sg00 (or higher) instead of 4Sg39. So we have to add 1°21' or higher to lagna. Lagna moves by 1°21' or 81' in 81x4 sec = 324 sec = 5 min 24 sec.

This means that the birthtime should be 9:10:24 instead of 9:05. Though we are told that the error in birthtime cannot be more than 5 minutes, it has to be more than 5 minutes in this case to explain known facts.

Please note that these calculations are made on the assumption that lagna moves uniformly. That is not the case in reality. So the actual rectified birthtime may be a little off. We can do approximate calculations first and then see if it has to be corrected further. For example, we may get lagna at 9:10:24 to be 5Sg59 instead of the expected value of 6Sg00. Then we have to add a few more seconds and see if we cross 6Sg00.

One may see from this example that an astrologer should know the details of the computation of divisional charts and be familiar with the longitudes at which lagna changes rasi in various divisional charts. That familiarity is a necessity for quick birthtime rectification.

Special Lagnas

Hora lagna moves twice as fast as lagna. Ghati lagna moves 5 times as fast as lagna.

***Lesson*:**

HL moves by 1° in 2 min. HL moves by 10' in 1/3 min (or 20 seconds). HL moves by 1' in 2 sec. HL moves by 10" in 1/3 sec.

GL moves by 1° in 4/5 min (or 48 seconds). GL moves by 10' in 4.8 seconds. GL moves by 1' in 0.48 sec (less than half a second).

Exercise 50: Suppose someone is born at 9:05 am and has GL at 20Le37. This puts GL in D-10 in Aq. Suppose we expect the D-10 GL in Ar to explain the native's periods of power and authority. What should the correct birthtime be?

32.2.2 *Das as*

Rasi dasas based on rasi chart change only if lagna changes rasi or a planet changes rasi. Because lagna changes rasi once in 2 hours, we do not have to deal with inaccuracies in rasi dasas in most cases.

Narayana dasa of divisional charts does not change in a small period of time, unless a planet changes rasi in the divisional chart of interest.

Sence, the dasa start dates in nakshatra, dasas change with small changes in birthtime. Let us say the complete duration (and not just the remainder at birth) of the dasa running at birth is n years. Let us say the birthtime is wrong by m minutes. Moon stays in the nakshatra for about 24x60 minutes (24 hours) and the error in the fraction of Moon's constellation that is yet to be traversed is $m/(24 \times 60)$. The error in the number of days of dasa left is $n \times 360 \times m/(24 \times 60) = (n \times m)/4$. If we add m minutes to the birthtime, we should subtract $(n \times m)/4$ days from dasa dates and vice versa.

If 7 years of Venus dasa remains at birth, then $n = 20$ and the approximate error in dasa dates is $20m/4 = 5m$ days, where m is the birthtime error in minutes. If the birthtime is wrong by 2 minutes, dasa dates are wrong by 10 days.

If the birthtime is wrong by 2 minutes and 3 years of Moon dasa were remaining at birth, then $n = 10$ and $m = 2$ and the error in dasa dates is 10x2/4 = 5 days.

In Kalachakra dasa, the error is more. If n years is the paramayush of the sequence corresponding to the navamsa of natal Moon and m minutes is the error in birthtime, the error in the dates of dasa is (n X m) days. If we add m minutes to the birthtime, we should subtract (n X m) days from dasa dates and vice versa.

For example, if the paramayush is 100 years and the birthtime error is 2 minutes, then the error in dates is 200 days. It is almost 7 months! For this reason, it is futile to use pratyantardasas in Kalachakra dasa unless one is absolutely confident of the birthtime.

32.2.3 *Tajaka Charts*

If the change in lagna in the natal chart due to a birthtime change is x, then the lagna in the Tajaka annual and monthly charts will also change by approximately x. However, we have to keep in mind that the list of divisional charts in which lagna is near rasi borders may change.

For example, let us say that natal lagna is at 23Sc30 and lagna in a Tajaka annual chart for 1980-81 is at 15Cn05. Let us say that the birthtime can have an error of upto 3 minutes (either way – plus or minus). Let us say that we are interested in the career of the native and especially in an event in career that took place in 1980-81. In natal D-10, lagna (23Sc30) is in the *middle* of the 8th dasamsa in Sc. Unless the birthtime changes by more than 6 minutes in either direction, lagna in D-10 will not change. However, lagna in 1980-81 Tajaka annual chart is close to a dasamsa border. If lagna is just below 15° in Cn, lagna in D-10 will be in the 5th from Pi. *i.e.* Cn itself. If lagna is just above 15° in Cn, lagna in D-10 will be in the 6th from Pi, *i.e.* Le. With the given birthtime, we get 15Cn05 and so lagna in D-10 in the Tajaka chart is in Le. But it could be Cn if the native's birth took place half a minute before the reported birthtime.

Thus, sometimes we cannot detect a birthtime error just by looking at the natal chart and dasas. Looking at the divisional charts of Tajaka annual charts can help in some cases.

The assumption here is that one casts Tajaka charts very accurately. This is not true with those who use the approximate method taught in this boo or those who find the exact solar return but use an approximate formula for Sun's motion or use a linear formula for ayanamsa.

The actual ayanamsa used matters only to a small extent, in the sense that it has the same impact on the longitude of lagna and the rasis occupied by lagna in various divisional charts, as it has in the natal chart. On the other hand, using an approximate linear formula for ayanamsa brings minor discrepancy in Sun's longitude which is multiplied by 360 in the longitude of lagna. This results in a serious error. Though we do not know exactly when Nirayana zodiac coincided with the Sayana zodiac, we do know the exact nonlinear formula of the precession. So one hoping to use Tajaka charts in birthtime rectification *must* use the correct *nonlinear* formula of the ayanamsa of one's choice. Unfortunately, many people use linear approximations. They are not good enough for Tajaka charts.

32.3 A Practical Approach

It is a good idea to first determine the correct D-9 lagna or D-10 lagna and then go to the other divisional charts. We should first determine that the birthtime is between 9:05 and 9:15. Then we can determine that it is between 9:07 and 9:11. Then we can use a more precise criterion and narrow down further. Thus we narrow down further and further with each criterion.

If one's marriage has already taken place, we can use D-9 to see it and fix D-9 lagna. If not, we can see one's general sense of duty, one's basic skills and one's interaction with others and fix D-9 lagna based on them. Then we can go to a higher divisional chart. However, in reality, sometimes it may become necessary to come back to D-9. For example, suppose someone can have lagna in D-9 in Li or Sc. Suppose we think that Li is also a good candidate but Sc is better. Then the candidates for D-24 lagna that we get with this choice may not make sense. It may make sense to place lagna in D-24 in another rasi and that may require lagna in D-9 to be in Li. In that case, we can revisit D-9 and change the lagna.

Trying to first do a broad rectification with D-9 and D-10 and then doing a fine rectification with high divisional charts like D-20 and Kalachakra dasa will provide a systematic approach to the problem, but we should be willing to come back to the first step if we are stuck in the second step.

After a couple of examples, this approach may become clearer.

32.4 Practical Examples

Example 130: Let us consider a gentleman whose birthdata is reported as: 30th November 1966, 10:36 am (IST), 77 E 47, 11 N 19. His D-4 and D-9 are shown in Chart 75 and his D-10 and D-24 are shown in Chart 76.

Lagna with the reported birthtime is at 13Cp16. Let us approach the problem of rectification in a pyramid-like approach. First let us verify D-4 lagna. The native left his motherland and went to USA in Jupiter dasa. In D-4, Jupiter owns 9th (flourishing abroad) and 12th (staying away from motherland) and he occupies the 7th house (long journeys). Rahu is the primary significator of foreign residence and he joins Jupiter. For these reasons, Jupiter dasa can certainly take him abroad. So lagna in D-4 is most probably correct.

D-4 lagna changes rasi at multiples of 7.5°. The lagna we used above (13Cp16) is between 7.5° and 15° in Cp. So we conclude that lagna is between 7Cp30 and 15Cp00.

Next, let us look at navamsa. In navamsa, lagna changes rasi at multiples of 3°20'. Here is changes at 13Cp20. The given lagna (13Cp16) is just below it. We see from Chart 75 that navamsa lagna is in Ar. However, with a very small error, it can be Ta also. Let us consider both.

If we take navamsa lagna in Ar, the native should be dynamic (Ar), spiritual and possibly short-tempered (Ketu). With Venus and Moon in trines, he should be skilled at singing or other arts. But he isn't. With Mercury in the 2nd house, he should be a skiled speaker. However, he isn't really a skillful speaker.

If we take navamsa lagna in Ta, the native should be a hard-working and sincere (Ta) intellectual (Mercury). He should be mild-mannered, liked by most people and learned in many subjects (Mercury). This description fits the native better. So probably lagna is above 13Cp20.

Chart 75

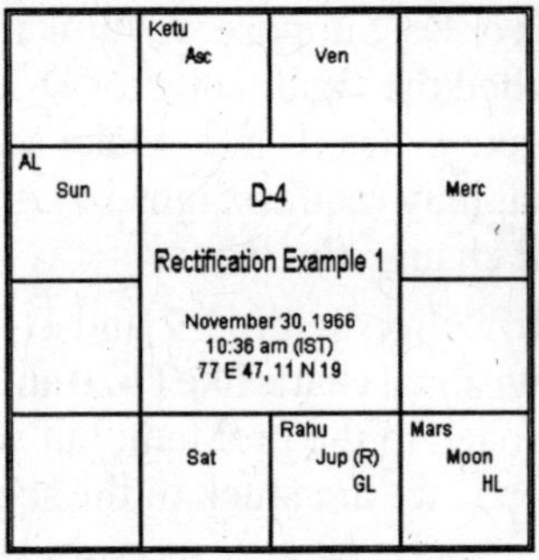

	Ketu Asc	Ven	
AL Sun	D-4 Rectification Example 1		Merc
	November 30, 1966 10:36 am (IST) 77 E 47, 11 N 19		
	Sat	Rahu Jup (R) GL	Mars Moon HL

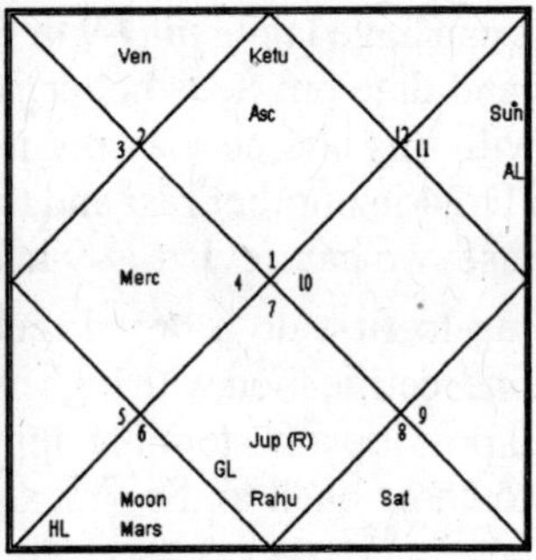

Ven, Ketu, Asc, Sun, AL, 3, 2, 12, 11, Merc, 4, 1, 10, 7, 5, 6, 9, 8, Jup (R), GL, Moon, Rahu, Sat, HL, Mars

Asc:	13 Cp 15	Sun:	14 Sc 09 (MK)	Moon:	9 Ge 32 (PK)	Mars:	4 Vi 32 (DK)
Merc:	24 Li 43 (AmK)	Jup (R):	10 Cn 57 (PiK)	Ven:	19 Sc 23 (BK)	Sat:	29 Aq 32 (AK)
Rahu:	21 Ar 36 (GK)	Ketu:	21 Li 36	HL:	21 Pi 03	GL:	1 Li 40

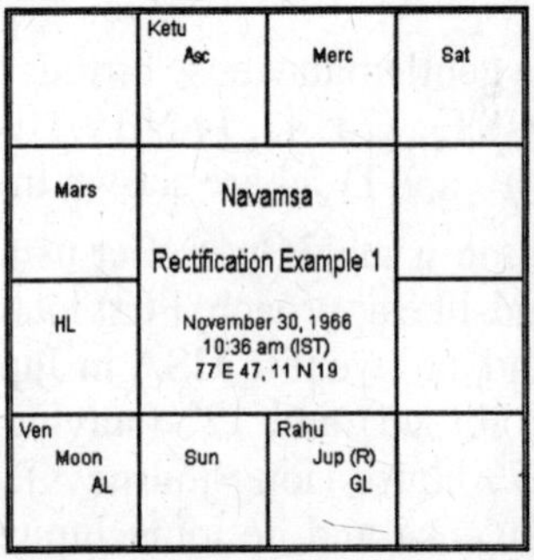

	Ketu Asc	Merc	Sat
Mars	Navamsa Rectification Example 1		
HL	November 30, 1966 10:36 am (IST) 77 E 47, 11 N 19		
Ven Moon AL	Sun	Rahu Jup (R) GL	

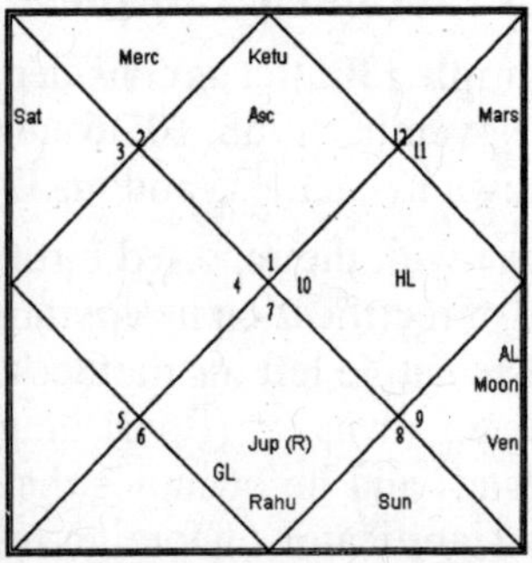

Merc, Ketu, Sat, Asc, Mars, 3, 2, 12, 11, 4, 1, 10, 7, HL, AL, Moon, 5, 6, 9, 8, Ven, Jup (R), GL, Rahu, Sun

Chart 76

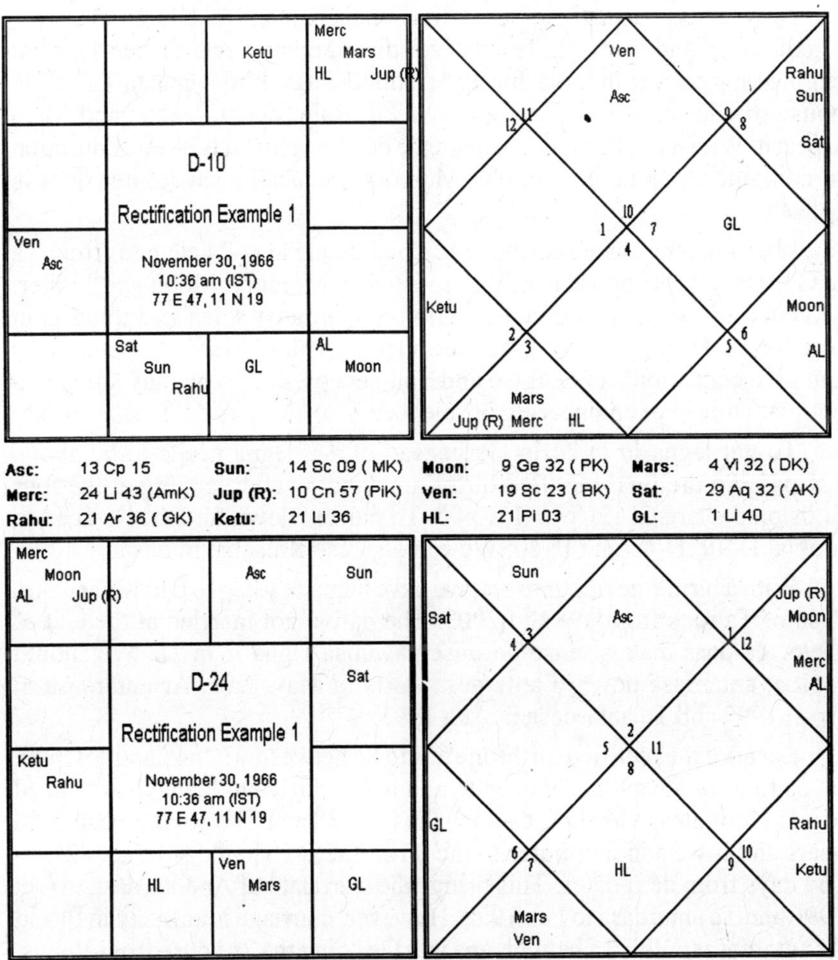

We have narrowed to the range 13Cp20-15Cp00, based on lagna in D-4 and D-9. Now let us consider D-10, the chart of career. The native is a dynamic software engineer. In D-10, AL shows one's status in career and how people perceive one. Here AL is in Virgo and its lord Mercury aspects it. So he is perceived in his career as an intelligent person (Virgo and Mercury). The 10th house from AL has Mercury and Mars and it can explain a career in software.

So probably lagna in D-10 is correct. This confirms that lagna is between 12Cp00 and 15Cp00. But we have no further narrowing down because of

D-10. We still have 13Cp20-15Cp00 as the rectified window.

Now let us go to a higher level divisional chart and take D-24, the chart of education and learning. The native studied computer science at a good engineering college in India during his Jupiter dasa. With lagna in Ta, the 4th house of education is in Le. Sun owns it. Rahu, Ketu, Venus and Mars aspect it. With this, education in medicine or management is likely. Education in computer science is unlikely. Moreover, education in Jupiter dasa is unlikely.

If we take the birthtime above 13Cp45, lagna in D-24 changes from Ta to Ge. Then the 4th house is in Vi, aspected by Mercury, Moon and Jupiter. Mercury and Virgo can give education in computer science. Jupiter is in own house. He aspects the 4th house and joins 4th lord Mercury. So his dasa can give education. A4 is in Ge and Sun occupies it. So he may study at a popular college of engineering or science.

To get lagna in D-24 in Ge instead of Ta, lagna needs to be above 13Cp45. So the final rectified birthtime window after looking at the four divisional charts is 13Cp45-15Cp00. To narrow down further, we need to look at D-40, D-45 and D-60. We can also use Kalachakra dasa.

With a birthtime of 10:36 am, we have lagna at 13Cp16 and Kalachakra dasa of Ta runs from 1987 to 2003. The native got married at the end of 1996. Ta dasa makes sense because navamsa lagna is in Ta. We should look at antardasa now. Pi antardasa starts in May 1995, Ar antardasa in April 1997 and Ta antardasa in Aug 1998.

Because the rectified birthtime has to be between 13Cp45 and 15Cp00, let us first try 13Cp45. We need to add half a degree to lagna. So we need to add 2 minutes to birthtime and make it 10:38 am. The paramayush is 86 years and if we add 2 minutes to the birthtime, we should subtract 82x2 = 164 days from dasa dates. This brings the start date of Ar antardasa to Oct 1996 and Ta antardasa to Feb 1998. However, marriage is unlikely in Pi and Ar antardasas. With Ta being lagna and Ge being the 7th house from Venus, marriage is most likely in Ta and Ge antardasas. So the start date of Ta antardasa must be moved from Feb 1998 to the end of 1996. We need to subtract about 400 days from the dasa dates. This requires further addition of 400/86=4.7 minutes to the birthtime. This will add another degree to lagna and lagna will be just below 15°. The rectified birthtime is around 10:42:30. The error in the reported birthtime can be due to errors in the clock used.

Of course, if we use the rectified birthdata and verify a few more events in the life of the native, we can be more confident that the rectification is correct.

Example 131: Suppose an astrologer friend of ours approaches us with the rasi chart of a gentleman, shown in Chart 77. Because the birth happened in 1939, we cannot rule out huge errors. The error need not be just 2 or 3 minutes. An error of even 10 minutes is possible.

Chart 77

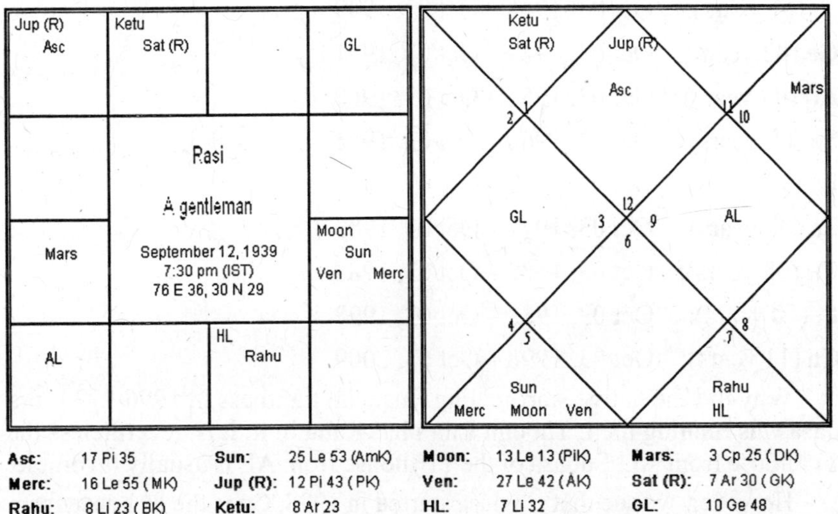

Asc:	17 Pi 35	**Sun:**	25 Le 53 (AmK)	**Moon:**	13 Le 13 (PiK)	**Mars:**	3 Cp 25 (DK)
Merc:	16 Le 55 (MK)	**Jup (R):**	12 Pi 43 (PK)	**Ven:**	27 Le 42 (AK)	**Sat (R):**	7 Ar 30 (GK)
Rahu:	8 Li 23 (BK)	**Ketu:**	8 Ar 23	**HL:**	7 Li 32	**GL:**	10 Ge 48

Let us say that the only thing our friend knows about this gentleman is that he thinks that 1978-79 was the golden period of life in terms of his finances and that he has been experiencing financial tightness since 1996-97. We have to rectify the chart just based on this information.

Which dasa should we use for financial matters? It is Sudasa. Let us find Sudasa.

Moon is at 13°13'25" in Leo. He is in Makha constellation, which runs from 0° to 13°20' in Le. His advancement in nakshatra is (13°13'25")/(13°20') = (793.4167')/(800') = 0.99177. The same fraction of the entire zodiac is 0.99177x360 = 357.0375° = 357° 2' 15". Adding this to lagna, we get Sree Lagna. Lagna is at 17°35'50" in Pi. So we get Sree Lagna at 14°38'5" in Pi. Sudasa starts from Pi. Because Sree Lagna is in an even rasi, Sudasa goes backward. We reckon quadrants, panapharas and apoklimas backwards and get Pi, Sg, Vi, Ge, Aq, Sc, Le, Ta, Cp, Li, Cn and Ar. Dasa periods are as in Narayana dasa. However, there is an exception for the first dasa. Because Jupiter is in Pi, Pi dasa is for 12 years. However, only a fraction of this is left at birth, based on the fraction of the rasi yet to be traversed by

Sree Lagna. This fraction is (30° – 14°38'5")/ 30° = 0.51218. So the remainder of Pi dasa at birth is 0.51218x12 years = 6 years 1 month 23 days.

We get dasas as

Pi (6.15 yrs): Sep 12, 1939 – Oct 03, 1945

Sg (03 years): Oct 03, 1945 – Oct 03, 1948

Vi (01 years): Oct 03, 1948 – Oct 03, 1949

Ge (02 years): Oct 03, 1949 – Oct 03, 1951

Aq (09 years): Oct 03, 1951 – Oct 03, 1960

Sc (05 years): Oct 03, 1960 – Oct 03, 1965

Le (12 years): Oct 03, 1965 – Oct 03, 1977

Ta (03 years): Oct 03, 1977 – Oct 03, 1980

Cp (08 years): Oct 03, 1980 – Oct 03, 1988

Li (10 years): Oct 03, 1988 – Oct 03, 1998

Cn (11 years): Oct 03, 1998 – Oct 03, 2009

Why did the native start feeling financial tightness in 1996-97? Libra dasa was running then. Though Libra has Rahu in it, it is nevertheless the 11th house from AL. Sudasa of the 11th house from AL is usually favorable.

However, we see that Cn dasa started in 1998. Cn is the 8th house from AL. The 8th house from AL stands for fall of status and material setbacks. It can certainly show financial tightness in Sudasa. Though two good upagrahas (Artha Prahara and Yamaghantaka – similar to Mercury and Jupiter in effects) are present in it, Cn contains two highly malefic upagrahas also – Indrachapa and Upaketu.

If the native has been experiencing financial tightness since Cn dasa started, it makes good sense. So probably Cn dasa should start in mid-1996 instead of Oct 1998. What is the required change in birth time for this change in Sudasa dates?

Exercise 51: We calculated the formulas for the approximate change in Vimsottari dasa and Kalachakra dasa dates if birthtime changes by *m* minutes. Do the same thing for Sudasa.

Complete the exercise before reading further. Based on the formula at the end of the exercise, dates of dasas in Sudasa move back by 6x12x*m* days if we add *m* minutes to the birthtime. We want it to move by 2 years or 720 days. So *m* should be 720/(6x12), *i.e.* 10. We should add 10 minutes to the birthtime and make it 7:40 pm. However, after calculating Sudasa for a birthtime of 7:40 pm, we realize that the dates of dasas have moved by almost 2.5 years instead of 2 years[92]. To get dasa start dates 2 years earlier, we just need to make the birthtime 7:38 pm.

With this new time, Cn dasa started in mid-1996. With Cn being the 8th house from AL, its dasa gave financial tightness.

Example 132: Suppose the rasi chart in Chart 78 is given to us as the chart of Microsoft company's Bill Gates. Suppose we have verified several divisional charts and they seem fine. Suppose we want to micro-rectify it.

The technique to be used for birthtime rectification varies from chart to chart. If one's D-10 lagna is close to a rasi border, we should use a technique that is sensitive to D-10 lagna and see which alternative makes better sense. If GL is close to a rasi border, we should use a technique that depends critically on GL and see which alternative makes better sense.

Here one can note that Sree Lagna (SL) is on a rasi border. With the birthtime of 9:15 pm, SL is at 28Ar15. If a few minutes are added to the birthtime, SL will be in Ta. We should use a technique that is sensitive to the rasi occupied by SL and see whether SL in Ar or Ta makes better sense.

Of course, Sudasa depends on SL and we should compute Sudasa.

Chart 78

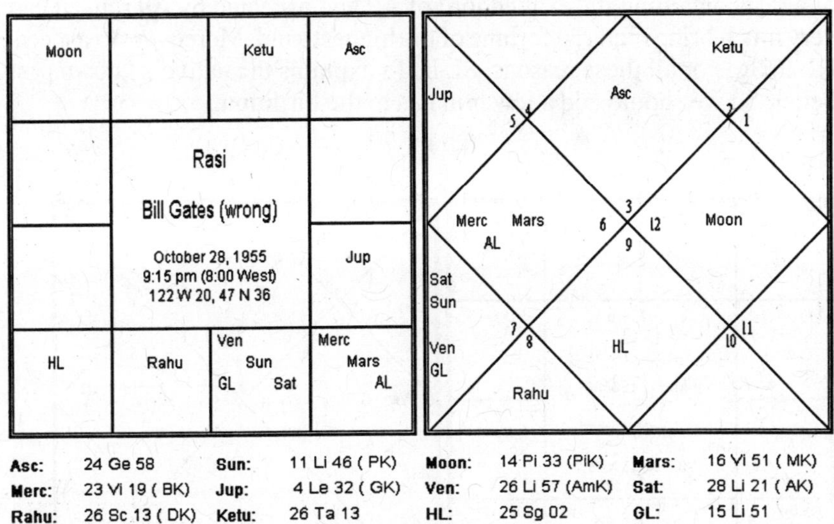

Asc:	24 Ge 58	**Sun:**	11 Li 46 (PK)	**Moon:**	14 Pi 33 (PiK)	**Mars:**	16 Vi 51 (MK)
Merc:	23 Vi 19 (BK)	**Jup:**	4 Le 32 (GK)	**Ven:**	26 Li 57 (AmK)	**Sat:**	28 Li 21 (AK)
Rahu:	26 Sc 13 (DK)	**Ketu:**	26 Ta 13	**HL:**	25 Sg 02	**GL:**	15 Li 51

92 The error in our approximations is due to assuming that lagna and Moon move at a certain uniform rate. The rate at which they move is not really linear/uniform. So the formulas given here should only be used for reference. One should finally compute charts and dasas for the rectified time and verify the rectification.

If SL is in Ar, Sudasa starts from Ar and goes as Ar, Cn, Li, Cp, Ta, Le, Sc etc. If SL is in Ta, Sudasa starts from Ta. Normally it will go as Ta, Aq, Sc, Le, Ar, Cp, Li *etc*, but Ketu's presence in Ta reverses the direction. So Sudasa goes as Ta, Le, Sc, Aq, Ge, Vi, Sg etc.

In the first case, one can see that Scorpio dasa runs from 1990 to 2000. In the second case, Virgo dasa runs during 1988-2000. Bill Gates was financially very successful and he became the world's richest man in late 1990's. Which dasa explains his financial success better?

Scorpio is the 3rd house from AL and upachayas from AL bring improvements in one's status. However, Scorpio has no aspect on HL. Moreover, it is afflicted by Rahu. So Scorpio dasa is not that great.

On the other hand, Virgo dasa can bring excellent results. It contains AL and its exalted lord. It is aspected by bhaagya pada (A9, arudha pada of the 9th house) and occupied by the exalted lord of bhaagya pada. The 9th house shows one's fortune. One may be fortunate to have a good guru and one may be fortunate to have a good leader. But the world's perceptions of one's fortune are driven by the recognition one gets and formal distinctions like being named in Forbes list of richest men. These are what drive the world's perceptions about one's fortune. A9 shows them the best. If Sudasa of a rasi containing the exalted lord of A9 and aspected by A9 runs, it can very much bring material fortune of the highest kind. Moreover, Vi aspects HL in Sg. For all these reasons, SL in Ta explains the native's known past better. So we should add a few minutes to the birthtime.

Chart 79

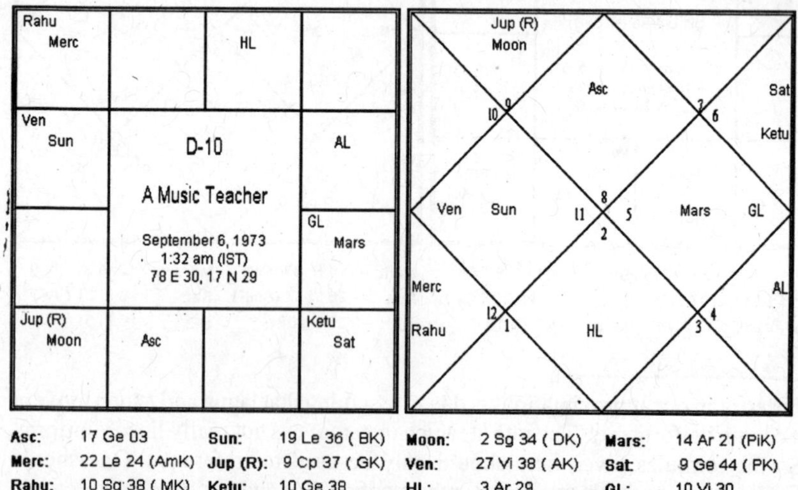

Example 133: Let us consider a lady whose D-10 is shown in Chart 79. She is a good singer and sang in some radio and television programs in India, but her career was cut down when she got married to an Indian engineer in USA and went to USA with him. In 1998, she started a music school in USA and started teaching Carnatic (south Indian classical) music.

In her D-10, Mars in the 10th house shows own ventures and enterprise. The 10th lord Sun joins Venus in the 5th house and shows fame as a singer. Sun-Venus combination can show music. Venus stands for creative activities. Sun and Moon stand for music. Sun stands for rhythm and Moon stands for melody. So a career in music is possible. As per Vimsottari dasa, Sun dasa started in 1998. This may be why her career was restarted in 1998. Let us check her Kalachakra dasa.

Kalachakra dasa of Aquarius started in October 1999. It may be noted that Aquarius contains Venus and 10th lord Sun. So Kalachakra dasa must have started just before she started her music institute. To get the Kalachakra dasas a little earlier, we need to add a little to the birthtime. So we should add a few minutes to the birthtime and make sure that Kalachakra dasa of Aquarius starts just before her career is restarted.

We have so far looked at 4 examples. In the first example, we had to look at several divisional charts to rectify the birthtime. In the second example, we rectified the birthtime based on a dasa. We did it because the past events given to us relate to an area of life (finances), for which there is an appropriate dasa. In the 3rd chart also, we used the same dasa, but for a different reason. We did it because a key parameter was on a rasi border. In the 4th example, we used Kalachakra dasa. Being a sensitive dasa, Kalachakra dasa is usually very useful in carrying out a fine birthtime rectification.

One should choose the approach on a chart-by-chart basis. The information provided by a client about past events should decide the techniques to be used. Birthtime rectification is an area in which one can become good only after considerable practice. **There are no hard and fast rules.**

32.5 Conclusion

There are two kinds of birthtime rectification – macro-rectification and micro-rectification. Macro-rectification is the case when you have two or more totally different birthdata from different sources and want to find out which is correct. For example, there are different versions of Sri A.B. Vajpayee's birthdata. If we want to find out which is correct, we have to look at various divisional charts and life events and see which one works better.

Micro-rectification is the one that we will need the most in practical consultations. The birthdata reported by clients usually has a little error and we have to rectify the birthtime.

Some people use some formula based techniques for birthtime rectification and assume that human births happen only in certain quanta of time. Most of those techniques do not work. The only correct way to rectify a birthtime is to correct it in such a way that one's nature and past life events are well explained. An astrologer should have an idea of the change introduced in various computations if the birthtime changes a little. Using lagna in D-9, D-10 etc, we can broadly rectify the birthtime. Then we can rectify it with a finer precision by going to higher divisional charts like D-20 and D-24 and using Kalachakra dasa. A couple of examples were provided in this book. Readers should understand the examples thoroughly and practice these techniques with as many charts as they can. The adage that practice makes one perfect is particularly true in this area. Readers should remember that correct birthtime rectification lays a solid foundation for the entire chart analysis – without correct birthtime rectification, all other fine techniques we learnt in this book are useless.

32.6 Answers to Exercises

Exercise 50:

GL in D-10 goes to the next rasi at multiples of 3°. Here it goes from Aq to Pi when GL crosses 21°. It goes from Pi to Ar when GL crosses 24°. So GL has to be at or above 24Le00. So the amount we have to add is 24°0' – 20° 37' = 3° 21' = 201'.

GL moves by 201' in 201 x 0.48 sec = 96.48 sec = 1 min 6.48 sec. So we should roughly add 1 min 7 sec and the birthtime should be 9:06:07 am or above.

There is an upper limit also. If it becomes too high, GL in D-10 will move from Ar to Ta. But we decided that GL in D-10 in Ar makes the best sense. So we cannot add another 3° to GL. GL moves by 3° in 3 x 4/5 = 12/5 min = 2 min 24 sec. Adding this to 9:06:07, we get 9:08:31. So the birthtime should be between 9:06:07 am and 9:08:31 am for GL in D-10 to be in Ar.

If we create several inequations like the above using lagna and special lagnas in various divisional charts, we can narrow down to the correct birthtime.

Exercise 51:

Lagna moves by 30° if the birthtime changes by 120 minutes. If the birthtime changes by *m* minutes, lagna changes by (*m*/120)x30 = (*m*/4)°. Moon moves by 3°20' (one quarter of a nakshatra) in 6 hours or 360 minutes. So, if the birthtime changes by *m* minutes, Moon's longitude changes by (*m*/

360)x(3°20'). So the fraction of the nakshatra occupied by Moon that is already traversed by Moon, changes by $(m/360)x(3°20')/(13°20')=m/(360x4)$. When we find this as a fraction of the zodiac, the change is $360°xm/(360x4)$ = $(m/4)°$. The error in Sree Lagna is the sum of the error in lagna and the error in this fraction of zodiac. So Sree Lagna changes by $(m/4)° + (m/4)° = (m/2)°$.

Lesson: Sree Lagna moves twice as fast as lagna. Hora lagna and Sree lagna, which move twice as fast as lagna, show the matters related to the 2nd house, *i.e.* money (HL is useful in death also). Ghati lagna, which moves 5 times as fast as lagna, shows the matters related to the 5th house, *i.e.* fame, power and authority.

If Sree Lagna increases by $(m/2)°$, then (30° – Sree Lagna) decreases by $(m/2)°$. The fraction (30° – Sree Lagna)/30° decreases by $(m/60)$. If the complete length of the first dasa is n years, then the remainder of the first dasa at birth decreases by nx$(m/60)$ years = (6 x n x m) days. If the remainder of the first dasa at birth decreases by these many days, all dasas come these many days *earlier*.

Formula: If the complete Narayana dasa length of the first dasa in Sudasa is n years and the birthtime changes by m minutes, all the dasa and antardasa dates change by approximately (6 x n x m) days. If the birthtime is earlier, dasas will come later and vice versa.

CAUTION: When we consider a change in birthtime by m minutes, it is possible that Moon changes nakshatra during the time. The above calculations still hold. When Moon is at the end of a nakshatra, the amount added to lagna to get Sree Lagna is just below 360°. When Moon moves to the next nakshatra, it changes to 0°. Though we have a big change in numbers, it is a continuous change and 360° = 0°. So we need not worry and we can use the above formula. However, if Sree Lagna changes rasi during the m minutes, Sudasa calculation changes completely and the above formula is no longer valid. For example, if Sree Lagna is at 29° in Ar and we consider adding 4 min to the birthtime, it changes Sree Lagna by (4/2)° and it goes to 1° in Ta. The whole dasa sequence changes now and we cannot use the above formula.

33. Rational Thinking

33.1 Introduction

Astrology lovers insist that it is a science. But any conscientious person familiar with the modern definition of "science" will agree that it is not a science. It *may* have been a science a few thousand years back, but it is no longer a science. A lot of astrological knowledge of Vedic times became corrupt in the last few hundred years, because of the degeneration of Indian culture precipitated by foreign invasions. The correct knowledge of the science of Vedic astrology is broken into parts and hidden in small corners of India. There are a lot of traditional families in India, which guard some special astrological techniques as "family secrets". The knowledge that is explicitly taught in most books – including this book – is either incomplete or simply incorrect. Gathering the correct knowledge from the remote corners of India and consolidating it is a daunting task.

It makes no sense to start from scratch and develop this subject completely. The best approach is to understand the teachings of sages correctly and then experiment to confirm our understanding. However, it is easier said than done. Astrologers don't agree even on the basics – such as the zodiac to be used and the ayanamsa. There are just too many things that are ambiguous and not completely clarified in classics. To complicate things further, some modern savants are making their own ill-considered departures from the teachings of sages and foolishly popularizing them. That only adds to the corruption of this knowledge.

The bottom line is — things are in a mess and astrology is far from being a science. However, readers need not despair. It is this author's prediction that astrology research will flourish in the coming century and a lot of long-standing issues will be resolved conclusively.

Understanding and accepting that a problem exists is the first step in fixing it. This author's intention is to make the readers aware of the problems. While we certainly want to keep the sanctity of the subject of astrology intact and not unduly worry about having it accepted as a science, it can only do good to apply the paradigms of modern science and approach astrology with a rational outlook.

33.2 Irrational Explanations

Because of the corruption that is rampant in astrological knowledge, people often use wrong principles to explain an event and fail in presenting straight-forward and sound logic. They beat around the bush to explain an event sometimes.

Example 134: We may hear people making a typing mistake and saying,"Mercury is retrograde. That is why people are making mistakes these days". Pray, do these mistakes happen only when Mercury is retrograde? Or, do they happen with a considerably higher frequency when Mercury is retrograde? Mercury's retrogression may last a couple of weeks and do the mistakes happen exactly during those two weeks?

If not, how can we correlate Mercury's retrogression and the typing mistakes? Probably the mistakes happen all the time, but they are more frequent during a few days. But the reason has to be a sookshma dasa or a praana dasa or a Bhrigu transit during that time, rather than Mercury's retrogression.

We should look at the nature of the event and the time period of its effectiveness and look for an astrological factor with almost the same period of effectiveness. One may make typing mistakes everyday, but a particular day may be worse than usual. In that case, the period of effectiveness of the event (*viz* making too many typing mistakes) is that day. A month-long retrogression or a year-long transit cannot be its reason. If we correlate it with an astrological factor with the same period of effectiveness (*e.g.* a sookshma dasa of Narayana dasa or Mercury's D-27 transit in a sign occupied in natal rasi chart by Rahu), it is plausible. But if we attribute the event to retrograde Mercury or debilitated Jupiter, it is not logical.

Example 135: Someone may have a very bad time at his office on a particular afternoon. He may say,"oh, it's because I am running the Vimsottari dasa of the 8th lord in D-10."

It is true that the 8th lord in D-10 can give the results experienced, but that doesn't mean his dasa was responsible for an isolated event in an afternoon. If one has similar experiences frequently, during the entire period of a dasa, then we can blame that dasa. After all, a dasa shows the overall mood in a long period of time.

However, if that is not the case and the experience is an isolated incident, then it is irrational to explain it using a dasa. Some other astrological factor with a smaller period of effect may have caused the event. For example, Moon may be transiting in D-10 in a rasi occupied by Saturn and Rahu in natal rasi chart. Moon, Sun and lagna lord in D-10 may be transiting in kakshyas without a rekha. The latter may show a bad period of a few days and the former factor with a period of effectiveness of about 6 hours may have triggered the event.

We will find the correct factor behind an event only if we search for it without compromising. A true researcher never compromises. Of course, there may be many astrological factors contributing to the manufacturing of an event and we may not be able to find all of them because we don't know all the possible techniques. Nevertheless, we should try to find the right factor within the limits of our knowledge. Accepting a wrong factor as the reason for an event is illogical. Attributing an isolated incident in a day to a dasa that runs for 10 years is irrational.

Some astrologers may make a correct prediction based on illogical thinking, due to luck (or spiritual strength). We should not be blinded by the success of a prediction. Success of a prediction does not prove the validity of the methods used. We may try to enhance our predictive success through good spiritual practices, but we should also try to identify the right factors behind various events and consolidate the scientific aspects of Vedic astrology. The scientific and spiritual aspects of astrology should go together and strengthen each other.

33.3 Known Past vs Future

Some authors present some principles in their books and present many examples that show the efficacy of the principles.

However, one finds many times that these principles are too vague to be useful in practice. They are good enough to explain known past, but not good enough to predict future.

An extreme example will make this clearer. Suppose someone presents us with a principle: "Someone born with lagna in an airy sign gets married when Venus transits in an own sign or a friendly sign or a watery sign or a trine from natal 7th house". It may make sense to us, because Venus is the significator of marriage and being in an own sign or a friendly sign or a watery sign makes this watery planet strong. Also, Venus transiting in a trine from natal 7th house may seem favorable for marriage to occur.

We may test this principle against as many examples as we want and we will find it to be satisfied in 100% cases. Does that mean that this is an excellent principle?

No! This is *not* a meaningful or useful principle at all. Why? The list given covers the entire zodiac. Ta and Li are own signs of Venus. Ge, Vi, Cp and Aq are friendly signs. Cn, Sc and Pi are watery signs. Ar, Le and Sg are trines from the 7th house for any person with lagna in an airy sign. If you count the signs, you will find that all the twelve signs are covered! So the principle indirectly means, "someone born in an airy sign gets married when Venus transits in one of the 12 signs". Of course, Venus transits one of the 12 signs always and this is a trivially correct statement. So it will be satisfied in the case of all people with lagna in an airy sign.

But, can we use it to make any predictions? If we get the chart of someone with lagna in an airy sign, can we predict using this principle when he will get married? No!

This is the problem with vague astrological principles. True, this is an extreme example, but didn't "Venus in own or friendly or watery sign or a trine from the 7th house" make some sense to us? However, it turned out to be too general (or vague) to help us in making a precise prediction.

Constructors like the above are commonly found in astrological literature. We talk about the 7th lord giving marriage or a planet aspecting or occupying 7th or 7th lord. Or a planet having an argala on 7th or 7th lord. If it is still not enough, we can add the nakshatra lord of 7th lord or his dispositor or someone else. As we add conditions, we finally cover all the planets. We can always explain the known past this way. Of course, if we have a standard procedure for finding the strongest candidate among all those planets and if his dasa always gives the results, then it is logical. But, if there are 6 candidates and we explain an event by simply showing the candidacy of the planet involved, it is irrational. We are in trouble when making predictions about future in that approach – which of the umpteen candidates will give the result?

The root cause of the problem is that we often use the wrong tool to analyze a matter. Sages explained hundreds of dasa systems and yet we use only a handful. When we use the correct technique, probably the strongest candidate gives the result. When we use a wrong technique, we are forced to give a vague justification.

For example, we saw in Example 58 that Mercury (8th lord in 7th) and Rahu (malefic in 2nd) were the strongest killer planets. By taking a variation of Vimsottari dasa that starts from the 8th star from Moon's star, we found that the native passed away in Rahu's antardasa in Mercury's dasa. However, one relying on standard Vimsottari dasa always will find that Venus dasa is running and he will explain the event based on the situation of Venus in the 7th house. But, if we take yogakaraka Venus to be a maraka because he is in the 7th house, we can take 6 planets (occupants and lords of 2nd and 7th) as marakas. With 6 planets out of 9 qualifying as marakas, how can we predict when the native passes away? On the other hand, by using the most appropriate dasa, we see that the event was given by the strongest candidates.

Because of the corruption in astrological knowledge, many contemporary astrologers don't use the most appropriate techniques always. Due to this, they have to deal with a lot of vagueness and they rely on spiritual strength for correct predictions. When explaining the past, a vague principle is fine. But predicting the future becomes difficult. One needs luck or spiritual strength.

33.4 Probability Analysis[93]

The point made above can be expressed mathematically. Let us say that event A denotes the occurrence (satisfying) of an astrological combination. Let us say that event B denotes the occurrence of an event. Let us say that we want to correlate and link A with B. For example, event A can be "Venus transits in a trine from the 7th house" and event B can be "the native gets married".

Now the conditional probability P(A|B) denotes the probability (or chance) that A occurs, given that B occurred, *i.e.* the chance that the combination is satisfied given that one gets married.

And P(B|A) denotes the probability (or chance) that B occurs, given that A occurred, *i.e.* the chance that one gets married given the combination is satisfied.

The two are different. When making predictions in real life, we are concerned with P(B|A). However, when explaining a known event in a book, we are concerned with P(A|B). If A is a large composite of many small conditions joined by "or" (*e.g.* Venus trnasits in a trine from the 7th house or Jupiter aspects UL in transit or dasa of UL lord runs or dasa of 7th lord runs), we maximize P(A|B). In other words, A is satisfied in most charts when B (marriage) occurs. So we think that A is an excellent principle with a good correlation with event B. However, making A very large makes P(B|A) very low and we can't predict B just because A occurred.

So we should stop unduly worrying about P(A|B) and we should worry more about P(B|A). High P(A|B) helps us in giving nice examples in books. It doesn't help us in predictions. We should not make our principles vague combinations of many components (*e.g.* if combinations x or y or z or w or v or u is satisfied, then event B occurs). We should always identify the strongest candidate to give an event. If an event is given by one of the six or seven weak candidates, we should reject the logic and search for an alternative technique in which the event is given by the best candidate. Only with an uncompromising rational approach and dedicated research into the teachings of great sages can we ever appreciate the subject of astrology in its fullest glory.

93 Some knowledge of the probability theory will be assumed in this discussion. Readers can refer to standard high school/college mathematics textbooks.

33.5 Statistical Research

When we come across an astrological principle, we can evaluate its worth using statistical research. We can take as many examples as we can and find out in what percentage of examples the principle is satisfied. Sometimes the result attributed to an astrological combination may be vague and subjective. But sometimes, we have clearly defined events as results and we can use statistical research in such cases.

Example 136: Suppose we want to evaluate the principle: "one gets married when the dasa *and* the antardasa as per Navamsa Narayana dasa belong to one of the four – lagna, upapada, 3rd from upapada and 8th from upapada". It is clearly defined. We can take 200 charts of married people and find the dasa and the antardasa running at the time of marriage. We can find the number of charts in which both dasa and antardasa belong to the 4 signs mentioned. Suppose the number of such charts is 90. So the success rate of the principle is 90x100/200 = 45%.

This means that the predictions made just using this principle will not have 100% success. However, the question is — is 45% good enough for this principle or not?

Assuming that there is really no correlation between getting married and this combination, we can find the expected success rate. If the real success rate is considerably higher, it means that there is a correlation. It will become clearer after we make some calculations.

Suppose there is no correlation between the above combination and getting married. Then let us find the probability of the dasa and the antardasa being one of the four signs on a random date. We have 4 signs. To maximize this probability (*i.e.* go to the worst case), let us say that lagna is not in the same sign as UL or the 3rd/8th from UL. So we have 4 signs out of 12. The probability that the dasa on any day belongs to these 4 signs is 4/12=1/3. Similarly, the probability that the antardasa on any day belongs to these 4 signs is 4/12=1/3. These two events are independent and the probability that the dasa *and* the antardasa on any day belong to these 4 signs is (1/3)x(1/3) = 1/9. Expressed as a percentage, this is 11%.

What this means is — if we find the dasa and the antardasa on any day, *both* belong to lagna or the 1st, 3rd or 8th from UL in only 11% cases on average. However, if the dasa and the antardasa on the day of marriage belong to these 4 signs in 45% cases, it is 4 times the expected success rate. That clearly shows that there is a link between the combination and marriage. This shows a statistically significant correlation.

Analysis as above does not directly help us in making predictions, but it helps us in validating atleast a part of astrology as a probabilistic science.

Astrology researchers who have the resources and skills should intelligently formulate well-defined principles, test them statistically and find the success rate and compare it with the expected success rate as above. Instead of lamenting the rejection of astrology by the scientific community, we should engage in this exercise and convince ourselves first.

This author is confident that exercises like this will establish parts of Vedic astrology as a science in the coming decades. Such statistical studies were conducted by some scientists and western astrologers in the past, but those people did not use the right factors. They did not have a proper grounding in serious Vedic astrology. Divisions, houses, arudhas, argalas, multiple dasas etc will enable us to conduct more meaningful and fruitive statistical research. Fuzzy logic theory will also be helpful.

Exercise 52: Suppose we evaluate the principle: "Chara dasa of a rasi occupied or aspected by the 3rd house or a rasi occupied or aspected by the 3rd lord or a rasi occupied or aspected by BK results in the birth of a brother". Suppose it is correct in 75% charts we examine. Evaluate the worth of this principle.

[HINT: If events A, B and C are independent, P(A or B or C) = P(A) + P(B) + P(C) – P(A).P(B) – P(B).P(C) – P(C).P(A) + P(A).P(B).P(C)]

33.6 Why Astrology Works

While we discuss rational thinking, we may as well address this most asked question: "Why does astrology work? How can planets have an impact on us? Isn't it irrational to think they do?"

Unfortunately we don't know exactly why planets influence us. We may not find that out in near future. Nevertheless, the subject of astrology becomes valid and justified if we prove some correlations statistically. Even if we cannot explain why planets influence us, we can still study the correlations between planetary motion and events in our lives. While it will be nice to be able to answer the fundamental question raised above, it is not necessary for astrology to be accepted as a statistical science. Some pseudorational people argue that astrology cannot be a science as long as we cannot explain why planets influence us. But that is not logical.

Sometimes we cannot explain new observations on the basis of old models and we have to come up with new theories and postulates. We may not be able to explain the influence of planets on us on the basis of the scientific model of the universe we have today. But that does not trivialize the statistical study of the correlations between planetary combinations and events in the lives of individuals.

33.7 Conclusion

Many astrologers lament the fact astrology is not accepted as a science. But they do not realize that a lot needs to be done before astrology is accepted as a science. A few common problems are discussed in this chapter. It is this author's hope that atleast some readers are motivated to evaluate astrology using the tools given by modern science. Spirituality, respect for Sages and scientific temper can co-exist.

33.8 Answers to Eexrcises

Exercise 52:

Let event A be: "dasa rasi is occupied or aspected by 3rd house". Let event B be: "dasa rasi is occupied or aspected by 3rd lord". Let event C be: "dasa rasi is occupied or aspected by BK". A rasi is aspected by 3 rasis (by rasi aspect). So P(A), P(B) and P(C) are all equal to 4/12=1/3 here.

So the combined probability is (1/3)+(1/3)+(1/3)–(1/9)–(1/9)–(1/9)+(1/27) = 19/27 or 70%. Though 75% is higher than 70%, it is not considerably higher. So there isn't any statistically significant correlation.

[Basically, combinations that are satisfied in 70% cases on average are poor candidates for our studies. Even if the combination is satisfied in 90% of the cases when the event occurred, we cannot correlate the combination with the event with confidence. On the other hand, if a combination is satisfied only in 5% cases on average, we can suggest a good correlation even if the combination is satisfied in 25% cases when the event occurred. Because 25 is 5 times 5, there is a strong correlation between the combination and the event in that case.]

34. Remedial Measures

34.1 Introduction

After stressing the importance of rational thinking in astrological analysis, let us come to an important topic that has no rational explanation. **Those who have *no* belief in Vedic remedies may skip this chapter**.

An expert astrologer may be able to predict bad times and setbacks successfully. But what good is it for, if something cannot be done to avert the setbacks and bad times? A doctor not only identifies the disease one is suffering from, but prescribes drugs to cure it. Can we do the same thing in astrology?

In this chapter, we will take a look at remedial measures. Remedial measures are the measures that are taken to remedy the unfortunate situations that a native is going through or is expected to go through.

The pattern to be followed by one's life is decided at the time of one's birth by the of planetary position then, which is in turn decided by the *karma* (actions) accumulated in past lives. However, it only decides the basic 'pattern' and not all the minute details. Though the basic pattern cannot be easily altered, the exact details can be altered by exercising free will. For example, one may be destined to have a vehicular accident on a particular day, but it can be a minor accident or a major one. Actions taken by one's free will have a role, along with the accumulated actions (karma) of past lives, in deciding the exact details. Remedial measures are the measures we take in order to manipulate the exact details to be relatively favorable to us.

34.1.1 *Commonsense Remedies*

When we anticipate good happenings, we can afford to take a few risks. On the other hand, we can take extra precautions when we anticipate bad happenings. If an accident is possible in a period, we can drive very carefully or even avoid travel if possible. If quarrels with authorities are possible in a period, one can be extra careful and consciously try to restrain oneself.

In this manner, we can take commonsense precautions to avert, or to reduce the impact of, the bad events anticipated.

34.1.2 *Pacifying Planets*

In Hinduism, we can remedy a bad result by the pacification of planets. There are 4 ways to make planets happy:

(1) *Wearing a gemstone*: This works only for planets that are favorable in one's horoscope. We can wear the gemstones of such planets to protect us.

(2) *Good deeds*: By committing good deeds, we can pacify planets.

(3) *Planetary Propitiation*: By reciting the mantras and stotras of planets, we can pacify them. Mantra is a combination of sounds with a special power to produce beneficial spiritual waves within us. Stotras are hymns in praise of planets.

(4) *Propitiation of Deities*: By propitiating various deities, we can pacify various planets.

34.2 Gemstones

One can wear the gemstones of favorable planets to get the blessings of those planets and tide over troubles. Look at the functional benefics in one's rasi chart and prescribe their gemstones. If a planet's dasa is running or if a planet is taking part in a favorable yoga, we may choose that planet. Wearing the gemstone of a planet speeds up the fructification of the good results promised in a chart by that planet.

If one wants good results in a particular area of life, we may strengthen favorable planets in the relevant divisional chart. For example, suppose someone wants improvement in career. We can prescribe the gemstone of a yogakaraka in D-10 then. If a functional benefic is badly placed or weak, its gemstone can still be used. For example, if one has lagna in Cp, Venus is a yogakaraka. Suppose Venus is in the 8th house (Le). Then he may not give good results in his dasa despite being a yogakaraka. In such a case, wearing diamond (gemstone of Venus) makes Venus powerful enough to give good results. On the other hand, gemstones of functional malefics in a chart should be avoided as far as possible. In addition, the gemstones of marakas should be avoided when one is running maraka dasas. A list of the gemstones and metals of various planets are given in Table 77. A ring made of the suggested metal with the suggested gemstone can be used for strengthening the planet.

Table 77: Gemstones of planets

Planet	Gemstone	Metal
Sun	Ruby	Gold
Moon	White pearl	Gold
Mars	Red coral	Copper
Mercury	Emerald	Silver/Platinum

Planet	Gemstone	Metal
Jupiter	Yellow sapphire	Gold
Venus	Diamond	Silver/Plantinum
Saturn	Blué sapphire	Iron (or silver)
Rahu	Hessonite (gomedh)	Silver
Ketu	Cat's eye	Silver

The ring must be worn for the first time on the weekday of the planet. The planetary strength should be good at that time. The planet ruling the gemstone should be strong at that time.

We can combine two gemstones and wear them, if the corresponding planets are friends and functional benefics. This is particularly recommended when the two planets form a yoga. Suppose someone has lagna in Virgo. If 10th lord Mercury and 9th lord Venus are together, they form dharma-karmadhipati yoga. A ring consisting of emerald and diamond may be advised. Similarly, if Sun and Moon conjoin in the chart of a person with Aries lagna, they form a raja yoga and a ring with ruby and pearl may be recommended.

Traditionally, astrologers assign the index finger to Jupiter, middle finger to Saturn, ring finger to Sun and little finger to Mercury. Traditionally, gemstones of Mercury and Venus are worn on the little finger; gemstone of Saturn is worn on the middle finger and so on. However, some astrologers suggest that the ring finger, middle finger, little finger and index finger show the four purushaarthas – dharma, artha, kama and moksha (respectively). They suggest wearing a ring on the finger representing the purushaartha of interest. One desiring marriage may wear the ring of his 7th lord on the little finger. One desiring good results in career may wear the ring of a yogakaraka in his D-10 on the middle finger and so on. Index finger represents moksha and it is usually left ringless.

34.3 Good Deeds

One can pacify planets by good deeds. Good deeds of this life can compensate for the sins of past lives. One can commit a good deed in an area ruled by a planet to please it. Some examples are listed below:

To please Sun, one may go to a temple or donate money to a temple or help in the administration of a temple. To please Moon, one may donate money to a music institute or help a fair lady. To please Mars, one may engage in physical exercise or donate money to a school gym. To please Mercury, one may donate money to an organization of scholars or get blessings from a scholar. To please Jupiter, one may respect and donate money to a learned Brahmin or a priest. Or one may donate cows to a priest. To please Venus, one may read poetry or help a poet. To please Saturn, one may perform some physical labor or help some people who live on manual labor. To please Rahu, one may donate some money to a research organization or go on a pilgrimage. To please Ketu, one may do meditation.

One can also give away (as charity) the grains ruled by different planets, to propitiate them. Sun rules wheat, Moon rules rice, Mars rules toor daal (a dark yellow lentil), Mercury rules moong daal (smaller yellow lentils of a lighter shade – they have a dark green skin), Jupiter rules chick peas, Venus rules a whitish grain, Saturn rules sesame seeds and Rahu rules black gram daal (white lentils with a black skin). For example, one can please Jupiter by giving away a big bowl of chick peas on a Thursday morning.

Fasting is also a popular remedial measure. By punishing ourselves by denying the basic necessity of food, we reduce other punishments. Fasting on the weekday ruled by upapada lord in rasi chart, for example, mitigates troubles in one's marriage. Fasting on the weekday ruled by rajyapada lord may mitigate troubles in career.

34.4 Propitiation of Planets

We can propitiate planets by reciting mantras and stotras. Mantra is a combination of sounds with a special power to produce beneficial spiritual waves within us.

A mantra should be recited with an accurate pronunciation and intonation. Some mantras do not have any intonation, but the pronunciation of sounds must be perfect. Some saattwik mantras are self-correcting, in the sense that one reading it will eventually be forced to learn the correct pronunciation and intonation. Some other mantras can produce negative effects with improper recitation. So one should be careful with mantras.

These days, people misuse the term "mantra" and refer to many stotras as mantras. Stotras are hymns in praise of planets and God. There is no correct intonation to read a stotra and devotion is important when reciting a stotra. Recitation of a stotra gives results very slowly. Interested readers can read the 108 names of various planets everyday. As lagna is the most important house in a chart and lagna lord shows the vitality of the chart, one may worship the planet owning lagna in the divisional chart representing the area of life that one wants to improve. For example, if one wants spiritual progress, lagna lord in D-20 should be worshipped. If one wants pleasures and comforts, lagna lord in D-16 should be worshipped.

There are different mantras for propitiating planets. In addition, there are kavachas, stotras and 108 names of all planets.

One popular mantra of each planet is listed below. One should read the stanza given first a few times and then repeat the basic mantra thousands of times. The recommended repitition count is also listed. The weekday ruled by a planet is ideal for repeating its mantra.

Note: The stanzas and mantras are being given *only in Devanagari script used* by Sanskrit and Hindi languages. Those who cannot read this script should consult a competent astrologer or a Hindu priest to learn these stanzas and mantras. This may cause an inconvenience to non-Indian readers of this book, but the purpose is to discourage mis-pronunciation. Giving an approximate transliteration in the Roman script can only encourage mistakes.

34.4.1 *Sun*

जपाकुसुमसकाशम् काश्यपेयम् महाद्युतिम्।
तमोरिम् सर्वपापघ्नम् प्रणतोऽस्मि दिवाकरम्।।
ॐ ह्रीं ह्रीं सूर्याय नमः (6,000 times)

34.4.2 *Moon*

दधिशंखतुषाराभम् क्षीरोदार्णवसंभवम्।
नमामि शशिनम् सोमम् शंभोर्मकुटभूषणम्।।
ॐ क्लीं सोमाय नमः (10,000 times)

34.4.3 *Mars*

धरणीगर्भसंभूतम् विद्युत्कांतिसमप्रभम्।
कुमारम् शक्तिहस्तम् तम् मंगलम् प्रणमाम्यहम्।।
ॐ हूं श्रीं मंगलाय नमः (7,000 times)

34.4.4 *Mercury*

प्रियंगुकलिकाश्यामम् रुपेणाप्रतिमम् बुधम्।
सौम्यम् सौम्यगुणोपेतम् तम् बुधम् प्रणामाम्यहम्।।
ॐ ऐं स्त्रीं बुधाय नमः (7,000 times)

34.4.5 Jupiter

प्रियंगुकलिकाश्यामम् रुपेणाप्रतिमम् बुधम्।
सौम्यम् सौम्यगुणोपेतम् तम् बुधम् प्रणामाम्यहम्।।
ॐ ऐं स्त्रीं बुधाय नमः (17,000 times)

34.4.4 Mercury

देवानाम् च ऋषीणाम् च गुरुम् कांचनसन्निभम्।
बुद्धिभूतम् त्रिलोकेशम्तम् नमामि बृहस्पतिम्।।
ॐ क्लीं बृहस्पतये नमः नमः (16,000 times)

34.4.4 Venus

हिमकुंदमृणाळाभम् दैत्यानाम् परमम् गुरुम्।
सर्वशास्त्रप्रवक्तारम् भार्गवम् प्रणमाम्यहम।।

ॐ ह्रीं श्रीं शुक्राय नमः (20,000 times)

34.4.7 *Saturn*

नीलांजनसमाभासम् रविपुत्रम् यमाग्रजम्।
छायामार्तांडसंभूतम् तम् नमामि शनैश्चरम्।।

ॐ ह्रीं श्रीं शनैश्चराय नमः (19,000 times)

34.4.8 *Rahu*

अर्धकायम् हमावीर्यम् चन्द्रादित्यविमर्दनम्।
हिंहिकागर्भसंभूतम् तम् राहुम् प्रणमाभ्यहम्।।

ॐ ऐं ह्रीं राहवे नमः (18,000 times)

34.4.9 *Ketu*

पलाशपुष्पसंकाशम् तारकाग्रहमस्तकम्।
रौद्रम् रौद्रात्मकम् घोरम् तम् केतुम् प्रणमाम्यहम्।।

ॐ ऐं क्लीं केतवे नमः (7,000 times)

There are many other mantras and one can refer to other books for the details. When reading a stotra, devotion is of utmost importance. When reading a mantra, devotion as well as the correct pronunciation are important.

34.5 Propitiation of Deities

Instead of propitiating planets directly, we can propitiate the ruling deities. Propitiating the deity corresponding to lagna lord in a particular divisional chart brings excellent results in the area of life shown by divisional chart. Propitiation of the deity corresponding to the strongest planet occupying or owning or aspecting the 12th house from AK in D-9 takes one's soul closer to liberation.

Table 78: Planets and deities

Planet	Deity
Sun	Shiva, Rama
Moon	Gauri, Lalita, Saraswati, Krishna
Mars	Hanuman, Rudra, Kartikeya (Subrahmanya), Narasimha
Mercury	Vishnu, Narayana, Buddha
Jupiter	Hayagreeva, Vishnu, Parameswara, Dattatreya, Any gurū
Venus	Lakshmi, Parvati
Saturn	Vishnu, Brahma
Rahu	Durga, Narasimha
Ketu	Ganesa

A list of commonly suggested deities for each planet is given in Table 78. "Prasna marga" gives some additional deities. Elders also intuitively prescribe deities based on the particular planetary combination in a chart. For example, Mercury and Saturn usually denote a Vaishnava deity. Sun denotes a Shaiva deity. Moon and Venus denote a goddess. Mars denotes a fiery form. Rahu denotes an aggressive deity. Based on the planetary combinations in a chart, we can choose the right deity.

For example, let us say we need to please Rahu in a chart. Let us say Mars and Rahu are in Ge, with Saturn and Mercury aspecting them. Rahu can denote Durga, but Saturnine and Mercurian influence suggests a Vaishnava deity. Martian influence on Rahu shows an angry deity. So "Ugra Narasimha", an angry form of Vishnu, may be worshipped to please Rahu. Rahu in Cancer may denote Durga in another chart. In another example, Mars may be in a fiery rasi in all vargas and Mercury may join him and it may show "Jwala Narasimha". Mars with Rahu (serpent) may show Subrahmanya (Kartikeya) in another chart. Mars with Saturnine influence may show Hanuman, as Saturn shows a Vaishnava deity and he has humility and the spirit of a servant.

The guidelines given in books are merely guidelines. The exact application depends on an astrologer's knowledge of mythology and classics and familiarity with the natures of various deities. By propitiating a deity who closely represents the spirit of a planet in a particular chart, one can please the planet more effectively.

34.6 Conclusion

This book is only an introductory textbook of integrated Vedic astrology. While an effort is made to cover a variety of topics, no topic has been covered exhaustively. The coverage of the topics in the current part ("Special Topics") is particularly brief. The purpose of this part is just to make the readers familiar with some practical aspects of Vedic astrology. Readers should refer to other books for more details on these topics. Readers may take advantage of *Vedic Remedies in Astrolog* by Pt. Sanjay Rath.

35. Mundane Astrology

35.1 Introduction

In this book, we have so far concentrated on predicting the fortune of individual human beings based on their birthcharts. We sometimes have to predict the collective fortune of large groups of people. An example is the fortune of a nation. To predict the fortune of a nation, we can use the birthchart of the leader of the nation, the swearing-in chart of the leader and the birthchart of the nation, if available. When these are not available, we can use lunar and solar new year charts and new month charts. Solar charts are good at showing some matters and lunar charts are good at showing some other matters. There are also some techniques based on transits. We can map different nations to different rasis and constellations and take transits with respect to those rasis and constellations. This approach needs a lot of further research and it is beyond the scope of this textbook.

Study of the collective fortune of groups of people using planetary charts is called "mundane astrology" and birthcharts of nations, swearing-in charts, lunar charts, solar charts and other charts used in mundane astrology are known as "mundane charts".

35.2 Re-interpreted Significations

In mundane charts, we can still use arudha padas, divisional charts etc, but we have to reinterpret the significations of various charts, houses and arudha padas judiciously. For example, D-9 may show relations with other nations and the role played in international polity. D-30 may show internal disturbances and violence. D-11 may show wars and terrorist activities. D-8 may show unexpected and sudden external troubles like natural calamities. D-10 may show political activity. D-24 may show universities, science, technology, arts, research and activities of intelligentsia. Arudha lagna may show how a nation is perceived in the world. A3 may shows its weapons. A6 may shows its enemies. A7 may show its allies. Significations of various houses are given below:

First house: General state of affairs in the nation, public health, cabinet.

Second house: State revenue, wealth, imports, commerce, allies, aristocracy.

Third house: Telecommunications, transportation, journalism, media.

Fourth house: Educational institutions, students, real estate, general feeling of well-being, trade, agriculture.

Fifth house: Children, new births, crime, parks, mentality of leaders.

Sixth house: State loans, debt, diseases, armed forces, territorial attacks.

Seventh house: Health of women, immorality, infant mortality, war, relations with other nations.

Eighth house: Death rate, state treasury, unexpected troubles, instability.

Ninth house: Temples, righteousness, judiciary, fortune.

Tenth house: The ruler, politics, parliament, foreign trade, exports, revolution and political instability.

Eleventh house: Gains from other nations, gains in trade, friendship.

Twelfth house: Secret enemies, plots, secret crime, hospitals, wars, losses.

35.3 Using Birthcharts

When a new leader takes command of a nation, it signals a new beginning for the nation and hence the chart cast for the moment of swearing-in is important. However, the beginning of a new *order* is more important than the beginning of a new *command*. When a nation re-organizes itself based on new philosophies and thought, it signals the beginning of a new order. Chart cast for the beginning of a new order is more important than a swearing-in chart.

For example, the nation of India existed for more than 5,000 years. However, it took a new identity when it won independence on 15th August 1947. The independence chart of India shows the beginning of a new order in India. Though several princely states joined India after her independence, there was no major change in the identity of India. When India formed its constitution and declared itself a Sovereign Replublic on 26th January 1950, its identity was only *consolidated* and not *changed*. So the independence chart (15th August 1947, midnight, Delhi) is the birthchart of India and it is the most important one for predicting India's fortune.

We can use Vimsottari dasa as well as Narayana dasa with a nation's birthchart. An example of the interpretation of Narayana dasa for a nation was given in Example 69. Another technique prominently used with the birthcharts of nations is Tajaka. We can cast Tajaka annual charts to predict the fortune of a nation in a year and use it with Sudarsana Chakra dasa[94].

Example 137: Let us consider India's independence chart and Tajaka annual chart of 1997-98 (see Chart 80). India surprised the international community by conducting a series of nuclear tests in May 1998. Let us look at D-24 (the chart of technology and research) and find Tajaka annual chart and Sudarsana Chakra dasa.

In natal D-24, lagna in Cp is stronger than Moon and Sun. In 1997, India finished 50 years and started the 51st year. We get 3 by subtracting multiples of 12 from 51. So Sudarsana Chakra dasa of the 3rd house runs in the year. So dasa belongs to Pi[95]. We should cast the annual chart when the 51st year starts and judge the chart w.r.t. Pi.

The most prominent placement is that Sun, Rahu and Ketu are in the 3rd house from Pi. This makes the 3rd house very strong and activities related to aggressive wepon development make sense. Situation of exalted Mars in the 11th house with two other planets is also favorable for technical growth. However, the presence of debilitated Venus in the 7th house from Pi may have resulted in bad relations with other nations in technical matters. After the nuclear tests, a lot of curbs were imposed by the western world on Indian institutions of science and technology.

35.4 Lunar charts

When Sun and Moon have an exact conjunction in every sign, it starts a new lunar month. When Sun and Moon conjoin in Pisces, it starts a new lunar year. We can cast a chart at the exact moment of Sun-Moon conjunction at the capital of a country and use it to predict the fortune of the nation in the upcoming month or year. We can use rasi chart as well as divisional charts. For timing events, we can compress Vimsottari dasa from 120 years

---

94 Sudarsana Chakra dasa and Tajaka annual charts are treated this book as two closely linked topics. When we say that Tajaka annual charts should be used, we automatically mean that Sudarsana Chakra dasa should be used.

95 We can also say that muntha is in Pi in D-24.

Chart 80

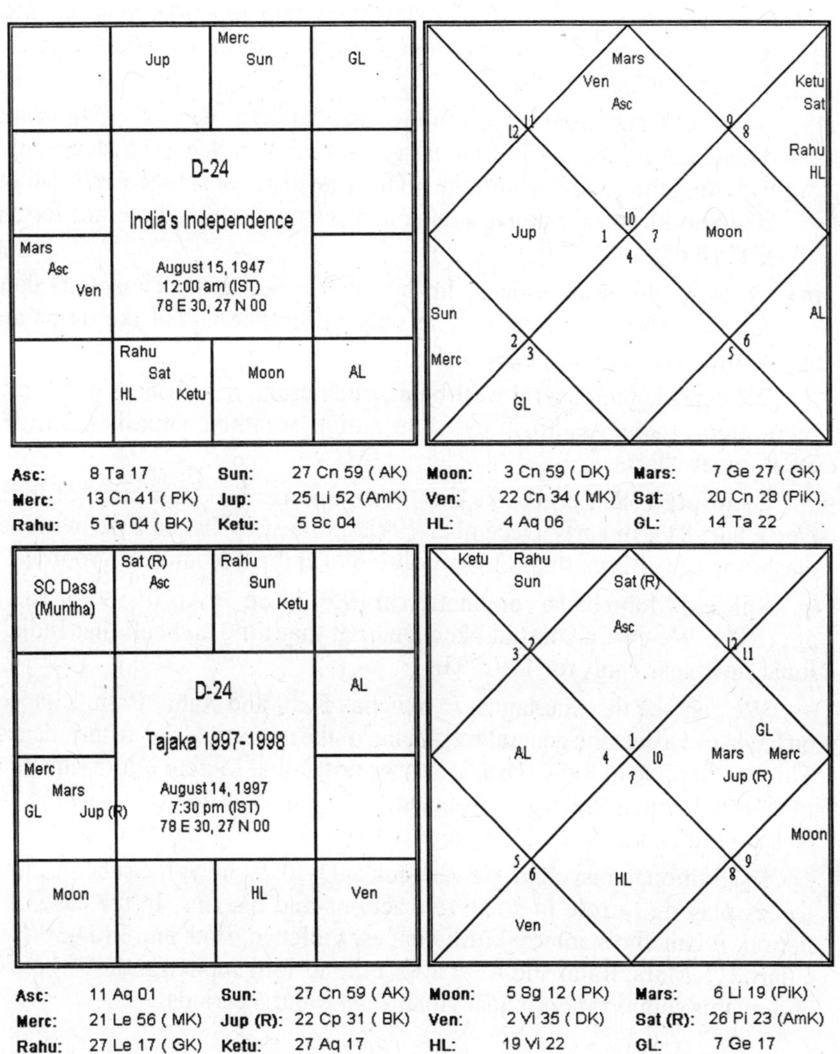

to a lunar month or a lunar year. To compress Vimsottari dasa, follow this procedure:

(1) Find the constellation occupied by Moon and find its lord. His dasa comes first.

(2) If we are compressing from 120 years to 360 days (approximately a lunar year), each year is compressed to 3 days. So Sun dasa becomes

18 days, Moon dasa becomes 30 days and so on. If we are compressing from 120 years to 30 days (approximately a lunar month), 1 year becomes 0.25 days. So Sun dasa becomes 1.5 days, Moon dasa becomes 2.5 days and so on.

(3) We do *not* take the fraction of the constellation traversed by Moon and decide the remainder in first dasa based on that. We get better results by letting the complete duration of the first dasa come together. If Moon is in Sun's constellation in a lunar new year chart, Sun dasa runs for the first 18 days.

(4) Go through the nine dasas in the same order as in Vimsottari dasa computed for natal charts. The only difference is that the dasas are compressed as mentioned above.

We can see the general well-being of a nation, restlessness of people, revolutions, trade, wealth, mood of the nation, weather, natural calamiities etc in lunar charts.

Example 138: Let us take the 1992-93 lunar new year chart of India (see Chart 81). In early December 1992, India was shaken by communal clashes in the aftermath of the demolition of Babri Mosque in Ayodhya[96].

Sun and Moon had a conjunction at 19 Pi 57 on 3rd April 1992 at 10:32 am (IST). We cast a chart at New Delhi at that time and call that India's lunar new year chart for 1992-93.

We can see that the lagna-7th axis has Ketu and Rahu. Rahu's aspect on lagna can affect the general well-being of the nation and create turbulence. This can happen in Rahu dasa. It may be noted that Mercury dasa runs first in this chart and Rahu dasa runs in early December. With Rahu owning the 9th house, it had to do with religious places.

In addition to rasi chart, we can look at D-30. It shows the subconscious forces playing a role in a native's actions and his sins. In the case of a nation, it can show internal turbulences, violence, riots *etc*. In D-30 (see Chart 81), Mars, Rahu and Ketu afflict the 9th lord Jupiter in the 9th house. Again, this supports communal violence in Rahu's periods.

---

96 Ayodhya is the birthplace of Lord Rama. According to a group of Indian scholars, Babri mosque was originally a temple of Lord Rama in the sacred city and Muslim invader Babar converted it to a mosque a few centuries ago. A political party wanted a Rama temple there. Though the mosque was unused for a long time, its demolition was unacceptable to Muslim leaders. Against court orders, activists of that party demolished the mosque in early December 1992 and it led to communal violence in different parts of India.

Chart 81

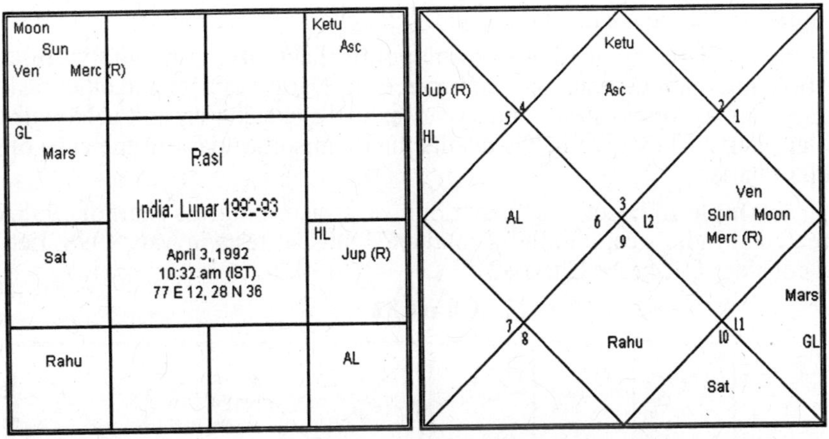

Moon Sun Ven Merc (R)			Ketu Asc
GL Mars	Rasi India: Lunar 1992-93		
Sat	April 3, 1992 10:32 am (IST) 77 E 12, 28 N 36		HL Jup (R)
Rahu			AL

Ketu
Asc
Jup (R)
HL
AL
Ven
Sun Moon
Merc (R)
Mars
GL
Rahu
Sat

Asc:	4 Ge 35	**Sun:**	19 Pi 56 (BK)	**Moon:**	19 Pi 57 (AmK)	**Mars:**	11 Aq 00 (PK)
Merc (R):	6 Pi 38 (GK)	**Jup (R):**	12 Le 01 (PiK)	**Ven:**	1 Pi 12 (DK)	**Sat:**	22 Cp 21 (AK)
Rahu:	11 Sg 07 (MK)	**Ketu:**	11 Ge 07	**HL:**	0 Le 35	**GL:**	16 Aq 50

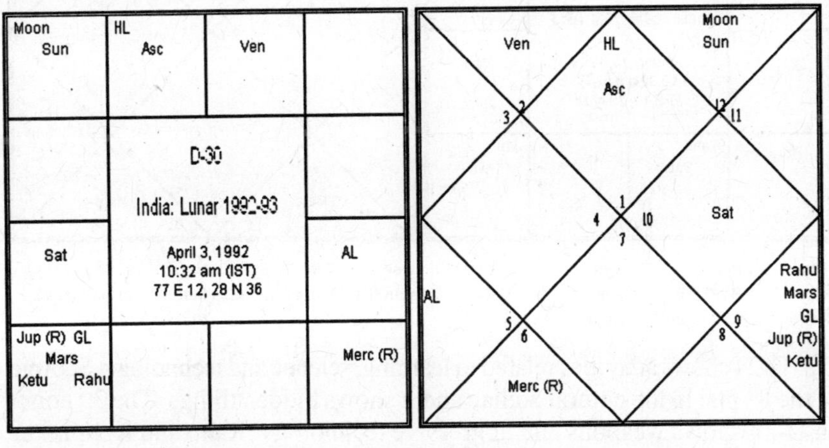

Moon Sun	HL Asc	Ven	
	D-30 India: Lunar 1992-93		
Sat	April 3, 1992 10:32 am (IST) 77 E 12, 28 N 36		AL
Jup (R) GL Mars Ketu Rahu			Merc (R)

Ven
HL
Asc
Moon
Sun
Sat
AL
Rahu
Mars
GL
Jup (R)
Ketu
Merc (R)

35.5 Solar charts

When Sun enters a rasi, it starts a new solar month. We can cast a chart for that moment and analyze the fortune of a nation during the solar month. In particular, charts cast when Sun enters the movable signs (Ar, Cn, Li and Cp) are important and they are used by some astrologers to predict a nation's fortune during a 3-month period.

We can cast the solar new year chart when Sun enters Aries, the first sign of the zodiac. This solar new year is celebrated in some parts of India. A chart cast at a nation's capital when Sun enters Aries can be used for predicting the nation's fortune for one year.

However, some astrologers prefer to use the chart when Sun enters Cp for predicting the fortune for a year. They consider the solar ingress into Capricorn[97] to be the most important solar chart in Kali Yuga.

Solar charts are good at showing political activity, wars, vitality of a nation, international relations, commerce etc. Narayana dasa and other rasi dasas can be compressed to one year (as in Tajaka charts) and used with solar charts. They give better results than Vimsottari dasa in the case of solar charts.

Example 139: Let us consider Sun's Capricorn ingress chart of 1998, erected at India's capital. India conducted nuclear tests in May 1998. Let us consider D-24 (see Chart 82).

Chart 82

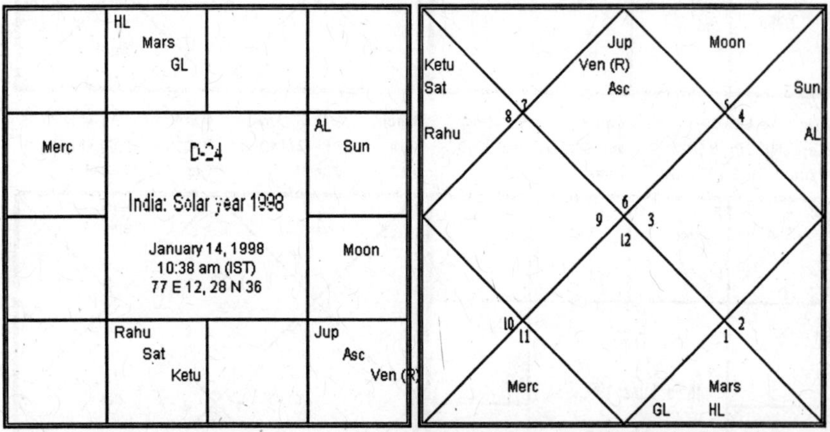

	HL Mars GL		
Merc	D-24		AL Sun
	India: Solar year 1998 January 14, 1998 10:38 am (IST) 77 E 12, 28 N 36		Moon
	Rahu Sat Ketu		Jup Asc Ven (R)

Jup Ven (R) Asc
Moon
Ketu Sat Rahu
Sun AL
8 7 5 4 6 9 3 12
10 11 1 2
Merc
GL Mars HL

Asc:	2 Pi 53	**Sun:**	0 Cp 00 (DK)	**Moon:**	17 Cn 27 (BK)	**Mars:**	27 Cp 21 (AK)
Merc:	8 Sg 07 (PiK)	**Jup:**	1 Aq 16 (GK)	**Ven (R):**	3 Cp 40 (PK)	**Sat:**	20 Pi 27 (AmK)
Rahu:	19 Le 11 (MK)	**Ketu:**	19 Aq 11	**HL:**	10 Ar 49	**GL:**	12 Vi 16

D-24 shows activities related to learning, science and technology. Scorpio is the 8th rasi in the natural zodiac and it shows hidden things. The 3rd house in D-24 shows weapons and aggressive technology. Rahu and Ketu in the 3rd house in Scorpio in D-24 of the solar new year chart suggest hidden activities related to aggressive weapon development technology. Lagna lord Mercury is in the 6th house and he shows enmity and poor relations with other nations in the matters of knowledge. This along with the debilitation of Venus can explain India's isolation in the scientific world following the nuclear tests.

---

97 This is celebrated in south India as "Makara Sankraanthi" or "Makara Sankramanam" or "Pongal".

35.6 Swearing-in Charts

We can cast a chart when a new leader (the chief of the executive wing of government) is sworn-in in a nation. That chart also has an impact on the nature of results experienced by the nation during the leader's tenure. We can find Narayana dasa of rasi chart and divisional charts of the swearing-in ceremony. We have to compress Narayana dasa from 120 years to the expected maximum length of the tenure.

Example 140: Let us take Indian Prime Minister Sri A.B. Vajpayee's swearing-in ceremony of March 19, 1998. Let us study D-9 and look at the relations with other nations (Chart 83).

Chart 83

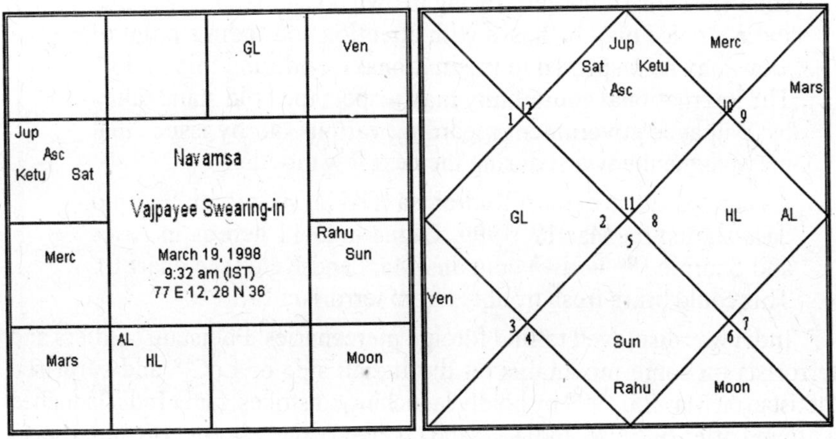

		GL	Ven
Jup Asc Ketu Sat	Navamsa Vajpayee Swearing-in March 19, 1998 9:32 am (IST) 77 E 12, 28 N 36		
Merc			Rahu Sun
Mars	AL HL		Moon

Jup Sat Ketu Asc 12 · Merc Mars 10 9 · 1 · 11 2 8 5 · GL · HL AL · Ven · 3 4 Sun Rahu · 7 6 Moon

Asc:	4 Ta 01	**Sun:**	4 Pi 31 (DK)	**Moon:**	9 Sc 46 (GK)	**Mars:**	17 Pi 20 (MK)
Merc:	22 Pi 53 (AmK)	**Jup:**	16 Aq 23 (PiK)	**Ven:**	18 Cp 21 (BK)	**Sat:**	26 Pi 21 (AK)
Rahu:	15 Le 48 (PK)	**Ketu:**	15 Aq 48	**HL:**	6 Ge 27	**GL:**	24 Li 33

An Indian Prime Minister's tenure can be a maximum of 5 years. If we compress 120 years of Narayana dasa to 5 years = 60 months, *i.e.* compress each year to half a month, we get dasas as given below:

Aq (06 years):	Mar 1998 -	Jun 1998
Cn (10 years):	Jun 1998 -	Nov 1998
Sg (02 years):	Nov 1998 -	Dec 1998
Ta (01 years):	Dec 1998 -	Jan 1999
Li (08 years):	Jan 1999 -	May 1999
Pi (01 years):	May 1999 -	May 1999
Le (12 years):	May 1999 -	Nov 1999

With Cn being the 6th house, its dasa brought bad relations with other nations. India was isolated in the international community after the nuclear tests. Li is the 9th house and it shows good diplomacy and excellent relations in navamsa. Its lord Venus is in a trine. So Libra dasa saw Vajpayee promoting peace with a nation shown by Libra – Pakistan – and the Lahore bus trip materialized in Li dasa.

About Le dasa, the following was written by this author in a magazine article[98]:

> "Leo dasa of six months will run from May 19, 1999. Leo has unobstructed argalas from two diplomatic planets – Moon and Venus. Leo is the 7th house and it contains Sun and Rahu. Rahu's presence may indicate unpleasant confrontation with some countries, but Sun is very strong in own house. This means that India's voice may be heard with attention and India's point of view may be respected in international fora during this period. The international community may respect the bold stand taken by Vajpayee government regarding various thorny issues that may plague the world during the next few months.
>
> As per Narayana dasa of Rudramsa (D-11), six-month Scorpio dasa started on Mar 19, 1999. Lagna in D-11 here is in Aries and Scorpio (8th house) contains Mars and Ketu (see chart 6). This could bring fresh troubles from terrorism."

India was dismayed to find foreign mercenaries, Pakistani soldiers and terrorists on some mountains on the Indian side of LoC[99] and surprised Pakistan on May 25, 1999 by boldly launching air strikes. Later India launched a ground offensive also. India's stand received excellent support and respect from the international community. After an emergency visit to US on a US holiday, an embarrassed Pakistani Prime Minister "requested" the intruders to withdraw into Pakistan and India ended the offensive triumphantly.

35.7 Conclusion

When we have the birthdata of a nation, we can use its birthchart. By the birth of a nation, we mean the start of a new order and the recognition of a new national identity. We can cast charts at a nation's capital when a new solar or lunar year or month starts and use them to predict the fortune of a nation during the year or month.

---

98 It was written one month before the Kargil offensive, but there was a delay of 3 months in publishing.

99 Line of Control, that divdes the parts of Kashmir controlled by India and Pakistan

Lunar new year charts are free from errors due to ayanamsa. However, solar new year charts are prone to heavy errors if ayanamsa is erroneous. If ayanamsa has an error of 1 arc-minute, this results in an error of 360 arc-minutes (*i.e.* 6°!) in lagna of the solar new year chart. This is because lagna moves 360 times as fast as Sun. In the time Sun takes to move by an angle of ?, lagna moves by an angle of (360x?). So the divisional charts of solar new year charts will not give consistent results until our ayanamsa is exact. It is not wise to assume that the ayanamsa one uses is perfect and free from any error.

One last word — The purpose of this small chapter is only to *introduce* mundane astrology to readers. Interested readers may refer to the writings on mundane astrology by great authors such as Varahamihira and Dr.B.V.Raman. This chapter should only be a starting point.

36. Muhurta or Electional Astrology

36.1 Introduction

When a person is born, the planetary position at that time decides how his/her life progresses. Similarly, when a new task is freshly started, the planetary position at that time decides how the task progresses. For example, the planetary position at the time one joins in a new job decides how one's new job goes. The planetary position at the time one starts a new company decides the fortune of the company. The planetary position at the time of a wedding decides how the marriage goes.

For this reason, believers choose an auspicious time when starting new ventures. The time when a new task is undertaken is called "muhurta". One can select a good muhurta for a variety of tasks – getting married, joining a new job, swearing-in ceremonies (in the case of political leaders), starting a new company, starting a kid's formal education, giving cooked rice to a baby for the first time, buying a vehicle, buying a house, housewarming, babyshowers etc. The list is endless. In India, old people choose a good muhurta even for getting a haircut or for cutting nails.

The topic of muhurta has a lot of controversies. Different guidelines are given in different classics and different conventions are in vogue in different regions of India. Out of the modern books on muhurta in English language, the one by Dr. B.V. Raman is very good.

36.2 Definition of Muhurta

Asrologers set nice muhurtas for the tasks of their clients, but they don't always verify that their clients know exactly what to do at the time of the muhurta. For example, if we set an auspicious muhurta for someone to join in a new job, what should he do at the time? Should he sign the job offer letter? Or, should he sign the employment contract (if applicable)? Or, should he sit in front of his computer and power it on? Or, should he read a document describing the work he has to do? What exactly should one do at the time of the muhurta set for joining in a new job?

What is the definition of the time of marriage? What is the definition of the time of joining in a new job? What is the definition of entering a new house? All these questions are not clearly answered in classics and we have to draw conclusions intelligently.

Accepting a job offer is like conception. Starting the work is akin to a baby coming out of mother's womb and starting to breathe on its own. Depending on what one does in a job, we can decide what "starting the work" means. It is not enough to sign some papers, but one has to start some work at the time of a muhurta. In the case of a marriage, the purpose of marriage is living together. Mangal sutra worn by a lady symbolizes it in Hindu culture. So the time when the bridegroom ties the knot is the most appropriate. In the case of a Christian marriage, the time when the bride and the bridegroom are pronounced a man and a wife after saying "I do" may be the most appropriate time. In the case of entering a new house (housewarming), the correct time of entering the house is when one starts "living" in the house. One may not start living in a house at the exact moment one enters a house with some suitcases. In the Hindu way of life, only a house where cooking is done is a place of living. So, traditionally, people warm milk on a stove at the time of muhurta. If milk is warmed for making sweet rice for offering Gods as a prasaad, that symbolizes the starting of life in the house. We have to decide intelligently on a case by case basis.

36.3 Basics of Muhurta

Tithi, yoga, karana, weekday and nakshatra form the 5 limbs of "panchaanga"[100]. When deciding a muhurta, we try to choose a good tithi, weekday, yoga, karana, nakshatra and lagna. For each task, there are certain tithis, weekdays, nakshatras and lagnas that are preferred. The nakshatra occupied by Moon at the time of a muhurta should be a good tara with respect to janma nakshatra. In addition, lord of the running hora (hour) should be a favorable planet in the natal chart, especially with respect to the house to which the activity belongs. For example, hora at the time of wedding should belong to a favorable planet in the natal chart with respect to the 7th house and upapada. Hora at the time of moving to a new house should belong to a favorable planet in the natal chart with respect to the 4th house and A4. If a planet owns the 8th house from the 4th house and occupies a badhaka sthana from A4, then it may be disastrous to move into a new house in his hora. Hora is a very important quantum of time.

100 Panchaanga means an almanac that lists auspicious and inauspicious times. It literally means "one with five limbs".

Table 79: Muhurta guidelines

Task	Tithis	Weekdays	Lagnas	Tithis
Construction of a new house	2, 3, 5, 7, 11, 13, 15	Mon, Wed, Thu, Fri	Ta, Ge, Vi, Sg, Aq, Pi (Le, Sc also)	2, 3, 5, 7, 11, 13, 15
Nakshatras: Aswini, Rohini, Mrigasira, Punarvasu, Uttaraphalguni, Hasta, Chitra, Swati, Anuradha, Uttarashadha, Sravanam, Dhanishtha, Satabhisha, Uttarabhadra, Revati				
Entering a new house	2, 3, 5, 7, 10, 11, 13, 15	Mon, Wed, Thu, Fri	Ta, Ge, Le, Vi, Sc, Sg, Aq, Pi	2, 3, 5, 7, 10, 11, 13, 15
Nakshatras: Rohini, Mrigasira, Uttaraphalguni, Chitra, Anuradha, Uttarashadha, Dhanishtha, Satabhisha, Uttarabhadra, Revati				
Naming a child	2, 3, 5, 7, 10, 11, 13	Sun, Mon, Wed, Thu, Sat	Benefic planet owned	2, 3, 5, 7, 10, 11, 13
Nakshatras: Aswini, Rohini, Mrigasira, Punarvasu, Pushyami, Uttaraphalguni, Hasta, Chitra, Swati, Anuradha, Uttarashadha, Sravanam, Dhanishtha, Satabhisha, Uttarabhadra, Revati				
Baby's first eating of rice	2, 3, 5, 7, 10, 13, 15	Sun, Mon, Wed, Thu, Fri	Benefic planet owned	2, 3, 5, 7, 10, 13, 15
Nakshatras: Aswini, Rohini, Mrigasira, Punarvasu, Pushyami, Uttaraphalguni, Hasta, Chitra, Swati, Anuradha, Uttarashadha, Sravanam, Dhanishtha, Satabhisha, Uttarabhadra, Revati				
Teaching alphabet	2, 3, 5, 7, 10, 11, 12	Mon, Wed, Thu, Fri	Ge, Vi, Sg, Pi	2, 3, 5, 7, 10, 11, 12
Nakshatras: Aswini, Punarvasu, Hasta, Chitra, Swati, Anuradha, Sravanam, Revati (Mrigasira, Ardra, Dhanishtha, Satabhisha)				
Sacred thread ceremony	2, 3, 5, 10, 11 (6, 12)	Mon, Wed, Thu, Fri	Benefic planet owned	2, 3, 5, 10, 11 (6, 12)

	Nakshatras: Aswini, Rohini, Mrigasira, Punarvasu, Pushyami, Uttaraphalguni, Hasta, Chitra, Swati, Anuradha, Uttarashadha, Sravanam, Dhanishtha, Satabhisha, Uttarabhadra, Revati			
Wedding	2, 3, 5, 7, 10, 11, 12, 13, 15	Mon, Wed, Thu, Fri	Benefic planet owned	2, 3, 5, 7, 10, 11, 12, 13, 15
	Nakshatras: Rohini, Mrigasira, Makha, Uttaraphalguni, Hasta, Swati, Anuradha, Moola, Uttarashadha, Uttarabhadra, Revati			
Placing new idols in pooja	2, 3, 5, 7, 8, 10, 11, 12, 13	Sun, Mon, Wed, Thu, Fri	Ta, Ge, Le, Vi, Sc, Sg, Aq, Pi	2, 3, 5, 7, 8, 10, 11, 12, 13
	Nakshatras: Aswini, Rohini, Mrigasira, Punarvasu, Pushyami, Uttaraphalguni, Hasta, Chitra, Swati, Anuradha, Uttarashadha, Sravanam, Dhanishtha, Satabhisha, Uttarabhadra, Revati			

A list of the common guidelines is given in Table 79. These are merely guidelines and not final recommendations. The recommendation in the case of a wedding muhurta, for example, is to keep the 7th house empty. However, expert astrologers flout these norms often, with considerable success.

The basic point in keeping the 7th house empty in a wedding muhurta is to avoid afflictions there. On the other hand, if the 7th house is occupied by benefics giving great yogas, how can that cause problems in marriage? Planetary strength is more important than strictly following these thumbrules.

36.4 Planetary Strength

Though a lot of thumbrules are given in literature, an intelligent astrologer gives more importance to the strength of planets in the muhurta chart than those thumbrules. Not only should the rasi chart be strong, but also the concerned divisional chart should be strong. For example, for joining a new job, lagna, 6th house and 10th house should be strong in rasi and D-10 charts. When starting a child's education, 1st, 2nd, 4th and 5th should be strong in rasi and D-24 charts. When buying a new vehicle, 1st and 4th houses (and A4) should be strong in rasi and D-16 charts. When entering a new house, the 1st and 4th from lagna and Venus in D-4 should be strong. When buying some real estate, the 1st and 4th from lagna and Mars in D-4 should be strong.

We can use Vimsottari dasa to time the progress of a task started at a muhurta. If we know the maximum time period for which the task started at a muhurta can last, we can compress Vimsottari dasa to that period. Details of the computation can be found in topic 35.4 in the chapter on "Mundane Astrology". If the task started at a muhurta has no fixed time period of effect, we can take Vimsottari dasa of 120 years.

In addition to planetary strength, we should ensure that the first dasa as per Vimsottari dasa belongs to a favorable planet in the chart. The effect of a muhurta lasts only for a few months or a couple of years and the strength of one's natal chart is more important in the long-run. So the first dasa as per Vimsottari dasa is important. For example, we may select a muhurta with excellent rasi and D-10 charts for joining in a new job and yet bad results may be experienced if the first dasa belongs to the 8th lord in D-10.

Example 141: Let us consider the muhurta chart used by Sri A.B. Vajpayee for swearing-in as India's Prime Minister in May 1996 (see Chart 84).

Chart 84

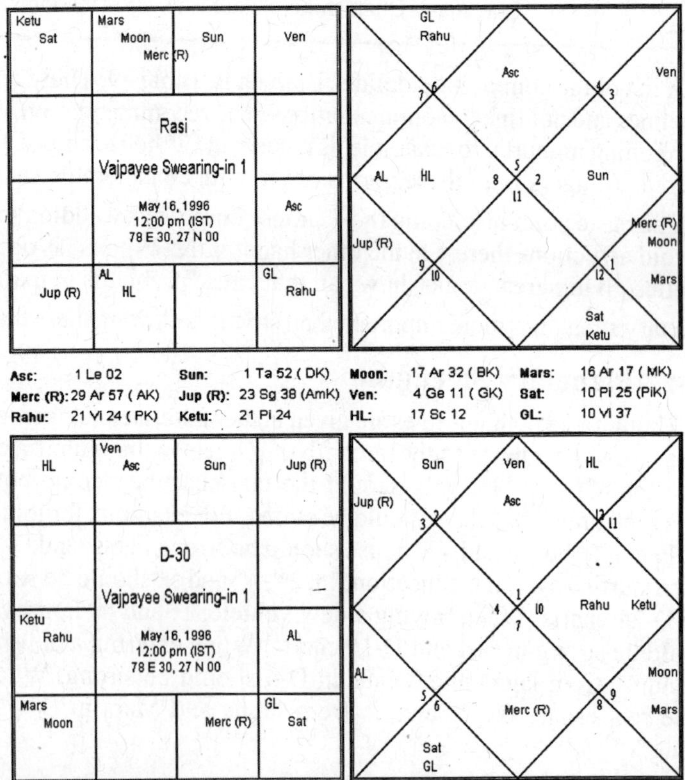

Asc:	1 Le 02	**Sun:**	1 Ta 52 (DK)	**Moon:**	17 Ar 32 (BK)	**Mars:**	16 Ar 17 (MK)
Merc (R):	29 Ar 57 (AK)	**Jup (R):**	23 Sg 38 (AmK)	**Ven:**	4 Ge 11 (GK)	**Sat:**	10 Pi 25 (PiK)
Rahu:	21 Vi 24 (PK)	**Ketu:**	21 Pi 24	**HL:**	17 Sc 12	**GL:**	10 Vi 37

In rasi chart, lagna lord Sun is in 10th and 10th lord Venus is in 11th. The 5th house is important for power and it contains its lord Jupiter. The 9th house of fortune is also very strong. On the whole, the chart is strong. Unfavorable sakuna karana was running at the time. Chaturdasi tithi (14th lunar day) is usually not considered auspicious, but its ruler Venus owns the 10th house here and it is acceptable. Overall, rasi chart is acceptable.

However, D-30 is weak. D-30 shows past and present evils and the punishment. To see an early death, it is an apt chart. Venus owns the 2nd and 7th houses in D-30 here. He is a strong maraka (killer). He afflicts lagna. Lagna lord of rasi chart (Sun) is in the 2nd house in D-30. Because of these, there was a premature end. The fact that Venus dasa was running at muhurta – Moon was in a Venusian constellation – did not help either. Sri Vajpayee remained in power only for 13 days. However, the strength of rasi chart ensured his return within a couple of years.

Example 142: Sri Vajpayee returned to power in March 1998. Let us consider the swearing-in muhurta used this time (see Chart 85).

Chart 85

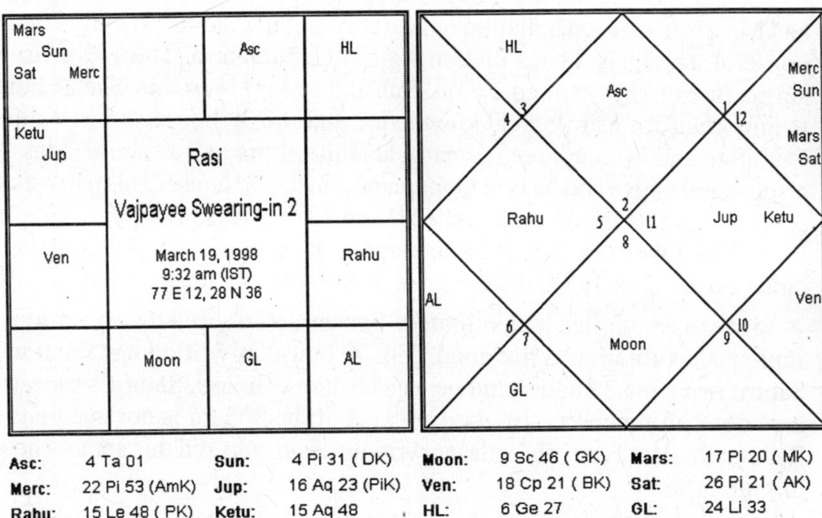

Lagna lord is in 9th with Uttamaamsa. Saturn owns 9th and 10th and he is in 11th with Uttamaamsa. The chart is basically strong. However, 3rd lord Moon is debilitated in 7th and that is not conducive to a long life. Situation of Gulika within 1° from lagna is also undesirable.

Because of the drawbacks, Sri Vajpayee lost the vote of confidence in April 1999. However, the opposition parties could not offer an alternative and Vajpayee remained as the caretaker Prime Minister. The position of his party improved in the October 1999 elections and he continued as PM. Let us time the setbacks of April 1999 using Vimsottari dasa compressed to 5 years. We can see that the 8th constellation Satabhisha falls in Aq and it is stronger than Moon's constellation, as Jupiter and Ketu occupy it. For matters related to longevity, we can use Vimsottari dasa started from the 8th constellation as it is stronger. Using this dasa, Ketu antardasa in Jupiter dasa ran during April 3-17, 1999. Venus antardasa ran for the next 40 days. With Jupiter owning the 8th house, Jupiter dasa was full of troubles. Ketu is the co-lord of the 7th house and he afflicts 8th lord. This resulted in the fall of the government. However, the next antardasa belonged to lagna lord Venus, who is the lord of Sanjivani mantra[101] . So Sri Vajpayee wasn't replaced by another leader and he remained as the caretaker PM.

Example 143: Let us consider the muhurta at which this author started writing this book (see Chart 86). Tithi is Saptami – an auspicious tithi. Yoga is Vriddhi yoga (growth). Karana is Vanija.

In rasi chart, lagna lord Moon occupies lagna in Paarijaataamsa. Lagna and Moon are in a constellation of Mercury, significator of writing. The 11th house of gains has Venus in own sign in Gopuraamsa. The 10th house of karma (action) has exalted 2nd lord Sun and 3rd lord Mercury. The 2nd house is important for astrological knowledge and the 3rd house shows writing. Both Sun and Mercury are in Paarijaataamsa. Lord of 10th house (Mars) is a yogakaraka here and he is in Gopuraamsa in the 2nd house. This parivartana (exchange of houses) between the 2nd and 10th lords is favorable for karma related to astrology. Jupiter is the significator of astrology and he has a close aspect on lagna and Moon. He aspects the 3rd house of writing also.

However, Jupiter is debilitated. For an activity related to astrology, Jupiter's debilitation is not good. The 3rd house of writing has Rahu in it. Saturn owns the 8th house and he aspects the 3rd house. Saturn's aspect on the house of interest is not good. Aspect of the 8th lord is not good either. Rahu in 3rd also shows obstacles in writing. Then, why did this author choose this muhurta?

(1) Lagna, 2nd, 5th, 10th and 11th are strong. The 3rd lord has a good placement, though 3rd is afflicted.

(2) Jupiter's aspect is always good in astrological activities. If Jupiter is weak, it can denote initial setbacks. But Jupiter's close aspect on lagna and lagna lord can only be beneficial in the long run.

---

101 This mantra can bring a dead person to life.

Chart 86

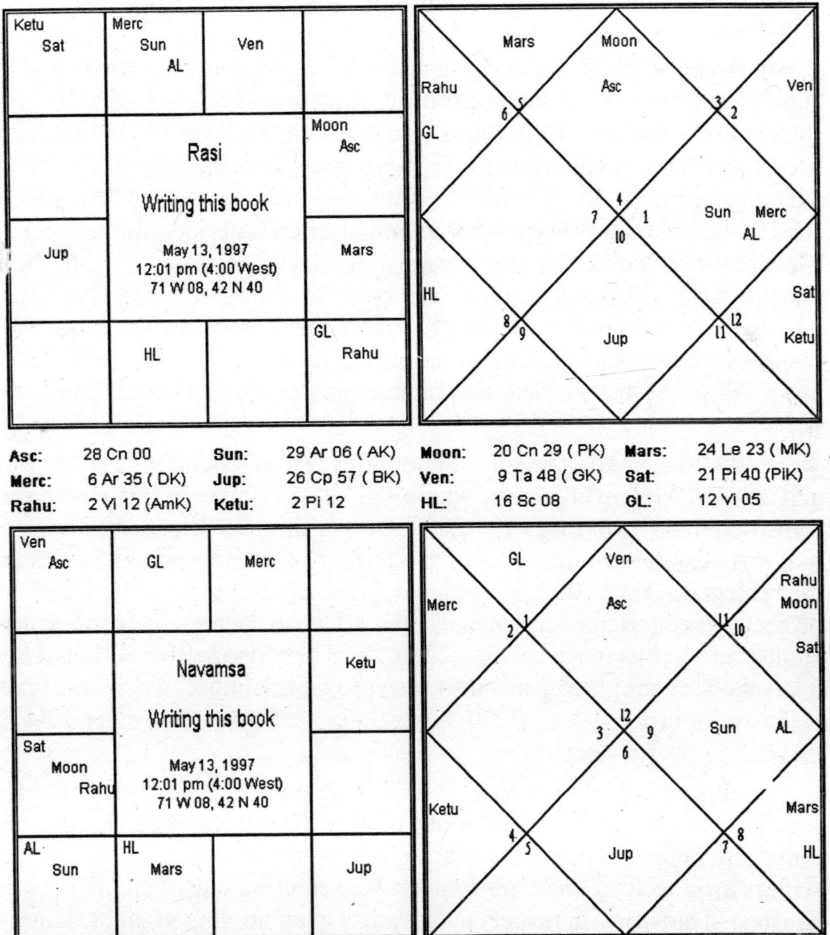

(3) Hora of Jupiter runs at the time of muhurta. Jupiter occupies the 2nd house of speech in this author's natal chart. In his natal D-24, Jupiter occupies Pi (10th house) and shows saattwik activities in society related to fine knowledge. A3 is in Pi in natal D-10 and Jupiter owns it. From A3 in D-24, he is the 2nd and 5th lord and occupies the 5th house (in own rasi). So Jupiter's hora is very favorable for starting astrological writing.

(4) More importantly, the Navamsa chart is strong.

If one's aim in writing a textbook on Vedic astrology is to contribute to a renaissance in Vedic astrology and to serve astrology researchers, then Navamsa is more important than Rasi. Navamsa is the chart that shows how one follows one's dharma (duty). So the strength of Navamsa is very important.

In navamsa (see Chart 86), lagna is in Pisces, a saattwik sign owned by Jupiter. Jupiter aspects lagna from 7th. Navamsa lagna is in the 9th from Rasi lagna. Exalted 3rd lord Venus is in lagna and he owns the 11th house in Rasi chart. This is favorable to fulfilling one's dharma related to writing. Mercury occupies the 3rd house in Navamsa and he owns the 3rd house in Rasi. This again shows using good communication skills in fulfilling dharma. Mars is strong in the 9th house in own sign. The 9th house must be strong in Navamsa for a dharmik activity. Sun is in 10th in both Rasi and Navamsa and that shows some recognition. Ketu is in the 5th house in Navamsa. This combination, if present in a natal Navamsa, makes one good at mathematics as per Jaimini Maharshi. Here, this combination makes an analytical approach possible.

In the Rasi chart, Aries is an important rasi as it contains 2nd lord Sun and 3rd lord Mercury. Saturn, who owns the 8th house in this chart, was transiting in Aries during 1998-2000. During this transit, progress was not made. After Jupiter entered Aries, this author became determined to restart the project. In April 2000, Sun entered Aries, his muhurta position, and the project was restarted with newfound vigor. Due to the presence of Mercury, Jupiter and Venus in Aries, May 2000 was a very productive period. After 3 years of contemplation and slow (no) progress, almost 40% of this book was written in April-May 2000. After Saturn left Aries, the other 60% of this book was finished.

As this example illustrates, we can use transits with muhurtas. Rasi is the chart of physical manifestation; navamsa is the chart of dharma and inner self; and, dasamsa is the chart of achievements in society. So transits with respect to Rasi chart are important in figuring out when the book is finished. Transits with respect to Navamsa chart are important in figuring out when and whether the book serves its intended purpose. Transits with respect to Dasamsa chart are important in figuring out how the book is received and when and whether it becomes popular. Thus we can adapt the meanings of divisional charts to muhurtas.

36.5 Conclusion

For standard principles related to muhurtas, readers can refer to other books. In this book, the importance of analyzing planetary positions as in natal charts is emphasized, as many books leave out this important aspect. One should analyze the rasi and relevant divisional charts of a muhurta just as in the case of natal charts.

37. Ethical Behavior of a Jyotishi

Jyotisha is the Sanskrit name of Vedic astrology. One who practices Jyotisha is called a Jyotishi. Vedas are the sacred scriptures of Hinduism. Veda simply means "Knowledge". Jyotisha is called a "Vedaanga" (a limb of Vedas). In particular, Jyotisha is called the eye of Vedas. It is the science of light and the eye of knowledge.

To its believers, Vedic astrology is not just another subject like mathematics and physics. It is considered a sacred subject. It gives its knower a *special power* to see the past, the present and the future. Such fine knowledge cannot reach an irresponsible person. So Maharshis have set some guidelines for the ethical behavior of Jyotishis. This author hopes that the readers of this book abide by those guidelines.

One should give this knowledge to worthy, honest and god-fearing students who have great respect for their teacher and who speak truth always. In Indian culture, one's relationship with a giver of knowledge is that of a servant with one's master. Just as a servant obeys each command of his master, a student obeys each command of his teacher. A wealthy man may give his servant only some money, but a teacher gives his students knowledge and knowledge is considered to be the most valuable asset in Indian culture. So teachers are treated with utmost respect. This may be tough to understand and appreciate, for readers from western cultures where knowledge is a commodity with a limited value.

Maharshis advised that one benefits by teaching Jyotisha to god-fearing students who treat their teacher with utmost respect and speak truth. On the other hand, one becomes sad everyday by teaching Jyotisha to atheists, liars and deceitful people.

In Kali Yuga, it may be difficult to find ideal students for this subject. Nevertheless, one should not teach this subject to unwilling people and unbelievers. This knowledge should be given only to the worthy students.

Jyotishis should also maintain dignity when offering astrological consultations. They should approach astrological consultations with the spirit of service. They possess special knowledge of a sacred subject and they should help those who need guidance. Jyotishis should be spiritually oriented and they should realize that their knowledge is priceless. Instead of running after material possessions, they should be happy with their knowledge and help people in need without expecting anything in return.

Accumulating wealth and material possessions gives only temporary happiness. It may make one happy for 10 years or 50 years or 100 years.

But when one dies and takes birth again, one loses all that. All these material possessions cannot be carried with one. A greedy person will only struggle in the infinite cycle of life, death and rebirth. Things can get only worse for a greedy person with each new life.

Just as one who does not exercise accumulates a lot of body fat which is a liability, a greedy person accumulates a lot of sin which becomes a liability in the cycle of life, death and rebirth. On the other hand, an austere person who punishes himself by denying comforts burns away the sins of past lives, just as one who troubles his body with regular exercise burns the body fat. So a wise person doesn't run after material possessions and tries to be austere.

An austere Jyotishi who serves humanity with his/her divine knowledge of Jyotisha burns away past sins and gets closer and closer to liberation from the cycle of life, death and rebirth.

One should always be positive when making predictions. Negative predictions should be made with a restrained tone. A Jyotishi may gently caution the clients about an impending danger and suggest remedial measures and precautions, but he should not scare the clients. Negative predictions should be made only when some preventive action is suggested. Negative predictions made just for fame or the sensation value bring unhappiness to the Jyotishi. Jyotishis should try to bring spiritual awareness in their clients and try to promote righteousness. Jyotisha should never be a business. It should be a spiritual service.

With deep respect for my gurus and maharshis, I shared my limited knowledge with the readers. May the readers of this book use the privileged knowledge of the divine subject of Jyotisha in the spirit of compassionate and selfless service and work for the uplifting of humanity!

Part 6: Real-life Examples

The "exercises" one encounters in real life can be considerably more complicated than the tailor-made exercises given in this bock. The exercises given in this book familiarize the reader with various techniques, but making real-life predictions requires more than that.

To illustrate the process of making predictions, some real-life situations that this author faced in his experience will be given. The process of synthesizing a prediction will be illustrated in as much detail as possible. These examples are meant for giving some guidance and inspiration to those who are new to the process of making predictions.

Real-life Example 1:

Birthdata of a lady is given in Chart 87. Her parents consulted the author in early 1997 and wanted to know exactly when she would get married.

For marriage, we should see rasi and navamsa charts (see Chart 87). Vimsottari dasa of Jupiter started in mid-1996. Can Jupiter give marriage? Well, he must. Because this dasa started at an age of 23, it will run till an age of 39. So Jupiter must give marriage. Being lagna lord in 11th, he can give all-round progress. Moreover, he aspects the 7th house Virgo and 7th lord Mercury here. So he can give marriage.

Who is the 7th lord? In rasi, 7th lord is Mercury. In D-9, 7th is in Cp and its lord Saturn aspects it from Sc. So Saturn antardasa can give marriage. When is it? It starts in the second half of 1998. But her parents already started looking for a match and Saturn antardasa is too late. Can Jupiter antardasa itself give marriage? It is not very likely.

Where will Jupiter be in late 1998? He will be transiting in Aq. Can Jupiter's Aq transit give marriage? It doesn't look too interesting. Pi transit is a better candidate. As Pi is natal lagna, Jupiter's Pi transit can bring all-round progress. From Pi, Jupiter will aspect Vi, the 7th house. He will also aspect Cn. Note that Cn contains 7th lord Mercury in rasi chart. In D-9, it contains lagna & Mercury. So Jupiter's Pisces dasa in 1999 can bring marriage.

The pratyantardasa running then is Mercury's (Jan-May 1999). With Mercury owning the 7th house in rasi and occupying lagna in D-9, his PD can give marriage. He is also DK.

To be sure, check Sudarsana Chakra dasa. On her birthday in 1998, she finishes 1998 – 1973 = 25 years and starts the 26th year. Subtracting multiples of 12 from 26, we get 2. So dasa of the 2nd house runs. In navamsa, it is Leo. At the time of the start of this dasa (*i.e.* Tajaka annual chart of 1998-99), Jupiter occupies Leo and Venus occupies Aquarius (see Chart 74). That is favorable. So marriage can take place in the year (1998-99).

Chart 87

Mars Asc		Moon	Ketu Sat
	Rasi A lady		Merc (R) Sun
Jup (R)	July 26, 1973 9:41 pm (IST) 80 E 28, 16 N 13		Ven
Rahu	GL HL AL		

Mars Asc 1 2 Moon 11 10 Jup (R) Ketu Sat 3 12 9 6 Rahu Sun AL HL 4 5 Merc (R) 8 7 GL Ven

Asc:	3 Pi 18	**Sun:**	10 Cn 01 (PiK)	**Moon:**	26 Ta 39 (AmK)	**Mars:**	28 Pi 12 (AK)
Merc (R):	0 Cn 13 (DK)	**Jup (R):**	14 Cp 12 (MK)	**Ven:**	8 Le 25 (PK)	**Sat:**	5 Ge 48 (GK)
Rahu:	12 Sg 48 (BK)	**Ketu:**	12 Ge 48	**HL:**	6 Sc 15	**GL:**	1 Sc 32

Mars		Jup (R)	Ven
	Navamsa A lady		Merc (R) Asc GL Rahu
Ketu	July 26, 1973 9:41 pm (IST) 80 E 28, 16 N 13		HL Moon
	Sat	Sun	AL

HL Moon Merc (R) Ven Rahu GL Asc AL Jup (R) 5 6 3 2 Sun 4 7 1 10 Sat Mars 8 9 12 11 Ketu

In Tajaka annual chart, lagna lord and 2nd lord have an exchange. The 2nd house shows family. Vivaha saham is in Sc. Mars owns it. Mars is also muntha lord. He has a very close ithasala with Venus, the natural significator of marriage and upapada lord. In navamsa, Mars is very strong in his moolatrikona Aries. He is in the 2nd from lagna and 9th from muntha. Patyayini dasa of Venus runs during Dec 98 and Jan 99. Patyayini dasa of Mars runs during Feb-Mar 99.

In 1999, the lunar month of Maagha ends in mid-February. It brings the season of marriages in India, because it is thought to be an auspicious month for marriages. So probably marriage will take place in that month.

So the final prediction given was – "she may get married in the first half of February 1999". Because upapada is in Li in rasi chart, she was advised to pray to goddess Lakshmi everyday and especially on Fridays.

She got married at the end of Jan 1999 and went to USA with her husband in early Feb 1999.

Real-life Example 2:

A noted Vedic astrologer of the west was expecting a child in November 1999. At the end of October 1999, he mentioned on an internet-based forum for Vedic astrology discussions[102] that his child would be born in a few weeks. He did not mention how many children he already had or what the due date for this new child was.

Later he expressed a desire on the forum to learn the computation of Narayana dasa for divisional charts. This author wanted to illustrate the computation using the gentleman's D-7, as he was expecting a child. His birthdata and natal D-7 are given in Chart 88.

Lagna in rasi chart is in Sc. The 7th house is in Ta. Its lord is Venus. He is in Ge in D-7 and Ge is stronger than Sg. So dasas start from Ge. Because Ge is a dual sign, we use the trinal progression of Vishnu. Because the 9th from Ge (*i.e.* Aq) is an even-footed sign, we go backward. So dasas go as Ge, Aq, Li, Vi, Ta, Cp, Sg, Le, Ar, Pi, Sc and Cn. It can be seen that Le dasa runs during 1988-2000.

It can be seen that exalted Jupiter is stronger than lagna in D-7 and he can be used as a reference. The 1st, 2nd and 5th lords from him are Moon, Sun and Mars and they are all conjoined in Leo. So Leo is a very important sign in this D-7. Its dasa can give children.

---

102 http://www.egroups.com/group/vedic-astrology

Chart 88

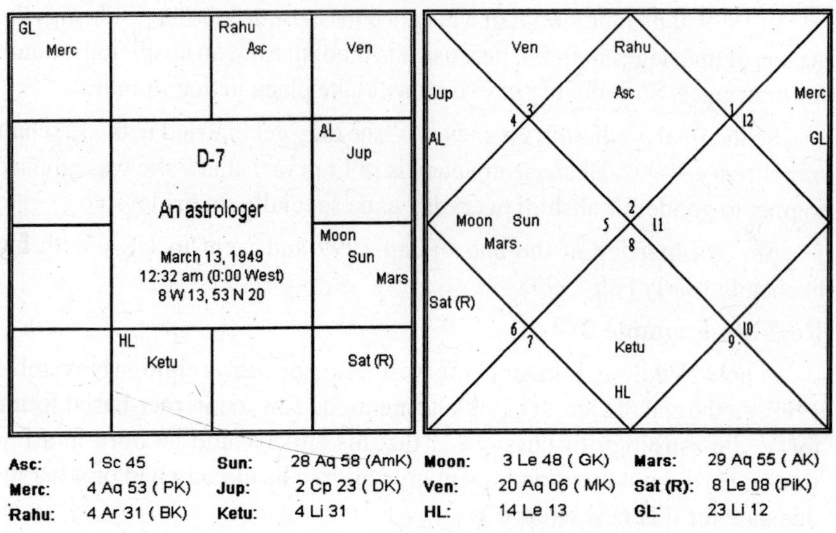

Let us find antardasas. Because Le is stronger, antardasas start from its lord Sun. He is in Le, an odd sign. So antardasas go as Le, Vi, Li, Sc *etc*. During 1999-2000, the 12th antardasa of Cn runs. It contains exalted Jupiter and it can give a child.

Pratyantardasas in Cn dasa start from Moon and again they go as Le, Vi, Li, Sc *etc*. March 13-April 13 is the first pratyantardasa. October 15-November 15 is the 8th pratyantardasa of Pisces. From November 15, Aries pratyantardasa runs. Which is more likely to give a child?

Pisces is the 11th house and contains the 5th lord Mercury. Mercury is also PK. He is in a trine from exalted Jupiter. So Pisces pratyantardasa is more likely to give a child.

Before it can be mentioned in public, it can be quickly cross-checked using the Tajaka annual chart of 1999-2000 (see Chart 89).

Chart 89

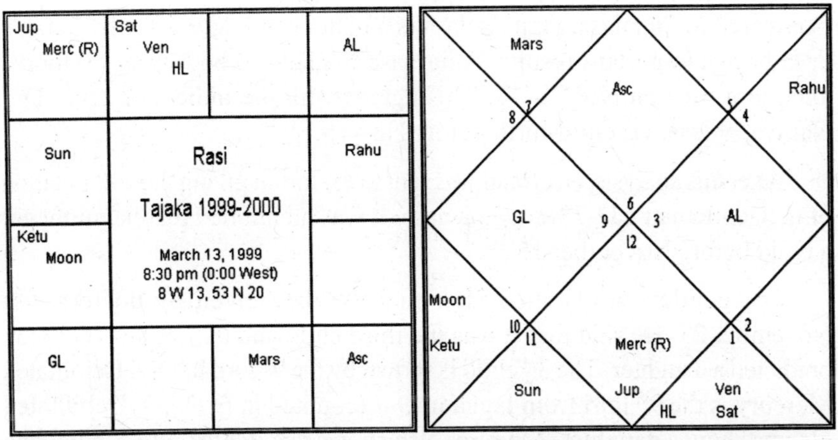

Jup Merc (R)	Sat Ven HL		AL
Sun	Rasi Tajaka 1999-2000 March 13, 1999 8:30 pm (0:00 West) 8 W 13, 53 N 20		Rahu
Ketu Moon			
GL		Mars	Asc

Mars
Asc
Rahu
8 7 5 4
GL
6
9 3
12
AL
Moon
10
11
Ketu
Merc (R)
2
1
Sun
Jup
HL
Ven
Sat

Asc:	20 Vi 11	**Sun:**	28 Aq 58 (AK)	**Moon:**	8 Cp 50 (PiK)	**Mars:**	18 Li 13 (AmK)
Merc (R):	9 Pi 21 (MK)	**Jup:**	12 Pi 48 (BK)	**Ven:**	0 Ar 38 (DK)	**Sat:**	7 Ar 29 (PK)
Rahu:	26 Cn 44 (GK)	**Ketu:**	26 Cp 44	**HL:**	14 Ar 40	**GL:**	24 Sg 04

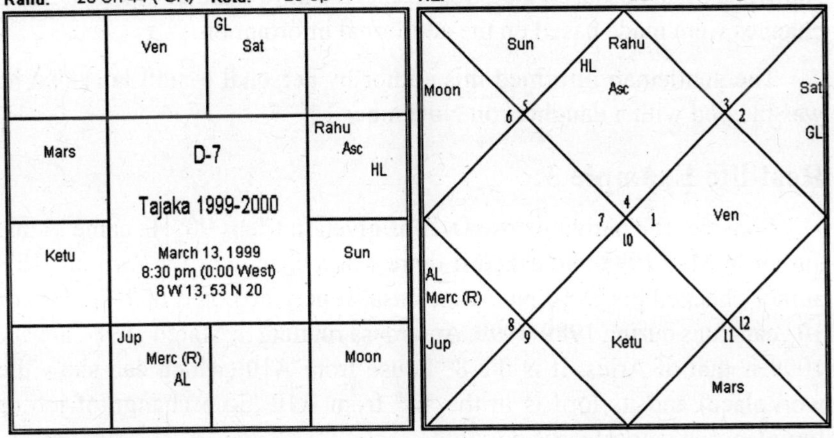

	Ven	GL Sat	
Mars	D-7 Tajaka 1999-2000 March 13, 1999 8:30 pm (0:00 West) 8 W 13, 53 N 20		Rahu Asc HL
Ketu			Sun
	Jup Merc (R) AL		Moon

Sun
Rahu
HL
Asc
Moon
Sat
GL
6 5 3 2
4
7 1
10
Ven
AL
Merc (R)
8
9
Jup
Ketu
12
11
Mars

In this chart, putra saham is in Cancer. Its lord Moon is in the 5th house of children. He has a very close half-degree ithasala with lagna lord Mercury. He also has an ithasala with Jupiter, natural significator of children. In D-7, the 5th house is occupied by Mercury and Jupiter. Moon owns lagna and occupies 3rd (11th from 5th, showing the gain of a child).

All these factors suggest a child in the dasa of Moon, who emerges as an important planet in rasi and D-7. However, Moon's dasa comes during

June-July. Lagna's Patyayini dasa runs during Oct 29-Nov 23 and Sun's dasa comes after it. This gentleman said on Oct 29 that he was expecting a child in a few weeks. So it has to be either lagna's dasa or Sun's dasa. Compared to Sun dasa, lagna's dasa is a better candidate. Usually lagna's dasa brings important results. Antardasa is likely to be Moon's. Moon's antardasa runs on Nov 14-15. This agrees with the indication from D-7 Narayana dasa, *viz* child-birth before Nov 15.

After this analysis, an e-mail was sent to the forum giving the computation of the gentleman's D-7 Narayana dasa. It was mentioned that he might get a child before November 15.

The gentleman clarified later that the date given by doctors was November 23. He said that it was the third child and the ultra-sound scan predicted a daughter. The 3rd child is shown by the 9th lord in D-7. Debilitated Mercury is the 9th lord from lagna in D-7 (counted in reverse). Debilitated planets show a daughter. Mercury also shows a daughter. We can now be more confident about child-birth in the pratyantardasa of Pisces as per D-7 Narayana dasa, because Pisces represents the third child in this D-7. So no changes were made based on the additional information.

The gentleman informed this author by personal e-mail later that he was blessed with a daughter on November 14.

Real-life Example 3:

Consider the native whose D-10 is given in Chart 90. He came to this author in May 1998 and asked if there was a change of job for him. This author checked his D-10 Narayana dasa. It may be noted that Cp dasa of 10 years runs during 1989-1999. Antardasa running in March 1998-January 1999 is that of Aries. It is the 8th house from A10 (which can show the workplace) and its lord is in the 12th from A10. So a change of job or turbulence at workplace is possible.

Because Ar contains AL and it is a trine from lagna, its antardasa is likely to be good for career and status. However, its lord Mars is with Rahu in the 8th house from the dasa rasi Cp. So this indicates pressures and undesirable developments too. This seems to suggest worries at the current job and then move to a new job with higher status.

This can be cross-checked with D-10 of Tajaka annual chart of 1998-99 (see Chart 91). AL in D-10 contains its lord Rahu and the other lord

Chart 90

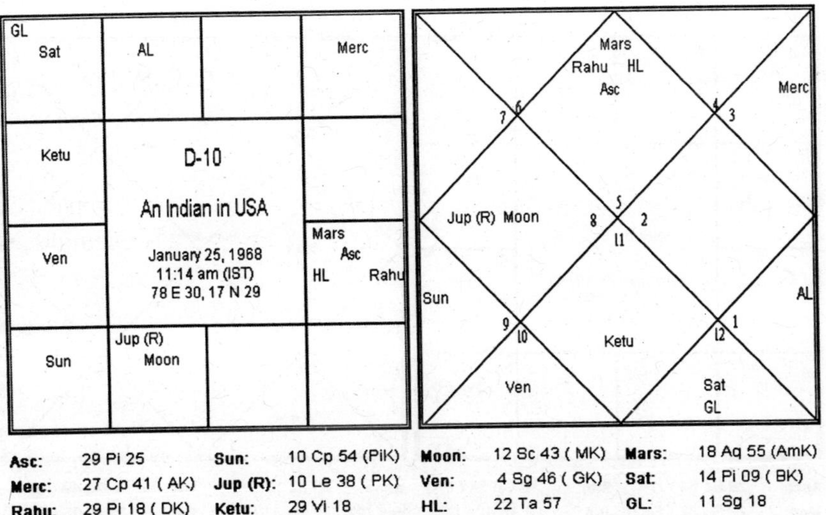

Asc:	29 Pi 25	**Sun:**	10 Cp 54 (PiK)	**Moon:**	12 Sc 43 (MK)	**Mars:**	18 Aq 55 (AmK)
Merc:	27 Cp 41 (AK)	**Jup (R):**	10 Le 38 (PK)	**Ven:**	4 Sg 46 (GK)	**Sat:**	14 Pi 09 (BK)
Rahu:	29 Pi 18 (DK)	**Ketu:**	29 Vi 18	**HL:**	22 Ta 57	**GL:**	11 Sg 18

Saturn is in the 5th house from it. These factors suggest good status in career in the year. However, Venus owns the 7th from lagna (dealings with others) and the 9th from AL (fortune) and he is debilitated. This does suggest some setbacks. Moreover, Saturn and Sun aspect each other in D-10. This shows trouble from authorities.

Let us check Tajaka monthly charts (Chart 92). In Tajaka monthly chart of May 26-June 26, 1998, lagna lord in D-10 is Venus and he is in the 12th house with exalted Sun, again supporting trouble from authorities. Moon and Mercury are with Ketu and Rahu respectively and it does not suggest a happy mental and emotional state, as far as work is concerned. However, in D-10 of the next month's chart, lagna lord Jupiter is in 10th in moolatrikona. Despite other weaknesses, this brings strength to D-10. In rasi chart also, 10th lord Mercury is in own rasi Ge (7th house) with 9th lord Sun and this shows good developments in career.

Based on all these factors, it was predicted that the native's relationship with his managers could deteriorate, he could be frustrated in June, he could be forced out of his job and he would join a better job in July.

Chart 91

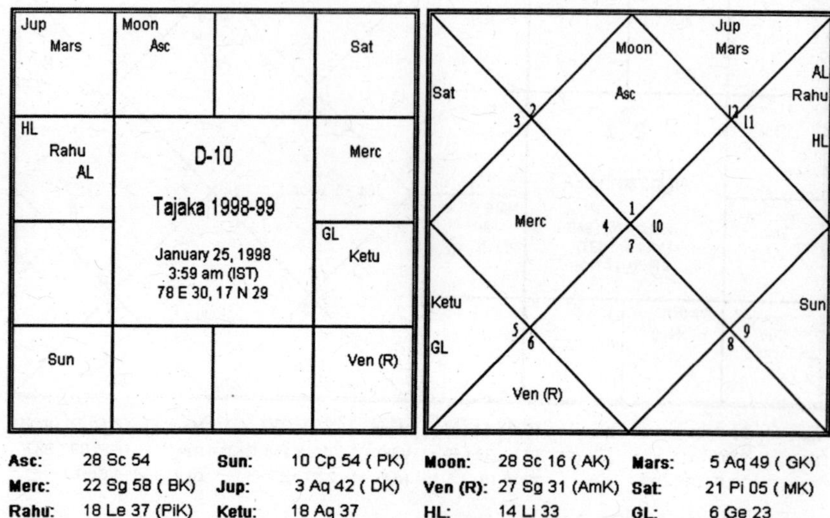

Asc:	28 Sc 54	**Sun:**	10 Cp 54 (PK)	**Moon:**	28 Sc 16 (AK)	**Mars:**	5 Aq 49 (GK)
Merc:	22 Sg 58 (BK)	**Jup:**	3 Aq 42 (DK)	**Ven (R):**	27 Sg 31 (AmK)	**Sat:**	21 Pi 05 (MK)
Rahu:	18 Le 37 (PiK)	**Ketu:**	18 Aq 37	**HL:**	14 Li 33	**GL:**	6 Ge 23

It happened as predicted. At the time of the original prediction, this author looked at Narayana dasa only upto antardasas. After he knew that the prediction came true, he checked pratyantardasas (PD) in retrospect. Scorpio's PD was running in June. Because of the presence of 8th lord and debilitated Moon, its PD brought pressures and frustration. The conjunction of 8th and 12th lords can give a Viparita Raja Yoga, but that can be effective only when the planets are in a dusthana in weakness or in a quadrant/trine in strength. Here Moon is debilitated and they are in a quadrant.

After the frustration in Sc dasa given by debilitated Moon, next PD of Sg during July brought success. He joined a better job. Because Sun is lagna lord and the lord of 5th from AL and because he occupies a trine from AL, this PD can be good for professional status. Because of his rasi aspect on Pi (GL), Sun can give a promotion also. Moreover, Sun is the planet of authority. So Sg antardasa gave a new job with a higher status.

The native came to this author again in May 1999. He was planning to buy a house in USA and wondered if his career would be stable or if it would be a mistake to buy a house.

Le dasa runs during 1999-2007. Because Le is lagna and the 5th from AL, its dasa has to be good. Antardasa of Sg was running till Sept 1999 and

Chart 92

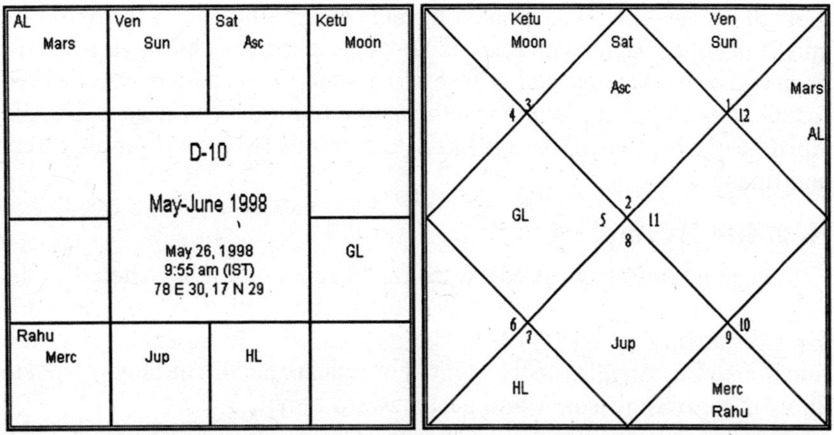

AL Mars	Ven Sun	Sat Asc	Ketu Moon
	D-10 May-June 1998 May 26, 1998 9:55 am (IST) 78 E 30, 17 N 29		
			GL
Rahu Merc	Jup	HL	

Ketu Moon 3 4 · Sat Asc · Ven Sun 1 12 Mars AL · GL 5 2 11 8 · 6 7 HL · Jup · 9 10 Merc Rahu

Asc:	8 Cn 43	**Sun:**	10 Ta 54 (MK)	**Moon:**	15 Ta 59 (BK)	**Mars:**	7 Ta 37 (PiK)
Merc:	24 Ar 14 (AK)	**Jup:**	0 Pi 02 (DK)	**Ven:**	1 Ar 46 (GK)	**Sat:**	4 Ar 41 (PK)
Rahu:	12 Le 12 (AmK)	**Ketu:**	12 Aq 12	**HL:**	17 Vi 32	**GL:**	27 Pi 44

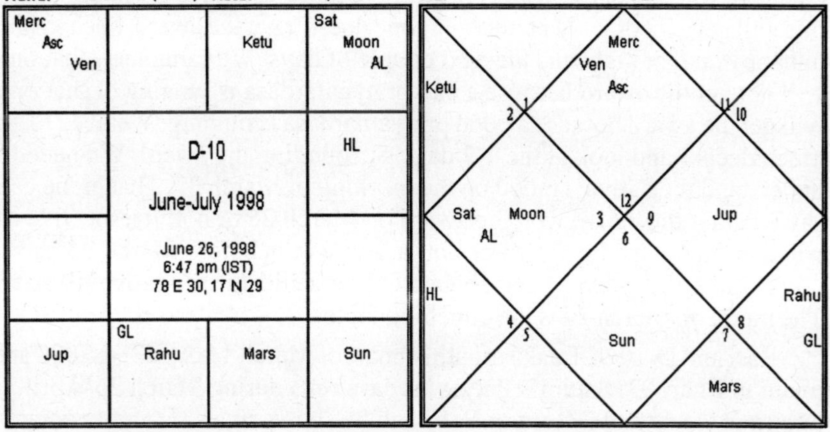

Merc Asc Ven		Ketu	Sat Moon AL
	D-10 June-July 1998 June 26, 1998 6:47 pm (IST) 78 E 30, 17 N 29		HL
Jup	GL Rahu	Mars	Sun

Merc Ven Asc · Ketu 2 1 · 11 10 · Sat Moon AL 3 12 9 6 · Jup · HL · Rahu GL · 4 5 · Sun · 7 8 · Mars

Asc:	10 Sg 22	**Sun:**	10 Ge 54 (PiK)	**Moon:**	11 Cn 16 (MK)	**Mars:**	29 Ta 29 (AK)
Merc:	28 Ge 36 (AmK)	**Jup:**	3 Pi 29 (DK)	**Ven:**	8 Ta 35 (PK)	**Sat:**	7 Ar 42 (GK)
Rahu:	10 Le 32 (BK)	**Ketu:**	10 Aq 32	**HL:**	12 Cn 21	**GL:**	0 Pi 18

it would be excellent for reasons already mentioned. So the native was told that there was nothing to worry about and he might in fact have a promotion in the next few months. That came true and his position improved at his new company.

Before we close this example, readers may note one thing. Lagna is in Pi, GL is in Sg and HL is in Ta in his natal rasi chart. So Venus owns HL, occupies GL and aspects lagna (by rasi aspect). For these reasons, Venus is a yogada (giver of yoga). His dasa must be excellent from the point of view of power as well as money. In rasi chart, Venus owns the 8th house and he occupies lagna with Rahu in D-4. These factors can suggest that his yoga will be in a foreign land. Vimsottari dasa of Venus started in April 1997 (using 360-day savana years) and the native left India and went to USA in April/May 1997. Venus dasa is likely to continue to be good for his career and finances.

Real-life Example 4:

On an internet-based Vedic astrology discussion forum, a noted Vedic astrologer of west gave the birthdata of her friend's son, who was nominated for an academy award (Oscar). The awards were to be announced at a function in Los Angeles on the night of March 26, 2000. The lady wanted to know if her friend's son would get an award or not.

For someone in the entertainment business, an Oscar nomination itself is a major achievement. We cannot look at the dasas one is running and conclude whether one will win the award or not. Because of the nomination, one will get a lot of good publicity. If one doesn't get the award, one may be unhappy on that night and the next couple of days. We cannot say that one will not get the award because a bad pratyantardasa is running or that one will get the award because a good pratyantardasa is running. We need to go much deeper and look at the 1-2 days surrounding the award. We need to understand the native's mood on the morning of March 27. That alone can say whether the native won the award on March 26 or not. Irrespective of whether one wins the award or not, a few weeks before March 26 and a few months after March 26 are bound to be excellent in the native's career. The mood on March 27 is the clinching factor.

Rasi and D-10 of Tajaka monthly chart of March 14-April 14, 2000 are given in Chart 93. Saturn's Patyayini dasa runs during March 26-April 3. Saturn is the 6th and 7th lord in D-10 and he shows rivals (6th) and contacts (7th) in the entertainment business. His exaltation may show meeting some important people. However, exaltation of 6th lord is not favorable. Moreover Saturn is debilitated in 6th in rasi chart. That can show disappointments. So meeting with important people, getting disappointed and making important contacts may be the results given by Saturn. However, we should focus on the 60-hour period for a better idea.

Rasi and D-10 of Tajaka sixty-hour chart of March 26-28, 2000 are given in Chart 94. This chart covers the period that starts in the afternoon of March 26 and lasts 2.5 days. In rasi chart, lagna has Rahu in it. Lagna lord is debilitated in 5th, the house of emotions. The strength of the 10th house

Chart 93

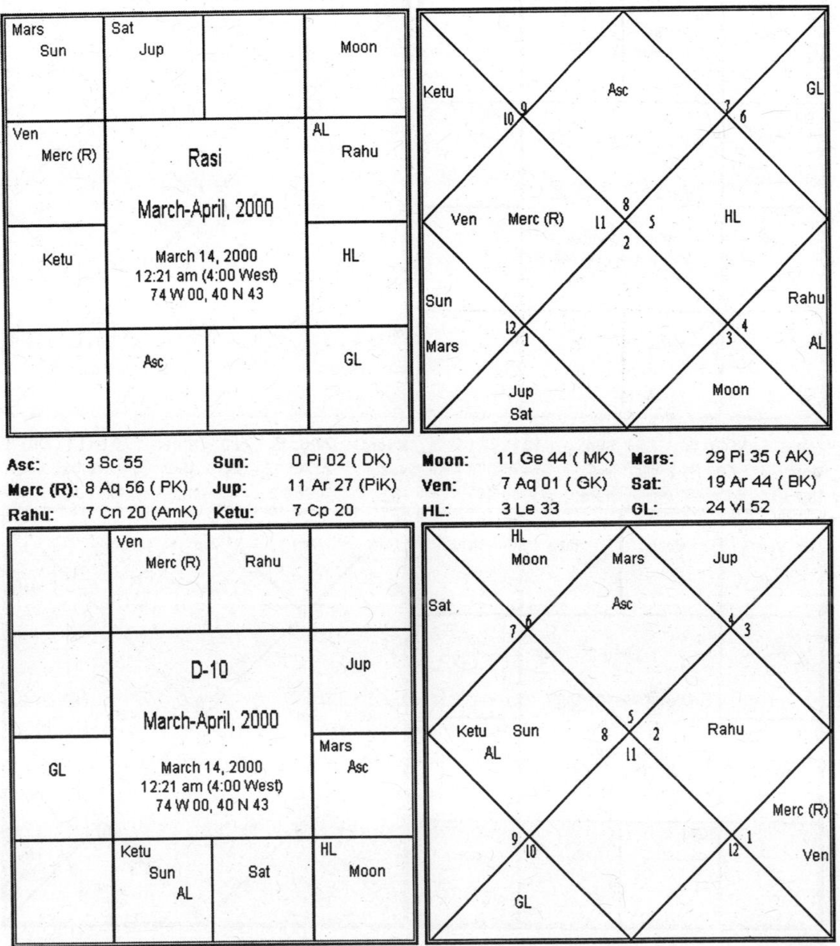

shows a good development in career (attending the Oscar night), but the weakness of lagna lord shows a disappointment. In D-10, lagna lord is in 8th and 8th lord is in lagna.

So it was predicted on the forum that the native was unlikely to win the award. Later, the lady who gave this chart informed the forum that her friend's son did not win the academy award.

Chart 94

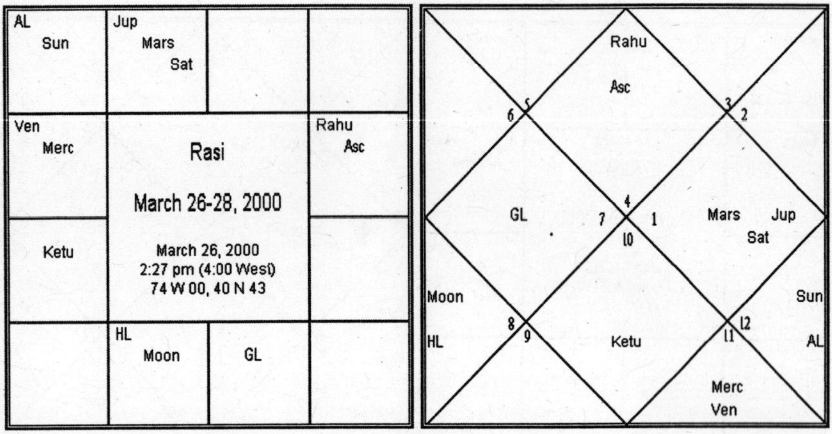

AL Sun	Jup Mars Sat		
Ven Merc	Rasi March 26-28, 2000		Rahu Asc
Ketu	March 26, 2000 2:27 pm (4:00 West) 74 W 00, 40 N 43		
	HL Moon	GL	

Rahu Asc
6 5 3 2
GL 7 4 1 10 Mars Jup Sat
Moon Sun
8 9 12 11
HL Ketu AL
Merc Ven

Asc:	16 Cn 54	**Sun:**	12 Pi 32 (GK)	**Moon:**	29 Sc 02 (AK)	**Mars:**	8 Ar 52 (DK)
Merc:	14 Aq 51 (PiK)	**Jup:**	14 Ar 09 (PK)	**Ven:**	22 Aq 33 (BK)	**Sat:**	21 Ar 03 (MK)
Rahu:	6 Cn 40 (AmK)	**Ketu:**	6 Cp 40	**HL:**	0 Sc 22	**GL:**	12 Li 35

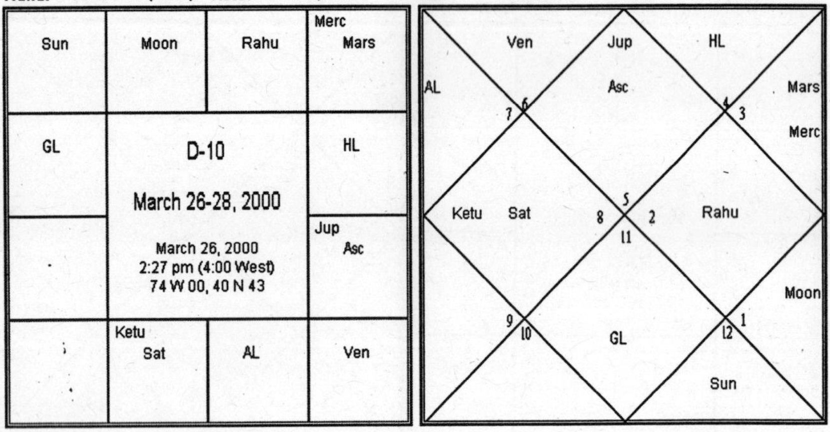

Sun	Moon	Rahu	Merc Mars
GL	D-10 March 26-28, 2000		HL
	March 26, 2000 2:27 pm (4:00 West) 74 W 00, 40 N 43		Jup Asc
	Ketu Sat	AL	Ven

Ven Jup HL
AL Asc Mars
7 6 4 3
Merc
Ketu Sat 8 5 2 11 Rahu
Moon
9 10 12 1
GL
Sun

Real-life Example 5:

When working on the birthtime rectification of a lady whose navamsa chart is given in Chart 95, this author wanted to guess when her marriage took place. He first looked at Vimsottari dasa. Mercury dasa runs during 1983-1999. Because Mercury is the 7th lord in 7th in navamsa, his dasa can give marriage. Because Mars owns the 2nd house and upapada and joins lagna lord, his antardasa can give marriage. Jupiter's antardasa can also give marriage.

Chart 95

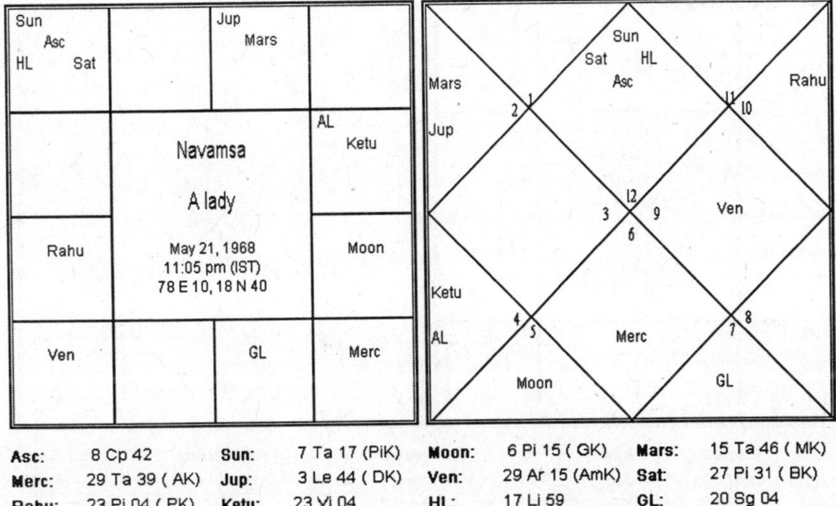

We can cross-check with Kalachakra dasa. Sg dasa runs from 1988-1998. For an Indian girl, this is the normal age of getting married. So irrespective of planets, this must be the dasa of marriage. In any case, Venus occupies Sg here and it can give marriage. Antardasa can belong to the 7th house Virgo containg Mercury. It can also be Gemini owned and aspected by the 7th lord. Gemini is the 7th house from Venus and from dasa rasi. Gemini antardasa runs from Sept 1991 to Aug 1992.

Next, this author checked the Tajaka annual chart of 1991-92 (see Chart 96). Vivaha saham is at 22Ge54, *i.e.* in the 7th house. Venus is the significator of marriage and he is at 21Ge11. The situation of Venus in the 7th house very close to vivaha saham very strongly indicates marriage in the year, perhaps in the Patyayini dasa of Venus.

Mercury is the 7th lord and vivaha saham lord. He is at 13Ar37. Lagna lord Jupiter is at 13Cn52. There is a square aspect between the two planets. Because Mercury is behind Jupiter by one quarter of a degree, there is a very "poorna (complete) ithasala" between them. This also makes marriage extremely likely in the year.

Chart 96

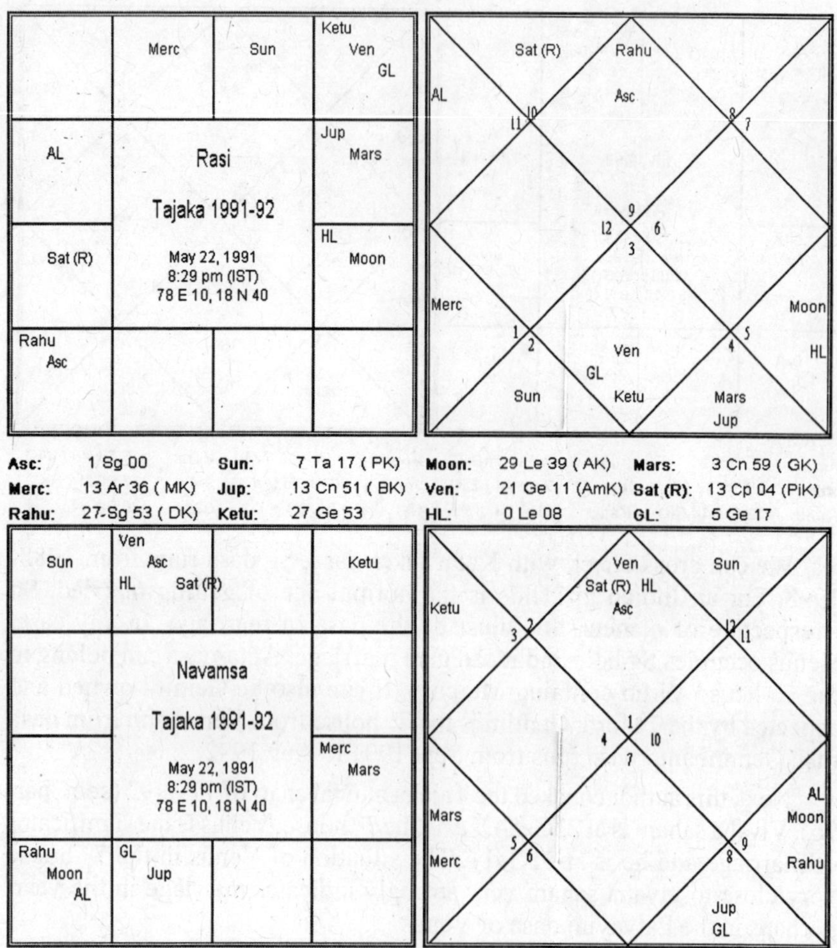

In navamsa, Venus owns the 7th house and occupies lagna. Mercury, lord of 7th in rasi chart, occupies a trine in navamsa and joins navamsa lagna lord. (Note: If the 7th lord in rasi chart is well-placed in navamsa, it is good. The 7th lord in rasi shows the partner in physical life and navamsa shows inner self and dharma.)

Venus dasa as per annual Patyayini dasa runs from 9th Nov 1991 to 7th Feb 1992. Venus-Mercury antardasa runs during February 5-7, 1992. So this author asked the lady, “did you get married in the first week of February 1992?” The lady was not a great believer in astrology and she was amazed. She said yes.

At that time, this author did not compute compressed Narayana dasa, but readers can verify that compressed D-9 Narayana dasa of Cn runs during Feb 5-20, 1992. Her marriage took place then and Cn contains upapada in navamsa (see Chart 96).

One Last Word

The purpose of these examples is not to brag about some correct predictions. Every astrologer makes hundreds or thousands of correct predictions and possibly hundreds of wrong predictions too. I also made many correct predictions and many wrong predictions. The purpose of the above examples is to illustrate the process of making predictions and to give guidance to those who are new to the process of making predictions.

I earnestly hope that readers pursue this divine subject in the right spirit, master it, serve their clients sincerely and contribute to a renaissance in Jyotish.

I again humbly request elders and scholars to correct my mistakes. May I be forgiven for my mistakes and excesses.

I bow with gratitude before Lord Jagannatha for making me write this book. May He continue to stand in the path of my eyes!

ॐ श्री जगन्नाथस्वामी नयनपथगामी भवतु में

सर्वे जनाः सुखिनो भवन्तु

May all people be happy!

असतो मा सद्गमय
तमसो मा ज्योतिर्गमय
मृत्योर्मा अमृतम् गमय
ॐ शांति शांति शांतिः

May we find Truth from Falsehood!
May we find Light from Darkness!
May we find the Nectar of Immortality from Death!
Let there be Peace, Peace, Peace!!

ॐ तत् सत्

:: *Om Tat Sat* ::